A Practitioner's Guide to
DIRECTORS' DUTIES AND
RESPONSIBILITIES

Consultant Editor
Tim Boxell
Slaughter and May

Fourth Edition

Published in 2010 by
Thomson Reuters (Legal) Limited (Registered in England & Wales,
Company No 1679046. Registered Office and address for service:
100 Avenue Road, Swiss Cottage,
London NW3 3PF) trading as City & Financial.

For further information on our products and services, visit
www.cityandfinancial.com

Typeset by LBJ Typesetting Ltd of Kingsclere
Printed and bound in Great Britain by CPI Antony Rowe,
Chippenham and Eastbourne

ISBN: 978 0 414 04311 4

No natural forests were destroyed to make this product;
only farmed timber was used and replanted.

A CIP catalogue record of this book is available
for the British Library.

Crown copyright material is reproduced with the permission of the Controller of
HMSO and the Queen's Printer for Scotland.

Biographies

Tim Boxell is a partner at Slaughter and May. Tim's practice mainly involves corporate, corporate finance, mergers and acquisitions and private equity work. A substantial part of his practice is of a cross-border nature. He has extensive experience of international transactions involving a number of overseas jurisdictions in a variety of business sectors.

He is a member of the Law Society's Company Law Committee and is also a member of the Policy & Technical Committee of the Association of Corporate Treasurers.

Chris Hale is a partner in Travers Smith LLP and head of the firm's Corporate Department. For the last 17 years he has specialised in UK and international buyout work, acting for both institutional investors and management teams on investments and divestments, as well as private equity-backed companies on mergers and acquisitions and other corporate matters. He writes and lectures regularly on company law and private equity in particular and is on the editorial boards of The Company Lawyer and Amicus Curiae.

Richard Slynn is a corporate partner in the London office of Allen & Overy LLP. His practice involves advising the boards of companies, building societies and other entities on directors' duties and on statutory, constitutional, corporate governance and regulatory issues and advising on strategic transactions, including mergers and acquisitions, joint ventures, and demutualisations.

Richard's clients include banks, building societies, insurance companies and asset managers. He monitors regulatory developments and advises clients on compliance issues and the strategic importance of regulatory change.

Michelle de Kluyver is Of Counsel at Norton Rose LLP. Michelle acts for banks, corporates and private equity funds primarily in complex cross-border mergers and acquisitions and joint venture disputes, shareholder disputes and investigations. Michelle was closely involved in providing advice relating to the Companies Act 2006, in particular the changes relating to shareholder derivative claims under Part 11 and also advises on collective redress. Michelle is a qualified solicitor advocate. Her litigation experience covers the High Court (Commercial and Companies Courts), Court of Appeal and House of Lords and on the ADR side, mediations and expert determinations. Her arbitration experience includes disputes under the LCIA, ICC, SCCI and UNCITRAL Rules and she has acted for an investor in relation to its claim under a bilateral investment treaty under the ICSID Rules.

Elliot Shear is a partner in the Corporate Group at Nabarro LLP. Elliot specialises in mergers and acquisitions for public and private companies and undertakes a full range of transactional and advisory work for corporate clients and financial institutions. His experience includes advising on corporate law and corporate governance – as well as mergers and acquisitions, flotations and joint ventures. Elliot's sector expertise is particularly in the defence industry – and also financial services. The strength of Elliot's growing reputation was recognised through his inclusion in "The Lawyer" magazine's recent "Hot 100" lawyers.

Vanessa Knapp is a principal consultant of Freshfields Bruckhaus Deringer LLP. In 2007 she was awarded an Order of the British Empire (OBE) for her services to corporate law. She specialises in company law, and mergers and acquisitions. Vanessa was closely involved in the review of company law leading to the Companies Act 2006. She is a member (and former Chairman) of The Law Society Company Law Committee and the CLLS Company Law Sub-committee. She has been a member of the EU expert advisory group providing advice on corporate governance and company law and is the UK representative of the Company Law Committee of the Council of the Bars and Law Societies of the European Union (CCBE).

John Farr was head of the Employment Group at Herbert Smith and a partner from 1982 until 2009. Since then he has been an active consultant at Herbert Smith. He is well-known for his representation of companies and senior individuals in contentious matters. His work covers corporate governance and boardroom disputes; bonus disputes; dismissals and redundancies; pension disputes; High Court applications in connection with restrictive covenants, confidential information and group defections; discrimination and harassment claims. Advisory and corporate work covers, *inter alia*, business transfers; reorganisations and collective redundancies; the devising and introduction of new terms of employment; and the implementation by clients of new UK and European employment and trade union legislation. He has been involved in the employment aspects of various large transactions.

Jemima Coleman advised on a wide range of employment issues, both contentious and non-contentious, as an associate at Herbert Smith before becoming a professional support lawyer. She writes regular client bulletins on developments in employment law, speaks at in-house client seminars and provides tailored client training on recent and forthcoming legislation. Experience of contentious work includes Employment Tribunal claims such as unfair dismissal, disability and sex discrimination and High Court proceedings involving injunctive relief for the enforcement of restrictive covenants. Non-contentious experience includes dealing with the employment aspects of corporate or real estate transactions, in particular the application of the Transfer of Undertakings Regulations to disposals, acquisitions and outsourcings as well as general advisory work.

Paul Lester is a partner in the Corporate Department of Lawrence Graham LLP. He specialises in corporate finance, stock exchange issues, public company takeovers, mergers and acquisitions, joint ventures, partnerships and LLPs, structured property transactions and property investments and funds.

Paul has extensive experience of advising corporate and institutional clients on the full range of corporate transactions both in the UK and internationally.

Caroline Carter has been a partner at Ashurst since 1998. She specialises in non-contentious and contentious employment law, advising listed companies and private equity houses on employment aspects of transactions including public takeovers, IPOs, mergers and acquisitions, restructuring and outsourcing exercises. Her advisory experience encompasses documentation and policy drafting in conjunction with clients' risk management strategy, corporate governance and boardroom issues, senior executive appointments and terminations, advice to remuneration committees and non-executives, and training for directors; dispute resolution experience includes protecting confidential information and enforcing post-termination restrictions, team moves, bonus and incentives disputes, high level workplace and other mediation; recent employment and employment appeal tribunal experience includes whistleblowing, equality and discrimination cases. BA (Hons) University of London.

Jonathan Marks has been a partner at Slaughter and May since 1997. He has a corporate and corporate finance practice and has been involved in a wide range of domestic and cross-border transactions including demutualisations, fund-raisings, IPOs, joint ventures and private and public acquisitions. Jonathan has advised a number of listed and other clients on constitutional, corporate governance and regulatory matters. He also has experience of advising on the corporate aspects of banking, capital markets and other financing transactions and outsourcing and other commercial agreements.

Michael Hatchard is practice leader of the English law facility at Skadden. The UK practice areas mirror those of Skadden's international practice generally, focusing on cross-border mergers and acquisitions, anti-trust, acquisition finance, corporate finance, project development, taxation, arbitration and litigation.

He has extensive experience in mergers, strategic investments and divestments including transactions governed by the Takeover Directive and Member State implementation legislation. His practice has also included financial restructurings and reorganisations. Michael has been identified as a leading rainmaker in European M&A and has consistently ranked in the top performance levels of European M&A league tables. His background in global securities transactions includes primary representation in connection with many of the UK privatisations and a broad range of primary and secondary securities offerings.

He is a member of the CLLS Company Law Sub-Committee.

Hamish Anderson is a partner in the banking department at Norton Rose LLP, specialising in insolvency. Hamish qualified as a solicitor in 1973 and has been a licensed insolvency practitioner since 1987. He is a past president and former council member of the Insolvency Lawyers' Association and a former council member of the Association of Business Recovery Professionals. Hamish is currently the chairman of the City of London Law Society Insolvency Committee and a member of both the Insolvency Practices Council and the Editorial Board for "Insolvency Law & Practice". He is also a Visiting Senior Research Fellow, Centre for Insolvency Law and Policy, Kingston University, a Visiting professor at Nottingham Trent University and a regular speaker and writer on insolvency matters.

Angela Hayes is a partner at Mayer Brown International LLP. She is a leading practitioner in FSA investigations and proceedings, financial services litigation and white collar crime and also has a financial regulation advisory practice.

She speaks and writes regularly on financial services regulatory topics and edits the leading textbook on FSA investigations, "*A Practitioner's Guide to FSA Investigations and Enforcement*" published by City & Financial.

Stephen Robins is a barrister at 3–4 South Square. He was called to the Bar in 2001. He has a general commercial practice with a focus on insolvency and company law.

David Allison is a barrister at 3–4 South Square. He was called to the Bar in 1998. His practice encompasses all aspects of general commercial and business litigation; corporate restructuring and insolvency; banking and financial services; insurance and reinsurance; and professional negligence.

Contents

5 Fair Dealing and Connected Persons
Vanessa Knapp
Principal Consultant
Freshfields Bruckhaus Deringer LLP

6 Service Contracts and Remuneration
John Farr
Partner
Jemima Coleman
Professional Support Lawyer
Herbert Smith

Chapter 1

Introduction

Tim Boxell

Partner

Slaughter and May

This Guide for practitioners – company directors and their professional advisers – is now in its fourth edition. Practitioners are only too aware that there is no simple model role for the company director. This is partly because of the way in which company law and the codes of corporate governance have developed in the UK, but also because of the diverse nature of the purposes and interests which corporate structures serve. Practitioners will want to master all aspects of the regulatory regime, both legal and voluntary, which prescribe the conduct to be expected of directors, as the consequences for breach can be serious. Further, practitioners need to be aware of, and be in a position to react to, changes which occur in the regulatory regime with which they are faced.

The roles of directors and their duties and responsibilities will vary according to the type of company they serve and, to some extent, to the nature of their position, as well as the level of regulation. But as a preliminary, practitioners may ask whether there is any underlying framework to which they may refer for guidance and from which they may infer what is expected of them.

Since the third edition of this Guide was published, almost all of the Companies Act 2006 ("CA 2006" or the "Act") has now come into force. The CA 2006 applies to all UK companies, small or large, private or public. The CA 2006, when enacted,[1] consisted of

---

[1] Subsequent amendments have been made by statutory instruments.

1,300 sections and 16 schedules with a view to meeting the previous government's promise to simplify company law and deregulate small companies. Some of the provisions simply restated the existing law, but many brought about a fundamental change in how companies would need to be governed in the future. Perhaps the most notable change for directors was that their duties were codified for the first time (Part 10 of the Act).

Other changes in the legislative and regulatory landscape have also occurred – for example, an updated version of the Combined Code, or the UK Corporate Governance Code as it is now known, has been published, which applies to listed companies for accounting years beginning on or after 29 June 2010. Moreover, the Financial Reporting Council has published a new Stewardship Code[2] which aims to enhance the quality of engagement between institutional investors and boards of listed companies and is seen as complementary to the UK Corporate Governance Code. It is hoped that the principles in the Stewardship Code will encourage better dialogue between investors and boards as well as promote greater transparency of how investors oversee investee companies. At European level, the Transparency Directive imposes obligations on listed companies to make further notifications to the market in a bid to improve market transparency. For companies regulated by the Financial Services Authority ("FSA"), new developments have affected the way in which firms and the conduct of their directors are supervised.

The abolition of the FSA and regulatory reform was announced by the Chancellor of the Exchequer in a recent Mansion House speech[3] and further details were subsequently given to the House of Commons by the Financial Secretary to the Treasury. The proposals include the creation of a new prudential regulator (the Prudential Regulatory Authority), as a subsidiary of the Bank of England, a Consumer Protection and Markets Authority and a Financial Policy Committee (responsible for macro-prudential regulation). The transition is to be completed in 2012. It remains to be seen exactly what the effects will be, but

---

[2] The UK Stewardship Code, 2 July 2010.
[3] Speech at the Lord Mayor's Dinner for Bankers and Merchants of the City of London by the Chancellor of the Exchequer, 16 June 2010.

one can expect "more intense supervision"[4] as part of the new government's promise to preserve the UK's reputation for transparency and efficiency in business and the UK's position as one of the world's leading global financial centres.

1.1 CA 2006 reforms

The CA 2006 is a complex piece of legislation, the consideration of much of which is outside the scope of this Guide. The following chapters, however, pick out and examine a number of areas of particular relevance to directors' duties and responsibilities, a few of which are highlighted in this introduction. It may still be a little too early to assess the full impact the provisions in the CA 2006 have had on company law – much of its effect remains uncertain. However, some practical guidance has been published and there has also been a steady stream of cases testing new sections. Together, these should, for the time being, give some indication and a degree of comfort to practitioners on how the CA 2006 should be applied in practice.

1.1.1 *Codification of directors' duties*

When the CA 2006 was enacted, Chapter 2 of Part 10 introduced, for the first time in the UK, what appeared to be an authoritative statement given by statute of what directors' duties actually are. The general duties owed by directors had been built up over many years by case law. The Company Law Review ("CLR") (commissioned in 1998 and comprising an independent group of experts, practitioners and business people) believed that there was a need to make the law in this area more consistent, certain, accessible and comprehensible, and recommended that there should be a statutory statement of directors' general duties.[5] The Law Commission and the Scottish Law Commission also recommended that there should be a statutory statement of a director's

---

4 Response by the Chairman of the FSA, Lord Turner, 16 June 2010.
5 The Company Law Review Steering Group presented its Final Report (*Company Law Reforms: Modern Company Law for a Competitive Economy*) to the Secretary of State for Trade and Industry on 26 July 2001.

main fiduciary duties and his duty of care and skill.[6] The CLR recommended that the statutory statement should largely be a codification of current law. However, the CLR also wanted greater clarity on what is expected of directors and to make the law more accessible, as well as to make development of the law in this area more predictable (but without hindering development of the law by the courts).

The previous government accepted the recommendations and, thereby, set itself a challenge: as the government acknowledged in the Explanatory Notes to the CA 2006, codification is not just a matter of transposing wording taken from judgments into legislative propositions; judgments are directed at particular cases and any principles which may be stated will rarely be exhaustive. The previous government considered it important that the connections with other areas of the law (such as trusts and agency) should not be lost, so that company law may continue to reflect developments elsewhere. Simply put, the challenge was to balance precision against the need for continued flexibility and development.

The Act specifies in Sections 171 to 177 the general duties that are owed by a director to the company. These duties are set out in more detail in Section 1.2 below. As for the interrelationship with the common law rules and equitable principles, the Act provides:

> "(3) The general duties are based on certain common law rules and equitable principles as they apply in relation to directors and have effect in place of those rules and principles as regards the duties owed to a company by a director.
> (4) The general duties shall be interpreted and applied in the same way as common law rules or equitable principles, and regard shall be had to the corresponding common law rules and equitable principles in interpreting and applying the general duties."[7]

---

[6] Joint report *Company Directors: Regulatory Conflicts of Interest and Formulating a Statement of Duties*, September 1999 (Law Com No 261, Scot Law Com No 173).
[7] Section 170 CA 2006.

That these duties are to be interpreted in the same way as the common law duties which the specified general duties have effect in place of may cause some difficulties, as the wording of the new statutory duties does not necessarily correlate exactly with how those duties were previously expressed or understood.

The majority of the sections of the CA 2006 imposing the general duties came into force on 1 October 2007, but the duty to avoid conflicts of interests did not come into force until 1 October 2008, to give companies more time to amend their articles of association to reflect the new provisions.

Of course, the specified general duties do not cover all the duties that a director may owe to the company. They are the general duties for a director to have in mind in carrying out his duties but there are other specific duties imposed (such as the duty to file accounts and reports with the registrar of companies[8]).

The CA 2006 makes changes to the manner in which a breach, or possible breach, of a director's duty may be ratified. The Act abolishes the right of a director to ratify his own breach of duty by providing that the necessary majority must be obtained disregarding votes in favour at the shareholder meeting by the director and any member connected with him.[9] Curiously though, it does not abolish the right for directors to vote in their capacity as shareholders to authorise in advance acts which may be in breach of their duties. Directors will therefore have an incentive to seek prior authorisation of acts which would otherwise constitute a breach of their duties. Helpfully, the CA 2006 does confirm that a substantial property transaction with a director may be entered into conditional upon shareholder approval; previously there was some doubt as to whether this was allowed, or whether the approval had to be obtained before the transaction could be entered into.[10] The Act also allows loans to be made by a company to its directors, provided that they are first approved by shareholder resolution.[11]

---

[8] Section 441 CA 2006.
[9] Section 239 CA 2006.
[10] Section 190 CA 2006.
[11] Section 197 CA 2006.

1.1.2 Derivative claims

Closely linked to the codification of directors' duties is the provision introduced by the CA 2006 putting derivative claims by shareholders onto a statutory footing.[12] A derivative claim is a claim by a member in respect of a cause of action vested in the company and seeking relief on behalf of the company. These claims can be brought only in respect of a cause of action arising from an actual or proposed act or omission involving negligence, default, breach of duty or breach of trust by a director of the company (including the duty to exercise reasonable care, skill and diligence). Once a shareholder has commenced a derivative action, he will have to apply to the court for permission to continue the action. If it appears to the court that the application and the evidence filed in support of it do not disclose a *prima facie* case for giving permission, the court must dismiss the application and may make any consequential order that it considers appropriate.[13] Permission must be refused if the court is satisfied that:

(a) a person acting in accordance with Section 172 CA 2006 (duty to promote the interests of the company) would not seek to continue the claim;

(b) the act or omission has not yet occurred and has been authorised by the company; or

(c) the act or omission has occurred, but was authorised before it occurred or has since been ratified by the company.[14]

The court must also consider further factors before deciding whether or not to grant permission, including whether the member is acting in good faith and whether the relevant act or omission could be authorised or ratified by the company. The court is required to have particular regard to any evidence before it as to the views of members of the company who have no personal interest in the matter.

There had been some concern that these new provisions would encourage activist shareholders to commence (or at least to

---

[12] Section 260 CA 2006.
[13] Section 261 CA 2006.
[14] Section 263(2) CA 2006.

threaten to commence) proceedings more readily. However, since these provisions have come into force, there has not been a huge raft of derivative action claims and, in fact, the attitude of the courts has prevented any significant increase in the number of derivative actions. Five major cases have involved derivative claims, where the court had to consider under Section 263(2) whether a hypothetical director, acting in accordance with Section 172, would continue the action.[15] The five decisions have not signalled any great renaissance of derivative claims: the permission of the courts to continue the case was refused in three of the these cases and in the two other cases the issue was adjourned pending a resolution of various disputes relating to the derivative claims, such as a dispute over the ownership of the company. These cases illustrate the judicial control over shareholder claims and the general reluctance of the courts to entertain derivative claims. Little use has been made of this new statutory procedure and so it seems that the status quo has been maintained.

1.1.3 Directors' reports

Some years ago, the then government announced that quoted companies would be required to prepare and publicise an operating and financial review. However, this was dropped in November 2005, as part of the previous government's drive to stop "gold plating" European legislation. Instead, companies, other than small companies,[16] must prepare a "business review" as part of their directors' report under the CA 2006. The Act imposes miscellaneous requirements in respect of reports that are required to be produced. Section 416 CA 2006 states that the reports must state:

(a) the names of the persons who, at any time during the financial year, were directors of the company; and
(b) the principal activities of the company in the course of the year.

---

[15] *Mission Capital Plc* v *Sinclair* [2008] BCC 866; *Fanmailuk.com Ltd* v *Cooper* [2008] BCC 877; *Franbar Holdings Ltd* v *Patel* [2008] BCC 885; *Stimpson* v *Southern Landlords Association* [2009] EWHC 2072 (Ch); *Iesini* v *Westrip Holdings Ltd* [2009] EWHC 2526 (Ch).

[16] If a company is entitled to the small companies exemption in relation to the directors' report, its directors' report does not need to contain a business review (Section 417(1) CA 2006).

Companies, other than small companies, must also state the amount (if any) that the directors recommend should be paid as dividend. Further detailed content to be included in the directors' report is set out in regulations made under Section 416(4) CA 2006, the applicability of which depends on the company's size.[17] Listed companies are also subject to the Disclosure and Transparency Rules, which require a corporate governance statement to be made either in the directors' report or separately elsewhere.

The Act also provides that a director is liable to compensate the company for any loss suffered by it as a result of any untrue or misleading statement in the directors' report, the directors' remuneration report or a summary financial statement derived from such report, or any omission from such reports. Importantly, however, a director is only so liable if he knew the statement to be untrue or misleading or was reckless as to whether the statement was untrue or misleading or he knew the omission to be dishonest concealment of a material fact (the "safe harbour").[18] Moreover, the director will not be subject to any liability to any person other than the company resulting from reliance by that person or another on information in respect to which the section applies (although this does not affect liability for a civil penalty or for a criminal offence). There is, it would seem, consequently much to be gained by ensuring that as much of the narrative reporting of the company as possible is brought within this safe harbour by including it within the directors' reports.

The "safe harbour" provided in Section 463 CA 2006 operates as a matter of English law and it may not be effective to exclude liability for a claim brought outside the UK; for example, where a claimant receives a company's reports containing misleading statements outside the UK. In light of this, companies have been giving consideration to including disclaimers of liability (except for that under English law). Such a disclaimer may not be effective but it would not be prejudicial and it has become increasingly

---

[17] The Large and Medium-sized Companies and Groups (Accounts and Reports) Regulations 2008 (SI 2008/410); the Small Companies and Groups (Accounts and Directors' Report) Regulations 2008 (SI 2008/409); the Companies Act 2006 (Amendment) (Accounts and Reports) Regulations 2008 (SI 2008/393).

[18] Section 463 CA 2006.

the market practice to include a "forward looking statement" disclaimer in connection with companies' financial reporting.

Directors of companies which have their securities traded on a UK regulated market[19] should also bear in mind that there is a separate liability under Section 90A Financial Services and Markets Act 2000 ("FSMA") for misleading statements. Section 90A(6) provides that only the company, and not its directors, will be liable to the acquirers of the companies' securities, for misleading statements in, or omission of any matter required to be published in, the relevant reports. However, Subsection (8) of Section 90A provides that this does not preclude liability that may attach to the individual directors by virtue of a court order,[20] restitution required by the FSA[21] and liability for a civil penalty or a criminal offence.[22] As of 1 October 2010, a new regime extends the Section 90A FSMA liability to all information which is published, or the availability of which is published, by means of a recognised information service.[23] This extension clearly means that directors of all relevant companies should be more alert to the potential Section 90A FSMA liability, when they are publishing any information in relation to the company.

1.1.4 Shadow directors

A shadow director is any person in accordance with whose directions or instructions the directors of the company are accustomed to act, although a person is not deemed to be a shadow director by reason only that directors act on advice given by him in a professional capacity.[24] Under the Act, the general directors' duties are expressed to apply to shadow directors where, and to the extent that, they would have applied previously under the corresponding common law rules or

---

[19] This currently covers companies with securities traded on the Main Market of the London Stock Exchange but not AIM. However, starting 1 October 2010 (*see* note 23 below), the regime is extended to all other multilateral trading facilities such as AIM, PSM and PLUS.

[20] Section 382 FSMA.

[21] Section 384 FSMA.

[22] Section 90A(8) FMSA.

[23] The Financial Services and Markets Act 2000 (Liability of Issuers) Regulations 2010 (SI 2010/1192).

[24] Section 251 CA 2006, restating the definition in Section 741(2) and (3) Companies Act 1985.

equitable principles.[25] This means that the laws relating to shadow directors are not comprehensively dealt with in the Act itself, but instead practitioners are forced to fall back on the previous, uncertain common law in this area. Recent cases such as *Holland v Commissioners of Revenue and Customs*[26] and *Secretary of State for Industry v Hall*[27] continue to develop the less than certain common law rules on the circumstances in which a person will be considered a *de facto* or shadow director. Nevertheless, there is still little to be told of precisely how the common law rules and equitable principles relating to shadow directors will sit alongside the codified directors' duties.

1.1.5 Register of directors' addresses

Previously, directors who were subject to the risk of violence or intimidation were permitted to keep their home addresses confidential. The CA 2006 contains broader protections for all directors. The Act permits a director to provide a service address for the public record rather than his home address and this service address may be the company's registered office. The directors must also provide their usual residential addresses to the company, and the company must maintain a new register of directors' usual residential addresses, which will not be open to public inspection. The Act imposes an obligation on the Registrar of Companies not to disclose information as to a director's usual residential address as part of the material available for public inspection.[28]

1.2 Duties and responsibilities

Previously, this area of the law has been fragmented and difficult, owing in large part to its common law origins superimposed by statutory (and even self-regulatory) provisions. The CA 2006 now provides a list of the general duties of directors, namely:

---

[25] Section 170(5) CA 2006.
[26] [2009] EWCA Civ 625.
[27] [2009] BCC 190.
[28] Section 242 CA 2006.

(a) to act in accordance with the company's constitution and only exercise powers for the purposes which they are conferred;[29]
(b) to promote the success of the company;[30]
(c) to exercise independent judgment;[31]
(d) to use reasonable care, skill and diligence;[32]
(e) to avoid conflicts of interest;[33]
(f)   not to accept benefits from third parties;[34] and
(g) to declare an interest in a proposed transaction or arrangement.[35]

As mentioned above, these general duties are based on certain common law rules and equitable principles and apply in place of those rules and principles as regards the duties owed to a company by its directors.[36] However, the general duties are to be interpreted and applied in the same way as the previous common law rules or equitable principles, and regard is to be had to the corresponding common law rules and equitable principles in interpreting and applying the general duties.[37] Hence, the extent to which they actually increase clarity is debatable. The obvious benefit for directors is that they now have a list of their general duties available in one place.

All of the above duties came into force on 1 October 2007, aside from the duty to avoid conflicts of interest which did not come into force until 1 October 2008 to enable companies to make provision in their articles of association to allow conflicts of interest to be authorised. Exactly how these duties are to be interpreted is not entirely certain. However, since the last edition of this book, some practical guidance on how these duties should be applied has been offered by institutional bodies such as the Institute of Chartered Secretaries and

---

[29] Section 171 CA 2006.
[30] Section 172 CA 2006.
[31] Section 173 CA 2006.
[32] Section 174 CA 2006.
[33] Section 175 CA 2006.
[34] Section 176 CA 2006.
[35] Section 177 CA 2006.
[36] Section 170(3) CA 2006.
[37] Section 170(4) CA 2006.

Administrators ("ICSA").[38] Although these duties will be examined in more detail in other Chapters, it is worth touching briefly on some aspects.

1.2.1 The duty to promote the success of the company

This requires a director to "act in the way he considers, in good faith, would be most likely to promote the success of the company for the benefit of its members as a whole".[39]

The concept of the members as a whole is discussed in more detail later in this Chapter. A useful starting point was given during the Company Law Review, when the Attorney-General stated in the House of Lords:

> "... what is success? The starting point is that it is essentially for the members of the company to define the objectives that they wish to achieve. Success means what the members collectively want the company to achieve. For a commercial company, success will usually mean long-term increase in value. For certain companies, such as charities and community interest companies, it will mean the attainment of the objectives for which the company has been established. But one can be more refined than that. A company's constitution and the decisions that a company makes can also go on to be more specific about what is the appropriate success model for the company. I have indicated that usually for a company it will be a long-term increase in value, but I can imagine commercial companies that would have a different objective as to their success."[40]

1.2.2 The duty to avoid conflicts of interest

A director of a company must avoid a situation in which he has, or can have, a direct or indirect interest that conflicts with the

---

[38] ICSA Guidance on Directors' General Duties, 18 October 2007. The guidance is intended primarily for public or listed companies but much of it can be applied to private companies as well.
[39] Section 172(1) CA 2006.
[40] House of Lords, Hansard, 6 February, 2006.

interests of the company. There will, however, be no breach of duty if the situation cannot reasonably be regarded as likely to give rise to a conflict of interest.[41] This duty has been controversial as it raised the question of whether directors who hold multiple directorships would be in breach of their duties as a result of this new express duty.

The duty will also not be infringed if the matter has been authorised by the directors.[42] There is an argument that authorisation obtained ahead of a director's appointment in respect of possible future conflicts would be sufficient authorisation, but it seems that the better view is that a specific authorisation will be required in respect of a matter arising after the appointment.

For private companies whose constitution does not prevent it, authorisation may be given by directors who have no interest in the matter giving rise to the conflict.[43] This represents a departure from the previous law, which required that any such matter had to be authorised instead by the members of the company. A public company's constitution must include a provision enabling the directors to authorise the matter and the authorisation must be given by directors who have no interest in the matter.[44]

Some guidance on directors' conflicts of interest has been published by the GC100 which concludes that most companies (including public companies) will want to amend their articles of association to include a general power for directors to authorise conflicts of interest.[45] The GC100 paper, among other things, highlights potential situations of conflict and it also provides suggested procedures for authorising conflict situations and reviewing authorisations.

---

[41] Section 175(4)(a) CA 2006. Applied in *Re Allied Business & Financial Consultants Ltd, O'Donnell v Shanahan* [2009] 1 BCLC 328.
[42] Section 175(4)(b) CA 2006.
[43] Section 175(5)(a) CA 2006.
[44] Section 175(5)(b) CA 2006.
[45] The Association for the General Counsel and Company Secretaries of FTSE 100 companies (GC100), Companies Act 2006 – Directors' Conflicts of Interests, 18 January 2008.

1.2.3   The level of reasonable care, skill and diligence

Directors are required to exercise reasonable care, skill and diligence.[46] This begs the question "what does that mean?" Traditionally, it was thought that the level of care and skill required to be a director was fairly minimal. Directors need no qualification to hold their post, and so the test appeared to be a subjective one against each individual director's own level of knowledge and skill. This has found less favour with time, and is now completely replaced by a dual (objective and subjective) standard of care, skill and diligence in the CA 2006. The Act expressly provides:[47]

> "[t]his means the care, skill and diligence that would be exercised by a reasonably diligent person with–
>
> > (a)   the general knowledge, skill and experience that may reasonably be expected of a person carrying out the functions carried out by the director in relation to the company, and
> >
> > (b)   the general knowledge, skill and experience that the director has."

This replicates the test set out in Section 214 Insolvency Act 1986 and consequently the case law in relation to that area will remain of great importance in setting the scope of the new duty. Hoffmann LJ had previously held that the duty of care for a director was set out accurately in Section 214, and applied that principle more widely in relation to directors' duties generally.[48] Cases under the Company Directors Disqualification Act 1986 may also be helpful in determining whether a director is in breach of his duty of reasonable care, skill and diligence. A notable case is *Re Continental Assurance Co of London Plc,*[49] where a non-executive director was disqualified, even though he did not know of the wrongful conduct in question. It was held that any competent director in his position would have known what was going on and, by virtue of the fact of his ignorance of what

---

[46]   Section 174 CA 2006.
[47]   Section 174(2) CA 2006.
[48]   *Re D'Jan of London Ltd* [1993] BCC 646.
[49]   [1996] BCC 888.

was going on, he was incompetent. It seems that this would also lead to a breach of his duty to exercise reasonable care, skill and diligence under the CA 2006.

In *Re Barings Plc (No 5)*,[50] it was established that there is a continuing obligation on directors to acquire and maintain a sufficient knowledge and understanding of the company's business for the proper discharge of their duties. It is therefore critical that a person accepting the office of director is aware not only of the nature of the duties that he owes to the company and its members and keeps up to date with the nature of the duties, but also acquires and maintains an appropriate knowledge of the company's business.[51] Exact parameters will vary according to the nature of the company and the individual experience and skill that the director in question possesses.

1.3 Further regulation

Although the codification of directors' duties in the CA 2006 is helpful in bringing certain duties together, it should be remembered that it is not an exhaustive list of directors' duties. As well as the specific duties and obligations imposed elsewhere in the CA 2006, there are numerous other regulatory requirements. Thus, for example, directors of listed companies are required to comply with a series of other sets of rules, such as the Listing Rules, the Takeover Code, the Disclosure and Transparency Rules (which implement the Transparency Directive into UK law) and the UK Corporate Governance Code. The new UK Corporate Governance Code was published in May 2010 and applies to reporting periods on or after 29 June 2010.

The growth in the number of companies listed on the Alternative Investment Market ("AIM") has meant that the AIM Rules for Companies now apply to a significant number of companies,

---

[50] [1999] 1 BCLC 433.
[51] Indeed, as regards to listed companies, Section B of the Main Principles of the UK Corporate Governance Code requires that all directors "should receive induction on joining the board and should regularly update and refresh their skills and knowledge".

and these also contain various regulations and duties of which directors of AIM listed companies need to be aware.

The emphasis of these rules and codes remains on the need for transparency and accountability. The rules are increasingly being put on a statutory footing – for example, Part 28 CA 2006 gave the Takeover Panel statutory authority to make rules and regulations in relation to takeovers and mergers of companies, and gives it the power to demand information from companies and to impose sanctions for non-compliance.

The FSA is moving increasingly towards more principles-based regulation, which will require directors of companies regulated by the FSA to take a more active role in how their business is run. The FSA operates an approved persons regime, whereby people wishing to be directors or controllers of regulated companies need to apply to the FSA for approval. Such people will need to demonstrate that they have the necessary skill, expertise and integrity to take on such a role. It would be an understatement to say that one of the effects of the recent banking crisis is the pro-active approach of the FSA when it comes to monitoring the approved persons regime. The economic crisis has made the FSA review the corporate governance of the regulated sector very closely and the FSA has certainly tightened its control over the conduct of such companies' directors. This is highlighted, for example, by the new Financial Services Act 2010 which contains a provision that gives the FSA the power to penalise any person found to have been performing controlled functions without being an approved person.

1.4 The company's interests

The established common law rules provide that directors owe their duties to their company. There was much debate at the beginning of the Company Law Review process as to whether directors' duties should continue to be owed solely to the company, except in limited cases, or whether directors should be required as a matter of law to account directly to third parties (e.g. suppliers, local communities, the environment, employees, etc.). The conclusion was that the existing position should remain, and this was confirmed by the CA 2006.[52] However, as part of their duty to promote the success of the company, as outlined above, directors must have regard to what the previous government termed "enlightened shareholder value". Consequently, a director must act in the way that he considers, in good faith, would be most likely to promote the success of the company for the benefit of its members as a whole, and in doing so have regard (amongst other matters) to:

(a)   the likely long-term consequences of any decision;
(b)   the interests of the company's employees;
(c)   the need to foster business relationships with suppliers, customers and others;
(d)   the impact of the company's operations on the community and the environment;
(e)   the desirability of the company maintaining a reputation for high standards of business conduct; and
(f)   the need to act fairly as between members of the company.[53]

The previous government's desire to introduce this list gave rise to considerable debate during the process. The government made it clear that directors have to do more than merely pay lip service to each of these factors, but must give each due and careful consideration when making decisions. Critics have consequently argued that this will make decision making more onerous, result in an increase in documentation and an increased likelihood that directors' decisions come under the scrutiny of the courts. The concern here was that the potential increase in bureaucracy may lead directors to be more risk-averse, which in turn may not be in the interests of their company.

However, there is considerable support for the argument that directors of well-run companies already have regard to these sorts of factors in their decision making in any event, and that having them listed in statute will not have much effect on such

---

[52]   Section 170(1) CA 2006.
[53]   Section 172 CA 2006.

companies. The Attorney-General, Lord Goldsmith, confirmed that he felt it was unlikely that the duty to have regard to these factors would have much practical effect on well-run companies and, when pressed as to why they were to be included in the CA 2006, stated:

> "If there are people at the moment who do not have regard to these factors then – on the basis of the best business practices that we have had explained to us by some of the best business leaders in this country – they should."[54]

Further, directors are only required to *have regard* to these factors; a director is entitled to take a decision that would, for example, inevitably have an adverse environmental impact, provided that he had regard to the impact and weighed up what he considered, in good faith, would be most likely to promote the success of the company. There will be no breach of statutory duty unless the directors fail to have regard to the factors listed. Indeed, as the director's duty is owed to the company, there may be situations where a decision would need to be taken for the success of the company as a whole despite it having such an adverse impact. It would seem prudent for directors to ensure that their decisions are appropriately documented, reflecting the due regard paid to the list of factors set out above. That said, one should guard against turning compliance into a "box-ticking" exercise. Practice will naturally develop, but it seems unlikely that practice for well-run companies will necessarily have changed dramatically.

So far, the practical effect on the boardroom has varied, quite naturally, for different companies based on the facts of each case. A paper trail may be appropriate in some cases where very significant decisions are made. However, arguably in some cases, if the reference to specific duties in the board minutes has not been part of the relevant company's ordinary practice, referring to the duties on an ad hoc basis may suggest that the directors may not have had regard to their duties at other times. One relatively easy practical step is to circulate with board papers an aide-memoire to directors' duties; one should thereby be able to

---

[54] House of Lords, Hansard, 9 May 2006.

demonstrate that the directors were aware of their duties at the time of the resolution.

The GC100[55] has issued best-practice guidelines for those concerned about the potential increase in bureaucracy. Where the nature of the decision being taken by the directors is such that it is supported by a formal process, that process need only specifically record consideration of the duties where the particular circumstances make it particularly necessary or relevant. The default position should be not to include any references to the specific CA 2006 directors' duties in the board minutes.

The general duty owed by a director to the company is to act in the way he considers, in good faith, would be most likely to promote the success of the company for the benefit of the members as a whole. Maximising value for shareholders over the long-term may well be the primary aim, but it is possible that the constitution of a company provide that the company should have different aims, such as achieving a particular goal (e.g. completing a construction project) or even maximising dividend revenues in the short term. It would be for the members of the company to set the purposes of the company, and these could be amended subsequently by special resolution passed at an annual general meeting ("AGM") or general meeting ("GM"). Where, or to the extent that, the purposes of the company consist of or include purposes other than the benefit of its members, the reference to promoting the success of the company for the benefit of its members can be taken as a reference to achieving those purposes.[56]

Certain situations may qualify these general principles. For example, on a takeover offer, the best price available to current shareholders may be the primary concern for the current board of directors of the target company. While the relationship between director and shareholder does not of itself give rise to direct responsibility, directors may assume a responsibility to shareholders directly when the circumstances require. An

---

[55] GC100's guidance on the Companies Act 2006 (Directors' Duties), 7 February 2007.
[56] Section 172(2) CA 2006.

example would be where a director makes a personal represen-tation to shareholders to induce them to transfer shares in his company and the director has a high degree of inside knowl-edge in relation to the shareholders.[57]

When a company is in financial difficulties, the interests of cred-itors become paramount. Directors will still need to have regard to the matters (and those stakeholders) set out above (e.g. the company's members and its employees), but the duty to promote the success of the company is expressly stated to have effect subject to any enactment or rule of law requiring directors, in certain circumstances, to consider or act in the best interests of the creditors of the company.[58] It will not always be easy for directors to see when the "tipping point" is reached, and the company is no longer able to trade its way out of trouble but must instead prepare for the onset of insolvency. In the wake of the recent banking crisis, the need for directors to consider the interests of the company's creditors and be mindful of the "tipping point" has been in sharper focus. There has been an increasing number of companies facing financial difficulties and such companies have benefited from insolvency and debt restructuring tools such as pre-pack administrations and credi-tors' voluntary arrangements, highlighting the relevance of the need for directors to give due attention to the interests of the company's creditors. In practice, directors of companies of doubtful solvency are faced with some very difficult decisions in order to attempt to minimise the loss to creditors but still act to promote the success of the company as a whole.

1.5   Nature of companies

General principles and the background to their development provide a good framework for practitioners determining the duties and responsibilities of directors. However, it has always been important to apply these general principles in the context of the type of company and of the particular role of that director. As the general duties under the CA 2006 are to be

---

[57]   This was the situation in *Platt and another* v *Platt* [1999] 2 BCLC 745.
[58]   Section 172(3) CA 2006.

interpreted by using common law and equitable principles, it would seem that this should still be the case even now that the duties have been codified.

The majority of companies in the UK are private limited companies. Many are owner-managed, in some cases effectively housing a sole trader, in others operating more like partnerships. For many of these companies, there will be little practical need to distinguish between the interests of directors and shareholders. However, there remains a need for legal safeguards to be in place should things go wrong. The luxury of limited liability enjoyed by the owners of these companies calls for at least minimum standards of behaviour for the benefit of third parties. The CA 2006 specifies what many of these standards are, and the duties under the Insolvency Act 1986 will also apply for the protection of creditors when things go wrong.

The previous government attempted to deregulate small, private companies in the course of drawing up the CA 2006. The idea was that certain minimum standards should apply to all companies, and as companies get larger, becoming listed or otherwise, further standards should then be imposed. Private companies will benefit from:

(a) shorter *pro forma* articles of association;
(b) the removal of the requirement for a company secretary;
(c) the removal of the requirement to hold an AGM;
(d) the removal of the requirement for unanimity in respect of written resolutions;
(e) the relaxation of the prohibition on granting financial assistance; and
(f) the introduction of a streamlined procedure for capital reductions.

In companies in which there are numerous shareholders, especially those that are listed, there is much more of a distinction between management and ownership. The duties and responsibilities of directors are not blurred by the coincidence of ownership. Directors will have substantial freedom to carry on the business of the company, but will find that there are many regulatory potholes into which they could potentially fall. By way of example, the CA 2006 imposes personal liability on directors should they knowingly or recklessly allow untrue or misleading statements to be published in certain directors' reports (although as mentioned above, there is a potentially useful safe harbour as a director will only be liable if he knew or was reckless as to whether the statement was untrue or misleading and he is only liable to compensate the company and not any other party).[59]

In addition, in the context of regulated entities, the FSA has the power to remove its approval of a director if it considers that the director is no longer a fit and proper person to carry on a regulated business, effectively preventing such a person from being the director of any regulated entity. Regulated and listed companies must comply with very high standards of disclosure and transparency in their dealings with the public, and the responsibility for these high standards rests with the directors and managers of those companies. The recent banking crisis has had its part in making the FSA more interventionist in various areas, including on occasions in respect of directors. It is expected that this regulatory trend will continue with a view to restoring public confidence and trust in the market.

1.6   The particular role of non-executive directors

The role of non-executive directors remains the subject of much discussion and debate, particularly in relation to listed and FSA-regulated companies. Similar to the position prior to its enactment, the CA 2006 makes no distinction between the duties owed to a company by its executive directors and its non-executive directors,[60] and so all directors owe similar duties. As mentioned above, developments in the law (both through the courts and statutory reform) as well as corporate governance developments have meant that the duties of the non-executive director now go far beyond simply attending board meetings. Their duty of care has arguably expanded along with this, and they will clearly owe duties to the company according to their role on the board and committees of the board, as well as having

---

[59] Section 463 CA 2006.
[60] Section 250 CA 2006 states that "director" includes any person occupying the position of director, by whatever name called.

the general CA 2006 duties, including the duty to exercise reasonable care, skill and diligence. Pursuant to Section 174(2) CA 2006 the duty to exercise reasonable care, skill and diligence is tested against the care, skill and diligence that would be exercised by a reasonably diligent person with:

(a) the general knowledge, skill and experience that may reasonably be expected of a person carrying out the functions carried out by the director in relation to the company (an objective test); and

(b) the general knowledge, skill and experience that the director has (a subjective test).

There appears to be a tendency towards non-executive directors taking on the crucial role of preserving good governance standards on the board of any major company, listed or otherwise, as evidenced by the UK Corporate Governance Code. For example, the main principle and supporting principle to paragraph A4 provides that:

> "As part of their role as members of a unitary board, non-executive directors should constructively challenge and help develop proposals on strategy. Non-executive directors should scrutinise the performance of management in meeting agreed goals and objectives and monitor the reporting of performance. They should satisfy themselves on the integrity of financial information and that financial controls and systems of risk management are robust and defensible. They are responsible for determining appropriate levels of remuneration of executive directors and have a prime role in appointing, and where necessary removing, executive directors, and in succession planning."

The banking crisis prompted the FSA to call for more of an active involvement from the non-executive directors of companies in the banking or regulated sector. The Turner Review of October 2008 identified the skill level and time commitments of non-executive directors as one of the key dimensions of required improvement in corporate governance. This spurred on the review by Sir David Walker, commissioned by the previous government, which re-evaluated the role of non-executive directors for those companies performing regulated activities.[61] Furthermore, the FSA's chief executive, Hector Sants, called for "a different calibre of non-executive directors, with a different mindset."[62]

The courts have clarified that the duties of non-executive directors do not require them to overrule specialist directors (like the finance director) in their specialist fields.[63] However, what is expected of a particular director will generally depend on the facts and circumstances of the particular matter in hand. Lord Woolf (in his extrajudicial capacity) recently suggested that non-executive directors should act like a guard dog that is prepared to bark when necessary.[64]

1.7 Group company directors

Directors of companies which are members of groups of companies often find themselves having to consider their position with great care when intra-group transactions or group interests are in issue, the more so when they are directors of more than one of the companies involved. A director of any company within a group owes a duty to act in the best interests of that company, whatever the competing interests of a subsidiary, parent, group holding company or sister company. While, in certain circumstances, European legislation is framed so as to hold a group as a single economic entity in relation to creditors, as well as in the regulation of competition and employment issues and for capital adequacy purposes, there remains no English law doctrine which permits the directors of one company to take into account the interests of other group companies as such. Given the advantages of limited liability enjoyed by each company within the group, it seems that the previous government and the courts were keen to ensure that the assets of each company are protected for their individual creditors.

---

[61] Walker Review, 26 November 2009.

[62] Speech by Hector Sants, chief executive, FSA Securities & Investment Institute Conference 2009, 7 May 2009.

[63] *Re Continental Assurance of London Plc* [2007] 2 BCLC 287 at paragraph 399.

[64] In response to a question from the audience following the COMBAR Annual Lecture 2008, "Global companies can and should have the highest ethical standards", 21 October 2008.

The statutory duty to avoid conflicts of interest came into force on 1 October 2008 and has led many companies to amend their articles of association to deal with such possible conflicts as well as to give thought as to how their ratification procedures work. Independent directors have been appointed to some boards, which facilitates the ability to take advantage of the CA 2006 provisions for ratification by fellow directors for certain acts. The issue surfaces most frequently in relation to two situations: financings, where the lender often seeks to achieve exposure on a group basis for contractual arrangements, with the obtaining of cross-guarantees and the like; and in intra-group reorganisations, whether undertaken for taxation or other purposes. In the latter context, transactions at an undervalue and the practice of transferring assets intra-group for a nominal consideration give rise to particular difficulties, notwithstanding the relaxation of the rules prohibiting financial assistance for private companies.[65] Some acts are not capable of ratification by either fellow directors or shareholders, and so directors may find themselves with difficult decisions to be made. The position remains that the directors of a subsidiary company (or parent company) owe a duty to that company, even if they owe duties to other companies within the group by virtue of their fellow directorships. They may have regard to the interests of the group if, but only if, it is in the interests of the relevant company to do so.

1.8　Conclusion

Although the codification of directors' duties in the CA 2006 had the stated aim of reflecting in statute the common law position, there have been some significant changes. Moreover the codified duties are not all the duties a director may owe to a company. Directors continue to owe their duties solely to the company (except in limited cases, such as in an insolvency), but the CA 2006 provides a statutory basis for shareholders to bring derivative claims.

The following chapters go into more detail in areas touched on above and other areas.

---

[65] CA 2006 Chapter 2 of Part 18.

Chapter 2

Appointment and Vacation of Office

Chris Hale

Partner

Travers Smith

2.1   Introduction

The Companies Act 2006 ("CA 2006") adopts the same approach as its predecessor, the Companies Act 1985 ("CA 1985") in being largely silent on the issue of how directors are to be appointed, although Sections 154 and 155 set out the basic requirements that companies must have a minimum number of directors, and that at least one must be a natural person. Sections 157 to 159 also deal with minimum age requirements for directors. For more on the qualification of directors *see* Section 2.3 below. For the benefit of shareholders and others, CA 2006 also imposes obligations in relation to the disclosure and publication of the identity of directors and certain personal details (*see* Section 2.5.1 below), and reserves the right for shareholders (regardless of any provision in any agreement between the company and the director) to remove the director and to elect their own replacement (*see* Section 2.4.5 below). Otherwise, CA 2006 leaves the shareholders to define their preferred procedures in the company's articles of association ("the articles") and/or in a shareholders' agreement.

The articles of most companies contain provisions along the same lines as those contained in the model articles for private companies and for public companies (i.e. the Regulations made pursuant to Section 19 CA 2006[1]) (the "Model Articles") which permit the appointment of directors either by an ordinary resolution of the shareholders or by a decision of the board and provide a standard list of circumstances in which a director's appointment will terminate automatically. Companies incorporated prior to 1 October 2008 (when the CA 2006 Model Articles came into force) under CA 1985 or earlier statutes (a "pre-CA 2006 company") may still have articles based on Table A[2] but the provisions of Table A as to the appointment of directors and the circumstances in which a director's appointment will terminate automatically are substantially the same as those in the Model Articles.

In practice, for most companies, decisions relating to the appointment of new directors (after incorporation) will be a matter primarily for the existing directors rather than the shareholders. In this way the existing directors, acting properly, are able to identify the skills required within the boardroom and find the right personality fit. However, in larger companies, shareholders will wish to monitor the performance of the directors after their appointment, and institutional shareholders of listed companies are now required by our corporate governance regime to do so. The articles of such companies usually contain retirement by rotation provisions which require a board appointment to be approved by shareholders at the first annual general meeting ("AGM") following the appointment and enable shareholders to vote on the directors' re-election when they retire by rotation, typically, every three years or so thereafter (but *see* Section 2.4.2 below on the new UK Corporate Governance Code requirements). Generally, retirement by rotation provisions are less common in private companies' articles.

Even in private companies the shareholders may in some circumstances take a more active role in the appointment and removal of directors. So, where a company is the wholly-owned subsidiary of another company, the parent company will usually control appointments to the board of that company and any other subsidiaries. A private company with institutional

---

[1] The Companies (Model Articles) Regulations 2008 (SI 2008/3229).
[2] SI 1985/805 as amended by SI 1985/1052.

shareholders, such as a private equity-backed company, will usually have one or more nominees on the board who are appointed by the institutional shareholders or, more unusually, lenders. Such directors fall into the sub-category known as "nominee directors" (*see* Section 2.8 below), although there is no recognition in statute of this role. Nominee directors are simply directors like any other in the eyes of the law.

In fact, CA 2006 contains no clear definition of the term "director", merely stating (Section 250) that for the purposes of the Act generally a "director" includes any person occupying the position of director, by whatever name called. This means that someone who acts as a director, even though they have never been appointed as such, may be deemed to be a "director" for the purposes of CA 2006 (i.e. a *de facto* director – *see* Section 2.7 below). Modern business practice has given rise to a number of sub-categories of director, not all of which are formally recognised in CA 2006. For example, directors may be executive or non-executive, or they may be acting as a *de facto* director, shadow director or alternate. Only the term "shadow director" is defined in CA 2006 (Section 251). Sections 2.6, 2.7 and 2.8 below deal with the manner in which such "directorships" are created, and in which they may be terminated.

2.2 Method of appointment of directors

2.2.1 The first director(s)

In order to effect registration of a new company under the CA 2006, a number of documents need to be delivered to the Registrar of Companies. The application for registration required under Section 9 CA 2006 must contain the name(s) and certain required particulars of the person or persons who is/are to be the company's first director(s). These particulars include, in the case of an individual, his names and any former name (i.e. a name by which the individual was formerly known for business purposes), a service address (for more on this, *see* Section 2.5.3 below) and the country or state (or part of the UK) in which he is usually resident, his nationality, business occupation (if any) and his date of birth. The application must also contain a consent by each person named as a director to his acting as such. When the Registrar of Companies issues the certificate of incorporation, those persons named as directors in the application are deemed to have been appointed as the first directors of the new company (*see* Section 16(6) CA 2006). No separate notice of appointment is needed under Section 167 CA 2006.

Companies can be incorporated electronically, that is to say that certain of the documents required to be sent to the Registrar of Companies on incorporation may be submitted electronically, and Companies House has arrangements in place to verify the authenticity of any signatures on such documents. *See* Section 2.5.2 below for more on electronic filing.

CA 2006 is silent on the procedures for the appointment of further directors following incorporation of the company (other than in certain specific circumstances, such as the appointment of a director to replace one removed by the shareholders under Section 168 CA 2006). These procedures are left as a matter for shareholders to determine in the company's articles. In every instance when considering the appointment (or removal – *see* Section 2.4 below) of a director it is, therefore, necessary to check the company's articles and any relevant shareholders' agreement.

2.2.2 *Appointment by the board*

The most common method of appointment of a director after the company's incorporation is by a decision of the board itself. Regulation 19 of the Model Articles for public companies contains a simple power for the directors to appoint further directors by a decision of the board. There is a similar power in the Model Articles for private companies, at Regulation 16.

The board will usually appoint a director in accordance with the standard procedure for directors' decision making as set out in the company's articles. The provisions governing decision making by directors are slightly different in the Model Articles for public and private companies. For public companies, Regulations 7 to 19 of the Model Articles enable directors to take decisions by a resolution passed either at a board meeting or in writing. For private companies, under Regulations 7 to 16 of the Model Articles, directors' decisions may be taken either at a meeting or more informally, by a unanimous "decision", which may or may not take the form of a written resolution, although it must still be recorded in writing. The articles should be checked for special arrangements relating to directors' decisions and particularly those relating to the appointment of directors. Special provisions apply in the Model Articles where the number of directors has fallen below the requisite quorum for directors' meetings in that the continuing director(s) may still act for the purposes of filling vacancies by appointing additional directors or convening a general meeting to enable shareholders to do so (Regulations 11(2) and 11(3) of the Model Articles for public companies and Regulation 11(3) of the Model Articles for private companies).[3] *See* also Sections 2.2.6 and 2.3.2 below on dealing with a situation where there are insufficient or no continuing directors.

2.2.3   Board appointments – UK Corporate Governance Code requirements

The UK Corporate Governance Code published in May 2010 (the "Code") has additional requirements as regards directors' appointments. Listed companies (i.e. those whose securities have been admitted to the Official List) are required by the Disclosure and Transparency Rules to include a corporate governance statement in the directors' report (*see* DTR 7.2.1). Compliance with Listing Rule 9.8.6R(6) (the "comply or explain" rule), which requires listed companies to state in their annual report how they have applied the Code, satisfies this DTR requirement. AIM-listed companies are not subject to the Code but in practice many AIM-listed companies seek to comply with the Code and larger AIM-listed companies are encouraged to do so by the Quoted Companies Alliance. The QCA has itself produced a simpler set of corporate governance guidelines (the "QCA Guidelines"), whose provisions on board appointments are similar in substance to those in the Code, and which the QCA treats as the minimum standard for AIM-listed companies.

---

[3] If Table A-based articles are relevant, Regulation 90 of Table A fulfils the same purpose.

Main Principle B.2 of the Code states that "There should be a formal, rigorous and transparent procedure for the appointment of new directors to the board". Code Provision B.2.1 requires companies to appoint a nomination committee which should lead the process for board appointments and make recommendations to the board. ICSA has published standard terms of reference for the nomination committee (*see* www.icsa.org.uk/assets/files/pdfs/guidance/071013.pdf) which are widely used by listed companies. Accordingly, for listed companies seeking to comply with the Code, the appointment of a new director by the board involves first a recommendation of a particular candidate by the nomination committee and secondly (unless, unusually, the power of appointment has been delegated to the nomination committee) a resolution of the board itself.

The Code requirement on the composition of the nomination committee is that a majority of its members should be independent non-executive directors, and the chairman should be either the chairman of the board or an independent non-executive director. The chairman and members of the nomination committee should be identified in the annual report. The Code also requires the committee's terms of reference to be made available to shareholders and others, for example by publishing it on the company's website (Code Provision B.2.1), and for the work of the committee to be disclosed in a separate section of the annual report (Code Provision B.2.4).

PIRC's requirement as regards the composition of the nomination committee is even more prescriptive. PIRC's 2010 Shareholder Voting Guidelines state that *all* of the directors on the committee should be independent, to avoid undue "personal patronage", and the chairman of the board should not be a member of the committee at all, to preserve the independence of his role.

The QCA Guidelines for AIM-listed companies also require board appointments to be made following a recommendation by a nomination committee and Appendix E to those Guidelines sets out a summary of the duties of the nomination committee which may be followed where the Code and the relevant ICSA terms of reference are not being applied.

As any appointment of a director by the board in a listed company context will be put before the shareholders at an AGM by virtue of the retirement by rotation provisions (as to which *see* Section 2.4.2 below), the Code also has additional requirements as to disclosure of the biographical details of directors submitted for election or re-election by shareholders, and the terms and conditions of appointment of non-executive directors. For more on these requirements, *see* Section 2.2.5 below. The Code also has strict criteria preserving the independence of the chairman and non-executive directors on the board, a topic which is addressed in Section 2.3.7. Performance evaluation for directors, a topic of key significance in today's economic and business climate, is also addressed in Section 2.3.7.

2.2.4 *Shareholder protection as regards board appointments*

In order to provide the shareholders with further protection against the board appointing unsuitable candidates as directors, listed companies are also subject to the retirement by rotation requirements of Main Principle B.7 of the Code, which states that all directors of FTSE 350 companies should be subject to annual election by shareholders and all others should be submitted for re-election at intervals of not more than three years, subject to continued satisfactory performance. Also, many listed companies' articles contain provisions similar to those set out in Regulation 20(2) of the Model Articles for public companies,[4] and required by the Code, which require a director to retire at the next following AGM after his appointment and to seek reappointment at that meeting by the shareholders (for more on retirement by rotation, *see* Section 2.4.2 below).

For private companies, there are no retirement by rotation provisions in the Model Articles and even where Table A still applies, Regulation 79, which deals with retirement by rotation, is often disapplied. Limited protection for shareholders in all companies is provided by the fact that, in exercising their powers of appointment, the directors must have regard to their general duties under Part 10, Chapter 2 CA 2006. These duties

---

[4] In the case of Table A-based articles, Regulation 79 makes similar provision.

will apply to all aspects of the decision to appoint a new director, including the timing of the appointment, the selection of the candidate and the resulting balance of power which the directors seek to create within the boardroom.

2.2.5 *Appointment by shareholders – general considerations*

The shareholders as a whole have an inherent power to appoint directors by shareholders' resolution unless this power has been restricted in the company's articles. Regulation 19 of the Model Articles for public companies and Regulation 16 of the Model Articles for private companies, for example, confirm this power, stating that the company may, by ordinary resolution, appoint a person who is willing to act as a director and is permitted by law to do so.[5]

Where any shareholders' resolution for the appointment of a director is originally proposed by the board, as with any other resolution proposed by the directors, it will be necessary for the directors to include with the notice of that resolution sufficient information to enable shareholders to make a proper judgment as to whether and, if so, how they wish to vote. The nature and amount of information required to discharge this duty will depend upon the circumstances and particular provisions apply for listed companies (*see* below). It would also probably be a breach of the directors' general duty under Section 172 (to promote the success of the company for the benefit of its members as a whole) to propose a candidate for improper purposes. For companies with Table A-based articles, Regulations 76 and 77 of Table A require biographical details of any director who is put forward for appointment or re-appointment by shareholders to be made available to shareholders in advance of the meeting, for shareholder protection purposes, but the Model Articles do not replicate Regulations 76 and 77 of Table A. It was thought, when

---

[5] A similar power is set out in Regulation 78 of Table A. Until 1985, earlier versions of Table A provided that the number of directors should be determined by the subscribers to the company's memorandum of association. On that basis, the number of directors was fixed and it is therefore for this historical reason that Regulation 78 refers to the appointment of new directors as "filling a vacancy or appointing an additional director". This language has been dropped in the CA 2006 Model Articles.

CA 2006 was passed, that Part 13 of the Act provided an adequate framework for appointments of directors by shareholders, and the requisition provisions set out in Sections 292, 303 and 338 do provide members with the opportunity to propose candidates for the office of director independently of anyone put forward by the company's management. However, the articles of most listed companies still contain provisions similar to Regulations 76 and 77 since the Code (Provision B.7.1) requires biographical details of proposed directors to be made available to shareholders voting on their election or re-election.

A public company in general meeting may not consider a single motion for the appointment of two or more directors (whether a first appointment or re-election), unless it has first been agreed by the meeting, without any vote being cast against the proposal, that a single resolution is acceptable (Section 160 CA 2006[6]). In the absence of such unanimous agreement, a separate resolution must be proposed for the appointment of each candidate. Any resolution moved in contravention of the requirement is void, whether or not any objection was raised at the time. Section 160 is designed to ensure that shareholders are given a genuine choice as to the composition of the board and shareholders can vote down the appointment of a particular director without having to reject the entire board.[7] For listed companies, Listing Rule 9.3.7 has the same effect.

Although a resolution moved in contravention of Section 160 is void, it may still have some consequences, namely:

(a) Section 161(1)(a) CA 2006 states that the acts of a director are valid notwithstanding any defect that may be discovered in his appointment afterwards;[8] and

(b) the second part of Section 160(2) will prevent the application in these circumstances of any provision which states that, if at the meeting at which a director retires by rotation the company does not fill the vacancy, the retiring director

---

6 This provision replaced Section 292 CA 1985.
7 The requirements of Section 292 CA 1985, which were replaced by Section 160 CA 2006, were considered in *PNC Telecom Plc* v *Thomas* [2002] All ER (D) 315.
8 *See* Section 2.3.9 on the effect of invalid appointments.

shall (if willing to act) be deemed to have been reappointed. (There is such a provision in Regulation 75 of Table A, but there is no equivalent in the Model Articles.)

It should be noted that nothing in Section 160 prevents a resolution altering the company's articles (*see* Section 160(4)). Accordingly, it would be possible, although highly unusual (and subject to the unfair prejudice protection regime set out in Section 994 CA 2006), for the general meeting to pass a special resolution adopting an article providing that two or more named persons be directors of the company without first obtaining uncontested consent to the proposing of such a resolution.

In order to avoid the cumbersome nature of the statutory procedures for calling or requisitioning meetings or resolutions (*see* Section 2.2.6 below), a company's articles or a shareholders' agreement may contain provisions granting certain shareholders special rights to appoint directors to the company's board. Such provisions are common in a private company context where the structure of the board or the identity of the directors is important to certain shareholders and where it may be important for such shareholders to effect board changes quickly to enable them to take control with a view to protecting their investment in the company. Examples would be where the company is private equity-backed or is the vehicle for a joint venture or a wholly-owned subsidiary of another company.[9] In such circumstances, the articles will also usually specify a simple procedure for the appointment without the need for a shareholders' resolution, such as the deposit at the registered office of the company of a written notice of appointment and consent to act. Care is required when drafting or interpreting such provisions in order to distinguish between a power to appoint and a power to nominate a candidate to be considered by the directors or by the company in general meeting. If the latter, the candidate may be voted down by the directors or shareholders.

Where a director is appointed by the shareholders, the moment at which he assumes office is determined by the time at which

---

[9] *See* Section 2.8 on nominee directors.

the resolution appointing him is passed. Where the resolution is taken at a meeting and is to be determined by a poll, it will be effective not from the moment that the poll is taken but from the moment that the result of a poll is declared or ascertained.

It is not unusual for resolutions appointing directors to specify that the appointment will take effect at a particular date and time or upon the happening of a specified event (e.g. completion of a transaction whereupon new directors are to be appointed). In an acquisition context, if two parties have entered into a conditional agreement for the sale and purchase of a company, the buyer occasionally requests the right to appoint someone to the board of the target company during the period between exchange of contracts and completion of the sale in order to give the buyer some control over the business it has contracted to acquire. For reasons of commercial sensitivity and confidentiality, the seller may object to such a request and there may instead (or in addition) be a list of matters requiring the consent of the buyer or the buyer's representative during such a period. If this list is very extensive, the buyer's representative may be deemed to be a shadow director of the target company in any event (for more on shadow directors *see* Section 2.7 below).

2.2.6   Appointment by shareholders – requisitions

Sections 292 and 303 CA 2006 enable shareholders either to require circulation of a written resolution (in the case of a private company only), or to require the directors to call a general meeting. In either case, these rights could be used to put forward a resolution to appoint one or more new directors, provided there is sufficient support for the requisition amongst the shareholders. Both Sections 292 and 303 require members representing at least 5 per cent of the paid-up voting shares to make the requisition. (In the case of Section 303, the percentage was reduced from 10 per cent to 5 per cent by the Shareholders' Rights Regulations.)[10] Section 338 CA 2006 also makes provision for shareholders of public companies to require the circulation of a resolution in advance of the AGM provided it is not

---

[10]   The Companies (Shareholders' Rights) Regulations 2009 (SI 2009/1632).

defamatory or otherwise "frivolous or vexatious", although they can still use the powers in Section 303 CA 2006 to requisition a general meeting if they consider that their proposed appointment of a new director cannot wait until the next AGM. Both are useful powers, particularly for a substantial shareholder who does not control the board and who may wish to secure control by appointing additional directors.[11] The requisition route was rarely used under the CA 1985 regime because of the level of formality involved. However, in this new era of shareholder activism in listed companies, there have been a number of high-profile examples recently of the Companies Act requisition procedures being used by hedge funds and other shareholders seeking to put a representative on the board or replace the incumbent board altogether. Listed company shareholders are now actively encouraged to take action where they believe that the directors are not managing the company in the best interests of shareholders as a whole. The concept of active share ownership was placed centre stage by the Walker Review, published in November 2009, which recommended that the Institutional Shareholders' Committee's Code on the Responsibilities of Institutional Investors be ratified by the FRC and should operate as the Stewardship Code under the auspices of the FRC, alongside the Corporate Governance Code. The Combined Code on Corporate Governance, the predecessor to the Code, has, since 1998, contained a section (Section E) which contained various recommendations addressed to institutional investors in listed companies which were designed to encourage them to make considered use of their votes. The Code replicates these recommendations in Schedule C but the FRC intends to remove Schedule C in view of the overlap with the new Stewardship Code. Principle 4 of the Stewardship Code requires institutional shareholders to "establish clear guidelines on when and how they will escalate their activities as a method of protecting and enhancing shareholder value". The underlying guidance on Principle 4 suggests that requisitioning a general meeting, possibly to change the board, should be considered if boards do not respond constructively to

---

[11] These provisions replace Section 386 CA 1985 which provided for shareholders' rights to requisition an extraordinary general meeting.

shareholder intervention. Principle 5, which recommends that institutional investors should be willing to act collectively with other investors where appropriate, is also relevant in this context, since the requisition route requires shareholder cooperation, both in making the requisition (*see* above) and in getting the relevant resolution(s) passed.

In practice what may happen is that one or more shareholders would write to, or otherwise enter a dialogue with the company as regards proposed board changes and if no action is taken by the board, the shareholder may proceed to requisition a general meeting to remove incumbent directors under Section 168 and appoint one or more new directors using the shareholders' power to do so by ordinary resolution under the articles. Few institutional shareholders will be willing to embark on the requisition route without a reasonable chance of success in view of the potential cost and adverse publicity involved in a failed attempt. For this reason it is common for the lead shareholder(s) to appoint proxy solicitation agents to carry out an analysis of the company's shareholder profile and solicit support for the resolutions.

Shareholders considering the requisition route for the appointment of new directors should also take account of (i) the provisions of CA 2006 on directors' conflicts of interest and (ii) the UK Corporate Governance Code requirements and the shareholder bodies' views on non-executive directors' independence criteria. There is inherent potential for a conflict of interest where a director is appointed to the board by or on behalf of a shareholder or group of shareholders, which is the same issue confronted by a nominee director in a private company context (*see* Section 2.8 below). In essence a nominee director is not permitted by company law to prefer the interests of his appointor over the interests of the company as a whole – *see* Sections 172 and 175 CA 2006. Also, a shareholder nominee for a board appointment will automatically give rise to an issue under the independence criteria in Code Provision B.1.1. That provision states that the board should, in the annual report, give reasons for their judgment that a particular director is deemed to be independent notwithstanding the existence of a whole range of relationships or circumstances, one of which is a relationship with a significant shareholder. Both the NAPF and PIRC take the view that a shareholder nominee will not automatically infringe the independence criteria, but the candidate will have to be able to demonstrate the absence of a material link with the relevant shareholder and should be able to satisfy the remaining criteria. Listing Principle 5 of the Listing Rules would also come into play. This requires all holders of the same class of securities to be treated equally, and is designed to ensure a listed company is not overly-dominated by a significant shareholder. For more on dealing with conflicts of interest generally *see* Chapter 3.

If the requisition is made by the shareholders of a public company, the written resolution route is not available, so the incumbent board must respond to the requisition under Section 303 by convening a general meeting. Even if the requisition is aimed at replacing board directors, the directors are obliged to act on it under Section 304. If they do not do so, Section 305 allows the members to do so at the company's expense and the cost may ultimately be collected from the defaulting directors out of their fees or other sums due to them (Section 305(7)).

Occasionally, the requirement for a general meeting gives rise to practical difficulties. If there are no surviving directors or if there is an insufficient number of directors to make up a quorum in order to convene a general meeting under Section 302 CA 2006, then the company's articles may enable any director or a certain percentage or number of members to convene the necessary general meeting. Regulation 28 of the Model Articles for public companies and Regulation 37 of Table A deal with such a situation but there is no equivalent provision in the Model Articles for private companies.

If there is no such provision in the company's articles, or if for any other reason it is impractical to call or hold the necessary general meeting, the shareholders of a private company with at least one director or a company secretary could rely on Section 292 to make the appointment by written resolution (although the written resolution could not be used for a resolution to remove a director under Section 168 CA 2006, which may be proposed at the same time). Alternatively, if the written resolution route is unavailable, any director or member entitled to vote may apply to the court pursuant to Section 306 CA 2006 for it to order a meeting to be called, held and conducted in the manner the court sees fit. Section 306 replaced Section 371 CA 1985 without substantive amendment and there were several cases considering the extent to which Section 371 could be relied upon in circumstances in which a director or shareholder or body of shareholders was using his or its position to frustrate the holding of a general meeting in order to effect changes at board level. In *Re Woven Rugs Ltd* [2002] 1 BCLC 324, a director threatened with dismissal refused to attend board meetings convened to call a general meeting to table a resolution to remove him as a director. His presence was required at the meeting to make up a quorum. It was held that a meeting could be ordered under Section 371, despite submissions of unfairness by the director. In *Union Music Ltd and another v Watson and another* [2003] 1 BCLC 453, the Court of Appeal ruled that Section 371 CA 1985 was intended to ensure that a company is not frustrated in its affairs by the impracticability of calling a meeting in the manner prescribed by its constitution. In that case, the shareholders' agreement required the prior written consent of both the minority and majority shareholder for the holding of a general meeting. The shareholders were in dispute and when a director resigned, the majority shareholder applied under that Section 371 for an order that a general meeting be held to appoint a replacement. The Court of Appeal held that where there are unequal shareholdings, the court is under no obligation to assume the parties had intended a veto for either shareholder and a meeting was ordered to take place.

2.2.7 Appointment by third parties

It is fairly unusual for directors to be appointed by third parties (i.e. other than by the board or the shareholders). The board or the nomination committee of the board may, in practice, seek assistance from third parties in identifying potential candidates and this is thought not to be prohibited under the terms of Section 173 CA 2006 which requires the directors to exercise independent judgment. It is possible for the company to adopt articles which confer the power to appoint directors on a third party, although the Model Articles contain no such provision.[12] Such delegation through the articles could be in favour of, for example, a seller of a company who is to receive consideration based upon the performance of the target business after the completion of the sale and is granted the right to appoint a director of the company during the period of the "earn-out" so as to monitor and/or control the company during that period.

A third party to whom the articles give a right to appoint and remove directors should be aware that he cannot enforce that right against the company. Whilst the provisions of a company's constitution bind the company and its members to the same extent as if there were covenants to observe those provisions on the part of the company and each member (*see* Section 33 CA 2006[13]), they do not have the effect of conferring rights on third parties which are directly enforceable against the company. This is confirmed by Section 6(2) of the Contracts (Rights of Third Parties) Act 1999 which specifically excludes a company's constitution from the scope of that Act. If a third party wishes to ensure that his right to appoint or remove a director is always respected, that party should seek a direct contractual undertaking from the shareholders in the company to act on his instructions. The third party should also be aware that there are circumstances in which his appointee could be removed by the shareholders or by the board of the company. The shareholders have a statutory right (in Section 168 CA 2006) to remove a director by ordinary resolution and the shareholders (or a particular group or class of shareholders) may have a right in the articles to remove a director without going through the Section 168 procedure. The directors may also be entitled to remove a director under a provision in the articles (although there is no such provision in the Model Articles). Again, the third party should consider seeking an undertaking from the shareholders and the directors (as relevant) not to exercise their rights to remove a director nominated by the third party unless the third party has requested or agrees to his

---

[12] Table A contained no such provision either.
[13] This section replaced Section 14 CA 1985 from 1 October 2008 without a change of substance.

removal (*see* also Sections 2.2.10 (Entrenchment) and 2.4.5 (Removal pursuant to Section 168 CA 2006) below).

2.2.8 Appointment by the court

Theoretically, it is possible, on application by a member to the court pursuant to Section 994 CA 2006 (unfair prejudice),[14] that the court may exercise the extremely wide powers granted to it by Section 996 to make "such order as it thinks fit" for giving relief in respect of the matters complained of, and order the appointment of one or more directors. In practice, however, even in extreme cases, in the exercise of their powers under Section 461 CA 1985 (the predecessor to Section 996), the courts were reluctant to interfere in the management of a company's affairs in this way, preferring instead to order the acquisition of one party's shares by another and for the resulting shareholders to appoint whomsoever they wish to act as the ongoing directors. There is nothing so far to suggest the attitude of the courts will be any different under the CA 2006 regime.

2.2.9 Appointment by the Secretary of State

Section 156 CA 2006 contains a new provision enabling the Secretary of State to direct the company to appoint one or more directors if it appears that the company is in breach of the statutory requirements as to the number of directors set out in Section 154 CA 2006, or that a company should have at least one director who is a natural person, under Section 155. The direction made by the Secretary of State (who would usually act through Companies House in these circumstances) will specify what the company must do in order to rectify the breach and the period within which it must do so, which must be not less than one month nor more than three months after the date on which the direction is given. If in the meantime the company has rectified the breach, it must give notice of the relevant appointment or appointments under Section 167 before the end of the period specified in the direction. There is a criminal penalty for failure to comply with a direction made under

---

[14] This section replaced Section 459 CA 1985 from 1 October 2008 without a change of substance.

Section 156 which may be levied on the company and every officer of the company in default (as defined in Section 1121 CA 2006). For these purposes, a shadow director is an officer of the company.

2.2.10 Entrenchment

It used to be relatively difficult under English law to entrench the appointment of a director, largely in view of Section 303(1) CA 1985, which provided that the shareholders' right to remove a director by ordinary resolution could not be overridden by anything in the articles or any agreement between the company and the director in question. Consequently a director was always vulnerable to removal by shareholders' resolution. Section 168 CA 2006, which replaced Section 303 CA 1985 on 1 October 2007, applies "notwithstanding anything in any agreement between [the company] and [the director]" and although it is no longer specifically expressed to override any contrary provision in the company's articles, such a provision, or any exclusion of the shareholders' rights under Section 168 CA 2006, would probably still constitute an unlawful fetter on the company's statutory powers (*Russell* v *Northern Bank Development Corp Ltd* [1992] 3 All ER 161) and therefore be unenforceable against the company. *See* further Section 2.4.5 below.

CA 2006 introduced statutory rights of entrenchment for provisions of the articles, ensuring that certain provisions of the articles, including those relating to directors' appointments, can only be amended or repealed if certain conditions are met, or procedures complied with, that are more restrictive than a special resolution (*see* Section 22 CA 2006[15]). There does not appear to be any restriction either on an agreement between shareholders *inter se* whereby they agree not to exercise their rights to remove a director nominated by a particular shareholder or class of shareholders or indeed a third party, unless the appointor has requested or agreed to his removal. Such an agreement could not bind the company (and could not

---

[15] Section 22(2) is not yet in force. The implementation of this section was delayed as a result of concern that provisions in companies' articles relating to variation of class rights might be caught by Section 22(2) and this was not the intention.

therefore appear in the articles) without falling foul of the *Russell* v *Northern Bank* principle. The agreement will, though, bind the shareholders who are party to it. In *Thomas and others* v *York Trustees Ltd* [2001] All ER (D) 179 it was held that a special resolution to remove directors under Section 303 CA 1985, which would be in breach of a provision of a shareholders' agreement providing for a shareholder with the right to appoint a director at all times and until expiry of the agreement, could not be put to shareholders. *See* also *Criterion Properties Plc* v *Stratford UK Properties LLC and others* [2002] EWCA Civ 1783, in which a company sought to entrench the appointment of two directors as part of a poison pill arrangement to deter a hostile takeover offer. *See* also Section 2.4.5 below on *Bushell* v *Faith* clauses and similar weighted voting rights provisions in articles, which are designed to protect a director in the event of a shareholder motion to remove him, and which are not outlawed by CA 2006.

2.3 Qualification

As we have seen, the Act defines a "director" as including any "person" occupying the position of director, by whatever name called. Schedule 1 Interpretation Act 1978 states that a "person" includes a body of persons corporate or unincorporated. Accordingly, any individual (subject to the age limits discussed in Section 2.3.1 below) or corporation is currently eligible to be a director.[16]

Although the position of director is one of considerable importance to the effective management of the company, there is no statutory requirement that a director should hold any form of qualification or take any examination in order to enable him to take up his office. Nevertheless there are certain safeguards designed to reduce the risk that inappropriate persons become directors or, if they do, to ensure that on the occurrence of certain events they should vacate their office automatically or shareholders should have the opportunity to remove them.

---

[16] Although corporate directors are still permitted under CA 2006, Section 155 requires companies to have at least one director who is a natural person.

Apart from those safeguards which are inherent in the mechanism for appointment, for example:

(a) references above to the general duties of directors contained in Part 10, Chapter 2 of CA 2006, when exercising their powers to appoint additional or replacement directors;

(b) the requirement that a separate shareholders' resolution is required for the appointment of each director of a public company;

(c) the general duty of directors who propose a resolution for appointment of a director at a general meeting to provide sufficient information about the proposed appointee to shareholders to enable them to make an informed decision; and

(d) for listed companies, the nomination committee procedure set out in the UK Corporate Governance Code,

there are a number of additional relevant provisions, as follows.

2.3.1 Age limit

It used to be the case under CA 1985 for a public company (or, a private company which is a subsidiary of a public company or of a body corporate registered as a public company in Northern Ireland), that no person was capable of being appointed a director if, at the time of his appointment, he had attained the age of 70. Further, any director of such a company was required to vacate his office at the conclusion of the AGM following his seventieth birthday and was not then eligible for automatic reappointment in default of another director being appointed in his place (Section 293 CA 1985). Section 293 CA 1985 was repealed on 6 April 2007,[17] largely due to concerns that the age limit might infringe age discrimination legislation. Despite the repeal of Section 293 CA 1985, it is worth checking a company's articles for any specific age limitations for directors, although such provisions are not common, and are likely to be less so since the introduction of the Employment Equality (Age) Regulations 2006 with effect from 1 October 2006.

---

[17] *See* Section 4(2)(c) Companies Act 2006 (Commencement No 1, Transitional Provisions and Savings) Order 2006 (SI 2006/3428).

Section 157 CA 2006 prescribes 16 as the minimum age for a director,[18] although it would be possible to appoint a person younger than 16 as a director provided the appointment did not take effect until that person attained the age of 16 (*see* Section 157(2)). Regulations may in future be made under Section 158 CA 2006 providing exceptions to the underage directors rule, but no such regulations have yet been proposed. Assuming therefore that no exceptions apply, any person who was under the age of 16 on 1 October 2008 who had been appointed as a director would automatically have ceased to be a director on that date, by virtue of Section 159 CA 2006. No notification of the revocation of the appointment was required to be filed at Companies House but any affected companies should have made the necessary arrangements for the appointment of a replacement if appropriate, and recorded the changes in the company books. The statutory prohibition on underage directors in Section 157 will not prevent a person who is younger than 16 but who acts as a shadow or *de facto* director from incurring liability as such (Section 157(5)). There was no equivalent provision to Section 157 CA 2006 in the CA 1985. Under Scottish law, however, where Section 1 Age of Legal Capacity (Scotland) Act 1991 states that a person under the age of 16 years shall have no capacity to enter into any transaction and the expression "transaction" includes "the giving by a person of any consent having legal effect", it is possible that a person under the age of 16 is incapable of consenting to be appointed a director.

2.3.2 Number of directors

As was the case under CA 1985, CA 2006 does not prescribe the maximum number of directors that a company may have and neither do the Model Articles.[19] A company's articles may contain some provision on this, although a prescribed maximum would be unusual in a private company context other than, for example, in a joint venture company where it

---

[18] Section 157 came into force on 1 October 2008.
[19] Regulation 64 of Table A states that, unless otherwise determined by an ordinary resolution of the company in general meeting, the number of directors (other than alternate directors) shall not be subject to any maximum.

may be important to specify the precise number of directors and who may appoint them to preserve a balance between the joint venture partners. When considering any appointment of a new director it is wise, however, to check if there is any maximum fixed by or under the authority of the relevant articles and, if so, that it will not thereby be exceeded.

With the exception of situations like joint ventures, most private companies maintain maximum flexibility in respect of board appointments. For example, a private equity-backed company will rarely have a maximum limit on the number of directors, so that the private equity house can "flood" the board by appointing such number of additional directors as would give it control of the board in order to safeguard its investment if the company is under-performing.

The Institutional Shareholders' Committee recommended, in a Statement of Best Practice ("The Role and Duties of Directors – A Statement of Best Practice" available from www.ivis.co.uk), that the articles of listed companies should provide for a maximum as well as a minimum number of directors, although not all listed companies' articles prescribe a maximum and if they do, the limit is set at a fairly high level to preserve flexibility. In terms of the number of directors, the UK Corporate Governance Code simply provides (in Supporting Principle B.1) that the board should be of sufficient size that the requirements of the business can be met and that changes to the board's composition and that of its committees can be managed without undue disruption, and should not be so large as to be unwieldy. The Code is more concerned with the balance of executive and non-executive directors on the board, and the independence of the chairman and the non-executive directors. For more on this *see* Section 2.3.7 below.

In its 2010 UK Shareholding Voting Guidelines, PIRC observes that the average board size for companies in the All Share Index is seven or eight, and this will be taken by it as the benchmark in assessing compliance with Supporting Principle B.1 of the Code.

More commonly, a company's articles may set a minimum number of directors. Table A stated (in Regulation 64) that, unless otherwise determined by ordinary resolution, the number of directors shall not be less than two. The Model Articles contain no such provision, although CA 2006 itself prescribes a minimum number of directors for both private and public companies (one and two respectively – *see* Section 154 CA 2006). CA 1985 provided that where the company has only one director, that individual could not also be the company secretary (Section 283(2) CA 1985). Since CA 2006 makes no provision for the company secretary of a private company (only public companies are required to have a company secretary – *see* Sections 270 and 271 CA 2006) and public companies must have two directors as a minimum, Section 283(2) CA 1985 was not replicated in CA 2006. This means that if a private company with a sole director chooses to have a company secretary, there will be no statutory prohibition on them being the same person.

If for any reason a company which should have more than one director ends up with a sole director, the company's articles will usually determine what the sole director can and cannot do until such point as a new director is appointed to comply with the minimum requirement. For example, Regulation 11(3) of the Model Articles for private companies states that if there are fewer directors than required for a quorum, the directors can only act to appoint more directors or call a general meeting to enable shareholders to do so. Regulation 11 of the Model Articles for public companies enables a sole director to appoint sufficient directors to make up the quorum or call a general meeting to enable shareholders to do so. It also provides for a situation where there is more than one director (but fewer than the quorum requirement) enabling a directors' meeting to be held in any event to appoint more directors.[20]

If a company finds itself with no directors at all, it will be in breach of Sections 154 and 155 CA 2006 and could be directed to appoint directors by the Secretary of State under Section 156 (*see* Section 2.2.9 above). To rectify the situation, either before or in response to any such direction, the shareholders should exercise

---

[20] Regulation 90 of Table A provides that a sole director may act only for the purpose of filling vacancies or of calling a general meeting (e.g. at which a resolution to appoint new directors is to be proposed).

their rights to appoint directors. For a private company, the easiest way to do this, in the absence of directors to call a general meeting, would be by written resolution. Regulations 17(2) and (3) of the Model Articles for private companies also make provision for the situation where there are no directors or shareholders as a result of death, enabling personal representatives to appoint directors. A public company, for whom the written resolution procedure is unavailable, will have to rely on the shareholders' right to call a general meeting under Section 305 CA 2006, or petition the court to convene a shareholders' meeting under Section 306 CA 2006.

2.3.3 *Qualifications specific to certain types of company*

In some instances, legislation specific to particular types of company may contain provisions requiring directors to have certain qualifications or provide that the appointment of a particular individual may result in the company losing the right to conduct certain types of business. For example, before an investment company with variable capital (otherwise known as an open-ended investment company) can be formed, the Financial Services Authority ("the FSA") must be satisfied that the proposed directors are fit and proper persons to act as directors of it and, if there are two or more directors, that the combination of their experience and expertise is such as is appropriate for the purposes of carrying on the business of the company.[21] These are ongoing requirements, failure to comply with which is a ground for revocation of the authorisation of the OEIC by the FSA.

2.3.4 *Shareholding qualification*

Neither the CA 2006 nor the Model Articles[22] require a director to hold any shares in the company of which he or she is a director. It used to be common for a company's articles to require directors to have a shareholding qualification while in office, to ensure that the director had a personal financial interest in the success of the company beyond his salary. Today this sort of

---

[21] *See* paragraphs 15(5) to (7) Open-Ended Investment Companies Regulations 2001.
[22] Table A had no such requirement either.

provision is extremely rare.[23] Although not a requirement as such, it is, however, common practice for directors of larger companies to be awarded shares or options over shares as performance-related remuneration. To ensure such awards are designed to promote the long-term success of the company, the UK Corporate Governance Code requires that shares should not vest and options should not be exercisable within three years of grant, and that directors should be encouraged to hold their shares for a period following vesting or exercise (*see* Schedule A of the Code). It is also usual for directors of private equity-backed companies to hold shares as a means of incentivising them to manage the company successfully, and for there to be a prohibition in the company's articles on directors transferring shares, to ensure they maintain a stake in the company.

2.3.5 Other qualifications contained in the company's articles

It is possible for companies to place further qualifications in their articles on who may act as a director, although care needs to be taken to ensure that any such provisions do not contravene any rules against discrimination contained within UK or EC law (e.g. if qualification was on the grounds of race or religion). Such provisions are not common.

2.3.6 Disqualification

It is possible that an individual may, from time to time, be disqualified from acting as a director. Such disqualification may arise by virtue of provisions in the relevant company's articles.

---

[23] The provisions of Section 291 CA 1985 required a director who was subject to qualification shares provisions to obtain his qualification shares within two months after his appointment (or such shorter time as may be fixed by the relevant articles). Section 291 was repealed with effect from 1 October 2009. If the articles require the director merely to "hold" the qualification shares, this is satisfied by the director being the registered holder and he does not also have to own the shares beneficially. However, the precise wording of the relevant article must be considered carefully.

The articles may provide that the director will cease to hold office automatically if he does not, within the required period, obtain his qualification shares. He may also cease to be a director automatically if at any subsequent date he ceases to hold his qualification shares and will be incapable of being reappointed as a director of that company until he has reacquired the necessary qualification shares. Unless the articles state that a director is required to obtain his qualification shares in the form of new shares issued by the company, he would usually be free to acquire them from any source and on any terms.

For example, there are often provisions in articles designed to ensure the removal of an existing director who is disqualified under statute or bankrupt or becomes physically or mentally ill or suffers some other event which makes their position untenable. Regulations 18 and 22 of the Model Articles for private and public companies (respectively) contain the standard list of such events (*see* Section 2.4.4 below for more details).

Disqualification may also arise, and this is the sense in which the term "disqualification" is usually employed, as a result of an order made by the court or a disqualification undertaking given by a director under the Company Directors' Disqualification Act 1986 ("CDDA 1986").

Any person against whom the court has made a disqualification order or from whom a disqualification undertaking has been accepted under CDDA 1986 shall not, without the leave of the court, be a director, liquidator, administrator, receiver or manager of a company's property or be in any way, whether directly or indirectly, concerned or take part in the promotion, formation or management of a company for the period specified within the relevant order or undertaking (*see* also Section 2.4.4 below). The court does have a discretion to permit a person to continue as a director of a specified company notwithstanding the grant of a disqualification order or acceptance of a disqualification undertaking if it is satisfied that the circumstances do not require disqualification from acting as a director of that particular company and the interests of third parties, such as creditors, are adequately protected. The use of disqualification orders and undertakings is increasing in an attempt to reduce the number of dishonest and/or incompetent persons holding the office of director within the UK.

Directors may also be disqualified for breaches of competition law pursuant to certain provisions of the Enterprise Act 2002. Under these provisions, a disqualification order may be made or a disqualification undertaking accepted in respect of a director who is in breach of competition law and whose conduct as a director is considered to make him unfit to be a director of a company. The effect of Competition Disqualification Orders and Competition Disqualification Undertakings are broadly similar to a disqualification order or undertaking made or accepted under the CDDA 1986. The OFT has published guidance on the Enterprise Act disqualification provisions, which can be found at www.oft.gov.uk/shared_oft/business_leaflets/enterprise_act/oft510.pdf.

2.3.7 Listed companies – corporate governance requirements

For listed companies, further provisions apply, driven by the need to ensure that high standards of corporate governance and management suitability and competence are imposed upon the directors of companies listed on the London Stock Exchange. First, the UK Corporate Governance Code contains the principle (Main Principle A.1) that every company should be headed by an effective board, which is collectively responsible for the long-term success of the company.

Main Principle B.4 requires that all directors should receive induction on joining the board and is supplemented by the Code Provision B.4.1 which states that the chairman should ensure that such induction is "full, formal and tailored" and that directors should avail themselves of opportunities to meet major shareholders. Main Principle B.4 further requires directors to regularly update their skills and knowledge. Main Principle B.6 requires the board to undertake a "formal and rigorous annual evaluation of its own performance and that of its committees and individual directors", and in the case of FTSE 350 companies, that the performance evaluation should be externally facilitated at least every three years. A recent ICSA report suggested that only 16 per cent of the top 200 listed companies carried out some form of external board evaluation in 2009.

In addition, the Code has rigorous requirements for the requisite skills, experience and independence of judgment among board members. For example, Main Principle B.1 requires that the board and its committees should consist of directors with the appropriate balance of skills, experience, independence and knowledge of the company to enable them to discharge their duties and responsibilities effectively. One of the Supporting Principles to Main Principle B.1 also requires a strong presence of both executive and non-executive directors (in particular, independent non-executives), such that no individual or small group of individuals can dominate the board's decision taking. Code Provision B.1.1 contains detailed independence requirements. In addition Code Provision A.2.1 requires that the chairman and chief executive role should not be combined.

Pressure from institutional shareholder bodies such as the ABI, NAPF and PIRC and from the press for listed companies to observe these provisions began to intensify in the aftermath of highly-publicised corporate failures such as Enron where lack of independent scrutiny of executive directors' actions was severely criticised. Boards have been subject to even greater scrutiny in the light of the recent financial crisis, particularly as regards collective board performance and remuneration (*see* Section 2.2.5 on activist shareholders seeking to make board appointments, and Sections 2.4.2 and 2.4.5 on directors being removed by shareholder resolution or voted down on being proposed for re-election). For example the most recent NAPF Corporate Governance Policy and Voting Guidelines suggest that shareholders may voice disapproval of shortcomings in the board evaluation process by abstaining on the re-election of the chairman or senior independent director, whose job is perceived to be to ensure effective performance evaluation at board level, and to vote down the re-election of poorly performing directors. PIRC also states in its 2010 UK Shareholder Voting Guidelines that companies should disclose details of continuing profes-sional development programmes for its directors and evidence that they have been reviewed during the year.

Both the NAPF and PIRC are also particularly concerned with the criteria for independence of the chairman and non-executive directors. The NAPF highlights length of tenure, cross-directorships and links to a significant shareholder as factors which will be seen as compromising independence. PIRC will only assess a director as independent if they can satisfy the additional criteria in PIRC's 2010 Shareholder Voting Guidelines over and above those set out in the Code.

Whilst it is no longer the case (since July 2005) that the Listing Rules explicitly require the directors and senior management of an applicant for listing to have appropriate expertise and experience, in July 2005 the FSA introduced six broad Listing Principles (*see* LR 7.2.1). The purpose of the principles, which now apply to companies with a premium listing, is to ensure that such companies pay due regard to the fundamental role they play in maintaining market confidence. In relation to directors, Principle 1 requires a premium-listed company to take reasonable steps to enable its directors to understand their responsibilities and obligations as directors. Principle 5 requires all holders of the same class of securities to be treated equally. This is designed to address the pre-July 2005 requirement for companies to demonstrate that the company and its directors are free from any potential conflicts of interest, particularly where the company has a significant shareholder who might be able to exercise influence over the company.

When a company publishes a prospectus, the Prospectus Rules require disclosure of certain information about its directors, their interests, remuneration, management expertise and experience, other directorships and details of any personal bankruptcy, convictions, sanctions or disqualifications and of receiverships or liquidations of any company of which the individual has been a director (*see* Section 14 of Annex 1, Appendix 3 to the Prospectus Rules). The same disclosure requirements apply in relation to prospectuses or admission documents published under the AIM Rules.

A premium-listed company's sponsor must also be satisfied, before any application for listing is made, that the directors of the issuer have established procedures which enable the company to comply with the Listing Rules and Disclosure and Transparency Rules on an ongoing basis (LR 8.4.2) and understand the nature and extent of their responsibilities under the Listing Rules and Disclosure and Transparency Rules (LR 8.3.4). The sponsor will be required to confirm that it is satisfied about such matters in its Declaration on an Application for Listing which it makes to the FSA.

2.3.8 Training for directors

In response to a desire by some of its members to improve their skills and to provide a solution for outside observers seeking to ensure the presence of certain skills at board level, in 1999 the Institute of Directors introduced a voluntary training and assessment programme leading to qualification as a chartered director. The qualification process is a very rigorous one, and those who attain the qualification must also undertake continuing training to maintain and develop their knowledge and skills.

Since the chartered director qualification was introduced in 1999 more than 840 directors have been chartered (up to April 2010), and as the UK Corporate Governance Code strongly advocates training for all listed company board directors, it seems likely that the use of the qualification will increase.

See also Section 2.3.7 above on the induction and performance evaluation provisions of the Code.

2.3.9 Effect of invalid appointment

Section 161 CA 2006 provides that the acts of a director are valid, notwithstanding any defect that afterwards may be discovered in his appointment or eligibility to act as a director or that he had ceased to hold office at all, or was not entitled to vote on the matter in question. This would be so even if the appointment had been void under Section 160 (appointment of public company directors to be voted on individually). A similar provision was contained in Table A at Regulation 92 and this provision, or something similar, may still be incorporated in the articles of many companies although the Model Articles under CA 2006 do not replicate Regulation 92, relying instead on Section 161 of CA 2006 itself. All that said, it is likely that the provisions of Section 161 and any equivalent provisions in a company's articles relating to defective appointment offer only limited protection to a person dealing with the company because their application appears to be restricted to a procedural defect in the appointment only. *See Morris* v *Kanssen* [1946] 1 All ER 586 (HL) 459, 471, which is authority for a number of propositions:

(a) that neither Section 143 Companies Act 1929 (and therefore presumably its successors, Section 180 Companies Act 1948, Section 285 CA 1985 and Section 161 CA 2006), nor Article 88 Companies Act 1929 Table A (or its successors,

Regulation 105 Companies Act 1948, Table A or Regulation 92 of Table A) validate an appointment which is contrary to the Companies Acts or the articles of association of the relevant company;

(b) that neither the Section nor the articles can assist a party if that party had knowledge of the facts giving rise to the invalidity;

(c) it cannot assist the party if that party is put on enquiry and does not enquire;

(d) it cannot avail anyone where there is no appointment at all.[24]

2.4 Vacation of office

Once appointed, there are then a number of ways in which a director's term of office may be brought to an end.

2.4.1 Voluntary resignation

A director may resign his office at any time, despite the fact that he may also be employed by the company and have a service agreement with it which requires him to serve for a fixed term or to give a period of notice of resignation. An executive director's service agreement (and therefore his employment with the company) may continue notwithstanding his resignation from the office of director. If the director terminates his service agreement at the same time and without giving the notice required by the service agreement he may be liable to the company in damages for breach of contract. Sometimes a company's articles will specify a procedure to be followed for giving effect to a resignation from the office of director. Regulation 18(f) of the Model Articles for private companies and Regulation 22(f) of the Model Articles for public companies,[25] for example, provide that the office of a director shall be vacated upon the company receiving notice that he is resigning or retiring and such notice coming into effect. Any notice to be given by any person pursuant to those provisions will be governed by the notices provisions in the articles (e.g. *see* Regulation 46 of the Model Articles for private companies and

---

[24] *See* also *Re New Cedos* [1994] 1 BCLC 797.
[25] Regulation 81(d) of Table A contains similar provision.

Regulation 82 of the Model Articles for public companies). In addition to any such procedural measures in the articles, Section 1139 CA 2006 enables a notice of resignation to be served on the company by leaving it at, or sending it by post to, the company's registered office.[26] A resignation once made cannot be withdrawn except with the consent of the company and, unless the articles provide otherwise, it is not necessary for a resignation to be accepted by the board before it becomes effective.

The articles of private equity-backed companies commonly discourage directors from resigning voluntarily by requiring them to sell any shares in the investee company held by them or their family members for a sum which can be well below the full market value if they resign (known as "leaver" provisions). Such provisions are designed to incentivise managers to see the investment through to a successful exit for both the private equity investors and management.

In the unusual circumstances where a share qualification exists (*see* Section 2.3.4 above), a director may resign voluntarily simply by disposing of his qualification shares.

2.4.2 Retirement by rotation and potential re-election

The Model Articles for private companies do not (unlike Table A) contain retirement by rotation provisions, and even if they are operating with Table A-based articles, many private companies disapply the retirement by rotation provisions because they are considered unnecessary and cumbersome for a small, closely-held company, particularly where there may be a shareholders' or other agreement giving shareholders the right to review directors' appointments. Indeed private companies are no longer required to have an AGM under CA 2006, and the retirement by rotation provisions generally operate by reference to the AGM cycle.

By contrast, most listed and many other public companies have provisions in their articles requiring a proportion of the directors to retire at each AGM. The rationale behind these retire-

---

[26] Section 725 CA 1985 contains a similar provision.

ment by rotation provisions, which are reinforced by the UK Corporate Governance Code (*see* below), is to ensure that an individual director's appointment as a director is not wholly entrenched and shareholders have an opportunity to review that appointment periodically.

By way of example of the way retirement by rotation works, the Model Articles for public companies[27] contain provisions (at Regulation 21) to the effect that at a company's first AGM all of the directors shall retire from office and, at every subsequent AGM, any director appointed since the last AGM or who was not appointed (or re-elected) at either of the previous two AGMs shall retire from office and may offer himself for reappointment. A director who retires by rotation is normally eligible for reappointment and would (until the recent focus on corporate governance) normally be re-elected as a matter of formality. Table A (Regulation 75) provided that if the retiring director is willing to continue, he is deemed to have been reappointed unless, at the meeting, it is resolved not to fill the vacancy, or unless a resolution for his reappointment is put to the meeting and lost, but there is no corresponding provision in the Model Articles under CA 2006. If the director is not reappointed then he will usually continue to hold office until the end of the meeting at which he is due to retire. For details about persons eligible for appointment in his place *see* Section 2.2.3 above.

Any person appointed as a director in place of a person removed from office under Section 168 is treated, for the purposes of determining the time at which he or any other director is to retire as if he had become a director on the day on which the person in whose place he is appointed was last appointed a director (Section 168(4)).

---

[27] The corresponding provision of Table A is slightly different. Regulation 73 provides that at every AGM subsequent to the first one, one-third of directors subject to retirement by rotation (or if their number is not three or a multiple of three, the number nearest one-third) shall retire from office and may put themselves up for re-election. In order to determine which of the directors are to retire at any particular AGM from amongst those eligible, it is normal for companies to select for retirement those directors who have been in office longest since their last appointment or reappointment (but *see* Section 2.3.1 above where a director has been appointed to replace another director who is retiring due to age). Where more than the required number were last appointed or reappointed at the same time, then those to retire are to be determined by lot, unless they agree amongst themselves who is to stand for re-election in that year (Regulation 74 of Table A).

If there is provision in a public company's articles to require that a director appointed initially by the board must retire at the first AGM following his appointment (e.g. Regulation 21(2)(a) of the Model Articles for public companies[28]), this provision can, at times, create practical difficulties. For example, if the board appoints a new director after the dispatch of notice of the company's AGM but before the meeting itself takes place, many companies' articles would require (as in the case of Regulation 21 of the Model Articles) that the director concerned must, nevertheless, still retire at the AGM and, if not reappointed at that meeting, vacate office at the end of it. In these circumstances the board will need to consider carefully the other provisions of the company's articles and the precise wording of the notice convening the meeting. Possible courses of action may include:

(a) proposing a resolution at the AGM to reappoint the relevant director under a provision in the company's articles if they enable such a resolution to be included within the "ordinary business" of the AGM, for which no specific notice is required in the notice of the meeting;[29]

(b) sending a further notice to shareholders including details of the additional resolution and, if necessary, adjourning the AGM to enable the necessary notice period to elapse; or

(c) allowing the new director's appointment to lapse at the end of the AGM and then reappointing him immediately by further resolution of the board.

In this last situation, the director will have to retire again at the next AGM and proper notice of his proposed re-election should be given.[30]

---

[28] *See* also Regulation 79 of Table A and Code Provision B.7.1 (referred to in more detail later in this Section).

[29] If, as is common, the notice of AGM contains full particulars of the directors retiring by rotation and submitting themselves for reappointment, it is doubtful whether the company could rely on the ordinary business provisions to table the resolution for the reappointment of a director who had not been named in the notice.

[30] A further possible solution for a company with Table A-based articles would be for the director to retire at the AGM and for the board then to recommend his appointment to the AGM, thus taking advantage of the provisions of Regulations 76(a) and 78 of Table A (if they apply). Not less than seven days' notice must be given to all who are entitled to receive notice of the meeting of the intention so to recommend and including details of the relevant director, all as required by Regulation 77 of Table A (if it applies).

It is effectively not open to listed companies to opt out of retirement by rotation provisions in view of the corporate governance requirements applicable to them. Historically, the Combined Code always imposed retirement by rotation requirements on directors of listed companies. The financial crisis in 2008 to 2009 triggered widespread reappraisal of the UK corporate governance regime, including the FRC's review of the Combined Code (now the UK Corporate Governance Code). One of the most controversial suggestions made by the FRC was that all directors should be subject to annual re-election (rather than every three years), in order to increase accountability to shareholders. Many commentators felt that annual re-election of the entire board would risk uncertainty and short-termism in the company's governance and create the potential to destabilise the board. Nevertheless Provision B.7.1 of the UK Corporate Governance Code (the "Code") requires all directors of FTSE 350 companies to be subject to annual election by shareholders. Provision B.7.1 then goes on to require directors of all other listed companies to submit themselves for re-election at the first AGM after their appointment and thereafter at intervals of no more than three years. PIRC's 2010 UK Shareholder Voting Guidelines stipulate annual re-election as good practice for all companies and where annual re-election is not adopted, PIRC recommends that any change in a director's role during the period between re-elections should be submitted to shareholders for approval.

Code Provision B.7.1 also requires that the names of all directors subject to election or re-election should be accompanied by sufficient biographical details and other relevant information to enable shareholders to make an informed decision as to their election. Consistent with Section 160 CA 2006, which effectively requires a separate resolution for each director, to enable shareholders to cast their vote on each director individually, Listing Rule 9.3.7 requires that the proxy form for re-election of retiring directors allows votes to be cast for or against the re-election of each director individually.

Companies to which the Code applies generally adopt articles which are compliant with the Code but many FTSE companies' articles are, at least in the short term, likely to be out of step with the new annual re-election requirements of the Code. The preface to the Code recognises that companies may need a transitional period before they introduce annual re-election and that companies may explain, rather than comply, if they believe that their existing arrangements ensure proper accountability. So, any departure from the Code's requirements must be highlighted in the next following annual report and accounts, as required under Listing Rule 9.8.6(6)(b). Shareholders are unlikely to go along with the removal of, or exemption from, retirement by rotation provisions. PIRC, for example, states that companies must remove provisions in their articles which have the effect of exempting directors from re-election. The shareholder bodies regard it as fundamental to good corporate governance that directors are required to seek regular re-election by shareholders, and the retirement by rotation provisions provide shareholders with an opportunity to express disapproval without having to go through the potentially costly and cumbersome requisition procedures.

For listed companies, the corporate governance climate has also evolved such that nowadays directors can no longer assume that their re-election is a formality, and directors are more accountable than ever to shareholders for their performance. As noted in Section 2.2.6, institutional shareholders are under a positive obligation under the FRC's new Stewardship Code to monitor the performance of their investee companies and their directors and senior management. The ultimate weapon for institutional shareholders who are dissatisfied with the company's performance would be to requisition a separate shareholders' meeting to change the composition of the board (as explained in more detail in Sections 2.2.5 and 2.4.5 below), but more commonly directors of listed companies are experiencing shareholder opposition to their re-election at the AGM, often as a result of concerns as to over-generous remuneration and severance arrangements and/or insufficiently stringent performance criteria attached to the award of bonuses and other incentive arrangements.

Many of the recent shareholder revolts have reflected opposition to the company's remuneration policy as set out in the remuneration report which companies are required to submit to shareholders for approval by Sections 420 to 422 CA 2006. The ABI regularly updates its remuneration guidelines in line with the expectations of the market to help boards of listed companies better understand institutional shareholders' concerns that remuneration should be linked to performance, and the ABI has frequently placed "red top" or "amber top" warnings on listed companies who are considered in breach of corporate governance requirements, which encourage opposition among shareholders. According to the IVIS Review 2009, five remuneration reports were voted down in 2009, including Punch Taverns which was red-topped, and Royal Dutch Shell and RBS which were amber-topped. Whilst a negative vote in respect of the directors' remuneration report will not affect the appointment or terms of appointment of individual directors (other than by exerting moral pressure and to avoid the risk of adverse publicity and "blacklisting" by the major institutional shareholders), one of the ways in which institutional shareholders can actively express their disapproval for an individual director's performance and/or remuneration package is by voting down his or her re-election.

The NAPF Corporate Governance Policy and Voting Guidelines state that shareholders may choose to vote against the re-election of a director in the absence of a supporting statement from the Board or where there is clear evidence of poor performance by the individual or the company. NAPF also recommends a vote against the chairman of the remuneration committee in the case of severe or persistent infringements of good practice in the company's remuneration arrangements.

In 2003, the government threatened legislation to control excessive severance payments to directors, but was persuaded for the time being to allow further time for the market to regulate itself based on the then Combined Code (now the UK Corporate Governance Code) and the ABI and other guidelines. The government did however take a reserve power in the CA 2006 (Section 1277) to make regulations requiring institutional shareholders to disclose information about the exercise of their voting rights, a measure designed to reinforce the level of engagement of shareholders with their companies. The last Labour government stated that it had no intention of making these regulations but was continuing to monitor developments.

2.4.3 Age

Section 293 CA 1985, which set a maximum age limit of 70 for directors of public companies, was repealed in April 2007 but, as referred to in Section 2.3.1 above, it may be worth checking a company's articles for age limits which may apply to terminate a director's period of office. For a discussion on the minimum age limit for directors *see* also Section 2.3.1 above.

2.4.4 Vacation of office pursuant to the company's articles

Most companies' articles contain provisions pursuant to which directors must vacate office automatically. The most common provisions are similar to those contained in Regulation 17 of the Model Articles for private companies and Regulation 22 of the Model Articles for public companies, both of which state that a person ceases to be a director as soon as:

(a) that person ceases to be a director by virtue of any provision of the Companies Act 2006 or is prohibited from being a director by law;

(b) a bankruptcy order is made against that person;

(c) a composition is made with that person's creditors generally in satisfaction of that person's debts;

(d) a registered medical practitioner who is treating that person gives a written opinion to the company stating that that person has become physically or mentally incapable of acting as a director and may remain so for more than three months;

(e) by reason of that person's mental health, a court makes an order which wholly or partly prevents that person from personally exercising any powers or rights which that person would otherwise have;

(f) notification is received by the company from the director that the director is resigning from office as a director and such resignation has taken effect in accordance with its terms.

These provisions update the corresponding provisions in Regulation 81 of Table A.[31] In one of the more significant changes, a director's failure to attend directors' meetings for a certain period was treated as a termination event under Table A, whereas there is no corresponding provision in the Model Articles. Early drafts of the Model Articles had a more general provision under which the director's appointment would terminate when all the other directors decided that a director should be removed from office, providing greater flexibility as to the circumstances in which non-attendance may arise. However that provision gave rise to concern that the directors could use it to overturn the appointment of a director by shareholders, so it was dropped. That said, there are often provisions in a company's articles enabling the board to remove a director by resolution of a particular majority or by unanimous resolution of the directors (excluding the director concerned).[32] Such provisions are usually designed to enable the board to deal with a disruptive director without the publicity and procedural difficulties of Section 168 CA 2006 in circumstances where a director, who no longer has the support of his fellow directors, refuses to resign.

---

[31] Regulation 81 of Table A states that the office of a director shall be vacated if:

  (a) he ceases to be a director by virtue of any provision of CA 1985 or he becomes prohibited by law from being a director;

  (b) he becomes bankrupt or makes any arrangement or composition with his creditors generally;

  (c) he is, or may be, suffering from mental disorder and either:

    (i) he is admitted to hospital in pursuance of an application for admission for treatment under the Mental Health Act 1983 or, in Scotland, an application for admission under the Mental Health (Scotland) Act 1960, or

    (ii) an order is made by a court having jurisdiction (whether in the UK or elsewhere) in matters concerning mental disorder for his detention or for the appointment of a receiver, *curator bonis* or other person to exercise powers with respect to his property or affairs;

  (d) he resigns his office by notice to the company; or

  (e) for more than six consecutive months he shall have been absent without the permission of the directors from meetings of directors held during that period and the directors resolve that his office be vacated.

[32] An August 1993 Statement of Principles from the Institutional Shareholders Committee ("Role and Duties of Directors – A Statement of Best practice", available from www.ivis.co.uk) suggests that listed companies' articles should provide that a director should only be dismissed by written resolution (unanimous) of the board or, at the very least, a majority of 75 per cent of co-directors. The Statement also suggests that the articles should provide that a director may be dismissed from office by his fellow directors for failing to attend a specified number of board meetings or board meetings held in a specified period.

The Model Articles also adopt a more generic approach in relation to mental illness in paragraph (e), avoiding specific references to mental health legislation that may change over time. The Model Articles provisions incorporate the consequences of the CDDA 1986 and the Enterprise Act 2002, pursuant to which a director may be prohibited by court order or pursuant to a disqualification undertaking from being a director for a specified period, unless he first obtains leave of the court. Such orders may be granted (or undertakings given) following general misconduct in connection with companies (such as conviction for indictable offences, persistent breaches of companies legislation or fraud); or for reasons of unfitness to hold the office of director (if the court is satisfied that the individual has been a director of a company which has, at any time, become insolvent and his conduct as a director of that company makes him unfit to be concerned in the management of a company); or, in the case of disqualification under the Enterprise Act 2002, for breach by the company of which the individual is a director of EC or UK competition law. (*See* also Chapter 13.)

In addition to these "standard" provisions, specific provisions on termination of a director's appointment may be found in a company's articles or in a shareholders' agreement. For example, where a director has been appointed by a particular interest group, the company's articles may provide for his appointor to remove the director in a similar manner to which the appointment was made (e.g. a private equity investor may be entitled to appoint and/or remove a specified number of directors, or sometimes any and all directors, by depositing a notice to that effect at the company's registered office). Similarly a director's period of office may terminate on some event specified in the articles (e.g. the end of an earn-out period where a particular director was appointed by the vendor and where the appointment was to be limited to the duration of the earn-out period).

2.4.5 Removal pursuant to Section 168 CA 2006

As a safeguard for shareholders a company may, pursuant to Section 168 CA 2006, by ordinary resolution remove a director before the expiration of his period of office. This provision overrides any agreement or arrangement between the company and the director, although it does not prevent the director from seeking compensation for breach (by reason of the operation of the Section) of any contractual rights which he may hold. Section 168 can be helpful if the board is unwilling to operate the provisions (if any) contained in the company's articles (*see* Section 2.4.4 above) or in the relevant director's service agreement (*see* Section 2.4.6 below) entitling them to remove a director, provided the director to be removed controls fewer than 50 per cent of the voting rights in issue.

As noted in Section 2.2.6 above, activist shareholders in listed companies have in recent years been more inclined to use their powers to propose resolutions at the company's AGM or requisition a general meeting in order to force board changes, removing incumbent directors and putting forward their own nominees. The Stewardship Code does suggest that if boards do not respond constructively to behind-the-scenes intervention on the part of institutional investors, then one of the ways in which shareholders can escalate their action is to requisition a general meeting or resolution to change the board. However the NAPF and other corporate governance voting guidelines for shareholders in listed companies still mainly focus on voting on re-election at the AGM rather than the more aggressive step of implementing the Section 168 procedure.

The Section 168 procedure may be used where the directors who are being targeted by the shareholders for removal are not retiring by rotation at the AGM, or the action cannot wait until the AGM so the general meeting requisition route is used. In the well-publicised case of *Mitchells & Butlers* in January 2010, a shareholder with a 22.8 per cent stake used a combination of all of the statutory powers available to it to replace the board, putting forward resolutions to appoint new directors and remove the former chairman and leading a revolt which resulted in several incumbent directors being voted down on re-election. (That case was the subject of a Takeover Panel investigation into allegations that certain shareholders had acted in concert, but the Panel found that no breach of the Takeover Code had occurred (*see* Panel Notice 2010/1 on the Panel's website at www.thetakeoverpanel.org).)

However, cases such as this are still relatively rare, and it may be that often companies agree to a behind-the-scenes compromise before the matter comes before a general shareholders' meeting. In a sense this may be achieving the intention behind the previous government's efforts to make boards more accountable to their shareholders, whilst not putting the company's fortunes at risk by publicising the shareholders' dissatisfaction.

Another reason why the Section 168 procedure can be unattractive or impracticable is that special notice of a Section 168 resolution is required, essentially to enable the director concerned to protest against his removal. Pursuant to Section 312 CA 2006, a Section 168 resolution is not effective unless notice of the intention to table it has been given to the company at least 28 days before the meeting at which it is to be considered and the company has given its members notice of any such resolution at the same time and in the same manner as it gives notice of the meeting. If that is not practicable, the company must give members notice, either by advertisement in a newspaper having an appropriate circulation or by any other mode allowed by the company's articles, at least 14 days[33] before the meeting at which the resolution is to be considered. If, after notice of the intention to table such a resolution has been given to the company, a meeting is called for a date 28 days or less after the notice has been given to the company, the notice is deemed properly given, even though the notice was not actually given within the time required.[34]

On receipt of the notice of an intended resolution to remove a director under Section 168 the company must, forthwith, send a copy of the notice to the director concerned. The director is entitled to be heard on the resolution at the meeting at which it is put, whether he is a member of the company or not. The

---

[33] Previously the limit was 21 days under Section 379 CA 1985. The change was made to bring it into line with Section 307 CA 2006, which provides that 14 days' notice will be sufficient for all general meetings except an AGM of a public company which still requires at least 21 days' notice.

[34] In view of the special arrangements for notice of a resolution to remove a director, under Section 288(2)(a), the written resolution procedure available to private companies under Section 288 CA 2006 does not apply to Section 168 resolutions.

director is also entitled to make written representations to the company (not exceeding a reasonable length) and to request that they be notified to members. The company must then (unless the representations are received by it too late for it to do so):

(a) in any notice of the resolution given to members of the company, state the fact that the representations have been made; and
(b) send a copy of the representations to every member of the company to whom notice of the meeting is sent (whether the notice is sent to members before or after the company receives the director's representations).

If a copy of the representations is not sent as required above because they were received too late or because the company failed to do so, the director may, in addition to being able to speak at the meeting, require that his written representations be read out at the meeting. Copies of the director's representations need not be sent out and they need not be read out at the meeting if, on the application of either the company or any other person who claims to be aggrieved, the court is satisfied that the director's rights to have his statement circulated are being abused.[35] Even if the director is not a party to such an application, the court may order the company's costs on the application to be paid by him.

As to whether it is possible to contract out of these provisions, Section 303 CA 1985 applied "notwithstanding anything in [the company's] articles". Although this saving has not been carried over into Section 168, Explanatory Note 68 CA 2006 states in general terms that a company's articles cannot contain anything that is contrary to the provisions of the Act. In any event such a provision or exclusion would in all likelihood constitute an unlawful fetter on the company's statutory powers, as outlined in the case of *Russell v Northern Bank Development Corp Ltd* [1992] 3 All ER 161. A company's articles

---

[35] Section 304 CA 1985 previously required the court to be satisfied that the director's rights were being abused "to secure needless publicity for defamatory matters". It is now sufficient under Section 169(5) for the court to be satisfied that the director's rights are being abused.

would not, therefore, be able to exclude the ability of a company to remove its directors by ordinary resolution. However, as was the position under the CA 1985, a company should be able to provide in its articles for another removal mechanism, for example removal by the majority shareholder(s) on written notice – a provision which is not uncommon in the articles of private equity-backed companies. Section 168 does not provide that removal by ordinary resolution is the *only* permissible method but simply that a company *may* use this method.

It was generally considered that nothing in the CA 1985 prevented the operation of any provision in the articles of the company, pursuant to which the director concerned (or any other person) is granted enhanced voting rights entitling him to defeat any resolution proposed pursuant to Section 303 (*Bushell v Faith* [1970] AC 1099) and there seems no reason why this should not be the case under CA 2006.[36] However, such provisions do need to be drafted carefully if they are to provide effective protection for the director concerned and if they are not to be circumvented. For example, the provisions need to create enhanced voting rights not only in respect of the Section 168 resolution itself but also any resolution which may first be proposed to change the articles in order to remove or dilute the article by which his voting rights are enhanced.

The provisions of Section 168 and the *Russell v Northern Bank* case should not prevent there being an agreement between a company's shareholders (outside the articles of association), enforceable as between shareholders, that they will not exercise their rights under Section 168 to remove a particular director, provided the agreement is not binding on the director or the company. This might be useful to secure the position of a director appointed by a particular shareholder or class of shareholder, for example, a private equity investor (*see* also Section 2.2.10 above for more on entrenchment). In private equity-backed companies, the appointment and removal of nominee

---

[36] There is some doubt, however, as to whether *Bushell v Faith* provisions would be upheld in the articles of association of a public company, as a result of *obiter dicta* the judgment of the House of Lords in the *Bushell v Faith* case which indicate that the principle is most appropriate to small, family-owned private companies.

directors of such investors is usually, as mentioned above, within the power of the private equity investor itself acting on its own (*see* also Section 2.8 below on nominee directors).

Shareholders should, however, consider the risk of a claim for unfair prejudice from a director who is also a shareholder, particularly if such a provision is to be added to a company's articles specifically in order to remove the director in question. There were several cases under the CA 1985 regime considering a petition for relief under Sections 459 to 461 CA 1985 (the predecessors to 994 to 998 CA 2006) as a result of allegations of unfair prejudice in relation to the removal of directors. It appears from the case law on the old Section 303 CA 1985 that the circumstances in which a petition under Section 994 (Section 459 CA 1985) would be most likely to succeed are where the director is a "founder", or the company is a family company, and where the individual would have some reasonable expectation of involvement in management. In a quasi-partnership context the House of Lords decision in *Ebrahimi v Westbourne Galleries Ltd and others* [1972] 2 All ER 492 may be relevant. *See* also *Brownlow v GH Marshall* [2001] BCC 152 and *Parkinson v Euro Finance Group Ltd and others* [2001] 1 BCLC 720. Conversely, in the case of *Re Astec (BSR) Plc* (unreported May 1998), Chancery Division, it was held that unfair prejudice could not be established simply because there was no reason for the removal of directors, nor were "legitimate expectations" relevant.[37] The cases on alteration of the company's articles to the detriment of the minority suggest that the majority shareholders should be particularly careful if a provision entitling them to remove a director summarily on written notice (effectively disapplying the special notice provisions of Section 168) is added to the articles after incorporation, where they may be perceived to be acting other than in good faith and in their own interests rather than those of the company as a whole. *See* for example, *Allen v Gold Reefs of West Africa Ltd* [1900]1 Ch 656 and *Greenhalgh v Arderne Cinemas Ltd* [1951] Ch 286 and, more recently, the Privy Council case of *Citco Banking v Pusser's Ltd and another* [2007] All ER (D) 369.

---

[37] *See* also *Woolwich v Twenty Twenty Productions Ltd* [2003] All ER (D) 211.

2.4.6 Vacation of office pursuant to a provision in a service contract

Provisions are often contained in a director's service contract with the company which require, as a matter of contract, a director to resign his office as director of the company if his employment with the company is terminated. Such provisions would usually also grant a power of attorney[38] in favour of one or more of the remaining directors, enabling such other directors to sign his letter of resignation on his behalf should he fail to do so as required by the terms of the service contract. Care needs to be taken when operating such provisions in a service contract to ensure that the service contract is terminated lawfully and that the events which give rise to the requirement for the director to resign have arisen.

In the case of many private equity-backed companies, it is not unusual to find provisions in the service contract providing for termination of the director's employment (and therefore triggering dismissal as a director) for breach of the director's undertakings (or covenants or warranties), qua shareholder, in any shareholders' agreement or the company's articles of association.

2.4.7 Vacation by order of the court

The court's powers on an application under Section 994 CA 2006 (unfair prejudice) are, in theory, wide enough for the court to order that a director cease to hold office. In practice, however, the courts are extremely reluctant to interfere in the direct management of a company in this way.

2.5 Notification obligations and returns to regulators

On a director's appointment to, or removal from, office, and upon any change in the identity or details of a director of a

---

[38] To be valid the power of attorney must be properly executed as a deed in accordance with the Law of Property (Miscellaneous Provisions) Act 1986. So, either the power of attorney should be contained in a separate document or the service contract should be executed as a deed.

company, in addition to any requirements specific to a particular type of company (*see* Section 2.3.3 above), a number of notifications must be made and returns filed with regulators, as follows.

2.5.1 Notifications to the company

On the appointment of any director, the company must record, in the register of directors maintained pursuant to Section 162 CA 2006, the details of the director specified by Section 163 CA 2006 or in the case of a corporate director, Section 164 CA 2006. Section 162 CA 2006 requires that a company's register of directors is open to public inspection. In the case of a director who is an individual, the register of directors will contain details of the director's service address rather than his home address, and the company must now maintain a separate register of directors' residential addresses under Section 165, which is not available for public inspection, in order to preserve confidentiality for a director who has chosen to file a service address which is not his or her usual residential address. Section 240 of CA 2006 makes the details of a director's home address (or an indication that the director's service address is his home address) "protected information" which means that it may be disclosed only in limited circumstances.

For more on this *see* Section 2.5.3 below.

For the purposes of Section 1144 CA 2006, the service address must be a place where service of documents can be effected by physical delivery and delivery of documents is capable of being recorded by the obtaining of an acknowledgement of delivery.[39] For this reason, a PO Box address or similar will not be suitable. Many directors have opted to use the company's registered office or principal place of business as their service address.

Pursuant to Section 228 CA 2006 the company must keep a copy of any written service contract between the director and the company (or a subsidiary) or, where it is not in writing, a written

---

[39] *See* paragraph 10 Companies (Annual Return and Service Addresses) Regulations 2008 (SI 2009/3000).

memorandum setting out its terms. As a result of the expanded definition of "service contract" set out in Section 227, the requirement also now extends to contracts for services and letters of appointment. Such copies must be kept available for inspection at the company's registered office or such other place as may be specified in the Regulations made under Section 1136 CA 2006.[40] Those Regulations apply to the company registers and other records, as well as directors' service contracts, which must be available for inspection, and enable a company to designate a single alternative location for inspection of service contracts and other company registers and records, for example, the company's principal place of business. Such documents must be open to inspection by any member of the company without charge under Section 229(1). Section 228(3) also requires service contracts to be retained and available for inspection for at least one year after they have expired.

As referred to above a director's home address is now "protected information" under section 240 CA 2006 and the disclosure restrictions will apply equally to a director's home address appearing in a service contract. In practice, a director may consent to his home address appearing in his service contract and therefore becoming publicly available by virtue of section 228, but if he withholds his consent or his consent has not been sought, the company may be obliged under Section 241 CA 2006 to remove details of the home address from the relevant service contract, and a service address should be used in the service contract. This should be the same service address as appears in the company's register of directors.

Section 324 CA 1985, which required a director, on his appointment, to notify his interests (and those of certain connected persons) in the share capital of, and any debentures issued by, the company and any other body corporate and thereafter, while he remained a director to notify any changes to such interests, was repealed on 6 April 2007. However directors of listed companies will have obligations under the Disclosure and Transparency Rules to notify the company of dealings

---

[40] The Companies (Company Records) Regulations 2008 (SI 2008/3006).

in shares and similar obligations apply to directors of AIM companies under the AIM Rules.

2.5.2 *Notifications to the Registrar of Companies*

As mentioned in Section 2.2.1 above, on the application for the incorporation of a new company under CA 2006, the registration details which are delivered to the Registrar of Companies under Section 9 CA 2006 must contain the names and required particulars of the first directors. The same details, including a consent to act from the new director, must be delivered to the Registrar of Companies, under Section 167 CA 2006, on the appointment thereafter of any new director. Similarly, any vacation of office for whatever reason and any change in the director's registered particulars (including residential address) must be notified to the Registrar of Companies. All such notifications must be made to the Registrar of Companies within 14 days after the relevant event. In addition, any changes must be properly recorded in any subsequent annual return filed under Section 855.

Under CA 2006, the Registrar of Companies is obliged, under Section 1068(5), to ensure that various documents (the full list is set out in Section 1078) can be delivered to the Registrar in electronic form. Advice on how documents can be filed electronically with Companies House can be found on the Companies House website at https://ewf.companieshouse.gov.uk.

2.5.3 *Disclosure of directors' residential addresses*

Following a number of much-publicised cases of harassment of directors of companies involved in particular sectors of commerce or industry (e.g. Huntingdon Life Sciences), CA 1985 was amended in 2002 to permit directors to apply for a confidentiality order whereby their usual residential address would be kept on a confidential register and the public register would contain details of a service address only. Until 1 October 2009, when the relevant provisions of the CA 2006 came into force, these provisions[41] applied only to directors who were threatened

---

[41] Inserted into CA 1985 by the Companies (Particulars of Usual Residential Address) (Confidentiality Orders) Regulations 2002 (SI 2002/912)).

with violence or intimidation. Since 1 October 2009, the relevant provisions of the CA 2006 have effectively extended the confidentiality provisions to all directors. So, on first appointment (and thereafter) directors are required to file only a service address for the public register at Companies House, and in the company's register of directors. The company must, though, keep a separate register of directors' residential addresses (Section 165). When a director is appointed, Companies House must be notified under Section 167 of the particulars of the director, including his residential address, but the residential address is "protected information" for the purposes of Sections 240 to 246 of CA 2006. As such, a company must not use or disclose that protected information except:

(a)   in communications with the relevant director;
(b)   to comply with any filing requirements under the Companies Acts; or
(c)   under court order,

unless the director consents to the use or disclosure of his home address details. Similarly, the address may not be disclosed by Companies House, with limited exceptions (e.g. if the Registrar of Companies is obliged to disclose it to a credit reference agency or under a court order). Under the transitional provisions,[42] for a director of a pre-CA 2006 company, whatever address the company had in the register of directors for that director (usually the home address unless a Confidentiality Order under CA 1985 had been granted) will have been deemed to be the service address. As such the director's home address will not be "protected information"[43] unless and until the director notifies the company that he wishes to use a service address, whereupon the company will be obliged to amend the register of directors and notify Companies House of the change. Some directors of pre-CA 2006 companies will not have filed a service address thus far, either because there is no particular sensitivity surrounding disclosure of their home address or possibly because they have taken the view that there is no advantage

---

[42]   *See* paragraph 27 of Schedule 2 Companies Act 2006 (Commencement No 8, Transitional Provisions and Savings) Order 2008 (SI 2008/2860).
[43]   *See* paragraph 33 of Schedule 2 Eighth Commencement Order.

to be gained from doing so since there is a rather obvious loophole under the CA 2006 regime whereby historic filings which contained the director's home address (e.g. the original Form 288) will still be on the register even if a subsequent change of address notification has been filed. Directors wishing to have these details removed must apply to the Registrar of Companies under the regulations made under Section 1088 of CA 2006.[44] These regulations only permit directors at risk of violence or intimidation to make an application under them to remove their existing home address details from the register.

2.5.4 The UK Listing Authority

Where the company is a listed company, Listing Rule 9.6.11 requires that the company notifies an RIS[45] of any change to the board as soon as possible and no later than by the end of the business day following the decision or receipt of notice about the change by the company. Such a notification must also be made if there are significant changes to the role, functions or responsibilities of an incumbent director, as well as in the event of directors' appointments and removals. However, no such notification is required where a director retires by rotation and is reappointed at a general meeting. The notification must state the effective date of change if it is not with immediate effect. If the effective date is not known at the time of the announcement, or has not been determined, the announcement should state that fact and the company must notify an RIS when the effective date has been decided. In the case of the appointment of a new director, the company's notification must state whether the position is executive, non-executive or as chairman and the nature of any specific function or responsibility to be undertaken by the director.

In addition, Listing Rule 9.6.13 requires listed companies to notify to an RIS the following information in respect of any new director appointed to the board:

---

[44] Companies (Disclosure of Address) Regulations 2009 (SI 2009/214).
[45] References in the Listing Rules to "RIS" or "Regulatory Information Service", are defined under the Listing Rules as a service listed in Appendix 3 to the Listing Rules. Appendix 3 contains a list of the names of the various commercial operations set up in competition with the Regulatory News Service of the London Stock Exchange following deregulation. The RNS is one of the approved services.

(a) the details of all directorships held by such director in any other publicly quoted company at any time in the previous five years, indicating whether or not the individual is still a director; and

(b) the details of any unspent convictions, relevant insolvencies or public criticisms by regulatory bodies (all as detailed in Listing Rule 9.6.13(2) to (6)),

or, if there are no such details to be disclosed, that fact.

The information required must be notified as soon as possible and in any event within five business days following the decision to appoint the director being made. In addition, under Listing Rule 9.6.14, an RIS must be notified as soon as possible if there is any change in any of the information in relation to current directors which has already been notified under Rule 9.6.13, including any new directorships.

2.5.5 Information on company stationery

Paragraph 8 of the regulations made under Sections 82 and 1051 CA 2006[46] (which replaced Section 305 CA 1985 on 1 October 2008) requires the names of all directors to be stated on business letters if any director's name is included somewhere on the letter (other than in the text or as a signatory). Therefore, any change in the identity of the directors of the company would also need to be reflected in the company's notepaper as required by Section 305 CA 1985 if the notepaper sets out the names of the directors. The regulations retain the old CA 1985 prohibition on companies cherry-picking which directors' names appear on the company stationery and, as under CA 1985, the option will be to include all or none.

2.6 Alternate directors

There is nothing in CA 2006 itself in relation to alternate directors, but it is common for companies, in their articles, to make

---

[46] The Companies (Trading Disclosures) Regulations 2008 (SI 2008/495).

provision for a director to appoint an alternate to stand in his place as a director of the company when he is not available. Table A had standard provisions allowing for the appointment of alternates (Regulations 65 to 69) but provision for alternates only appears in the Model Articles for public companies under CA 2006. It was assumed when CA 2006 was enacted that few private companies would want or need a provision for alternates, but there is nothing to prevent a private company adopting articles which allow for alternates.

It is necessary to look carefully at the wording of the particular company's articles to identify the precise detail of any procedures to be followed for the appointment and removal of an alternate.

Where the Model Articles for public companies apply, Regulation 25 enables a director to appoint any other director or any other person approved by a resolution of the directors as his alternate to exercise his powers and carry out his responsibilities in relation to the taking of decisions by the directors. This provision reflects the narrower view adopted by the then government in introducing the Model Articles that it is in relation to formal decision-making processes that alternates are most likely to be useful, as this is probably the only context in which it is critical to have a particular number of directors involved. Regulations 25 and 26(1), therefore, envisage that alternates will only act in relation to formal decision making rather than exercising all the same rights and responsibilities as the appointors have as directors.

Regulation 27 of the Model Articles for public companies sets out the circumstances in which an alternate's appointment will terminate, for example when the appointor revokes the appointment by notice to the company, upon his appointor ceasing to be a director (unless he retires by rotation and is then reappointed at the same general meeting), upon the death of the appointor or upon the occurrence of any event in relation to the alternate which, had it applied to his appointor, would result in the appointor ceasing to be a director (if, for example, the provisions on termination of a director's appointment set out in

Regulation 22 of the Model Articles for public companies apply to the alternate).[47]

Regulation 15 of the Model Articles for public companies deals with alternates' voting powers and provides that an alternate director has an additional vote on behalf of any appointor who is not participating in the meeting and would have been entitled to vote had they participated. Otherwise, if the appointor is present, the alternate is not entitled to vote. The same would normally be true of a directors' written resolution, although there is no explicit provision to this effect in the Model Articles for public companies (as was the case in Regulation 93 of Table A).

Under the Model Articles for public companies, the alternate is not entitled to receive any remuneration from the company for his services as an alternate (as was the case under Table A) except such part of the appointor's remuneration as he shall direct.

Apart from administrative arrangements, the actual status of the alternate is also governed by the company's articles. In the case of the Model Articles for public companies, Regulation 26 provides that an alternate is deemed for all purposes to be a director of the company and shall alone be responsible for his own acts and omissions. However, an alternate is not deemed to

---

[47] Where Table A applies, Regulations 65 to 69 state that any director may appoint any other director, or any other person approved by a resolution of the directors and willing to act, to be his alternate, and may remove his alternate from office at any time. Appointment and removal are by notice to the company, signed by the director, or by any other manner approved by the board. Under Table A, the board retains control over the identity of the alternate.

Regulation 66 goes on to detail certain administrative provisions. For example, an alternate is entitled to:

(a) receive notice of all meetings of directors and all meetings of committees of directors of which his appointor is a member;
(b) attend and vote at any such meetings at which his appointor is not personally present; and
(c) generally perform all of the functions of the appointor as a director, in his absence.

Regulation 67 provides that a person shall automatically cease to be an alternate if his appointor ceases to be a director. If his appointor retires by rotation or otherwise but is reappointed or deemed to have been reappointed at the meeting at which he retires, any appointment of an alternate made by him which was in force immediately before the retirement of the director continues after his reappointment.

be the agent of or for his appointor.[48] Given that the position of an alternate is defined by the articles of the particular company, great care needs to be taken in drafting and in interpreting the relevant regulations to identify the precise boundaries of an alternate's powers and the nature of his responsibilities.

As a general rule, it is likely that an alternate will be treated as a director for the purposes of CA 2006[49] and the company would, therefore, have to complete and file a return to Companies House under Section 167 on his appointment. In those circumstances, his details should also be entered into the Register of Directors and the Register of Directors' Residential Addresses and he will be subject to all of the statutory duties of directors under Part 10 CA 2006, so far as relevant to the scope of his appointment, including those relating to conflicts of interest.

As regards whether alternates can sign Companies House forms, the Registrar's Rules made under Section 1117 CA 2006 do not address alternates specifically. In most cases the form itself will specify by whom the form should be signed, or in the case of a statement of compliance required under CA 2006, by whom the statement should be made. Where the signature of a director is required, Companies House has advised that only an alternate who was on the register at Companies House as a director of the relevant company (*see* above) would be treated as a director for these purposes. Where a statutory declaration is required of directors, the accepted view is that an alternate can swear a statutory declaration in place of (but not in addition to) his appointor.

It is also thought that an alternate can act as a director for the purposes of signing contracts on behalf of the company, and witness the company seal, if the company has one, and its articles provide that documents to which the company seal is affixed may be signed by a director (as is the case with Regulation 81 of the Model Articles for public companies and Regulation 9 of the Model Articles for private companies).[50]

---

[48] Regulation 69 of Table A made similar provision.
[49] This is supported by the definition of director in Section 250 CA 2006.
[50] Or *see* Regulation 101 of Table A.

However, in respect of documents executed as a deed without the company seal, under Section 44(2) CA 2006, it is less certain that an alternate is entitled to sign as a director because the Section seems to envisage personal signature by the directors and/or secretary in question (as did its predecessor, Section 36A(4) CA 1985). If a director is not going to be available to execute a document as a deed under Section 44(2) CA 2006, rather than the director appointing an alternate to execute the document in place of the director, the better route would be for the company to appoint an attorney in advance to execute the document as a deed on its behalf. The appointment of either a corporate or individual attorney to act on behalf of the company would be valid, provided the power of attorney itself was validly executed by the company as a deed.

2.7   Shadow directors and *de facto* directors

Where a person exerts control over a board of directors to the extent that the directors (as a whole) are accustomed to acting in accordance with his directions or instructions then (unless the directors are merely acting on advice given by him in a professional capacity) Section 251 CA 2006 states that he will be treated as a "shadow director" of the company.[51]

The purpose of the shadow director provisions is to ensure that those persons who seek to control the affairs of a company without accepting a formal appointment as a director of it are, nevertheless, caught by the relevant parts of the legislation. So, by definition there is no question of a person being "appointed" as a shadow director. The appointment as such will happen by default.

Those Sections of CA 2006 which expressly apply to shadow directors include the general duties of directors in Sections 171 to 177, the provisions relating to transactions with directors (Section 223) and Section 231 (contract with sole member who is also a director). However, Section 251(3) CA 2006 states that, in relation to these Sections, a body corporate is not to be treated

---

[51] The definition was the same under Section 741(2) CA 1985.

as a shadow director of any of its subsidiary companies by reason only that the directors of the subsidiary are accustomed to acting in accordance with its directions or instructions.

The application to shadow directors of the general duties of directors set out in Sections 171 to 177 is subject to Section 170(5) which states that they will only apply where and to the extent that the corresponding common law rules or equitable principles so apply. The scope of the application of the general duties to shadow directors is not entirely clear, therefore, although in the Explanatory Notes to the CA 2006, the then government tried to assist by stating that Section 170(5) is intended to limit the application of the general duties to shadow directors to the circumstances in which the common law rules or equitable principles replaced by the statutory duties applied to shadow directors. So, where the common law rule or equitable principle does not apply to a shadow director, the statutory duty replacing that rule or principle will not apply either. The Hansard record of the debate on this particular provision provides some further clarification in that Lord Goldsmith confirmed that the intention was not to crystallise the law as it relates to shadow directors as at the date on which the general duties came into force (1 October 2007), but that the then government's intention was to allow the law to develop further (Lords Hansard text for 6 February 2006, column GC 248). The uncertainty will no doubt remain until the law has bedded down.

In addition, some provisions of other legislation are expressly stated to apply to shadow directors. *See* Sections 6 to 9 CDDA 1986 (in relation to disqualification for unfitness) and the wrongful trading provisions of Section 214 Insolvency Act 1986.

Whether or not a particular person is held to be a shadow director will depend on the precise nature of the relationship and the facts of each individual case.[52] As noted above, because of the very nature of the position, there is no formal appointment or

---

[52] In the case of *Secretary of State for Trade and Industry* v *Deverell* [2000] 2 All ER 365, the Court of Appeal gave a broad definition to the term "shadow director". The judgment in that case stressed that the primary purpose of including the concept of shadow directors in legislation is to protect the public and therefore the term should be construed broadly.

removal process and, therefore, it will be necessary for any person engaged in a relationship with the board of directors of a company to consider very carefully whether he is likely to fall within the definition, and to act accordingly.

A *de facto* director is a person who acts as a director without having been duly appointed as such, or who continues so to act after his formal appointment has been terminated or expired. This definition of *de facto* director does not appear in CA 2006, but derives from the common law. In the case of *Re Kaytech International Plc, Secretary of State* v *Kaczer* [1998] All ER (D) 655, the Court of Appeal adopted a flexible and practical approach to the determination of whether a person is a *de facto* director. In that case, the Court of Appeal stated that the crucial issue in determining *de facto* directorship was whether the individual in question had assumed the status and functions of a company director so as to make himself responsible as if he had been formally appointed as a director. The general duties of directors set out in Sections 171 to 177 CA 2006 are owed by a *de facto* director in the same way and to the same extent as a properly appointed director. In addition, certain provisions of the CDDA 1986 and the Insolvency Act 1986 also apply to *de facto* directors.

2.8   Nominee directors

The term "nominee director" generally means a director appointed by one of the shareholders or a lender to look after the interests of the appointor or some other third party, but again there is no statutory definition of nominee director, or recognition of his role as nominee as distinct from any other director and, for Companies Act purposes, a nominee director is simply a director like any other. A nominee director may be executive or non-executive. However, the role of the nominee director is potentially complex. He represents the interests of his appointor and reports to him on the activities of the company, but he may also be required to act as an "independent" director or as adviser to the board, and he must also bear in mind his general duties as a director to the company itself under Sections 171 to 177 CA 2006, which will be paramount. Except where the interests of his appointor and the company coincide, the nominee director should not identify the interests of the company with those of his appointor (*see Scottish Co-operative Wholesale Society Ltd* v *Meyer* [1999] BCLC 351). This does not mean, though, that the nominee may not pay any attention to the concerns and interests of his appointor, or that he should not, in appropriate cases, have special regard to such interests. What he must not do is subordinate the company's interests to those of his appointor. The introduction of the statutory, general duties of directors set out in Sections 171 to 177 CA 2006 is not thought to have changed this position, except that Section 172 makes it even clearer that directors are to act in the interests of the company's members as a whole, which has particular relevance to the position of nominee directors.

Chapter 3

Directors' Duties

Richard Slynn

Partner

Allen & Overy LLP

Michelle de Kluyver

Of Counsel

Norton Rose LLP

3.1   Introduction

This Chapter focuses on the general duties which directors owe to their company. Part 10 Companies Act 2006 ("CA 2006") includes a statutory statement (codification) of these general duties. They are set out in Sections 171 to 177 CA 2006 under the following headings:

(a)   duty to act within powers;
(b)   duty to promote the success of the company;
(c)   duty to exercise independent judgment;
(d)   duty to exercise reasonable care, skill and diligence;
(e)   duty to avoid conflicts of interest;
(f)   duty not to accept benefits from third parties; and
(g)   duty to declare interest in proposed transaction or arrangement.

The key aim of codification was to make the law regarding directors' duties more accessible. With a couple of exceptions (relating to declarations of directors' interests in transactions or arrangements with the company and conflicts of interest), the stated intention was principally to restate rather than change the previous law.

The general duties as codified do not cover all the duties that a director may owe to the company. Many of these are imposed by other provisions in the legislation (for example, directors need to take into account the obligations on them that arise as a result of the unfair prejudice regime contained in Part 30 CA 2006) and other duties remain uncodified, such as the duty to consider the interest of creditors in times of threatened insolvency and the duty of confidentiality which a director owes to his company. It is interesting to note that, under the law prior to CA 2006, the duty of confidentiality was generally accepted as taking priority over other duties. For example, in the Australian case of *Harkness* v *CBA* (1993) 12 ACSR 165, it was held that the duty of confidentiality owed by a director to a company is greater than the duty he owes to the appointing shareholder to report information to that shareholder.

At the time of enactment, there was a concern as to whether the statutory duties would effectively preserve the pre-existing law. One of the key reasons for this concern was that the statutory language used in CA 2006 does not in all cases concur with the decisions of the courts in interpreting the common law and equitable principles applying to the comparable duty prior to codification. In commenting on the Company Law Reform White Paper (Cm 6456), the Law Society's Company Law Committee, the Company Law Sub-Committee of the City of London Law Society and the Law Reform Committee of the General Council of the Bar raised certain concerns as to the potential lack of flexibility resulting from enshrining the general duties in a statutory code. Two cases were cited as examples of the benefits of the flexibility of case law. These were *Newgate Stud Co* v *Penfold* [2004] EWHC 2993 and *Item Software* v *Fassihi* [2004] EWCA 1244 (CA). In the *Item Software* case, Arden LJ considered it to be unhelpful to fragment duties into particular categories because this reduced flexibility. In fact, the case law generated since the implementation of the CA 2006 does not suggest that there has been a loss of flexibility and the concerns do not seem to be being borne out in practice; however, the post-implementation jurisprudence is still relatively limited.

3.2 Continuing relevance of common law and equitable principles applicable prior to CA 2006

Regard will continue to be had to the corresponding common law and equitable principles (both as applied to directors' duties before codification and as developed in other areas of law on an ongoing basis) when interpreting and applying the general duties.

CA 2006 states in Section 170 that:

> "The general duties are based on certain common law rules and equitable principles as they apply in relation to directors and have effect in place of those rules and principles as regards the duties owed to a company by a director."

It also provides that:

> "The general duties shall be interpreted and applied in the same way as common law rules or equitable principles, and regard shall be had to the corresponding common law rules and equitable principles in interpreting and applying the general duties."

These provisions were intended to ensure continuity of law and a smooth transition to the codified duties, although the need to refer back to the previous common law rules and equitable principles did bring into question the extent to which the codified law met its stated objective of being more accessible and comprehensible than the previous position at law.

The other noteworthy feature of Section 170 is that it recognises that common law and equitable principles will continue to develop in other areas (such as those applying to trustees, agents and other fiduciaries). The effect of this is that the courts may continue to have regard to developments in the common law and equitable principles applying to such other types of fiduciary relationships.

The combined effect is that the courts can interpret the statutory general duties in a flexible and evolving manner, having regard not only to pre-existing common law and equitable principles at the time of enactment, but also to developments in those principles in other fiduciary relationships over time.

In addition, as there has been no codification of the remedies for breach of the general duties, the consequences of breach will be the same as they would have been for breach of the previous corresponding duties.

3.3   To whom do the general duties apply?

The general duties are owed by a director of a company to the company. It follows that only the company can enforce the duties. However, Part 11 CA 2006 (which is considered in Chapter 10) covers the circumstances where members of the company may be able to enforce the duties on behalf of the company by way of a derivative claim. Part 11 CA 2006 does not, however, operate to give shareholders direct rights of recovery against the company for breaches of directors' duties.

A "director" is defined in Section 250 CA 2006 to include any person occupying the position of director, by whatever name called. It is accepted that the term "director" is wider than simply including a person who has been validly appointed as a director and that the duties of a director may be assumed by a person who acts as a director, a *de facto* director, without having been appointed validly, or at all.

The provisions regarding the duties owed by shadow directors were the subject of much debate. A shadow director is defined as a person in accordance with whose directions or instructions the directors of the company are accustomed to act. For the purposes of the general duties of directors, Section 251(3) CA 2006 expressly exempts a body corporate from being a shadow director of any of its subsidiary companies by reason only that the directors of the subsidiary are accustomed to act in accordance with its directions or instructions. CA 2006 provides in Section 170(5) that: "The general duties apply to shadow directors where, and to the extent that, the corresponding common law rules or equitable principles so apply". The intended effect is that where a common law rule or equitable principle applied to a shadow director prior to CA 2006, the statutory duty replacing the common law rule or equitable principle will now apply to the shadow director instead. Where the position was that certain common law rules and equitable principles did not apply to shadow directors, the effect is that the statutory duty replacing those rules or principles will not apply either. This approach was taken because the law prior to CA 2006 was unclear as to the extent to which the common law duties and equitable principles applied to shadow directors. Case law, culminating in the case of *Ultraframe* v *Fielding and others* [2005] EWHC 1638 (Ch), differed on the extent to which shadow directors were subject to directors' duties. In the *Ultraframe* case, the court concluded that simply falling within the definition of a shadow director was not enough to impose on a person the same fiduciary duties as owed by the company's *de jure* or *de facto* directors, this was especially the case where the shadow director did not deal with, or claim the right to deal directly with, the company's assets. However, if the acts of a shadow director went beyond indirect influence, he could then be subject to specific fiduciary duties (particularly where he sought to further his own interests, as opposed to those of the company). Given that the position was unclear, the decision to preserve the status quo rather than to attempt to codify the duties applicable to shadow directors gives the courts flexibility to continue to develop the law in this area.

In the case of *Secretary of State for Trade and Industry* v *Hall* [2009] BCC 190 the question arose as to when a director of a corporate director could be characterised as a shadow (alternatively, *de facto*) director for the purpose of disqualification proceedings under the Company Directors Disqualification Act 1986 ("CDDA"). The court analysed those issues by applying the principle set out in *Re Hydrodam (Corby) Ltd (in liq.)* [1994] BCC 161 that a shadow directorship would arise where an individual gave instructions based on which the company (through its directors) was accustomed to act. In *Secretary of State for Trade and Industry* v *Hall* a company called Legal Directors Ltd ("LDL") was appointed as a corporate director of a company called Mercury Solutions UK Ltd ("Mercury"), which later went into insolvent liquidation. The Secretary of State sought to have Mr Nuttall, a director of LDL, disqualified under the CDDA on the basis that he was responsible for the inactivity of the corporate director which in turn had contributed to Mercury's failure.

Mr Nuttall successfully challenged the proceedings on the basis that he had no role in the management of LDL or LDL's management of Mercury; nor had he held himself out as a *de facto* director. A director of a corporate director of a company is therefore unlikely to be characterised as a shadow or *de facto* director of the underlying company unless he exercises the requisite degree of control required by the Hydrodam test. Thus although complete inactivity by a director can constitute unfitness; some activity amounting to sufficient control is required to constitute that person as a shadow director (or indeed *de facto* director) of a company in the first place.

In two specific cases, the duties continue to apply after a person ceases to be a director. First, this applies in relation to the duty to avoid conflicts of interest concerning the exploitation of any property, information or opportunity of which he became aware at a time when he was a director. Secondly, it applies to the duty not to accept benefits from third parties relating to things done or permitted by him before he ceased to be a director.

3.4   The general duties

Set out below is an analysis of each of the statutory general duties. In respect of each, there is an outline of the duty and consideration of particular issues that arise in interpreting it (including, where appropriate, consideration of how the developed case law regarding the corresponding old duty may be relevant when the courts are asked to consider the meaning of the codified duty).

It should be noted that CA 2006 states that, unless otherwise provided, more than one of the general duties may apply in relation to any particular set of facts. Thus, for example, taking a bribe from a third party would fall within the codified duty not to accept benefits from third parties but could also be a breach of the duty to promote the success of the company for the benefit of its members or represent a failure to exercise independent judgment.[1] In other words, the duties are cumulative

---

[1] Bribery of private persons will also be an offence under the Bribery Act 2010 when it comes into force.

and directors must take care to ensure that they comply with every duty that could apply on any particular set of facts. One specific exception to this general proposition is that the duty to avoid conflicts of interests is expressly stated not to apply to a conflict of interest arising in relation to a transaction or arrangement with the company. In this situation, the duty to declare an interest in a proposed transaction or arrangement or, alternatively, the requirement to declare an interest in an existing transaction or arrangement, will apply instead of the duty to avoid conflicts of interests.

In relation to charitable companies, Section 181 CA 2006 modifies certain aspects of the general duty to avoid conflicts of interests and the application of certain exceptions to such general duty and the general duty not to accept benefits from third parties.

Directors must also bear in mind that the codified general duties are not exhaustive and they must comply with all other applicable laws, which include non-codified fiduciary and common law duties as well as a vast number of obligations and attendant sanctions imposed by statute. These include a large number of criminal offences within CA 2006 as well as under other legislation of particular relevance to directors, including environmental and health and safety legislation, the Financial Services and Markets Act 2000, the Anti-Terrorism, Crime and Security Act 2001 and the Enterprise Act 2002, as a few examples. Attention has already been drawn to the unfair prejudice regime contained in Part 30 CA 2006.

3.5 Duty to act within powers

The duty set out in Section 171 CA 2006, requires a director to act in accordance with the company's constitution and only to exercise powers for the purposes for which they are conferred.

The reference to a company's constitution is given a wide meaning. Under Section 257 CA 2006, the constitution includes resolutions or decisions come to in accordance with the constitution and any decision of the company or a class of members that is treated as equivalent to a decision by the company (under any enactment or rule of law). It also includes the company's articles

93

(2)

and any resolutions or agreements covered in Section 29 CA 2006. These are the specified resolutions and agreements which must be filed with the Registrar of Companies. Of course, the consequence of the broad definition of the constitution is that directors must ensure that they are aware of all resolutions, decisions and agreements that comprise the constitution for these purposes to ensure that they act in accordance with this general duty.

What constitutes a proper purpose in relation to the exercise of powers must be ascertained in the context of the specific situation under consideration and regard may be had to previous case law. For instance, directors must not exercise their powers to protect their own positions or to make life difficult for particular shareholders or potential shareholders or in order to obtain a particular outcome in a takeover situation. This is the case even if the manner in which they exercise their powers happens to be in the best interests of the company. The authoritative case on the issue is *Howard Smith v Ampol Petroleum* [1974] AC 821, in which a company (Millers) had two shareholders together holding 55 per cent of the shares. A third shareholder (Howard Smith) announced its intention to make an offer which the board of Millers wanted to succeed but which the two principal shareholders opposed. The board allotted additional shares to Howard Smith, which diluted the two principal shareholders' interest to a minority interest. The court held that, although the board acted *bona fide* and the directors believed it was in the best interests of Howard Smith to raise funds by the issue of shares, the substantial purpose of the allotment was to favour one shareholder over others. The allotment was therefore set aside. It was not necessary for the plaintiffs to prove that the directors acted out of self interest or to preserve their own control of the management. It was sufficient that the directors had exercised their powers for an improper purpose. The court set out the judicial approach as follows:

> "Having ascertained, on a fair view, the nature of this power, and having defined, as can best be done in the light of modern conditions, the, or some, limits within which it may be exercised, it is then necessary for the court, if a particular exercise of it is challenged, to examine the substantial purpose for which it was exercised and to reach a conclusion

whether that purpose was proper or not. In doing so it will necessarily give credit to the *bona fide* opinion of the directors, if such is found to exist, and will respect their judgment as to matters of management; having done this, the ultimate conclusion has to be as to the side of a fairly broad line on which the case falls."

The real issue, therefore, relates to the directors' substantial purpose. It does not matter if a consequence of a particular course of action by the directors is that their own interests are advanced if that was not their principal or substantial purpose (*Hirsche v Sims* [1894] AC 654 at page 660, and restated in the case of *CAS (Nominees) Ltd v Nottingham Forest FC Plc* [2002] BCC 145).

The principle could be invoked in relation to any power whose purpose could be clearly discerned from the articles. For example, in *Re a Company, Ex parte Glossop* [1988] BCLC 570, the principle was applied to the directors' power to recommend dividends.

3.6 Duty to promote the success of the company

Section 172 CA 2006 provides that a director "must act in the way he considers, in good faith, would be most likely to promote the success of the company for the benefit of its members as a whole", and in doing so have regard to a non-exhaustive list of factors. The list covers the following:

(a) the likely consequences of any decision in the long term;
(b) the interests of the company's employees;
(c) the need to foster the company's business relationships with suppliers, customers and others;
(d) the impact of the company's operations on the community and the environment;
(e) the desirability of the company maintaining a reputation for high standards of business conduct; and
(f) the need to act fairly as between members of the company.

Sub-section (2) of this section provides that, where the purpose of the company is something other than the benefit of its members,

[handwritten margin top: of its other then companies' members benifit.]

[handwritten left margin: judgmat in by good faith]

the directors must act in the way they consider, in good faith, would be most likely to achieve that purpose. The explanatory notes to CA 2006 state that it is a matter for the good faith judgment of the directors as to what those purposes are, and where the company's purposes are partly for the benefit of its members and partly for other purposes, the extent to which those other purposes apply in place of the benefit of the members.

[handwritten: In case of insolvency duty is displaced and codified law leaving the duties in this situation on previous law Common law to develop this area]

Sub-section (3) recognises that (amongst other things) the duty to promote the success of the company is displaced when the company is insolvent. Rather than specifying the duties that apply in that situation, the sub-section leaves the previous law intact with a view to allowing the existing common law to develop in this area. Chapter 11 deals with the duties of directors facing insolvency.

Section 172 enshrined in statute the principle of enlightened shareholder value. The reference to directors' good faith judgment is designed to ensure that business decisions on, for example, strategy and tactics are for the directors, and not subject to decision by the courts, provided the directors were acting in good faith.

Prior to enactment CA 2006, the Government made a number of important clarificatory remarks when the Bill was debated in Parliament. The Minister for Industry and the Regions made statements to the following effect:

(a) the words "have regard to" mean "think about" or "give proper consideration to";

(b) while a director must have regard to the various factors stated, that requirement is subordinate to the overriding duty to promote the success of the company. A director will not be required to consider any of the factors beyond the point at which to do so would conflict with this overriding duty;

(c) directors are subject to the "good faith business judgment" test and not the reasonableness test;

(d) "the decisions taken by a director and the weight given to the factors will continue to be a matter for his good faith judgment";

(e) "there is no particular reason that a director would have to provide written evidence proving that in taking a particular decision he or she had had regard to these factors; that evidence would not be required for him or her to defend themselves against such action";

(f) the provision "does not impose a requirement on directors to keep records . . . in any circumstances in which they would not have to do so now" – "the onus will be on the company to prove that the director has not complied, rather than on the director to show that he has"; and

(g) "we do not intend a director to be required to do more in having regard to the factors than acting in good faith and in accordance with the duty of care and skill. It will, for example, be for the director to make a judgment on the likely longer-term consequences of his decisions in good faith and in compliance with his duty to exercise reasonable care, skill and judgment".

In the House of Lords, the Attorney-General made the following remarks on the interpretation of certain words and phrases:

(a) on the meaning of "success", Lord Goldsmith stated "it is essentially for the members of the company to define the objectives that they wish to achieve. Success means what the members collectively want the company to achieve. For a commercial company, success will usually mean long-term increase in value. For certain companies, such as charities and community interest companies, it will mean the attainment of the objectives for which the company has been established";

(b) ". . . it is for the directors . . . by reference to the objectives of the company . . . to judge and to form a good faith judgment about what is to be regarded as success for the benefit of the members as a whole . . . and they will need to look at the company's constitution, shareholder decisions and anything else that they consider relevant in helping them reach their judgment"; and

(c) on the meaning of "members as a whole", Lord Goldsmith stated that this means: "for the members as a collective body – not only to benefit the majority shareholders, or any particular shareholder or section of shareholders . . ."

Although these Parliamentary statements give some helpful guidance as to the intended interpretation of the statutory provisions, it will remain to be seen whether disaffected shareholders will seek to use the derivative action provisions contained in Part 11 CA 2006 (*see* Chapter 10) in circumstances where they allege that directors have failed to have regard to relevant factors in reaching their decision. There is no evidence of such a trend to date.

in *West Coast Capital (Lios) Ltd* [2008] CSOH 72 at paragraph [21], Lord Glennie in the Court of Session observed that Section 172 CA 2006 did "little more than set out the pre-existing law on the subject". It remains to be seen whether the English courts will adopt a similar view.

When making a decision, a director should give proper consideration to the listed factors, along with any other factors which are relevant to the matter in question. This requirement to have regard to these factors is, however, subordinate to the overriding duty to promote the success of the company.

It has been observed that the non-exhaustive list of factors that directors are required to take into account reflect the wider expectations in the community as to what constitutes responsible business behaviour and that this approach to business decisions has already found some recognition in company law.[2] The Court of Appeal made a passing reference to the Section 172 CA 2006 duty in the employment case of *Rolls-Royce Plc* v *Unite the Union* [2009] EWCA Civ 387 where the court referred to the need for an employer to judge a situation from the wider perspective of "enlightened self-interest" rather than his own self-interest. The former included the employer taking into account the interests of the employees as one of the factors in determining the needs of the business. The court indicated that this approach should be compared with the duty of directors in Section 172 CA 2006. The use of the term "enlightened self-interest" is almost certainly drawn from, and echoes, the concept of "enlightened shareholder

---

[2] *See* the discussion at pp 617 to 618 of J Lowry, "The Duty of Loyalty of Company Directors: Bridging the Accountability Gap through Efficient Disclosure", [2009] *The Cambridge Law Journal* 607 and p 157 and citing the judgment in *Teck Corp* v *Millar* (1972) 33 DLR (3d) 288.

value" and seems to indicate an acceptance in the court that business decisions based on pure self-interest alone belong to a different time.[3]

In line with the enlightened shareholder value concept, CA 2006 links the duty to promote the success of the company to the narrative reporting requirements. Section 417(2) CA 2006 provides that: "The purpose of the business review is to inform members of the company and help them assess how the directors have performed their duty under Section 172 (duty to promote the success of the company)". Directors must, therefore, demonstrate in the business review that they have had regard to the factors (including the various stakeholders referred to) set out in that section. The decision as to what information is provided and the level of disclosure is left to the directors' discretion. If directors consider that they have breached their duties, the breach would be disclosable under their Sections 171 to 177 CA 2006 duties and, by extension, in the business review.[4]

The duty to promote the success of the company also encompasses the previous fiduciary duty to act fairly as between members of the company. This duty was spelt out in *Mutual Life Insurance v Rank Organisation Ltd* [1985] BCLC 11, where US shareholders of Rank brought an action on the grounds that the directors had excluded them from participating in a rights issue by Rank. The directors justified the exclusion on the grounds of the cost and effort which would be incurred in meeting US registration requirements if the offer had been extended to all shareholders. The action failed as the court held that the directors had exercised their powers in good faith in the interests of the company and that they had, in fact, exercised them fairly as between the different shareholders.

Most of the case law considering Section 172 CA 2006 to date relates to applications by shareholders for permission to continue

---

[3] One of the members of the Appeal Court was The Rt Hon Lady Justice Arden DBE Court of Appeal, who was a member of the Steering Group for the Company Law Review.

[4] *See* the discussion at pp 618–619 of J Lowry, "The Duty of Loyalty of Company Directors: Bridging the Accountability Gap through Efficient Disclosure", [2009] *The Cambridge Law Journal* 607.

derivative claims. This arises because the court has to refuse permission for a derivative claim to proceed if a director acting in accordance with the Section 172 CA 2006 duty to promote the success of the company would not continue the derivative claim. In *Dimitri Giacobbe Iesini others outers* v *Westrip Holdings Ltd and others* [2009] EWHC 2526 (Ch) the court held that it would only bar a derivative claim on this ground if none of the directors would have continued the derivative claim themselves. Where directors were likely to disagree among themselves, the court would not apply the mandatory bar.

On 7 February 2007, The Association of General Counsel and Company Secretaries of the FTSE100 (GC100) published guidance setting out the GC100's view on best practice guidelines for compliance with directors' duties under CA 2006. It is the view of the GC100 that while it is mandatory for directors to take into account the various factors set out in the non-exhaustive list in Section 172 CA 2006, they are subsidiary to the overall duty under Section 172. The GC100 considers that directors should not be "forced to evidence their thought processes whether that is with regard to the stated factors or any other matter influencing their thinking. Apart from the unnecessary process and paperwork this would introduce into the boardroom, it would inevitably expose directors to a greater and unacceptable risk of litigation". The GC100 has therefore advised against directors recording in the minutes, at least as a default position, that they have taken each of these factors into consideration.

It seems clear that having regard to the list of factors should not be a box ticking exercise, and there is nothing to be gained by a company in creating a paper trail simply stating that the directors considered the list of six factors. Equally, directors will not be absolved from their duty to take account of the relevant factors simply because management has been tasked with preparing detailed supporting papers referring to the relevant factors. However, in circumstances where one or more of the factors is particularly relevant to a significant decision, it may be appropriate to record the board's considerations. Evidencing consideration of the factors (e.g. in board minutes) may be of particular benefit in circumstances where the directors anticipate a problem or wish to have on record a demonstration that they have carried out their duties. One reason for wishing to have such a record, particularly for major decisions, relates to the preparation of the company's business review (as mentioned above).

3.7 Duty to exercise independent judgment

Section 173 CA 2006 provides that a director must exercise independent judgment. It is expressly stated that this duty is not infringed by his acting either:

(a) in accordance with an agreement duly entered into by the company that restricts the future exercise of discretion by its directors; or
(b) in a way authorised by the company's constitution.

The intention of this duty is to codify the principle that directors must exercise their powers independently and not subordinate their powers to the will of others (either by delegation or otherwise) unless authorised under the constitution. This does not prevent a director from taking proper advice from lawyers, accountants or other advisers; it is only the director's judgment that must be independent, in the sense that it must be his judgment, not that of someone else. A director may also adopt someone else's judgment if he considers that that judgment is in the best interests of the company.

The section is silent on the powers of directors to delegate. The powers of delegation will, therefore need to be clearly set out in the articles. Directors may delegate the performance of their functions and the exercise of their powers if the company has given them the power to do so.

One of the exceptions to the duty to exercise independent judgment is where the directors are authorised by the "constitution". As referred to in Section 3.5 above, the constitution is given an extended meaning for the purposes of Part 10 CA 2006. This seems to include ordinary resolutions passed by the members of the company. Prior to CA 2006 the position was that only a resolution passed as a special resolution could constitute a direction to the directors, leaving the directors free to exercise their own judgment in matters of management in other circumstances. The consequence is that the directors' powers of management may be subject to more interference from shareholders than was previously the case.

Section 173 permits the status of the nominee director (a concept which is of particular significance in the context of joint ventures) to be enshrined in the company's constitution with the effect that a nominee is able to follow the instructions of the person who appointed him. However, the director must still comply with the other duties, such as promoting the success of the company.

Prior to CA 2006, the law relating to the fettering of a director's discretion had been developed in a number of cases which are still likely to be of relevance in interpreting the general duty. The duty not to fetter his discretion meant, in practice, that a director must not bind himself to vote on board resolutions (or to fulfil other functions as a director) in a particular predetermined way; when voting (or fulfilling such other functions) he must consider all the circumstances at the time and decide then what is in the best interests of the company. If he were to agree in advance how to exercise his votes (or fulfil other functions), he would have deprived himself of the ability to exercise proper judgment.

Thus, under the law prior to CA 2006, it was not open for a director (even one who had been appointed by a shareholder or other third party under a special power in the company's constitution) to agree to vote, etc. in accordance with the directions of another person. Shareholders could insert into a company's memorandum or articles provisions limiting the matters on which the directors could reach decisions or take actions (or on which directors may do so without shareholders' approval) but any restrictions on the directors' powers agreed by directors outside the company's constitution would be in breach of their fiduciary duties and unenforceable.

However, this would not have prevented the directors from causing their company to enter into a contract and undertaking to exercise their powers in such a way as to ensure the proper fulfilment of the contract. If it was in the best interests of the company to enter into the contract, it was open to the directors to agree to exercise their powers to ensure that the contract was carried out. This was decided in *Fulham Football Club Ltd v Cabra Estates Plc* [1994] 1 BCLC 363 at page 392, where the Court of Appeal approved a rule established in an Australian case (*Thorby v Goldberg* (1964) 112 CLR 597):

> "If, when a contract is negotiated on behalf of a company, the directors *bona fide* think it in the best interests of the company as a whole that the transaction should be entered into and carried into effect, they may bind themselves by the contract to do whatever is necessary to effectuate it."

Two earlier cases (*Rackham v Peek Foods Ltd* [1990] BCLC 895 and *John Crowther Group Plc v Carpets International Plc* [1990] BCLC 460) held (at first instance) that undertakings by directors to recommend proposed transactions to shareholders for their approval were unenforceable. The court in the *Fulham Football Club* case stated that, whilst these cases may be justified on their particular facts, they should not be read as laying down a general proposition that directors can never bind themselves as to the future exercise of their powers. Each of these cases involved an agreement by a company to sell a subsidiary to a purchaser with the agreement being conditional on the approval of the shareholders; in one case these were the seller's shareholders and in the other case they were the purchaser's shareholders. The directors of the relevant companies agreed with the other side to recommend the transactions to their shareholders, or to use their best endeavours to procure the fulfilment of the condition. Before the meeting of the shareholders other events occurred which caused the sale/purchase to be seriously disadvantageous to the relevant companies, and the directors refused to recommend the relevant transaction to their shareholders. The courts held that the directors were under a fiduciary duty to make full and honest disclosure to their shareholders and not to give bad advice. The courts upheld the directors' actions in each case.

These cases support the principle that directors should not give an unqualified undertaking in advance to recommend a course of action to shareholders in case, at the time of the recommendation, the directors are no longer of the view that the proposed course of action is in the best interests of the company; the recommendation could not then be made honestly. Nor should the directors give an unqualified undertaking to make statements to shareholders in the future which might amount to a misrepresentation, for example as to the supposed merits of a proposal compared with the merits of any available alternative. If pressed to give such undertakings, directors should make it clear that their obligations are subject to the proper fulfilment of their duties to the company and to its shareholders.

3.8 Duty to exercise reasonable care, skill and diligence

This duty provides that a director must exercise reasonable care, skill and diligence. This is defined in Section 174(2) as follows:

> "This means the care, skill and diligence that would be exercised by a reasonably diligent person with:
>
> (a) the general knowledge, skill and experience that may reasonably be expected of a person carrying out the functions carried out by the director in relation to the company, and
>
> (b) the general knowledge, skill and experience that the director has."

This duty mirrors the test laid down in Section 214 Insolvency Act 1986.

The objective test, set out in (a) above, represents the minimum standard required by the duty on all directors. However, if the particular director possesses greater general knowledge, skill or experience than may reasonably be expected of a director carrying out the same functions, he will have to meet the higher standard of care, skill and diligence appropriate to his general knowledge, skill and experience as referred to in (b) above. This does not mean, however, that a professional on the board is expected to use all his skills. So, for example, a lawyer does not have to research a particular point but can rely on external advisers, although he must use his general knowledge, skill and ability when considering the matter. The Government also stated that a non-executive director will not be expected to have all the knowledge about the internal workings of the business that an executive director has, and so the law will take account of individuals' different perspectives.

The statutory duty reflects very closely the position developed under the common law prior to CA 2006 as stated in *Re D'Jan of London Ltd* [1993] BCC 646. Under principles developed under case law it is dangerous for a person to accept a directorship when he is not sufficiently qualified or experienced to be able to fulfil the functions he is expected to carry out. A director of a rubber company is unlikely to be able to claim as a defence his complete ignorance of the rubber industry, nor will a finance director of a FTSE 100 company be able to claim as a defence the fact that he is innumerate. On the other hand, whilst a director of a small building firm may not normally be expected to have a sophisticated grasp of the foreign exchange markets, he would be expected to have such knowledge (and to have exercised it) if he was also a senior employee of a bank engaged in that sphere of activity. This was illustrated by *Re Continental Assurance Co of London Plc (in liq.) (No 1)* [1997] 1 BCLC 48, where a senior executive of a bank was appointed a non-executive director of the company and its subsidiary. In breach of Section 151 Companies Act 1985, the subsidiary made a loan to the holding company to enable it to service its bank loans. When the subsidiary became insolvent, the director was disqualified – his ignorance about the purpose of the upstream loan was held not to be a defence but evidence of his failure to exercise the appropriate degree of competence, especially in the light of his experience as a banker and his ability to understand the accounts of the holding company.

The moral of the cases is that a person should not accept a directorship where he is out of his depth and, further, that a highly qualified person should remember to continue to exercise his skills even when he is acting as a director in a role where the exercise of such skills would not normally be expected. Once appointed, a director cannot discharge himself from his responsibilities by maintaining a negligible actual involvement in the affairs of the company. For example, in *Re Galeforce Pleating Co*

Ltd [1999] 2 BCLC 704, it was held that, for as long as an individual continued to hold office as a director, and in particular to receive remuneration from it, it was incumbent on that person to inform himself as to the financial affairs of the company and to play an appropriate role in the management of its business.

In *Bairstow v Queens Moat Houses Plc and others* [2000] 1 BCLC 549, the court held that an executive director who is paid substantial remuneration is expected to know the requirements that must be satisfied before a payment of dividends may be made.

However, a director is entitled, in the absence of suspicious circumstances, to rely on the experience and expertise of his co-directors and other officers of the company. Directors may also rely on the opinions of outside experts and, indeed, they may be negligent if they do not obtain an outside opinion in appropriate circumstances (*Re Duomatic Ltd* [1969] 2 Ch 365). Boards do, however, need to exercise care to ensure that they do not permit directors who may have a conflict of interest to instruct the external advisers on whose advice they wish to rely: *Dimitri Giacobbe Iesini and others v Westrip Holdings Ltd and others* [2009] EWHC 2526 (Ch).

Directors cannot absolve themselves entirely of responsibility by delegation to others. In *Re Bradcrown Ltd* [2001] 1 BCLC 547, a finance director who relied solely on professional advice received without making his own independent judgment was found to be unfit. Lawrence Collins J stated that a director is obviously entitled to rely on legal advice, but in this case he had asked no questions and sought no advice while approving transactions that removed substantially all of the assets from the company. The director had simply done what he was told and abdicated all responsibility: "In these circumstances he cannot seek refuge in the fact that professional advisers were involved in the transactions".

By contrast, in *Re Stephenson Cobbold Ltd (in liq.), Secretary of State for Trade and Industry v Stephenson and others* [2000] 2 BCLC 614, the court refused to disqualify a non-executive director as, although he was a cheque signatory, he was not involved in deciding which creditors should be paid where preferential treatment had been given. On the evidence, the defendant, an experienced businessman, was not a party to any policy of non-payment of Crown debts as he relied on professional accountants. The fact that he was a cheque signatory did not make him a party. Again, on the facts, his being a signatory did not amount to permitting a breach of fiduciary duties by the managing director in relation to the misuse of the company's funds. He had queried the payment and received assurances from the auditors. He was not disqualified.

The extent to which non-executive directors could be liable for failures within the company will depend on the circumstances, including the part which the director could be reasonably expected to play. There is no difference between the tests to be applied to non-executives and those applied to executives; the difference will lie in the functions they fulfil and the extent of the care and diligence that they can be reasonably expected to exercise. For instance, failure to ensure that proper controls are exercised over management (and by management) could be evidence of breach of duty, though the extent to which directors are expected to investigate whether proper controls are exercised will vary in the circumstances.

Re Continental Assurance Co of London Plc (in liq.) [2001] BPIR 733 (also referred to as *Singer v Beckett* [2001] BPIR 733) involved a trial of an application made by the liquidators against eight former directors (two executive and six non-executive) alleging wrongful trading and misfeasance. The liquidators' case with respect to the misfeasance was that the non-executive directors had failed to exercise the requisite skill and care as directors in relying on the management accounts and other financial information as presented to them from time to time. It was held in this case that the non-executive directors had not followed blindly the advice of the finance director and auditors but had been in the habit of probing and testing the financial information provided from time to time, and it had been reasonable and proper for them to have relied on such financial information.

In *Re Barings Plc and others (No 5)* [1999] 1 BCLC 433, the chief executive of a bank faced disqualification proceedings following the insolvency of the bank caused by unauthorised securities trading of an individual employee. The executive chairman sought (unsuccessfully) to defend himself by claiming that his expertise was in the corporate finance side of the business, that he had very little understanding of the activities in which the trader was involved (despite its representing a significant proportion of the bank's reported profits) and that he relied on the internal audit department and external auditors. The judge's summary of the duties of directors includes the following (at p 489):

> "(i) Directors have, both collectively and individually, a continuing duty to acquire and maintain a sufficient knowledge and understanding of the company's business to enable them properly to discharge their duties as directors.
>
> (ii) Whilst directors are entitled (subject to the articles of association of the company) to delegate particular functions to those below them in the management chain, and to trust their competence and integrity to a reasonable extent, the exercise of the power of delegation does not absolve a director from the duty to supervise the discharge of the delegated functions.
>
> (iii) No rule of universal application can be formulated as to the duty referred to in (ii) above. The extent of the duty, and the question whether it has been discharged, must depend on the facts of each particular case, including the director's role in the management of the company."

The judge also stated (at p 488):

> "Where there is an issue as to the extent of a director's duties and responsibilities in any particular case, the level of reward which he is entitled to receive or which he may reasonably have expected to receive from the company may be a relevant factor in resolving that issue."

Although the decision in the *Barings* case was on the question of disqualification, it does not require much imagination to conclude that, if a director has conducted himself in a manner which renders him unfit to be a director, the company may have a claim against him for not exercising proper skill, care or diligence if it has suffered a loss as a result.

A test of the law in this area was the claim brought by the Equitable Life Assurance Society against 15 of its former directors. The proceedings as originally filed sought £3.9 billion in damages, making the claim one of the largest ever brought before the English courts. The Society alleged that its former board had failed to seek legal advice prior to instituting a differential bonus policy which was subsequently found to be unlawful by the House of Lords in *Equitable Life Assurance Society v Hyman* [2002] 1 AC 408. It alleged further that the board had failed to take precautions against losing the *Hyman* litigation by cutting bonuses and warning policyholders about the risks of losing. The non-executive directors sought to have the claim against them struck out (*Equitable Life Assurance Society v Bowley and others* [2003] EWHC [2003] BCC 829), arguing that it was fanciful to contend that no reasonable non-executive director would have failed to challenge the advice of the executive directors in these circumstances. They relied upon the comments of Romer J in *Re City Equitable Fire Insurance Co Ltd* [1925] 1 Ch 407 that a director was entitled, in the absence of grounds for suspicion, to assume that an employee of the company would perform their duties honestly. Langley J in *Bowley* did not accept that this represented the modern law insofar as it was suggested that directors were entitled to place unquestioning reliance on others to do their job. Instead, he indicated that the extent to which a non-executive director may reasonably rely on the executive directors would be fact sensitive. For this and other reasons he declined to strike out the claim. It should be noted, however, that the claims were eventually withdrawn at the end of a six month trial, suggesting that the Society had encountered significant difficulties in showing that the directors had actually been negligent.

In *Lexi Holdings (in admin) v Luqman and others* [2009] All ER (D) 269 (Feb), the court found that sibling directors had been in breach of this duty by their total inactivity in relation to notifying anyone that their brother, who was also a director of the company, had a conviction for fraud. The brother had appropriated money from the company. The court found that had advice been sought and the auditors informed, the subsequent misapplications could not have been perpetrated.

3.9 Duty to avoid conflicts of interest

This duty replaces the former no conflict rule applying to directors. It covers all conflicts, actual and potential, between the interests of the director and the interests of the company. It includes in particular conflicts relating to the exploitation of the company's property, information or opportunity for personal purposes. The only conflicts not covered by this duty are those relating to transactions or arrangements with the company, which have to be declared and which are covered separately in Sections 177 and 182 CA 2006. Any reference in Section 175 to a conflict of interest includes a conflict of interest and duty and a conflict of duties.

Section 175(1) CA 2006 states that "A director of a company must avoid a situation in which he has, or can have, a direct or indirect interest that conflicts, or possibly may conflict, with the interests of the company". Where the conflict involves the exploitation of property, information or opportunity, it is immaterial whether the company could take advantage of the property, information or opportunity. It will therefore address a situation where the directors could create the (false) impression that the company could not take advantage of the property, information or opportunity, and it is prudent to operate from a working assumption that if a conflict of interest exists, the obligation will be breached.[5] The reference to "indirect interest" means that it is likely that interests of anyone connected with a director will be considered in deciding whether or not a director has a conflict. It should be noted that the categories of persons "connected" with a director were broadened under Section 252 CA 2006.

Section 175(4) provides that the duty is not infringed:

> "(a) if the situation cannot reasonably be regarded as likely to give rise to a conflict of interest; or
> (b) if the matter has been authorised by the directors."

---

[5] For a less severe approach in relation to an opportunity that a director took up post his resignation *see Island Export Finance Ltd* v *Umunma* [1986] BCLC 460.

Sub-sections (5) and (6) provide further detail on authorisation by the directors. In the case of a private company incorporated on or after 1 October 2008, authorisation may be given by the directors so long as the company's articles do not prohibit this. In the case of a private company incorporated before 1 October 2008, authorisation may be given by the directors if the company either passes an ordinary resolution permitting this (assuming the articles have not already been amended so as to prohibit it) or if the company amends its articles to expressly allow it. In the case of a public company, authorisation may be given by the directors only if the company's articles expressly allow this. In each case, the authorisation will only be effective if:

(a)   the meeting at which authorisation is given is quorate without counting the director concerned or any other interested director; and
(b)   the authorisation was given without any such director voting or would have been agreed to if their votes had not been counted.

It appears that sub-section (4)(b) (which provides that the duty is not infringed "if the matter *has been* authorised by the directors") requires director authorisations to be given in advance (and not retrospectively).

Authorisation by shareholders also remains possible.

A number of issues were highlighted in discussions relating to the enactment of this duty. One issue was that the duty is framed as a positive rather than negative duty. The law prior to CA 2006 was generally regarded as giving rise to a disability rather than imposing a duty in this area, although this was challenged by the Solicitor-General who referred to the cases of *Movitex* v *Bulfield* [1988] BCLC 104 and *Gwembe Valley Development Co* v *Koshy* [2003] EWCA Civ 1048. The Solicitor-General noted that the courts were moving to the conclusion that, whether viewed as duties or disabilities, all such incidents are aspects of the fiduciary's primary obligation of loyalty.

Particular concern has arisen in relation to people holding multiple directorships. Under the previous law there was scope for sensible management of conflicts by directors, such as absenting themselves from meetings at which a particular matter was to be discussed. In the House of Lords, the Attorney-General indicated that a director who obtains his board's consent to another appointment would be entitled to assume that that consent "franks" any subsequent conflicts which arise in practice. However the language of the section refers to the "matter" being authorised.

Some use may be made of the safe harbour in Section 175(4)(a) CA 2006 (sometimes referred to as the "materiality test") which applies where the situation cannot reasonably be regarded as likely to give rise to a conflict of interest (but this, in itself, gives rise to some difficulties as to interpretation). In the Parliamentary debate prior to enactment of CA 2006, the Solicitor-General stated that, "For as long as that remains true, the director will not be in breach of the duty . . . if he [the director] cannot foresee a situation, it cannot reasonably be regarded as being likely to give rise to a conflict of interest. If a person can foresee a situation, the directors or members of the company should be informed about that and can then act accordingly". The duty to avoid a situation where interests or duties are in conflict come into play only where there is a real possibility of such conflict. In the Scottish case of *Eastford Ltd* v *Gilliespie* [2009] CSOH 119 two directors asked the board to ratify their prior decision to raise an action in the name of the company alleging a breach of duty against another director. The court accepted that on the facts of the case the directors could exercise their voting power to ratify their own conduct because on the particular facts of the case there was no conflict of interest between them and the company.[6]

To what extent can the constitution of a company contain provisions to facilitate dealing with conflicts? Section 180(4)(b) CA 2006 provides that the general duties are not infringed by

---

[6] The two directors risked being personally liable for commencing an action without the authority of the board but in this case that risk remained as the company was impecunious: ratification did not improve the directors' position in that regard.

anything done (or omitted) by the directors, or any of them, in accordance with provisions in the company's articles for dealing with conflicts of interest. Section 232(4) CA 2006 (relating to protecting directors from liability) states that: "Nothing in this section prevents a company's articles from making such provision as has previously been lawful for dealing with conflicts of interest". So these provisions clearly envisage that the articles can address dealing with conflicts (although the precise extent to which this is possible is the subject of some debate).

The position prior to CA 2006 is illustrated by the *Movitex* case where it was held that shareholders could exclude or modify the application of the self-dealing rule by including a provision in the articles that provided that a director could be interested in a contract with his company provided he made full disclosure of his interest. Provisions which have been commonly included, such as abstaining from voting or not attending meetings, provided a practical solution under the pre-existing law. Another example of what was previously capable of being addressed in the articles was the situation where a director had two competing directorships. In this situation the company's constitution could include provisions to relieve the director of his duty not to divert away business opportunities. The law relating to the position of nominee directors in relation to the conflict of interest duty is not particularly developed. As a general rule, the court will assume that the nominee is obliged and able to ignore the instructions of his or her nominator when necessary.

The powers of shareholders to authorise conflicts and to prevent a breach of duty are preserved by Section 180(4) CA 2006 but, as was the case under the pre-existing law, care is needed to ensure that sufficient information is given to shareholders to enable them to make an informed decision. Authorisation and ratification are dealt with further below in Section 3.13.

Insofar as remedies are concerned, the position under CA 2006 is discussed below in Section 3.12. The courts will draw on the remedies which applied to breaches of the no conflict rule in existence prior to CA 2006 (although the fact that the law has changed in this area means that, over time, case law will develop to reflect the statutory duty).

The following principles under the law prior to CA 2006 will still be of relevance in interpreting the statutory provisions (at least until new case law develops). If there was a conflict between an interest of the company and another interest (or a duty) of the director in any transaction, the director must account to the company for any benefit he received from the transaction (unless, by reason of the company's constitution or an informed approval given by the shareholders, he was permitted to retain the benefit). For example, in the case of *JJ Harrison (Properties) Ltd* v *Harrison* [2002] 1 BCLC 162, a director of a company acquired some land from the company at a price which reflected the fact that planning permission had been refused to develop the land. At the time of the acquisition, the director was aware that, for various reasons, the prospect of planning permission being granted had improved. This fact was not disclosed to the board at the meeting to approve the transaction. The court found that the director was in breach of his fiduciary duties to the company and held the property upon trust for the company. Accordingly, he was liable to account for the profits he made from the subsequent sale by him of the land.

If the company suffered a loss by virtue of the conflict (e.g. because the director directed a benefit to go to another entity rather than to the company), the director would be liable to account for the loss. This is so even though the director did not derive any benefit personally and was under a duty to that other entity to promote its interests. For example, in *Scottish Co-operative Wholesale Society Ltd* v *Meyer* [1959] AC 324, directors of a partly owned subsidiary acquiesced in a policy of its holding company to deprive the subsidiary of business contracts, which were diverted to the parent company. In an action by minority shareholders in the subsidiary, those directors of the subsidiary who were "nominees" of the holding company (and also directors of the holding company) were held to be in breach of their duties to the subsidiary by their inaction in failing to protect that company from the loss of business.

3.10   Duty not to accept benefits from third parties

This duty stems from the fiduciary duty existing prior to CA 2006 prohibiting the exploitation of the position of director for personal benefit (sometimes referred to as the duty not to make secret profits).

Section 176 CA 2006 provides that a director must not accept a benefit from a third party conferred by reason of him being a director or his doing (or not doing) anything as a director. For these purposes a third party is defined as meaning "a person other than the company, an associated body corporate or a person acting on behalf of the company or an associated body corporate". Bodies corporate are associated if one is a subsidiary of the other or both are subsidiaries of the same body corporate (which means, for example, that a 50/50 joint venture company will not be an associated body of the joint venture parties). Where a director provides services to the company through another person, benefits received by the director from that person are not regarded as conferred by a third party.

The term benefit is intended to be construed widely. In the Parliamentary debate prior to the enactment of CA 2006, the Solicitor General stated that: "A benefit for the purposes of this duty includes benefits of any description, including non-financial benefits. In using the word 'benefit', we intend the ordinary dictionary meaning of the word. The Oxford English Dictionary defines it as "a favourable or helpful factor, circumstance, advantage or profit".

Although, there is no provision for authorisation by independent directors, the duty will not be infringed if the acceptance of the benefit cannot be reasonably regarded as likely to give rise to a conflict of interest. It is not considered appropriate to attempt to deal with the acceptance of third party benefits in a company's articles (for example, by specifying that *de minimis* amounts of up to a specified level may be accepted); the appropriate test is whether or not acceptance of the benefit can reasonably be regarded as likely to give rise to a conflict.

In relation to the law prior to CA 2006, the duty not to make a secret (or, rather, unauthorised) profit can be illustrated by the following case of *Regal (Hastings) Ltd* v *Gulliver* [1942] 1 All ER 378. In that case four directors and Regal's solicitor subscribed for shares in a subsidiary of Regal to give it sufficient additional funds to acquire extra cinema leases. Regal did not have sufficient resources itself to provide the funds to the subsidiary. When the shares in the subsidiary were sold at a profit, Regal (controlled by new owners) claimed the profits from the directors and the solicitor. The court held that, as fiduciaries, the directors were liable to account to the company for the profit that they had made (in fact, the solicitor was held not to be liable). It was held in the House of Lords that:

> "The rule of equity which insists on those who by the use of a fiduciary position make a profit, being liable to account for that profit, in no way depends on fraud or absence of *bona fides*; or upon such questions or considerations as whether the profit would or should otherwise have gone to the plaintiff, or whether he took a risk or acted as he did for the benefit of the plaintiff, or whether the plaintiff has in fact been damaged or benefited from his action."

The directors were liable even though Regal could not have made the profit itself (because of lack of resources) and even though they had acted in the best interests of the company and had not caused it loss. However, the directors could have kept the profit if they had obtained the approval of the company's shareholders in general meeting.

At common law, the duty not to make secret profits often intertwined with the common law no conflict rules, particularly in the area of exploiting opportunities, diverting business away from the company and the duty to account arising from the position of trust. One advantage of the common law was that it gave a degree of flexibility to the judges to decide cases upon the merits of the parties in particular factual situations. For example, the Court of Appeal's judgment in *Bhullar and others* v *Bhullar and another* [2003] EWCA Civ 424 (concerning the diversion by a director of a business opportunity to himself) considered the test for determining what constitutes an opportunity for the company. The court affirmed that the test would be satisfied if a reasonable man looking at the facts would think there was a real, sensible possibility of conflict between the director's personal interest and the interests of the company. Another example is the case of *Wilkinson v West Coast Capital and others* [2005] EWHC 3009 (Ch), where it was held, on the facts, that directors who discovered an opportunity and pursued it for their own benefit were not in breach of fiduciary duty to their company. A shareholders' agreement (which was expressed to take precedence over the company's articles) required a specified majority consent before the company could buy any business. As the directors were party to the shareholders' agreement and had power to block the company from pursuing the opportunity, they were held not to be in breach of the no conflict rule in pursuing the opportunity through another company to their own advantage.

3.11 Duty to declare interest in proposed transaction or arrangement

This general duty (contained in Section 177 CA 2006) replaced the equitable rule that directors may not have an interest in transactions with the company unless the interest has been authorised by the members.

In practice, the equitable rule was usually modified by provisions in the articles which provided for disclosure and abstention from voting at board meetings. The statutory duty removes the requirement for authorisation but requires a director to disclose the nature and extent of any interest, whether direct or indirect, that he has in relation to a proposed transaction or arrangement with the company. The reference to indirect interests means that the director himself does not need to be a party to the transaction for the duty to apply; another person's interest could amount to an interest on the part of the director. As stated in Section 3.9 above, the categories of persons "connected" with a director were broadened under Section 252 CA 2006.

Disclosure is required before the company enters into the transaction or arrangement and can be made at a meeting of the directors, by notice in writing sent to the other directors, or by way of a general notice to the effect that the director has an interest in a specified body corporate or firm and is to be regarded as interested in any transaction or arrangement that may be made with that body or firm after the date of the notice, or that the director is connected with a specified person and is to be regarded as interested in any transaction or arrangement that may be made with that person.

The nature and extent of the interest must be declared and if, after disclosure, the declaration proves to be or becomes inaccurate or incomplete, a further declaration must be made correcting the earlier one, assuming that the company has not yet entered into the transaction or arrangement.

There are various circumstances specified where there is no requirement to make a declaration. No declaration is required where the director is not aware of having an interest or is not aware of the transaction or arrangement in question. However, it is expressly provided that the director is to be treated as being aware of matters of which he ought reasonably to be aware. In the Parliamentary debate prior to enactment of CA 2006, the Attorney-General considered these words and stated that it should be judged objectively whether the director ought reasonably to be aware of a particular matter. From a practical point of view, this gives rise to directors having to undertake a certain amount of due diligence regarding their potential interests in order to avoid breaching the duty inadvertently.

Other situations where no declaration is required are: if the interest cannot reasonably be regarded as likely to give rise to a conflict of interest; if, or to the extent that, the directors are already aware or ought reasonably to be aware of it; and if the interest concerns the terms of a director's service contract that are considered by a meeting of the directors or a committee appointed for the purpose.

Section 180(4)(b) CA 2006 provides that the company's articles may contain provisions for dealing with conflicts of interest compliance which will prevent a breach of the general duty. The explanatory note to CA 2006 provides that conflicted directors may, subject to the company's articles, participate in decision taking relating to such transactions with the company although the articles may require that the directors must disregard the views of an interested director.

It should be noted that Section 182 CA 2006 deals separately with declarations of interest in existing transactions or arrangements. This provision is dealt with in Chapter 5. While a breach of Section 182 is a criminal offence, a breach of Section 177 is not. The Attorney-General explained the distinction by referring to the fact that a breach of Section 182 cannot affect the validity of the existing transaction or arrangement whereas a failure to declare an interest in a proposed transaction or arrangement could lead to other consequences such as voidability. This raises the issue (which is considered further below) that CA 2006 does not expressly set out the remedies applying to the general duties and therefore gives rise to some uncertainties, particularly where the statutory duty departs from the concepts developed by prior case law and in relation to common law and equitable duties.

In relation to the relevance of case law prior to CA 2006, the Solicitor-General confirmed that the general duty replaces the equitable principle that directors may not enter into contracts with their company or have an interest in any of the company's contracts. The authorities include *Aberdeen Railway Co v Blaikie Brothers* [1854] 2 Eq Reg 128, [1843–60] All ER 249 and reflect the same principle that prevents an agent from contracting with his principal and a trustee from contracting with his trust (as determined in *Keech v Sandford* [1726] Sel Cas Ch 61).

3.12 Consequences of breach of general duties

Section 178 CA 2006 provides that the consequences of breach (or threatened breach) of the general duties are the same as would apply if the corresponding common law rule or equitable principle applied. Each of the general duties (with the exception of the common law duty to exercise reasonable care, skill and diligence) are stated to be "enforceable in the same way as any other fiduciary duty owed to a company by its directors".

This leaves some uncertainty as to how the civil remedies will apply in all cases where the general duties concerned are not identical to those established by case law. Prior to enactment of CA 2006, the Solicitor-General stated that "where those duties have been codified the courts will be able to identify the relevant rule or principle. Where they have been changed the courts will

119

need to find the rule or principle that covers the same subject matter as the general duty contained in the statutory statement ... the fact that the general duties might depart from common law rules and equitable principles in certain ways will not alter the circumstances flowing from their breach. The question will not be whether the rule or principle has been breached but what the consequences should be once it has been breached. The consequences of a breach of the fiduciary duty can include damages, compensation, restoration of a company's property, rescission of a transaction or a requirement of a director to account for any profits made as a result. They may also include injunctions or declarations, although those matters are primarily employed when a breach is threatened but has not yet occurred. The consequences of a breach of the duty of care and skill may include the court awarding compensation or damages".

It will remain to be seen whether, in practice, the courts will have any difficulty in deciding the appropriate remedy for a breach of general duty and in their interpretation of Section 178 CA 2006. This issue has not been tested to date.

3.13 Consent, approval or authorisation by members

Section 180 CA 2006 contains various provisions relating to the general duties concerning board approval, shareholder authorisation and circumstances where approval or authorisation is not required if certain other approvals have been obtained or if certain matters are dealt with in the articles. This section should also be read with the provisions relating to ratification by a company of conduct by a director amounting to negligence, default, breach of duty or breach of trust in relation to the company, which are set out in Section 239 CA 2006.

First, Section 180 makes it clear that, unless the company's constitution requires otherwise, the consent or approval of members of the company is not required in relation to:

(a) the duty to avoid conflicts of interest where authorisation has been duly obtained by the directors in accordance with Section 175; and

(b) the duty to declare an interest in a proposed transaction or arrangement, where the declaration is duly made in accordance with Section 177. This was a change from the common law rules and equitable principles which could have required a transaction or arrangement to be set aside if the consent or approval of the members of the company had not been obtained.

Secondly, there are circumstances where it is expressly stated that it is not necessary to comply with the provisions relating to the duty to avoid conflicts of interest (Section 175) or the duty not to accept benefits from third parties (Section 176). This is the case where the provisions of Chapter 4 of Part 10 CA 2006 apply and, either approval is given under that Chapter, or where it is provided that approval is not needed. Chapter 4 (which is considered in Chapter 5 of this edition) deals with the requirements for member approval in relation to four different types of transaction by a company:

(a) long-term service contracts;
(b) substantial property transactions;
(c) loans, quasi-loans and credit transactions; and
(d) payments for loss of office.

For each type of transaction, the basic requirement for member approval is set out followed by express exceptions to the basic rule and finally the consequences of breaching that rule.

Thirdly, Section 180(4)(a) preserves "any rule of law" enabling the company to give authority, specifically or generally, for anything to be done (or omitted) by the directors, or any of them, that would otherwise be a breach of duty. Under the common law rules, breaches of fiduciary duty could be authorised by ordinary resolution, although unlawful acts (such as unlawful dividends, unlawful returns of capital or acts otherwise in breach of statute or the general law) could not be authorised. This reflects the principle that those to whom duties are owed may release fiduciaries from their legal obligations provided there is full disclosure in advance of the decision. Where breaches of fiduciary duties have been lawfully authorised (or ratified), the court will be obliged to refuse permission to a shareholder who has brought a derivative claim under Part 11 CA 2006 to continue that claim.

Section 180(4)(b) provides that, where the articles contain provisions dealing with conflicts of interest, provided a director acts in accordance with those provisions, then he or she will not be held to be in breach of any of the general duties by acting in accordance with those provisions.

Save for these express exceptions, Section 180(5) provides that the general duties will have effect (unless otherwise provided or the context otherwise requires) notwithstanding any enactment or rule of law. An example of a situation where CA 2006 does provide otherwise is Section 247 which enables directors to make provision for employees on the cessation or transfer of a company's business even if this would otherwise constitute a breach of the general duty to promote the success of the company.

As to ratification, the provisions in Section 239 CA 2006 made significant changes to the pre-existing law. Previously, the common law allowed an interested shareholder to vote his or her shares on a matter in which he or she was interested. For this reason, the courts stopped short of accepting that *all* breaches of directors' duties could be ratified by ordinary resolution – as directors in breach could vote to forgive themselves in respect of the breach. The dividing line as to which breaches could be ratified and which could not is not easy to draw. For example, in *Daniels v Daniels* [1978] Ch 406, directors' negligence was not ratifiable, whereas in *Pavlides v Jensen* [1956] Ch 565, it was ratifiable. The distinction may lie in the fact that in the former case there was a misappropriation of corporate property while in the latter there was not. Under the statutory provision, any decision by a company to ratify conduct by a director amounting to negligence, default, breach of duty or breach of trust in relation to the company must be taken by the members without reliance on the votes of the director concerned (if a member of the company) and any member connected with him (although such person may attend and be counted in the quorum and otherwise take part in the proceedings of a shareholders' meeting). For these purposes a director includes a former director and "connected person" is given a very wide meaning. This concept of disqualification may have the benefit that breaches of all directors' duties are, in principle, ratifiable, compared with the common law position where the courts decided that not all breaches could be ratified, particularly where dishonesty or expropriation of corporate property was involved. However, it is unclear whether the courts will in fact adopt such an approach.

Section 239(6) makes it clear that the law on unanimous consent is expressly preserved. The explanatory notes to CA 2006 state that this has the effect that the restrictions imposed by this section as to who may vote on a ratification resolution will not apply when every member votes (informally or otherwise) in favour of the resolution. Also, the powers of the directors to agree not to sue, or to settle or release a claim made by them on behalf of the company are expressly preserved.

Finally, the section provides that any other enactment or rule of law imposing additional requirements for valid ratification or any rule of law as to acts that are incapable of being ratified by the company are not affected by this section. So, for example, unlawful acts or breaches of statute may not be ratified.

3.14 Direct duties of director to shareholders

Earlier within this Chapter there have been references to areas where CA 2006 provisions on general duties of directors do not attempt to address the legal principles existing at the time of its enactment. These include: the law relating to shadow directors; duties to creditors on impending insolvency; those fiduciary duties not covered by the general duties; the duty of confidentiality; and the remedies applying to breach of the general duties. This Chapter concludes with a further category of duty which applies to directors, namely, the direct duty owed in certain circumstances to shareholders.

There will be occasions when directors, particularly of public companies, will be communicating with their shareholders. They owe a general duty to those shareholders to be honest and not to mislead (*Gething* v *Kilner* [1972] 1 WLR 337) or (when seeking their approval of transactions or recommending particular courses of action) to make full (as well as honest) disclosure

(*Normandy* v *Ind Coope & Co* [1908] 1 Ch 84). In addition, quite apart from the liability that can arise in respect of the general duty of disclosure in relation to prospectuses, directors could be personally liable for the tort of negligent misstatement, that is if shareholders were to suffer loss by relying on negligent misstatements made by the directors (*Re Chez Nico (Restaurants) Ltd* [1992] BCLC 192). Such statements do not necessarily have to be made in writing (as in circulars); they can be made orally, as may be more likely in the case of dealings with shareholders in private companies with few shareholders.

It was formerly considered that directors owed no direct fiduciary duty to shareholders, as opposed to their company. This stemmed from the decision in *Percival* v *Wright* [1902] 2 Ch 421 where the headnote states that, "The directors of a company are not trustees for individual shareholders, and may purchase their shares without disclosing pending negotiations for the sale of the company's undertaking". The decision has been doubted in a number of cases both in the UK and elsewhere where it has been held that, in certain special circumstances, directors can be placed under fiduciary duties, including a duty of disclosure, vis-à-vis shareholders individually. In *Re Chez Nico (Restaurants) Ltd*, Nico Ladenis (a high-profile restaurateur) had sought to exercise powers of compulsory acquisition of minority shares under Section 429 of the Companies Act 1985. A minority of shareholders objected and the court decided that, as a matter of law, the powers were not in fact exercisable in the light of the particular events. However, the court noted with disapproval the failure of Mr Ladenis to give the minority shareholders sufficient or accurate information, but commented that, as the powers of compulsory acquisition were not exercisable, it was unnecessary to hold whether Mr Ladenis was, under the general law, under a fiduciary duty to disclose the true position to the minority shareholders; obiter, however, it confirmed its approval of the decision of the New Zealand Court in *Coleman* v *Myers* [1997] 2 NZLR 225, in which directors were held to be under such a duty to shareholders.

In *Platt* v *Platt* [1999] 2 BCLC 745 a director (who was also a shareholder) was held liable for negligent misrepresentation and breach of his fiduciary duties owed directly to his fellow shareholders. In that case, a director persuaded his brothers to transfer their shares to him for £1 to enable the business to be sold to the main supplier – the alternative, the director said, was to call in the receivers. When the sale to the supplier failed to materialise and no receivers were appointed, the brothers called for their shares to be returned to them. The director refused and subsequently sold all of the shares at a profit. The director had failed to give his brothers adequate or up-to-date financial or trading information about the company and had made it diffi-cult for his brothers to check the facts with the supplier. It was held that in the circumstances the director was under a fidu-ciary duty to disclose matters which he knew or had reason to believe would be material to his brothers' decision to transfer their shares. The director was held liable for the loss of value of the brothers' shares.

In *Peskin and another* v *Anderson and others* [2001] 1 BCLC 372, former members of the RAC Club, who did not benefit from payments made on the disposal of a motoring services business, unsuccessfully alleged that the directors were in breach of fidu-ciary duty in not informing them of the proposed sale and thereby deprived them of the opportunity to be readmitted as members in order to be eligible for the windfall. The Court of Appeal examined the duties owed to shareholders. Mummery LJ stated:

> "The fiduciary duties owed to the company arise from the legal relationship between the directors and the company directed and controlled by them. The fiduciary duties owed to the shareholders do not arise from that legal relationship. They are dependent on establishing a special factual rela-tionship between the directors and the shareholders in the particular case. Events may take place which bring the directors of the company into direct and close contact with the shareholders in a manner capable of generating fidu-ciary obligations, such as a duty of disclosure of material facts to the shareholders, or an obligation to use confiden-tial information and valuable commercial and financial opportunities, which have been acquired by the directors in that office for the benefit of the shareholders, and not to prefer and promote their own interests at the expense of the

125

shareholders ... There are, for example, instances of the directors of a company making direct approaches to, and dealing with, the shareholders in relation to a specific transaction and holding themselves out as agents for them in connection with the acquisition or disposal of shares; or making material representations to them; or failing to make material disclosure to them of insider information in the context of negotiations for a take-over of the company's business; or supplying to them specific information and advice on which they have relied. These events are capable of constituting special circumstances and of generating fiduciary obligations, especially in those cases in which the directors, for their own benefit, seek to use their position and special inside knowledge acquired by them to take improper or unfair advantage of the shareholders."

Whilst these decisions show that English law recognises the duties of directors to shareholders in certain circumstances, it does not mean directors must at all times reveal all they know to shareholders or risk incurring liability. Frequently, directors will be under duties (e.g. regulatory duties or duties of confidentiality, whether owed to third parties or to the company itself) not to reveal information prematurely nor to reveal it selectively. The courts will respect the *bona fide* views of directors as to the best interests of the company (as long as they are not unreasonably held) and will not seek to substitute their own views. But the courts have been increasingly reluctant to allow companies (and their shareholders or creditors) to suffer as a result of directors failing to conduct themselves in accordance with others' reasonable expectations of them or as a result of directors putting their own interests or other outside interests ahead of the company's interests. In the era of codified duties, and the emphasis given to enlightened shareholder value, over time it will become clearer just how significantly CA 2006 has increased the exposure of directors to claims for breach of duty and how often shareholders will seek to test and develop the law through the medium of the derivative claims procedure in Part 11 CA 2006. The fears of some commentators (as articulated in the press at the time that CA 2006 was being debated) that Part 11 CA 2006 would open the floodgates to tactical shareholder litigation have not been realised.

3.15 Directors' statutory liability for false and misleading statements: the Davies Review

Although the focus of this Chapter is on the general duties of directors under CA 2006, it is worth touching on the issue of directors' responsibilities in respect of statements to the market. This is an area that has received considerable attention since late 2006 when HM Treasury appointed Professor Paul Davies QC to undertake a review of issuer liability for false and misleading statements.

The Davies Review considered the case for extending the statutory damages regime (including the availability of a safe harbour) for disclosures required by the Transparency Directive (2004/109/EC). Section 90A Financial Services and Markets Act 2000 ("FSMA") was introduced by Section 1270 CA 2006 and came into force on 8 November 2006. Professor Davies published his final report on 4 June 2007, noting the various limitations of the Section 90A FSMA regime. He recommended that HM Treasury should exercise its powers under Section 90B FSMA to extend the Section 90A FSMA regime to other disclosures to the market and to issuers on exchange-regulated markets and other multilateral trading facilities. On 17 July 2008, HM Treasury published a Consultation Paper responding to the Davies Review and setting out the government's proposals to extend the Section 90A FSMA regime. The consultation closed in October 2008. On 9 March 2010, HM Treasury published its response to the responses to the consultation, broadly accepting the recommendations of the Davies Review.

On 8 April 2010, the Financial Services and Markets Act 2000 (Liability of Issuers) Regulations 2010 (SI 2010/1192) ("Regulations") were published together with an explanatory memorandum. They insert a new Section 90A FSMA which refers to a newly inserted Schedule 10A, which together considerably expand the current statutory liability regime. The Regulations come into force on 1 October 2010 and will apply in relation to information first published on or after 1 October 2010.

Fraud will remain the basis of liability under the Regulations. The issuer's liability will arise where there is an untrue or misleading statement and a person discharging managerial responsibilities within the issuer knew the statement to be untrue or misleading or was reckless as to that fact. In respect of omissions of information, liability will arise where the person discharging managerial responsibilities knew the omission to be a dishonest concealment of a material fact.

The Regulations will apply to securities that are admitted to trading on a securities market that is situated or operating in the UK (with the issuer's consent) or where the UK is the issuer's home state. This gives the Regulations potential extraterritorial reach. The extended regime will apply to most transferable securities. It includes interests in securities but excludes depositary receipts, derivative instruments or other financial instruments representing securities unless they have been admitted to secondary trading with the issuer's consent. The Regulation will extend the issuer liability regime to all information that the issuer publishes by means of a recognised information service whether or not the information is required to be published. The issuer will also be liable for any dishonest delay in publishing information.

An issuer may be liable to pay compensation to a person who has acquired, sold or continues to hold securities in reliance on published information and who has suffered loss as a result of an untrue or misleading statement in that published information. This represents a considerable extension of the previous regime which restricted the issuer's liability to acquirers of securities. It will, nonetheless, be more difficult for mere "holders" to establish rights to compensation as they will need to demonstrate reliance; this should in practice be very difficult for passive holders to do.

The Regulation will not prevent shareholders from bringing claims, *inter alia*, under Section 90 FSMA or for breach of contract or liability under the Misrepresentation Act 1967. Additionally, an issuer will remain liable for negligent misstatements where the *Caparo Industries* v *Dickman* [1990] 2 WLR 358 doctrine would apply to found such negligence.

Although the Regulations do not extend to directors, they may still be liable to the company in negligence (although *see* Section 463 CA 2006 for certain exclusions from liability and the exceptions to those).

Chapter 4

Potential Liabilities

Elliot Shear

Partner

Nabarro LLP

4.1 Introduction

It is the very essence of English company law that a limited company is a separate legal entity from its shareholders – and yet it acts through persons appointed as directors. Directors are responsible for the day-to-day running of the company and for making decisions on the management of the company's business and control of its assets and yet their acts or omissions ordinarily expose the company to liability rather than the directors personally.

However, directors boast a complex and contrasting variety of characteristics – and these ensure that there are still circumstances in which directors may be personally liable to third parties for their acts or omissions as directors. These characteristics include the fact that a director is an agent of the company; however unlike any other agent, a director determines how his principal (the company) acts. Also, a director is similar to a trustee in the sense that a director owes the company fiduciary duties in the same way a trustee owes duties to the beneficiaries of a trust (however, a director does not hold property like a trustee because the company can own and hold its own assets). A director is an officer, but not necessarily an employee, of the company. Finally, although generally directors are appointed as such, a person who acts as a director without ever being appointed as one (a shadow director or *de facto* director) can be subject to the same duties and liabilities as a validly appointed director.

Whether on a contractual, tortious or criminal basis; based on statute, various rules or miscellaneous codes; or in the potential minefield of a liquidation, directors must remain vigilant to protect their own personal position as directors, as well as fulfilling all of their duties to the company. While most of English company law is based on the obligations, responsibilities and potential liabilities faced by the company itself, this Chapter makes clear that there are a host of specific areas where personal liability for directors is a real issue. These include very precise areas of contract law, as well as more general areas of tort and criminal law. Directors of public companies are faced with an abundance of further potential personal liabilities – particularly where the company is listed.

Finally, directors need to note that not all of their conduct can be subsequently ratified by shareholders and that the circumstances in which their personal liability can be indemnified by the company are strictly limited. Consequently, the areas in which a director can be personally liable are likely to be far more extensive than many, even highly risk-averse, directors are aware.

4.2　Liability for exceeding authority

A director's authority is generally derived from both the company's articles of association and the express or implied terms of his service contract. He has authority to carry out expressly or impliedly authorised acts and his authority extends to any subordinate acts that are necessary, or reasonably incidental, to carrying out the authorised acts. The management of the company is generally entrusted to the directors through the articles. Although the articles are not automatically binding between a company and its officers, they may be expressly or impliedly incorporated into the contract between the company and a director.[1]

Other sources of a director's authority could include effective resolutions of the company or particular classes of shareholders

---

[1] *Globallink Telecommunications Ltd v Wilmbury and others* [2003] 1 BCLC 145.

and shareholders' agreements. A director's authority may also be implied by the particular office or job to which the director is appointed.[2] Finally, the director can derive authority from the subsequent ratification of his acts (discussed in Section 4.8 below).

Third parties who deal with directors acting in excess of their authority are protected by Section 40(1) Companies Act 2006 ("CA 2006") which provides that:

> "... [i]n favour of a person dealing with a company in good faith, the power of the directors to bind the company, or authorise others to do so, is deemed to be free of any limitation under the company's constitution."

These include limitations that derive from a resolution of the company, or class of shareholders, and from any agreement between the members of the company or of any class of share-holders.

In order to take advantage of Section 40(1) CA 2006, third parties will not have to investigate whether the director was authorised to bind the company, or to authorise others to bind it.[3] In addition, there is a presumption that the third party will be acting in good faith unless the contrary is proved. The presumption is further strengthened by a provision that an act will not be regarded as being in bad faith simply because the third party knows the act is beyond the powers of the director under the company's constitution. These provisions provide strong protection for third parties transacting with companies through their directors.

Directors who exceed their actual authority expose themselves to personal liability.[4] They may be liable for breach of fiduciary duty and therefore liable to indemnify the company against any losses incurred by it in consequence of the transaction entered into. If the parties to the transaction include a director of the

---

[2] *Hely Hutchinson* v *Brayhead Ltd* [1968] 1 QB 549.
[3] Section 40(2)(b)(i) CA 2006.
[4] Section 40(5) CA 2006.

131

company or of its holding company, or a person connected with any such director, the transaction will be voidable at the instance of the company. The director, or any persons associated with him, may be liable to account to the company for any gain he has made directly or indirectly by the transaction and may be required to indemnify the company for any loss or damage resulting from the transaction.

4.3 Potential contractual liability

A director is not generally personally liable for the company's contracts even where the director has signed on the company's behalf. However, there are certain very specific circumstances in which a director should be aware that he may be liable on company contracts.

4.3.1 Pre-incorporation contracts

As companies do not exist prior to their incorporation, pre-incorporation contracts are null and void. Pre-incorporation contracts are unenforceable either by or against the company because the company is not a party to the contract.[5] It is not possible to ratify pre-incorporation contracts because the company had no capacity to make them in the first place.[6]

A director will be personally liable at common law under the pre-incorporation contract if the counterparty can show that although the director ostensibly contracted as an agent of the company, he intended to be a party to the contract himself. The court will examine a range of factors such as how the (future) director signed the contract and the terms of the contract itself. As the only way in which a pre-incorporation contract can be given effect at common law is if the director contracted as a principal, the courts will fairly readily interpret the factual circumstances as having this legal result.[7]

---

[5] *Newborne v Sensolid (GB) Ltd* [1954] 1 QB 45.
[6] *Kelner v Baxter* (1867) LR 2 CP 174; *Natal Land and Colonisation Co v Pauline Syndicate* [1904] AC 120.
[7] *Newborne v Sensolid (GB) Ltd* [1954] 1 QB 45.

The position, is, however, even stronger under legislation. Section 51(1) CA 2006 provides that a director is personally liable if he enters into a pre-incorporation contract purportedly on behalf of the company prior to its incorporation. The terms of the section will apply even if all parties to the contract knew that the company had not been formed at the date of the contract.[8] The section applies "subject to any agreement to the contrary". This allows for the possibility of the pre-incorporation contact being novated to the company once it is formed.[9] If the director is personally liable, he can sue as well as be sued on the pre-incorporation contract.[10]

4.3.2 Pre-trading certificate contracts

A private company may transact business as soon as it is incorporated, but a company that was registered as a public company when it was originally incorporated is not permitted to transact any business or exercise any borrowing powers until it has either been issued with a *"trading certificate"* by the registrar under Section 761(1) CA 2006 or re-registered as a private company.

The consequence of transacting or borrowing without a trading certificate is that the company and the defaulting officer will be guilty of a criminal offence under Section 767(2) CA 2006. The defaulting officer will either be liable to a fine on indictment or to a fine not exceeding the statutory maximum on summary conviction.

If the company enters into a transaction without a trading certificate, the transaction will remain valid.[11] However, if the company fails to comply with its obligations under the transaction within 21 days from being called upon to do so, the directors of the company are jointly and severally liable to indemnify the other party to the transaction in respect of any loss or damage suffered by him by reason of the company's failure to

---

[8] *Phonogram Ltd* v *Lane* [1982] QB 938.
[9] *Howard* v *Patent Ivory Mf Co* (1888) 38 Ch D 156.
[10] *Braymist Ltd and others* v *Wise Finance Co Ltd* [2002] EWCA Civ 127, [2002] 1 BCLC 415.
[11] At common law, a contract entered into in such a case where the trading certificate was never granted did not bind the company and was unenforceable against it (*Re Otto Electrical Manufacturing Co (1905) Ltd, Jenkins's Claim* [1906] 2 Ch 390).

comply with those obligations. The directors who will be liable are those who were directors at the time the company entered into the transaction.

4.3.3 Contracts without proper disclosure of company details

Under CA 2006, provisions regarding the disclosure and display of a company's name are largely dealt with in the Companies (Trading Disclosures) Regulations 2008 (SI 2008/495), which came into force on 1 October 2008 (the "2008 Regulations"). These were amended by the Companies (Trading Disclosures) (Amendment) Regulations 2009, in force from October 2009.

Where a company is seeking to enforce a contract that does not comply with the 2008 Regulations, those proceedings will be dismissed if the defendant can show that company has breached the 2008 Regulations or the defendant has otherwise suffered some loss as a result of the breach.

Section 84 CA 2006 sets out the criminal consequences of any breach and provides that the company and any defaulting officer are guilty of an offence and are liable to a fine on summary conviction not exceeding level 3 on the standard scale and, in the event of a continued contravention, a daily fine not exceeding one tenth of level 3 on the standard scale.

The 2008 Regulations require a company to disclose its registered name in characters that can be read with the naked eye in or on all:

(a) business letters, notices and other official publications and order forms of the company;
(b) bills of exchange, promissory notes, endorsements and order forms;
(c) cheques purporting to be signed by or on behalf of the company;
(d) orders for money, goods or services purporting to be signed by or on behalf of the company;
(e) bills of parcels, invoices and other demands for payment, receipts and letters of credit;
(f) applications for licences to carry on a trade or activity;

(g) all other forms of its business correspondence and documentation;

(h) its websites.

Historically, the trading disclosures provision has been strictly enforced by the courts. Its object is to protect persons who deal with the company in ignorance of the fact that they are dealing with an entity with limited liability.[12] However, its scope has been extended by the courts to include not only those cases in which the words indicating the company's limited liability status are omitted but to cases where the word "limited" appeared but the company's name has been misstated by the omission of a word,[13] where the words in the company's name are transposed[14] and where additional words have been added to the name.[15] By contrast, misspelling a company's name will not amount to a breach of the section provided that no danger of confusion arises from this.[16]

Section 85 CA 2006 provides that minor variations in the company's name are not to be taken into account. Thus, no account is to be taken of whether: upper or lower case characters (or a combination of the two are used); whether diacritical marks or punctuation are present or absent; or whether the name is in the same format or style as is specified under Section 57(1)(b) CA 2006 for the purposes of registration, provided there is no real likelihood of names differing only in those respects being taken to be different names.

---

[12] *Penrose* v *Martyr* (1858) E1B1 & E1 499; *Atkin* v *Wardle* (1889) 5 TLR 734; *British Airways Board* v *Parish* [1979] 2 Lloyd's Rep 361; *Blum* v *OCP Repartition SA* [1988] BCLC 170.

[13] *Hendon* v *Adelman* (1973) 117 SJ 631, LR Agencies Ltd rather than L & R Agencies Ltd; *Barber and Nicholls Ltd* v *R and G Associates Ltd* (1981) 132 NLJ 1076, "(London)" omitted from the company name R and G Associates (London) Limited. The abbreviations "Co" and "Ltd" are acceptable substitutes for company and limited respectively (*Banque de l'Indochine et de Suez* v *Euroseas Group Finance Co Ltd* [1981] 3 All ER 198 and *Stacey & Co Ltd* v *Wallis* (1912) 106 LT 544). Other abbreviations may be accepted where the abbreviation is one generally accepted and where no other word is similarly abbreviated – not, e.g. where "M" was substituted for "Michael" in the name Michael Jackson (Fancy Goods) Limited (*Durham Fancy Goods Ltd* v *Michael Jackson (Fancy Goods) Ltd* [1968] 2 QB 839).

[14] *Atkins* v *Wardle* (1889) 61 LT 23 (the company name, South Shields Salt Water Baths Company Limited, misstated as Salt Water Baths Company Limited, South Shields and South Shields Water Baths Company).

[15] *Nassau Steam Press* v *Tyler* (1894) 70 LT 376, "Old Paris and Bastille Syndicate Ltd" rather than "Bastille Syndicate Ltd".

[16] For example, "Primkeen" rather than "Primekeen" (*Jenice Ltd* v *Dan* [1994] BCC 43).

4.4   Potential tortious liability

4.4.1   *Negligent acts and omissions of the company*

In the majority of cases, a company's directors will not be responsible for the company's negligence, or other tortious acts or omissions, simply because they are officers of, and direct, the company.[17] This is the case even where the company is small and the director necessarily has a lot of power over its affairs; and also where the director is the sole director and shareholder of the company.[18] English law is mindful to preserve the principle that the company is separate and distinct in law from its directors, shareholders and officers and should therefore enjoy the benefit of limited liability.

> "Commercial enterprise and adventure is not to be discouraged by subjecting a director to such onerous potential liabilities."[19]

English law will, however, attach liability to the director where he has effectively made the tortious conduct his own, as opposed to the company's. Where it is sought to make a director liable for his company's tort, there will be a careful examination of the role personally played by the director in respect of the act complained of. A director will be liable with the company as a joint tortfeasor if:

(a)   the director authorises, orders, directs or procures the commission of the tort; or
(b)   the director assumes responsibility for the negligent act or omission.

4.4.1.1   *Authorise, order, direct or procure*

If a director personally commits a tort, he will of course be liable for it and cannot escape liability merely because he has carried

---

[17]   *Rainham Chemical Works Ltd* v *Belvedere Fish Guano Co Ltd* [1921] 2 AC 465 at 476.
[18]   *British Thomson-Houston Co Ltd* v *Sterling Accessories Ltd* (1924) 41 RPC 311, referred to in *Evans (C) and Sons Ltd* v *Spritebrand Ltd* [1985] 1 WLR 317 at 325.
[19]   *PLG Research Ltd* v *Ardon International Ltd* [1993] FSR 197 at 238.

out the tort in the course of his duties as a director of a company.[20] Equally, if a director forms a company for the express purpose of doing a wrongful act, or expressly directs that the company do a wrongful act, the director will be individually responsible.[21]

However, for the director to be liable for his company's tort, express direction is not a necessity. A lesser form of control can attract liability. A director may be personally liable if he directs or procures the commission of a negligent act. The direction and procurement can be either express or implied.[22]

The question of what kind of participation in the act of the company will give rise to personal liability on the part of the director has been described as "an elusive question".[23] It will involve a careful examination of the personal involvement of the director and may raise difficult questions of degree about whether a director had ordered or procured the relevant acts to be done. Broad policy considerations may also be taken into account in deciding whether the conduct is of such a nature as to make the director personally liable.[24]

Although express and implied direction and procurement may attract personal liability, a director who merely "facilitates" a tort is not personally responsible for it. His conduct must at least amount to conduct that would render him liable as a joint tortfeasor if the company had not existed.[25] For example, selling materials for the purpose of infringing a patent to the man who is going to infringe it, even knowing that the buyer is going to do so, may not amount to procuring a tort.

A director may be made jointly liable for a company's torts regardless of his state of mind. It may not be necessary for the

---

[20] *Evans (C) and Sons Ltd* v *Spritebrand Ltd* [1985] 1 WLR 317 at 323.

[21] *Rainham Chemical Works Ltd* v *Belvedere Fish Guano Co Ltd* [1921] 2 AC 465.

[22] *Performing Right Society Ltd* v *Ciryl Theatrical Syndicate Ltd* [1924] 1 KB 1 at 14–15, quoted in *Evans (C) and Sons Ltd* v *Spritebrand Ltd* [1985] 1 WLR 317 at 328.

[23] *Mentmore Manufacturing Co Ltd* v *National Merchandising Manufacturing Co Inc* (1978) 89 DLR (3d) 195 referred to in *Evans (C) and Sons Ltd* v *Spritebrand Ltd* [1985] 1 WLR 317 at 325–326.

[24] *Evans (C) and Sons Ltd* v *Spritebrand Ltd* [1985] 1 WLR 317 at 330. *See Mancetter Developments Ltd* v *Garmanson Ltd* [1986] 1 All ER 449 and *AP Besson Ltd* v *Fulleon Ltd* [1986] FSR 319 for examples of cases where directors have been found liable as joint tortfeasors.

[25] *PLG Research Ltd* v *Ardon International Ltd* [1993] FSR 197 at 238–239.

director to know or have been reckless as to whether his acts were likely to be tortious.[26] The exception is where a particular mental state would be an element of the tort. If the claimant has to prove a particular state of mind or knowledge on the part of the defendant as a necessary element of the tort alleged, the state of mind of the director will be relevant. However, it is not a precondition of liability that there be a "knowing, deliberate, wilful quality" to the director's actions in order for liability to attach.[27]

4.4.1.2 Assumption of responsibility for the negligent act or omission

A director will be jointly liable with the company where he assumes responsibility to the victim, expressly or by implication, for the act or omission that constitutes the tort.[28] This will usually require the director to put himself into a special relationship with the victim, for example, writing letters or issuing invoices suggesting that the director, rather than the company, was personally answerable for the services owed in the particular circumstances.[29]

4.4.2 Negligent misrepresentation

A company may become liable in tort for negligent statements[30] for the economic loss suffered by a claimant on *Hedley Byrne* principles, namely where the company creates a special relationship with the claimant by assuming responsibility towards him, for example, by giving advice to the claimant in a professional capacity in the knowledge that that advice will be reasonably relied on.[31] The assumption of responsibility principle extends beyond the making of statements to the provision of services. In order to establish a cause of action the claimant will need to show that he relied on the assumption of responsibility by the

---

[26] *Evans (C) and Sons Ltd* v *Spritebrand Ltd* [1985] 1 WLR 317 at 329–330. This is at least the case in relation to infringements of Section 1(2) Copyright Act 1956.

[27] *Evans (C) and Sons Ltd* v *Spritebrand Ltd* [1985] 1 WLR 317 at 330.

[28] *Fairline Shipping Corp* v *Adamson* [1975] QB 180.

[29] *See* also *Yuille* v *B&B Fisheries (Leigh) Ltd, The Radiant* [1958] 2 Lloyd's Rep 596 at 619–620.

[30] Even where there is a contractual duty in the same respect.

[31] *Hedley Byrne & Co Ltd* v *Heller and Partners* [1964] AC 465.

company. In considering what amounts to an assumption of responsibility, the courts will apply an objective test. The primary focus is not on what the defendant thought or intended personally, but on whether what he said or did in his dealings with the claimant as judged in the relevant context, means that the defendant assumed responsibility towards the claimant for the advice or services.

It is possible for a director to be personally liable in respect of a company's negligent misrepresentations or services. As with other forms of tortious conduct, a director will not be personally liable for negligent misrepresentations just because he is an officer of the company. In a small company, the director will almost inevitably have qualities and skills that are core to the advice or services offered by the company but that does not mean that the director will have assumed personal responsibility to the customers of the company. A director's personal liability will arise where the director, or someone on his behalf, conveyed, directly or indirectly, to the claimant that the director assumed personal responsibility towards him. In deciding whether a director has assumed responsibility to the claimant, the courts will investigate the oral and written exchanges between the director and the claimant to see whether they "cross the line". The claimant will also have to establish reliance as a matter of fact and it must have been reasonable for the claimant to have relied on an assumption of personal responsibility by the individual director. It is not sufficient for the company to have a special relationship with the claimant. There must have been an assumption of responsibility that creates a special relationship with the director himself.

4.4.3 Statutory liability

Section 2(2) Misrepresentation Act 1967 provides that where a person has entered into a contract after a misrepresentation made to him otherwise than fraudulently, and he would be entitled to rescind that contract, then the court may award damages in lieu of rescission if it appears to the court that it would be equitable to do so. Damages may be recovered under Section 2(3) Misrepresentation Act 1967.

4.4.4 Fraudulent misrepresentation

The elements of the tort of deceit will be satisfied where a person makes a false representation to another person intending that they be induced to act on it and they do in fact rely on it, as a result of which they change their position to their detriment.[32] The representation may be oral, in writing or arise by implication from words or conduct. The representor must know or believe the representation to be untrue, or be careless, reckless, or indifferent as to its truth. Based on these principles, a director responsible for a prospectus (for example) will be liable in the tort of deceit if he signs or authorises the issue of a prospectus knowing or believing it to contain a false statement for the purpose of inducing the claimant to take up shares which the claimant does, and then subsequently suffers loss as a consequence.[33] The company will also be liable in respect of the director's act if it is within the scope of his authority but the director's liability remains. The claimant can combine the claim for deceit with a claim for statutory relief (e.g. under Section 90 Financial Services and Markets Act 2000 ("FSMA")) and a claim against the company for rescission,[34] although generally relief is either by way of damages or rescission.

The principles that apply to the assessment of damages payable where the claimant has been induced by a fraudulent misrepresentation to buy property are set out in the judgment of Lord Browne-Wilkinson in *Smith New Court Securities Ltd* v *Scrimgeour Vickers (Asset Management) Ltd* [1997] 4 AC 254. They are that the defendant is bound to make reparation for all the damage flowing directly from the transaction, even if not foreseeable although it must have been directly caused by the transaction. The claimant is entitled to recover the full price paid by him but must give credit for any benefits received as a result of the transaction, which generally include the market value of the property at the date of acquisition, unless the application of this rule would prevent full compensation. The general rule will

---

[32] *See* per Lord Herschell *Derry* v *Peek* (1889) 14 App Cas 337.
[33] *Andrew* v *Mockford* [1986] 1 QB 372; cf. *Peek* v *Gurney* (1873) LR 6 HL 377; also *Al-Nakib Investments (Jersey) Ltd* v *Longcroft* [1990] 3 All ER 321.
[34] *Frankenburg* v *Great Horseless Carriage Co* [1900] 1 QB 504.

usually not apply where the misrepresentation has continued to operate after acquisition and has induced the claimant to retain the asset or if the claimant is by reason of the fraud locked into the property. The claimant is also entitled to recover consequential losses caused by the transaction. The usual principle of mitigation applies. Lord Browne-Wilkinson considered that it would be an over-elaboration to cross-check the computation by comparing what the value of the business would have been if the misrepresentation had not been true with the value of the contract price. This approach to the measure of damages can be contrasted with the law of negligence where the claimant's entitlement to recover losses will depend on what was foreseeable by reference to the scope of the duty owed by the defendant.

4.4.5 Misstatements in company reporting

Theoretically, a director can be liable for misstatements in the company's accounts. However, it would be unlikely to result in liability for investment decisions because the element of reliance in the tort of deceit would be difficult to establish. This is because (unlike with a selling document like a prospectus) there is no intention to induce reliance in respect of securities trading. A similar difficulty arises in relation to negligent misstatements in the company's accounts. Based on the principles in *Caparo Industries Plc v Dickman* [1990] 1 All ER 568, HL, there is no general duty of care owed to shareholders who rely on the company's statutory accounts to make investment decisions. This is because the purpose of the statutory accounts is to assist shareholders to exercise their corporate governance rights. Following the implementation of the Transparency Directive, concerns were raised that the distinction drawn in *Caparo* between corporate governance rights and investment decisions might be undermined in relation to company reporting required by the Transparency Directive because the directive focuses on (and is indeed "animated by" the objective of) investor protection. Subsequently, the government enacted Section 90A FSMA to deal with these concerns.

Section 90A FSMA creates a statutory liability scheme in relation to all disclosures made by a listed company through a recognised information service. Section 90A FSMA creates a liability on listed issuers for fraudulent or reckless misstatements or from omissions amounting to a dishonest concealment of a material fact. From 1 October 2010 the liability under Section 90A FSMA is extended to dishonest delays in publishing information, pursuant to amendments made by the Financial Services and Markets Act 2000 (Liability of Issuers) Regulations 2010.

Holders, as well as acquirers and sellers, of securities may rely on Section 90A. The section does not require issuers to intend acquirers to rely on the reported information and in that sense is broader in scope than the tort of deceit. It is a requirement that the investor must have reasonably relied on the information. Although the section does not extend liability to directors, directors may still be liable to the company in negligence. Section 463 CA 2006 excludes directors from liability for negligence in relation to the directors' report and directors' remuneration report (and summary financial statements derived from them). However, it does not excuse directors where they know that the statement is untrue or misleading or are reckless as to those matters, or where directors know that an omission was a dishonest concealment of a material fact.

4.5   Potential criminal liability

Apart from crimes of strict liability, a person will only be convicted of a crime if he has committed the elements that constitute the crime, including the requisite state of mind, or *mens rea*. Accordingly, a director may be criminally liable in respect of any criminal acts of a company if the requisite *mens rea* can be proved against him individually. For example, a director may be guilty of conspiring with, or aiding and abetting, a company to commit a wrong.

Legislation may make it an offence for a director of a company to enable the company to commit an offence in some way. Any number of formulations may be used. Common examples are formulations that make directors liable if they "cause or knowingly permit" the commission of an offence by a company, or if the offence occurred with the director's "consent or connivance" or as a result of his "neglect". In each case, the requisite conduct and mental element will need to be independently proven against the director.

Further, companies are obliged to comply with judgments and orders of the court and undertakings given by them to the court. RSC Order 45, Rule 5(1) Civil Procedure Rules relevantly provides that:

> "... [w]here a person required by a judgment or order to do an act within a time specified in the judgment or order refuses or neglects to do it ... or a person disobeys a judgment or order requiring him to abstain from doing an act, then, subject to the provisions of these rules, the judgment or order may be enforced by one or more of the following means, that is to say ... where that person is a body corporate, with the permission of the court, a writ of sequestration against the property of any director or other officer of the body; subject to the provisions of the Debtors Act 1869 and 1878, an order of committal against that person or, where that person is a body corporate, against any such officer."

In spite of the broad words of the Rule, the courts will not make an order for committal for contempt against a director merely because he holds office and has knowledge of the order. An order for committal can only be made against an officer of a company where he can be shown to be in contempt[35] or where he is responsible for the company's breach of the order or judgment, whether by his actions or wilful failure to ensure the company's compliance with its obligations.[36] Directors cannot, however, be passive in the face of orders made, or undertakings given, restraining a company from doing certain acts. A director who is aware of the terms of such an order or undertaking is under a duty to take reasonable care to secure the company's compliance with it. Even if the director has not participated in the company's breach, he will be exposed to committal for contempt if the company breaches the order in circumstances where the director wilfully failed to take adequate and continuing steps to ensure

---

[35] *Director General of Fair Trading* v *Buckland* [1990] 1 WLR 920.
[36] *Re British Concrete Pipe Association's Agreement* [1982] ICR 182 at 195.

that those to whom compliance had been delegated had not misunderstood or overlooked the obligations.[37]

4.6 Potential liabilities when issuing securities

Directors need to be aware of their responsibilities, obligations and potential liabilities as directors in connection with a proposed application for admission of a company's shares to the Official List of the Financial Services Authority and to trading on the London Stock Exchange's Main Market for listed securities. Attention should be drawn in particular to the personal liability to which a director may be exposed in relation to the contents of a prospectus prepared in accordance with FSMA, the prospectus rules made under Part VI FSMA (the "Prospectus Rules") and the European Commission's Prospectus Regulation (809/2004) (the "Prospectus Regulation").

It is important to note that some of the requirements in the context of preparing a prospectus have a continuing effect on a company's activities and those of the directors after admission. This applies particularly to the obligations imposed by Section 397 FSMA, which are discussed below.

Under the FSMA, personal liability for a prospectus will not extend to an admission document for which a director of a company to be admitted to the AIM Market of the London Stock Exchange will be responsible. However, directors of AIM Market companies will still need to be conscious of their potential criminal liabilities under Section 397 FSMA – and also the contractual and tortious liability they have expressly assumed by means of the responsibility statement they will have entered into.

4.6.1 *Requirement for prospectus*

Section 85 FSMA requires that (unless one of a small number of exceptions apply) a prospectus approved by the FSA be made available to the public before:

---

[37] *AG for Tuvalu v Philatelic Distribution Corp* [1990] 1 WLR 926.

(a) shares in a UK company are offered to the public in the UK; or

(b) a request is made for the admission of such shares to trading on the London Stock Exchange's Main Market for listed securities.

The prospectus must be produced, approved and published in accordance with the detailed requirements of FSMA, the Prospectus Rules and the Prospectus Regulation. The Prospectus Regulation prescribes the detailed information requirements of the prospectus. The CESR Recommendations give guidance on the practical interpretation of the Prospectus Regulation.

In addition to those specific requirements, there is a general requirement under Section 87A(2), (3) and (4) FSMA that the prospectus contain all information which is necessary to enable investors to make an informed assessment of the assets and liabilities, financial position, profits and losses and prospects of the company and of the rights attaching to the shares to be listed. The necessary information must be presented in a form which is comprehensible and easy to analyse and having regard to the particular nature of the shares to be listed and the company.

If, after the date of approval of the prospectus by the FSA and before the start of trading in the company's shares, there arises or is noted any significant new factor, material mistake or inaccuracy relating to the information included in the prospectus, the company must submit a supplementary prospectus containing details of the new factor, mistake or inaccuracy to the FSA for its approval. Section 87Q(4) FSMA provides that an investor who has already agreed to buy or subscribe for the relevant shares may withdraw his acceptance within two working days after the date of publication of any such supplementary prospectus.

4.6.2 Responsibility for prospectus

The Prospectus Rules set out the persons responsible for a prospectus. These include the company, each director of the company and also each person who has accepted (and is stated in the prospectus as having accepted) responsibility for the whole or any part of it or who has authorised any part of the prospectus.

Any liability may, therefore, be shared jointly among a number of persons. The Prospectus Rules do not specify exactly how the liability will be shared amongst those who are jointly responsible but if, for example, a director were sued by a disgruntled investor, he could be liable for the full amount of any loss, although he would be able to claim a right of contribution from the other persons who are jointly responsible under the Civil Liability (Contribution) Act 1978.

The Prospectus Regulation requires the prospectus to contain details of those who are responsible for the information contained in it and a responsibility statement to the following effect:

> "The Company and each of the Directors whose names appear on page [   ] of this document accept responsibility for the information contained in this document. The Company and the Directors declare that, having taken all reasonable care to ensure that such is the case, the information contained in this document is to the best of their knowledge in accordance with the facts and contains no omission likely to affect its import."

4.6.3 Civil liability under FSMA

Under Section 90 FSMA the persons responsible for a prospectus are liable to pay compensation to any person who acquires shares in the company and who suffers loss in respect of them as a result of any untrue or misleading statement contained in the prospectus or the omission from it of any matter required to be included pursuant to the general duty of disclosure imposed by Section 87A FSMA.

Liability exists to initial subscribers for or purchasers of shares in the context of fundraisings carried out in connection with a prospectus. In addition, although the position is not free from doubt, liability under FSMA probably also exists to persons who buy shares in the market who can demonstrate that their loss resulted from statements in or omissions from a prospectus. There is no need to show reliance on the misstatement, provided the loss resulted from it. In broad terms, the measure of compensation will be calculated by comparing the value which the shares would have had if the prospectus had been correct with their actual value.

There are formal defences to this potential liability (and these are set out in Schedule 10 FSMA) which include the defence that a director will not be liable if at the time the prospectus was submitted to the FSA he had made such enquiries as were reasonable and reasonably believed that the particular statement was true and not misleading or that the matter the omission of which caused the loss was properly omitted.

Another defence arises in respect of a statement made by or on the authority of an expert and included in the prospectus with the expert's consent, and where the director reasonably believed, at the time the prospectus was submitted to the FSA, that the expert was competent to make the statement and had consented to its inclusion in the form and context in which it was included, and in either case the director continued in this belief until the shares were acquired; or the shares were acquired before it was reasonably practical to bring a correction to the attention of those likely to acquire them; or before the shares were acquired the director took all reasonable steps to secure that a correction was brought to the attention of persons acquiring shares; or he continued in this belief until after commencement of dealings and the shares were acquired after such a lapse of time that he ought reasonably to be excused from liability.

A director shall also not be liable if the person suffering the loss acquired the shares in question knowing that the statement was false or misleading or knowing of the omitted matter or of the change or new matter.

Finally, even if a director cannot demonstrate reasonable belief in the accuracy of the prospectus at the time it was published, there is still a defence if he can show that:

(a) before the shares were acquired a correction had been published in a manner calculated to bring it to the attention of potential investors; or

(b) he took all reasonable steps to secure such publication and reasonably believed that it had taken place before the shares were acquired.

4.6.4 Criminal liability under FSMA

Section 397 FSMA imposes potential criminal liability on a director. It provides that a person is guilty of an offence punishable by imprisonment and/or a fine if he:

(a) makes a statement, promise or forecast which he knows to be misleading, false or deceptive in a material particular; or
(b) dishonestly conceals any material facts; or
(c) recklessly makes (dishonestly or otherwise) a statement, promise or forecast which is misleading, false or deceptive in a material particular.

A director would also be guilty of an offence if he does any of the above for the purposes of inducing, or is reckless as to whether it may induce, another person (whether or not the person to whom the statement, promise or forecast is made) to enter or offer to enter into, or to refrain from entering or offering to enter into, an investment agreement (which, broadly speaking, includes an agreement to buy, sell or underwrite shares). Recklessness in this context means either not caring whether a statement is true or closing one's eyes to the possibility that it may be false. The wording is sufficiently wide to include misstatements in or dishonest concealment of material facts from a prospectus.

Section 397 FSMA also provides that a person is guilty of an offence punishable by imprisonment and/or a fine if he does any act or engages in any course of conduct which creates a false or misleading impression as to the market in or the price or value of any investments, if he does so for the purpose of creating that impression and of thereby inducing another person to acquire, dispose of, subscribe for or underwrite those investments or to refrain from doing so or to exercise, or refrain from exercising, any rights conferred by those investments.

It is a defence for the person concerned to prove that he reasonably believed that his act or conduct would not create an impression that was false or misleading as to the matters mentioned above.

The maximum period of imprisonment for conviction of an offence under Section 397 FSMA is six months in the case of a summary conviction and seven years in the case of conviction on indictment. Fines on summary conviction are subject to the statutory maximum from time to time, but on indictment are not subject to any limit.

It is also an offence (under Section 398 FSMA) for a person to provide information to the FSA which he knows to be, or to provide information recklessly which is, false or misleading in a material particular, in connection with an application for admission to the Official List or for approval of a prospectus or otherwise in purported compliance with any other requirement imposed by or under FSMA (which would include the Listing Rules, Prospectus Rules and Disclosure and Transparency Rules). Fines may be imposed for breach of this section.

Under Section 400 FSMA, a director, member of the committee of management, chief executive, manager, secretary or similar officer of the company, or a person purporting to act in any such capacity, may also be guilty of an offence (punishable with imprisonment and/or a fine) committed by the company under FSMA if it is found to have been committed with his consent or connivance, or to be attributable to any neglect on his part.

4.6.5   Other criminal liability

Under Section 19 Theft Act 1968, a director is liable to imprisonment if he publishes or concurs in publishing a written statement or account (which includes a prospectus) which to his knowledge is or may be misleading, false or deceptive in a material particular, with the intent to deceive shareholders or creditors.

It is an offence under Section 2 Fraud Act 2006 to make a false representation (by words or conduct as to any fact, law or state of mind of any person) whether express or implied either: knowing that the representation is false or misleading, or being

149

aware that it might be. The victim of the representation need not actually rely upon it. A false representation in a prospectus could therefore lead to a criminal fraud charge if accompanied by the appropriate guilty intent.

It is an offence under Section 3 Fraud Act 2006 to fail to disclose information where there is a legal duty to do so (e.g. statutory, contractual, custom from a trade or market, or a fiduciary relationship). Those who fail to make full disclosure pursuant to legal obligations will therefore be at risk from prosecution. This could include a deliberate failure to make disclosures in a prospectus in breach of the FSMA or Prospectus Rules requirements.

4.6.6   Other civil liability

4.6.6.1   Negligent misstatement

Where a director has been negligent in making a statement contained in the prospectus he may be liable under a claim for damages brought by a claimant who has suffered loss through acting in reliance on that statement.

This liability is reinforced by the inclusion of the responsibility statement in the prospectus. On the face of it this statement establishes a duty of care by the directors to persons who rely on statements in the prospectus and who suffer loss, where the loss was a reasonably foreseeable consequence of the negligent misstatement. Although the position is not free from doubt, case law has established that it is at least arguable that the duty of care extends to persons who buy shares in the market (i.e. it extends beyond persons who buy shares in a fundraising carried out on the admission of a company's shares to the Official List).[38]

4.6.6.2   Deceit

If a director has been fraudulent in misrepresenting facts stated (including a misleading omission) in the prospectus by making

---

[38] *Possfund Custodian Trustee Ltd* v *Diamond* [1996] 1 WLR 1351 (Ch D).

a statement either with knowledge of its falsity or being reckless as to whether it is true or false, he could be liable for damages to a shareholder or purchaser deceived by it. The measure of damages in an action for deceit is the actual damage suffered by the claimant.

A director will not be liable in an action for deceit if he can prove that he held an honest belief in the facts stated even though his belief was not based on reasonable grounds. He may not be liable if he can prove that the person suing him was not in fact misled by the statement. It is, however, no defence to the director that the claimant might easily have ascertained that the statement was untrue by independent enquiry.

4.6.6.3 *Contract and the Misrepresentation Act 1967*

If a prospectus contains an untrue or misleading statement or if there is an omission which renders any statement in the prospectus misleading, a person suffering loss from subscribing for or purchasing shares may have a remedy under the Misrepresentation Act 1967 which provides the remedies of rescission of the contract and/or damages.

In connection with an admission of a company's shares, the company will enter into an agreement with the financial adviser acting as its sponsor. Under that agreement the company will give to the sponsor certain warranties and indemnities. The warranties and indemnities from the company to the sponsor will relate to the accuracy and completeness of financial and other information concerning the group as contained in the prospectus and compliance by the company with other relevant legal requirements, including the Companies Act, FSMA, the Listing Rules, the Prospectus Rules, the Disclosure and Transparency Rules, the Admission and Disclosure Standards and the Prospectus Regulation.

If an action were to be brought against the sponsor by purchasers of the company's shares, the sponsor would rely on the warranties and indemnities given by the company and, in the event of a breach of warranty, would institute action against the company in relation to loss suffered by the sponsor as a result of any such claim. This is rare in practice but if such a claim was successful, the company may have a claim in turn against the directors.

4.6.6.4 *Duty of care*

The directors also owe to the company at common law a duty to exercise reasonable care and skill in the performance of their duties. If a breach of this duty results in a misstatement in the prospectus and the company is required whether under statute or at common law to compensate third parties who rely on the misstatement, the company may be able to recover its loss from the directors.

4.7 Potential Takeover Code liabilities

The City Code on Takeovers and Mergers (the "Code") imposes another layer of responsibilities on all members of the board of directors of a public company involved in a takeover, in addition to their statutory and other responsibilities outlined in this Chapter. In the context of a takeover situation directors will need, in particular, to have regard to their duties under the CA 2006 to exercise independent judgment, to avoid conflicts of interest or duty, not to accept benefits from third parties, and to declare interests in proposed transactions or arrangements with the company. Directors on the board of target who are involved in a management buy-out, or who will remain involved with the business after completion of the takeover, will need to have particular regard to these statutory duties as well as their duties under the Code.

As the Code has now been placed on a statutory footing, directors need to be even more aware of their responsibilities under the Code. The Panel on Takeovers and Mergers (the "Panel"), is the supervisory authority which polices the Code and the conduct of takeovers and now has certain statutory powers of enforcement under the CA 2006. For example the Panel can ask the court to enforce compliance with its rulings (Section 955 CA 2006) or require the payment of compensation to shareholders where there has been a breach of specific rules of the Code that deal with the offer price to be paid to target shareholders (Section 954 CA 2006 and paragraph 10(c), Introduction to the Code).

It is a general principle of the Code that directors should act in the interests of the company as a whole and ensure, so far as they are reasonably able, that the Code is complied with in the conduct of an offer. The Code requires the target board to give its opinion on the offer to all target shareholders; however the duties of the target directors in giving their views cannot always be easily reconciled with their general duty to promote the success of the company. In general, directors do not owe any duty to shareholders directly. However, in the context of a takeover some duties are owed directly to shareholders, particularly when it comes to deciding whether or not to recommend the offer to them. In summary, directors must not mislead shareholders and must form an honest opinion on the merits of the offer.

The Panel has accepted that the responsibility for supervising and monitoring an offer can rest with a committee of the board of a company. Nevertheless, every member of the board of directors will be required to accept responsibility for each document issued in connection with an offer and the individual responsibility of each director is not removed by delegation to a committee. This principle is emphasised in guidance notes on the responsibility of all the directors of a company during the course of an offer contained in Appendix 3 to the Code. Arrangements should, therefore, be made to ensure, among other things, that the entire board is provided promptly with copies of all documents and announcements issued by or on behalf of a company involved in a takeover which bear on the offer and that each director receives promptly details of other relevant matters.

Rule 19.1 of the Code creates a requirement for documents, advertisements or statements made in connection with a takeover to satisfy the highest standard of accuracy and to present information adequately and fairly. Rule 19.2 provides that each document (subject to certain exceptions found in Rule 19) issued to shareholders or advertisement published in connection with an offer must state that the directors of the bidder (and where appropriate the target) accept responsibility for the information contained in the document or advertisement for which they are responsible and that, to the best of their knowledge and belief (having taken all reasonable care to ensure that such is the case), the information contained in the document or advertisement is in accordance with the facts and, where appropriate, that it does not omit anything likely to affect the import of such information.

The notes to Rule 19.2 contain guidance on the application of the rule and expressly state that a responsibility statement extends to expressions of opinion as well as of fact. The inclusion of a responsibility statement in a takeover document (including a scheme document) or advertisement could expose the directors to a civil action in tort if he has failed to take reasonable care. For this reason alone no such document should be dispatched or issued unless each director has confirmed in writing that he or she accepts responsibility in terms of the responsibility statement contained in the document. The responsibilities which directors have as regards the standards of care and accuracy required in the preparation of documents and announcements under the Code are in addition to those responsibilities contained in statute and common law.

Directors will need to be particularly alive to Section 953 CA 2006 which creates offences in relation to offer and response documents prepared in relation to takeover bids. If an offer document published in respect of the bid does not comply with the document offer rules then the person making the bid will commit an offence. Where the person making the bid is a body of persons (i.e. a board of directors) that body who caused the document to be published will be liable for committing the offence. Directors will only be liable if they knew that the offer document did not comply, or were reckless as to whether it complied, and failed to take all reasonable steps to ensure that it did comply. Directors may be liable on conviction on indictment to a fine or, on summary conviction, to a fine not exceeding the statutory maximum.

4.8   Ratification

The CA 2006 does not codify the common law on ratification of directors' breaches, and the common law restrictions on ratification are preserved by Section 239(7).

Not all conduct by directors is capable of ratification by shareholders, but the law on which types of breach of duty are capable of ratification is unclear and the cases are difficult to reconcile. However, it is clear that shareholders cannot ratify (or authorise) breaches of duty which are fraudulent or are outside the powers of the company. On the other hand, it appears that an act which is merely negligent is ratifiable, even when it causes loss to the company. It also appears that if the directors exercised their powers in good faith but for improper purposes, that is also ratifiable.

Section 239 provides that ratification by a company of conduct by a director amounting to negligence, default, breach of duty or breach of trust in relation to the company must be by resolution of the members (Sections 239(1) and 239(2)).

Sections 239(3) and 239(4) also set out new requirements as to who can vote on a resolution to ratify a director's conduct. Section 239(3) provides that where the ratification resolution is proposed as a written resolution, the director himself (if a member) and any person connected with him are not eligible to vote on it. At a meeting where a resolution to ratify the conduct of a director is to be proposed, votes in favour of the resolution cast by the director concerned (if a member) and the votes of any member connected with him must be disregarded in determining whether the resolution is passed. The director and any member connected with him can still attend the meeting and be counted in the quorum (*see* Section 239(4) CA 2006). The definition of "connected person" for the purpose of Section 239 is modified by Section 239(5) and may also include other directors. However, nothing in Section 239 affects the validity of a decision taken by unanimous consent of the members of the company, or any power of the directors to agree not to sue, or to settle or release, a claim made by them on behalf of the company (Section 239(6)).

These new requirements mark a significant change from the position under the common law. The position is different when giving authorisation to directors before they take a particular action. In that case, the director concerned and any connected persons are not excluded and their votes will be counted.

4.9   Indemnity and insurance against liability

Section 232 CA 2006 sets out the basic prohibition on provisions (in service agreements, letters of appointment, the articles of association or elsewhere) protecting directors from liability in connection with any negligence, default, breach of duty or breach of trust in relation to the company. Any provision that purports to exempt the director of a company (to any extent) from such liability is void (*see* Section 232(1)) and any provision by which a company directly or indirectly provides an indemnity (to any extent) for a director of the company, or of an associated company, against such liability in relation to the company of which he is a director is void (*see* Section 232(2)).

There are certain exceptions to the basic prohibition: the provision of insurance, qualifying third-party indemnity provisions ("QTPIPs") and qualifying pension scheme indemnity provisions ("QPSIPs").

Section 233 provides that the general prohibition does not prevent a company from purchasing and maintaining for a director of the company, or of an associated company, insurance against negligence, default, breach of duty or breach of trust in relation to the company.

Section 234 sets out what constitutes a QTPIP. A third-party indemnity provision is a provision for indemnity against liability incurred by the director to a person other than the company or an associated company. Such a provision will be a QTPIP if the requirements set out in Section 234(3) are met:

(a)   the provision must not indemnify the director against any liability to pay a fine imposed in criminal proceedings or a sum payable to a regulatory authority by way of a penalty in respect of non-compliance with any requirement of a regulatory nature (however arising); and

(b)   the provision must not provide any indemnity against any liability incurred by the director:

   (i)   in defending criminal proceedings in which he is convicted; or

(ii) in defending civil proceedings brought by the company, or an associated company, in which judgment is given against him; or

(iii) in connection with an application for relief in which the court refuses to grant him relief.

Section 234(4) sets out how "conviction", "judgment" and "refusal of relief" are to be interpreted and Section 234(5) sets out when the conviction, judgment or refusal are to be interpreted as "final".

The applications for relief caught by Section 234(3) are applications under Section 661(3) or (4) CA 2006 (power of the court to grant relief in case of acquisition of shares by an innocent nominee) and Section 1157 CA 2006 (the general power of the court to grant relief in the case of honest and reasonable conduct).

Section 235 provides that the general prohibition does not apply to QPSIPs. This exemption only applies to directors of a company where the company is a trustee of an occupational pension scheme (i.e. it does not cover directors who themselves are trustees of such schemes). In such circumstances provision may be made to indemnify the director against liability incurred in connection with the company's activity as a corporate trustee of the pension scheme. The permitted indemnity under a QPSIP can be wider than a QTPIP. The provision must not provide any indemnity against any liability of the director to pay a fine imposed in criminal proceedings or a sum payable to a regulatory authority by way of penalty in respect of non-compliance with any requirement of a regulatory nature (however arising). The provision must also not provide any indemnity against any liability incurred by the director in defending criminal proceedings in which he is convicted. Therefore unlike a QTPIP, a QPSIP can cover a director's liability to the pension trustee company itself, or to an associated company incurred in connection with the company's activities as a corporate trustee of the pension scheme.

Sections 205 and 206 CA 2006 are also relevant. Generally, companies are prohibited from granting loans to their directors unless the transaction is first approved by a resolution of the members (*see* Section 197). There are exceptions to this general rule. Subject to certain conditions, these exceptions include expenditure for defending proceedings (*see* Section 205) and expenditure in connection with regulatory action or investigations (*see* Section 206).

4.10 Statutory relief

In any proceedings against a director where negligence, default, breach of duty or breach of trust is established, the court may relieve the director of liability, either in whole or in part, if it is satisfied that the director acted honestly and reasonably, and that having regard to all the circumstances of the case, including those connected with his appointment, he ought fairly to be excused.[39] A company is entitled to elect whether to claim damages or an account of profits against a director for breach of his fiduciary duty and Section 1157 CA 2006 applies whichever remedy is elected.[40] Section 1157 only applies to proceedings against a director by, on behalf of or for the benefit of his company for breach of his duty to the company as a director. It also applies to penal proceedings for the enforcement of specific duties imposed by the Companies Acts on the company's officers, but it cannot be used against strangers to the company.[41]

The section can be used to excuse a director from liability for negligence.[42] Conduct that is *ultra vires* the company may also be excused[43] depending on the circumstances because the provision is designed to protect honest directors and is "*not to be construed in a narrow sense*".

Where a director anticipates proceedings he may apply to the court for relief under Section 1157(2) CA 2006. If proceedings are already pending, then only the court seised of those proceedings may grant the relief sought.[44]

---

[39] Section 1157 CA 2006.
[40] *Coleman Taymar Ltd v Oakes* [2001] 2 BCLC 749: liability to account being just as much a liability for this purpose as liability to pay damages, per Judge Robert Reid QC at 770.
[41] *Customs and Excise Commissioners v Hedon Alpha Ltd and others* [1981] 2 All ER 697.
[42] *Re D'Jan of London Ltd* [1994] 1 BCLC 561; *Barings Plc (in liq.) v Coopers & Lybrand (a firm), Barings Futures (Singapore) Pte Ltd (in liq.) v Mattar* [2003] All ER (D) 294 (Oct).
[43] *Claridge's Patent Asphalte Co Ltd* [1921] 1 Ch 543.
[44] *Re Gilt Edge Safety Glass Ltd* [1940] Ch 495.

When exercising its discretion under Section 1157 CA 2006, all three requirements of Section 1157(1) CA 2006 must be satisfied.[45] The director therefore has the onus of showing that he acted honestly, that he acted reasonably and that having regard to all the circumstances of the case he ought fairly to be excused. The test imposed by Section 1157 CA 2006 is an "essentially" subjective one, requiring an examination of all the circumstances of the case to ascertain whether the director concerned has acted honestly and reasonably and deciding whether on those grounds he ought to be excused. The subjective approach is limited to the "honesty" element of "honestly and reasonably" since reasonableness tests are by nature objective.[46] It follows that the court has no jurisdiction to grant relief from liability under Section 1157 CA 2006 where the claim made against the officer involves the application of an objective standard to his behaviour.[47] The standard of reasonableness to be satisfied in the context of Section 1157 CA 2006 is that of "a man of affairs dealing with his own affairs with reasonable care and circumspection" in such a case.[48] The question of what is reasonable may be assessed by reference to the company's past conduct.[49] Given the scope of the analysis that has to be undertaken, it is unlikely that an application for relief under Section 1157 CA 2006 would succeed on a summary judgment application.[50]

4.11 Insolvency*

When a company is insolvent or verging on insolvent, the common law requires a shift in its directors' duties, away from shareholders towards creditors and what is in their best interests.[51] From the case law, it is not clear exactly when this shift in duty first occurs. In practice, it is both prudent and typical for

---

[45] *Coleman Taymar Ltd* v *Oakes* [2001] 2 BCLC 749.
[46] *Coleman Taymar Ltd* v *Oakes* [2001] 2 BCLC 749.
[47] *Re Produce Marketing Consortium* [1989] 1 WLR 745.
[48] *Re Duomatic Ltd* [1969] 2 Ch 365, 377, per Buckley J.
[49] *Re Duomatic Ltd* above at 375 and 170, per Buckley J.
[50] *Equitable Life Assurance Society* v *Bowley and others* [2004] 1 BCLC 180.
* The author thanks Glen Flannery, partner in Nabarro LLP's restructuring and insolvency team, for his work on this Section 4.11.
[51] *West Mercia Safetywear Ltd* v *Dodd* [1988] BCLC 250 (CA); *Kinsela* v *Russell Kinsela Pty Ltd* (1986) 4 NSWLR 722; *Re MDA Investment Management Ltd* [2004] 1 BCLC 217, at paragraph 70.

directors to assume that the shift first occurs at around the time that the company first becomes unable to pay its debts by reference to the tests set out in Section 123 Insolvency Act 1986 ("IA 1986"). Under Section 123 IA 1986, a company is deemed to be unable to pay its debts if:

(a) the company fails, within three weeks after its service on it, to pay or settle a statutory demand (a form of written demand for sums over £750);

(b) execution or other process issued on a court judgment or order obtained against the company, is returned unsatisfied in whole or in part;

(c) the company is unable to pay its debts as they fall due and this is proved to the court's satisfaction. This is commonly referred to as the cash-flow insolvency test; or

(d) the value of the company's assets is less than the amount of its liabilities, taking into account its contingent and prospective liabilities, and this is proved to the court's satisfaction. This is commonly referred to as the balance sheet insolvency test.

The duty to act in the best interests of creditors is owed to the company, but in the event of a formal insolvency it is enforceable by the company's liquidator.[52] If the duty is not properly discharged and this causes creditors to suffer loss, a subsequently appointed liquidator can bring a claim against any culpable director to compensate the company's estate for the loss. Section 212 IA 1986 provides a mechanism for bringing this kind of claim, as explained in more detail below.

A number of other potential causes of action against directors can arise where a company is insolvent and it enters into a formal insolvency process under IA 1986. These are summarised below as well.

4.11.1 Misfeasance

In the course of winding up a company, the liquidator or any affected creditor, or with permission of the court, any contribu-

---

[52] *Re Horsley & Weight Ltd* [1982] 3 All ER 1045.

tory, may bring an action against a person who is or has been a director of the company who has "misapplied or retained, or become accountable for, any money or other property of the company, or been guilty of any misfeasance or breach of any fiduciary or other duty in relation to the company".[53]

This captures a wide range of conduct. By way of example, the breach of "fiduciary or other" duty could include a breach of the director's duty to the company to act in the best interests of the company's creditors when the company was insolvent by reference to the tests set out above. The "other" duty may include negligence,[54] but it does not extend to all cases in which the company has a right of action against the officer of a company. It is limited to cases where there has been something in the nature of a breach of duty by an officer of the company and does not include a claim for repayment of an ordinary debt.[55] In addition, the liquidator can only sue in respect of a cause of action vested in the company.[56]

The director may be examined and if found liable, the court may order the director personally to restore the company to its former position or otherwise compensate it for the consequences of his misconduct.[57] The remedy under Section 212 IA 1986 is discretionary[58] such that the court may award a lower damages sum than that required to remedy the misfeasance in full.[59] The court also has a discretion where remedies sought go beyond those available at common law.[60] The court may relieve a director from liability under Section 212 IA 1986 where the provisions of Section 1157 CA 2006 apply, that is, where it appears to the court that the director acted honestly and reasonably and ought fairly to be excused.[61]

---

[53] Section 212(1) IA 1986.
[54] *Kyrris v Oldham* [2003] EWCA Civ 1506.
[55] *Re Etic Ltd* [1928] Ch 861.
[56] *Re Ambrose Lake Tin & Copper Mining Co Ex Parte Taylor Ex Parte Moss* [1880] 14 Ch D 390.
[57] Section 212(3) IA 1986.
[58] *Re Westlowe Storage and Distribution Ltd (in liq.)* [2000] 2 BCLC 590.
[59] *The Commissioners of Inland Revenue v Richmond, Jones* [2003] EWHC 999 (Ch).
[60] *Re Continental Assurance Co of London Plc* [2001] BPIR 733.
[61] *Re Westlowe*, above note 58.

Although the shareholders can ratify breaches of duty by the directors where the company is solvent, if the breach occurs when the company is insolvent or becomes so as the result of the breach, the ratification will be ineffective.

It is well established that Section 212 IA 1986 does not create new liabilities. It merely provides a simpler procedure for the recovery of property or compensation in a winding up. Sums or property recovered under Section 212 IA 1986 are the product of a chose in action vested in the company prior to the liquidation and are accordingly considered to be assets of the company which are capable of being made the subject of a charge[62] or of being assigned by the company or the liquidator.[63] This contrasts with the proceeds of contribution orders against directors for fraudulent or wrongful trading which are held for creditors but not as assets of the company. They are not, therefore, capable of being made the subject of a charge or of being assigned by the company.

4.11.2 Fraudulent trading

Directors are exposed to both civil and criminal liability for fraudulent trading.

Civil liability can arise under Section 213 IA 1986, if in the course of the winding up of the company, it appears that any business of the company has been carried on to defraud its creditors, to defraud creditors of any other person, or for any fraudulent purpose.[64] This provision only applies if the company goes into liquidation.

On the application of the liquidator, the court may declare any person, including a director, knowingly party to the carrying on of business in this way liable to contribute to the company's assets as it thinks proper.[65]

The first element of Section 213 IA 1986 requires the court to be satisfied that there was an intention to defraud creditors.

---

[62] *Re Anglo-Austrian Printing & Publishing Union (No 3)* [1895] 2 Ch 891.
[63] *Re International Championship Management Ltd* [2006] EWHC 768 (Ch).
[64] Section 213(1) IA 1986.
[65] Section 213(2) IA 1986.

This requires actual dishonesty on the part of the defendant.[66] The test for intention to defraud is subjective,[67] although the standard of dishonesty will be what reasonable and honest people consider to be dishonest, provided that the defendant realised that by those standards his conduct was in fact dishonest.[68]

The second element of Section 213 IA 1986 requires the defendant to have participated in carrying on the business with intent to defraud. The defendant will not be liable for fraudulent acts of the company in which he did not participate; they are irrelevant to the claim against him.[69] However the concept of participation is widely construed.[70] A defendant may be liable under the section even if a single creditor was defrauded by a single transaction, provided that the transaction could properly be described as a fraud on a creditor in the course of carrying on business.[71] Participation requires some form of positive act; passivity is not sufficient. There are circumstances in which a transaction that is dishonest will not amount to carrying on of the business for that purpose.[72] The phrase "carrying on business" does not require active trading and may include the collection of assets and distribution of their proceeds to discharge liabilities of the company.[73] A person who performs certain duties to the company, such as a secretary, may not be found to be "concerned in carrying on the business of the company" by performing the duties appropriate to their office and so may avoid liability.[74] The knowledge of a particular person in an organisation may be attributed to the board so rendering the company liable to a claim for fraudulent trading. This will happen where a company delegates sufficient authority to that person, such as giving them the ultimate decision-making power in respect of a transaction.[75]

---

[66] *Re Augustus Barnett & Son Ltd* [1986] 2 BCC 98904, at 98907.
[67] *Bernasconi and another* v *Nicholas Bennett & Co (a firm) and another* [2000] BCC 921.
[68] *Twinsectra Ltd* v *Yardley* [2002] UKHL 12.
[69] *Re Bank of Credit and Commerce International SA and another* [1999] BCC 943.
[70] *Re Augustus Barnett & Son Ltd* [1986] 2 BCC 98904.
[71] *Re Gerald Cooper Chemicals Ltd* [1978] 2 All ER 49.
[72] *Re Gerald*, above note 71.
[73] *Re Sarflax Ltd* [1979] 1 All ER 529.
[74] *Re Maidstone Building Provisions* [1971] 1 WLR 1085.
[75] *Morris* v *Bank of India* [2005] EWCA Civ 693.

The contribution that the defendant may be required to make should reflect and compensate for the loss which has been caused to creditors by the carrying on of the business in the fraudulent manner. Although under the predecessor law it was held appropriate to include a punitive as well as a compensatory element in the court's order, this is no longer the case.[76] To the extent that Parliament intended a punitive element, this is to be found in the criminal sanctions for fraudulent trading under 993 CA 1986 (*see* below). Where two or more individuals are found liable under Section 213 IA 1986, their respective liability is not automatically joint and several. Instead, a court can apportion liability on the basis of the degree of control each defendant had over the affairs of the company and the extent to which each defendant benefited from the fraud. This is similar to the approach taken in the context of wrongful trading – *see* below.[77] Any contribution payable by the director will be held for the benefit of its creditors generally rather than any particular creditor.

Criminal liability for fraudulent trading can arise under Section 993 CA 2006 if a director knowingly carries on the business of a company with intent to defraud creditors of the company or for any other fraudulent purpose.[78] Unlike the civil sanctions under Section 213 IA 1986, this applies whether or not the company is in the process of being wound up.[79]

The court will not construe the words "or any fraudulent purpose" as applying only to creditors. The section is wide and is intended to protect against "fraudulent trading and not fraudulent trading just in so far as it affects creditors".[80] Dishonesty is a necessary element of fraudulent trading and the same general standard of dishonesty applies as for criminal cases.[81]

The penalties for fraudulent trading are severe. Section 993 CA 2006 provides that a person is liable to imprisonment or

---

[76] *Morphitis v Bernasconi* [2002] EWCA Civ 289.
[77] *Re Continental Assurance Co* [2001] BPIR 733.
[78] Section 993(1) CA 2006.
[79] Section 993(2) CA 2006.
[80] *R. v Kemp* [1988] QB 645.
[81] *R. v Lockwood* [1986] 2 BCC 99333.

a fine, or both.[82] The punishment will depend on whether the conviction for fraudulent trading is summary or on indictment. A person who is guilty of fraudulent trading on conviction on indictment is liable to an imprisonment term not exceeding ten years or an unspecified fine (or both).[83] A person who is summarily convicted of fraudulent trading in England and Wales is liable to imprisonment for a maximum of 12 months or a fine (or both).[84] In Scotland and Northern Ireland the period of imprisonment is slightly shorter, being six months.[85]

In addition to the civil and criminal sanctions above, a person who is declared to have traded fraudulently, or found guilty of fraudulent trading, may be made the subject of a disqualification order under Sections 4 and 10 Companies Directors Disqualification Act 1986 ("CDDA 1986"). The maximum period of disqualification is 15 years.

4.11.3 *Wrongful trading*

Wrongful trading under Section 214 IA 1986 was introduced as a mechanism for providing a civil remedy against directors whose mismanagement of the company had caused loss to creditors. An important difference between fraudulent and wrongful trading is that the basis of liability for wrongful trading is more akin to negligence than to dishonesty.[86]

Where a director knew or ought to have concluded that there was no reasonable prospect of the company avoiding an insolvent liquidation (the "wrongful trading point") and he did not take every step available to him to minimise the potential loss to the company's creditors,[87] the court can require the director to contribute to the company's assets as it thinks proper.[88] These wrongful trading provisions only apply if the company goes

---

[82] Section 993(3) CA 2006.
[83] Section 993(3)(a) CA 2006.
[84] Section 993(3)(b)(i) CA 2006.
[85] Section 993(3)(b)(ii) CA 2006.
[86] *Morris*, above note 75.
[87] Sections 214(2) and 214(3) IA 1986.
[88] Section 214(1) IA 1986.

into insolvent liquidation[89] and only the company's liquidator can bring the action.

Only persons who are or have been directors of the company are exposed to claims for wrongful trading. This can include shadow directors[90] and *de facto* directors.[91] This potentially brings a number of outsiders within the ambit of Section 214 IA 1986, for example, turnaround specialists, lending banks, and parent companies, where they have exercised sufficient influence for them to be considered a shadow or *de facto* director.[92]

Section 214(7) IA 1986 expressly states that shadow directors are treated as directors for the purpose of the wrongful trading provisions. A shadow director is someone in accordance with whose directions or instructions the directors of the company are accustomed to act.[93] A person is not to be regarded as a shadow director by reason only of providing advice in a professional capacity.[94]

A *de facto* director is a person who acts as a director without having been validly appointed. A *de facto* director can also be caught by the wrongful trading provisions.[95] In determining whether a person is caught, the crucial issue is whether that person has assumed the status and functions of a company director so as to make himself responsible as if he were a *de jure* director. Where there is a *de jure* corporate director of the insolvent company, a person who acts as *de jure* director of that corporate director would not automatically be considered a *de facto* director of the insolvent company simply by virtue of mere performance by him of his duties as a *de jure* director of the corporate director.[96] Something more will be required. The degree of control which the director of the corporate director exercised over that company would be relevant as

---

[89] Section 214(2) IA 1986.
[90] Section 214(7) IA 1986.
[91] *Re Hydrodan (Corby) Ltd (in liq.)* [1994] BCC 161.
[92] *Re Tasbian Ltd (No 3)* [1992] BCC 358.
[93] Section 251 IA 1986 and Section 251 CA 2006.
[94] Section 251(2) CA 2006.
[95] *Re Tasbian*, above note 92.
[96] *Revenue and Customs Commissioners* v *Holland and another: in Re Paycheck Services 3 Ltd and others* [2009] EWCA Civ 625.

would shareholder control of the corporate director.[97] It will not be sufficient to constitute someone as a director on the basis that he was in a position to control the actions of a company notwithstanding that he did not actually exercise the powers pertinent to his position.[98]

In addition, the section almost certainly extends to foreign directors, resident abroad, of a foreign company being wound up in England and Wales under the IA 1986.[99] A claim may also be made against the estate of a deceased director.[100]

The director is judged on the basis of what he knew or ought to have known, the conclusions he should have reached and the steps he should have taken, as against a reasonably diligent person having both:

(a)   his general knowledge, skill and experience; and
(b)   the general knowledge, skill and experience that might be reasonably expected of someone carrying out the same functions as he did.

This is a combined objective and subjective test. It is objective in the sense that the director must exercise the general knowledge, skill and experience that a reasonable director would. Thus an inexperienced director cannot escape liability on the basis that he personally did not realise the company could not avoid insolvency in circumstances where a reasonable director would have done so.[101] The subjective part of the test takes into account the particular skills of the director in question. These particular skills are in addition to the skill set that the reasonable director is meant to have. So if a director has particular financial expertise that means he would have been aware of the unavoidable insolvency at an earlier point in time than a director who did not have that expertise, he will be held to the higher standard. A non-executive director is

---

[97]   *Secretary of State for Trade and Industry* v *Hall* [2006] EWHC 1995 (Ch).
[98]   *Hall*, above note 97.
[99]   *Re Howard Holdings Inc* [1998] BCC 549.
[100]   *Re Sherborne Associates Ltd* [1995] BCC 40.
[101]   *Re Purpoint Ltd* [1991] BCC 121.

not expected to possess the same skill set as an executive director.[102]

In *Re D'Jan of London Ltd* the court held that the test set out in Section 214(4) IA 1986 encapsulates the duty of directors at common law.[103] That position is also reflected in Section 174 CA 2006, which codifies a director's duty to exercise reasonable care, skill and diligence in *Re D'Jan* terms.

The knowledge to be imputed to a director in testing whether or not he knew or ought to have concluded that there was no reasonable prospect of the company avoiding insolvent liquidation is not limited to the documentary material actually available at the given time. The words "ought to know or ascertain", indicate that facts which, given reasonable diligence and an appropriate level of general knowledge, skill and experience, are capable of being ascertained, must be included.[104]

The steps that are required to minimise the potential loss to creditors so as to avoid liability in any particular case will depend on all the circumstances of that case at the relevant time. In deciding whether the steps taken were sufficient, the same objective and subjective standards discussed above will be applied. What is unlikely ever to be appropriate once the wrongful trading point has been reached, is for the director to simply ignore the situation and continue as normal, or to continue trading with some distant (unrealistic) hope that fortunes might change. If a director has in fact done all he can to minimise potential loss to creditors then he will not be liable for wrongful trading.

There is little guidance as to how any contribution order should be calculated. The cases decided so far indicate that it should be compensatory rather than penal, calculated with reference to the amount of the company's assets that have been depleted by the director's conduct.[105] Loss which could not have been reasonably foreseen as a consequence of continued trading

---

[102] *Equitable Life Assurance Society* v *Bowley* [2003] EWHC 2263 (Comm).
[103] [1993] BCC 646.
[104] *Re Produce Marketing Consortium (in liq.) Ltd (No 2)* [1989] 5 BCC 569.
[105] *Re Produce Marketing Consortium Ltd* [1989] 5 BCC 569 at 597, Knox J.

should not be taken into account, nor should loss attributable to other causes which would have been incurred in any event.[106] Where two or more individuals are found liable under Section 214 IA 1986, their respective liability is not automatically joint and several – a court can apportion liability between them.[107] Any contribution payable by the director will be held for the benefit of its creditors generally rather than any particular creditor. Accordingly any receipt will not be caught by a charge over the company's assets and it is incapable of assignment.[108]

The defence under Section 1157(1) CA 2006, that the director has acted honestly and reasonably and ought fairly to be excused does not apply to a wrongful trading claim as it is inconsistent with the objective standard imposed on the director.[109]

A person who is declared to have traded wrongfully may also be made the subject of a disqualification order under Section 10 CDDA 1986. As with a declaration of fraudulent trading, the maximum period of disqualification is 15 years.

4.11.4   Re-use of company name on "phoenix company"

Section 216 IA 1986 restricts a director of a company that goes into insolvent liquidation from re-using the company's name or a similar name for a period of time following the insolvency of the first company in circumstances where he is a director or otherwise involved in the promotion, formation or management of the second or "new" company. The section is aimed at preventing directors of insolvent companies from simply rolling over the business into a new, undercapitalised company with the same or a similar name, without some protection for creditors who may (mistakenly) believe that they are still dealing with the "old" insolvent company when in fact they are dealing with the "new" company.

The section applies to any person who was a director or shadow director of the insolvent company at any time in the period of

---

[106] *Lexi Holdings Plc (in admin)* v *Luqman* [2009] EWHC Civ 117.
[107] *Re Continental Assurance Co* [2001] BPIR 733.
[108] *Re Oasis Merchandising Services Ltd* [1996] 1 All ER 1009.
[109] *Re, Produce Marketing*, above note 104.

12 months before the day on which it went into liquidation. For a period of five years beginning with the day on which the company went into liquidation, any such director or shadow director cannot, except in exempted circumstances:

(a) be a director of any other company that is known by a prohibited name; or

(b) in any way, whether directly or indirectly, be concerned or take part in the promotion, formation or management of any company known by a prohibited name; or

(c) be concerned or take part in the promotion, formation or management, whether directly or indirectly, in any business (not carried on by a company) known by a prohibited name.[110]

A prohibited name is one by which the company in liquidation was known (or by which any business carried on by that company was known) at any time in the period of 12 months before the day on which the company went into liquidation, or is a name so similar so as to suggest an association with that company.[111]

In considering whether the second name is sufficiently similar to the first to suggest an association between the two, the court will examine all the circumstances in which they were actually used or likely to be used, including such matters as the types of product dealt in, the location of the business, the types of customers dealing with the companies and those involved in the operation of the two companies.[112] The test is whether the similarity between the two names is such that it is probable that members of the public, comparing the names in the relevant context, would associate the two companies with each other.[113]

A director whose conduct contravenes Section 216 IA 1986 is guilty of an offence and is liable to imprisonment or a fine, or both. In addition, he may be personally liable, jointly and

---

[110] Section 216(3) IA 1986.
[111] Section 216(2) IA 1986.
[112] *Christopher Ricketts v Ad Valorem Factors Ltd* [2003] EWCA Civ 1706.
[113] *Commissioners of HM Revenue and Customs v Sean Gerard Walsh* [2005] EWCA Civ 1291.

severally with the company and any other person so liable, for the debts of the "new" company known by the prohibited name if he is involved in the "management" of that company, and those debts were incurred at a time when he was so involved.[114] A person does not have to be a director to be held personally liable for debts under this section. It is sufficient if he, whether directly or indirectly, takes part in the management of the company.[115]

A director can avoid liability under Section 216 IA 1986 by obtaining leave of the court, or, where the new company is acquiring the whole or substantially the whole of the business of the company in liquidation under arrangements with an insolvency practitioner acting as its liquidator, administrator, administrative receiver or supervisor of a company voluntary arrangement, by giving a prescribed notice to creditors.[116]

4.11.5   Other actions

Other possible criminal causes of action against directors of insolvent companies under IA 1986, which are outside of the scope of this chapter, include:

(a)   swearing a statutory declaration of solvency without having reasonable grounds for forming the requisite solvency opinion;[117]
(b)   fraud in anticipation of winding up;[118]
(c)   transaction(s) in fraud of creditors;[119]
(d)   misconduct in the course of the winding up;[120]
(e)   falsification of the company's books;[121]
(f)   making material omissions from the statement relating to the company's affairs;[122] and
(g)   making false representations to creditors.[123]

---

[114]   Section 217(1)(a) and Section 217(3)(a) IA 1986.
[115]   Section 217(4) IA 1986.
[116]   Section 216(3) IA 1986 and Rule 4.228 Insolvency Rules 1986.
[117]   Section 89 IA 1986.
[118]   Section 206 IA 1986.
[119]   Section 207 IA 1986.
[120]   Section 208 IA 1986.
[121]   Section 209 IA 1986.
[122]   Section 210 IA 1986.
[123]   Section 211 IA 1986.

Chapter 5

Fair Dealing and Connected Persons

Vanessa Knapp

Principal Consultant

Freshfields Bruckhaus Deringer LLP

5.1　Introduction

This Chapter looks at some of the provisions in Part 10 Companies Act 2006 which deal with fair dealings between a director and his company (or another company in the same group) and between such companies and anyone connected with a director. It does not deal with the various obligations to disclose details of certain transactions or arrangements in the company's accounts. These provisions replaced the provisions of Part X Companies Act 1985.

5.1.1　Background to the provisions

This area of law was reviewed by the Law Commission in 1998 (*see* Law Commission Consultation Paper No 153) at the request of the Department of Trade and Industry ("the DTI") in connection with the review of company law. The Law Commission said that many of the provisions represented a "hasty legislative response" to a number of financial scandals in the 1970s. It identified the many inconsistencies between the various provisions in the Companies Act 1985 – for example whether a particular act was prohibited absolutely, was not prohibited provided disclosure had taken place or was not prohibited provided consent was given, and whether approval had to be given beforehand or could be given afterwards.

In September 1999, the Law Commission published a report (Law Commission No 261) which considered the responses it had received to the earlier Consultation Paper. This recommended that most of the provisions of Part X should be retained as a supplement to the protection provided by the general law. It also recommended some specific changes to some of the provisions and the introduction of a coherent code of civil remedies. The Consultation Document on Modern Company Law published by the Company Law Review Steering Group in March 2000 accepted most of these proposals. The *Final Report on Modern Company Law* published by the Company Law Review Steering Group in June 2001 did not propose any further major changes to the existing regime.

The Act has broadly followed the approach suggested and most of the inconsistencies have been ironed out. In particular, shareholder approval can now be given for all the areas covered. Originally, it was proposed that the provisions relating to loans, quasi-loans and credit transactions should apply to all companies, removing the difference of approach where a company is associated with a public company. At a late stage, the government reversed this policy so that only companies that are public companies or are associated with a public company have to worry about the provisions relating to quasi-loans, credit transactions and loans to persons connected with a director.

5.1.2   Companies subject to the provisions

Before looking at various provisions in Part 10, it is helpful to understand some of the defined terms which are used in those provisions. All of the provisions of Part 10 apply to a "company". This means a company formed and registered under the Companies Act 2006, the Companies Act 1985, the Companies Acts 1948 to 1983, the Companies (Northern Ireland) Order 1986 or under certain earlier Acts (*see* Section 1).[1] It includes unlimited companies. In contrast, "body corporate" includes bodies incorporated outside the UK, but

---

[1]   In this Chapter, all section references are to the Companies Act 2006 unless otherwise stated.

not a corporation sole or a partnership that is not regarded as a body corporate under the law by which it is governed (*see* Section 1173).

5.1.3 Directors and their connected persons

The Part 10 provisions apply to a "director". This is defined (*see* Section 250) to include any person who occupies the position of director, "by whatever name called". This means that someone whom a company thinks it has appointed as a director is a director even if the appointment proves to be invalid. It also includes someone who acts as a director, even though the company has never appointed them as such. In some cases, it can also include an alternate director. A shadow director is treated as a director for the purposes of the relevant provisions (Section 223), although if a person stops being treated as a shadow director this is not treated as a loss of office. A shadow director is a person in accordance with whose directions or instructions the directors of the company are accustomed to act. Someone is not, however, a shadow director only because the directors act on their advice in a professional capacity. Also, a body corporate is not a shadow director of its subsidiaries only because the subsidiaries' directors are accustomed to act in accordance with the holding company's instructions or directions (Section 251). Some of the provisions also apply to a person connected with a director. Those who come within this category are set out in Section 252. As this is a fairly complicated provision, it is dealt with separately at the end of this Chapter in Section 5.10. For the purposes of the various provisions dealt with in this Chapter, it does not matter what law governs the transaction or arrangement in question (*see* Section 259).

5.1.4 Subsidiaries, holding companies and wholly-owned subsidiaries

Some of the provisions in Part 10 also relate to subsidiaries, holding companies and subsidiaries of holding companies. Section 1159 (and *see* Section 1160 and Schedule 6) sets out the definition of "subsidiary", "holding company" and "wholly-owned subsidiary". In each case, the definition extends to bodies corporate as well as Companies Act companies and to sub-subsidiaries and holding companies of a holding company. A company is a subsidiary of another (which is therefore the holding company of that subsidiary) if one of three tests is satisfied. The first is if the holding company holds a majority of the voting rights in the subsidiary. The second is if the holding company is a member of the subsidiary and has the right to appoint or remove a majority of the directors. The third test is if the holding company is a member of the subsidiary and controls alone a majority of the voting rights, pursuant to an agreement with other shareholders or members.

5.1.5 Charities

There are particular rules for companies which are charities – *see* Section 66 and Section 66A Charities Act 1993 as substituted by Section 226. The Charity Commission must give its prior written consent where the members of the company give an approval under Section 188, 190, 197, 198, 200, 201, 203, 217 or 218 and where the members give an affirmation under Section 196 or 214. Without the Commission's prior written consent, the approval or affirmation is ineffective (*see* Section 226). Prior written consent must also be obtained where the company does not need to obtain approval because it is a wholly-owned subsidiary (*see* Section 226). If the company does not obtain prior written approval, it is treated as if the exemption for wholly-owned subsidiaries did not apply.

5.1.6 Where approval is needed under more than one provision

In some cases, approval may be required under more than one section in Chapter 4 of Part 10 of the Act. For example, a director might sell a substantial asset in return for a loan. In such cases, the requirements of each applicable section must be met, but a company can pass one resolution giving all the necessary approvals (*see* Section 225).

5.2 Loss of office and retirement from office

The Companies Act 2006 requires companies to disclose payments to directors for loss of office or as consideration for retiring from office or in connection with their retirement from office. Such payments are unlawful unless they have been disclosed and approved by shareholders.

(a) Section 217 deals with payments by a company for loss of office to a director of the company or a holding company. Payments are prohibited unless they have been approved by the members of the company and, where payment is to a director of a holding company, by the members of the holding company.

(b) Section 218 deals with payments for loss of office made by any person to a director of a company in connection with the transfer of all or any part of the company's under-taking or property or of the undertaking or property of any subsidiary of the company. It prohibits any payments (i.e. not just those made by the company), unless details of the proposed payment (including its amount) are disclosed to members of the company (and each other company whose approval is needed) and the proposal is approved by the members of the company (or, where the transfer is the transfer of all or part of the undertaking or property of a subsidiary, by the members of each of the companies).

(c) Section 219 deals with any payments (again, not just those made by the company) made in connection with a transfer of shares in the company or in a subsidiary of the company, resulting from a takeover bid. A payment is prohibited unless it has been approved by a resolution of the holders of the shares to which the bid relates and any other holders of that class of shares. "Takeover bid" is not defined (the definitions in Section 943(7) and Section 953(9) only apply for the purposes of those respective Sections). Section 219 applies as much to offers for private companies as to offers for public companies which are subject to the City Code on Takeovers and Mergers. If the City Code applies, the company will also need to consider Rules 21 (restrictions on frustrating action) and 24.5 (special arrangements), as well as any Listing Rule requirements (*see* Section 5.6 below).

Where a payment falls within more than one section, the requirement of each applicable section must be met. However, the company does not need to pass a separate resolution to give approval under each section (Section 225(3)).

5.2.1 Payment for loss of office

Section 215 sets out a definition of "payment for loss of office" for the purposes of Chapter 4 of Part 10. It catches a payment to a director or past director of a company:

(a) by way of compensation for loss of office as director of the company;

(b) by way of compensation for loss of any office or employment in connection with the management of the affairs of the company or any subsidiary undertaking, either while the person is a director of the company or in connection with ceasing to be a director;

(c) as consideration for, or in connection with, their retirement from office as director of the company; or

(d) as consideration for, or in connection with, their retirement from any office or employment in connection with the management of the affairs of the company or any subsidiary undertaking, either while the person is a director of the company or in connection with ceasing to be a director.

The section makes it clear that compensation and consideration include non-cash benefits (confirming Lord Macfadyen's view in *Mercer v Heart of Midlothian Plc*).[2] The section also makes it clear that payments to a person connected with a director or to any other person on the direction of the director or a connected person or to another person for the benefit of a director or a connected person are all treated as payment to the director, and so are caught by the requirements. The section also makes it clear that a person cannot avoid the relevant requirements by directing someone else to make a payment or getting someone else to make a payment for them.

---

[2] [2001] SLT 945.

5.2.2 Exception for payments in discharge of a legal obligation

A company does not need to obtain members' approval for payments which discharge a legal obligation. Section 220 makes it clear that a payment does not need to be approved if it is made in good faith:

(a) in discharge of an existing legal obligation;
(b) by way of damages for breach of an existing legal obligation;
(c) by way of settlement or compromise of any claim arising in connection with the termination of a person's office or employment; or
(d) by way of pension in respect of past services.

In order to be an "existing legal obligation", the obligation must be an obligation of the company or any body corporate associated with it. In addition, the obligation must not have been entered into in connection with, or in consequence of, the event giving rise to the payment for loss of office, where the company is making a payment for loss of office to a director or to a director of a holding company (i.e. within Section 217). Where the company is making a payment for loss of office in connection with the transfer of the company's undertaking or property, or in connection with a share transfer (i.e. within Section 218 or Section 219), an existing legal obligation means an obligation of the company or a body corporate associated with it that was not entered into for the purposes of, in connection with, or in consequence of, the transfer. If a payment falls within both Section 217 and Section 218 or within both Section 217 and Section 219 (payments in connection with a transfer of shares resulting from a takeover bid), the test for payments within Section 217 applies to determine whether there is an existing legal obligation. If there is a payment only part of which falls within the exception and part of which does not, the payment is treated as if each part is a separate payment.

Section 220 broadly follows the position which applied before the Companies Act 2006 (under which *bona fide* payment by way of damages for breach of contract or by way of pension for past service was excluded – *see* Section 316(3) Companies Act 1985). In practice, companies will often be able to rely on this exclusion to avoid having to disclose payments and seek shareholder approval. Companies have sometimes been criticised for taking a generous view of what constitutes a *bona fide* payment by way of damages. In February 2008 the Association of British Insurers ("ABI") and National Association of Pension Funds ("NAPF") issued a joint statement on Executive Contracts and Severance and the ABI issued guidelines on policies and practices on executive remuneration in December 2009 which also include guidance on severance. It can often be difficult to agree what reduction is appropriate to reflect the director's chance of finding another directorship. The Law Commission suggested (*see* Law Commission Consultation Paper No 153) that directors would have the protection of Section 316(3) Companies Act 1985 (which is similar to Section 220) if they relied on proper legal advice, even if it were wrong.

Section 220 also reflects the Privy Council case of *Taupo Totara Timber* v *Rowe*,[3] which considered whether Section 191 New Zealand Companies Act 1955 (which was identical to Section 312 Companies Act 1985, which dealt with payments to a director for loss of office) applied to payments which a company has agreed to make to a director when he retires or loses office, before the retirement or loss of office occurs. The question in that case was whether a provision in the service contract of a managing director, which required the company to pay an amount of money to the director on resignation or dismissal, had to be approved by the company under Section 191. The agreement did not fix the amount of the payment and the Privy Council held that Section 191 only applied to payments which the company had not previously agreed to pay or which the company did not have a legal obligation to make. Accordingly, no disclosure to members or approval was needed.

---

[3] [1978] AC 537, PC.

The *Taupo Totara* case was followed in a case before the Outer House of the Court of Session, *Lander* v *Premier Pict Petroleum Ltd*.[4] In that case, Mr Lander, who was a company director, became entitled to a golden parachute payment under the terms of his service agreement if there was a change of control of the company and he gave notice to terminate his employment. He resigned in the circumstances envisaged by the contract, but the company refused to make the payment and argued that the payment was unlawful as it had not been disclosed and approved under Section 312 Companies Act 1985. Lord Osborne rejected the company's argument. Following the Privy Council decision, he decided that the Sections only apply to proposed payments, that is, that payments which the company was already legally obliged to pay were not covered by the Sections. Section 220 reflects the decisions in the *Taupo Totara* case and *Lander* v *Premier Pict Petroleum Ltd*.

The position is, however, less clear where an obligation to make a payment is entered into shortly before a director loses his office. In *Mercer* v *Heart of Midlothian Plc*, Lord Macfadyen's statements suggested that where a contractual payment was agreed just before resignation in order to ensure that Section 312 Companies Act 1985 would not apply, it was not clear that the payment did not need approval. Lord Macfadyen thought it was likely that an agreement which is entered into on the basis that there will be a further period of continuing office would fall to be treated as a covenanted payment and so would fall outside the scope of the Section. The position under Section 220 is slightly different. The question to be asked is whether the legal obligation is entered into "in connection with, or in consequence of" the event giving rise to the payment or the transfer. These are wider tests, and so will make it harder for companies to argue that a legal obligation taken on about the time of the event or transfer is not connected and so is exempt from the need for approval.

---

[4] [1997] SLT 1361.

5.2.3 Memorandum setting out particulars and approval requirements

Where a payment needs to be approved, a memorandum setting out particulars of the proposed payment, including its amount, must be made available to the members of the company whose approval is being sought (Sections 217(3), 218(3) and 219(3)). If approval is being given by written resolution, the memorandum must be sent or submitted to every eligible member at or before the time when the proposed resolution is sent or submitted to him. An accidental failure to send or submit the memorandum to one or more members is disregarded unless the articles provide otherwise (Section 224(1)). If approval is being given by passing a resolution at a meeting, the memorandum must be made available for inspection by members at the company's registered office for at least 15 days ending with the date of the meeting and at the meeting itself.

If the approval is for a payment in connection with a share transfer within Section 219, if the person making the offer or any associate of that person (as defined in Section 988) is a member, they are not entitled to vote on the resolution. If they would otherwise be entitled to do so, they are, however, entitled to receive a copy of any written resolution and to be given notice of the meeting at which the resolution is to be proposed and to attend that meeting, speak and, if present in person or by proxy, to count towards the quorum (Section 219(4)). Also for payments in connection with a share transfer within Section 219, a payment will be deemed to be approved for the purposes of Section 219 if a quorum is not present at the meeting and a quorum is again not present at an adjournment of the meeting at a later date (Section 219(5)). There is no equivalent provision for payments which need approval under Section 217 or Section 218.

As explained above, in some cases approval may be required from the members of a holding company or a subsidiary as well as from the company itself. There are some helpful provisions (in Sections 217(4), 218(4) and 219(6)) which provide an exception in two cases. The first is that no approval is required if the body corporate is a wholly-owned subsidiary of another body corporate. The second is that no approval is required for a body corporate that is not a UK-registered company, that is, a company registered under the Companies Acts 2006 (*see* Section 1158). The effect is broadly that companies incorporated outside the UK are exempt from the need for shareholder approval.

5.2.4 *Exception for small payments*

There is also an exception for small payments which applies to all three Sections requiring approval (Section 221(1)). A company does not need approval if the company or one of its subsidiaries makes the payment and the amount or value of the payment, together with the amount or value of any other relevant payments, does not exceed £200. What counts as an "other relevant payment" varies depending on whether the payment falls within Section 217, Section 218 or Section 219. Where Section 217 applies, the "other relevant payments" are payments for loss of office by the company or any of its subsidiaries to the same director in connection with the same event. Where Section 218 or 219 applies, the "other relevant payments" are payments for loss of office paid in connection with the same transfer to the same director by the company or any of its subsidiaries.

5.2.5 *Civil consequences of breach*

The consequences of breaching Sections 217 to 219 vary slightly (Section 222). In all three cases, the recipient holds any payment received on trust.

(a) Payments made in contravention of Section 217 are held on trust for the company making the payment. Any director who authorised the payment is jointly and severally liable to indemnify the company that made the payment for any loss resulting from it.

(b) Payments made in contravention of Section 218 are held on trust for the company whose undertaking or property is being transferred (apparently, even if the payment was made by another person).

(c) Payments made in contravention of Section 219 are held on trust for the persons who have sold their shares as a result of the offer made (again, rather than for the person who made the payment). In addition, the person who receives the payment must bear any expenses he incurs in distributing the payment to those shareholders himself, and cannot deduct them from the payment. There is no guidance as to how the payment is to be divided between the shareholders.

If a payment contravenes Section 217 and Section 218, only the civil consequences applying to payments which contravene Section 218 apply. If a payment contravenes Section 217 and Section 219, only the civil consequences applying to payments which contravene Section 219 apply, unless the court directs otherwise.

5.2.6   Anti-avoidance provisions

The Sections contain some anti-avoidance provisions. These apply where a director is to cease to hold office or to hold any office or employment in connection with the management of the affairs of the company or any of its subsidiary undertakings in connection with a transfer falling within Section 218 or 219. In such a case, if a director is paid more per share than other shareholders or is given any valuable consideration by someone other than the company in either case in connection with a transfer subject to Section 218 or 219, the excess price or the money value of the consideration is deemed to be a payment for loss of office (Section 216).

5.2.7   Relationship with Section 190

Section 190(6) makes it clear that a payment for loss of office is not also subject to the requirements in Section 190 for substantial property transactions with directors or connected persons to be approved (*see* Section 5.5 below).

5.3   Disclosure of interests in existing transactions or arrangements

As explained in Chapter 3, Section 177 sets out, as part of the statement of the general duties of directors, a director's duty to declare an interest in a proposed transaction or arrangement with the company to the other directors. This replaces the equitable rule that directors may not have an interest in transactions with the company unless the interest has been authorised by the members. This duty is enforceable in the same way as any other fiduciary duty owed to the company and the consequences of breach are the same as would apply if the corresponding common law rule or equitable principle applied. In addition, Section 182 requires a director to declare any interest in an existing transaction or arrangement the company has entered into. The section does not apply if, or to the extent that, the interest has been declared under Section 177. Failure to comply with the requirements of Section 182 is a criminal offence and a person guilty of an offence is liable to a fine (Section 183).

A director who is in any way, whether directly or indirectly, interested in a transaction or arrangement that has been entered into by the company must declare the nature and extent of that interest to the other directors of the company. The declaration can be made in one of three ways:

(a)   at a meeting of the directors;
(b)   by notice in writing in accordance with Section 184; or
(c)   by a general notice in accordance with Section 185.

In *Guinness Plc v Saunders and another*,[5] when considering the requirements of Section 317 Companies Act 1985 which required a declaration of interest to be made at a meeting of the directors, it was held that declaration to a committee of the board was not enough. It seems likely the same will be true for Section 182 except for declarations relating to a director's own service contract (*see* below).

If a declaration is made by notice in writing, the director must send the notice to the other directors. It can be sent in hard copy form by hand or by post. If the recipient has agreed to receive notices in electronic form and by electronic means, it can be sent by agreed electronic means in an agreed electronic form. Where

---

[5]   [1988] 1 WLR 863.

a director declares an interest in accordance with Section 184, the making of the declaration is deemed to form part of the proceedings at the next meeting of the directors after the notice is given. Section 248 requires companies to keep minutes of directors' meetings for at least 10 years from the meeting and that section applies as if the declaration had been made at the next directors' meeting.

A director can also give a general notice in accordance with Section 185. In that case, the notice must be given to the directors of the company to the effect that the director has an interest (as member, officer, employee or otherwise) in a specified body corporate or firm and is to be regarded as interested in any transaction or arrangement that may be made with that body corporate or firm after the date of the notice. A notice can also be given to the effect that the director is connected with a specified person (other than a body corporate or firm) and is to be regarded as interested in any transaction or arrangement that may be made with the specified person after the date of the notice. The notice must state the nature and extent of the director's interest in the body corporate or firm or the nature of his connection with the specified person. A general notice is not effective unless either it is given at a meeting of the directors or the director takes reasonable steps to secure that it is brought up and read at the first directors' meeting after the general notice is given.

The requirements also apply to shadow directors, with some adaptations (Section 187). "Shadow director" is defined in Section 251 as any person in accordance with whose directions or instructions the directors of the company are accustomed to act. However, there is an exception for someone who gives advice in a professional capacity, such as a solicitor or accountant, provided the only reason that person would be treated as a shadow director is because of that advice. There is another exception for the purposes of some Sections in the Companies Act 2006 (but not Sections 182 to 187). Under this exception, a body corporate is not treated as a shadow director of any of its subsidiaries only because the directors of the subsidiary are accustomed to act in accordance with the holding company's directions or instructions.

Shadow directors can only declare their interests in a contract by a notice in writing to the directors or by general notice. A shadow director cannot make a declaration of interest at a meeting of the directors. A general notice given by a shadow director is not effective unless it is given by notice in writing in accordance with Section 184. The requirements of Section 185(4) (which require a general notice to be given at a directors' meeting or require the director to take reasonable steps to secure the general notice is brought up and read at the next meeting of the directors after it is given) do not apply.

The director's duty is not merely to disclose that he has an interest: he must disclose "the nature and extent of the interest". His declaration must make his colleagues "fully informed of the real state of things" (*see Imperial Mercantile Credit Association* v *Coleman*[6]). The fact that the interest is the same as other employees' or that it is an interest in another group company does not mean that it does not have to be disclosed.

The section does not require disclosure of interests which the director is not aware of or where the director is not aware of the transaction or arrangement in question. (This is a change from the position under Section 317 Companies Act 1985.) However, a director is treated as being aware of matters of which he ought reasonably to be aware. This will prevent directors burying their heads in the sand to avoid a disclosure obligation. A director also need not disclose an interest under Section 182 if it cannot reasonably be regarded as likely to give rise to a conflict of interest or if, or to the extent that, the other directors are already aware of the interest. The other directors are treated as being aware of anything of which they ought reasonably to be aware. A director need not declare an interest if, or to the extent that, it concerns the terms of his service contract which have been, or are to be, considered at a directors' meeting or by a board committee appointed to consider those terms. These provisions make changes to the position under Section 317 Companies Act 1985 which should be helpful in practice to directors and companies.

---

[6] [1873] LR 6 (HL) 189 at 216, per Lord Chelmsford.

Any declaration required by Section 182 must be made as soon as reasonably practicable. There is still a duty to make a declaration, even if this timing requirement has not been met (Section 182(4)). If a declaration proves to be inaccurate or incomplete or becomes inaccurate or incomplete, a further declaration must be made (Section 182(3)).

There are special requirements which apply if a company has a sole director, but is required to have more than one director (Section 186). In this case, the declaration of interest must be recorded in writing and the making of the declaration is deemed to form part of the proceedings at the first meeting of the directors after the notice is given. The requirements of Section 248 as to making and keeping of minutes apply as if the declaration had been made at that meeting. There are also separate requirements where a company which has a sole director enters into a contract with that sole director (*see* Section 231).

Sections 182 to 187 do not contain any provisions setting out what the effect is on a contract if a director fails to declare an interest. This has, however, been considered by the courts in relation to Section 317 Companies Act 1985, which contained an obligation on a director to declare an interest in a contract or a proposed contract. There does not seem to be any reason why the conclusions reached in relation to Section 317 Companies Act 1985 should not be relevant to Section 182.

If a director failed to comply with Section 317 Companies Act 1985 this did not make the contract in which the director was interested unenforceable. In *Hely Hutchinson* v *Brayhead*[7] Lord Pearson said that Section 317 merely created a statutory duty of disclosure and imposed a fine for non-compliance. This approach was approved, obiter, in *Guinness Plc* v *Saunders*.[8] Harman J also took this view in *Lee Panavision Ltd* v *Lee Lighting Ltd*,[9] concluding that remarks by Lord Templeman in the *Hely Hutchinson* case that suggested a contract was voidable where there was a breach of contract were incorrect.

---

[7] [1968] 1 QB 549.
[8] [1990] 2 AC 633.
[9] [1991] BCC 620.

In *Craven Textile Engineers Ltd* v *Batley Football Club Ltd*[10] the Court of Appeal held that the court did not have a general discretion to do what seemed "fair and just" if a director was in breach of Section 317. In that case, a director claimed payment for work done and goods supplied to the company. He had failed to disclose his interest in the contract to the company. The Court of Appeal said it was impossible to restore the parties to their original positions and so rescission of the contract was not possible. The director was entitled to payment of his invoices notwithstanding the breach of Section 317.

In *Runciman* v *Walter Runciman Plc*,[11] a question arose as to the position where a director failed to disclose an interest in a contract and a variation to that contract, but all the affected parties were aware of the director's interest in the contract. In that case, the director failed to disclose his interest in his own service contract in accordance with Section 199 Companies Act 1948 (which was replaced by Section 317). The director was wrongfully dismissed. The company conceded the claim but argued it was not bound by the contract because of the breach of Section 199. Simon Brown J held that there was no suggestion that the director or his fellow directors had abused their position. Even if the Section had not been complied with, the contract was not automatically invalid. The decision in this case was that the balance of justice did not require a "technical breach" of the section to render the variation unenforceable. This case shows that the courts have not necessarily been sympathetic to companies seeking to avoid obligations as a result of a technical breach of an obligation to declare an interest in a contract. Under Section 182(6)(c) the position in relation to declarations of interest in a director's service contract is, in any case, now different. However, it is probably not safe to assume that the *Runciman* case means a company cannot ever avoid a contract where an interest has not been properly disclosed.

---

[10] unreported 7 July 2000.
[11] [1992] BCLC 1085.

5.4 Contracts with directors who are sole members

If a limited company which has only one member enters into a contract with that member, there are particular requirements that the company must follow if the sole member is a director or shadow director of the company (*see* Section 231). Section 231 applies to companies limited by shares or by guarantee, but not to unlimited companies. It does not apply to contracts entered into in the ordinary course of the company's business. There is no case law on what is the ordinary course of business in the context of Section 322B Companies Act 1985 (which Section 231 replaces). However, in other contexts it has been held to mean "part of the undistinguished common flow of business done . . . calling for no remark and arising out of no special or particular situation" (*Broome* v *Speak*[12]). The question will be one of fact which will depend on what the company does.

Unless the contract is in writing (in which case, the company need do nothing more), the company must ensure that the terms of the contract are either set out in a written memorandum or are recorded in the minutes of the first meeting of the directors of the company after the contract is made (*see* Section 231(2)). If the company fails to meet this requirement, every officer who is in default is liable to a fine (*see* Section 231(3)), but the validity of the contract is not affected (*see* Section 231(6)). These requirements are in addition to any other statutory or other requirement which may apply to the contract (*see* Section 231(7)).

5.5 Substantial property transactions involving directors

Companies are prohibited from entering into certain arrangements to transfer non-cash assets above a certain value to or from directors (or people connected with them), unless certain shareholder approvals have first been obtained or the arrangement is conditional on obtaining those approvals. Section 190 applies to transfers (both direct and indirect) to or from a

---

[12] [1903] 1 Ch 586.

director of the company or a director of any holding company of the company or to or from any person connected with such a director. Shadow directors are treated as directors for the purposes of the Section (Section 223(1)).

Section 190 differs from Section 320 Companies Act 1985 in various ways. Under Section 190, companies can enter into a contract with a director or connected person conditional upon obtaining the necessary approvals. This brings the Act's requirements into line with the Listing Rules requirements (*see* Section 5.6) and is helpful. The *de minimis* threshold has been raised from £2,000 to £5,000 and there is a new exemption for transactions with administrators.

"Non-cash asset" is defined in Section 1163 as "any property or interest in property other than cash". For this purpose, cash includes foreign currency. Section 1163(2) extends the meaning of transfer or acquisition of a non-cash asset to include creating or extinguishing an estate or interest in any property or a right over property. It also includes the discharge of any person's liability other than a liability for a liquidated sum.

The section does not apply to a transaction so far as it relates to anything to which a director is entitled under his service contract or to payment for loss of office as defined in Section 215 (Section 190(6)).

In *Re Duckwari Plc (No 1)*,[13] a company acquired either the benefit of a contract or a beneficial interest in the property which was the subject of the contract. The Court of Appeal held that the asset acquired was a non-cash asset for the purpose of Section 739(2) Companies Act 1985 (now replaced by Section 1163). In *Gooding* v *Cater*, the court held that where a company discharged its own liability for damages for breach of a director's service contract, it did not have to obtain prior approval under Section 320 Companies Act 1985 (which Section 190 replaces).[14] In *Mercer* v *Heart of Midlothian Plc*, Lord Macfadyen thought it was

---

[13] [1997] 2 BCLC 713.
[14] *See Gooding* v *Cater* (unreported 13 March 1989) Chancery Division.

"questionable" whether the benefits received by the former director (including seats in the director's box at Tynecastle Stadium on match days, access to the boardroom and a car park pass) amounted to a non-cash asset as they were a personal right against Heart of Midlothian rather than a right over property. In *Ultraframe (UK) Ltd v Fielding (No 2)*[15] it was held that an exclusive licence of design right was a "non-cash asset".

Transfers of non-cash assets only need to be approved if the value of the asset exceeds £100,000 or (if less) it exceeds 10 per cent of the company's asset value (although transfers of assets valued at £5,000 or less do not need to be approved) (Section 191). The company's asset value is its net asset value determined by reference to its most recent statutory accounts. Where no accounts have been prepared when the arrangement is entered into, the company's asset value is treated as being the amount of the company's called-up share capital. The non-cash asset must be valued when the arrangement in question is entered into. A company's statutory accounts are its annual accounts prepared in accordance with Part 15 of the Act and its "most recent statutory accounts" are the accounts for which the time for sending them out to members (in accordance with Section 424) is most recent. In *Micro Leisure Ltd v County Properties and Developments Ltd*,[16] the Scottish Court of Session held that the value of the asset can be the special value of the asset to the director and not the objective market value of the asset. The case related to Section 320 Companies Act 1985, but there appears to be no reason why the same approach should not apply to Section 191.

If there is an arrangement which involves more than one non-cash asset or if the arrangement is one of a series involving non-cash assets, the arrangement is treated as if it involved a non-cash asset of a value equal to the aggregate of all the non-cash assets involved in the arrangement or the series (Section 190(5)). This prevents companies from splitting an arrangement into different parts to avoid the requirements applying to it.

---

[15] [2005] EWHC 1638 (Ch).
[16] *The Times*, 12 January 2000.

There are various exceptions from the requirement to obtain approval. Section 190 only applies to companies as defined in Section 1, but not to other bodies corporate. If the company is a wholly-owned subsidiary of another body corporate (as defined in Section 1159(2)), no approval is needed wherever its holding company is incorporated (*see* Section 190(4)(b)). No approval is needed for transfers between members of the same wholly-owned group: that is, from a holding company to a wholly-owned subsidiary or vice versa, or from one wholly-owned subsidiary to another wholly-owned subsidiary in the same group (Section 192(b)).

Approval is required if an arrangement is entered into when the company is in a members' voluntary winding up but not otherwise if the company is being wound up (Section 193(1)(a)). It is also not required if the company is in administration within the meaning of Schedule B1 Insolvency Act 1986 or the Insolvency (Northern Ireland) Order 1989 (SI 1989/2405 (NI 19)). Approval is not required if the director acquires the non-cash asset in his capacity as a member (Section 192(a)), for example where a director receives bonus shares in common with other members or shares under a scrip dividend arrangement. Finally, no approval is needed if the director or a connected person effects a transaction on a recognised investment exchange (as defined in Part 18 Financial Services and Markets Act 2000), such as the London Stock Exchange, through an independent broker as defined in Section 194(2).

Section 190(1) provides that where approval is needed the arrangement must be approved "by a resolution of the members of the company". If the arrangement is with a director of a holding company (or a connected person of such a director), it must also be approved "by a resolution of the members of the holding company" (Section 190(2)). This wording differs from Section 320 Companies Act 1985, which required a resolution of the company or holding company in general meeting. In relation to Section 320, the requirement was held to be satisfied where all the shareholders of a company had unanimously agreed, at a meeting, to the transfer of company property to certain of those shareholders and directors, even though the meeting was described as a "board meeting" and no shareholders' resolution giving prior approval was passed.[17] In another case, an approval of a transaction subject to Section 320 of the company without any formal resolution was held to be sufficient, applying *Re Duomatic Ltd* [1969] 2 Ch 365.[18] There does not seem to be any reason why a court would come to a different conclusion in the light of the requirements of Section 190.

The consequences of entering into an arrangement in breach of Section 190 are set out in Section 195. The company can avoid the arrangement and any transaction entered into in pursuance of the arrangement, unless one of a number of conditions has been satisfied. These are:

(a) that it is no longer possible to return the money or asset which was the subject of the arrangement or transaction;

(b) the company has been indemnified in pursuance of Section 195 by some other person for the loss or damage it has suffered;

(c) a person who is not a party to the arrangement or transaction has acquired any rights in good faith, for value and without actual notice that Section 190 had been breached, and those rights would be affected if the arrangement or transaction were avoided; or

(d) the members of the company affirm the arrangement by resolution within a reasonable period and, if the arrangement involves a transfer of an asset to or by a director of its holding company (or someone connected with that director), the arrangement is also affirmed by a resolution of the members of the holding company (Section 196).

A transaction was not illegal just because Section 320 Companies Act 1985 had been breached (*see Niltan Carson Ltd* v *Hawthorne*)[19] and the same would appear to be the case if Section 190 is breached. Section 190(3) provides that a company is not subject to any liability by reason of a failure to obtain

---

[17] *See Re Conegrade Ltd* [2002] All ER (D) 19.

[18] *NBH Ltd* v *Hoare* [2006] EWHC 73.

[19] [1988] BCLC 298, 322.

approval required by Section 190. Also the transaction is not void *ab initio*. However, directors (both the director who enters into the arrangement or transaction and the directors who authorise it) and connected persons who enter into the transaction or arrangement are liable to account to the company for any gains made, directly or indirectly, as a result and to indemnify the company for any resulting loss or damage (Section 195(3)). The liability to indemnify is a joint and several liability with anyone else who is liable under Section 195. The liability arises whether or not the company avoids the arrangement or transaction and is in addition to any other liability. However, a director can avoid liability for an arrangement between the company and a person connected with him if he can show that he took "all reasonable steps" to secure the company's compliance with Section 190 (Section 195(6)). A person connected with a director and a director who authorised the arrangement or transaction can avoid liability if he can show that he did not know the relevant circumstances constituting the contravention when the relevant arrangement was entered into (Section 195(7)). In *Re Duckwari Plc (No 1)*[20] it was held that the liability to indemnify the company extends to a decline in the market value of an asset after it has been acquired. In *Re Duckwari Plc (No 2)*,[21] it was held that the director was not liable for the costs of borrowing that the company incurred to buy the asset in question. In *Murray* v *Leisureplay Plc*,[22] Lady Justice Arden said that the costs of obtaining a due diligence report were a direct result of the arrangement for acquiring the relevant asset and could be recovered. However, the costs of hiring an additional director were not foreshadowed by the acquisition and could not be recovered under Section 322(3)(b) Companies Act 1985 (reproduced in Section 195(3)(b)).

5.6 Transactions with related parties

Companies that have a premium listing of equity securities by the Financial Services Authority ("FSA") and are therefore

---

[20] [1999] Ch 253.
[21] [1999] Ch 268.
[22] [2005] EWCA Civ 963.

subject to the Listing Rules are also subject to restrictions on transactions and arrangements between the listed company or any of its subsidiary undertakings and certain group directors or an associate of such a director. Under Chapter 11 of the Listing Rules, if a listed company (or any of its subsidiary undertakings as defined in the FSA glossary) wishes to enter into a transaction or arrangement with a director or his associate or where the company or subsidiary undertaking and the director or associate are each investing in, or providing finance to, another undertaking or asset, broadly speaking it must meet certain disclosure requirements and obtain shareholder approval for the transaction, unless an exception applies. The rules also apply to any other similar transaction or arrangement between a listed company or subsidiary undertaking with any other person if the purpose and effect is to benefit a director or associate.

The company must ensure that the director does not vote on the resolution to approve the transaction and that the director takes all reasonable steps to ensure his associates do not vote. The Listing Rules contain guidance as to the approach to take where someone who is a party to a transaction or arrangement which is subject to shareholder approval becomes a related party after the notice of meeting has been sent out but before the meeting takes place. The company must send a further circular to shareholders containing additional information that would have been required if the person had been a related party when the transaction was entered into, which must be received at least one clear business day before the last time for lodging proxies for the meeting. The requirements do not apply to transactions of a revenue nature in the ordinary course of business.

The directors who are subject to the Listing Rules requirements are the directors and shadow directors of the company, any of its subsidiary undertakings, any parent undertaking or any subsidiary undertaking of a parent undertaking (*see* the FSA glossary). Anyone who was a director of a group company in the 12 months before the date of the transaction or arrangement is also caught by the requirements. "Associate" is widely defined to mean:

(a) that individual's spouse, civil partner or child (who together are referred to as "the individual's family");
(b) the trustees (acting as such) of any trust of which the individual or any of the individual's family is a beneficiary or discretionary object. There are exceptions for a trust which is an occupational pension scheme, as defined in article 3(1) of The Financial Services and Markets Act 2000 (Regulated Activities) Order 2001, or an employees' share scheme, as defined in Section 1166 of the Act, provided, in each case, the trust does not have the effect of conferring benefits on persons all or most of whom are related parties;
(c) any company if the individual or any member or members (taken together) of the individual's family, or the individual and any such member or members (taken together), are directly or indirectly interested in the company's equity securities (or have a conditional or contingent entitlement to become interested) so that they are (or would be if the condition were met or the contingent interest became an interest) able:
   (i) to exercise or control the exercise of 30 per cent or more of the votes able to be cast at general meetings on all, or substantially all, matters, or
   (ii) to appoint or remove directors holding a majority of voting rights at board meetings on all, or substantially all, matters.

For the purpose of (c), where more than one director of the listed company, its parent undertaking or any of its subsidiary undertakings is interested in the equity securities of another company, then the interests of those directors and their associates will be aggregated when determining whether that company is an associate of the director.

If a listed company (or any of its subsidiary undertakings) proposes to enter into a transaction which might be a related-party transaction, the company must obtain guidance from a sponsor to assess the potential application of LR 11. If the company enters into a related-party transaction, the company must make a notification in accordance with LR 10.4.1R. Chapter 10 of the Listing Rules contains rules dealing with transactions by listed companies where the requirements depend upon the size of the transaction. LR 10.4.1R requires the company to notify certain details to a Regulatory Information Service as soon as possible after the terms of the transaction are agreed. The details are those that would be required for a Class 2 transaction, and also the name of the related party (i.e. the director or associate) and details of the nature and extent of the related party's interest in the transaction or arrangement.

The listed company must send a circular to shareholders containing certain prescribed information (*see* LR 11.1.7R). This includes full particulars of the transaction together with the related party's name and the nature and extent of his interest in the transaction. Where an asset is being acquired or disposed of under a "related party" transaction where any percentage ratio (for the purpose of deciding what class the transaction is under Chapter 10 of the Listing Rules) is 25 per cent or more, there must be an independent valuation of the asset if "appropriate" financial information is not available. The directors of the listed company must state in the circular that the transaction is fair and reasonable as far as the security holders of the company are concerned, and that the directors have been advised that this is the case by an independent adviser acceptable to the FSA. The director who is a party to the related transaction (or whose associate is a party to the related transaction) must not take part in the board's consideration of the matter, and the circular must state this (*see* LR 13.6).

If a company (or any of its subsidiary undertakings) varies or novates an existing agreement with a director or associate, the variation or novation is caught, whether or not the original agreement was made when the director or associate was a related party.

There are various exceptions to the requirements, which are set out in LR 11.1.6R. These include:

(a) small transactions – this is defined by reference to various percentage ratios used for classifying transactions for Listing Rules purposes. Where all of these do not exceed 0.25 per cent, the exception applies. If one or more ratio exceeds 0.25 per cent but is less than 5 per cent, the normal rules (including having to obtain shareholder approval) do not apply. Before the company enters into the transaction or arrangement it can, instead of the normal rules applying, provide the FSA with written details of the proposed transaction or arrangement and provide a written confirmation from an independent adviser acceptable to the FSA that the proposed terms are fair and reasonable as far as the company's shareholders are concerned. The company must undertake to include details of the transaction or arrangement in its next published annual accounts. These details must include, where relevant, the identity of the related party, the value of the consideration for the transaction or arrangement and all other relevant circumstances.

If a company enters into more than one related party transaction or arrangement with the same director (or any of his associates) in a 12-month period, the transactions must be aggregated unless they have been approved by shareholders. If the transactions in aggregate would be treated as a Class 2 transaction (because any percentage ratio is 5 per cent or more) or Class 1 transaction, the company must follow the usual requirements for the latest transaction and give details of all the transactions being aggregated in the circular to shareholders. If one or more of the percentage ratios for the aggregated small transactions is more than 0.25 per cent but all the percentage ratios for the aggregated small transactions are less than 5 per cent, the company must provide written confirmation from an independent adviser that the terms of the latest small transaction are fair and reasonable and provide the FSA in writing with the details of all the aggregated small transactions and undertake to include the relevant details of all the aggregated small transactions in the next published annual accounts;

(b) certain issues of new securities or sales of treasury shares to a related party;

(c) exceptions for certain benefits in accordance with the terms of an employees' share scheme or a long-term incentive scheme;

(d) granting credit to a related party on normal commercial terms or of an amount and on terms no more favourable than those offered generally to group employees or a grant of credit by the related party on normal commercial terms on an unsecured basis;

(e) granting an indemnity to a director to the extent specifically permitted by the Act or maintaining an insurance contract for a director to the extent allowed by the Act or a loan or assistance to a director if specifically permitted by the Act;

(f) a related party underwriting an issue of securities provided certain conditions are met;

(g) a related party co-investing in, or providing finance to, another undertaking or asset with the listed company if, broadly, the related party's investment is no more than 25 per cent of the company's and an independent adviser has confirmed in writing to the FSA that the company's terms are no less favourable than those applying to the related party; and

(h) where the related party is (or was) a director (or shadow director) of an insignificant subsidiary or is (or was) a substantial shareholder in an insignificant subsidiary. This is a subsidiary undertaking which has contributed less than 10 per cent of the profit of the listed company and has represented less than 10 per cent of the assets of the listed company in each of the three financial years preceding the date of the transaction for which accounts have been published. (There are different rules if the subsidiary undertaking has been part of the group less than three years.)

For exceptions falling within paragraphs (b) to (h) the transaction or arrangement must not have any unusual features.

If a director of a listed company is knowingly concerned in a breach of the Listing Rules requirements, the FSA can impose a fine on him or publish a statement censuring the director (Section 91 Financial Services and Markets Act 2000).

5.7 Loans to directors and related transactions

5.7.1 Loans

Subject to various exceptions, companies are prohibited from making loans to directors and persons connected with them and entering into similar transactions unless the transaction has been approved by shareholders' resolution. The provisions are very detailed and quite complex; they contain various anti-avoidance provisions. Under the relevant sections of the Companies Act 1985 (Sections 330 to 342) the requirements varied depending, broadly, on whether or not there was a public company in the company's group. When the Companies Act 2006 was originally introduced as a Bill it was proposed that this distinction should be abolished, so all companies should be subject to the same requirements. However, at a late stage the Bill was amended so that the provisions relating to quasi-loans, loans to persons connected with a director and credit transactions only apply to public companies or companies associated with a public company. A company is associated with a public company if either it is a subsidiary of a public company or it has a public company as its subsidiary or if both companies are subsidiaries of the same body corporate (Section 256).

The basic prohibition applies to all companies. A company must not:

(a) make a loan to a director or to a director of its holding company; or
(b) give a guarantee or provide any security in connection with a loan made by anyone to a director of the company or its holding company (*see* Section 197(1)).

The prohibition does not apply if the transaction has been approved by a resolution of the members of the company. If the director is a director of the company's holding company, the transaction must also have been approved by a resolution of the members of the holding company (Section 197(2)).

If the company is a public company or is associated with a public company, there is an additional restriction on loans to persons connected with a director of the company or a director of its holding company. In this case the company also must not make a loan to such a connected person, or give a guarantee or provide any security in connection with a loan made by any person to such a connected person. As for loans to directors, the prohibition does not apply if the transaction has been approved by a resolution of the members of the company and, if the connected person is connected with a director of the company's holding company, also by a resolution of the members of the holding company (Section 200).

For the purposes of Sections 197 to 214 a director includes a shadow director (*see* Section 223(1)) but, for these purposes, a body corporate is not treated as a shadow director of any of its subsidiaries only because the directors of the subsidiary are accustomed to act in accordance with the holding company's directions or instructions (*see* Section 251(3)). It appears from the section that it does not matter whether the director is entering into the loan in another capacity, for example as a trustee of an employee share trust.

A "loan" is not defined. Generally, this involves a payment of money to or for someone on condition that it will be repaid in money or money's worth. It is not essential for interest to be paid on the money lent. In *Currencies Direct Ltd* v *Peter Simon Ellis*,[23] there was a dispute as to whether monies paid by the company to a director were a loan or remuneration for work and services. At first instance, Gage J found, on the facts, that most amounts were remuneration but that some amounts were loans. In the case of the amounts which were loans there was an express written acceptance by the director of his liability to pay the sum on demand whereas there was no evidence that the other amounts were paid to the director as advances, subject to an express or implied term that they be repaid. The Court of Appeal upheld this approach. In the case of *In the Matter of Ciro Citterio Menswear Plc sub nom (1) Ciro Citterio Menswear Plc (in admin) (2) Johal (3) Feakley* v *Thakrar and others*,[24] the court found that there was a loan of company funds where it was only evidenced by a debit entry in the company's computerised nominal ledger. The case considered an arrangement between the directors of the company to make unused credit balances on the directors' accounts available to other directors. However, on the facts, the court held that the arrangements between the

---

[23] [2002] EWCA Civ 779.
[24] [2002] All ER 717.

directors had not created a loan by the directors in favour of the director in question. It was the company which had partly funded the transfer of property. Agreeing to make money available probably does not, of itself, amount to making a loan until the money is actually advanced. In *Champagne Perrier – Jouet SA v Finch*,[25] the court held that a company which had paid a director's bills and supplied goods to a company he controlled, on credit, had not made a loan to him. However, such an arrangement would fall within the definition of a quasi-loan (*see* Section 5.7.2 below). Providing security is also not defined. However, it seems fairly clear that the section would catch a situation, for example, where a bank or other third party lends money to a director and the company enters into an agreement where, if the loan or interest is not repaid, the lender has rights against some or all of the company's assets or undertaking to recover the amount not paid.

Before a resolution is passed a memorandum must be made available to members setting out the nature of the transaction, the amount of the loan and the purpose for which it is required and the extent of the company's liability under any transaction connected with the loan. If the resolution is to be passed as a written resolution the memorandum must be sent or submitted to every eligible member when the proposed resolution is sent or submitted to him (or beforehand). Accidental failure to send or submit the memorandum will be disregarded unless the articles provide otherwise (*see* Section 224). If the resolution is to be passed at a meeting, the memorandum must be made available for inspection at the company's registered office for at least 15 days ending with the date of the meeting and at the meeting itself (Section 197(3) and (4) and Section 198(4) and (5)).

The requirement for approval under Section 197 does not apply to wholly-owned subsidiaries (as defined in Section 1159(2)) or to bodies corporate that are not UK-registered companies (as defined in Section 1158) (Section 197(5)).

---

[25] [1982] 1 WLR 1359.

5.7.2 Quasi-loans

Unless the transaction has been approved by shareholders' resolution, a public company or a company associated with a public company must not:

(a) make a quasi-loan to a director of the company or a director of its holding company or to a person connected with such a director; or

(b) give a guarantee or provide any security in connection with a quasi-loan made by anyone to such a director or a person connected with him (*see* Section 198 and Section 200).

The prohibition does not apply if the transaction has been approved by a resolution of the members of the company. If the director is a director of the holding company or if the connected person is a person connected with a director of the company's holding company, it must also be approved by a resolution of the members of the holding company.

A quasi-loan is defined in Section 199(1). It is a transaction under which one party (the creditor) agrees to pay a sum for another (the borrower) or in fact pays a sum for the borrower other than under an agreement. It also includes situations where the creditor agrees to reimburse expenditure incurred by a third party for the borrower or in fact reimburses such expenditure other than under an agreement. The terms of the transaction must include that the borrower (or a person on his behalf) will reimburse the creditor or that the borrower incurs a liability to reimburse the creditor. Examples of quasi-loans include a company paying for goods on behalf of a director, even if the director subsequently reimburses the company, and a company allowing a director to use a company credit card for private expenditure.

As for loans (*see* Section 5.7.1 above), there is a requirement to make a memorandum available to members giving prescribed details of the proposed quasi-loan before the written resolution or resolution at a meeting is passed (*see* Section 198(4) and (5) and Section 200(4) and (5)). The matters to be disclosed are the nature of the transaction, the amount of the quasi-loan and the purpose for which it is required and the extent of the company's liability under any transaction connected with the quasi-loan. The memorandum must be sent or submitted to every eligible member when the proposed written resolution is sent or submitted to them (unless it has already been sent or submitted). Accidental failure to send or submit the memorandum will be disregarded unless the articles provide otherwise (*see* Section 224). If the resolution is to be passed at a meeting, the memorandum must be made available for inspection by members of the company at the company's registered office for at least 15 days ending with the date of the meeting and at the meeting itself. Also, as for loans, the requirement for approval does not apply to wholly-owned subsidiaries (as defined in Section 1159(2)) or to bodies corporate that are not UK-registered companies (as defined in Section 1158) (Section 198(6) and Section 200(6)).

5.7.3　Credit transactions

Unless the transaction has been approved by shareholders' resolution, a public company or a company associated with a public company is also prohibited from entering into a credit transaction as a creditor for the benefit of a director or a director of its holding company or a person connected with such a director (*see* Section 201(2)(a)). Also, it cannot give a guarantee or provide any security in connection with a credit transaction made by anyone for the benefit of such a director or a person connected with him (*see* Section 201(2)(b)). The prohibition does not apply if the transaction (i.e. the credit transaction, the giving of the guarantee or the provision of the security) has been approved by a resolution of the members of the company and by a resolution of the members of the holding company if the director or connected person is a director of the holding company or a person connected with such a director.

Credit transaction is defined in Section 202(1). It is a transaction under which one party (the creditor):

(a)　supplies any goods or sells any land under a hire-purchase agreement or a conditional sale agreement (defined in the Consumer Credit Act 1974 – *see* Section 202(3)); or

(b) leases or hires any land or goods in return for periodical payments.

It also includes transactions where the creditor otherwise disposes of land or supplies goods or services on the understanding that payment is to be deferred. For this purpose, services means anything other than land or goods, and it does not matter whether payment is made in a lump sum, instalments, periodical payments, or in any other way.

Before a resolution approving a credit transaction is passed, a memorandum must be made available to members setting out the nature of the transaction, the value of the credit transaction and the purpose for which the land, goods or services sold or otherwise disposed of, leased, hired or supplied under the credit transaction are required and the extent of the company's liability under any transaction connected with the credit transaction. If the resolution is to be passed at a meeting, the memorandum must be made available for inspection by members at the company's registered office for at least 15 days ending with the date of the meeting and at the meeting itself. In the case of a written resolution, the memorandum must be sent or submitted to every eligible member when the written resolution is sent or submitted to him (or beforehand) (Section 201(4) and (5)). Accidental failure to send or submit the memorandum will be disregarded unless the articles provide otherwise (*see* Section 224).

As for loans and quasi-loans (*see* Sections 5.7.1 and 5.7.2 above), there is no need for shareholder approval if the company is a wholly-owned subsidiary or unless the company is a UK-registered company (as defined in Section 1158) (Section 201(6)).

5.7.4 *Transactions or arrangements on behalf of another*

Section 212 sets out when a transaction or arrangement is made "for" a person. In the case of a loan or a quasi-loan, it is made for him if it is made to him. In the case of a credit transaction, it is made for him if he is the person to whom goods, land or services are supplied, sold, hired, leased or otherwise disposed of under the transaction. A guarantee or security is made for a person if it is entered into in connection with a loan or quasi-loan made to him or a credit transaction made for him. In the case of a related arrangement falling within Section 203 (*see* Section 5.7.5), it is made for him if he is the person for whom the transaction is made to which the arrangement relates.

5.7.5 Anti-avoidance provisions: related arrangements

Section 203 contains some anti-avoidance provisions which are relevant to the transactions which are prohibited under Sections 197, 198, 200 or 201 unless the arrangement in question has been approved by a resolution of the members of the company and, if the director or connected person for whom the transaction is entered into is a director of its holding company or a person connected with such a director, also by a resolution of the members of the holding company. Section 203(1)(b) prohibits a company from assuming any rights, obligations or liabilities under a transaction or arranging for any rights, obligations or liabilities under a transaction to be assigned to it which it could not have entered into itself without shareholder approval under Section 197, 198, 200 or 201. So, for example, a company cannot take an assignment of a loan made by a third party to one of its directors and cannot assume obligations under a guarantee made in connection with a quasi-loan to a person connected with one of its directors or a director of one of its holding companies. In such cases, to decide whether the transaction would have required approval under Section 197, 198, 200 or 201 if it had been entered into by the company, the transaction is treated as being entered into on the date the arrangement is made for the company to assume the rights, liabilities or obligations (Section 203(6)).

Section 203(1)(a) deals with more complicated avoidance techniques. Unless shareholder approval has been obtained, a company cannot take part in any arrangement under which someone else ("A") enters into a transaction which the company itself could not have entered into without obtaining approval under Section 197, 198, 200 or 201 and that person A obtains any benefit from the company or a body corporate associated with it pursuant to the arrangement. It does not matter whether it is the company, one of its subsidiaries or holding companies or a subsidiary of any of the company's holding companies which provides the benefit. The prohibition does not apply if the arrangement has been approved by a resolution of the members of the company and of the members of the holding company if the director or connected person for whom the transaction is entered into is a director of its holding company or a person connected with such a director. This section would stop a company entering into a "back-to-back" arrangement with a totally unconnected company to make loans to that company's directors in return for that company making loans to its directors or directors of its holding company. It would also stop an arrangement under which a third party provides a guarantee or security for a loan to a company's director under an arrangement for another group company to place business with that third party.

"Arrangement" is not defined. Arguably it is intended to catch something which is not a legally binding agreement, although the Law Commission has said that it is thought it must be legally enforceable and refers to *Re British Basic Slag Ltd's Application*[26] (*see* paragraph 6.11 of Law Commission Consultation Paper No 153). In the parliamentary debates when the section was first enacted the government stated that the section was intended to apply only where the benefit provided by the company or another group company was the quid pro quo for the transaction entered into by the third party. This makes it clear that if there is a usual course of dealing between the company and the third party, unconnected to the transaction between the third party and the director, this is not prohibited by the section. According to the parliamentary debates the burden of proof for proving there is an arrangement is on the person who alleges it exists.

Before a resolution approving an arrangement within Section 203 is passed a memorandum must be made available to members setting out the matters that would have to be disclosed if the company were seeking approval of the transaction to which the arrangement relates, the nature of the arrangement and the extent of the company's liability under the arrangement

---

[26] [1963] 1 WLR 727.

or any transaction connected with it. If the resolution is to be passed at a meeting, the memorandum must be made available at the company's registered office for at least 15 days ending with the date of the meeting and at the meeting itself. If the resolution is a written resolution, the memorandum must be sent or submitted to every eligible member no later than the time the proposed resolution is sent or submitted to him.

An approval is not needed under Section 203 if the company is a wholly-owned subsidiary, or if it is not a UK-registered company as defined in Section 1158 (Section 203(5)).

5.7.6 Exceptions

Given the breadth of the provisions in Sections 197, 198, 200 and 201, it is not surprising that there are a large number of exceptions.

5.7.6.1 *Exceptions for expenditure on defending proceedings, regulatory actions and investigations*

A company does not need shareholder approval to provide funds to a director of the company or holding company or a person connected with them to meet expenditure incurred in defending certain proceedings if certain conditions are met (*see* Section 205). The company can provide funds to meet expenditure incurred in defending any criminal or civil proceedings in connection with any alleged negligence, default, breach of duty or breach of trust by the director in relation to the company or an associated company or in connection with any application to the court by the director for relief under Section 1157 (relief in a case of honest and reasonable conduct) or Section 661(3) or (4) (relief in a case of an acquisition of shares by an innocent nominee). Funds can also be provided to meet expenditure to be incurred for those purposes or to enable a director to avoid incurring such expenditure. It must be a term of the loan that it is to be repaid, or (as the case may be) the company's liability is to be discharged, if the director is convicted in the proceedings, judgment is given against him in the proceedings or the court refuses to grant relief. It must also be a term that it is to be repaid or discharged not later than the date when the conviction, judgment or refusal of relief becomes final. This happens either when the period for bringing an appeal ends without the appeal being brought, or if an appeal or further appeal is brought and is disposed of. The section makes it clear that this happens when any appeal is abandoned or ceases to have effect or if the appeal is determined and the period for bringing any further appeal has ended without the appeal being brought.

The provisions of the Companies Act 2006 differ from those of Section 337A Companies Act 1985 which allowed a company to meet any expenditure incurred or to be incurred by a director in defending any criminal or civil proceedings – not just those in connection with any alleged negligence, default, breach of duty or breach of trust by him in relation to the company or an associated company.

Section 206 also makes it clear that a company does not need approval under Section 197, 198, 200 or 201 for anything it does to provide one of its directors or a director of its holding company with funds to meet expenditure incurred in defending an investigation by a regulatory authority or against action proposed to be taken by a regulatory authority. This is also the case for anything done to provide funds for expenditure to be incurred for such purposes or to enable the director to avoid incurring such expenditure. The Explanatory Notes to the Companies Act 2006 state that this is a new exception.

5.7.6.2 *Intra-group loans*

Because the provisions of Sections 197, 198 and 200 are widely drawn, they could prevent one company in a group making a loan or quasi-loan to another company in the same group or entering into a guarantee or providing security in connection with a loan or quasi-loan by a third party to another group member without the relevant approvals. This could arise, for example, because a director of one group company is connected with another group company – for example, because the director holds 20 per cent of its equity share capital (*see* Section 5.10 below). Approval under Sections 197, 198 or 200 is not required to make a loan or quasi-loan to an associated body corporate or to give a guarantee or provide security in connection with a loan or quasi-loan made to an associated body corporate (Section 208(1)). Similarly, approval is not required under Section 201 to enter into a credit transaction as creditor for the benefit of an associated body corporate or to give a guarantee or provide security in connection with a credit transaction entered into by any person for the benefit of an associated body corporate (Section 208(2)). Bodies corporate are associated if one is a subsidiary of the other or both are subsidiaries of the same body corporate (Section 256).

5.7.6.3   *Minor/business transactions*

A company can make a loan or quasi-loan, give a guarantee or provide security in connection with a loan or quasi-loan without needing approval under Sections 197, 198 or 200 if the aggregate of the value of the transaction and of any other relevant transactions or arrangements does not exceed £10,000 (*see* Section 207). The previous exception for small loans only applied to loans (and not quasi-loans, guarantees or security) and the aggregate amount was £5,000. Section 210 sets out how "other relevant transactions or arrangements" are to be determined for the purposes of an exception to Section 197, 198, 200 or 201 (*see* Section 5.8 below). The requirement to aggregate certain transactions is intended to prevent the exception being used as a way of avoiding the basic prohibition – for example, by having a number of group companies making small loans to a director.

A company may enter into a credit transaction or enter into a guarantee or provide security in connection with a credit transaction without needing approval under Section 201 if the aggregate of the value of the credit transaction, guarantee or security and of any other relevant transactions or arrangements does not exceed £15,000 (*see* Section 207(2)). The previous exception for such credit transactions, guarantees and securities had an aggregate limit of £10,000. If the relevant amounts are more than £15,000, the exception can still apply if:

(a)   the company enters into the transaction in the ordinary course of its business; and

(b)   the value of the transaction is not greater than the value it is reasonable to expect the company would have offered to someone unconnected with the company and of the same financial standing, and the terms of the transaction are not more favourable than it is reasonable to expect the company to have offered to such a person (*see* Section 207(3)).

5.7.6.4   *Exception for expenditure on company business*

Difficult questions can arise as to whether a company makes a loan to a director if it advances money to him to allow him to meet his business expenses. Although the better view is probably that normally there is not a loan to the director where money is provided in advance to meet expenses, it may be harder to reach this view if, for example, a director is advanced a large amount for a long period and can use this to meet personal expenditure, even if he subsequently repays his personal expenditure and any unused amounts. Section 204 provides an exception from the requirement for approval in Sections 197, 198, 200 or 201 as long as certain requirements are met. Where the requirements are met, the company can do anything to provide a director, a director of its holding company or a person connected with such a director with funds to meet expenditure he has incurred or will incur or to enable the director or the connected person to avoid incurring such expenditure. This means, for example, that the company can arrange for goods or services to be available to the director so that he does not have to arrange and pay for these himself. The requirements are as follows:

(a)   the expenditure must be incurred "for the purposes of the company" or "for the purpose of enabling him properly to perform his duties as an officer of the company". Following *Brady v Brady*,[27] there is a risk that the courts would adopt a narrow construction of what "for the purposes of the company" means; and

---

[27]   [1989] AC 755.

(b) the aggregate value of the transaction in question and any other relevant transactions or arrangements (calculated in accordance with Section 211) must not exceed £50,000.

5.7.6.5 Money-lending companies

Section 209 provides an exception from the prohibitions in Sections 197, 198 and 200 for "money-lending companies". A money-lending company is a company whose ordinary business includes making loans or quasi-loans or giving guarantees or providing security in connection with loans or quasi-loans. Provided certain conditions are met, a money-lending company can make a loan or quasi-loan to anyone, or enter into a guarantee, or provide security in connection with a loan or quasi-loan without needing approval under Section 197, 198 or 200. The exception does not, however, extend to credit transactions. The conditions are as follows:

(a) the company must enter into the transaction (the loan, quasi-loan, guarantee or security) in the ordinary course of its business; and
(b) the terms of the transaction must not be more favourable than the company could reasonably be expected to have offered to a person of the same financial standing who was unconnected with the company and the value of the transaction must not be greater than could reasonably have been expected to be offered to such a person.

The section does not define what constitutes the "ordinary course of the company's business". It is generally thought that this means that the transaction must be consistent with the normal course of the company's business and of a kind and on a scale normal for the company. It does not matter that the company's normal practice differs from the normal practice of other similar companies.[28] A decision as to whether the

---

[28] *See Steen* v *Law* [1964] AC 303 and, in contrast, *Countrywide Banking Corp Ltd* v *Dean* [1998] WLR 441.

conditions are met in any case will therefore involve some consideration of the company's usual approach.

There are special provisions which allow money-lending companies to give home loans to their directors or a director of one of their holding companies or to an employee on favourable terms or for a larger amount than would normally be the case (*see* Section 209(3) and (4)). The conditions to be satisfied are:

(a) the loan must be made to facilitate the purchase or improvement of all or part of any dwelling-house together with land occupied and enjoyed with that house or to replace a loan made by a third party which meets these requirements;

(b) the house must be the only or main residence of the person to whom the loan is made;

(c) the company ordinarily makes loans to its employees and the terms of the loan in question are no more favourable than those on which such loans are ordinarily made.

(The exception under the Companies Act 1985 did not allow a money-lending company to enter into a quasi-loan or guarantee or indemnity even if the conditions were met.) The conditions mean that a company can lend a director a larger amount than it would lend to a comparable third party provided the terms of the loan are no better than are ordinarily made available to the company's employees. Note that the company must, in fact, ordinarily make loans to its employees for the exception to apply. However, the amount must not be so large as to fall outside the company's ordinary course of business.

5.8 Other relevant transactions or arrangements

Sections 210 and 211 set out how to determine what are "other relevant transactions or arrangements" for the purpose of the various exceptions from Section 197, 198, 200 or 201 and their value. The company must first identify all the relevant transactions and arrangements for the director or for one of his connected persons which the company or one of its subsidiaries has entered into relying on the particular exception it proposes to rely on for the proposed transaction or arrangement. So, for example, if the company proposes to rely on the exception in Section 207 to make a loan to a director it must identify any other loans, quasi-loans, guarantees or security provided in connection with a loan or a quasi-loan under £10,000 that it or any of its subsidiaries has already made to the director or a connected person. The company must also identify any loan, quasi-loan, guarantee or security provided in connection with a loan or quasi-loan being entered into at the same time as the proposed transaction or arrangement. If the proposed transaction or arrangement is to be made for a director of a holding company or a connected person, the company must identify all the transactions for that director or a connected person entered into by the holding company or any of its subsidiaries (or being entered into at the same time as the proposed transaction or arrangement). If any of the earlier transactions were made by a company which was a subsidiary when the transaction was made but is no longer a subsidiary when the determination is being made, those transactions can be ignored.

Once all the relevant transactions or arrangements have been identified, the value of each must be determined in accordance with Section 211 and aggregated with the value of the proposed transaction or arrangement to see if the limit for the proposed transaction is exceeded. For loans, the value is the amount of its principal. The value of a quasi-loan is the amount, or maximum amount, that the person to whom the quasi-loan is made is liable to reimburse the creditor. Where a guarantee or security is to be given (or has been given) it is the amount guaranteed or secured. Where there is a Section 203 arrangement, the value is the value of the transaction to which the arrangement relates. The value of a credit transaction is the price that could reasonably be expected to be obtained for the goods, land or services to which the transaction relates if they had been supplied (at the time the transaction is entered into) in the ordinary course of business and on the same terms (other than price) as the terms on which they have been supplied, or are to be supplied. If it is impossible to express the value of a transaction or arrangement as a specific sum of money – whether because the amount of any liability is unascertainable or for any other reason and whether or not any liability has been reduced – the value is deemed to exceed £50,000, which means that the proposed transaction will not fall within any of the exemptions.

The value of any "other relevant transaction or arrangement" as determined is reduced by any amount by which the liabilities of the person for whom the transaction or arrangement was made have been reduced.

5.9 Civil consequences of contravening Sections 197, 198, 200, 201 or 203

If a company enters into a transaction or arrangement in contravention of Sections 197, 198, 200, 201 or 203, the transaction or arrangement is voidable at the company's instance except in four cases (Section 213). The first is where the money or asset which is the subject of the transaction or arrangement can no longer be restored. The second is where the company has been indemnified for any loss or damage resulting from the transaction or arrangement. The third case is where a third party has acquired any rights in good faith, for value and without actual notice of the contravention and those rights would be affected if the transaction or arrangement were avoided. The fourth case is where the transaction or arrangement is affirmed by the members of the company and, where necessary, by the members of its holding company "within a reasonable period" (Section 214).

As the position under Section 213 is the same as the position was under Section 330 Companies Act 1985 (i.e. as the terms of Section 213 provide that a transaction made in contravention of Sections 197, 198, 200, 201 or 203 is voidable at the instance of the company unless the provisions of Sections 213(2) or 214 apply), it follows that neither Section 213 nor public policy prevent a company from recovering a loan made to a director in contravention of Section 197.[29]

If a transaction or arrangement is made with a director of the company or a director of a holding company, the director incurs

---

[29] *See Currencies Direct Ltd v Peter Simon Ellis* [2002] EWCA Civ 779, CA.

liabilities. If the transaction or arrangement is made with a person connected with a director of the company or a holding company, both the person connected with the director and the director with whom that person is connected are liable under Section 213, although the director can escape liability in this case if he shows that he took all reasonable steps to make sure the company complied with the relevant section. In either case, any director of the company who authorised the transaction or arrangement is also liable. However a director who authorised a transaction or arrangement will not be liable if he shows that, at the time of the transaction or arrangement was entered into, he did not know the relevant circumstances constituting the contravention (Section 213(7)). The same is true for a person connected with a director of the company or of its holding company if he can show he did not know the relevant circumstances constituting the contravention when the transaction or arrangement was entered into. In each case the liability is incurred whether or not the transaction or arrangement is avoided (Section 213(3)).

The liability in each case is twofold. First, it is to account to the company for any gain the director or connected person has made directly or indirectly by the transaction or arrangement. Second, it is to indemnify the company for any loss or damage which results from the transaction or arrangement. The liability to indemnify is a joint and several liability with anyone else liable under Section 213. The liability does not prejudice any other liability a director or person connected with a director may incur. Also, nothing in Section 213 excludes the operation of any other enactment or rule of law by virtue of which the transaction or arrangement may be called into question (Section 213(8)). In *Neville and another* v *Krikorian and others*[30] (which considered the position under Section 341 Companies Act 1985) it was held that a director who knowingly allowed a practice to continue under which lending by the company to his co-director was treated as acceptable had authorised the individual payments which were made in accordance with that practice even though he did not have actual knowledge of

---

[30] [2006] EWCA Civ 943.

each individual payment when it was made. The director was held jointly and severally liable for the indebtedness of his co-director. In *Queensway Systems Ltd (in liq.) and others* v *Walker and another* [2006] EWHC 2006 (Ch) a co-director was found to be authorising an arrangement or transaction for the purposes of Section 341(2), even though she did not know the relevant payments were being posted to a loan account. She knew payments were being made and if she had applied her mind to the question of what payments were being made and whether there was any justification for them, she would have discovered there was no justification.

There is no longer any criminal liability for entering into a transaction or arrangement without the necessary approval. Under the Companies Act 1985, criminal liability could be incurred by the company, a director and anyone else who procured the transaction or arrangement if the company entering into the transaction or arrangement was a member of a group which included a public company.

In the case of *Ciro Citterio Menswear Plc*[31] the High Court held that in some cases breach of Section 330 Companies Act 1985 could give rise to a constructive trust even though neither Section 330 nor Section 341 Companies Act 1985 mentioned this. However, in that case the High Court held that a constructive trust had not arisen. The director was not in breach of his fiduciary duties and there was no straightforward misappropriation of the company's property.

5.10   Connected persons

Sections 252 to 255 set out when a person is connected with a director for the purposes of Part 10 Companies Act 2006. A person ("A") is connected with a director of a company if (but only if) A is:

(a)   a member of the director's family, i.e. the director's spouse, or civil partner, any other person (whether of the same or a

---

[31] *See in the matter of Ciro Citterio Menswear Plc sub nom (1) Ciro Citterio others* [2002] 2 All ER 717.

different sex) with whom the director lives as partner in an enduring family relationship, the director's children or step-children (of any age), the children or step-children aged under 18 (and who live with the director, but who are not children or step-children of the director) of the director's partner, and the director's parents (Section 253). Note that the director's grandparents, grandchildren, sisters, brothers, aunts, uncles, nephews and nieces are not connected with the director even if they live with the director. The categories caught are now wider than was the case under Section 346 Companies Act 1985;

(b) a body corporate with whom the director is connected (*see* below). As explained below, in two situations a body corporate connected with a director will not be treated as a connected person of that director;

(c) a person acting as a trustee of a trust if the beneficiaries of the trust include the director, anyone in (a) above or a body corporate with which the director is connected (*see* below) or if the trustees have a power under the trust that can be exercised for the benefit of any of those people or bodies. However, trustees acting as trustees of an employees' share scheme (as defined in Section 1166) or as trustees of a pension scheme will not be connected with a director merely because he is a beneficiary or potential object of the trust;

(d) acting as the director's partner or acting as a partner of anyone in (a), (b) or (c);

(e) a firm that is a legal person under the law by which it is governed in which the director is a partner;

(f) a firm that is a legal person under the law by which it is governed, if one of the partners of that firm is connected with the director as set out in (a), (b) or (c) above;

(g) a firm that is a legal person under the law by which it is governed ("X"), if the director is a partner in another firm which is a partner of X, or a person connected with the director as set out in (a), (b) or (c) is a partner in another firm which is a partner of X.

Put more simply, (e), (f) and (g) mean that if a director is a partner in a firm that is a legal person under the law by which it is governed, that firm and any other firm which the first firm is in partnership with are each connected with the director. Similarly, if a person connected with a director is a partner in a firm that is a legal person under the law by which it is governed, that firm and any other firm which the first firm is in partnership with are each connected with that director. The provisions in (e), (f) and (g) used only to apply to Scottish firms but now apply more broadly.

Section 254 sets out when a director is connected with a body corporate. There are two situations where this is the case. The first is if the director and persons connected with him are together interested in at least 20 per cent of the nominal value of the equity share capital of the body corporate. Equity share capital means the issued share capital but not share capital which only has a limited right to participate in a distribution for both dividends and capital (*see* Section 548). So, for example, preference shares with a fixed right to a dividend and a right only to the return of a fixed amount of capital, such as the amount paid on subscription of the shares, and no further right to participate in any surplus would not be equity shares. The second case where a director is connected with a body corporate is where he and the persons connected with him are together entitled to exercise more than 20 per cent of the voting power at any general meeting of that body corporate or control the exercise of such voting power.

A director is taken to control a body corporate if (but only if) he or any person connected with him is interested in any part of that body's equity share capital (as defined in Section 548 – *see* above) or is entitled to exercise (or control the exercise of) any part of the voting power at any general meeting of the body corporate and the director, his connected persons and any other directors of the relevant company together are interested in more than half of the equity share capital or can exercise (or control the exercise of) more than half the voting power at any general meeting of the body corporate (*see* Section 254). If a director controls a body corporate ("A") which can control the exercise of voting power at a general meeting of another body corporate ("B"), the director is treated as being able to exercise control over that voting power at B's general meetings (*see* Section 254(4) and 255(4)). If a company holds shares as treasury shares, those shares and the voting rights attached to them are disregarded for the purposes of working out if a director is connected with a body corporate or controls it (*see* Section 254(5) and 255(5)).

When working out whether a director is connected with a body corporate or is deemed to control it, there are special rules where a person connected with a director is:

(a)   a body corporate with which the director is connected; or
(b)   a trustee.

In the first case, the interests in shares or votes held by the body corporate are ignored unless the body corporate is also a connected person by virtue of being a trustee or a partner of the director or of someone else connected with him (*see* Section 254(6)(a)). The interests of shares or votes held by a trustee of a trust are ignored provided the only reason the trustee would be treated as a connected person is because the beneficiaries of the trust include (or may include) a body corporate which is connected with the director (*see* Section 254(6)(b)).

A person is not treated as being connected with a director if that person is himself or herself a director of the company (*see* Section 252(3)).

As will be seen from the above, the definition of connected person is extremely wide and catches people, companies, trustees, firms and partners (including those incorporated overseas) which would not, ordinarily, be thought of as being connected with a director. The definition is further broadened by the rules set out in the Companies Act 2006 Schedule 1 which apply when determining whether a director is connected with a body corporate or is taken to control a body corporate. Under this, any restrictions or restraints on the exercise of any right attached to an interest in shares are ignored, and a director will be treated as being interested in shares when he has agreed to buy them or has a right or obligation under which he can become entitled to exercise a right conferred by them (e.g. he has a call option or is subject to a put option). A director is also treated as being interested in shares if he can exercise a right conferred by holding the shares (such as voting) or can control that right, even though he is not the registered holder. The provisions of Schedule 1 should be considered carefully in each case to see whether the director has an interest.

Most of those who responded to the Law Commission's Consultation Paper on Part X Companies Act 1985 thought that the definition of "connected persons" caused difficulties in practice and should be amended. The Law Commission thought that they were justified in their concerns, particularly as to when a body corporate is treated as a connected person and the Company Law Review Steering Group agreed with this (*see* the Consultation Document on Modern Company Law published in March 2000). However the Companies Act 2006 has not dealt with this point and the definition is even broader than before.

Chapter 6

Service Contracts and Remuneration

John Farr

Partner

Jemima Coleman

Professional Support Lawyer

Herbert Smith

6.1 Introduction

The legal issues relevant to directors' service contracts and remuneration are considered in this Chapter, together with the relevant best practice guidance.

This Chapter examines the following issues:

(a) definition of a service contract;
(b) authorisation by the board of the company's entry into service contracts with directors;
(c) limits on the length of the term of a director's service contract;
(d) disclosure of service contracts, both to shareholders and the wider public;
(e) remuneration of directors;
(f) other benefits accorded to directors, for example pension arrangements and share option schemes; and
(g) compensation payable to directors for loss of office.

6.2 Definition of a service contract and key provisions

Chapter 5 of Part 10 Companies Act 2006 ("CA 2006") on "Directors' Service Contracts" sets out a definition of a director's "service contract" at Section 227:

> "(1) For the purposes of this Part [10], a director's 'service contract', in relation to a company, means a contract under which –
>
> (a) a director of the company undertakes personally to perform services (as director or otherwise) for the company, or for a subsidiary of the company, or
>
> (b) services (as director or otherwise) that a director of the company undertakes personally to perform are made available by a third party to the company, or to a subsidiary of the company."

The definition includes contracts of service (e.g. an executive service agreement), contracts for services and non-executive letters of appointment. The contract may relate to any services that a director undertakes personally to perform for the company or a subsidiary or where a director provides services through a third party (e.g. a personal services company) (Section 227(1)(b) CA 2006).

A shadow director (any person in accordance with whose directions or instructions the directors of the company are accustomed to act) (Section 251 CA 2006) is covered by Section 227, as are *de facto* directors (anyone who acts as if he is a director and is treated as such by the board but has not been validly appointed). For the purposes of the CA 2006, "director" is defined to include any person occupying the position of director, by whatever name called (Section 250 CA 2006).

6.3 Authorisation of service contracts – compliance with the company's constitution

Any service contract with a director must be authorised in accordance with the company's articles of association. The articles identify the responsibilities and duties of individual directors and the board as a whole. The articles usually prescribe that vacancies may be filled or additional directors may be appointed by the board of directors (subject to the articles' maximum number of directors) and will state the quorum required in order for a board meeting to take place. Provisions relating to directors' powers, remuneration, interests, voting rights, ability to count in the quorum as well as the procedure for removal of directors may also be contained in the articles of association. The consequence of a failure to follow the articles is that any purported agreement will be void. These principles apply equally to any changes to the terms of directors' service contracts.

The directors must also comply with the new codified directors' duties set out in CA 2006:

(a) a duty to act within powers (Section 171);
(b) a duty to promote the success of the company (Section 172);
(c) a duty to exercise independent judgment (Section 173);
(d) a duty to exercise reasonable care, skill and diligence (Section 174);
(e) a duty to avoid conflicts of interest (Section 175);
(f) a duty not to accept benefits from third parties (Section 176); and
(g) a duty to declare interest in proposed transaction or arrangement (Section 177).

These duties are discussed in more detail in Chapter 3 of this Guide.

In certain instances, the statutory duties provide for derogation where a director is acting in a way authorised by the company's constitution.

The position in relation to a director's obligation to disclose an interest in his own service contract changed with effect from October 2008. There is a general duty on directors to declare their interest in a *proposed* transaction or arrangement, breach of which is a civil offence. However, from October 2008, there is no need for a director to declare an interest if it concerns terms of his service contract that have been or are to be considered (i) by a meeting of the directors, or (ii) by a committee of the directors appointed for the purpose under the company's constitution (Section 177(6)(c) CA 2006). However, the articles of association may prescribe that directors should declare their interest in such circumstances.

The board should approve service contracts and changes to their terms formally only after a proper consideration of the company's interests and after ensuring compliance with the articles and the codified directors' duties mentioned above. The minutes of the board meeting should confirm compliance with these formalities and a copy of the minutes, signed by the chairman of the meeting, should be kept as evidence that the proper procedure has been followed.

6.4 Limits on the length of the term of a service contract

6.4.1 Statutory limits – Section 188 CA 2006

Executive and non-executive directors' service contracts where the guaranteed term of employment with the company or any subsidiary is, or may be, longer than two years, require member approval (Section 188 CA 2006). The terms of the contract must be made available for inspection for at least 15 days before the meeting to approve it, and at that meeting. Further, if more than six months before the end of the guaranteed term of a director's employment the company enters into a further service contract (otherwise than in pursuance of a right conferred by or under the original contract on the other party to it), then Section 188 CA 2006 will apply as if there were added to the guaranteed term of the new contract the unexpired period of the guaranteed term of the original contract (Section 188(4) CA 2006). If a service contract contains such a term and there has been no shareholder approval, the term will be void and the service contract deemed to be terminable on reasonable notice.

There are a couple of exceptions. Shareholder approval is not required for a long-term service contract between a wholly-owned subsidiary and one of its directors. Nor is shareholder approval required if the company is not a UK-registered company (Section 188(6) CA 2006).

The purpose of this section is to encourage the trend towards shorter length service contracts as contracts with a guaranteed term of over two years can be costly for the company to terminate early. These new provisions apply equally to non-executive directors' letters of appointment. It is expected that notice provisions will become much more common in non-executive letters of appointment as a result. Previously, institutional shareholders have voiced concerns that the presence of notice provisions could make it easier for executive directors to remove non-executive directors following a board-level disagreement. It may be that some organisations will prefer to obtain shareholder approval to obtain the safeguard of a long-term contract for their non-executive directors. A provision could even be inserted into such a contract in which the non-executive agrees not to bring a claim for damages for any early termination of his appointment. A contractual waiver of such claims at the outset should be binding.

6.4.2 *Corporate governance on service contract limits*

The new UK Corporate Governance Code ("the Corporate Governance Code") was published by the Financial Reporting Council ("FRC") in June 2010. It replaces the Combined Code. The Corporate Governance Code will apply to accounting periods beginning on or after 29 June 2010 and, as a result of the new Listing Regime introduced in April 2010, applies to all companies with premium listing of equity shares regardless of whether they are incorporated in the UK or elsewhere. Copies of the Corporate Governance Code are available from the website of the FRC www.frc.org.uk.

The revised Corporate Governance Code states the following in relation to Service Contracts and Compensation:

"D.1.4. The Remuneration Committee should carefully consider what compensation commitments (including pension contributions and all other elements) their directors' terms of appointment would entail in the event of

227

early termination. The aim should be to avoid rewarding poor performance. They should take a robust line on reducing compensation to reflect departing directors' obligations to mitigate loss." [Formerly B.1.5.]

Further, at paragraph D.1.5:

"D.1.5 Notice or contract periods should be set at one year or less. If it is necessary to offer longer notice or contract periods to new directors recruited from outside, such periods should reduce to one year or less after the initial period." [Formerly B.1.6.]

In relation to notice periods, the Association of British Insurers ("ABI") and the National Association of Pension Funds ("NAPF") revised Joint Statement on Executive Contracts (February 2008) provides that the one-year notice period referred to in the Corporate Governance Code should not be seen as a floor, and boards are strongly encouraged to consider contracts with shorter notice periods. If it is necessary to offer executives longer notice periods, for example for incoming executives at companies in difficulties, the ABI/NAPF Guidance indicates that the termination provisions and the length of the contract need to be justified and need to reduce on a rolling basis (paragraph 3.6).

The 2009 ABI Guidelines "Executive Remuneration – ABI Guidelines on Policies and Practices" state that the remuneration committee should ensure that contracts protect the company from being exposed to the risk of payment in the event of failure. Shorter notice periods are one mechanism for avoiding an excessive severance payment on termination. When drawing up contracts, remuneration committees should calculate the likely cost of any severance and determine whether this is acceptable (paragraph 3.2). The ABI Guidelines also suggest that the contract should make clear that if a director is dismissed following the use of a disciplinary procedure, a shorter notice period than that given in the contract would apply (paragraph 3.7). In reality, this may be difficult to negotiate.

The Listing Rules do not apply to companies quoted on AIM (previously called the Alternative Investment Market). The three key sources on corporate governance specific to AIM companies reflect much of the best practice guidance outlined in the Corporate Governance Code:

(a) the London Stock Exchange's AIM Rules for Companies;
(b) the voluntary Corporate Governance Guidelines for AIM Companies published by Quoted Companies Alliance ("QCA") on 13 July 2005 which is the representative body for small and mid-cap quoted companies (formerly known as CISCO); and
(c) the voluntary Corporate Governance Policy and Voting Guidelines for AIM Companies published by NAPF in April 2007.

In addition, all companies incorporated in England and Wales are bound by any corporate governance provisions contained in the Companies Act 2006.

6.5 Disclosure of service contracts

6.5.1 Statutory obligations

A company must keep copies of every director's service contract (or where there is no written contract, a memorandum of the terms) open to inspection by shareholders without charge (Section 288 CA 2006).

This obligation applies regardless of the length of any service contract and whether or not it is terminable within 12 months. The exception for contracts where the unexpired term of the contract was less than 12 months or where the company could terminate the contract within 12 months without payment of compensation that existed under Section 318(11) Companies Act 1985 ("CA 1985") was not retained.

All the copies and memoranda must be kept available for inspection at the company's registered office or a place specified in regulations under Section 1136 (Section 228(2) CA 2006). In a new provision, the copies and memoranda must be retained by the company for at least one year from the date of termination or expiry of the contract and must be kept available for inspection during that time (Section 228(3) CA 2006). As a result of the expanded definition of service contract in Section 227 CA 2006, this section will now apply to contracts for services and non-executive letters of appointment. These provisions apply equally to variations of a director's service contract and accordingly any documents amending the terms of a service contract must also be open to inspection by shareholders (Section 228(7) CA 2006). The company must give notice in the prescribed form to the registrar as to the place of inspection and of any change to that place unless they have at all times been kept at the company's registered office (Section 228(4) CA 2006). The disclosure requirements apply even where the director's contract requires him to work wholly or mainly outside the UK (the dispensation that previously existed under Section 318(5) CA 1985 was not retained). There are heavy financial penalties for a failure to comply with these requirements. It is a criminal offence for which every officer of the company who is in default may be held liable to pay a fine (currently up to £1,000) (Section 228(6) CA 2006). In a change from the previous position under Section 318 CA 1985, the company is no longer liable under the criminal offence.

Where a shareholder is denied inspection the court can compel inspection or direct that the copy required be sent to the person requiring it (Section 229(5) CA 2006).

In addition to members' right to inspect (without charge) the copies of service contracts held by the company mentioned above, a significant new development is that members will have the right, upon payment of the prescribed fee, to request copies of such directors' service contracts (or, if not in writing, a memorandum of its terms) (Section 229 CA 2006). The copy must be provided within seven days of the company receiving the request. Where a shareholder is denied inspection the court can compel inspection or direct that a copy be sent to the person requiring it (Section 229 CA 2006).

6.5.2 Corporate governance guidance on disclosure of service contracts

The Corporate Governance Code 2010 states that the terms and conditions of appointment for non-executive directors should be made available for inspection by any person at an annual general meeting for 15 minutes prior to and at the meeting and at the registered office of the company during normal business hours (paragraph B.3.2, formerly A.4.4 of the 2008 Combined Code).

Terms and conditions of appointment of non-executive directors should be made available by placing the information on a website that is maintained by or on behalf of the company (Schedule B: Disclosure of corporate governance arrangements). There is no comparable requirement to make executive directors' terms and conditions available for inspection.

The ABI/NAPF Joint Statement 2008 states that companies should clearly disclose key elements of directors' contracts on their website and summarise them in the remuneration report.

6.5.3 The Takeover Code guidance on disclosure

The Takeover Code aims to provide a framework within which takeovers of public companies are conducted and to ensure fair and equal treatment of all shareholders. The Takeover Code covers both takeovers by contractual offer from the bidder to purchase the target shareholders' shares and schemes of arrangement sanctioned by the court under CA 2006.

Rule 25.4 of the Takeover Code requires particulars of service contracts of directors and proposed directors of the target or any of its subsidiaries to be disclosed in the first major circular from the target board advising shareholders on an offer (whether recommending acceptance or rejection of the offer). If any of the contracts have been entered into or amended within six months of the offer document, details of the previous arrangements must be provided (and, if there have been none, this should be stated).

The particulars to be disclosed include:

(a) the name of the director under contract;
(b) the date of the contract, the unexpired term and details of any notice periods;

(c)   full particulars of the directors' remuneration including salary and other benefits;
(d)   any commission or profit-sharing arrangements;
(e)   any provision for compensation payable upon early termination of the contract; and
(f)   details of any other arrangements which are necessary to enable investors to estimate the possible liability of the company on early termination of the contract.

It is not acceptable to refer to the latest annual report, indicating that information regarding service contracts may be found there, or to state that the contracts are open for inspection at a specified place.

A criminal offence has been introduced where the offer document does not contain the required information (including certain employee information). This applies to bids covered by the directive (e.g. a bid for a company listed on the Official List); and to other bids (e.g. a bid for a company listed on AIM) or to schemes of arrangement from November 2006. It is therefore very important that the information disclosed in bid documents on employment matters is accurate and complete. Further discussion on these changes falls outside the scope of this Chapter.

However, Rule 26 of the Takeover Code which requires various documents to be made available for inspection and published on a website for inspection by the other party, or by any competing offeror or potential offeror, from the time that the offer document or offeree board circular, as appropriate, is published until the end of the offer period (and any related competition reference period), no longer includes a requirement for all service contracts of offeree company directors to be disclosed.

6.5.4   *Persons entitled to inspect*

As can be seen from the above, different provisions apply to who is entitled to inspect under the Companies Act 2006, the Corporate Governance Code and the Takeover Code. In summary the position is as shown in Table 6.1.

Table 6.1: Entitlement to inspect

What can be inspected?	Who can inspect? Who can request a copy?	Provision
Directors' service contracts or memorandum of terms (where no written directors' service agreement), contracts for services and letters of appointment. This obligation applies regardless of the length of any service contract or whether or not it is terminable within 12 months. It also applies where the director's contract requires him to work wholly or mainly outside the UK.	Shareholders only	Section 228 CA 2006
Right to request copies of directors' servic contracts (or, if not in writing, a memorandum of its terms), contracts for services and letters of appointment upon payment of prescribed fee.	Shareholders	Section 229 CA 2006
Non-executive terms and conditions of appointment.	Any member of the public	B.3.2 Corporate Governance Code Schedule B of the Corporate Governance Code
Various documents, including all service contracts of target company directors or proposed directors (and, where such contracts have been entered into or amended within the last six months, particulars must be given of any previous arrangements).	The offeror, any competing offeror or potential offeror from the time that the offer document or Target board circular is published to the end of the offer period.	Rule 25.4 Takeover Code

6.6   Remuneration of directors

6.6.1   Components of directors' remuneration

6.6.1.1   Salary

A significant part of a director's remuneration is likely to be his salary. In relation to listed companies, the salary level should be set by the remuneration committee in accordance with:

(a)   the principles contained in the Corporate Governance Code (*see* Section 6.6.2 below);

(b)   the ABI Guidelines on Executive Remuneration;

(c)   the new Financial Services Authority ("FSA") Remuneration Code of Practice applicable to FSA regulated firms from January 2010. This sets out principles against which the FSA will assess the quality of firms' remuneration policies and any linkage between these policies and excessive risk-taking by staff. Key objectives of the code include making firms' boards focus more closely on ensuring that the total amount distributed by a firm is consistent with good risk management and that individual compensation practices provide the right incentives; and

(d)   other best practice guidance including the CIPD guidelines on executive remuneration, the ICGN Non-executive Director Remuneration Guidelines and Policies (March 2010) and 2010 RiskMetrics Group UK Remuneration Guidance.

The NAPF wrote an open letter to the chairmen of FTSE 350 companies in December 2009 addressing issues about executive pay. In its letter, the NAPF urges restraint in executive pay. It recommends that companies create simpler remuneration structures which better align interests over the long term and expose management to significant financial risk if they fail to reach certain goals. It also recommends that boards should pay close attention to how profits are apportioned between capital, remuneration and dividends to shareholders and suggests that companies should in their annual reports explain how these different demands have been addressed. Whilst the NAPF accepts that given market conditions share plan performance conditions may no longer be realistic, and therefore need to be amended, it expects awards to be scaled down at the same time. The NAPF believes that the practice of deferring parts of bonus payments into shares is good and expects more companies to do this in future.

Further details of the factors influencing the level at which salaries should be set by the remuneration committee are set out below.

6.6.1.2   Bonus

In addition to his salary, a director may be entitled to a bonus under a scheme which is either discretionary or contractual. The nature of the scheme is crucial, particularly in assessing damages on an early termination of the service contract. If discretionary, the director will not be contractually entitled to the bonus even when any targets as to individual/company performance are met, though the company would be under the general duty not to act in breach of the duty of trust and confidence in the way it exercised the scheme – this means that it should not exercise its discretion in bad faith or capriciously. If truly contractual, the director is entitled to the bonus calculated in accordance with the bonus formula and the company cannot refuse to pay it or withhold any part of it. The Court of Appeal decision in *Keen v Commerzbank* [2006] EWCA Civ 1536 has confirmed that an employer can rely on a condition of a bonus scheme that the employee must be in employment at the payment date to be eligible for a bonus. Employers wishing to withhold a bonus from an employee who has left or is under notice on the bonus payment date should expressly provide this in the scheme rules. A recent case (*Rutherford* v *Seymour Pierce Ltd* [2010] EWHC 375 (QB)) has highlighted that it will be difficult to argue that such a term could be implied without evidence of a clear unvarying practice, at the time of entering into the contract, of not paying bonuses in this situation.

However, employers should be wary of pre-contractual statements or representations, for example by headhunters or recruitment consultants, which might be used as evidence of a contractual entitlement where the bonus is intended to be discretionary. Clearly, careful drafting of the scheme is essential where no contractual entitlement is intended.

Entitlement under the scheme will depend on the terms of the scheme, but common factors are the company's performance in the relevant financial year (or the performance of particular subsidiaries for which a director is responsible) by reference to profits and the individual director's performance. A recent High Court decision (*Fish* v *Dresdner Kleinwort* [2009] EWHC 2246 (QB)) confirmed that there is no duty on employees to give up contractual bonuses due to the employer's financial losses. The employer's argument that a senior employee's duty of trust and confidence, good faith or fiduciary duty obliged him to waive his right to a contractual bonus when the employer suffered significant financial losses failed. Employees cannot be obliged to forego their contractually promised remuneration simply because the employer's financial situation changes after the promise is made.

The bonus commonly takes the form of a cash payment, but some companies have adopted deferred share bonus plans whereby a part of the bonus is payable in shares which must be held by the director for a significant period. In many cases, the bonus is only payable on production of an auditor's certificate confirming that the amount is due. The decision in *Keen* v *Commerzbank* referred to above also confirmed that an employee wishing to challenge the amount of a discretionary bonus has a high evidential hurdle to clear. The fact that the employer had paid less than the line manager's recommendation and less than reflected the success of the employee's team was insufficient, given the employer's wide discretion in fluctuating market and labour conditions. An employee will need strong evidence of irrationality or perversity, supported by independent evidence, to be able to proceed with his claim.

6.6.1.3   Long-term incentive schemes

A long-term incentive scheme which offers a director the right to acquire shares in the parent company may be another component of a director's remuneration. Such arrangements will often take the form of a share option, where the director will benefit from any increase in share price, or the grant of a share award, where the director can acquire shares at nil or nominal cost. These awards will generally be dependent on the company's performance, assessed by reference to particular targets. Alternatively they may take the form of a deferred bonus award, whereby part of the director's annual cash bonus is taken in the form of shares and, if left with the trustees of the scheme for a certain period, will qualify the director for a matching allocation of additional free shares. Again, the level of the matching award will generally be dependent on the company's performance. Under the Listing Rules, long-term incentive schemes for directors (whether payable in cash, shares or any other security) have to be approved by the shareholders except in specified circumstances (LR 9.4). This principle is reiterated at paragraph D.2.4 (*see* below) of the Corporate Governance Code.

6.6.1.4   Golden hellos

Offer letters may provide for a cash bonus payable when the director commences employment. These are taxable as income in the normal way. They can take the form of an immediate cash payment or a guaranteed bonus for the first year/part year of employment when a discretionary bonus scheme would otherwise operate. An immediate cash payment would normally become repayable if the director left within a specified period of commencing employment. Such payments can be justified where they are needed to attract the best recruits.

6.6.2   Requirements of the Corporate Governance Code in relation to directors' remuneration

Section D.1 of the Corporate Governance Code (more or less replacing B1.1 to B1.6 of the previous version of the Combined Code) contains general guidance as to the level and components of directors' remuneration as follows:

(a)   Levels of remuneration should be sufficient to attract, retain and motivate directors of the quality required to run the company successfully, but a company should avoid paying more than is necessary for this purpose. A significant proportion of executive directors' remuneration should be structured so as to link rewards to corporate and individual performance (the "Main Principle").

(b) The performance-related elements of executive directors' remuneration should be stretching and designed to align their interests with those of shareholders and to promote the long-term success of the company. The remuneration committee should judge where to position their company relative to other companies. But they should use such comparisons with caution, in view of the risk of an upward ratchet of remuneration levels with no corresponding improvement in performance. They should also be sensitive to pay and employment conditions elsewhere in the group, especially when determining annual salary increases (the "Supporting Principle").

Remuneration policy:

(c) In designing schemes of performance-related remuneration for executive directors, the remuneration committee should follow the provisions in Schedule A to the Corporate Governance Code (D.1.1).

(d) Where a company releases an executive director to serve as a non-executive director elsewhere, the remuneration report should include a statement as to whether or not the director will retain such earnings and, if so, what the remuneration is (D.1.2).

(e) Levels of remuneration for non-executive directors should reflect the time commitment and responsibilities of the role. Remuneration for non-executive directors should not include share options or other performance-related elements. If, exceptionally, options are granted, shareholder approval should be sought in advance and any shares acquired by exercise of the options should be held until at least one year after the non-executive director leaves the board. Holding of share options could be relevant to the determination of a non-executive director's independence (as set out in provision B.1.1) (D.1.3).

(f) *See* also sections D.1.4 and D.1.5 set out above at Section 6.4.2.

Paragraph D.2 of the Corporate Governance Code provides that there should be a formal and transparent procedure for developing policy on executive remuneration and for fixing the remuneration packages of individual directors. No director should be involved in deciding his or her remuneration. The Corporate Governance Code provides that:

(a) The board should establish a remuneration committee of at least three, or in the case of smaller companies, two, independent non-executive directors. The company chairman may be a member of, but not chair, the committee if he or she was considered independent on appointment as chairman. The remuneration committee should make available its terms of reference, explaining its role and the authority delegated to it by the board (D.2.1).

(b) The remuneration committee should have delegated responsibility for setting remuneration for all executive directors and the chairman, including pension rights and any compensation payments (D.2.2).

(c) The board itself or, where required by the articles of association, the shareholders should determine the remuneration of the non-executive directors within the limits set in the articles of association (D.2.3).

(d) Shareholders should be invited specifically to approve all new long-term incentive schemes (as defined in the Listing Rules) and significant changes to existing schemes, save in the circumstances permitted by the Listing Rules (D.2.4).

Schedule A to the Corporate Governance Code sets out various provisions on the design of performance related remuneration for executive directors which the remuneration committee should follow. In summary these are:

(a) The remuneration committee should consider whether the directors should be eligible for annual bonuses. If so, performance conditions should be relevant, stretching and designed to enhance shareholder value and to promote the long-term success of the company. Upper limits should be set and disclosed. There may be a case for part payment in shares to be held for a significant period.

(b) The remuneration committee should consider whether the directors should be eligible for benefits under long-term incentive schemes. Traditional share option schemes should be weighed against other kinds of long-term incentive scheme. Executive share options should not be offered at a discount save as permitted by the relevant provisions of the Listing Rules.

(c) In normal circumstances, shares granted or other forms of deferred remuneration should not vest, and options should not be exercisable, in less than three years. Directors should be encouraged to hold their shares for a further period after vesting or exercise, subject to the need to finance any costs of acquisition and associated tax liabilities.

(d) Any new long-term incentive schemes which are proposed should be approved by shareholders and should preferably replace any existing schemes or, at least, form part of a well-considered overall plan incorporating existing schemes. The total rewards potentially available should not be excessive.

(e) Payouts or grants under all incentive schemes, including new grants under existing share option schemes, should be subject to challenging performance criteria reflecting the company's objectives, including non-financial performance metrics. Remuneration incentives should be compatible with risk policies and systems, and criteria for paying bonuses should be risk adjusted.

(f) Grants under executive share option and other long-term incentive schemes should normally be phased rather than awarded in one large block.

(g) Consideration should be given to the use of provisions that permit the company to reclaim variable components in exceptional circumstances of misstatement and misconduct.

(h) In general, only the basic salary should be pensionable. The remuneration committee should consider the pension consequences and associated costs to the company of basic salary increases and any other changes in pensionable remuneration, especially for directors close to retirement.

6.6.3 The ABI Guidelines on Executive Remuneration

The 2009 ABI Guidelines on Executive Remuneration Policies and Practices set out the following main principles:

(a) Boards are responsible for adopting remuneration policies and practices that promote the success of companies in creating value for shareholders over the longer term. The policies and practices should be demonstrably aligned with the corporate objectives and business strategy and reviewed regularly.

(b) Remuneration committees should be established in accordance with the provisions of the Combined Code (which has now been replaced by the Corporate Governance Code). They should comprise independent directors who bring independent thought and scrutiny to all aspects of remuneration. It is important to maintain a constructive and timely dialogue between boards and shareholders regarding remuneration policies and practices.

(c) Executive remuneration should be set at levels that retain and motivate, based on selection and interpretation of appropriate benchmarks which should be used with caution, in view of the risk of an upward ratchet of remuneration levels with no corresponding improvement in performance.

(d) Executive remuneration should be linked to individual and corporate performance through graduated targets, that align the interests of executives with those of shareholders. The resulting arrangements should be clear and readily understandable.

(e) Shareholders will not support arrangements which entitle executives to reward when this is not justified by performance. Remuneration committees should ensure that service contracts contain provisions that are consistent with this principle.

Boards should demonstrate that performance-based remuneration arrangements are clearly aligned with business strategy and market requirements, and are regularly reviewed. The overall arrangements should be prudent, well communicated, incentivise effectively and recognise shareholder expectations. Remuneration committees should maintain a constructive and timely dialogue with their major institutional shareholders on remuneration policy and practice, including issues relating to share incentive schemes. There should be transparency on all matters relating to the remuneration of present and past directors and, where appropriate, other senior executives.

Shareholders' attention should be drawn to any special arrangements and significant changes since the previous remuneration report.

The ABI Guidelines provide that remuneration committees are responsible for ensuring that the mix of incentives reflects the company's needs, establishes an appropriate balance between fixed and variable remuneration, and is based on targets that are stretching, verifiable and relevant and which take account of risk. Remuneration committees should satisfy themselves as to the accuracy of recorded performance measures that govern vesting of variable and share-based remuneration and establish effective procedures for disclosure and communication of strategic objectives, which enable shareholders to take an informed and considered view of remuneration policy and its implementation. Remuneration levels should properly reflect the contribution of executives and there should not be unjusti-fied windfalls and inappropriate gains arising from the opera-tion of share incentive schemes and other associated incentives. Legal redress should be considered where performance achievements are subsequently found to have been significantly mis-stated so that bonuses and other incentives should not have been paid. Particular attention should be paid to arrangements for senior executives who are not board members but have a significant influence over the company's ability to meet its strategic objectives. Boards should consider disclosure of those risks and how they are managed in accordance with the obligations of the Enhanced Business Review under Section 417 CA 2006.

Further, in relation to pay, bonus provision, contracts and sever-ance, the ABI Guidelines provide that remuneration committees should ensure that base pay reflects the contribution of the exec-utives concerned. Bonuses should reflect actual achievements against carefully chosen and monitored targets. Any material ex gratia payments should be fully explained, justified and subject to shareholder approval prior to payment. Shareholders are not supportive of transaction bonuses that reward directors and other executives for effecting transactions irrespective of their future financial consequences. Remuneration committees should scrutinise all other benefits, including benefits in kind and other financial arrangements to ensure they are justified, appropriately valued and suitably disclosed.

6.6.4 Role of the remuneration committee

It will be seen from the provisions of the Corporate Governance Code and the ABI Guidelines set out above that the remuneration committee plays a vital role in setting the levels and structure of directors' remuneration. *See* paragraph D.2 of the Corporate Governance Code and Section I of the ABI Guidelines in particular.

6.6.5 Disclosure requirements

6.6.5.1 Directors' report and directors' remuneration report – Part 15 (Accounts and reports) Companies Act 2006

All UK companies are required to prepare and file annual accounts and a directors' report and to have those accounts audited (subject to certain exemptions on grounds of size). The company may choose which accounting regime to apply – either Companies Act accounts prepared in accordance with the Companies Act 2006 or IAS accounts prepared in accordance with the International Accounting Standards ("IAS").

Every company must send a copy of its annual accounts and reports (which includes the remuneration report in the case of a quoted company) to every member of the company, every holder of the company's debentures and every person who is entitled to receive notice of general meetings (Section 423 CA 2006). Directors of a public company must lay before the company in general meeting, copies of its annual accounts and reports (Section 437 CA 2006). A quoted company must, prior to its accounts meeting, give its members notice of an ordinary resolution, approving the directors' remuneration report, although entitlement of a person to remuneration is not made conditional on the resolution being passed (Section 439 CA 2006). The directors of a quoted company must deliver a copy of the directors' remuneration report to Companies House (Section 439).

Requirements for Companies Act accounts are set out in Regulations:

(a) the Large and Medium-sized Companies and Groups (Accounts and Reports) Regulations 2008 (SI 2008/410); and

(b) the Small Companies and Groups (Accounts and Directors' Report) Regulations 2008 (SI 2008/409).

These Regulations set out the detailed requirements in relation to disclosure of directors' remuneration. Listed companies also have to comply with the Disclosure and Transparency Rules in relation to obligations imposed on them regarding periodic financial reporting.

It is the directors' duty to ensure that annual accounts are prepared in accordance with CA 2006, although they may delegate the detailed preparation activity to others. Directors should ensure that annual accounts give a true and fair view and so they must be satisfied with the methods adopted. The board must approve the accounts; the accounts should be signed on behalf of the board by a director. A parent company of a group or large or medium-sized companies must prepare group accounts. There are penalties for non-compliance (Section 419 CA 2006). Only small companies are not required to produce group accounts (Section 399 CA 2006).

Directors' report

Chapters 5 and 6 of Part 15 CA 2006 retain, in an amended form, many of the provisions from CA 1985 relating to the preparation of a directors' report. Directors must prepare a directors' report for each financial year of the company including the names of the directors and the principal activities of the company in the course of the relevant financial year (Sections 415(1) and 416(1) CA 2006). A parent company of a group which prepares group accounts must also prepare a group directors' report. The directors' report must be approved by the board of directors and signed on behalf of the board by a director or the company secretary. All companies (except small companies) must produce a business review as part of the directors' report.

However, as mentioned above, there are enhanced business review requirements for quoted companies (Section 417 CA 2006).

The purpose of the business review is to inform members of the company and help them assess how the directors have performed their duty under Section 172 (duty to promote the success of the company) (Section 417(2)). The business review must contain a fair review of the company's business and a description of the principal risks and uncertainties facing the company (Section 417(3)). A balanced and comprehensive analysis of the development and performance of the company's business during the financial year, and the position of the company's business at the end of the year is required consistent with the size and complexity of the business (Section 417(4)).

Under the new regime, unless the company is subject to the small companies' regime, quoted companies must include certain additional information in their business review including reference to the main trends and factors likely to affect the future development, performance and position of the company's business and information about environmental matters (including the impact of the company's business on the environment), the company's employees, social and community issues and essential contractual arrangements. Where directors of quoted companies have nothing to report on these matters, their review must identify this fact (Section 417(5) CA 2006). These new contents requirements for quoted companies under the CA 2006 are more onerous than those in relation to business reviews under the CA 1985. Quoted companies therefore have a forward-looking element to their business reviews, whereas unquoted companies may simply use their business reviews to report on past performance and achievement. Directors are not required to disclose information about impending developments or matters in the course of negotiation if the disclosure would, in the opinion of the directors, be seriously prejudicial to the interests of the company (Section 417(10) CA 2006). Directors may also omit from the business review information about a third party (e.g. essential contractual or other arrangements) where in the directors' opinion it would be seriously prejudicial to that third party and contrary to the public interest.

The Secretary of State is given power to make provisions by regulations as to other matters that must be disclosed in the directors' report including any provision that was formerly made by Schedule 7 CA 1985 (Section 416(4) CA 2006).

Directors' remuneration report

All quoted companies must publish a report on directors' remuneration (Section 420 CA 2006). All other companies are required to provide details of directors' remuneration in the notes to the financial statements, but the disclosure is far simpler than for a remuneration report. The remuneration report must be approved by the board of directors and signed on behalf of the board by a director or company secretary (Section 439 CA 2006).

The remuneration report forms part of the annual report and accounts. It must be sent to the quoted company's shareholders with notice of the AGM, laid before the meeting and a copy sent to Companies House.

It is an offence for directors of quoted companies not to produce a directors' remuneration report or to produce a report which does not comply with the requirements of the Companies Act 2006.

Directors' remuneration report: information not subject to audit

The remuneration report should include details of:

- The board's procedures relating to directors' remuneration and information about the role of the remuneration committee including who was on it, the names of external advisers appointed and further details about any advisers appointed to the committee who were not directors of the company.
- The company's remuneration policy, including details of performance criteria for share options or other long-term incentive plans ("LTIP").

- Details of each director's remuneration in the preceding financial year and how pay and employment conditions elsewhere in the company were taken into account in determining directors' remuneration. (Disclosure is required in relation to contract terms, notice periods, compensation, share options, LTIPs and pensions.)
- Performance graphs to provide historic information on the company's total shareholder return ("TSR") compared with the TSR of a broad equity market index over a period of the five most recent financial years (or, if fewer, the number of years since the company obtained its listing).

The disclosures required in the remuneration report to some extent duplicate the disclosures required under the Listing Rules and effectively put some of the requirements of paragraph 9.8.8R of the Listing Rules (*see* Section 6.6.5.2) into legislative form.

Directors' remuneration report: information subject to audit

The following information in the directors' remuneration report is subject to audit:

(a) details of directors' remuneration, splitting compensation into different elements: emoluments, bonuses and expenses plus any benefits in kind, compensation for loss of office or other termination payments;

(b) details of share option schemes setting out directors' share option entitlements including options granted, exercised and lapsed in the period;

(c) details of LTIPs and directors' LTIP entitlements;

(d) details of directors' pensions with separate disclosure for money purchase and final salary schemes;

(e) significant payments to past directors; and

(f) sums paid to third parties in respect of a director's services.

The auditors must confirm in their auditors' report whether the company has fulfilled the relevant disclosure requirements in relation to the auditable parts of the directors' remuneration report.

Directors' remuneration report: consequences of breach

Directors may be liable for fines for failure to:

(a) prepare the remuneration report;
(b) provide information to prepare the remuneration report;
(c) sign the remuneration report;
(d) give notice of the vote on the remuneration report to share-holders;
(e) put the resolution on the remuneration report to a vote.

A director is only liable to compensate the company for any loss it suffers as a result of any untrue or misleading statement in, or omission from, the directors' report, directors' remuneration report or summary financial statements, if the director knew or was reckless as to whether the statement was untrue or misleading or knew the omission to be dishonest concealment of a material fact (Section 463 CA 2006).

A safe harbour provision has been introduced by CA 2006 which sets out the statutory basis of directors' liability to the company in relation to the directors' report (including the business review) and the directors' remuneration report. A director will be liable only in relation to statements which are untrue or misleading and are made in bad faith or recklessly or if there is deliberate and dishonest concealment of material facts. The safe harbour also provides that liability of the director is only to the company and not to any third party.

The Financial Services Act 2010 received Royal Assent on 8 April 2010. Provisions empowering the Treasury to make regulations for authorised firms to prepare, approve and disclose remuneration reports covering their executives, officers, employees and consultants (and those of their corporate group) came into force with immediate effect. On 10 March 2010, HM Treasury published a draft of the Executives' Remuneration Reports Regulations 2010. They will be further amended in advance of a full public consultation. The new disclosure regime is due to come into force for annual reports in respect of 2010 that are issued in early 2011. The Regulations require disclosure of the number of relevant executives whose remuneration in the preceding financial year exceeded £500,000 and specify narrow disclosure bands which start from £500,000 and go up in £500,000 increments to £5 million, and then up from £5 million by £1 million increments.

6.6.5.2 The Listing Rules

Paragraph 9.8.8R of the Listing Rules requires the board of a listed company to include the following information on directors' remuneration in its annual report and accounts to shareholders:

(a) a statement of the company's policy on executive directors' remuneration (LR 9.8.8R(1));

(b) information presented in tabular form (if appropriate) on the amount of each element in the remuneration package of each director, by name (including basic salary and fees, the estimated money value of benefits in kind, annual bonuses, deferred bonuses, compensation for loss of office and payments for breach of contract or other termination payments) and the total remuneration for each director for the period under review and for the corresponding prior period; any significant payments made to former directors during the period under review; and any share options, including "save-as-you-earn" options, for each director, by name, in accordance with the requirements of the Directors' Remuneration Regulations (9.8.8R(2)(a) to (d));

(c) details of any long-term incentive schemes, other than share options as required by paragraph 9.8.8R(2)(d) above, including the interests of each director, by name in the long-term incentive schemes at the start of the period under review (9.8.8R(3));

(d) details of any entitlements or awards granted and commitments made to each director under any long-term incentive schemes during the period, showing which crystallise either in the same year or in subsequent years (9.8.8R(4));

(e) details of the monetary value and number of shares, cash payments or other benefits received by each director under any long-term incentive schemes during the period (9.8.8R(5));

(f)   details of the interests of each director in the long-term incentive schemes at the end of the period (9.8.8R(6));

(g)   an explanation and justification of any element of a director's remuneration, other than basic salary, which is pensionable (9.8.8R(7));

(h)   details of any directors' service contract with a notice period in excess of one year or with provisions for pre-determined compensation on termination which exceeds one year's salary and benefits in kind, giving the reasons for such notice period (9.8.8R(8));

(i)   details of the unexpired term of any directors' service contract of a director proposed for election or re-election at the forthcoming annual general meeting, and, if any director proposed for election or re-election does not have a directors' service contract, a statement to that effect (9.8.8R(9));

(j)   a statement of the listed company's policy on granting of options or awards under the employees' share schemes and other long-term incentive schemes, explaining and justifying any departure from that policy in the period under review and any change in the policy from the preceding year (9.8.8R(10));

(k)   for money purchase schemes, details of the contribution or allowance payable or made by the listed company in respect of each director during the period under review (9.8.8R(11)); and

(l)   for defined benefit schemes, information on the amount of the increase during the period (excluding inflation), and the accumulated total amount at the end of the period, in respect of the accrued benefit to which each director has become entitled over the year; and either the transfer value of the increase (less any directors' contributions); or sufficient information for a reasonable assessment of the transfer value to be made for each director (9.8.8R(12)).

6.7   Other benefits

6.7.1   *Pension arrangements*

Pension benefits may be a very significant element of a director's remuneration package. Benefits for directors may be provided through an existing company scheme set up for all employees (although often special sections may be appropriate offering a higher scale of benefits, a lower retirement age and special terms on early termination of employment), or through a separate pension scheme for executives, or via contributions to a director's personal pension arrangement.

Usually, benefits will be provided through registered pension schemes, in order to qualify for reliefs and exemptions from various taxes. However, since the government announced that tax relief for high earners will be restricted, there has been renewed interest in unregistered arrangements as a means of retirement benefit provision for executives and directors.

There are no limits on employer contributions to registered pension schemes. Tax relief on employer contributions to a registered pension scheme is given by allowing the contributions to be deducted as an expense in computing the profits of a trade, profession or investment business, and so reducing the amount of an employer's taxable profit. Employer contributions qualify for tax relief if they are made "wholly and exclusively for the purposes of the employer's trade".

Relevant UK individuals (broadly, those aged under 75, resident in the UK and with relevant UK earnings chargeable to income tax) who are active members of registered pension schemes will be entitled to tax relief on their contributions on an amount up to 100 per cent of their earnings. Contributions over 100 per cent of earnings are possible, although pension providers are not required to accept them and no tax relief would be available.

However, a 40 per cent tax charge (the "annual allowance charge") is payable where contributions made by, or on behalf of, a member (therefore, including employer contributions) in a year are in excess of the annual allowance. This annual allowance is set at £255,000 for 2010/11 and the Treasury has confirmed that this will be frozen for the tax years 2011/12 to 2015/16 inclusive.

In addition, a single lifetime limit on retirement savings for tax purposes applies. Pension savings in excess of this "lifetime allowance" will be subject, on vesting, to a recovery charge of 55 per cent if taken as a lump sum (and 25 per cent if taken as pension). The occurrence of certain "benefit crystallisation events" (including becoming entitled to a scheme pension and death) triggers the test of an individual's pension savings against his or her available lifetime allowance. The lifetime allowance is set at £1.8 million for 2010/11 and will be frozen at this amount for 2011/12 through to 2015/16 inclusive. Those whose retirement savings were close to, or in excess of, the lifetime allowance as at 6 April 2006 (the date when the pensions tax regime was overhauled and when the lifetime allowance was introduced) may have been able to take advantage of transitional protection.

Notwithstanding the relatively recent redesign of the pensions tax framework, the government has announced further changes to the rules applicable to high earners. With effect from 6 April 2011, tax relief on the pensions savings of high earners (broadly, those with taxable incomes in excess of £150,000) will be eroded, with the result that those whose taxable incomes exceed £180,000 will only receive tax relief at the basic rate of 20 per cent. Employer contributions (and the value of any benefit funded by the employer in a defined benefit scheme) will be included when calculating an individual's taxable income, provided that an individual's pre-tax income (including their own contributions and any charitable donations) is at least £130,000. This means that individuals whose pre-tax income is over £130,000 will need to establish the value of the pension benefit funded by their employer and will see the tax relief on their pension savings restricted if they exceed the £150,000 threshold.

The resulting tax charge will usually be collected via self-assessment. However, individuals with the highest charges (i.e. exceeding £15,000, will be able to opt for their pension scheme to pay the charge on their behalf, with the scheme reducing their pension pot or accrued pension entitlement for that year by an equivalent amount).

Anti-forestalling provisions already apply to prevent high earners from front-end loading contributions made by (or on behalf of) them, prior to the new restrictions taking effect.

The planned changes to the high earner tax regime have led to interest from employers in unregistered pension schemes (known as employer-financed retirement benefit schemes ("EFRBS")), which are thought likely to be outside of the ambit of the post-2011 tax restrictions. EFRBS are viewed as successor vehicles to pre-6 April 2006 "unapproved arrangements" (funded unapproved retirement benefit schemes ("FURBS") and unfunded unapproved retirement benefit schemes ("UURBS")).

EFRBS are subject to their own particular tax and National Insurance requirements (which are broadly more favourable to high earners when compared to the effects of the post-April 2011 tax relief restrictions). In essence, employer contributions to EFRBS are not subject to National Insurance charges/contributions or otherwise taxable at the time they are paid into the EFRBS; neither are they tax deductible until benefits start to be paid to the member. National Insurance charges will not be payable when benefits are paid out of the EFRBS where the benefits are within the limits which apply to registered pension schemes and where the employment relationship has come to an end (including any consultancy arrangement). The employee pays tax on any benefit he or she receives from the EFRBS; and the normal inheritance tax rules apply. Monies held in EFRBS will not count towards the individual's lifetime allowance.

However, there is some uncertainty as to whether EFRBS will be caught by anti-avoidance provisions. It is hoped that more clarity on this point will be provided in advance of the implementation of the new regime in April 2011.

6.7.2 Share schemes

6.7.2.1 Long-term incentive schemes

Another key component of a director's remuneration can be a long-term incentive scheme which typically offers the director the right to acquire shares in the company or its parent company. Such arrangements will often take the form of a share option, where the director will benefit from any increase in share price, or the grant of a share award, where the director can acquire shares at nil or nominal cost. These awards will generally be dependent on the company's performance, assessed by reference to pre-set targets.

Alternatively, they may take the form of a deferred and matching bonus award, whereby part of the director's annual cash bonus is taken in the form of shares and, if left with the trustees of the scheme for a certain period, will qualify the director for a matching allocation of additional free shares. Again, the level of the matching award will generally be dependent on the company's performance.

The main types of schemes for directors are set out below.

Discretionary share option schemes

This type of scheme normally gives the director the right to buy shares in the company at an exercise price equal to market value at the date of grant of the option. The option will normally be exercisable from the third anniversary of grant until the tenth anniversary of grant (provided the director is still in employment), although some companies will allow a proportion of the option to become exercisable where the director leaves in certain specified circumstances. These type of schemes are usually established in two parts – an approved part (which normally attracts income tax and National Insurance Contributions reliefs on options over shares with an aggregate value of up to £30,000 per participant at the original grant price, provided the options are not exercised for at least three years from grant) and an unapproved part (which provides for unapproved options in excess of this limit and which will usually be subject to PAYE and National Insurance Contributions).

Enterprise management incentive ("EMI") schemes

EMIs are another type of approved option designed to assist higher risk trading companies to attract key executives by offering them generous tax reliefs on share options over shares with a value of up to £120,000 at the date of grant. A company, whether quoted or unquoted, can qualify for an EMI provided its gross assets do not exceed £30 million, it has fewer than 250 full-time equivalent employees, it is not under the control of another company and it carries on a "qualifying trade" wholly or mainly in the UK (although this requirement is soon to be changed to the company having a "permanent establishment" in the UK). Most trades will qualify, but the following activities, amongst others, are deemed insufficiently high risk and therefore will not qualify:

(a) property development;
(b) shipbuilding;
(c) coal and steel production;
(d) hotel management;
(e) leasing;
(f) banking; and
(g) insurance and other financial services.

There is an aggregate £3 million limit on the total value of shares in the company over which unexercised options under an EMI may exist at any time.

There is no requirement under an EMI for a minimum period before exercise. Qualifying companies may consequently choose their own exercise periods provided the option is capable of being exercised within 10 years of grant. There will normally be no income tax or National Insurance Contributions to pay when an EMI option is exercised provided the option was granted at no less than market value (options can be granted at a discount to market value, but any such discount is taxable on exercise). When the shares are sold, capital gains tax will apply to any untaxed gains at the more favourable rate of 18 per cent.

Share award schemes

Share award schemes, unlike discretionary options, give the right to acquire shares at nil or nominal cost. The awards will generally be structured as a free share award, nil-cost option or as the award of restricted (forfeitable) shares. The extent to which those shares may be received, usually at the end of a three-year period, will depend on the company's performance, assessed by reference to pre-set targets. Share award schemes are unapproved schemes, and so the value of the shares received will be subject to income tax and National Insurance Contributions on vesting. Increasingly, companies are requiring their directors to defer part of their annual cash bonus which is then taken in the form of shares and, if not sold for a certain period, will qualify the director for a matching allocation of additional free shares. Again, the level of the matching award will generally be dependent on the company's performance.

"Phantom" share schemes

Phantom share schemes are cash bonus schemes made to look like a share option scheme, or other long-term incentive plan, with the amount of the cash bonus mirroring the gain which would have been made on a true share scheme. They are usually used where a share scheme is not possible, but where the company wishes to link part of the director's remuneration to the share price as an incentive.

Eligibility for participation in any such scheme will be determined by the particular scheme rules which may provide that the board or a board committee, namely the remuneration committee, shall determine whether an individual participates in a scheme in any given year, and the extent of that participation. It is therefore advisable not to refer to participation in incentive schemes in the director's service agreement, save to say that the director may be invited to participate in schemes, subject to their rules.

Share awards for directors usually involve significant numbers of shares and therefore often involve unapproved schemes in addition to schemes approved by HM Revenue and Customs, which benefit from tax advantages but have restrictive grant limits. Unapproved schemes have the benefit of limits set only by shareholders, but do not have the tax advantages of approved schemes.

Under the Listing Rules, any scheme which may involve the issue of new shares requires shareholder approval (LR 9.4). A scheme which uses existing shares may also require shareholder approval if one or more of the directors is eligible to participate and the scheme involves conditions in respect of service and/or performance to be satisfied over more than one financial year. This principle is reiterated at paragraph D.2.4 of the Corporate Governance Code (formerly B.2.4 of the Combined Code).

Listed companies (and companies considering a listing) will be keen to ensure that their share schemes are supported by institutional shareholders. Such companies will also need to take into account the guidelines issued by the ABI when drafting their share schemes. These guidelines provide recommendations on, for example, the maximum amount of new shares which may be used under the schemes and the use of performance targets to link remuneration to performance. The ABI Guidelines provide that share-based incentives should align the interests of executive directors with those of shareholders and link reward to performance over the longer term. Vesting should be based on performance conditions over a period (not less than three years) appropriate to the strategic objectives of the company. Any new share-based incentives should be subject to prior shareholder approval. Where any changes to share incentive award levels or remuneration structures are being proposed or new incentives, disclosures should be made to shareholders of such changes together with the remuneration committee's rationale for the changes and an explanation of the costs.

6.8 Compensation for loss of office

6.8.1 *Damages for early termination of a service contract*

In the absence of a liquidated damages, or payment in lieu, provision in the contract, or any misconduct or other contractual breach on the part of the director entitling the company to dismiss with immediate effect, the director will be entitled to damages for wrongful dismissal if he is dismissed summarily.

Before turning to the issue of how damages will be assessed, a brief word about the recent approach of HM Revenue and Customs to the tax treatment of termination payments. If there is a pay in lieu of notice ("PILON") provision expressly stated in the contract or implied by virtue of custom and practice, sums paid under this section or broadly equivalent to the monies due under it will be fully taxable unless the employer can show he has terminated in breach. A few years ago, the HM Revenue and Customs put forward a controversial argument that, even if there is no express or implied PILON provision, termination payments would nonetheless be taxable as emoluments from employment if the employer habitually made the termination payments unless there was contemporaneous proof that the payment was individually negotiated, for net rather than gross earnings, and mitigation was considered. This approach was initially rejected by the Special Commissioners and this decision was upheld by the High Court (on slightly different grounds). However, the High Court refrained from commenting specifically on HM Revenue and Custom's controversial hard line so there remains some uncertainty in this area (*SCA Packaging Ltd* v *Revenue and Customs Commissioners* [2006] UKSPC SPC00541, 23 May 2006, [2007] EWHC 270 (Ch)).

Damages for wrongful dismissal will otherwise be assessed by reference to the net loss the director has sustained as a result of the breach of contract for the balance of the term of the service contract or the notice period. The net loss is calculated by assessing the net salary that the director would have received during that period, plus a sum to represent the loss of any other contractual benefits (e.g. a car) for the period.

Genuine termination payments which are not taxable under Section 62 of Income Tax (Earnings and Pensions) Act 2003 ("ITEPA") as general earnings or under any other provision may be exempt from tax up to the first £30,000 pursuant to Section 401 ITEPA. (Section 401 applies to payments made in relation to offices or employment, so will cover termination payments made to non-executive directors.) Incidentally, it is interesting that the government has chosen not to increase the £30,000 threshold in recent years (it has remained static since 1988), thereby gradually eroding the benefit of this tax exemption. The balance over £30,000 will be subject to income tax in the normal way and a damages payment will need to be grossed up to take account of the tax that the director will have to pay on the excess over £30,000. (Incidentally, payments under Section 401 ITEPA are not generally liable to NICs, even if they exceed £30,000, as they are not "earnings".) Further, in assessing appropriate damages the board would be entitled to make a deduction for accelerated receipt, that is, a deduction to reflect that the director will receive the sum immediately rather than in monthly instalments had he remained in employment. The percentage deduction should be set by reference to what the director might reasonably be expected to earn by way of interest on the total sum.

Entitlement to damages is subject to the director's duty to attempt to mitigate his loss by seeking suitable alternative employment, thereby reducing the damages payable by the company by the amount that the director might reasonably be expected to earn. The courts will expect the departing director to do everything he can to find another job. Initially, the director would be entitled to restrict his search to positions at a similar level, offering equivalent salary and other benefits, but after a period he might be expected to look at a lower level. Clearly, if the director already has another job this can be taken into account by the company in assessing what it should pay the departing director – provided that the company knows about it. This is why a director may be required to warrant in any settlement documentation that he has not already obtained another job or been offered one.

In light of this, it will be clear that the unexpired length of the contract is especially significant, as companies cannot assume that mitigation will significantly reduce their liability. In deciding the level of damages payable, the board will have to consider carefully the director's prospects of finding alternative employment and it would not be exercising its powers in the best interests of the company if it failed to do so. To take expert advice from, for example, a recruitment consultant experienced in board-level prospects would assist the board in discharging this responsibility. Board minutes should record the board's consideration of the mitigation issue and how and why it reaches its conclusions. It will be interesting to see how the codification of directors' duties will impact on directors' existing duty to act in the best interests of the company in determining appropriate severance payments.

The revised 2009 ABI Guidelines place further emphasis on the board's role in approving termination payments. The remuneration committees should ensure that contracts protect the company from being exposed to the risk of payment in the event of failure. Annual bonuses should be contractually related to performance. In the event of early termination there should be no automatic entitlement to bonuses or share-based payments. If the service contract is simply to include a notice period, damages for breach of which would then be subject to the director's duty to mitigate his loss, shareholders will expect reassurance that the board has taken steps to ensure that the director has mitigated his loss to the fullest extent possible.

As mentioned above, the inclusion of a clause in the service contract providing for phased payments where the company continues to pay the departing executive on the usual basis for the outstanding term of the contract or, if earlier, until the executive finds new employment is supported by the ABI. Continued payment could be stated to be conditional on the executive making reasonable efforts to find other employment (and, possibly, providing the company with proof of this).

6.8.2 *Payments for loss of office – Sections 215 to 222 CA 2006*

Section 217(1) CA 2006 provides that:

> "A company may not make a payment for loss of office to a director of the company unless the payment has been approved by a resolution of the members of the company."

A payment for loss of office is defined in Section 215 CA 2006 as a payment made to a director or past director of a company as:

(a) compensation for loss of office as director of the company (Section 215(1)(a));

(b) compensation for loss of any other office or employment in connection with the management of the affairs of the company or of any subsidiary undertaking (Section 215(1)(b));

(c) consideration for or in connection with his retirement from office as a director (Section 215(1)(c)); or

(d) consideration for or in connection with retirement from any other "office or employment in connection with the affairs of the company" or any subsidiary undertaking while a director or in connection with ceasing to be a director (Section 215(1)(d)).

The new regime under the Companies Act 2006 for payments for loss of office is discussed in detail in Chapter 5, paragraph 5.2 "Loss of office and retirement from office".

Cash and non-cash benefits are expressly covered. Payments to a person connected with a director, or payments to any person at the direction of, or for the benefit of, a director or a person connected with him will be treated as payments to the director for the purposes of Sections 217 to 221 and therefore require members' approval (Section 215(3)). It is clear that a payment to a former director would be caught as there is an express reference to "past director" in Section 215 CA 2006. Extending the scope of the requirement to obtain members' approval to a payment to a director or former director in respect of loss of employment is limited to where the employment relates to the management of the affairs of the company. However, this still represents a significant change.

A company may not make a payment for loss of office to a director of its holding company unless the payment has been approved by a resolution of the members of the company making the payment (unless the subsidiary is wholly-owned) and the members of the holding company (Section 217(2) CA 2006). A memorandum setting out details of the proposed payment (including its amount) must have been made available to members of the company before approval is given.

Member approval is also required if the company wishes to make a payment for loss of office to a director of the company in connection with the transfer of the whole or any part of the undertaking or the property of the company or of the subsidiary of the company (Section 218 CA 2006). In the case of payment for loss of office to a director in connection with the transfer of shares in the company (or in a subsidiary of the company) resulting from a takeover bid, approval is required of the holders of the shares to which the bid relates and of any holders of shares of the same class (Section 219 CA 2006). Extending the requirement for members' approval to payments for loss of office in these circumstances is new. There is also a presumption that member approval will be required in respect of any payments made pursuant to an arrangement entered into as part of the agreement for the share transfer in question, or within one year before or two years after that agreement, and to which the company whose shares are the subject of the bid, or any person to whom the transfer is made, is privy (Section 219(7) CA 2006). Another change is the exclusion of persons making the offer for shares in the company (and any associate of them) from voting on any resolution to approve a payment for loss of office in connection with a share transfer (Section 219(4) CA 2006).

Shareholder approval is not required for a payment made in good faith in one of the following situations:

(a)   in discharge of an existing legal obligation (defined as an obligation "that was not entered into in connection with, or in consequence of, the event giving rise to the payment for loss of office");
(b)   by way of damages for breach of such an obligation;
(c)   by way of settlement or compromise of any claim arising in connection with the termination of a person's office or employment; or
(d)   by way of pension in respect of past services (Section 220(a) to (d) CA 2006).

Section 220 CA 2006 broadly follows the exception contained in Section 316(3) CA 1985 for *bona fide* payments made by way of damages for breach of contract, as discussed in Chapter 5, Section 5.2.2.

A payment made in accordance with a clearly drafted payment in lieu of notice, liquidated damages or change of control provision should not require shareholder approval under the Companies Act 2006 as it should fall within the exemption for payments made in discharge of an existing legal obligation.

It is likely that for a payment of damages to be made "in good faith" and to escape the need for shareholder approval, a deduction should be made to take account of mitigation and accelerated receipt. Similarly, in relation to the exception for compensation payable in respect of a settlement or compromise of claims arising from termination of employment, a sensible estimate of the amount of likely compensation for any statutory claims, together with an assessment of likely compensation for breach of contract and a careful consideration of the director's future prospects of employment will be needed if the proposed compensation is to fall within the exemption and avoid the need to obtain shareholder approval.

The final exemption which relates to "pension for past services" is intended to cover a payment made to a pension scheme on behalf of a director in connection with the loss of office or employment. However, the scope of the exemption is unclear and a cautious approach is advisable especially given the ABI guidance on ensuring that executives do not depart on special or preferential pension terms (e.g. with limited or no actuarial reduction).

The civil consequences of breaching these sections are set out at Section 222(1) to (3) CA 2006 and are discussed in Chapter 5, Section 5.2.5.

6.8.3   Golden parachutes and golden handshakes

A director's service contract may provide for an enhanced severance payment to be paid on early termination of the contract. This may be a liquidated damages clause providing for a payment to be made on a breach of contract (usually known as a golden handshake). Or it may be a contingency payment providing for a payment to be made on the occurrence of a particular event, such as change of control, for example, where the employing company is taken over or its business is transferred outside the group (known as a golden parachute). NB the 2009 ABI Guidelines state that shareholders are less supportive of the liquidated damages approach which involves agreement at the outset on the amount that will be paid in the event of severance. Further, the ABI Guidelines provide that contracts should not contain additional protection in the form of compensation for severance as a result of change of control. In order to be enforceable, the liquidated damages provision must be a genuine pre-estimate of the director's loss – if it is not, then it is likely to be unenforceable as a penalty. Best practice guidance encourages the drafting of liquidated damages clauses which provide for a reduction to take account of accelerated receipt and the duty to mitigate.

The clause will set out a formula as to how the director's entitlement is to be calculated. This is usually a multiplier of the number of years left to run under the service contract/the length of the notice period and the director's gross salary and, usually, a sum representing the other contractual benefits. A similar effect can be achieved by including a payment in lieu of notice or "PILON" clause in the contract.

The advantage of such provisions is that they avoid the uncertainties of quantifying the contractual damages for wrongful dismissal which would otherwise be payable. An advantage for the director is that no account is taken of the director's duty to mitigate his loss by seeking further employment. This, of course, can be a significant disadvantage to the employing company if it sees a former director walk straight into a new job following termination. The real advantage to the company of such a provision is the fact that, by paying out under the liquidated damages clause, the company will be acting in accordance with the service contract and will therefore be able to rely on any enforceable restrictive covenants in the service contract. By contrast, if it breaches the service contract in dismissing the director, it cannot rely on the restrictive covenants.

It is becoming less common to see liquidated damages clauses which do not provide for a reduction to take account of accelerated receipt and the duty to mitigate. However, the Court of Appeal upheld a liquidated damages provision in a chief executive's service contract providing for one year's gross salary, pension contributions and other benefits in kind, notwithstanding that no reduction was made for mitigation (*Murray* v *Leisureplay Plc* [2005] EWCA Civ 963). In considering whether the liquidated damages provision amounted to a penalty clause (i.e. representing more than a genuine pre-estimate of probable loss arising on termination), the majority of the Court of Appeal held that a clause will only be a penalty if the party seeking to avoid the terms can demonstrate that the sum payable on breach is "extravagant or unconscionable" compared with the greatest loss that could follow from the breach. Further, the commercial context could be taken into account. The fact that the executive, in this case, had agreed to significant post-termination restrictive covenants was relevant. Looking at the clause in its commercial context, it was considered appropriate for the employer to pay out the full liquidated damages payment without a reduction for mitigation in return for the executive's agreement to these important restrictions. Companies may now be more likely to be bound by liquidated damages provisions even where the provision permits a departing executive to receive more than they would have obtained in damages at common law.

Liquidated damages provisions are also unattractive from a tax perspective (fixed severance payments pursuant to a liquidated damages clause are subject to income tax and national insurance contributions which can lead to a 12.2 per cent uplift in the cost to the company). A liquidated damages payment will not attract the tax-free element of a termination payment referred to above (currently £30,000) as it is construed by the HM Revenue and Customs as a contractual payment and not a payment representing damages for wrongful dismissal.

6.8.4 Summary – key provisions in executive and non-executive contracts

The following key points should be considered in relation to an executive director's service contract (or contract for service):

(a) the board should approve service contracts and variations formally only after ensuring compliance with the articles and a proper consideration of the company's best interests and the new codified directors' duties;

(b) shareholder approval is required for contracts for a period of more than two years, otherwise the term will be void and the service contract deemed terminable on reasonable notice;

(c) the term or notice period should not normally be more than one year;

(d) shareholders may inspect directors' service contracts or memorandum of terms (where no written directors' service agreement) and request copies upon payment of a prescribed fee;

(e) remuneration should normally be partly linked to performance;

(f) no share option should be issued to directors at a discount (save as permitted by the Listing Rules);

(g) long-term incentive schemes are subject to restrictions; in normal circumstances, shares granted or deferred remuneration should not vest, and options should not be exercisable, in less than three years; and

(h) termination payments should be fair and not a "reward for failure".

The following key provisions should be considered in a non-executive director's letter of appointment:

(a) the time commitment expected to carry out the role should be disclosed;

(b) remuneration should reflect time commitment and responsibilities of the role; and

(c) no share options should be granted.

Chapter 7

Share Dealing by Directors and Connected Persons

Paul Lester

Partner

Lawrence Graham LLP

7.1   Introduction

Directors have a special relationship with the company of which they are officers, in part, because of their duties of good faith in their dealings with the company and, in part, because of the nature and amount of information they hold about the company and its business.

At common law, the duties of directors in relation to their dealings in shares were not particularly high. The case of *Percival* v *Wright* [1902] 2 Ch 421 is considered to be authority for the view that, in the absence of any misrepresentation on the part of the directors, since the duties of the directors were owed to the company, no action would lie in respect of a purchase of shares in a company by the directors even though the directors had information which, had it been known to the sellers, would have led them to put a higher value on their shares. This general approach is subject to there being no particular relationship between the directors and the shareholders in question which would lead to a fiduciary obligation existing (*see* comments made in *Re Chez Nico (Restaurants) Ltd* [1992] BCLC 192 and *Peskin* v *Anderson* [2001] 1 BCLC 372).

The intuitive feeling that it is wrong for directors (and other persons) to deal in shares with the benefit of price-sensitive information has led to provisions, both statutory and non-statutory, with a view to restricting the freedom which directors would otherwise appear to have at common law. This has meant that, in relation to directors, English law has not had to become involved in developing theories of liability based on, for example, misuse of company property (confidential information), as has happened in the US. In the absence of such theories of liability which rely on interpretations of directors' duties to the company, this also means that the provisions of Section 170 and following of the Companies Act 2006 (general duties of directors) are unlikely to apply to dealings in shares by directors. There are also other provisions, such as the market abuse offences introduced by the Financial Services and Markets Act 2000 ("FSMA"), that, while not specifically aimed at directors, may well have greater implications for directors than for other shareholders of a company because of directors' privileged access to information about the company, its business, its financial position and prospects.

Directors are, of course, almost always in a privileged position compared to outsiders when it comes to information about a company of which they are officers. It is not considered necessary or desirable to prevent directors from dealing in shares completely (indeed, share incentive plans of one sort or another are thought by many to be good since they are seen as a way of linking, at least in part, the fortunes of the directors to the fortunes of the company, although the policy guidelines of the National Association of Pension Funds consider that the independence of a non-executive director may be compromised where such director has a holding of more than 1 per cent in the case of a company admitted to the Official List or 3 per cent in the case of a company admitted to AIM). The relevant laws and regulations therefore operate so as only to prevent dealings when the information is material or significant. The disclosure obligations provide transparency, to ensure that dealings are subject to scrutiny by the public and by the regulators.

7.2 Restrictions on dealing

Insider dealing is a criminal offence and therefore requires the more onerous criminal burden of proof ("beyond reasonable doubt"), whereas market abuse is a civil offence with the corresponding lower burden of proof ("balance of probabilities"). The perceived difficulty in successfully proving the necessary component parts of the offence of insider dealing led to relatively few prosecutions under the criminal law in the 1980s and 1990s. This was part of the rationale behind the introduction of the civil market abuse regime.

Notwithstanding the differing standards of burden of proof, however, given the nature and gravity of an enforcement action brought under the market abuse regime, the Financial Services and Markets Tribunal and the courts will need to satisfy themselves fully that the individual in question is guilty of the conduct alleged. Consequently, in practical terms the burden of proof in the civil regime is unlikely to be materially different from that under the criminal law.

When the civil market abuse regime came into force on 1 December 2001, responsibility for criminal prosecutions of insider dealing was also handed to the FSA. In light of the perceived difficulties in bringing successful prosecutions for insider dealing, the FSA initially tended to focus its efforts on using its civil market abuse powers to safeguard the integrity of the markets. This gave the impression that the criminal insider dealing laws were unlikely to be used. This has changed significantly in recent years.

In its business plan for 2008/09 published in February 2008, the FSA stated its intention to take enforcement action in order to achieve "credible deterrence". With that came a willingness to use the full range of enforcement powers available to it, whether civil or criminal.

In her speech in September 2009 on the FSA's strategy and approach to fighting fraud, Margaret Cole (the FSA's Director of Enforcement) said:

> "Historically we had used our prosecution powers sparingly. But that changed three or so years ago with our commitment to taking a tougher stance on markets offences. With that commitment came the recognition that criminal prosecutions send a strong deterrent message. We

are determined to deliver this message confidently and to be a feared and respected criminal prosecutor . . ."

It is therefore clear that insider dealing and market abuse are both important weapons in the FSA's armoury in combating prohibited share dealings.

7.2.1 Insider dealing

The offence of insider dealing is contained in Part V Criminal Justice Act 1993 ("CJA"). The objective of the law is to prevent those with inside information from using this information to their advantage to make a profit when dealing with others. A breach of the law is a criminal offence. The relevant provisions depend on there being an individual (and not a body corporate) who is an "insider" who deals in securities of a company with the benefit of confidential information, or encourages somebody else to deal, or who improperly discloses that information to a third party. As will be seen below, a director who (as a director) has information about the company, will almost always be an insider. Therefore the key issues which need to be determined in relation to insider dealing by directors will tend to centre around the materiality or significance of the confidential information in question, or as to the availability of one of the exemptions, and not around whether the director is an "insider".

The CJA creates three main offences:

(a) dealing in price-affected securities, that is dealing in securities on the basis of information which would, if made public, be likely to have a significant effect on the price of the securities;

(b) encouraging another to deal in price-affected securities; and

(c) improperly disclosing information which a person holds as an insider.

To establish liability, a number of elements have to be present. There must be "inside information", which is information which:

(a) relates to particular securities or to a particular issuer, or particular issuers, of securities (including information affecting its business prospects);
(b) is specific or precise;
(c) has not been made public; and
(d) if it were made public would be likely to have a significant effect on the price (or value) of any securities.

In contrast to the interpretative guidance provided under the market abuse regime, the CJA gives little or no guidance as to the meaning of key words and expressions. For example, no indication is given in the CJA as to the scope of the words "specific or precise" or what is a "significant" effect on the price of securities, which has resulted in a degree of uncertainty, particularly in relation to "significant". Although some counsel have expressed the view that significance should be calculated by reference to a (small) percentage of the market value of a share, there is no certainty as to what the percentage might be or even whether it is a percentage at all or an absolute amount. There is no judicial decision on the point and, until there is guidance from the courts, directors who have inside information which might have an effect on a share price should only deal with caution. If there is doubt about whether any particular piece of information might be price-sensitive and, if so, to what extent, a director might be well advised to seek professional advice from a stockbroker (probably the company's broker or somebody else who follows the company closely). Although, as will be seen below, there is no defence of reasonable belief that information was not price-sensitive, a court is likely to look more favourably on a person who at least took reasonable steps to confirm that the information was not price-sensitive than one who did not.

Some guidance as to the meaning of "made public" is given in Section 58 CJA, which sets out four situations in which information *will* be treated as having been made public.

These are that:

(a) the information is published in accordance with the rules of a regulated market for the purpose of informing investors and their professional advisers (e.g. by making an announcement through a Regulatory Information Service);

(b) it is contained in records which are required by statute to be open to inspection by the public (e.g. at Companies House);

(c) it can be readily acquired by those likely to deal in any securities to which the information relates or of an issuer to which the information relates; or

(d) it is derived from information which has been made public.

If information is available otherwise than in the four circumstances listed above, it cannot be assumed that it has been made public for the purposes of the CJA. This is another area of uncertainty on which there is no judicial guidance.

However, Section 58 does provide that information *may* be treated as having been made public even though the information:

(a) can be acquired only by persons exercising diligence or expertise;

(b) is communicated to a section of the public and not to the public at large;

(c) can be acquired only by observation;

(d) is communicated only on payment of a fee; or

(e) is published only outside the UK.

To establish liability for insider dealing, it must be proved that the individual concerned knew that the information was, in fact, inside information and that he/she had that information from an inside source. This also applies to "secondary" insiders who must know that the person from whom they have obtained information is an insider and that the information is inside information.

The information must be from an inside source. A person has information from an inside source if (and only if):

(a) he/she has the information through:

(i) being a director, employee or shareholder of an issuer of securities; or

(ii) having access to the information by virtue of his/her employment, office or profession; or

(b) he/she receives the information directly or indirectly from a person who is a director, employee or shareholder of the issuer of securities.

Generally speaking, an individual who is a director of the company will fall squarely within (a) above, and will thereby satisfy the test as to requisite knowledge, so that if he/she holds inside information (as defined), his/her dealings will be caught by the CJA.

Once it has been established that an individual has satisfied the requirements described above (i.e. that he/she has inside information, with the requisite knowledge, from an inside source), it must then be established whether he/she has committed one of the three offences.

The meaning of the word "securities" in this context should be noted. The term "securities" can clearly cover a wide range of investments but the relevant securities for the purpose of the CJA are defined in Section 54(1) and Schedule 2. The securities may not just be shares, but include debentures, warrants, futures, options and contracts for differences. In general terms the CJA is concerned with securities dealt in, or under the rules of, markets specified for the purpose by order (primarily London Stock Exchange markets, including AIM and PLUS) together with derivatives of those securities which are traded off-market as well as on-market.

7.2.1.1 *Dealing in price-affected securities (Section 52(1))*

Price-affected securities are securities in relation to which there is information which would, if made public, be likely to have a significant effect on the price or value of those securities. A person deals in securities if he/she:

(a) acquires or disposes of them;
(b) agrees to acquire or dispose of them;
(c) enters into a contract which creates the securities (relevant to derivatives);
(d) procures, directly or indirectly, an acquisition or disposal of the securities by any other person (which will often be

his/her agent, nominee or a person acting under his/her instruction).

The dealing must take place on a regulated market or the individual must have relied upon (or have been himself/herself) a professional intermediary. "Professional intermediary" is a person who carries on a business of acquiring or disposing of securities (as principal or agent) or of acting as an intermediary between those taking part in any dealing in securities, or indeed any employees of such persons.

7.2.1.2   *Encouraging another to deal (Section 52(2)(a))*

It is also an offence for an individual who has information as an insider to encourage another person to deal in price-affected securities in relation to that information, knowing or having reasonable cause to believe that the dealing would take place on a regulated market or the individual was relying on (or was himself/herself) a professional intermediary.

The person receiving the information does not have to realise that the securities are in fact price-affected securities and the inside information does not actually have to be given to the recipient. It is the act of encouraging that is relevant (and, indeed, there need be no actual dealing).

7.2.1.3   *Disclosing information (Section 52(2)(b))*

An individual who has information as an insider will commit an offence if he/she discloses that information to another person otherwise than in the proper performance of his/her employment, office or profession.

7.2.2   **Defences**

The defences to the three offences outlined above are contained in Section 53 CJA. The defences vary depending on which of the three offences is alleged to have been committed and are as follows:

7.2.2.1 *Defences to dealing and encouraging another to deal*

An individual will not be guilty of an offence of dealing or encouraging another to deal if he/she can show that any one of the following applies:

(a) that he/she did not at the time of the offence expect the dealing to result in a profit attributable to the fact that the information in question was price-sensitive information in relation to the securities;

(b) that at the time he/she believed on reasonable grounds that the information had been or would be disclosed widely enough to ensure that none of those taking part in the dealing would be prejudiced by not having the information (the "equality of information" defence); or

(c) that he/she would have done what he/she did even if he/she had not had the information.

An individual will also not be guilty of an offence of dealing or encouraging another to deal by virtue of a special defence contained in Schedule 1 CJA, if:

(a) the information the individual has as an insider is "market information" and it was reasonable for a person in his/her position to have acted as he/she did despite having that information as an insider at the time; or

(b) he/she acted in connection with an acquisition or disposal which was under consideration or the subject of negotiation and with a view to facilitating the accomplishment of the relevant transaction, and the information he/she had was market information which arose directly out of his/her involvement in the particular transaction.

For the purpose of this defence, "market information" is information consisting of any of the following facts:

(a) the fact that securities of a particular kind have been or are to be acquired or disposed of, or that their acquisition or disposal is under consideration or the subject of negotiation;

(b) the number of those securities or the price (or range of prices) of those securities;

(c) the identity of the persons involved or likely to be involved in any capacity in an acquisition or disposal;

(d) the fact that securities of a particular kind have not been or are not to be acquired or disposed of.

In deciding whether it is reasonable for an individual to have acted as he/she did whilst in possession of market information, three issues have to be taken into account:

(a) the content of the information;

(b) the circumstances in which he/she first had the information and in what capacity; and

(c) the capacity in which he/she now acts.

7.2.2.2 *Defences to disclosing*

An individual will not be guilty of an offence of disclosing inside information if he/she can show that:

(a) he/she did not at the time expect any person to deal in the securities on a regulated market or in reliance on a professional intermediary because of the disclosure of the information; or

(b) although he/she did expect the above, he/she did not expect the dealing to result in a profit attributable to the fact that the information was price-sensitive information relating to the securities.

It will be seen that dealings by a director, or encouraged by a director, for the benefit of himself/herself or another person in circumstances in which the securities are price-affected securities, will generally not fall within any of the defences described above. One circumstance in which there might be a defence, however, is when a director is in the exercise period for an option or for the conversion of a convertible security where the final date for the exercise of the option or for conversion falls during a period when the director would otherwise be prevented from dealing by reason of his/her holding inside information. In this case, it may well be possible to argue that the director would have done what he/she did even if the director had not had the information. In addition, depending on the nature of the information, the director may also be able to claim that he/she had market information and that it was reasonable for the director in his/her position to have acted as he/she did despite having that information as an insider at the time. The occasions on which these defences will be available, however, are likely to be rare.

7.2.3 Jurisdiction

There are rules governing the territorial scope of the offence of insider dealing, which vary according to the particular offence:

(a) *the offence of dealing*: in order to commit this offence, the transaction does not have to take place within the UK. However, the following requirements must be satisfied:

    (i) the individual must have been within the UK at the time when he/she is alleged to have done any act which constitutes or forms a part of the dealing; or

    (ii) the market on which the dealing is alleged to have taken place is a market which is specified by order by HM Treasury as being regulated in the UK for the purposes of the CJA; or

    (iii) the professional intermediary was within the UK at the time when he/she is alleged to have done anything causing the alleged offence to have been committed;

(b) *the offences of disclosing and encouraging*: these offences can only be committed if:

    (i) the defendant was within the UK at the time when he/she is alleged to have committed the offence; or

    (ii) the alleged recipient of the information or encouragement was within the UK at the time when he/she is alleged to have received the information or encouragement.

7.2.4 Penalties

An individual convicted of the offence under the CJA is liable to a fine and/or imprisonment (for a term not exceeding six months on summary conviction, or seven years on a conviction on indictment).

A transaction in securities, which is effected in breach of the insider dealing provisions of the CJA, will not be void or unenforceable. There is no provision in the CJA to compensate a "victim" of insider dealing and there are no other civil remedies, but there are provisions for compensation or penalties in other statutes. For example, if a person who has suffered loss as a result of insider dealing can be identified, the Powers of Criminal Courts (Sentencing) Act 2000 allows a court to make a compensation order requiring the person convicted by that court to pay compensation for any loss suffered as a result of the insider dealing. In addition, the Crown Courts have the power under the Proceeds of Crime Act 2002 to make an order confiscating the proceeds of crime.

7.2.5 Market abuse

The market abuse regime was first introduced in the UK upon the coming into force of FSMA in 2001, and amended in 2005 by the Financial Services and Markets Act 2000 (Market Abuse) Regulations 2005 to implement the Market Abuse Directive ("MAD").

When FSMA was initially enacted, three types of behaviour constituted market abuse, namely, misuse of information, creating a misleading or false impression to the market and market distortion. With the implementation of MAD, there are now seven types of behaviour which fall within the definition of market abuse. This reflects a difference in approach in prohibiting abusive behaviour whilst still covering broadly similar ground. The original regime defined market abuse in broad terms, but limited its application to circumstances in which behaviour was regarded as abusive by a "regular user" of the market. MAD, however, defines instances of behaviour which would constitute market abuse far more specifically, and the "regular user" test has been removed in all but two of the types of behaviour (listed at (3) and (7) below). These "regular user" provisions are remnants of the original FSMA regime which go beyond the minimum requirements of MAD and consequently the definition of market abuse in the UK is wider than in many other EU countries.

MAD was implemented in the UK with effect from 1 July 2005. At that time, the "super-equivalent" provisions were made subject to a so-called "sunset" clause, such that they would automatically expire after three years, by which time an HM Treasury review on the effectiveness of the regime was expected to have been concluded. In June 2008 the sunset clause was extended to 31 December 2009 in the hope that the European Commission's own review of MAD would be completed and the UK could align its market abuse regime with the rest of the EU. However, the Commission had not published any proposals by 31 December 2009 and the UK extended the sunset clause again, this time until 31 December 2011.

The types of behaviour which constitute market abuse are listed in Section 118 FSMA and are:

(1) where an insider deals, or attempts to deal, in a qualifying investment or related investment on the basis of inside information relating to the investment in question;

(2) where an insider discloses inside information to another person otherwise than in the proper course of the exercise of his employment, profession or duties;

(3) where the behaviour (not falling within (1) or (2) above):

(i) is based on information which is not generally available to those using the market but which, if available to a regular user of the market, would be, or would be likely to be, regarded by him as relevant when deciding the terms on which transactions in qualifying investments should be effected, and

(ii) is likely to be regarded by a regular user of the market as a failure on the part of the person concerned to observe the standard of behaviour reasonably expected of a person in his position in relation to the market;

(4) where the behaviour consists of effecting transactions or orders to trade (otherwise than for legitimate reasons and in conformity with accepted market practices on the relevant market) which:

    (i)   give, or are likely to give, a false or misleading impression as to the supply of, or demand for, or as to the price of, one or more qualifying investments, or

    (ii) secure the price of one or more such investments at an abnormal or artificial level;

(5)   where the behaviour consists of effecting transactions or orders to trade which employ fictitious devices or any other form of deception or contrivance;

(6)   where the behaviour consists of the dissemination of information by any means which gives, or is likely to give, a false or misleading impression as to a qualifying investment by a person who knew or could reasonably be expected to have known that the information was false or misleading;

(7)   where the behaviour (not falling within (4), (5) or (6) above):

    (i)   is likely to give a regular user of the market a false or misleading impression as to the supply of, demand for or price or value of, qualifying investments, or

    (ii) would be, or would be likely to be, regarded by a regular user of the market as behaviour that would distort, or would be likely to distort, the market in such an investment,

and the behaviour is likely to be regarded by a regular user of the market as a failure on the part of the person concerned to observe the standard of behaviour reasonably expected of a person in his position in relation to the market.

The definition of "inside information" (in Section 118C FSMA) is formulated in a slightly different way from the definition in the CJA. The information, for what are described as "qualifying investments" (including shares and debentures, but not commodity derivatives), has to be of a precise nature and:

(a)   not be generally available;
(b)   relate directly or indirectly to an issuer of such investments or to a related investment; and
(c)   if generally available, would be likely to have a significant effect on the price of the relevant investments.

Section 118C(6) FSMA states that information would be likely to have a significant effect on price if, and only if, it is information of a kind which a reasonable investor would be likely to use as part of the basis of his investment decisions.

An "insider" for these purposes is defined (in Section 118B FSMA) as any person who has information:

(a) as a result of his membership of an administrative, management or supervisory body of an issuer of qualifying investments;
(b) as a result of his holding in the capital of an issuer of qualifying investments;
(c) as a result of having access to the information through the exercise of his employment, profession or duties;
(d) as a result of his criminal activities; or
(e) which he has obtained by other means and which he knows, or could reasonably be expected to know, is inside information.

There is a general "defence" to alleged market abusive behaviour based upon the person in question being able to demonstrate to the FSA that there are reasonable grounds for the FSA (or the Tribunal) to be satisfied that the person:

(a) believed, on reasonable grounds, that his behaviour did not amount to market abuse; and
(b) he took all reasonable precautions and exercised all due diligence to avoid behaving in a way which would amount to market abuse.

In contrast to the statutory provisions on insider dealing, FSMA does provide guidance on how the rules are to be interpreted. Section 119 FSMA obliges the FSA to issue a code containing "appropriate guidance" to those determining whether or not behaviour amounts to market abuse. The code may specify descriptions of behaviour that, in the FSA's opinion, do or do not amount to market abuse; factors that in the FSA's opinion should be taken into account in determining whether or not behaviour amounts to market abuse; and descriptions of behaviour which are or are not accepted practice in relation to one or more specified markets. The code has statutory force and provides "safe harbours" of conduct: if someone behaves in a way which is described in the code in force at the time as behaviour which does not amount to market abuse, that person's behaviour will be treated under FSMA as not amounting to market abuse.

The code for the purposes of Section 119 FSMA is the FSA's Code of Market Conduct (MAR1). The Code of Market Conduct sets out specific guidance and examples for each of the seven types of behaviour constituting market abuse. In addition to the Code of Market Conduct, there is a limited, but developing, body of case law created by the Financial Services and Markets Tribunal, but with the relatively recent amendments to the structure of the FSMA regime implemented by MAD, this case law is currently of limited assistance.

Two key decisions, however, have come from the European Court of Justice (in December 2009 in the case of *Spector Photo Group NV* v *Commissie voor het Bank-, Financie- en Assurantiewezen (CBFA)* (C-45/08)) and the Court of Appeal (in April 2010 in the case of *Winterflood Securities Ltd and others* v *Financial Services Authority* [2010] EWCA Civ 423). Those decisions have emphasised the fact that market abuse need not be intentional or deliberately abusive in order to be the subject of penalties, whether the regime is dictated by MAD or FSMA.

There is an overlap between market abuse and insider dealing because market abuse can cover conduct falling within the insider dealing regime. Conduct which amounts to insider dealing will almost invariably also amount to market abuse. In addition, the market abuse regime has a wider territorial scope than the insider dealing regime and applies to any instrument admitted to trading on an EEA regulated market. This can have significant practical implications; for example, a director of a UK Plc who is in the US discloses inside information about his company (traded on the London Stock Exchange) to a US shareholder with the aim of encouraging that person to buy shares in the company. This would not amount to insider dealing under the CJA because of the CJA's limited territorial scope. However, it would be market abuse as it would amount to "requiring or encouraging" another to commit market abuse as the behaviour is in relation to an investment traded on a UK market.

Owing to the overlap between the two regimes, there is a risk of multiple jeopardy. The FSA has the power to institute criminal proceedings in respect of insider dealing as well as to institute proceedings in respect of market abuse. However, the FSA has stated that it will bring either market abuse charges or insider dealing charges against any individual.

Interestingly, the FSA is prepared to bring different charges against different individuals in relation to the same case. In March 2010 Malcolm Calvert was convicted of five counts of insider dealing and sentenced to 21 months' imprisonment and, further, in May 2010 ordered to pay a £473,955 confiscation order and £50,000 towards the FSA's costs. The insider dealing offences involved Mr Calvert instructing a friend, Bertie Hatcher, to acquire shares and splitting the gains made between them. The FSA agreed to use its regulatory powers against Mr Hatcher, rather than bring a criminal prosecution, as Mr Hatcher had agreed to assist the FSA with its investigations and prosecution of Mr Calvert. Mr Hatcher was fined £56,098 for breaching the insider dealing behaviour provisions of the FSMA market abuse regime.

7.3 The Model Code

7.3.1 *Introduction*

The Model Code is to be found in the Appendix to Chapter 9 of the Listing Rules of the FSA. The provisions of the Model Code apply in addition to the requirements of the rules against market abuse and the CJA in relation to insider dealing. It is principally a code of conduct which forms part of the continuing obligations laid down in the Listing Rules.

The restrictions imposed by the Model Code are, in some respects, more onerous than the CJA. This is partly in order to ensure that directors are seen to be above suspicion in relation to their transactions in listed securities of the company of which they are a director. It can also cover dealings in certain circumstances not covered by the CJA. As the introduction to the Model Code states:

> "This code imposes restrictions on dealing in the securities of a listed company beyond those imposed by law. Its purpose is to ensure that persons discharging managerial responsibilities do not abuse, and do not place themselves under suspicion of abusing, inside information that they may be thought to have, especially in periods leading up to an announcement of the company's results."

With effect from 6 April 2010, a company's listing on the Official List of the UKLA is categorised either as a "premium" listing or as a "standard" listing. The ongoing compliance requirements of a standard listing follow the minimum standards of the EU directives that apply to listed securities, whereas the ongoing compliance requirements of a premium listing encompass the additional requirements of the UKLA's Listing Rules.

Consequently, compliance with the Model Code is a requirement only of those companies with a premium listing on the UKLA's Official List. Companies moving "down" to a standard listing from a premium listing, or moving "up" from AIM, will already have a share dealing code in place and it is likely that they will retain their share dealing code (at least initially) in order partly to demonstrate good corporate governance and partly to protect the directors' position. It remains to be seen whether, over time, companies with a standard listing will choose to operate such a code.

A company admitted to AIM is subject to the AIM Rules, Rule 21 of which requires the company to ensure that its directors and applicable employees do not deal in its securities during a close period. In order to ensure compliance with Rule 21, AIM companies will commonly adopt a share-dealing code in line with the Model Code. Accordingly, whilst the Model Code does not directly apply to AIM companies, in practice most AIM companies adopt it as their share-dealing code.

7.3.2   Restrictions on dealing

In relation to dealings by directors, Chapter 9 of the Listing Rules provides that a listed company must require its directors and appropriate employees, including persons discharging managerial responsibilities ("PDMRs"), to comply with a code of dealing in terms no less exacting than those of the Model Code and must take all proper and reasonable steps to secure such compliance. It is also made clear that companies may impose more rigorous restrictions upon dealings by directors and employees if they so wish.

The Model Code is narrower in its focus than the insider dealing provisions of the CJA in that it only regulates dealings by restricted persons (and their connected persons) in securities listed on the Exchange.

The following are the activities which the Model Code states are *included* in the definition of "dealings" (so the list is not exhaustive):

(a)   any acquisition or disposal or agreement to acquire or dispose of any securities of the company;

(b)   entering into a contract the purpose of which is to secure a profit or avoid a loss by reference to fluctuations in the price of any securities of the company;

(c)   the grant, acceptance, acquisition, disposal, exercise or discharge of an option (whether for the call, or put or both) to acquire or dispose of any securities of the company;

(d)   entering into, or terminating, assigning or novating any stock lending agreement in respect of the securities of the company;

(e)   using as security, or otherwise granting a charge, lien or other encumbrance over the securities of the company;

(f)   any transaction, including transfer for nil consideration, or the exercise of any power or discretion effecting a change in ownership of a beneficial interest in the securities of the company; or

(g)   any other right or obligation, present or future, conditional or unconditional, to acquire or dispose of any securities of the company.

A director or other restricted person must not deal in any securities of the company without obtaining clearance to deal in advance. A director or company secretary must always seek clearance from the chairman (or any other director(s) designated for this purpose) before any dealing. PDMRs (who are not directors) and other employee insiders must not deal in securities of the company unless clearance has been received from the company secretary or a designated director. The chairman or chief executive (or designated director(s)) must receive the appropriate clearance from the chief executive or chairman respectively. If the role of chairman and chief executive are combined, that person must receive clearance from the board.

A director or other restricted person cannot be given clearance for a dealing if:

(a)   the proposed dealing is of a short-term nature. An investment with a maturity of one year or less will always be considered to be of a short-term nature;

(b)   the proposed dealing will take place during a "prohibited period" which is:

(i)   any period when there exists any matter which constitutes inside information in relation to the company; or

(ii)   any "close period". Close periods are the periods immediately before the announcement of a company's results, that is, the 60-day period immediately before a preliminary announcement of the annual results, or, if there is no preliminary announcement, the period of 60 days before the publication of its annual financial report (or, if shorter, the period from the end of the relevant financial period to the date of publication), and, if the company reports half-yearly, the period from the end of the relevant financial period up to and including the time of the announcement or publication. Companies which announce results on a quarterly basis are subject to a 30-day close period prior to publication of quarterly results (or, if shorter, the period from the end of the relevant financial period to the time of announcement).

"Inside information" for this purpose is as defined for the purposes of the market abuse provisions of FSMA (Section 118C, *see* Section 7.2.5 above).

A company must respond to a request for clearance within five business days of the request being made and keep a written record of that response and of any clearances given. Any director or any other restricted person that has requested clearance must also be given a copy of the response to that request and a copy of the clearance if granted. If clearance is granted, the restricted person must deal as soon as possible and in any event within two business days of receiving clearance.

The Model Code also provides that, if a person is in severe financial difficulty or there are other exceptional circumstances, and the person himself is not in possession of inside information, clearance may be given for a director or other restricted person to sell (but not to buy) securities when he/she would otherwise be prohibited from doing so. The director responsible for deciding whether to give clearance must decide, having consulted with the FSA, whether such "exceptional circumstances" exist. One example stated in the Model Code of where "an exceptional circumstance" could exist is where there is "a pressing financial commitment that cannot be satisfied otherwise than by selling the securities". Where clearance to deal is given in exceptional circumstances in a close period, Listing Rule 9.2.10R states that the notification to a Regulatory Information Service required by Disclosure Rule 3.1.4R must also include a statement of the exceptional circumstances.

In addition to being prohibited from certain dealings himself/herself, a director is also required to seek to prohibit dealings in his/her company's securities by connected persons or by an investment manager acting on his/her behalf or on behalf of a connected person during a close period. In order for the director to comply with this obligation, the Model Code states that the director must advise the connected persons of the following:

(a) the name of the listed company of which he/she is a director;

(b) the close periods during which they cannot deal; and

(c) that they must tell the listed company immediately after they have dealt in the company's securities.

For the purpose of the Model Code, "connected persons" are defined in Section 96B(2) of and Schedule 11B FSMA. Schedule 11B uses the expression "manager", which means a person discharging managerial responsibilities within a company (which will include a director of the company). The following persons are "connected" with a manager:

(a) members of the manager's family – that is, a spouse or civil partner, any relative who on the date of the transaction had shared the same household as the manager for at least 12 months, the manager's children, and the manger's stepchildren under the age of 18;

(b) a body corporate with which the manager is associated – that is, either a body corporate where the manager (or a person connected with him) is a director or senior executive who has power to make management decisions affecting the future development and business prospects of that body corporate; or a body corporate in which the manager (together with his connected persons) is interested in shares comprising at least 20 per cent of the body corporate's equity share capital or they are entitled to exercise (or control the exercise) of more than 20 per cent of the voting power at any general meeting of that body corporate;

(c) a person acting as a trustee of a trust the beneficiaries of which include the manager (or any person connected with the manager pursuant to (a) or (b) above) or the terms of which trust confer a power on the trustees that may be exercised for the benefit of the manager (or any such connected person). For these purposes, an employees' share scheme trust and a pension scheme trust are not included;

(d) a person acting as partner of the manager or as partner of any person connected with the manager by virtue of (a), (b) or (c) above;

(e) a firm which is a legal person under the law by which it is governed and in which the manager is a partner, or in which a partner is a person who is connected with the manager by virtue of (a), (b) or (c) above, or in which a partner is a firm in which the manager is a partner (or in which there is a partner who by virtue of (a), (b) or (c) above is connected with the director).

References to a person connected with a manager do not include a person who is also a manager of the company in question.

Dealings by a director as a trustee will be covered by the Model Code but, if the director or other restricted person is not a beneficiary, the Model Code will not regard any dealing in his/her company's securities undertaken by the trust as a dealing, provided that the other trustees acted independently from the director in deciding whether or not to deal.

Another area in which the scope of the Model Code is wider than the scope of the CJA relates to the grant and the exercise of options, or the award of shares, under employee incentive plans. Directors and other restricted persons cannot be granted options or be awarded securities or given other rights or interests to acquire securities during a prohibited period unless:

(a)   the award or grant is made under the terms of an employee share scheme; and
(b)   the terms of the scheme set out the timing of the award or grant and such terms have either previously been approved by shareholders or summarised in a document sent to shareholders or the timing of the award or grant is in accordance with the timing of previous awards or grants under the scheme; and
(c)   the terms of the scheme set out the amount or value of the award or grant or the basis on which the amount or value is calculated and do not allow the exercise of discretion; and
(d)   the failure to make the award or grant would be likely to indicate that the company is in a prohibited period.

Similarly, the exercise of an option or the exercise of a right under an employee share scheme, or the conversion of a convertible security, is not permitted in a prohibited period unless the company has been in an exceptionally long prohibited period or had a number of consecutive prohibited periods, and the final date for the exercise of such option or right or conversion falls during a prohibited period and the director could not reasonably have been expected to exercise it at an earlier time when he/she was free to deal. It should be noted, however, that where exercise or conversion is permitted, a director must not be given permission to sell any of the securities he/she acquires, unless the sale is to fund the costs of the exercise or conversion and/or any tax liability arising from it and a binding undertaking to use the proceeds in this way was entered into when the company was not in a prohibited period.

The general restrictions applying to employee share schemes, do not apply to saving schemes under which the director or other restricted person is contractually bound to pay by way of regular standing order, direct debit or deduction from his/her salary or where securities are acquired by way of a standing election to reinvest dividends or other distributions or are acquired as part payment of a director or restricted person's remuneration without regard to the provisions of the Model Code. For this exemption to apply, there are a number of provisions which must be complied with, including the relevant person not entering into the scheme during a prohibited period or varying the terms of his/her participation or selling securities of a listed company within the scheme, during the prohibited period.

A number of common corporate transactions are expressly stated to be not subject to the provisions of the Model Code, including undertakings or elections to take up entitlements under a rights issue or other offer or the actual taking up of those entitlements or allowing entitlements to lapse. The Model Code does not apply to the sale of entitlements to take up shares in a rights issue nil-paid to allow take-up of the balance of the entitlements under the issue, to undertakings to accept, or the acceptance of, a takeover offer, to dealings between directors and their connected persons or to certain dealings in relation to shares in HMRC-approved share option schemes and share incentive plans.

7.3.3 Interaction with the market abuse regime

It should be noted that a director might fall foul of the market abuse provisions mentioned in Section 7.2.5 above even though his behaviour is in accordance with the Model Code. In relation to the offence of requiring or encouraging another to commit market abuse, however, the FSA has given guidance that a director of a company will not be regarded as having required or encouraged another person to engage in behaviour amounting to market abuse where the director acts in compliance with provisions of the company's code of dealing implemented in accordance with Rule 9.2.8R of the Listing Rules (equivalent to the requirements in paragraphs 20, 21 and 22 (dealings by connected parties and investment managers) of the Model Code).

7.4 The Takeover Code

The City Code on Takeovers and Mergers (the "Takeover Code") was established to ensure the fair and equal treatment of all shareholders in relation to takeovers and it contains a framework within which takeovers are conducted. The operation of the Takeover Code is overseen by the Panel on Takeovers and Mergers (the "Panel"), which draws its members from major financial and business institutions.

The Takeover Code will apply whenever a person makes an offer to the shareholders of certain types of company to acquire all or some of their shares, where the offeree company is:

(a) a listed public company resident in the UK, the Channel Islands or the Isle of Man; or
(b) a public company resident and with its place of central management and control in the UK, Channel Islands or Isle of Man that is not listed; or
(c) a private company resident and with its place of central management and control in the UK, the Channel Islands or the Isle of Man but only if there has been some public market for its shares, or it has filed a prospectus, at any time during the 10 years prior to the relevant date.

Residence for these purposes means the place where the company has its registered office. In determining where a company has its place of central management and control, the Panel will take into account (amongst other things) the country in which the majority of the directors (executive and non-executive) are ordinarily resident.

The Code also applies to:

(a) a company resident in the UK but admitted to trading on a regulated market in one or more Member States of the European Economic Area ("EEA") but not on a regulated market in the UK;

(b) a company resident in another EEA Member State and admitted to trading only on a regulated market in the UK; and

(c) a company resident in another EEA Member State and admitted to trading on a UK regulated market and at least one other regulated market in the EEA, provided that the securities of the company were first admitted to trading in the UK only, or were simultaneously admitted to trading on a UK regulated market and at least one other regulated market of the EEA (and the company notifies the Panel and the other regulatory authorities that it has chosen the Panel to regulate it), or the Panel is the supervisory authority pursuant to the second paragraph of Article 4(2)(c) of the Directive on Takeover Bids (2004/25/EC).

The introduction to the Takeover Code makes it clear that the "spirit" of the Takeover Code is important and must be observed as well as the precise wording and the Panel has decided that if the "spirit" of the Takeover Code is not observed, this can be viewed as a breach, regardless of whether a particular rule has been broken. It can be seen, therefore, that the Takeover Code is not black and white, and is open to interpretation. If in doubt as to the meaning of any provision, it is advisable to seek clarification by consulting the Panel.

Directors are covered by the Takeover Code like other persons and will usually be regarded as "acting in concert" with their company. The general consequences of this are not described in this Chapter, but there are a number of rules in the Code which specifically deal with share dealings and their consequences.

(a) *Rule 4.1*: this Rule prohibits dealings of any kind in securities of an offeree company by any person, other than the offeror, who is privy to confidential price-sensitive information about an offer or contemplated offer, prior to an announcement of the offer or contemplated offer or of the termination of discussions.

(b) *Rule 4.2*: this Rule restricts dealings by the offeror and persons acting in concert with it (such as directors), by providing that such persons must not sell any securities in the offeree company during an offer period, unless consent from the Panel is obtained and following 24 hours' public notice that such sales might be made. If any such sales are made, neither the offeror nor persons acting in concert with it will generally be permitted to purchase securities in the offeree thereafter.

(c) *Rule 5*: if a person (and persons acting in concert with him/her) is interested in shares carrying less than 30 per cent of the voting rights in a company, he/she must not acquire an interest in other voting rights which, when aggregated with the existing holding, would carry 30 per cent or more of the voting rights in the company. If a person (and his/her concert parties) already holds 30 per cent or more, but not more than 50 per cent of the shares carrying voting rights, then the person and his/her concert parties cannot acquire any further shares. The Rule is subject to a number of limited exceptions (e.g. the Rule does not apply if the shares are acquired from a single shareholder and no other acquisitions are made within any seven days of that acquisition).

7.5   Disclosure of interests

Under the Companies Act 1985, a director was required to give notice to the company of any dealings made by the director in the company's shares. This requirement was repealed by the Companies Act 2006 with effect from 6 April 2007. For companies admitted to the UKLA's Official List, the disclosure of directors' dealings in shares will be governed instead by the

Disclosure and Transparency Rules of the FSA (the "Disclosure Rules"). For companies admitted to AIM, the disclosure of directors' dealings in shares will be governed by the AIM Rules.

7.5.1 Disclosure under the Disclosure Rules

If a director of a listed company or a connected person deals in the securities of the company, the company must be notified within four business days of the dealing in accordance with Disclosure Rules 3.1.2R and 3.1.3R. For this purpose, the definition of connected person is the same as for the Model Code (*see* Section 7.3.2 above). The company must then notify an RIS of any information notified to it in accordance with Disclosure Rule 3.1.2R by the end of the business day following receipt of the information from the director or connected person, in accordance with Disclosure Rule 3.1.4R. The notification required by Disclosure Rule 3.1.2R must contain information on: the name of the director or, where applicable, the name of the person connected with such director; the reason for responsibility to notify; a description of the securities; the nature of the transaction (e.g. acquisition or disposal); the date and place of the transaction; and the price and volume of the transaction.

7.5.2 Disclosure under the AIM Rules

A company admitted to trading on AIM must notify an RIS without delay of any dealings by a director in the securities of the company (AIM Rule 17). The notification must contain information on: the identity of the director concerned; the date on which the disclosure was made to it; the date on which the deal was effected; the nature of the transaction; the nature and extent of the director's interest in the transaction; where a deal takes place when it is in any close period, the date upon which any previous binding commitment was notified or the date upon which the Stock Exchange granted permission to deal in order to mitigate severe personal hardship; and where the notification concerns a related financial product, the detailed nature of the exposure. AIM Rule 31 requires an AIM company to ensure that each director discloses to the company all information needed by the company in order to comply with its reporting obligations under Rule 17. For the purpose of Rule 17, dealings by a director include dealings by that director's spouse, civil partner or child under 18 years (and any trust in which such individuals are trustees or beneficiaries and any company over which they have control or more than 20 per cent of its equity or voting rights).

7.5.3 Disclosure under the Takeover Code

In the case of dealings covered by the Takeover Code, there are additional rules for disclosure of a director's dealings in the shares of the offeror and the offeree company.

Rule 8 of the Takeover Code provides for a disclosure regime whereby parties involved in a takeover are required to announce what holdings they have, and dealings they have made, in the shares of the other parties.

An "Opening Position Disclosure" is an announcement containing details of interests or short positions in, or rights to subscribe for, any relevant securities of a party to the offer (other than a cash offeror). A "Dealing Disclosure" is an announcement containing details of any dealing made in relevant securities of any party to the offer (other than a cash offeror). For the purpose of Rule 8, the expression "relevant securities" includes securities of the offeree company which are being offered for or which carry voting rights; equity share capital of the offeree company and an offeror; securities of an offeror which carry substantially the same rights as any to be issued as consideration for the offer; and securities of the offeree company and an offeror carrying conversion or subscription rights into any of the foregoing.

Rule 8.1 of the Takeover Code requires the offeror to make a public Opening Position Disclosure within 10 business days of the announcement that first identifies it as an offeror (and of any announcement first identifying a competing offeror, other than a cash offeror). The offeror must also make a Dealing Disclosure if it deals in any relevant securities during an offer period, and such disclosure must be made by 12 noon on the business day following the day of dealing.

Rule 8.2 requires the offeree to make a public Opening Position Disclosure within 10 business days of the commencement of an offer period (and of any announcement first identifying any offeror, other than a cash offeror). The offeree must also make a Dealing Disclosure if it deals in any relevant securities during an offer period, such disclosure to be made by 12 noon on the business day following the day of dealing.

Rule 8.3 requires any person who is interested in 1 per cent or more of any class of any relevant securities of any party to the offer (other than a cash offeror) to make a public Opening Position Disclosure and, if he deals during the offer period, a Dealing Disclosure.

Rule 8.4 requires any person who is "acting in concert" with any party to an offer to make a public Dealing Disclosure if he deals in any relevant securities of any party to the offer (other than a cash offeror) during an offer period, either for his own account or for the account of discretionary investment clients. For the purposes of the Takeover Code, the directors of a company (together with their close relatives and related trusts) will be presumed to be acting in concert with the company. "Close relatives" is not defined, but would at the least include spouse and infant children (and may, depending on the circumstances, be wider).

A person who is acting in concert with a party to an offer does not need to make an Opening Position Disclosure itself. Instead, details of the person's position must be included in the Opening Position Disclosure made by the party to the offer with which he is acting in concert.

Therefore, directors will need to ensure that:

(a) their holdings of relevant securities are included within any Opening Position Disclosure made by the company of which they are a director; and

(b) they make a Dealing Disclosure if they deal in relevant securities during the offer period.

Rules 24 and 25 provide for the detailed information that has to be given in offer documents and defence documents respectively. As well as much detailed financial information and general information about the offer, Rule 24.3 (in the case of offer documents) and Rule 25.3 (in the case of defence documents) require that a detailed list of shareholdings and of dealings be disclosed. Thus, in the offer document, there must be disclosed (*inter alia*):

(a) shareholdings in the offeror (in the case of a securities exchange offer only) and in the offeree company in which directors of the offeror are interested; and
(b) if a director has dealt for value in the shares in question during the period beginning 12 months prior to the commencement of the offer period (and ending with the latest practicable date before the posting of the offer document), details of the dealings, including dates must be stated. If no such dealings have occurred this must be stated.

In the case of a defence document, Rule 25.3 requires that the first major circular from the offeree company board advising shareholders on an offer must disclose (*inter alia*):

(a) the shareholdings in the offeree company and in the offeror in which directors of the offeree company are interested; and
(b) if any director has dealt for value in the shares in question between the start of the offer period and the latest practicable date prior to the posting of the circular during the period beginning 12 months before the start of the offer period and ending with the latest practicable date before the posting of the circular, the details of any dealings, including dates. If no such dealings have occurred this must be stated.

Chapter 8

Directors' Powers and Proceedings

Caroline Carter

Partner

Ashurst

8.1 A company's constitution – statutory provisions

What is the position where:

(a) a company acts beyond the limits of the objects clause within its constitution;
(b) a board acts beyond the limits of its collective authority; or
(c) individual directors or other employees act beyond the limits of their own individual authority?

Are resultant transactions enforceable? What is the position of the authorising director(s)?

Section 39(1) Companies Act 2006 ("CA 2006") provides that "the validity of an act done by a company shall not be called into question on the ground of lack of capacity by reason of anything in the company's constitution". This covers the situation where a company enters a transaction which is beyond the scope of its objects, for example starting a pig farm where the company's objects are limited to the financial services sector. Such transactions would previously have been *ultra vires* at common law and void. Now, under Section 39 CA 2006, they can be enforced in many cases by third parties to the transactions.

Section 39 CA 2006 makes reference to the company's constitution rather than (as under Section 35 Companies Act 1985 ("CA 1985") its memorandum. This is because, under CA 2006, the memorandum of association disappears for new companies.[1] There is no requirement for new companies to have an objects clause.[2] For existing companies, the current objects clause is treated as a provision of the articles of association (the "articles").[3] In order to make the objects unrestricted going forward, an existing company may amend its articles by special resolution to remove the restrictions in place (and many companies have in fact done so). In these circumstances, Section 31 imposes a new formality in requiring additions, alterations or removals of statements of objects in a company's articles to be notified to the Registrar of Companies (on form CC04). The changes will not have effect until that notification has been noted on the Companies House register (unlike the CA 1985, where changes took effect when the resolution to effect them was passed).

While a failure to comply with an explicit requirement in the constitution makes a transaction unauthorised, and consequently voidable, it is not of itself void. The third party, if acting in good faith (the concept of good faith is explored further below), can invoke Section 40 CA 2006 to prevent the company treating the transaction in question as void. It may enforce the legal obligations that arise from the transaction against the company as if there had been no limit on the company's powers specified in its constitution. The only time when a transaction entered into by a company is void automatically is where the transaction offends one of the provisions of CA 2006 and is considered illegal.[4]

---

[1] Under Sections 8 and 9 CA 2006 the new form of memorandum of association is a document which is delivered to the registrar of companies on incorporation saying that the subscribers wish to form the company. The memorandum no longer forms part of the company's "constitution", which is limited to the articles and certain other resolutions and agreements.

[2] Section 31(1) CA 2006.

[3] Section 28(1) CA 2006.

[4] For example, giving or receiving a bribe or other bribery offences under the Bribery Act 2010, or corporate manslaughter offences under the Corporate Manslaughter and Corporate Homicide Act 2007.

Can the company's shareholders do anything to stop such transactions? What if the company itself wants to enforce the legal obligations created with the third party? Previously, under Section 35(2) CA 1985, shareholders were allowed to seek redress in court to restrain the company from acting in a manner which, but for the impact of Section 35(1) CA 1985, would be beyond its capacity, provided that legal obligations had not yet been created.[5] In addition, under CA 1985, for the company to enforce the provisions of the transaction against the third party, it had first of all to ratify the transaction by special resolution of the company's shareholders.

These two powers no longer exist under CA 2006.[6] This is because they are now considered unnecessary provisions in light of the fact that first, under CA 2006, a company may have unrestricted objects (and where this is the case the directors' powers are correspondingly unrestricted), and second, there exists a specific duty for directors to act in accordance with the company's constitution.[7]

The director(s) responsible for the transaction in question remain liable for all consequent loss which the company may suffer as a result of such a transaction, unless and until a separate resolution is passed by the shareholders. Pursuant to Section 239 CA 2006, any breach of the codified directors' duties may be ratified by the shareholders by way of an ordinary resolution.

For this purpose, the directors should be very careful to ensure that the company's objects clause is always wide enough to cover the proposed transaction (*see* Sections 8.1.1 and 8.1.2 below).

---

[5] This right was limited almost to the point of disuse because it was extinguished as soon as legal obligations (which were created by virtue of acts beyond the company's capacity under Sections 35(1) and 35(A) CA 1985) arose from the purported act. Further, this right was of limited use as shareholders would frequently not have been aware of the relevant matters before legal obligations had been created and therefore the company would have been bound to proceed at the third party's behest.

[6] Although the right to seek redress in court to restrain the directors acting beyond their powers under Section 40(4) CA 2006 remains, subject to legal relations not yet being created. In addition, directors may be liable to shareholders for exceeding their powers under Section 40(5) CA 2006.

[7] Section 171 CA 2006.

Whose acts bind the company for the purposes of Section 39 CA 2006? The wording of Section 39 CA 2006 (previously Section 35 CA 1985), "an act done by a company", was originally thought likely to cover an act purported to be done by a company by any of the following:[8]

(a) the company's board;
(b) an individual to whom the board has purported to delegate authority; or
(c) an individual whom the board has held out to a third party as having authority to act on the company's behalf.

The waters were muddied considerably by a decision of the Court of Appeal[9] which dealt with decisions taken by improperly constituted boards (e.g. insufficient directors attending to achieve necessary quorum). It now seems to hinge on the identity of the third party trying to enforce the transaction in question against the company and whether they are an insider or an outsider.[10]

Let us look first at situations where a decision is taken by an inquorate board and where the third party is an outsider. Whether a third party who is an outsider can enforce a transaction against a company in such circumstances, depends on whether they obtain the protection of Section 40 CA 2006. This provision works in favour of a person dealing with a company in good faith and has the effect of disapplying fetters found within a company's constitution on directors' powers to bind the company.

When is a person deemed to be dealing in good faith? Sections 40(2)(b)(ii) and (iii) CA 2006 provide that: a person "is presumed to have acted in good faith unless the contrary is proved", and "is not to be regarded as acting in bad faith by

---

[8] A narrower interpretation is possible though this would deprive the section of the protection that the European Communities Act 1972 intended it to give innocent parties dealing with companies.
[9] *Smith* v *Henniker-Major & Co* [2002] EWCA Civ 762.
[10] The existing case law dealing with points of law under CA 1985 will continue to apply to the equivalent provisions of CA 2006.

reason only of his knowing that an act is beyond the powers of the directors under the company's constitution".

This does not mean that lack of knowledge automatically means that the person concerned is acting in good faith. There may be some other vitiating factor present, and/or the person dealing with the company may deliberately fail to enquire as to the provisions of the company's constitution. This can cause the person not to be acting in good faith and therefore not able to avail himself of Section 40(1) CA 2006. The extent of relevant vitiating factors is not clear, and there has been insufficient case law to clarify the extent to which the courts are willing to offer protection under this section to the dealing party.

Section 40(2)(b)(i) CA 2006 states that a third party dealing with a company "is not bound to enquire as to any limitation on the powers of the directors to bind the company". However, despite this provision, where there is the possibility of the existence of vitiating factors, consultation of the company's constitution, although not legally required, may be prudent.

What if the company is a charity? By Sections 39(2) and 40(6) CA 2006, the provisions of Sections 39 and 40 CA 2006 respectively are modified in relation to companies which are charities. They do not apply to acts of a company which is known to be a charity, except where they are normal commercial transactions, entered into for the full market consideration, with persons who have no knowledge that the act is beyond the company's constitution or beyond the powers of the directors.[11] Further, when considering a change in the company's objects clause, the directors must be sure that they seek prior approval from the charity commissioner.

Turning now to the second scenario – where a decision is taken by an inquorate board and where the third party is an insider, for example, a director of the company. The 2002 Court of Appeal decision[12] referred to above involved a director of a

---

[11] Section 42 CA 2006.

[12] The director, Mr Smith, was the chairman of the company and as such had a duty to ensure that the constitution was properly applied. He was personally responsible for the error on which he then tried to rely.

company attempting, at an inquorate meeting, to assign a legal right which was vested in the company to himself. The Court of Appeal found by a majority that he was unable to benefit from the provisions in Section 35A CA 1985 (now Section 40 CA 2006), but their reasoning was far from clear. They did not go so far as to say that no director could rely on this provision, but decided that someone in his specific position could not rely upon it.[13]

The decision seems to have been taken, at least in part, to get away from a clear and logical but otherwise unpalatable High Court ruling that a decision of an inquorate board was not a decision of the board at all and therefore that no third party, whether an insider or an outsider, could rely on its protection. In the meantime, directors should be aware that they will have difficulties enforcing a transaction where they contract with their own companies and where they purport to hold a board meeting, either alone or with other board members, which is inquorate or otherwise improperly convened, at which the transaction in question is approved.

Even if a director can rely on Section 40 CA 2006, this is not their last hurdle. Section 41 CA 2006 qualifies Section 40 CA 2006 by providing that a transaction with a director (or other connected person) is "voidable" at the company's instance where the board's constitutional limits have been exceeded. This section covers transactions both where the directors carry out acts beyond the company's powers under its constitution or where they exceed their own powers to act under the company's constitution. It is a provision designed to deprive "insiders" of the benefits otherwise afforded by Sections 39 and 40 CA 2006 (as described above) to persons who deal with a company. It takes effect where directors have exceeded any limitation on their powers within the company's constitution (whether in the constitution, a shareholder resolution[14] or an agreement between members[15]) in connection with a transaction where

---

[13] *Smith v Henniker-Major & Co* [2002] EWCA Civ 762.
[14] The shareholder resolution can be in a general meeting or a resolution by a particular class of shareholders.
[15] The agreement can be between all members or the shareholders of a particular class of shares.

one of the other parties is an insider. Insiders for this purpose are directors of either the company or of its holding company and persons connected[16] with those directors.

Section 41 CA 2006 applies to any director (or other insider) who deals with his company, whether or not he plays an active part in the company's decision to conclude that transaction. Such transactions are voidable at the insistence of the company unless the circumstances specified in Section 41(4) CA 2006 arise.[17]

The directors who authorised the transaction in question, whether or not the transaction is avoided by the company, must:

(a) account to the company for any gain (whether direct or indirect) under the transaction; and
(b) indemnify the company against any resultant loss or damage.

Insiders other than directors can avoid this liability in certain circumstances.[18]

8.1.1 Drafting and interpretation of objects clauses

As discussed above, the drafting of a company's objects clause may no longer affect whether or not a transaction is enforceable by a third party against a company. However, the scope of this clause is still crucial for determining whether director(s) authorising the transaction acted outside the company's scope and are thus subject to personal liability for any resultant loss that may be suffered by the company in relation to the transaction concerned.

---

[16] "Connected persons" are defined in Section 252 CA 2006 as a person who is not a director of the company who falls into one of five categories specified therein, including spouses, children, stepchildren, partners and also any body corporate with which the director is connected.

[17] One of these circumstances when a transaction cannot be avoided by the company would be if the legal rights of a third party, who has acted in good faith, for value, and without actual notice that the directors had exceeded their powers in entering the transaction on behalf of the company, would be affected (Section 41(4)(c) CA 2006).

[18] To avoid liability under Section 41(5) CA 2006, the insider must prove that at the time of the transaction he did not know that the directors were exceeding their powers.

Under CA 2006, unless the company's constitution specifically states otherwise, a new company's objects will be unrestricted. However, it may still be of importance to new and existing companies how any objects clause they adopt will be interpreted.

Many companies have taken to including very broad wording within their objects clause to try to increase its scope to cover any business that the company may want to be involved in. To give the intended interpretation to such general wording in the objects clause, it is advisable to state that each paragraph is to be read separately and without limitation by reference to other clauses.[19] This prevents the courts from limiting the ambit of the objects clause to matters related and auxiliary to those laid out expressly in the clause.

However, if the constitution authorises an act expressly to a limited extent, this by implication forbids any act outside of that limit. For example, a power to borrow up to £1,000 will be read so that borrowing in excess of £1,000 will be unlawful under the company's constitution.

Where the memorandum is unclear, or is contradicted by provisions in the articles, then the following rules of construction apply.

(a) the memorandum takes precedence over the articles;
(b) the articles cannot vary the memorandum by purportedly giving the memorandum powers inconsistent with it;
(c) however, if the memorandum is ambiguous or silent then contemporaneous articles may explain the meaning.

As discussed above, this scenario does not occur under CA 2006 as the memorandum is reduced to a document containing only basic information in relation to the company's incorporation and will no longer form part of its "constitution". For existing companies, the provisions that were once in the memorandum are treated as provisions in the articles. It is as yet unclear if any

---

[19] This interpretation can be seen in the case *Cotman* v *Brougham* [1918] AC 514 where it was held that, once the registrar of companies accepts the clause, it is conclusive that the company has all the powers set forth in its constitution, however dissimilar they may be from what appears to be the main object of the company.

internal inconsistencies that arise following this transfer will be resolved in favour of those provisions that were previously contained within the memorandum.

8.1.2 Directors' personal liability

A director is liable under Section 41 CA 2006 for any damages suffered by the company as a result of the transaction, unless and until the company ratifies the breach of the duty to abide by the company's constitution. There is no financial cap on the potential liability.

A director will also be liable where he deals with the company or its holding company in respect of which he holds a director-ship. Any director of the company who authorised the transaction is also liable, pursuant to Section 41(3) CA 2006.

It is not just the directors against whom the company can have legal recourse. If the matter in question has involved a breach of trust by a director[20] and company property has been misappropriated, then the court may find that there is a constructive trust and that the third party holds the property in question on trust for the company. Other remedies may also be open to the company, such as common law tracing or tortious remedies for having induced a breach of contract or fiduciary duty.

8.1.3 Limiting directors' personal liability

As described above, third parties can enforce agreements against a company, even if the directors of the company exceeded their authority or the nature of the transaction exceeds the company's objects under its constitution. Under CA 2006, the company must pass a shareholder resolution if it is to absolve the director(s) concerned from personal liability.

Prospective directors will often seek to limit the effects of this potential personal liability (before accepting their appointments

---

[20] Not all breaches of directorial duty are a breach of trust, though all breaches of trust are by necessity a breach of duty. Breach of trust requires misappropriation of company assets.

to a board), whether by way of an insurance policy or an indemnity agreement.

8.1.3.1 Indemnity agreements

Indemnity agreements are commonly entered into between a director and the company in respect of personal liability that may be incurred by the director during and as a result of his office. There were substantial relaxations on the restrictions in this area introduced by the Companies (Audit, Investigations and Community Enterprise) Act 2004 (the "C(AICE)A 2004").[21] C(AICE)A 2004 was inserted into CA 1985 and is substantially repeated in CA 2006 under Sections 232 to 238. Under these provisions, companies cannot exempt a director from any liability attaching to him in connection with negligence, default, breach of duty or breach of trust by him in relation to the company.[22] However, the new provisions mean that:

(a) Companies are able to indemnify directors in civil proceedings brought by third parties (including regulatory authorities such as the Financial Services Authority ("FSA") and the US Securities Exchange Commission ("SEC") or class or other shareholder actions) against both the claim itself, and against the cost of defending the proceedings, even if judgment is ultimately given against him, provided such "qualifying third party indemnity provision" ("QTPIP") does not indemnify a director against any liability he incurs:

    (i) to the company or to an associated company;

    (ii) to the payment of criminal fines or regulatory penalties (such as a fine imposed by the FSA);

    (iii) in defending civil proceedings brought by the company, or an associated company, in which judgment is given against him; or

    (iv) in an unsuccessful application for relief from liability under the Companies Act.[23]

---

[21] C(AICE)A 2004 came into force on 6 April 2005. Indemnities granted before that date are not rendered invalid by the new provisions introduced by C(AICE)A 2004, provided they were valid under the previous Section 310 CA 1985.

[22] Section 232 CA 2006.

[23] Section 234 CA 2006.

If the indemnity is deemed to cover any of these liabilities, the QTPIP will be void in its entirety. It must therefore be carefully drafted.

(b) Companies are able to pay a director's defence costs (in civil or criminal cases) as they are incurred, even if the action is brought by the company itself. The director would still be liable to pay any damages awarded to the company and to repay his defence costs if judgment is given against him. However, where the proceedings are brought by a third party, the company may waive such payment under a QTPIP.[24]

(c) Companies are still able to purchase directors' and officers' liability insurance (*see* Section 8.1.3.2 below).

(d) The restrictions on indemnifying directors only apply to indemnities given by the company (or a group company). They do not catch indemnities given by a third party.

CA 2006 introduces a new provision allowing companies to provide qualifying pension scheme indemnity provisions ("QPSIPs").[25] Under the provisions, pension trustee companies (and their associated companies) are able to indemnify a director of a pension trustee company against liability incurred in connection with the company's activities as trustee of the scheme.

The company must disclose the existence of any QTPIP or QPSIP in the director's report. All QTPIPs and QPSIPs must be retained by the company for at least one year after they have expired and shareholders have the right to inspect any QTPIP or QPSIP. There is criminal liability for every officer of the company in default of the requirement to retain and provide a

---

[24] Payment of costs as they are incurred is permitted by means of a loan under Section 205 CA 2006 to cover expenditure incurred by a director in defending criminal or civil proceedings. Loans for this purpose are however restricted to amounts incurred in defending criminal or civil proceedings in connection with any alleged negligence, default, breach of duty or breach of trust by the director in relation to the company. In addition, Section 206 CA 2006 allows for a company to provide a director with funds for expenditure incurred or to be incurred by him in defending himself in an investigation by a regulatory authority, or against action proposed to be taken by a regulatory authority, in connection with any alleged negligence, default, breach of duty or breach of trust by him in relation to the company.

[25] Section 235 CA 2006.

QTPIP or a QPSIP for inspection.[26] Companies should be wary of using shareholder funds to protect directors from their own misdeeds where this type of protection could be negatively perceived by investors.

Companies wishing to take full advantage of these indemnity provisions are likely to need to amend their articles in order to permit:

(a) the granting of indemnities under sections 232 to 238 CA 2006;[27]
(b) the lending of money to fund defence costs incurred by directors in defending themselves in civil or criminal proceedings (the ability to fund directors' defence costs in litigation is an entirely new concept which should be effected in the articles); and
(c) the voting of interested directors on (a) and (b).

8.1.3.2   Insurance policies against directors' personal liability

For over a decade now, it has been commonplace for employers to take out insurance policies in favour of their directors. The relaxation of the rules in respect of indemnities discussed above has not lessened the attraction for companies in taking out such policies. A directors' and officers' liability insurance policy (frequently referred to as "D&O insurance") typically comprises:

(a) directors' and officers' liability insurance; and
(b) companies' reimbursement insurance.

---

[26] Sections 237(6) and (7) and 238(3) and (4) CA 2006.
[27] Some existing articles may already cover the Sections 232 to 238 regime if they allow wide enough indemnities, for example, "subject to the provisions of the Companies Act in force from time to time". Arguably though, some existing articles could be construed to exclude third-party claims where the director's defence is unsuccessful or claims are settled as directors can now be indemnified in such circumstances. A company's articles which exclude such claims would need to be amended to take full advantage of the CA 2006 provisions. The uncertainty arises because existing articles often allow indemnification "in particular where judgment is given in favour of the director", implying that it is not allowed where the director loses the case.

Frequently, companies will buy D&O insurance policies covering both of these elements. Equally, directors' and officers' liability insurance can be purchased on its own by directors in an individual capacity.

What matters are typically covered by these policies? Typical policies on the market cover:

(a) liability arising from actual or alleged negligent acts;
(b) errors;
(c) omissions;
(d) misstatements;
(e) misleading statements;
(f) neglect; and
(g) breach of duty.

In addition, they are likely to extend to:

(a) damages;
(b) settlements;
(c) legal fees; and
(d) expenses.

Matters unlikely to be protected include:

(a) the consequences of defamation;
(b) injury or death;
(c) pollution;
(d) dishonest, fraudulent or criminal acts or omissions;
(e) payments for punitive or exemplary damages;
(f) criminal, civil or regulatory fines;
(g) penalties imposed by law; and
(h) taxes.

It is important to note that many policies do not protect directors where they are being sued by their own company.

Companies considering taking out such an insurance policy should make sure that:

(a) the company's constitution permits such policies to be effected. If they do not, or the ambit of the objects clause is

311

unclear, the objects clause should be altered (*see* Section 8.1.1 above);

(b) the company's articles do not limit the company to only giving certain types of indemnity or taking out certain types of insurance, in which case the articles may need to be amended;

(c) the company's articles require an independent quorum of directors when such matters are discussed, in which case the articles may need to be amended;[28] and

(d) the insurance policy proposed covers all liabilities, against which the company needs to protect the director, that may lawfully be insured against.

Clearly, the company must also make sure that a policy is renewed when required to prevent the cover lapsing. Where a company effects such a policy in respect of one of its directors, it must state this fact in the next directors' report.

Directors should scrutinise the terms of their company's D&O insurance policies in order to assess whether there are significant gaps and if so, whether they should take out personal cover. (The argument that not having cover makes directors less likely to be sued is cold comfort to those faced with lawsuits.)

Provision A.1.3 in the UK Corporate Governance Code (the "Corporate Governance Code")[29] states that companies should provide appropriate D&O insurance to directors. A further recommendation of the Higgs Review that companies should supply details of their insurance cover to potential

---

[28] If all the directors are intended to be covered by a single policy, it may not be possible to convene a board meeting with an independent quorum if the articles do not permit interested directors to count in the quorum and to vote on matters in which they have an interest, provided that they have disclosed their interest. Most public companies and some private companies would need to alter their articles inserting a new provision relaxing the quorum requirement in these circumstances if the policies are to be approved by resolution of the directors and not by the shareholders.

[29] The Corporate Governance Code applies to all companies with premium listing for reporting periods beginning on or after 29 June 2010. For reporting periods beginning before this date, the June 2008 Combined Code (the "Combined Code") will apply. The Combined Code will continue to be available on the FRC website at http://www.frc.org.uk/corporate/ukcgcode.cfm.

non-executive directors before they are appointed, was not included in the Combined Code.

The Institute of Chartered Secretaries and Administrators ("ICSA"), in conjunction with various bodies,[30] drew up a guidance note for companies to use when obtaining D&O insurance.

From an individual director's point of view, the ICSA recommends the following:

(a) when seeking to join a company, a director should ask for written confirmation that he will be included in the company's D&O insurance and notified of any changes in cover that might affect him;

(b) a director should ask the company to confirm that the appropriate notifications have been or will be made to the insurer in order to start the policy cover;

(c) it is important to check that the policy covers "past and present directors" to ensure that cover continues after the director's retirement; and

(d) a director seconded to, or given an additional role in, an associated or unrelated company should check that he will be covered either under the main policy or the associated/unrelated company's policies.

In respect of the extent of cover provided, the following important points were made by the ICSA:

(a) *Jurisdiction*: Some policies restrict cover to specific geographical areas or exclude certain jurisdictions. A director should consider carefully the possibility of a claim arising in any area excluded under the policy.

(b) *Tax*: This is rarely covered. A director should obtain confirmation of the tax treatment in relation to the policy and his personal position in order to ascertain whether his benefit under the policy is taxable as a benefit in kind.

---

[30] The City of London Law Society, the ICSA, the Association of British Insurers, the British Insurance Brokers' Association and the ICSA Company Secretaries Forum. Guidance note reference numbers 030925 and 081105.

(c) *Insured v insured*: This is the case where policies fail to cover actions between parties covered by the same policy – for example, an action taken by the company against a director or one director against another. It is vital for a director to be clear on whether the policy would cover him against claims from the company itself and/or another director covered by the same policy.

(d) *Other policies*: A director may be covered under, for example, employer's or public liability policies or prospectus liability policies. Where a director is covered by more than one policy, he should make a point of clarifying the precise position in case of any conflict.

(e) A director should clarify the amount of cover provided under the policy per claim (there may be sub-limits for different heads of claim) and per year.

Another pertinent point to make, in light of the derivative action provisions contained in CA 2006, is to ensure that the D&O insurance covers the costs and expenses of dealing with and defending shareholder litigation.

8.1.3.3   Court order

The court may relieve a director of his personal liability in respect of proceedings for negligence, default, breach of duty or breach of trust under the powers granted to it in Section 1157 CA 2006 where it finds that:

(a) the director has acted honestly and reasonably; and
(b) that having regard to all the circumstances of the case he ought fairly to be excused.

In such circumstances, the court may relieve the director, either wholly or in part, from his personal liability on such terms as the court thinks fit. A company may indemnify a director for the costs of bringing a successful claim under this section.

8.2   Related-party transactions

What is the position where a director or someone closely connected with him wishes to transact with the company of which he is a director? The position with regard to unlisted companies, whether private or public, is less regulated than that for companies listed with the UKLA, which are subject to the requirements set out under Chapter 11 of the Listing Rules.

8.2.1 Provisions applicable to all companies

8.2.1.1 General provisions

Under Section 177 CA 2006, directors are required to disclose interests in proposed contracts. Any such declaration must be made before the company enters into the transaction. Section 182 CA 2006 addresses disclosure in respect of existing contracts and stipulates that a declaration should be made as soon as is reasonably practicable. The CA 2006 provisions are broadly similar to those contained under Section 317 CA 1985. However, under CA 2006, there are the following differences:

(a) the director's declaration must be of both the nature and extent of his direct or indirect interest (rather than a declaration of only the nature of the interest);

(b) (by implication rather than express provision) no disclosure is required where a private company has only one director; and

(c) there is no need to disclose anything that the other directors already know about or ought reasonably to have known.

The requirements of disclosure are not fulfilled by disclosure to a committee of directors.[31] Inadequate disclosure can lead to conviction, an unlimited fine as well as the civil consequences for breach of the codified duties found under Sections 171 to 177 CA 2006. Under Section 178(1) the civil consequences for breach of these duties remain the same as under the corresponding common law fiduciary duty and consequently, existing case law continues to be relevant.

---

[31] *Guinness* v *Saunders* (1988) 4 BCC 377. Inadequate disclosure resulted in the director being a constructive trustee of the benefits transferred.

Under common law, a director is bound to disclose to shareholders his interest in a contract which the company is party to or is about to become a party to. Failure to do so has two main consequences:

(a) the contract is voidable at the option of the company against any party who has notice of the breach of duty;[32] and

(b) any profit the director derives from the transaction can be claimed by the company.[33]

Whether or not directors can count in quorum or vote on resolutions in board meetings concerning transactions in which they have an interest depends on the provisions within the company's articles. These must be checked carefully to see if the Model Articles that apply under CA 2006 have either been varied or excluded.[34]

The Model Articles[35] broadly repeat a number of the provisions of Table A in respect of directors voting on transactions in which they are interested. Under Model Article 14 (which mirrors Regulations 94,[36] 95 and 98 of Table A), save as otherwise

---

[32] This right to avoid the transaction can lapse if the company either affirms the contract or takes a long time deciding whether or not to avoid the transaction.

[33] This remains the case even if the director is able to show that the profit would have been made had he had made the required disclosure.

[34] The requirements in the Listing Rules with regard to the voting of a related party are likely to colour the articles in most listed companies, at least to the extent that the interested director may not vote in the particular board resolution in which he has an interest.

[35] Under Section 19 CA 2006, the Secretary of State has the power to make regulations prescribing model articles. This power has been used to implement three sets of model articles for all companies limited by shares: one for private companies limited by shares, one for private companies limited by guarantee and one for public companies. These Model Articles apply to any company of that type which is formed and registered under CA 2006, to the extent that it does not choose to modify or exclude the provisions of the relevant Model Articles in its own registered articles. The Model Articles for private companies are much shorter and simpler than Table A as they are intended to be suitable for use by small businesses. The Model Articles for public companies cover everything covered by Table A, except matters which are now dealt with in CA 2006 itself. They also incorporate provisions dealing with a number of matters not dealt with in Table A, but which the articles of public companies commonly cover.

[36] Regulation 94 contains exceptions relating to the giving of guarantees whether by the director or a third party or the subscription for shares. The Model Articles for public companies refer to both of these exceptions, and also to voting on contracts about employees' and directors' benefits which are not "special". The Model Articles for private companies refer to the giving of the guarantee exception only. Both sets of Model Articles also allow for a director to vote on a transaction in which he is interested where (a) the company has disapplied (by way of an ordinary resolution) the applicable provision of the articles which would otherwise have prevented him from doing so; and/or (b) where the director's interest cannot reasonably be regarded as likely to give rise to a conflict of interest.

provided for in the articles, a director shall not vote at a board meeting or a committee meeting on any matter in which he has directly or indirectly an interest or duty which is material and which conflicts or may conflict with the company's interests. For these purposes, the interest of a person connected with the director is to be taken as if it were the interest of that director. A director shall not be counted in the quorum of a meeting in relation to a resolution on which he is not entitled to vote. If there is a dispute over a director's eligibility to vote, then the chairman of that meeting, during the meeting in which the relevant resolution takes place, shall decide conclusively in relation to any director (other than himself) whether that director was entitled to vote.

Even if the articles do allow a director to vote on a matter in which he has an interest (which under Sections 177 and 182 CA 2006 he must disclose), then, under the common law he is still obliged to exercise that vote in the *bona fide* best interests of the company. The equivalent codified provision under Section 172 CA 2006 is the duty to act in the way the director considers, "in good faith, would be most likely to promote the success of the company".

Regulation 85 of Table A permits a director (provided he has disclosed to the other directors the nature and extent of any material interest) to be a party to the transaction with the company or to be a director of the other company which is party to the transaction, without being as a result liable to account to the company for any profits made out of these transactions. Such a transaction shall not be avoided by reason of this interest alone. If the director has no knowledge of the interest and it would be unreasonable to expect him to have such knowledge, then it shall not be treated as an interest under Regulation 86 of Table A. Neither Regulation 85 nor 86 are replicated in the Model Articles.

8.2.1.2   Directors' service contracts

Directors are clearly interested in their own service contracts. As this interest is so apparent, there is no need to declare it to the board.[37]

---

[37] Section 177(6)(c) CA 2006.

The Model Articles for both public (Article 23) and private (Article 19) companies provide that directors' terms of service, including the amount of remuneration given, may be determined by the other directors, subject to the provisions of CA 2006.

Remuneration is deemed to accrue from day to day if there is nothing further to rely upon in a service contract. It is clearly open to a director to negotiate a service contract with the company. Indeed this is crucial to protect the position of the director.

The company must disclose the remuneration of its directors in the annual accounts.[38] The annual accounts must show a breakdown of the constituent elements of each individual director's remuneration package.

The extent of disclosure increased as a result of the provisions within the Directors' Remuneration Report Regulations 2002 (the "2002 Regulations"), which came into force on 1 August 2002.

For accounting periods beginning on or after 6 April 2008, the 2002 Regulations are replaced by Schedule 8 Large and Medium-sized Companies and Groups (Accounts and Reports) Regulations 2008 (the "2008 Regulations"). Both sets of Regulations prescribe the content of the directors' remuneration report, which is required by Section 421 CA 2006. The specific disclosure requirements under the 2008 Regulations remained largely unchanged.

Under the 2008 Regulations, the following is required to be included in the remuneration report of quoted companies and is not subject to audit:

---

[38] Section 412 CA 2006 specifies what must be disclosed. The basic matters which a company must disclose are: (a) gains made by directors on the exercise of share options; (b) benefits received or receivable by directors under long-term incentive schemes; (c) payments for loss of office (as defined by Section 215 CA 2006); (d) benefits receivable, and contributions for the purpose of providing benefits, in respect of past services of a person as director or in any other capacity while director; and (e) consideration paid to or receivable by third parties for making available the services of a person as director or in any other capacity while director.

(a) details of the remuneration committee, including the name of any person who provided the committee with advice which materially assisted it in its deliberations and the nature of any other services that person provided to the company;

(b) a forward-looking statement of the company's policy on directors' remuneration for the following financial year and subsequent years, including a detailed summary of any performance conditions to which directors' share options or long-term incentive plans are subject and the company's policy on the duration of directors' service contracts, including the notice periods and termination payments under such contracts;

(c) a statement of considerations of conditions elsewhere in the company and group (applies to remuneration reports for financial years beginning on or after 6 April 2009);

(d) a performance graph comparing over a five-year period the total shareholder return on the company's shares with a hypothetical holding of shares of the same kinds and number as those by reference to which a broad equity market index is calculated; and

(e) details of directors' service contracts.

The following matters must be included in the remuneration report and are subject to audit:

(a) the amount of each director's emoluments and compensation in the relevant financial year;

(b) details of share options and interests in long-term incentive plans held by directors;

(c) details of directors' pension rights and excess retirement benefits;

(d) details of compensation paid to past directors; and

(e) details of sums paid to third parties in respect of a director's services.

The obligation to prepare a remuneration report in accordance with the regulations falls upon those who are directors of the company immediately before the end of the period for filing and delivering accounts and reports for the financial year in question. Any such director who fails to produce a report or to comply with the rules as to the contents of the report is guilty of an offence and liable to a fine, unless he can show that he took all reasonable steps for securing compliance with the regulations.[39]

The Small Companies and Groups (Accounts and Directors' Report) Regulations 2008 came into force on 6 April 2008 and apply to companies subject to the small companies regime under Part 15 CA 2006 for financial years beginning on or after that date.

8.2.1.3   Loans to directors[40]

CA 2006 has substantially changed the position in respect of loans to directors. Previously, under CA 1985, loans to directors were prohibited except in limited exceptional circumstances. CA 2006 replaces this prohibition with a requirement for shareholder approval (except in the broadly similar exceptional circumstances found under CA 1985) for loans to directors and persons connected with directors. As under the previous legislation, quasi-loans, whereby the company takes on a director's debts on the basis that the director will reimburse the company are also covered, as are credit transactions where the company supplies goods or services to a director on the basis that there will be a later payment and the giving of guarantees or securities for loans.[41]

The director concerned and his or her connected persons are not precluded from voting on the resolution. In addition to obtaining shareholder consent, a written memorandum is required to be made available to shareholders before the resolution is passed. The memorandum must set out the nature of the transaction, the amount of the loan, quasi-loan or credit transaction and the extent of the company's liability connected with it. If the director or connected person is a director of the holding company of the company making the loan, then the holding

---

[39] Section 421 CA 2006.
[40] "Loan" is not defined in the legislation but is understood as payment on understanding there will be repayment.
[41] Sections 197, 198 and 201 CA 2006.

company's shareholders must also give their approval by way of an ordinary resolution.

CA 2006, unlike its predecessor, applies the provisions and exceptions uniformly to public and private companies (by removing the definition of "relevant company").

There are exceptions to the requirement that shareholder approval must be obtained under CA 2006.[42]

Outside these exceptions, loans or credit transactions made without prior shareholder approval are voidable at the company's option unless the company has already been indemnified or if such voiding would affect a third party who had no notice of breach of statute. Directors in breach of the loan provisions are liable to account to the company for the benefits they have received irrespective of whether the company affirms or avoids the transaction. This penalty also applies to connected persons who have benefited from loans and to the directors who authorised the transaction on behalf of the company.[43] The CA 1985 criminal sanctions for breach of the loans to directors provisions are repealed under CA 2006.

Even if such a transaction is permitted, if the recipient party is one of the company's own directors, the director of its holding company or a connected person of such director, then

---

[42] The exceptions under CA 2006 are: (a) loans to meet a director's expenditure in carrying out company business. The loan cannot exceed £50,000 (Section 204 CA 2006); (b) loans to fund a director's expenditure incurred or to be incurred in defending any criminal or civil proceedings in connection with any alleged negligence, default, breach of duty or breach of trust by the director in relation to the company. This is more restrictive than was previously the case under Section 337A CA 1985, as it defines the permitted heads of claim for which a loan may be advanced (Section 205 CA 2006); (c) loans to fund a director's expenditure in relation to regulatory action or investigation in connection with any alleged negligence, default, breach of duty or breach of trust. This is a new exception not found previously under CA 1985 (Section 206 CA 2006); (d) £10,000 loans or quasi-loans. (Note that there is no longer any two-month repayment requirement for quasi-loans) (Section 207 CA 2006); (e) £15,000 credit transactions (Section 207(2) CA 2006); (f) credit transactions given on not more favourable terms and not for a greater value than would be offered to an unconnected person of the same financial standing (Section 207(3) CA 2006); and (g) loans and quasi-loans by money-lending companies lending in the ordinary course of their business. Under Section 209 CA 2006, the caps on maximum amounts allowed under this exception are removed and a new term of "home loans" is introduced to cover loans made to facilitate the purchase of an only or main residence.
[43] Section 213 CA 2006.

the transaction must be disclosed in the company's accounts. This disclosure is required even if the person concerned only held office for part of the financial year.

8.2.1.4 Substantial property transactions

A company cannot enter into an arrangement with either a director of the company or of its holding company whereby the director acquires from or provides to the company one or more non-cash assets of a "substantial" value,[44] unless:

(a) the transaction is approved in a general meeting of that company (or if the company is a wholly-owned subsidiary by a general meeting of its holding company); or

(b) the contract is conditional on receiving subsequent shareholder approval.[45] (This is the one significant change in this area introduced by CA 2006.)

Section 190 CA 2006 does not apply to a director's contractual right to compensation for loss of office or to "anything to which a director of a company is entitled under his service contract".

Transactions contravening Section 190 CA 2006 are generally voidable by the company apart from in exceptional circumstances[46] when the transaction will stand. Directors are liable to account for profits made and to indemnify the company for losses suffered under such transactions[47] unless the director took reasonable steps to secure the company's compliance with

---

[44] Sections 190 to 196 CA 2006. A non-cash asset is of substantial value if it is: (a) not less than £5,000; and (b) greater than £100,000 or 10 per cent of the company's net asset value as determined from the last annual accounts. Section 190(5) CA 2006 provides for an aggregation of non-cash assets that form part of an arrangement or series of arrangements in order to determine whether the financial thresholds have been exceeded so that shareholder approval is required.

[45] Section 190(1) CA 2006.

[46] The exceptions whereby a company may not void the transaction are: (a) where it is not possible to restore to the company the asset or cash which passed to the director; (b) where the company has already been indemnified for loss; (c) where a third party has acquired rights for value without notice and would be adversely affected by making the transaction void; or (d) where the transaction has been affirmed by the company's shareholders in a general meeting within a reasonable time.

[47] Section 195(3) CA 2006.

the requirements relating to substantial property transactions or was unaware of the circumstances causing contravention.[48]

8.2.1.5   *General disclosure requirements*

The company must disclose in its accounts all transactions in which one of its directors or a director of a holding company had a "material" interest. If the board thinks the relevant interest is not material, then it is not to be so treated.

8.2.2   *Provisions applicable to listed companies*

Listed companies have more stringent obligations than non-listed companies in respect of related-party transactions. These restrictions are laid out in the Listing Rules and are summarised below. The Listing Rules define "transaction with a related party"[49] to include transactions between the listed company or any of its subsidiary undertakings and a related party and an arrangement in which the listed company or any of its subsidiary undertakings and a related party invest in or provide finance to another undertaking or asset (thus covering joint ventures).

The definition of "related party" includes not only persons who are (or were in the 12 months preceding the date of the transaction) directors or shadow directors[50] of either the company, any of its subsidiary undertakings or its parent company, but also covers associates of these related parties. Associates in the context of directors includes the director's spouse, civil partner or child, trustees of trusts of which the aforementioned are beneficiaries or discretionary objects and also companies in which the related person and any member of that person's family are entitled to exercise direct or indirect control over at least 30 per cent of the votes.

Where any transaction is to be entered into between a listed company (or any of its subsidiary undertakings) and a related party:

---

[48] Sections 195(6) and (7) CA 2006.

[49] Chapter 11.1.5 of the Listing Rules.

[50] Under Section 251 CA 2006, a shadow director is a person in accordance with whose directions or instructions the directors of the company are accustomed to act.

(a)   the company must notify a Regulatory Information Service ("RIS") without delay after the terms have been agreed and provide the RIS with the name of the related party and details of the nature and extent of the related party's interest in the transaction or arrangement. The notification must be made in accordance with LR 10.4.1;[51]

(b)   a circular containing the matters required by LR 13.3 and LR 13.6 must be sent to the shareholders to give them sufficient information to evaluate the proposed transaction and its potential effects on the company. The circular must include a statement by the directors that the transaction is fair and reasonable so far as the shareholders of the company are concerned and that the directors have been so advised by an independent adviser acceptable to the UKLA;

(c)   shareholders must have given their prior approval[52] of the transaction in a general meeting; and

(d)   the company must ensure, where applicable, that the related party abstains from voting on the resolutions[53] on the related transaction and must take all reasonable steps to ensure that the related party's associates also abstain from voting on such resolutions.

Listed companies are required to aggregate all transactions they (or any of their subsidiary undertakings) enter into with the same related party (and any of its associates) in any 12-month period which have not been approved by the shareholders. If such aggregated transactions would be classified as a Class 2 or larger transaction,[54] then the UKLA will require the company to comply with the requirements listed above as stipulated under LR 11.1.7 in respect of the latest transaction. The consequent circular sent to shareholders will then need to detail all other transactions so aggregated. LR 11.1.7 will not apply in respect of smaller related party transactions.[55] However, the company

---

[51] Under LR 10.4.1, matters to be covered should include the value of the gross assets concerned and, if it is a disposal by the company, what will be done with the proceeds.

[52] Prior shareholder approval is not necessary where the related-party transaction is made conditional on it being obtained before completion.

[53] This requirement covers board resolutions as much as shareholder resolutions.

[54] Calculated in accordance with Chapter 10.2 of the Listing Rules.

[55] Transactions where each of the percentage ratios referred to in Chapter 10.2 of the Listing Rules is less than 5 per cent, but one or more exceeds 0.25 per cent, (e.g. the assets ratio whereby the gross assets involved in the transaction is compared to the gross assets of the listed company).

must contact the FSA, before entering into the transaction, with written information of the details of the transaction, written confirmation from an independent adviser that the terms are fair and reasonable as far as the shareholders of the company are concerned and a written undertaking to include details of the transaction in the company's next published annual accounts.[56]

These provisions also apply where a particular contract is either varied or novated, where the agreement will be between the company and a related party, even if, when the agreement was originally entered into, there was no such relationship.[57]

There are a number of exceptions to the requirements set out above where the transaction falls into a specific category. These categories include those involving employees' share schemes and long-term incentive schemes, credit transactions under normal business terms, small transactions[58] and the grant by the company of directors' indemnities. Legal advice should be sought before relying on these exceptions to ensure that the proposed transactions fall within the categories exempted.

8.3 Delegation

8.3.1 *General*

There is not a lot of express guidance on how a company actually carries out acts. Certain powers are reserved to the members by statute.[59] Otherwise, the starting point is that the company, unless otherwise expressly provided for in its constitution or by board resolution, can only act after proposals have been agreed by the passing of a board resolution at a board meeting by the majority of the directors attending, provided quorum requirements for the meeting are satisfied. Without

---

[56] LR 11.1.10.
[57] LR 11.1.9.
[58] Small transactions for these purposes are those where each of the percentage ratios is equal to or less than 0.25 per cent.
[59] Powers reserved to a company's shareholders include the power to change the objects of the company, the power to change the articles, the power to change the company name and the power to ratify actions by directors otherwise beyond the capacity of the company.

express delegation of authority having been given to a group of directors, it is inappropriate for such directors to act without first convening at a meeting, notice of which has been given to the whole body of directors. Decisions of a majority of the directors made at board meetings which are not duly convened will be invalid. An exception to the requirement to hold meetings may be permitted where all directors acquiesce and a decision is taken informally,[60] although this should not be relied upon unless absolutely necessary.

For each board meeting, reasonable notice must be given to all directors, unless they are out of the country. The articles will provide for the business of the company to be managed by the directors. If the company has Table A articles or adopts the Model Articles under CA 2006, then the directors will be permitted to manage the company's business by exercising the powers provided by the relevant Companies Act and the constitution. Directors do not have any power to act beyond that capacity.

Company affairs would grind to a halt if this were the only legal method of taking company decisions. Often therefore, there will be express provision for committees of directors or even solely executive directors to manage limited matters on behalf of the company. There are some matters which, in the interests of good corporate governance, should not be delegated down from a board level. For listed companies, the Corporate Governance Code requires boards of directors to produce a schedule of matters which are reserved for the approval of the main board.[61] Paragraph 4.24 of the Cadbury Report (from which the Combined Code originated) states that such a schedule should include at least:

(a) acquisitions and disposals of assets of the company or its subsidiaries that are material to the company; and
(b) management of investments, capital projects, authority levels, treasury policies and risk management policies.

---

[60] *Charterhouse Investment Trust Ltd* v *Tempest Diesels Ltd* (1986) BCLC 1 at 9.
[61] Code Provision A.1.1.

The Cadbury Report also recommended that rules to help determine the materiality of any transaction should be produced and used by boards. The materiality of a transaction under these rules should then dictate the number of board signatures required for the transaction, with more directors needed to be directly involved for more substantial transactions. This helps to minimise the scope for misjudgement and possible illegality.

The Cadbury Committee also stated that boards should agree the procedures to be followed when, exceptionally, decisions are required to be taken between board meetings.

In light of the above, listed companies should take care before delegating approval of any of the following:

(a) interim and final dividend recommendation;
(b) significant changes in accounting policies or practices;
(c) material circulars to shareholders and listing particulars;
(d) press releases concerning matters decided by the board;
(e) board appointments and removals; and
(f) terms of reference for executive directors.

8.3.2 *Delegation to committees*

A company must have express provision within its constitution before it may delegate any functions to a committee of directors. There will usually be a provision to this effect in the company's articles. Regulation 72 of Table A (and Model Articles 5 and 6) provide that the directors of the company may (by board resolution) delegate any of their powers[62] to any committee consisting of one or more directors. Such delegation may be subject to any conditions the directors may impose. The board, when resolving to make such delegation, must not only clearly define the ambit of the committee's authority, but also specify whether the powers granted to the committee are granted in exclusion or in addition to the board of directors' own powers.

---

[62] Whilst "any" powers can be delegated, bear in mind the comments on good corporate governance above, particularly for listed companies.

Even if powers are granted exclusively to a committee, the board in all cases retains the ability to alter or revoke any authority given.[63] Such revocation can be effected by the board passing a resolution expressly revoking the authority of the committee. It can also occur implicitly where the board exercises a power that has been delegated to the committee where the original delegation gave authority solely to the committee.

The membership of a committee must be set out by the board, specifying if membership is to be for a fixed period or for such period until the member resigns his position or is replaced. However, even if the appointment of a particular person to a committee was for a fixed period, it may be revoked immediately by the board.[64]

The ability to delegate some of the board's decision-making powers to committees is an invaluable way of facilitating company management. It allows directors to attend, overall, fewer management meetings each and thereby frees up more time to develop the commercial aspects of the company. Abuse of the committee structure as a means of excluding a particular director or minority of directors who are properly entitled and obliged to participate in the management, not just by voting but also by having general corporate financial and commercial information available to them, is not permitted.[65]

The aim of releasing some directors from the need to attend some meetings (as allowed by the committee structure) does not mean that it entitles a company to take matters discussed at committee meetings any less seriously. Minutes should be kept of all committee proceedings in the same way as is required by Section 248 CA 2006 for board meetings.

Good corporate governance recognises that some matters are better dealt with by committees, rather than by the whole board, particularly where factions of directors are bound to be

---

[63] Any agreement that purports irrevocably to delegate the directors' powers would be viewed by the courts to be contrary to public policy and unenforceable.

[64] *Manton v Brighton Corp* [1951] 2 KB 393.

[65] *Bray v Smith* [1908] 124 LT Jo 293.

interested in the outcome, for example, producing general company policy on directors' pay.

The Corporate Governance Code requires that companies maintain three committees:

(a) Audit committee[66]
     The audit committee's function is to establish formal and transparent arrangements for the application of corporate reporting, risk management and internal control principles and ensure an appropriate relationship with the company's auditors is maintained.
(b) Nominations committee[67]
     The nominations committee's aim should be to establish formal, rigorous and transparent procedures for the appointment of new directors to the board. Its duties include the constant evaluation of the make-up of the board, in terms of skills and experience, to assess where and what type of new appointments need to be made.
(c) Remuneration committee[68]
     The remuneration committee's duties should principally involve establishing a balance between putting together sufficiently attractive remuneration and benefits packages to retain and motivate directors and senior management of the quality required to run the company successfully and ensuring that such packages are not more generous than is necessary and are made up of a significant proportion of rewards linked to corporate and individual performance.

Independent non-executive directors should make up the entirety of the audit committee and the remuneration committee and the majority of the nominations committee. In the interests of transparency, the three committees should make available[69] their terms of reference, explaining their roles and the authority delegated to them by the board.

---

[66] Corporate Governance Code Provision C.3.
[67] Corporate Governance Code Provision B.2. Formerly Code Provision A.4 of the Combined Code.
[68] Corporate Governance Code Provision D.1. Formerly Code Provision B.1 of the Combined Code.
[69] This requirement to make the information available would be met by making it available on request and by including the information on the company's website.

If a board delegates power to a committee without any provision relating to the committee's quorum, all acts of the committee must be done in the presence of all members of the committee. In these circumstances (which would be unusual) the committee has no power to add to their number or to fill a vacancy.

Regardless of the nature and number of matters delegated to committee level for listed companies, the Corporate Governance Code requires that the board should still meet regularly.[70]

8.3.3 Delegation to individual executives

Delegation may be to individuals, particularly to executive directors of a company who have various areas of specialised business expertise. The usual executive posts that a reasonable sized company will fill include the managing director or chief executive officer, chairman, sales director and finance director. Regulation 91 of Table A (and Model Articles 12, 13 and 31) permits directors to appoint a chairman of the board who may be provided with a casting vote, where votes are otherwise evenly distributed in a directors' board meeting. The chairman by his title does not have any particular areas of responsibility other than those set out expressly.

The authority to delegate matters down to other individual directors comes from Regulations 72 and 84 of Table A (Public Company Model Articles 5 and 19) which, in addition to allowing delegation by the board to a managing director, also allow the appointment by the directors of the board of "one or more of their number ... to any other executive office". The Model Articles for public and private companies also give directors wide powers to delegate duties and decisions, to individuals and committees. If the company has not adopted Table A articles (or the Model Articles), then there must be an article expressly on this point. The board are unable to delegate to a managing director unless the articles or a resolution enable them to do so.[71] Any such delegation to an executive, as to a committee, may be made subject to any conditions the directors

---

[70] Code Provision A.1.1.
[71] *Nelson v James Nelson & Sons* [1914] 2 KB 770.

may impose and either collaterally with or to the exclusion of their own powers and may be revoked or altered. Executives other than the managing director are usually appointed with a restricted area of responsibility such as finance, marketing etc. Any such executive appointee may not have to retire by rotation, subject to the provisions of the company's articles of association.[72] In *Hely-Hutchinson* v *Brayhead Ltd*,[73] Justice Roskill disagreed that "mere status, derived from the holding of a particular office [. . .] of itself implies an authority which would not otherwise exist".[74] The case itself concerned a chairman acting as managing director.

The level of power that ought to be delegated to a particular individual is reflected partly by the executive status given in their service contract and partly by their area of expertise and past experience. Some executive posts have connotations of holding more power than others, though the exact remit in each case is a matter to be set by the board. The most important director of a company is often described as the "managing director" or as the "chief executive". In relation to listed companies, the Corporate Governance Code recognises the power that is frequently delegated to the chief executive and states that one person should not hold both the roles of chief executive and chairman. The board must agree in writing a clearly established division of responsibilities between the chairman and the chief executive.[75] The key is to have a strong and independent non-executive element, with a recognised senior member, on the board. Consequently, the Corporate Governance Code also provides that a chief executive officer should not become a chairman of his company even once he has stepped down from the former role.[76]

---

[72] Regulation 84 of Table A states that a managing director and a director holding any other executive office shall not be subject to retirement by rotation. By contrast, Model Article 21 for public companies requires that directors who have been appointed by the directors since the last AGM, or who were not appointed or reappointed at one of the preceding two AGMs, must retire from office and may offer themselves for reappointment. The Model Articles for private companies are silent on this point.

[73] *Hely-Hutchinson* v *Brayhead Ltd* [1968] 1 QB 549.

[74] However, he conceded such an implication might be made in some cases.

[75] Code Provision A.2.1.

[76] Where, in exceptional circumstances, the board decides that a chief executive should become chairman, the board should consult major shareholders in advance and should set out its reasons for the decision to shareholders at the time of the appointment and in the next annual report (Code Provision A.3.1). Formerly Code Provision A.2.2 of the Combined Code.

There can, in certain circumstances, be cases of implied delegation. These are generally argued for when something has gone wrong and the company has sought to limit its liability by claiming that a particular director had not had the requisite power delegated to him and that consequently the company was not bound. Where an individual has matters of authority impliedly delegated down to him, then the company can be held to any transactions completed with third parties in good faith (as discussed above in Section 8.1). In the *Charterhouse* case above, Hoffmann J found that there had been acquiescence by two of the three directors of a company in respect of the third director agreeing to surrender tax losses for the company. Such a finding was on the basis that the other two directors were content to acquiesce to whatever lawful terms were agreed between the third director and the other party. It did not matter that there had not been a formal board meeting delegating such power. This is not to say that there can be an implied delegation of all matters by acquiescence.[77]

8.3.4 Delegation by directors to non-officer employees and other parties

It was Romer J's view in *Re City Equitable Fire Insurance Co*[78] that the larger the business, the more numerous and the more important would be the matters that the directors would have to leave to the managers, the accountants and the rest of the staff.

In a similar way to the responsibility ministers take for the actions or omissions of any civil servant within their department, so directors will almost invariably pass down a certain level of responsibility and day-to-day running of aspects of the areas they oversee, whilst still retaining ultimate responsibility for the internal management of more junior members.

Directors are permitted to rely upon non-employee advisers in particular circumstances. In the case of *Stevens* v *Hoare*,[79] it was

---

[77] The case *Mitchell & Hobbs (UK) Ltd* v *Mill* [1996] 2 BCLC 102 is the authority that there is no unilateral right on the part of a managing director to take proceedings on a company's behalf in the absence of express delegation by the board.
[78] *Re City Equitable Fire Insurance Co* [1925] Ch 407.
[78] *Stevens* v *Hoare* (1904) 20 T.L.R. 407.

ruled that, in the context of the preparation of a prospectus, directors are entitled to rely upon the assistance and advice of the company's legal advisers. Indeed, for listed companies, the Corporate Governance Code provides that there should be a procedure agreed by the board of directors in the furtherance of their duties to take independent professional advice if necessary, at the company's expense.[80]

8.3.5 Continuing duties of a director towards matters delegated

A director is entitled, in the absence of any matters that should put him on notice, to trust his fellow directors and all other officers of the company to perform those matters which may be properly delegated to them. But whilst the board may make these delegations, they cannot abdicate responsibilities for these powers and cannot relieve themselves of the duty to continue to supervise the management of these matters. This principle was most publicly borne out in the trial of the various directors of the Barings group after the collapse of Barings Bank, with total losses of £927 million caused largely by a single trader, Nick Leeson.

In the *Barings*[81] case, it was accepted by the Companies Court that boards may delegate specific tasks and functions within the company or group to managers and/or employees. Jonathan Parker J emphasised however that this does not mean that directors (either individually or collectively) cease to bear any responsibility for discharging the delegated function. Directors have, collectively and individually, an ongoing duty to acquire and maintain a sufficient knowledge and understanding of the company's business, including supervision of the carrying out of delegated functions, to enable them properly to discharge their duties as directors. The judge did not attempt to formulate a rule of universal application as to directors' residual duties of monitoring and supervision referred to above. The extent of these duties, and the question of whether they have been discharged, depend upon the particular facts of each case,

---

[80] Code Provision B.5.1. Formerly A.5.2 of the Combined Code.
[81] *Re Barings Plc (No 5)* [1999] 1 BCLC 433.

including the director's role in the management of the company.

As a result of *Barings*, all directors, whatever their status, have a basic duty to keep themselves regularly informed of company affairs (especially finance matters) and to participate, at least to some degree, in the supervision and monitoring of their co-directors and other delegates. This duty continues to exist even if directors are kept very busy by other particular aspects of their work. The managing structure is not obliged to accommodate the amount of time a director may be spending doing the business of the company, for example winning deals.[82] Less time to spend on supervision does not lead to a lessening of the duty to supervise. Merely sitting in on meetings without making inquiries and without having acquired the background knowledge to understand at least a proportion of the content does not aid fulfilment of the duty.

Though previous law[83] had led to the conclusion that non-executive directors had an equivalent level of directorial responsibility, one implication of Barings is that more will be expected of executive directors than of non-executive directors. This does not of course mean that non-executive directors have no responsibility.

The level of the individual director's remuneration is now a relevant factor in determining the extent of his duty,[84] as more is expected of a highly paid director. Similarly, the standard of the basic duty may be scaled upwards to reflect the level of each director's skill and experience.[85] This will extend to the level of skill and experience which a director holds himself out as having, if different.

---

[82] The court rejected such a submission by one of the Barings directors, Mr Turkey.

[83] After the case of *Dorchester Finance Co Ltd* v *Stebbing* [1989] BCLC 498, a strong message was received that non-executive directors have the same legal responsibilities as any other director and will be subject to all the statutory restrictions affecting directors.

[84] Sir Richard Scott V-C in his judgment in *Barings* commented: "Status within an organisation carries with it commensurate rewards. These rewards are matched by the weight of the responsibilities that the office carries with it, and those responsibilities require diligent attention from time to time to the question whether the system that has been put in place and over which the individual is presiding is operating efficiently, and whether individuals to whom duties, in accordance with the system, have been delegated are discharging those duties efficiently".

[85] *Re Continental Assurance Co of London Plc* [1997] 1 BCLC 48.

The directors in the Barings case were disqualified under the Company Directors Disqualification Act 1986, following the failures of internal management controls. The controls were found to be "crass" and "absolute" in that they allowed Mr Leeson to operate in an entirely unacceptable manner. There was no challenge to the honesty or integrity of the three respondents, but as a result of such disqualification, they were nevertheless prevented from taking up directorships for considerable periods.[86]

What has been the impact of *Barings*? The Corporate Governance Code expressly requires listed companies' boards to maintain a sound system of internal control to safeguard shareholders' investment and the company's assets. The Financial Reporting Council ("FRC") also maintain further specific guidance on internal control, known as the Turnbull Guidance. The current version of the Turnbull Guidance has been in force since 1 January 2006, although the FRC are currently considering an updated version as part of its wider review of the Combined Code.[87]

In its current form, the Turnbull Guidance states that: "a company's system of internal control has a key role in the management of risks that are significant to the fulfilment of its business objectives". It indicates that the company's internal control system should:

(a) be embedded within its operations and not be treated as a separate exercise;
(b) be able to respond to changing risks within and outside the company; and
(c) enable each company to apply it in an appropriate manner related to its key risks.

The guidance requires companies to identify, evaluate and manage their significant risks and to assess the effectiveness of the related internal control system. Boards of directors are called on to review regularly reports on the effectiveness of the system of internal control in managing key risks, and to

---

[86] Under the 1986 Act the court can fix an appropriate period of up to 15 years.
[87] Now that the Corporate Governance Code has been published, the further review of the Turnbull Guidance has been scheduled for the second half of 2010.

undertake an annual assessment for the purpose of making their statements on internal control in the annual report.[88] The guidance encourages directors to use the annual report as a communication opportunity in order to relay a positive message to investors and shareholders alike in respect of the board's attitude towards risk management, internal control and the framework within which these are effectively managed and reviewed.

The current Turnbull Guidance can be found on the FRC's website.[89]

8.3.6   *Where there has been no official delegation of authority*

While Section 40 CA 2006 (as discussed above in Section 8.1) does not operate to extend directly the powers of anyone else other than the board of directors, such as a committee or any individual director, it is possible that, under the law of agency, the acts of an individual may still bind the company where there has been no official delegation of authority.

When can the third party rely on agreements it has made with this unauthorised person who acts beyond the bounds of his authority? The individual may bind the company to the agreement if it acts as the company's agent. The law of agency is complex but, essentially, the individual agent must have either actual authority (which clearly is not applicable here) or ostensible authority to do the thing which he does on behalf of the company (his principal).

When will an individual have ostensible authority? What amounts to ostensible authority will vary with circumstances. If a company (or a person with actual authority for a particular matter) represents that an individual has authority delegated down to him for that matter, then the company will, if the third party relies on this representation, be bound by the acts of the individual and prevented from claiming that the individual did not have such authority. There is no such thing as a

---

[88] As required by Corporate Governance Code Provision C.2.1 and LR 9.8.6.
[89] www.frc.org.uk/corporate/internalcontrol.cfm.

self-authorising agent. In some cases, ostensible authority arises not from a positive act, but from acquiescence by the company to an individual's assumed role, such as permitting a director or ex-director to continue to act as if he were still authorised to do so even though his authority had been terminated.

To determine what is usually or customarily within the scope of the authority of a particular agent, the relevant factors to consider include the principal's kind of business, the role of the office-holder in that business, current business practices and all other material circumstances. The main executive posts and the ostensible authority that a third party can generally attribute to them are set out below:

(a) Managing director/chief executive – a company's managing director/chief executive may generally be presumed to have wide authority to manage the company's ordinary business. An individual permitted to manage the company's day-to-day business may be treated as if he were a managing director.

(b) Chairman – the chairman, by virtue of that office alone, enjoys no special authority to act on behalf of the company in dealings with third parties.[90] He should be treated, in the absence of holding any particular executive posts, as any other director.

(c) Company secretary – while in the past, company secretaries had a limited role, nowadays the company secretary enjoys a wider range of responsibility for the company's administrative and legal activities.[91]

(d) Finance director – finance directors generally have ostensible authority for accounting and treasury matters.

(e) Other executive directors – other executive directors, in addition to their authority as ordinary directors, generally have such authority as is usual for somebody occupying

---

[90] *Hely-Hutchinson* v *Brayhead Ltd* [1968] 1 QB 549 – although in this case the chairman was held to have actual implied authority on the basis that he was also the *de facto* managing director.

[91] The earlier case law as regards the ostensible authority of a company secretary must be regarded with caution since the role of the secretary has blossomed. It is reasonable now to expect a wider scope of ostensible authority. However, it is worth noting that under Section 270 CA 2006, there is no longer a requirement for a private company to have a company secretary.

the position they hold as a result of their service contract with the company. This will therefore vary largely from domain to domain.

(f) Ordinary directors – unless the articles provide otherwise, a director does not have authority to bind the company unless he acts as part of the board passing resolutions. An individual director's ostensible authority to act for the company is as a result so limited as to be almost negligible.

8.4   Directors' access to company books

Directors have long had an acknowledged right to inspect the company's books, either at a board meeting or elsewhere. This right extends not just to the minutes of directors' meetings, and to the company's accounting records. In the case of *Conway* v *Petronius Clothing Co*[92] Slade J clarified that this right of inspection derived not from Section 147[93] Companies Act 1948 (now Section 386 CA 2006), but from common law. Slade J did however leave open the question "whether this right conferred on [the director] at common law is to be regarded on the one hand as a right incident to his office and independent of contract or on the other hand, as a right dependent on the express or implied terms of his contract of employment with the company, so that it may be excluded by express provision to the contrary". If the latter is found to be the case then express terms in directors' service contracts might limit or exclude this right in the event of a board resolution.

The court has discretion as to whether or not to order an inspection. It is clear from the cases that the right will be enforced, not for the directors own advantage, but to enable him to carry out his duties as a director.

In *Oxford Legal Group Ltd* v *Sibbasbridge Services Plc and another* [2008] EWCA Civ 387, the Court of Appeal refused to enforce the right to inspect a company's accounts, not only where the

---

[92] *Conway* v *Petronius Clothing Co* [1978] 1 WLR 72.
[93] Section 147 Companies Act 1948 was intended merely to impose sanctions if the books were not properly kept.

purpose for which the inspection was sought was to injure the company, but also where the purpose was improper. The court confirmed that the true nature of the right to inspect was in order to enable the director to carry out his role as such.

The courts will also intervene where a director is improperly excluded from board meetings by his fellow directors, by granting an injunction restraining the exclusion.[94]

As the right to inspect is for the benefit of the company, it terminates on a director's removal from office. Almost invariably in cases where directors are refused access to the company books, the majority of directors will be seeking to get those denied access removed expediently as directors. Where an application by those refused access comes before the court and a general meeting of the company has already been convened for the purpose of removing the applicant(s) as director(s), the court will normally intervene only if it considers such intervention necessary for the protection of the company. Such were the allegations in the *Petronius* case, where misconduct was alleged against the applicant director and the court ruled that the balance of convenience was against making the order before a meeting had been held to consider the director's removal.

It will often be argued in such cases that the applicant plans to abuse the inspection, if granted by the court, to damage the interests of the company. Though a court will not allow a director to abuse his right by disregarding the confidence his office imposes, in the absence of clear proof from the respondent, it will be assumed that the applicant will inspect in the company's best interests and for its benefit.

Where the court uses its discretion to enforce the right to inspect, particularly where the applicant is not a finance director, he is entitled to the assistance of an expert, for example an accountant (subject to the court's discretion to order otherwise or impose conditions). But the company in turn is entitled to a reasonable time to consider whether to object to the proposed expert.

---

[94] *Pulbrook v Richmond Consolidated Mining Co* [1878] 9 Ch D 610.

8.5 Third-party rights to view the company books

Section 8.4 above dealt with the rights of directors to view the company books. Directors must be aware of the circumstances in which third parties can insist on inspecting the company books so that they do not breach the relevant sections in CA 2006 and render themselves liable for a personal fine.

8.5.1 General viewing

This section gives a non-exhaustive list of various company books and related matters and their required circulation or "inspectability".

8.5.1.1 Register of charges

The register of charges must be open for inspection by members and creditors[95] daily at the company's registered office (or at such other location specified in regulations) (Section 877(2) CA 2006). Any refusal by an officer of the company to such inspection is liable to a penalty. On a winding up, however, no one may inspect this register without a court order.

8.5.1.2 Company accounts

A limited company is required to keep accounts sufficient to show and explain the company's transactions. These records[96] must be kept at the company's registered office, or such other place as the directors think fit, and must be open to inspection by the company's officers at all times.[97] The accounting records must be kept for at least six years (or a reduced minimum of three years for a private company) from the date on which they were made.[98] Under CA 2006, public companies must lay

---

[95] This right of inspection does not extend to prospective creditors.

[96] Section 1135 CA 2006 permits the records to be in hard copy or electronic form but if the latter, they must be capable of being reproduced in hard copy form.

[97] The directors are required to refer to the company accounts. Failure can amount to serious incompetence as in *Re Continental Assurance Co of London Plc* [1997] 1 BCLC 48 where an interest-free loan amounted to financial assistance prohibited under Section 151 CA 1985. The director's failure to appreciate what would have been obvious if he had viewed the accounts amounted to allowing the loans and this gross incompetence resulted in his disqualification.

[98] Sections 386 and 388 CA 2006.

accounts each year before shareholders in a general meeting. Private companies are not under an obligation to do so and will no longer need to pass a resolution (as under CA 1985) to dispense with the requirement. However, both public and private companies are required to send a copy of their annual accounts to all shareholders.[99]

8.5.1.3 The register of directors and secretaries

The company is obliged to keep a register of all directors and secretaries of the company, including shadow directors. The companies registrar must be notified of any changes made to the register.[100] The register must be open to members and any refusal to allow inspection leads to liability to a one-off fine or to a daily default fine in the case of continued refusal.

8.5.1.4 The register of directors' interests in shares and debentures

The requirement for companies to keep a register to record the information about interests in shares and debentures about which their directors are required to notify the company is no longer in force under CA 2006. However, there are equivalent provisions for public companies only under the FSA's Disclosure and Transparency Rules.[101]

8.5.2 Liquidation/receivership

When a company goes into liquidation, the appointed liquidator clearly has a right to view the company books as he will deal with the liquidation matters on the company's behalf with the sanction of the court or the liquidation committee if required. The court may also enforce delivery to the appointed liquidator of any of the books, property, paper and records to

---

[99] Sections 423 and 437 CA 2006.

[100] Sections 162 to 167 CA 2006 and Sections 275 and 276 CA 2006 (secretaries).

[101] The FSA's Disclosure and Transparency Rules came into force in January 2007 and deal with financial reporting requirements, disclosure of interests in securities and information to be provided to holders of shares in connection with general meetings. The Rules do not apply to all public companies but only to publicly traded companies, that is, companies with shares admitted to trading on the London Stock Exchange, the Alternative Investment Market and Plus Markets (traded companies).

which the company appears to be entitled,[102] though this power is exercisable by the liquidator himself. The liquidator's requirements must be complied with without any avoidable delay.

An administrative receiver has similar rights; amongst those who have a duty to co-operate with him are persons who have at any point been officers of the company concerned. The administrative receiver can apply to the court for a private examination of any officer of the company.[103]

---

[102] Section 234 Insolvency Act 1986.
[103] Section 236 Insolvency Act 1986.

Chapter 9

Corporate Governance

Jonathan Marks

Partner

Slaughter and May

9.1 Introduction

Corporate governance has received an unprecedented amount of attention from politicians, regulators and the media as a result of the recent financial crisis. Rarely have issues relating to corporate governance attracted so much national interest.

Sir David Walker was commissioned by the previous Labour government to investigate corporate governance failings at Britain's banks and similar financial institutions before the crisis. He produced his final recommendations in November 2009 (the "Walker Review"). The Walker Review placed a large portion of the blame for the crisis on boardroom behaviour and criticised boards for having failed to provide the necessary leadership to avert the crisis. It argued that boards too often lacked an effective challenge to dominant and over-ambitious executives. It also argued that boards too easily succumbed to arguments in favour of increased leverage and were complacent about low-frequency, high-impact risk factors.

Aside from debates about the causes of the financial crisis in the UK there are other reasons for a heightened public awareness of corporate governance issues:

(a) On a global level, the crisis has raised concerns about corporate governance in relation to a number of high-profile business failures. Recently, the spectre of Enron was revived in relation to Lehman Brothers' use of the accounting manoeuvre known as "Repo 105" to report an improved leverage position. The Chapter 11 Examiner's report of Anton Valukas, published in March 2010, accused Lehman's board of having misled counterparties, credit-rating agencies and its own shareholders.[1]

(b) There continues to be considerable popular anger at what many perceive as clear examples of boardroom greed. In Britain, the pay gap between the executives of top companies and the "shop floor" has doubled in the past decade. In 2008, the pay of the average chief executive of the UK's 100 largest companies was 94 times that of the average full-time worker.[2] Similarly, with studies showing that women number fewer than one in 10 FTSE 100 directors, board-rooms appear to some to be as much a "closed shop" as ever, although there are some high-profile success stories.[3]

(c) Attitudes about the interrelationship between large companies and society may be changing. Until now, the theory of corporate governance in the UK has mainly been predicated on the belief that what is good for the shareholder is good for the company and good for the economy in general. In the wake of a financial crisis that saw the UK taxpayer pick up the tab to avoid the collapse of the UK banking system, the Walker Review raised the idea of an implicit social contract between shareholders, the company and the general public at large.[4] The Walker Review's words also echo recent developments in other areas of law such as the attempt to introduce an "enlightened shareholder value" concept into directors' duties by the Companies Act 2006 ("CA 2006").

(d) Following the financial crisis, other low-frequency, high-impact events such as the Deepwater Horizon oil spill in

---

[1] Anton R. Valukas *Lehman Brothers Holdings Inc Chapter 11 Proceedings Examiner's Report*, 13 March 2010.

[2] Income Data Services data cited in Megan Murphy and Nicholas Timmins, "Boardroom pay gap doubles in a decade", *The Financial Times*, 28 November 2009.

[3] Sealy, Vinnicombe and Doldor, *The Female FTSE Board Report 2009*, Cranfield University, 2009, "Working as a non-executive director: Getting more women on board", *The Financial Times*, 11 March 2010.

[4] Sir David Walker, *A Review of Corporate Governance in UK Banks and Other Financial Industry Entities: Final Recommendations*, 26 November 2009, ("Walker Review"), paragraph 5.7, p 70.

the Gulf of Mexico and the disruption caused to the European aviation industry and wider economy by the volcanic ash cloud between March and May 2010 have served to re-emphasise the importance of having good governance in relation to risk management. Turnbull guidance on internal controls is due to be republished later in 2010 and there have been other reports to help boards improve risk management.[5]

Whilst the Walker Review is primarily directed at the future governance of financial institutions, it is also leading to changes in governance for other listed companies.

9.1.1   The Walker Review and the UK Corporate Governance Code

The Walker Review comprised 39 different recommendations proposing changes in the key areas of board function and composition, risk management, remuneration and the role of institutional shareholders.

An appeal for greater accountability unites these 39 recommendations. It is an appeal that operates on three key levels. First, within the boardroom, the Walker Review urged non-executive directors to do more to hold executives to account, particularly in managing risk and developing companies' overall strategy. It called for the creation of board-level risk committees, chaired by a non-executive director, which would have the power to scrutinise and block transactions where necessary. It recommended that non-executive directors be given personalised training under the regular review of the chairman. The Walker Review highlighted the need for non-executive directors to exercise a more rigorous "strength of character" in their dealings with executive directors. It proposed that "independence of mind" and an "atmosphere of challenge" should replace the current formal appearance of leadership, encouraging boards to contest undesirable executive decisions.

---

[5] *See* Deloitte's *Risk Intelligent governance: A practical guide for boards*, August 2009; ICAEW Foundation *Getting it Right: A report by Independent Audit Limited on risk governance in non-financial services companies*, October 2009.

Second, the Walker Review called for the annual re-election of chairmen to improve accountability to companies' shareholders. To aid shareholders in bringing boards to account, the Walker Review also encouraged boards to undertake a "formal and rigorous" evaluation of its performance. It proposed that these reviews be facilitated every two to three years by an independent and qualified external reviewer.

Finally, beyond the boardroom, the Walker Review examined the role of shareholders in taking positive action to bring boards to account. The Walker Review made clear that responsibility for enforcing good governance rested as much with financial institutions' shareholders as with their boards, calling on institutional shareholders to take a more active role as "owners" of their companies.

As a consequence, a new "Stewardship Code", was proposed by the Walker Review and has now been introduced for all companies as guidance on the way that institutional shareholders should engage with companies' boards.[6] The new Stewardship Code operates on a "comply or explain" basis along the lines of the old Combined Code. It is designed to be followed by those investment managers who pursue an "active" engagement model of investment.

The Financial Reporting Council ("FRC") published a report in December 2009 which identified those Walker Review recommendations that could be applied to all listed companies through changes to the Combined Code on Corporate Governance ("Combined Code"). As a consequence, the Combined Code was revised and republished as the UK Corporate Governance Code ("Governance Code") in May 2010. The change in name was itself proposed by the Walker Review. The new Governance Code applies to accounting periods beginning on or after 29 June 2010 and, as a result of the new Listing Regime introduced in April 2010, applies for the first time to foreign companies with a "premium listing" in the UK.

---

[6] Walker Review, Recommendation 16, p 17.

The FRC stopped short of introducing the Walker Review recommendations that were suitable only for banks and financial institutions, such as the proposal that remuneration committees be responsible for setting firm-wide pay, but went further in other areas: specifically, all directors of FTSE 350 companies are now recommended to put themselves up for annual re-election. Through key changes to the Combined Code, the FRC has stated that it hopes to encourage boards to be better balanced and avoid "group think", to promote proper debate in the boardroom, to improve risk management at board level, and to foster performance-related pay that is better aligned to the long-term interests of the company.[7] As such, the new Governance Code closely mirrors the Walker Review, particularly in its desire for greater board accountability. This drive for accountability is perhaps best represented by new recommendations on directors' annual re-election and the intro-duction of externally facilitated board reviews every three years for FTSE 350 companies.

9.1.2 Other developments in corporate governance

Apart from the Walker Review and the FRC's new Governance Code, there have been developments in corporate governance in other areas:

(a) The introduction of the Stewardship Code is the latest in a line of attempts to improve shareholder engagement in the last few years. A number of the changes in the CA 2006 were designed to improve shareholder involvement in corporate decision making. The CA 2006 was amended in 2009 by The Companies (Shareholders' Rights) Regulations 2009 which implemented the Shareholder Rights Directive. The Shareholder Rights Directive was developed by the European Commission to facilitate the cross-border exer-cise of voting rights by shareholders. It introduced throughout the EU minimum standards of 30 calendar days' notice of a general meeting, the abolition of share blocking (to be replaced by a record date), rights to ask

---

[7] FRC, *Revisions to the UK Corporate Governance Code (Formerly the Combined Code)*, May 2010.

questions at or before a meeting and simplified systems of proxy voting, voting in absentia and counting of votes.

(b) The Governance Code applies solely to listed companies, which is where corporate governance policy making has traditionally focused. Recently, however, there has also been an attempt to bring a degree of corporate governance regulation to unlisted companies as well. In April 2010 the Institute of Directors ("IoD") published a set of 14 corporate governance principles for unlisted companies, an initiative led by the European Confederation of Directors' Associations ("ecoDa").[8] The directors' duties codified by the CA 2006 apply equally to unlisted companies.

(c) Corporate governance policy is becoming increasingly international as governments and supranational organisations respond to the growing globalisation of investment and the rapid development of state-level regulation. The International Corporate Governance Network ("ICGN") published a revised set of global corporate governance principles in November 2009.[9] The European Union has been responsible for several initiatives, setting up a European corporate governance forum at the end of 2004[10] and sponsoring a RiskMetrics Group study on corporate governance monitoring and enforcement practices in Member States.[11] In June 2010 the European Commission published a Green Paper seeking views on a number of questions relating to corporate governance in financial institutions. Another Green Paper is set to follow in early 2011 reviewing corporate governance in listed companies more generally.

(d) There has also been the introduction of specialist governance codes in recognition of the unusual corporate governance circumstances applying in certain cases – for example, to private equity firms and investment management companies. The European Private Equity and Venture Capital Association ("EVCA") republished corporate governance

---

[8] ecoDa, *Corporate Governance Guidance and Principles for Unlisted Companies in Europe*, April 2010.

[9] ICGN, *Global Corporate Governance Principles: Revised (2009)*, November 2009.

[10] The European Corporate Governance Forum published a statement on 23 March 2009, "Cross-border issues of Corporate Governance Codes".

[11] RiskMetrics Group, *Study on Monitoring and Enforcement Practices in Corporate Governance in the Member States*, 23 September 2009.

guidelines for private equity firms in January 2009, while the Association of Investment Companies ("AIC") and the National Association of Pension Funds ("NAPF") have both produced guidelines for investment companies.[12]

(e) There have been other reviews aside from the Walker Review in response to the financial crisis. The Organisation for Economic Co-operation and Development ("OECD") set up a steering group on corporate governance and published its conclusions in February 2010. The OECD's proposals are aligned with many of the recommendations in the Walker Review, such as the recommendation that risk-management lines should go direct to the board, that there should be training programmes for board members, and the idea of introducing a code of investor steward-ship.[13] Similarly, the Pensions Investment Research Consultants Limited ("PIRC") published its "manifesto" for corporate governance reform in April 2009.[14]

9.1.3 *Corporate governance and its significance*

The changes in UK corporate governance (in particular, the new Governance Code and Stewardship Code, the CA 2006 and the amendments resulting from the Shareholder Rights Directive), taken together with the ongoing interest in other jurisdictions,[15] all suggest that there is going to continue to be considerable interest in corporate governance reform in years to come.

But what is corporate governance? In 1992, the Cadbury Report[16] defined corporate governance as the system by which companies are directed and controlled. In introducing the

---

[12] EVCA *Corporate Governance Guidelines: Guidelines and good practice in the management of privately held companies in the private equity and venture capital industry*, June 2005 (reprint January 2009); AIC, *The AIC Code of Corporate Governance: A framework of best practice for Member companies*, May 2007; NAPF, *Corporate Governance Policy and Voting Guidelines for Investment Companies*, April 2010.

[13] OECD Steering Group on Corporate Governance, *Corporate Governance and the Financial Crisis: Conclusions and emerging good practices to enhance implementation of the Principles*, 24 February 2010.

[14] PIRC, *Beyond the crisis: PIRC's manifesto for corporate governance and capital market reform*, April 2009.

[15] OECD, *Corporate Governance and the Financial Crisis*, February 2010; RiskMetrics, *Study on Monitoring and Enforcement Practices*, September 2009.

[16] *The Financial Aspects of Corporate Governance*, 1 December 1992.

report, it pointed out the effectiveness with which boards discharge their responsibilities as determining Britain's competitive position. It saw directors' freedom to drive their companies forward within the framework of effective accountability as being the essence of any system of good corporate governance. Boards of directors were regarded as responsible for the governance of their companies – with the shareholders' role in governance being to appoint the directors and the auditors and satisfy themselves that an appropriate governance structure was in place.

In its second White Paper on Company Law Reform dated March 2005, the government again stressed the economic importance of the UK's system of company law and corporate governance. It noted that:

> "Our system of company law and corporate governance . . . sets out the legal basis on which companies are formed, operated and managed. It provides the corporate vehicle which enables people to collaborate in business, and the legal structure through which companies are financed, ultimately by millions of savers and pensioners. It sets the rules for company boards and shareholders and for the exercise of decisions on business growth and investment. And, it is the means by which people are held to account for the exercise of corporate economic power.
>
> For these reasons, an effective framework of company law and corporate governance is a key building block of a modern economy. A genuinely modern and effective framework can promote enterprise, enhance competitiveness and stimulate investment. Conversely, an ineffective or outmoded framework can inhibit productivity and growth and undermine investment confidence. The high profile corporate collapses of recent years – including Enron, WorldCom and Parmalat – have demonstrated the critical importance to the modern global economy of robust frameworks for corporate activity, and the far-reaching economic consequences when these fail."

Research by Deloitte into the causes of the 100 largest one-month declines in the share price of the 100 largest international companies from 1994 to 2003[17] further illustrates the benefits of good corporate governance. The research identified a number of contributing causes of major losses of shareholder value. Deloitte noted that:

> "The consequences, in many cases, were surprisingly severe: Some of the value losses were so substantial that the effected companies never recovered . . ."

Four key areas of risk were identified – strategic risk, operational risk, financial risk and external risk – as well as a large number of contributing events which fell within the four main categories. Examples ranged from internal issues – such as accounting problems caused by fraud or manipulation of accounting information – to external matters such as terrorism.

Whilst good corporate governance cannot be expected to enable companies to avoid loss of shareholder value in all cases, it should nonetheless provide a means by which a company's directors can help take better decisions in the first place, minimise the risk of certain adverse events occurring, and also assist directors to respond to challenges which do occur, in a timely and effective manner.

9.2 Background

The separate roles of the board and the shareholders are long established. By the middle of the nineteenth century, it had become established practice for the shareholders to elect the directors and for the directors to run the company. If the members were unhappy with the running of the company they could, in theory, change the board but not intervene in the management. Until their removal, the existing board continued to have control over the management of the company.

This has been an enduring theme in company law, reinforced by the Cadbury Report:

---

[17] *Disarming the Value Killers: A Risk Management Study,* 2005 and cited in the Turnbull Review Group's *Review of the Turnbull Guidance on Internal Control, Proposals for updating the guidance,* 16 June 2005.

> "The formal relationship between the shareholders and the board of directors is that . . . the directors report on their stewardship to the shareholders and . . . the shareholders as owners of the company elect the directors to run the business on their behalf and hold them accountable for its progress."[18]

In the post-war years, some institutional investors took the view that it was cheaper to invest in successful companies and to avoid or divest from the unsuccessful ones. Where institutional intervention did take place, it was often on an informal basis rather than through representations or other action at formal shareholder meetings. If the company underperformed, shareholders just sold their shares. As the share price fell, it was at least possible that acquisitive and more successful companies might move in with takeover proposals. This environment provoked debate about the appropriate standards of corporate governance which it was desirable to promote.

The law currently provides a basic framework of corporate governance by specifying the minimum number of directors that companies may have, by regulating the conduct of directors in a limited way, by requiring disclosure of certain matters and by providing for certain decisions to be taken by the shareholders. Apart from these requirements, however, companies are generally free to establish their own systems of governance by means of provisions in their articles of association or by less formal internal rules. As a result, governance structures are not in the main prescribed by law but have developed out of business and commercial practice. The governance of listed companies is also influenced by the additional rules promulgated and administered by the UK Listing Authority of the FSA, which are mainly directed towards the protection of investors.

During the 1990s the codes of practice developed by three committees (which were set up to examine corporate governance issues) introduced a new dimension. The approach adopted in those codes was to use self-regulation as a means of promoting

---

[18] *The Financial Aspects of Corporate Governance*, 1 December 1992; paragraph 6.1.

and maintaining practices of good governance. The intention in each case was to establish a voluntary code, but with an emphasis on disclosure. The idea was to encourage transparency in corporate governance through disclosure obligations which would promote shareholder pressure to comply with best practice in appropriate cases.

The Cadbury Committee was set up in May 1990 as a result of public concern over high-profile corporate failures such as Polly Peck, BCCI and Maxwell. The objective of the Cadbury Committee was to help to raise the standards of corporate governance and the level of confidence in financial reporting and auditing by setting out clearly the responsibilities of the directors and their relationship with the auditors. The committee published its report, accompanied by its Code of Best Practice, in December 1992.[19]

Concern over what were considered to be excessive remuneration and compensation packages awarded to some directors resulted in the establishment of the Greenbury Committee in January 1995 to identify good practice in determining directors' remuneration. The committee published its report and Code of Best Practice in July 1995.[20]

Unlike the Cadbury and Greenbury Committees, the establishment of the Hampel Committee in November 1995 was not a reaction to public concern about the way in which companies regulated themselves, but rather to the two reports which had preceded it. The Hampel Committee was born out of the recommendation of Cadbury and Greenbury that a committee should follow up on the implementation of their findings. The aim was to draw up a set of principles and a code, based on Cadbury, Greenbury and its own conclusions.

Following the publication of the final report of the Hampel Committee, the London Stock Exchange ("LSE") issued the Principles of Good Governance and the Code of Best Practice

---

[19] *The Financial Aspects of Corporate Governance*, 1 December 1992; The Code of Best Practice, 1 December 1992.
[20] *Directors' Remuneration – Report of a Study Group chaired by Sir Richard Greenbury*, 17 July 1995.

(the Combined Code) in June 1998, which was derived from the reports of the three committees on corporate governance. At the same time, the LSE published a new listing rule. This required listed companies to include in their annual reports and accounts specified details as to how they had complied with the Combined Code during the year under review, but it did not require listed companies to comply with the Combined Code. This was the basis of the "comply or explain" philosophy that still underpins UK corporate governance.

The Turnbull Committee was set up by the Institute of Chartered Accountants in England and Wales ("ICAEW") to provide guidance for listed companies on how to implement the requirements in the Combined Code relating to internal control. Its report set guidelines for ensuring that companies have in place effective risk-management and internal control systems.[21] It followed a principles-based approach and did not include detailed prescription as to how to implement the guidance. The same approach was adopted when the guidance was revised in October 2005.

Following the collapse of Enron in 2001, the government appointed Derek Higgs in April 2002 to head a review of "the role and effectiveness of non-executive directors in the UK". This followed the Myners Review of institutional investment, *Institutional Investment in the United Kingdom, a Review*, March 2001. In addition, the FRC commissioned a report by Sir Robert Smith to clarify the responsibilities of audit committees and to develop the existing Combined Code guidance in this area.[22] The final reports from these exercises were published in January 2003 and included a revised version of the Combined Code which was due to take effect from 1 July 2003. However, following criticism of both the substance of certain findings of the Higgs Review and the speed at which its findings were to be implemented through the revised Combined Code, the FRC did not publish the final version of the revised Combined Code until 23 July 2003. The revised version took effect from

---

[21] *Internal Control: Guidance for Directors on the Combined Code*, September 1999.
[22] The Smith Report, *Audit committees: Combined Code guidance*, January 2003. A modified version dated July 2003 forms part of the related guidance accompanying the Combined Code.

1 November 2003. Following a review of the implementation of the Combined Code in 2005, the FRC consulted on a small number of changes to the Combined Code. These changes were incorporated in an updated version published in June 2006. Between April and July 2007 the FRC carried out a similar review of how the Combined Code was being implemented and proposed a small number of amendments in 2008. A revised Combined Code took effect in June 2008.

In response to the financial crisis in the last part of the previous decade, the Labour government appointed Sir David Walker to head an enquiry into banks' corporate governance. The Walker Review published its final report in November 2009. The report included a list of recommendations for how the Combined Code should be reformed. The FRC brought forward its review of the Combined Code scheduled for 2010 to accommodate the Walker Review's recommendations. While the Walker Review focused specifically on corporate governance in financial services firms, the FRC's remit was wider as the Combined Code applied to all listed companies regardless of industry sector. For this reason some recommendations were adopted while some were deemed inappropriate.

As a consequence of the Walker Review, the name of the Combined Code was changed from "The Combined Code on Corporate Governance" to "The UK Corporate Governance Code". It is hoped that this title will make its status as the UK's recognised corporate governance standard for companies clearer to foreign investors and to foreign companies listed in the UK which, as a result of changes to the FSA's Listing Regime, now need to report against the Governance Code if they have a premium listing.[23] The Governance Code was published in May 2010.

In terms of legislation, the key development in recent years has been the enactment and coming into effect of the CA 2006. The Companies Bill (formerly called the Company Law Reform Bill) received Royal Assent on 8 November 2006 and followed on

---

[23] *See* LR 9.8.7R.

from a review of company law begun as far back as 1998. The CA 2006 contains about 1,300 sections and is said to be the longest ever UK statute. The Act replaced virtually all the Companies Acts 1985 and 1989, much of the Companies (Audit, Investigations and Community Enterprise) Act 2004 and the Directors' Remuneration Report Regulations 2002.

The changes introduced by the CA 2006 include:

- the codification of directors' duties with an obligation to have regard to specific matters;
- various additional rights for shareholders, including the right for a registered member of a listed company to nominate a third party to receive information from the company and, in the case of all companies if their articles so provide, to exercise voting rights;
- a new statutory process for bringing derivative claims in the name of the company with additional rights for shareholders to those previously provided under the common law; and
- certain additional requirements for a company's business review (building on the provisions introduced previously in controversial circumstances).

Before considering the changes most directly relevant to corporate governance in more detail, further consideration is given to certain of the provisions of the FSA's Listing Rules and Disclosure and Transparency Rules, the Governance Code and the Stewardship Code.

9.3 The Listing Rules and Disclosure and Transparency Rules

The Listing Rules, Prospectus Rules and the Disclosure and Transparency Rules provide important protection to the holders of shares listed on the Main Market of the London Stock Exchange. Revised Listing Rules came into force in July 2005 but have been regularly updated since then to take account of changes in legislation and the introduction of new legislation. Most recently, the rules were amended in April 2010.

As part of the FSA's previous move towards "principles-based" regulation, the Listing Rules contain six listing principles (as well as more detailed rules and guidance).[24] These principles are that:

(a) A listed company must take reasonable steps to enable its directors to understand their responsibilities and obligations as directors (Principle 1).
(b) A listed company must take reasonable steps to establish and maintain adequate procedures, systems and controls to enable it to comply with its obligations (Principle 2).
(c) A listed company must act with integrity towards holders and potential holders of its listed equity shares (Principle 3).
(d) A listed company must communicate information to holders and potential holders of its listed equity securities in such a way as to avoid the creation or continuation of a false market in such listed equity shares (Principle 4).
(e) A listed company must ensure that it treats all holders of the same class of its listed equity shares that are in the same position equally in respect of the rights attaching to such listed equity shares (Principle 5).
(f) A listed company must deal with the FSA in an open and cooperative manner (Principle 6).

The Listing Rules include guidance in relation to Principle 2. The guidance states that Principle 2 is intended to ensure that the relevant listed companies have adequate procedures, systems and controls to enable them to comply with their obligations under the Listing Rules and Disclosure and Transparency Rules. The guidance goes on to note that, in particular, the FSA considers that listed companies should place particular emphasis on ensuring that they have adequate procedures, systems and controls in relation to identifying whether any obligations arise under LR 10 (significant transactions) and LR 11 (related-party transactions), and the timely and accurate disclosure of information to the market. Further guidance is provided in relation to the latter. The FSA notes that timely and accurate disclosure of information to the market is a key obligation of

---

[24] The listing principles are set out in LR 7.2.1R with the related guidance included at LR 7.2.2G and LR 7.2.3G. The GC100 published "Listing Rules Guidelines" in May 2007. They describe practices intended to represent "reasonable best practice" for large listed companies.

listed companies. The guidance then provides that, for the purposes of Principle 2, a listed company with a premium listing of equity shares should have adequate systems and controls to be able to ensure that it can properly identify information which requires disclosure under the Listing Rules or Disclosure and Transparency Rules in a timely manner. Such a company must also ensure that any such information identified is properly considered by the directors and that such a consideration encompasses whether the information should be disclosed.

The detail of the Listing Rules is outside the scope of this Chapter. Nonetheless, there are certain provisions of significance in this context. LR 9.8 contains various provisions relating to the publication of a listed company's annual report and accounts.[25] A company incorporated in the UK with a premium listing is required (amongst other things) to include the following in its annual report and accounts:

> "9.8.6 R (3) a statement made by the directors that the business is a going concern, together with supporting assumptions or qualifications as necessary, that has been prepared in accordance with "Going Concern and Liquidity Risk: Guidance for Directors of UK Companies 2009", published by the Financial Reporting Council in October 2009;
>
> (5) a statement of how the listed company has applied the Main Principles set out in the UK Corporate Governance Code, in a manner that would enable shareholders to evaluate how the principles have been applied;
>
> (6) a statement as to whether the listed company has:
>
> > (a) complied throughout the accounting period with all relevant provisions set out in the UK Corporate Governance Code; or

---

[25] The wording set out in this chapter reflects the revised wording of the FSA's Consultation Paper CP10/3: Effective corporate governance (Significant influence controlled functions and the Walker Review), Appendix 1 Annex G. The FSA intends to publish a policy statement with final rules in the third quarter of 2010. The revised wording is used here because it incorporates reference to the UK Corporate Governance Code as opposed to the Combined Code.

    (b) not complied throughout the accounting period
        with all relevant provisions set out in the UK
        Corporate Governance Code and if so, setting out:

        (i) those provisions, if any, it has not complied with;
        (ii) in the case of provisions whose requirements
            are of a continuing nature, the period within
            which, if any, it did not comply with some or
            all of those provisions; and
        (iii) the company's reasons for non-compliance . . ."

The Listing Rules were recently updated such that an overseas company with a premium listing must include in its annual report and accounts a statement of how it has complied with the Governance Code in the same way as for UK-incorporated companies with a premium listing.[26] It must also disclose the unexpired term of the service contract of any director proposed for election or re-election at its forthcoming annual general meeting. If any director for election or re-election does not have a service contract, a statement to that effect must be included.[27]

A company with a standard listing (either incorporated in the UK or overseas) is not required by the Listing Rules to state how it has complied with the Governance Code. However, it must publish a corporate governance statement detailing its approach to corporate governance.[28]

DTR Chapter 7 (corporate governance) was introduced in the previous government's implementation of the Eighth (and amendments to the Fourth and Seventh) Company Law Directives in June 2008.[29] DTR 7.2 requires all companies listed in the UK, whether with a premium or standard listing, incorporated in the UK or overseas, to make corporate governance statements in their directors' reports.[30] Alternatively, the corporate governance statement can be included in a separate report published together with the annual report, or on the issuer's

---

[26] LR 9.8.7R.
[27] LR 9.8.8R(9).
[28] *See* LR 14.3.24, LR 18.4.3(2) and DTR 7.2.
[29] The Statutory Audit Directive (2006/43/EC) and the Company Reporting Directive (2006/46/EC).
[30] DTR 7.2.1R.

website, in which case there must be a cross-reference to this in the directors' report.[31] Companies with a premium listing must refer to the fact that they are subject to the Governance Code.[32] As under the Listing Rules, a company must explain which parts of the Governance Code it departs from and its reasons for doing so.[33] Guidance states that compliance with the LR 9.8.6R (above) will satisfy this requirement.[34]

The Disclosure and Transparency Rules also set out the content requirements for this corporate governance statement. The corporate governance statement must contain a description of the main features of the company's internal control and risk-management systems in relation to the financial reporting process.[35] The Disclosure and Transparency Rules provide that the corporate governance statement must also contain the information required by paragraph 12(2)(c), (d), (f), (h) and (i) of Schedule 7 Large and Medium-sized Companies and Groups (Accounts and Reports) Regulations 2008 where the issuer is subject to the requirements of that paragraph.[36] In addition, the corporate governance statement must contain a description of the composition and operation of the issuer's administrative, management and supervisory bodies and their committees.[37] Guidance provides that where a company with a premium listing follows the recommendations on disclosure relating to particular provisions in the Governance Code,[38] this last requirement will be met.[39]

Under the Listing Rules, a company with a premium listing must ensure that the auditors review each of the following[40] before its annual report is published:

---

[31] DTR 7.2.9R.
[32] DTR 7.2.2R.
[33] DTR 7.2.3R(1)(b).
[34] DTR 7.2.3G.
[35] DTR 7.2.5R. DTR 7.2.10R states that an issuer which is required to prepare a group directors' report within the meaning of Section 415(2) Companies Act 2006 must include in that report a description of the main features of the group's internal control and risk-management systems in relation to the process for preparing consolidated accounts.
[36] DRT 7.2.6R.
[37] DTR 7.2.7R.
[38] e.g. Governance Code A.1.1, A.1.2, B.2.4, C.3.3, D.2.1.
[39] DTR 7.2.8R.
[40] LR 9.8.10R.

- LR 9.8.6R(3) (statement by the directors that the business is a going concern); and
- the parts of the statement required by LR 9.8.6R(6) (corporate governance) that relate to the following provisions of the UK Corporate Governance Code:

  (a) C.1.1;
  (b) C.2.2; and
  (c) C.3.1 to C.3.7.

The Auditing Practices Board has recently updated its bulletin providing guidance for auditors when reviewing a company's statement in relation to Governance Code compliance in accordance with LR 9.8.10R.[41]

In addition, the annual report and accounts of a UK-incorporated company with a premium listing must include a report to shareholders by the board which contains all of the matters set out in LR 9.8.8R. As well as requiring a statement of the listed company's policy on the executive directors' remuneration, this rule requires considerable detail on the remuneration of all of the directors, as well as an explanation and justification of any element (other than basic salary) which is pensionable, and a statement of the company's policy on the granting of options or awards under its employee share scheme and other long-term incentive schemes, with explanations and justifications of departures from the policy in the period under review.

The Governance Code and the related disclosure provisions under the Listing Rules and Disclosure and Transparency Rules seek to encourage both companies' boards and their shareholders to consider whether their companies are being governed in shareholders' best interests. LR 9.8.6R(5) requires companies with a premium listing to state how they have applied the "Main Principles" of the Governance Code, which represent certain broad concepts believed to underpin effective board governance. Beyond this, however, a degree of flexibility is allowed to companies in how they adhere to these Main Principles under LR 9.8.6R(6)(b). This is known as "comply or

---

[41] Developments in Corporate Governance Affecting the Responsibilities of Auditors of UK Companies, Bulletin 2009/4 December 2009.

explain": where a company with a premium listing does not apply the "Code Provisions", it must disclose how and why it has done things differently. Shareholders are then able to decide whether it is necessary to put pressure on the board to make changes to the way that the company is governed. Flexibility in the application of the Code Provisions is seen as being achievable by fostering an informed dialogue between the company and its shareholders. Companies are to review and explain their governance policies, including any special circumstances which in their view justify departure from generally accepted best practice, and shareholders and others should show flexibility in the interpretation of the Governance Code, taking into account the explanations they receive and judging them on their merits.

Notwithstanding that the Governance Code encourages such an approach, this has not always been how shareholders have responded in practice. The FRC canvassed the views of a number of chairmen at FTSE 100 and 250 companies as to the effectiveness of the old Combined Code.[42] While many chairman saw the lack of prescription of the Combined Code as a key strength, concern was expressed at the use of a box-ticking approach to governance evaluation. Some chairmen felt frustrated with the engagement process with shareholders generally. Equally, companies have not always met the standard of reporting that has been asked for. The FRC's final report in its review of the Combined Code stated that the quality of disclosure by companies was variable and that there were too many boilerplate and uninformative reports.[43] The Accounting Standards Board ("ASB") has highlighted the importance of effective shareholder communication in its report on good and bad practice in narrative reporting.[44]

9.4 The UK Corporate Governance Code

The UK Corporate Governance Code (the "Governance Code") is the new title for what was previously called the "Combined

---

[42] FRC, *Review of the Effectiveness of the Combined Code. Summary of the main points raised at meetings with the chairman of FTSE companies*, July 2009.

[43] FRC, *2009 Review of the Combined Code: Final Report* ("Final Report"), December 2009.

[44] Accounting Standards Board, *Rising to the challenge: A review of narrative reporting by UK listed companies*, October 2009.

Code on Corporate Governance". When first established by the Hampel Committee, the Combined Code was designed as a statement of "broad principles" that should be applied "flexibly and with common sense to the varying circumstances of individual companies".[45] The philosophy behind the Combined Code was always to serve as a general guide to good practice rather than as a checklist of "hard and fast" rules.[46]

The Walker Review in the wake of the financial crisis heralded potentially the biggest shake-up of corporate governance since the Combined Code was first introduced. Many argued that the crisis exposed identifiable weaknesses in companies' systems of corporate governance, such as a failure to give proper risk oversight at board level and a failure appropriately to hold executives to account or to rein in the remuneration incentives that helped allow a culture of short-termism to develop.

Nevertheless, in spite of these failings, the Walker Review endorsed the UK's unitary board system and affirmed that the Combined Code remained broadly fit for purpose. Its opinion was that the financial crisis was more the result of a failure of behaviour than a failure of process and that the "comply or explain" approach of the Combined Code was well-suited to the task of bringing into effect the necessary behavioural change for reform of corporate governance. Indeed, a prescriptive, "box-ticking" approach to governance was firmly rejected, and the flexibility offered by a code of practice was held up as having distinct advantages over other regulatory or legislative solutions. Eschewing a radical restatement of principles, the Walker Review focused instead on trying to reform board culture through key changes in the Combined Code's emphasis.

The FRC conducted a review of the Combined Code in parallel with the Walker Review in 2009 to see how best to incorporate its recommendations. The FRC review's main conclusion echoed the Walker Review's call for behavioural change by stating that more attention needed be paid to "following the spirit of the Code as well as its letter". The changes it introduced focused on

---

[45] Hampel Report, paragraph 1.11.
[46] Phrase comes from the Hampel Report, paragraph 1.11.

altering the "tone" of the Combined Code by making limited but significant changes to the code's principles and provisions in order to guide board behaviours. Chairmen are now encouraged to report personally in their annual statements how the principles have been applied in order to try to challenge what the FRC calls the "fungus" of "boiler-plate reporting". By doing so, the FRC hopes to encourage genuine engagement with the "spirit" of the new Governance Code.

The FRC's revisions have resulted in significant structural adjustments to the Combined Code, particularly to Section A on "Directors", which has been divided into two sections called "Leadership" (Section A) and "Effectiveness" (Section B). This division was designed to give more prominence to some of the factors that underpin an effective board. The orders of the sections dealing with remuneration and accountability were reversed, such that "Accountability" is now Section C and "Remuneration" is Section D. The structure and content of the Preamble to the Combined Code was also updated to form a new introductory section. With the introduction of the Stewardship Code, Section E on "Institutional Shareholders" was regarded as redundant and was removed. The old Combined Code Schedule B on the liability of non-executive directors was also removed as it was felt that there was more comprehensive guidance available from other sources, in particular the updated good practice guidance from the Higgs Review which is set to be issued to the FRC by the Institute of Chartered Secretaries and Administrators ("ICSA") and published at the end of 2010.

Despite this structural overhaul, most of the content of the Governance Code is the same as it was under the Combined Code. Two new Main Principles were added (B.1 and C.2) that make explicit certain elements of good practice implied by the old Combined Code: specifically, having an appropriate balance of skills, experience, independence and knowledge on the board and making it clear that boards have a responsibility for a company's strategic risks and internal controls. Most of the changes apply to what were Sections A and B and are adjustments to the wording or alterations to the position in which principles and provisions were previously ordered. Three Supporting Principles in Section A were upgraded to

Main Principles (A.3, A.4 and B.3), and Main Principle A.5 on "Information and professional development" was divided into separate parts. The most significant Walker Review recommendations were incorporated through changes to the Code Provisions. Accordingly, chairmen are now to oversee personal training for each director (B.4.2), an external evaluation of the board of every FTSE 350 company should be facilitated every three years (B.6.2), and directors of FTSE 350 companies should stand for re-election every year (B.7.1). The main purpose of such changes is to improve board accountability to shareholders, to emphasise the importance of having non-executive directors who can provide an effective "challenge" to executive leadership, and to elevate the board's role in risk management.

The Governance Code as it stands still remains true to the content of the original Combined Code introduced by the Hampel Committee in 1998. "The Code has been enduring, but it is not immutable", the introduction observes. The success of the Combined Code has so far rested on its ability to evolve to suit ideas of best practice in an ever-changing business environment. Whether its successor will be so successful will depend on its ability to continue do so.

9.4.1 Leadership

"Leadership", the new heading of the first section of the Governance Code, attempts to bring into focus the most important role that boards are expected to provide. Like many revisions to the Combined Code, this change in title is one of emphasis rather than substance. As noted above, the old Section A on "Directors" was split into two parts, "Leadership" and "Effectiveness", in order to give prominence to factors believed to underpin an effective board, but the content of this section has largely remained the same, albeit in a restructured format.

Nevertheless, the new heading does emphasise the point that it is the board, as opposed to simply the management, that is required to govern a company and dictate its strategy. A fundamental statement of the role of the board is provided in the first Supporting Principle:

"The board's role is to provide entrepreneurial leadership of the company within a framework of prudent and effective controls which enables risk to be assessed and managed. The board should set the company's strategic aims, ensure that the necessary financial and human resources are in place for the company to meet its objectives and review management performance. The board should set the company's values and standards and ensure that its obligations to its shareholders and others are understood and met."[47]

Effective leadership by the board requires leadership from within it, and this is a role expressly provided to the chairman by the Governance Code in a new Main Principle.[48] The chairman is key to setting the board's agenda. He should ensure enough time and appropriate information is available for strategic discussion. The chairman should also ensure that the right culture is fostered and that the board is marshalled such that all directors contribute effectively and that appropriate checks and balances are in place to executive power.

In effect, the chairman's role is to be responsible for the working of the board, for the balance of its membership and for ensuring that all directors, executive and non-executive alike, are able to play their full part in its activities. By contrast, the role of the chief executive is to run the business and to implement the policies and strategies adopted by the board. Effective division between chairman and chief executive was always central to the Combined Code[49] and goes back to the Cadbury Report which recommended separating the two roles to "ensure a balance of power and authority, such that no one individual has unfettered powers of decision".[50]

The importance of having a strong chairman who is independent of the chief executive has been highlighted by the governance failings brought to light by the financial crisis, where, with some notable exceptions, chief executives were

---

[47] Governance Code A.1.
[48] Governance Code A.3.
[49] Now Governance Code A.2.
[50] The Cadbury Report, paragraph 4.9.

insufficiently held to account at some financial institutions. The Walker Review called the role of the chairman "paramount" and changes to the Combined Code are designed to encourage chairmen to play a more positive role in boardrooms.[51] The ability of the chairman to head up a strong non-executive presence on the board is considered equally important.

The Walker Review was very critical of the failure of non-executive directors to provide an effective "challenge" to executive power. As a consequence, a new Main Principle was introduced to the Governance Code setting out the role of non-executive directors.[52] Previously a Supporting Principle, this version elevates a part of the old Combined Code to further emphasise the importance of the role that non-executive directors are expected to provide on the board. Non-executives are considered vital to the proper operation of a unitary board system. They are there to provide an effective challenge to the potential short-termism and self-interest of executive directors and to promote the long-term success of the company.[53]

The Governance Code also recommends that, even where the roles of chairman and chief executive are held by different people, there should be a recognised senior independent non-executive director, who must meet the test of independence, other than the chairman, and to whom concerns can be conveyed.[54] The Higgs Review concluded that the senior independent non-executive director should be available to shareholders if they have reason for concern that contact through the normal channels (i.e. the chairman or chief executive) has failed, although this conclusion was criticised as undermining the role of the chairman.[55] The Governance Code recommends that the senior independent non-executive director attend sufficient meetings with shareholders to obtain a balanced understanding of their concerns.[56]

---

[51] ICSA Guidance Note, *The Roles of Chairman, Chief Executive and Senior Independent Director under the Combined code*, September 2004.
[52] Governance Code A.4.
[53] *The role and effectiveness of the non-executive director*, by Derek Higgs, published January 2005. A revised version of this guidance for non-executive directors is expected to come out later in 2010.
[54] Governance Code A.4.1.
[55] The Higgs Report, paragraphs 7.4 and 7.5; Governance Code A.4.1.
[56] Governance Code E.1.1.

Changes to the Governance Code have added an extra dimension to the role of the senior independent non-executive director. The Walker Review called for the position not only to be an alternative channel of communication for the expression of dissatisfaction from outside the board but also to perform a similar role within it. Senior independent non-executive directors should act as an intermediary and arbitrator, if need be, between the chairman and chief-executive, or the chairman and the non-executive directors, ensuring that the non-executive directors are able to contribute effectively. Senior independent non-executive directors should be the "lightening conductor" for non-executives to express their concerns, when necessary, and, given the "inevitable tendency towards collegiality in boards" which can lead to "excessive deference in colleagues" that "stifles critical enquiry and challenge", the senior independent non-executive director "should be the potentially negative charge on the board".[57] The senior independent non-executive director should also provide critical support as a "sounding board" to the chairman.[58]

9.4.2 Effectiveness

The importance of having appropriate input from non-executives on the board to protect the company's interests has been brought into sharper focus by the financial crisis. One of the ways in which the Hampel Committee recommended that the board of a company can achieve its role effectively was to ensure that the board was not dominated by one individual or a group of individuals. To promote this end, the Combined Code provided that the board should include non-executive directors of sufficient calibre and number for their views to carry significant weight in the board's decisions. The Hampel Committee recommended that non-executive directors should comprise not less than one-third of the board. The Higgs Review went further, putting particular emphasis on greater non-executive presence. The Higgs Review version of the Combined Code stated that at least half of the board, excluding the chairman, should be non-executive directors, and that the board should identify in its

---

[57] Walker Review, paragraphs 4.27 and 4.28.
[58] Governance Code A.4.1.

annual report the non-executive directors that it determines to be independent.[59] The Governance Code currently requires an "appropriate combination" of executive and non-executive directors on the board.[60] Following concern about the ability of smaller companies to recruit sufficient independent non-executive directors to meet this requirement, the FRC made an amendment to the Combined Code which provides for companies below FTSE 350 level to have at least two independent non-executive directors.[61]

The independence of non-executives has long been viewed as a key issue in assessing their ability to perform their role. However, concerns at the lack of banking qualifications and industry experience of non-executives at Northern Rock, the Royal Bank of Scotland and elsewhere has resulted in refinement to this approach. The Walker Review questioned whether independence should be the overriding concern when recruiting non-executive directors: boards should sometimes give greater weight to experience over independence and should be ready to depart from independence criteria where required.[62]

In this respect the Combined Code has not been altered, but the phraseology of the new Main Principle has ensured that the emphasis on the independence of non-executives has been set in a broader context. The board must now comprise directors with the appropriate balance of "skills, experience, independence and knowledge of the company".[63] Nevertheless, independence still remains very important and a non-executive should ideally be expected to show an "independence of mind and spirit, of character and judgement".[64] The board should still identify in the annual report each non-executive it considers to be independent.[65]

---

[59] Combined Code (June 2008) A.3.1.
[60] Governance Code, Supporting Principle to B.1.
[61] Governance Code B.1.2. PIRC does not consider that a public company's market capitalisation should determine its approach to corporate governance.
[62] Walker Review, paragraph 3.8, p 44. *See* also Grant Thornton, *Are they experienced? A review of FTSE 350 non-executive director experience*, 2009.
[63] Governance Code B.1.
[64] Walker Review, p 44.
[65] Governance Code B.1.1.

The criteria for independence are based largely on a joint statement issued by the Association of British Insurers ("ABI") and the National Association of Pension Funds ("NAPF") in 1999.[66] Whilst the Governance Code leaves the final judgment as to whether a director can be considered independent in the hands of the board, it lists a number of circumstances that may lead the board to conclude that a director should not be considered independent. In essence, a director is considered independent when the board determines that the director is independent in character and judgment, and there are no relationships or circumstances which could affect, or appear to affect, the director's judgment. Relationships or circumstances which may affect judgment include where the director:

(a) has been an employee of the company or group within the last five years;

(b) has, or has had within the last three years, a material business relationship with the company either directly or as a partner, shareholder, director or senior employee of a body that has such a relationship with the company;

(c) has received or receives additional remuneration from the company apart from a director's fee, participates in the company's share option or a performance related pay scheme, or is a member of the company's pension scheme;

(d) has close family ties with any of the company's advisers, directors or senior employees;

(e) holds cross-directorships or has significant links with other directors through involvement in other companies or bodies;

(f) represents a significant shareholder; or

(g) has served on the board for more than nine years from the date of his or her first election.

Whilst the board is free to disregard the presence of any of these relationships or circumstances, it must explain in the annual report why it considers a director to be independent notwithstanding their existence.

---

[66] A joint ABI/NAPF Statement, *Responsible Voting*, July 1999, Appendix 1, 19.

The various corporate governance reports suggest that one way of promoting an effective and balanced board is for there to be a transparent policy and system for recruiting new directors. This is advocated in the Governance Code which provides that the board should make new appointments on the recommendation of a nomination committee.[67] The members of the nomination committee and the process by which nominations are made should be identified in the annual report, and a majority of them should be independent non-executives.[68] The aim of the nomination committee is to promote objectivity in the appointment of directors, which is crucial in guaranteeing a balanced board not dominated by a particular individual or group of individuals. If a chairman chairs the nomination committee they should stand down when the recruitment of a new chairman is under discussion.[69]

The Higgs Review stressed the importance of considering candidates from a wide range of backgrounds and looking beyond the "usual suspects". The Tyson Report on the Recruitment and Development of Non-Executive Directors of June 2003 supported this approach, calling on boards to consider candidates from a diversity of backgrounds, skills and experiences and look to "new pools of talent". The Walker Review offered a mild correction to this emphasis, in that it stressed that relevant industry and professional experience should be an important factor when assessing the suitability of new directors. Nevertheless, the Walker Review still implicitly supported the idea of recruiting from as wide a pool as possible while bearing industry experience in mind. Indeed, the Walker Review was concerned that increasing demands placed on directors and an increase in their legal liabilities might have the effect of reducing the pool from which directors can be chosen. Another of the Walker Review's concerns was that greater demands placed on non-executive directors' time might deter talented candidates and curb the enthusiasm or ability of companies to allow executives to take up non-executive positions elsewhere.[70]

---

[67] Governance Code B.2.
[68] Governance Code B.2.4 and B.2.1.
[69] Governance Code B.2.1.
[70] Walker Review, paragraphs 2.20 to 2.22, 3.9 and 3.20.

Some respondents to the FRC's consultation thought that there should be specific reference to gender diversity in the Governance Code. This point resonated with the FRC's self-stated intention to foster cultural change in company boards. The FRC was critical of the low number of women involved in corporate governance, as was the previous Labour government which launched an inquiry, "Women in the City", in July 2009. A recent report showed that in 2009 women accounted for only 12 per cent of all directors at FTSE 100 companies, and 7 per cent in FTSE 250 companies.[71] The FRC argued that more women can bring greater diversity to the boardroom, which in turn can improve the quality of decision making and reduce the risk of "group think".

The Walker Review called for a substantial increase of time commitment from non-executives at banks and financial institutions, from 25 to around 35 days a year.[72] This recommendation was not adopted into the new Governance Code as it was felt that it was too prescriptive outside the financial services sector. The FRC has nevertheless introduced a new Main Principle stating that directors must be able to allocate sufficient time to the company to perform their responsibilities effectively.

As a result of the Higgs Review and the Tyson Report, a new Main Principle was added to the Combined Code that directors undergo an induction to the board and further training to continually update their skills and knowledge of the business.[73] The supporting principles and provisions have been further developed by the latest revisions. Non-executives' lack of understanding of the affairs of their companies was seen by the Walker Review as a major governance failing before the crisis. As part of an effort to increase non-executive directors' involvement in businesses an amendment has been made to the Governance Code such that directors are required to gain appropriate knowledge of the company and access to its operations and staff.[74] Where newly appointed non-executives are

---

[71] Sealy, Vinnicombe and Doldor, *The Female FTSE Board Report 2009*, Cranfield University, 2009.
[72] Walker Review, Recommendation 3, pp 48 to 49.
[73] Previously Combined Code A.5, now Governance Code B.4.
[74] Governance Code, Supporting Principle to B.4.

chosen for their leadership but lack experience, then training is all the more important to get them familiar with the industry and the company's business. A Code Provision has been introduced that chairmen regularly review every director's training and development needs.[75]

Chairmen are also responsible for ensuring that directors receive accurate, timely and clear information.[76] Again, it is especially important in the light of the Walker Review to ensure that non-executives are properly informed of the company's operations and business concerns going into meetings in order to engage effectively with the executives. It is the company secretary's role to coordinate information flows between directors and directors' committees.[77] The board should also ensure that directors have access to independent professional advice at the company's expense.[78]

A major Walker Review proposal that the FRC has included in the Governance Code is the provision that an external evaluation should be conducted on boards of FTSE 350 companies at least every three years.[79] This Code Provision was designed to introduce more objectivity in the board review process.[80] The Walker Review suggested that an evaluation statement should underline the independence of the process by indicating any other business relationships between the external reviewer and the company and, where a relationship does exist, that the board is satisfied that any potential conflict has been appropriately managed. The Walker Review also said that it would be desirable for the statement to provide some indication of the outcomes of the evaluation process, but at the same time appreciated that the sensitivity of information might make publication of the results undesirable. It seems as if any statement made public will not need to go far beyond basic information in view of the fact that an evaluation has been conducted, that conclusions on how to improve the functioning of the board have been

---

[75] Governance Code B.4.2.
[76] Governance Code B.5.
[77] Governance Code, Supporting Principle to B.5.
[78] Governance Code B.5.1.
[79] Walker Review, Recommendation 12, Governance Code B.6.2.
[80] FRC, Final Report, paragraph 3.41.

drawn from it and are being implemented. The statement should include confirmation that directors have had an opportunity to raise questions and concerns and that the necessary actions to remedy any weaknesses identified have been taken.[81]

This Code Provision has been addressed to FTSE 350 companies as opposed to all companies as was initially proposed in the FRC's first draft Governance Code. It was decided to limit the provision to FTSE 350 companies because of concerns that the market for board evaluation services is still new and currently not developed enough to meet the increase of demand that would result from the provision immediately applying to all companies. The FRC has said that it will consider whether to extend this provision to smaller companies at its next review.

Another significant alteration to the Combined Code is the provision that all directors of FTSE 350 companies should be put up for annual re-election.[82] This proposal was subject to much debate. The Walker Review recommended that only chairmen should be put up for annual re-election as it felt that this would emphasise the "special accountability" of chairmen within the board and increase their attentiveness to communication with major shareholders.[83] It stated that it preferred this option to bringing in re-election for all directors but that banks' boards should keep under review the possibility of transitioning to annual re-election of all directors at a later date.

In response to the Walker Review, the FRC set out two alternative proposals in its draft Governance Code. The first was for an annual re-election of all directors, the second was to have annual election of the chairman alone. Many respondents to the FRC's consultation expressed concern that giving the chairman ultimate responsibility for corporate governance was inconsistent with the concept of a unitary board and risked undermining the chairman's position. Equally, there was strong support from institutional shareholders for annual re-election

---

[81] Walker Review, paragraphs 4.33, 4.34 and Recommendation 12, p 65.
[82] Governance Code B.7.
[83] Walker Review, Recommendation 10, paragraphs 4.23 to 4.26, pp 60 to 62.

of all directors as it was believed this would enhance the board's accountability and promote better engagement between the board and shareholders.

Objections were raised by some respondents that the annual re-election of directors might have a destabilising effect on the boards of smaller companies, which could potentially be exposed to disagreements between a few large shareholders, and might encourage short-termism among directors. Some respondents also believed that it might make it harder to recruit directors concerned about their security of tenure. The FRC was not persuaded by many of these concerns as it pointed to the record of companies who had already introduced the measure. It also favoured giving shareholders the chance to vote on directors without waiting for up to two years to do so. Nevertheless, in the end, a compromise position was adopted. The Code Provision now applies only to FTSE 350 companies in order to avoid the risk of destabilising smaller companies envisaged by some respondents. Companies below FTSE 350 level are recommended to have shareholder election for every director in the first year after their appointment, and re-election thereafter at intervals of no more than three years, as was the case under the Combined Code. Even so, the FRC encourages companies outside the FTSE 350 to consider their policy on director re-election carefully with a view to introducing annual re-elections for all directors.

The preface of the Governance Code points out that FTSE 350 companies are:

> "free to explain rather than comply if they believe that their existing arrangements ensure proper accountability and underpin board effectiveness, or that a transitional period is needed before they introduce annual re-election".

9.4.3 *Financial and business reporting*

> "The board should present a balanced and understandable assessment of the company's position and prospects."[84]

---

[84] Governance Code C.1.

The Governance Code emphasises the need for directors to report that the business is a going concern in the company's annual or half-yearly financial statements, with supporting assumptions or qualifications as necessary.[85] This Code Provision has been updated to make it consistent with the terminology used in the Disclosure and Transparency Rules on half-annual reports.[86] The FRC provides guidance that sets out the process directors should follow when assessing whether the company is a going concern, the period covered by the assessment and the disclosures ongoing concern and liquidity risk.[87] As previously mentioned, this provision is reinforced by LR 9.8.6R(3) which requires a UK-incorporated company with a premium listing to include in its report and accounts a statement made by the directors that the business is a going concern, together with supporting assumptions or qualifications as necessary, that has been prepared in accordance with this guidance.

The presumption that a company is a going concern – namely that the company will continue in operational existence for the foreseeable future – is one of the fundamental accounting concepts[88] upon which the preparation of a company's accounts is based. It is presumed that a company is a going concern unless the published accounts contain a clear statement to the contrary. In any case, the directors are under a duty to ensure that the accounts present a true and fair view of the financial affairs of the company, and so the application of this basic principle would require disclosure in the accounts if there are factors which cast doubt on the going concern presumption.

The board's responsibility to present a balanced and understandable assessment of the company's position and prospects

---

[85] Governance Code C.1.3.

[86] The Disclosure and Transparency Rules were themselves brought into line with the EU Transparency Directive, as implemented by the Transparency Obligations Directive (Disclosure and Transparency Rules) Instrument 2006 and the International Accounting Standard (IAS) 34 "Interim Financial Reporting" (*see* Accounting Standards Board statement "Half-Yearly Financial Reports" February 2007).

[87] FRC, *Going Concern and Liquidity Risk: Guidance for Directors of UK Companies 2009*, October 2009.

[88] International Standard on Auditing (UK and Ireland) (ISA) 570 "Going Concern" (April 2009). *See* also, APB's guidance to auditors in assessing companies' Corporate Governance and Going Concern Statements, Bulletin December 2009.

also extends to interim and other price-sensitive public reports and reports to regulators.

The Governance Code has introduced a new Code Provision that directors should include in the annual report an explanation of the company's business model and overall financial strategy. This was added in response to a House of Commons Treasury Committee recommendation for companies to set out "in a short business review, in clear and jargon-free English, how the firm has made (or lost) its money and what the main future risks are judged to be".[89] The aim is both to help shareholders and potential investors understand the company's business risks and also to serve as another prompt to the board to consider their long-term business model.[90] The Governance Code also states that this explanation should be located in the same part of the annual report as the business review required by Section 417 CA 2006.

9.4.4   Risk management and internal control

> "The board is responsible for determining the nature and extent of the significant risks it is willing to take in achieving its strategic objectives. The board should maintain a sound system of risk management and internal control systems."[91]

A major theme of the Walker Review was the need for boards to take more responsibility for a company's risks. This is reflected in the new Governance Code. The FRC has expanded its Main Principle (above) to make explicit the board's role in managing risk.

However, two of the Walker Review's main proposals for improving the management of risk in financial institutions – the compulsory introduction of board risk committees and "Chief Risk Officers" – were not adopted by the FRC in its changes to

---

[89] House of Commons Treasury Committee, *Banking Crisis: reforming corporate governance and pay in the City*, May 2009.
[90] FRC, Final Report, p 26.
[91] Governance Code C.2.

the Combined Code. Responses to the FRC's review, including a report of the ICAEW, expressed the view not only that most financial institutions' risk control processes are inappropriate for the majority of non-financial companies, but also that the risk committees and Chief Risk Officers suggested by the Walker Review would be unhelpful or even damaging as they would segregate risk management and dilute boards' overall responsibility for risk oversight.[92]

As currently envisaged by the Governance Code, the role of boards in managing risk is essentially twofold. The board must make decisions as to the strategic risk that a company is prepared to take and must also involve itself in monitoring a company's risk management and internal control systems. In fulfilling the latter, the Governance Code recommends that directors conduct a review, at least annually, of the effectiveness of the system of internal controls, and that the directors report to shareholders that they have done so. The review should cover all material controls, including financial, operational and compliance controls and risk-management systems. This contrasts with Section 404 Sarbanes-Oxley Act which is concerned only with internal controls over financial reporting.[93]

The Turnbull Committee first issued guidance for directors on how to comply with this aspect of the Combined Code in 1999. After the FRC established the Turnbull Review Group in 2004, the Turnbull guidance was re-published in October 2005 to incorporate a small number of changes. Among other things, the re-published guidance encouraged boards to use the internal control statement as an opportunity to help shareholders understand the risk and control issues facing a company.

The FRC is expected to republish the Turnbull guidance some time in 2010 with minor amendments to ensure that it adequately addresses some of the specific issues raised during

---

[92] ICAEW, *Getting it Right: A Report by Independent Audit Limited on Risk Governance in Non-Financial Services Companies*, October 2009. The report also contains practical guidance for risk management at board level.

[93] This was a factor in the Turnbull Review Group deciding not to follow the model of requiring a company's management to make a statement on the effectiveness of internal controls over financial reporting and the external auditor to issue an attestation report.

the FRC review, such as processes for ensuring that emerging risks are brought to the board's attention in a timely manner. The updated Turnbull guidance will be particularly relevant to company boards in view of the financial crisis and other low-frequency, high-impact risks that have affected many companies in recent years. ICAEW's report stated that the Turnbull principles still remain relevant but are prone to a "box-ticking" approach to compliance and, as such, their usefulness is dependent on how boards implement them. ICAEW also concluded that it should be a priority for the FRC to encourage better application of existing guidance rather than to introduce more rules and regulations.

The Turnbull guidance is based on the adoption by a company's board of a risk-based approach to establishing a sound system of internal control and to reviewing its effectiveness. The guidance notes that this should be incorporated by a company into its normal management and governance processes – and should not be treated as a separate exercise to meet regulatory requirements.

The guidance puts responsibility for a company's systems and controls onto the directors. They must set appropriate policies and seek regular assurance to satisfy the board that the system is functioning effectively and managing risks in the manner approved. The guidance states that the board should take various factors into account when determining what would constitute a sound system of internal control for their particular company:

(a) the nature and extent of the risks facing the company;
(b) the extent and categories of risk which the board regard as acceptable for the company to bear;
(c) the likelihood of the risks concerned materialising;
(d) the company's ability to reduce the incidence and impact on the business of risks that do materialise; and
(e) the costs of operating particular controls relative to the benefit thereby obtained in managing the related risks.[94]

---

[94] Internal Control, Revised Guidance for directors on the Combined Code, October 2005, paragraph 16.

The Turnbull guidance outlines certain matters which should be encompassed within an internal control system. The guidance also states characteristics which an effective system of internal control should have. The system should:

(a) be embedded in the operations of the company and form part of its culture;

(b) be capable of responding quickly to evolving risks to the business arising from factors within the company and to changes in the business environment; and

(c) include procedures for reporting immediately to appropriate levels of management any significant control failings or weaknesses that are identified together with details of corrective action being undertaken.[95]

Although the board formulates the company's policies on internal control, it is the role of management to implement the policies by identifying and evaluating risks for consideration by the board and designing, operating and monitoring a suitable system of internal control. All employees have some responsibility for internal control, and they should collectively have the necessary knowledge, skills, information and authority to carry out this responsibility effectively.

The guidance indicates the responsibilities within companies for reviewing the effectiveness of internal controls:

(a) it sees this as an essential part of the board's responsibilities stating that the board needs to exercise reasonable care, skill and diligence in forming its view based on the information and assurances provided to it;

(b) where tasks are delegated to designated board committees, the results should be reported to and considered by the board. It is the board that takes responsibility for the disclosures in the annual reports and accounts;

(c) effective monitoring on a continuous basis is stated to be an essential component of a sound system of control. The board should regularly receive and review reports on

---

[95] ibid., paragraph 21.

internal control, and should also make an annual assessment for the purpose of making its public statement on internal control; and

(d) management is accountable to the board for monitoring the system of internal control and for providing assurance to the board that it has done so.

The Turnbull guidance provides further suggestions as to the approach that should be adopted by management in preparing reports for the board and their contents. The guidance also provides for how the board should go about reviewing the reports provided, what it should consider in making a public statement on internal control and the content of this statement. It is a requirement of the guidance that the statement includes confirmation that necessary actions have been or are being taken to remedy any significant failings or weaknesses identified from the board's review.

The Securities and Exchange Commission ("SEC") identified the Turnbull guidance as a suitable framework within which non-US companies which are SEC-registered can address the requirements of Section 404(a) Sarbanes-Oxley legislation. The FRC issued guidance to help those companies who elect to adopt the Turnbull guidance as such a framework.[96]

9.4.5 Audit committee and auditors

"The board should establish formal and transparent arrangements for considering how they should apply the corporate reporting and risk management and internal control principles and for maintaining an appropriate relationship with the company's auditor."[97]

The Governance Code recommends that this objective should be achieved by establishing an audit committee of at least three members (or, in the case of companies below FTSE 350 level, at least two members), who should all be independent

---

[96] FRC, The Turnbull Guidance as an evaluation framework for the purposes of Section 404(a) Sarbanes-Oxley Act, 16 December 2004.
[97] Governance Code C.3.

non-executive directors. At least one member should have recent and relevant financial experience. A company that applies these recommendations will also satisfy the requirements of Chapter 7 Disclosure and Transparency Rules.[98]

The role of the audit committee includes monitoring of financial statements, reviewing financial reporting judgments and reviewing the company's internal audit function and financial controls.[99] The audit committee is responsible for making recommendations to the board concerning the appointment of the external auditor and for monitoring the external auditor's independence, objectivity and effectiveness. The audit committee should also develop and implement policy on the engagement of the external auditor to supply non-audit services.

The FSA has stated that a company that applies the Governance Code's recommendations will meet the minimum requirements set out by the Disclosure and Transparency Rules.[100] The Disclosure and Transparency Rules also require an issuer to make a statement available to the public disclosing which body carries out the audit committee functions, but provide that this can be included in the corporate governance statement in the annual report under DTR 7.2 (*see* "Listing Rules" above).[101]

ICAEW,[102] ICSA[103] and the FRC[104] have all published guidance for audit committees.

9.4.6 Remuneration

A perennial source of debate, remuneration has been the subject of two major reviews. The Greenbury review was set up to

---

[98] DTR 7.1.1R provides that at least one member of the audit committee must be independent and at least one member must have competence in accounting and/or auditing.
[99] Governance Code C.3.2.
[100] DTR 7.1.3R. DTR 7.1.7G states that the FSA believes that application of the Code's recommendations will result in compliance with the DTRs.
[101] DTR 7.1.5G and 7.1.6G.
[102] The ICAEW produce a number of guidance documents for audit committees. Titles in the series are: Whistleblowing arrangements (March 2004); Monitoring the integrity of financial statements (March 2004); The internal audit function (March 2004); Company reporting and audit requirements (November 2003); Evaluating your auditors (November 2003); Reviewing auditor independence (November 2003); and Working with your auditors (November 2003).
[103] *ICSA Guidance Note: Terms of Reference – Audit Committee* (March 2009).
[104] FRC, *Challenges for Audit Committees Arising from Current Economic Conditions*, November 2008.

produce guidelines to combat what was perceived to be excessive remuneration practices. It established the idea of having a remuneration committee staffed by non-executive directors. What are now Section D and Schedule A to the Governance Code came out of proposals from the Greenbury Committee. More recently, remuneration has again faced calls for reform and has resurfaced by way of the Walker Review. The Walker Review produced proposals to curb excessive pay in the financial sector and attempt to tie it more closely to risk and discourage short-termism, introducing concepts like bonus "clawback". The Walker Review has come up with recommendations on remuneration alongside recommendations from other institutions: the FSA has issued a Code of Practice, the UK government passed legislation including the Finance Act 2010 and the bank payroll tax, and there have been significant actions taken at European[105] and international level.

The FRC preferred not to be too prescriptive for remuneration at non-financial firms. It rejected some Walker recommendations, such as the suggestion that remuneration committees should set the parameters of firm-wide pay, saying that such recommendations were not appropriate beyond the financial sector. To an extent, it argued, financial sector remuneration, with its large number of high earners below board level whose activities could have a material impact on the company's risk exposure, is unique to the issues and concerns facing the financial sector.

Nevertheless, the FRC has made some significant changes to the Combined Code in relation to remuneration. The new Governance Code includes a clearer statement of the need for performance-related elements of executive directors' pay to be aligned to the "long-term success of the company". Amendments to Schedule A to the Governance Code mean that consideration should now be given to "non-financial performance metrics where appropriate" and remuneration should be tied more closely to risk policies. Reference to the concept of having remuneration "clawback" is also made in Schedule A in

---

[105] e.g. EC Recommendation May 2009 proposes that the directors' remuneration report sets out how employee pay conditions have been taken into account.

"exceptional circumstances of misstatement or misconduct". Unfortunately, the Governance Code provides no further guidance on how to approach the difficulties associated with implementing clawback in practice.

The title of Schedule A has been amended to make more explicit the fact that performance-related remuneration should only apply to "executive directors". The Governance Code now more clearly expresses the differences between ideal executive and non-executive pay structures and new wording has been included in Code Provision D.1.3 that non-executive directors' pay should not include share options "or other performance-related elements". In this way, non-executive pay should not risk compromising non-executive independence and objectivity.

The ABI, RiskMetrics and the ICGN have published guidelines on executive and non-executive remuneration respectively.[106] The ABI recently republished an updated version of its guidelines on executive pay. The new guidelines contain relatively few amendments, mainly relating to a new acknowledgement of risk management as one of the key considerations relevant to executive remuneration and incentives, and appear to reflect some of the conclusions of the Walker Review. This is broadly consistent with RiskMetrics guidance which says that remuneration should be clearly linked to key performance indicators. New ICGN guidelines on non-executive remuneration, on the other hand, put forward radical proposals by recommending that non-executive pay should be designed to align non-executive directors' interests with those of shareholders through the use of equity-based remuneration.

9.4.7 Communication

"The board should use the AGM to communicate with investors and to encourage their participation."[107]

---

[106] ABI, *Executive Remuneration – ABI Guidelines on Policies and Practices*, 15 December 2009; *See* also, Executive Remuneration – ABI Position Paper, 15 December 2009; RiskMetrics, *2010 RiskMetrics UK Remuneration Guidance*, February 2010; ICGN, *ICGN Non-executive Director Remuneration Guidelines and Policies*, March 2010.

[107] Governance Code E.2.

There has been no shortage of commentary on the role of share-holder meetings in the governance of companies. In 1995, with the encouragement of the Department of Trade and Industry ("DTI"), as it then was,[108] a joint City/industry working group was established[109] "to suggest practical ways in which the relationship between UK industry and institutional shareholders can be improved as a stimulus for long-term investment and development".

Virtually all participants in the working group's consultation exercise viewed the AGM as then constituted as an "expensive waste of time and money". Criticisms referred to poor attendance by institutional shareholders and to the hijacking of proceedings by special-interest groups or by individuals with questions irrelevant to most people attending the meeting.

The solution recommended by the working party was to change the format of the AGM to make it a more interesting and rewarding event so that major investors saw value in attending. Thus:

(a) an updated trading statement would be provided at the meeting and operational managers would make presentations;
(b) shareholders would be encouraged to submit their questions in advance;
(c) questions which were not of general interest would be referred to the relevant director or manager after the meeting; and
(d) institutions should accept their responsibilities to take an active and involved interest in constitutional governance.

In 1996, the DTI issued a consultative document[110] raising a number of specific questions in this context:

(a) Should the Companies Act be amended to render it easier for shareholders to requisition resolutions?

---

[108] Since June 2009, the DTI has been known as the Department for Business, Innovation and Skills ("BIS").
[109] *Developing a Winning Partnership – How Companies and Institutional Investors are Working Together* (The Myners Report), February 1995.
[110] Shareholder Communications at the General Meeting, April 1996.

(b) Should there be additional provisions to allow and regulate questions asked by members, both private and corporate, at AGMs?

(c) Should the law make it easier for the beneficial owners of shares (particularly with the introduction of CREST) to attend shareholder meetings when their shares were held by nominees?

ICSA, with support from the DTI, established a working party to deal with the issues raised by the responses to the DTI's consultative document. The working party issued a guide to what was considered best practice in the conduct of AGMs.[111] The guide sets out 24 principles as to best practice at AGMs.

The guide emphasises the importance of good communication with shareholders, including in relation to questions at the AGM (which should be encouraged) about past performance, results and intended future performance. The guide also advocates the provision of an updated trading statement at the AGM, together with a report from at least one executive director. Given the length of time which can elapse between the release of the preliminary announcement and the holding of the annual meeting, this may be a useful way in which to encourage attendance.

The Hampel Committee had two main recommendations in this area:

(a) the practice of some companies in mounting a full business presentation with a question and answer session should be examined and perhaps followed by other companies; and

(b) without a poll being demanded, companies should announce the total proxy votes for and against each resolution, once it has been dealt with by the meeting on a show of hands. The Committee was of the view that this would be likely to encourage an increase in shareholder voting.

---

[111] A Guide to Best Practice for AGMs, September 1996.

The Governance Code contains provisions relating to AGMs.[112] Boards should use the AGM to communicate with private investors and encourage their participation. In addition:

(a) separate resolutions should be proposed on each substantially separate issue, and there should be a resolution on the reports and accounts;
(b) companies should indicate the level of proxies lodged on each resolution after it has been dealt with on a show of hands setting out the number of votes for and against the resolution and the number of shares in respect of which the vote was directed to be withheld;
(c) chairmen of the audit, remuneration and nomination committees should be available to answer questions at the AGM; and
(d) at least 20 working days' notice of the AGM should be given.

In March 2010 the LSE published a practical guide to investor relations which emphasised the importance of shareholder meetings for good communication, saying that shareholder meetings should be used as a discussion forum where management is as transparent as possible about the running of the business.[113] The continuing attention paid to shareholder communication highlights the importance for the good governance of a company of maintaining a sound relationship with its shareholders.

9.5 The Stewardship Code

While the Governance Code provides guidelines for ideal board governance, it can do little to regulate the extent to which shareholders enforce good governance in practice. Shareholders have received almost as much criticism as boards for their failure to monitor properly the companies they owned before and during the crisis. The then City Minister Lord Myners blamed an "absence of an effective voice of ownership" for

---

[112] Governance Code E.2.
[113] LSE, *Investor Relations: A Practical Guide*, 15 March 2010, p 49.

banks' failings. Spiralling executive pay and employee bonuses were for him "iconic" of shareholders' inability to hold boards to account.[114] Myners was a prominent figure in accusing many shareholders of short-termism: having been too focused on making quick gains from movements in banks' share prices, he argued, shareholders neglected and possibly did not care about the long-term consequences of boardroom strategy. Similarly, the Walker Review expressed the belief that a situation in which feedback is given to a company solely through movements in its share price "cannot be regarded as a satisfactory ownership model".[115]

The Walker Review called for a fundamental change in investor behaviour. It argued that before the crisis investors were at best uninterested in burdening themselves with the task of engaging with banks' boards and at worst exacerbated management errors by taking short-term views and encouraging banks to accumulate ever more leverage in a bid to improve balance sheet efficiency.[116] The Walker Review proposed a Stewardship Code to operate in parallel to the Governance Code and to be monitored by the FRC. To this end, the Walker Review recommended that the FRC adopt as the Stewardship Code the "Code on the Responsibilities of Institutional Shareholders", prepared by the Institutional Shareholders' Committee ("ISC"). The FRC published a consultation paper in January 2010 inviting respondents to comment on the ISC text, the disclosure requirements of the Stewardship Code, and exactly which institutional shareholders should be encouraged to subscribe to it.[117] Subsequently, the ISC Code was adopted with only a few minor amendments and published by the FRC as "The UK Stewardship Code" ("Stewardship Code") in July 2010. The Stewardship Code applies to institutional investors and is

---

[114] e.g. speech by Financial Services Secretary to the Treasury, Paul Myners, at the NAPF Corporate Governance Seminar, Cheapside, London, 9 February 2010.

[115] Sir David Walker, *A review of corporate governance in UK banks and other financial industry entities: Final recommendations* ("Walker Review"), paragraph 5.7, p 70; *see also The Financial Times*, "Sir David Walker: Conformity not compliance", 12 April 2010.

[116] Walker Review, Chapter 5 "The role of institutional shareholders: communication and engagement", pp 68 to 89.

[117] FRC, *Consultation on a Stewardship Code for Institutional Investors*, January 2010.

designed to set out a model of responsible long-term investor engagement.[118]

Concerns about stewardship are not new but date back to when a code on corporate governance was first suggested. The principle of "comply or explain" hinges on shareholders taking sufficient interest in the disclosures that companies make. When the Cadbury Committee proposed the idea of a corporate governance code in 1992, it acknowledged that such a code could only succeed if sufficient interest was shown by investors in how boards chose to apply it.[119] A key aspiration of the Stewardship Code is to encourage investors to take a long-term perspective on their investments and by doing so commit time and resources to considering corporate governance issues and developing relationships with investee companies.

As well as bettering corporate governance, it is hoped the Stewardship Code will improve the investment process for end investors. Originally, the Combined Code was designed to fix what might be described in economics as the "agency problem", where the alignment of interests of principal (the shareholders) and agent (the board) is sometimes obscured because of the information gap and the self-interest of directors.[120] The Stewardship Code is an attempt to fix another agency problem: that between end investors (be they pension funds, insurance companies or the general public) and investment managers.[121] By encouraging greater transparency in requiring managers to state openly their policies on engagement, as well as publishing how they have voted and the activities they have conducted, it is hoped the Stewardship Code will help investors differentiate managers and scrutinise their commitment to corporate governance and long-term value creation.[122] Hence, the Stewardship

---

[118] Note that the ISC definition of "institutional investor" in the introduction to the Stewardship Code includes "pension funds, insurance companies, and investment trusts and other collective investment vehicles and any agents appointed to act on their behalf".

[119] Report of the Committee on the Financial Aspects of Corporate Governance, 1 December 1992, paragraph 2.5.

[120] Walker Review, paragraph 1.12, p 26.

[121] Walker Review, paragraph 5.2, p 68.

[122] *See* the section "Clear mandates" to ISC paper *Improving Institutional Investors' Role in Governance*, June 2009. The Stewardship Code requires disclosure of the information listed under Principles 1, 5, 6 and 7.

Code attempts to deal with Myners' criticism of "ownerless corporations" on another level by strengthening the relationship between companies and their ultimate owners.

The introduction of a Stewardship Code has two goals, therefore: to improve long-term value creation for end investors and to enhance corporate governance oversight. In the Stewardship Code's own words its aim is to "enhance the quality of engagement between institutional investors and companies to help improve long-term returns to shareholders and the efficient exercise of governance responsibilities".[123] The idea behind having a Stewardship Code was supported by a RiskMetrics study for the European Commission and also by a steering group paper for the Organisation for Economic Co-operation and Development.[124] There is already a global code called the ICGN Statement of Principles on Institutional Shareholder Responsibilities.

9.5.1 The stewardship principles

The Stewardship Code does not amount to a totally new endeavour; rather, the Stewardship Code is a collection of principles that have been developed over the course of the last 20 years.

In 1991, at the time of the Cadbury Review, the ISC published a statement on "The Responsibilities of Institutional Shareholders in the UK". When the Combined Code was established in 1998 it contained a section (Section E) that comprised a number of non-binding recommendations addressed to institutional shareholders. The March 2001 Myners Review of shareholder activism recommended that those responsible for pension scheme investments should have a duty actively to monitor and communicate with the management of investee companies and

---

[123] FRC, The UK Stewardship Code, July 2010, Preface.

[124] Risk Metrics, *Study on Monitoring and Enforcement practices in Corporate Governance in the Member States*, September 2009; Organisation for Economic Co-operation and Development Steering Group on Corporate Governance *Corporate Governance and the Financial Crisis: Conclusions and emerging good practices to enhance implementation of the Principles*, pp 26 to 27.

to exercise shareholder votes where those would enhance the value of the investment. The Department of Work and Pensions jointly with the Treasury then issued a Consultation Paper in February 2002, "Encouraging Shareholder Activism".[125] In response to this, the ISC issued a Statement of Principles on 21 October 2002, which was a voluntary code of practice setting out the responsibilities of institutional investors in relation to the companies in which they invest.[126] The Higgs Review recommended that institutional investors apply the ISC Statement of Principles and as a consequence it was explicitly referred to in Principle E.1 of the Combined Code.

The ISC Statement of Principles was updated in September 2005 and June 2007, when it was released alongside a framework for voting disclosure. In response to recommendations of the Walker Review, the ISC converted its Statement of principles into a code in November 2009, which was adopted by the FRC's January 2010 Consultation Paper as the draft Stewardship Code. The ISC Pripciples now form the seven principles of the Stewardship Code. These provide that institutional investors should:

(a) publicly disclose their policy on how they will discharge their stewardship responsibilities;
(b) have a robust policy on managing conflicts of interest in relation to stewardship and this policy should be disclosed;
(c) monitor their investee companies;
(d) establish clear guidelines on when and how they will escalate their activities as a method of protecting and enhancing shareholder value;
(e) be willing to act collectively with other investors where appropriate;
(f) have a clear policy on voting and disclosure of voting activity;
(g) report periodically on their stewardship and voting activities.

---

[125] *Encouraging Shareholder Activism – A Consultation Document*, 4 February 2002.
[126] ISC *The Responsibilities of Institutional Shareholders and Agents in the UK.*

The Stewardship Code operates like the Governance Code on a "comply or explain" basis. Unlike the Governance Code, however, there is no absolute obligation to have regard to the Stewardship Code's recommendations as a matter of course. The Walker Review recognised that the willingness of institutional investors to involve themselves in active engagement is dependent on the investment mandates under which they operate.[127] To accommodate this, the Walker Review recommended that institutional investors have a responsibility to disclose the business model they are using and, where they do adhere to an active engagement business model, state this on their website along with the extent to which they commit to the Stewardship Code. The Walker Review proposed that the FSA consult on introducing a new rulebook requirement to bring this into effect.[128] It is hoped that the disclosure of the business model will assist beneficial shareholders in making an informed choice when placing fund management mandates. Foreign investors are also encouraged to commit to the Stewardship Code on a voluntary basis.

Regulators had to deal with several regulatory issues when considering the introduction of the Stewardship Code. The Stewardship Code encourages investors to engage in collective action with other investors to secure more influence over boards. Concerns were raised in the July Consultation Paper to the Walker Review that such action might breach concert party provisions of Rule 9 of the Takeover Code and the "acting in concert" rules of the FSA's controllers regime which derives from the EU Acquisitions Directive (and which requires persons "acting in concert" to notify the FSA of an intention to acquire an aggregate holding exceeding 10 per cent of the shares in a financial institution).[129] In response, the Walker Review called for the

---

[127] Walker Review, paragraph 5.2, p 68. The ISC's "Improving institutional investors' role in governance" (June 2009) recommended that mandates clearly express the type of commitment to corporate governance.

[128] In the FSA's January 2010 Consultation Paper CP10/3: Effective corporate governance (Significant influence controlled functions and the Walker Review) and in the speech by Sally Dewar at the FSA City Corporate Governance and Remuneration Summit, 30 March, the FSA stated its intention to introduce a new COB disclosure rule. The FSA intends to publish a policy statement with final rules in the third quarter of 2010.

[129] Walker Review, Annex 7, pp 151 to 152.

creation of "safe harbours", saying there was a need to recognise the distinction between collective action that is designed to achieve a degree of control on a continuing basis and that which sets out to achieve "a limited, specific and relatively immediate objective". As a result, the Takeover Panel issued a statement which made clear the circumstances in which collective action would not be deemed "control seeking".[130]

The Walker Review also acknowledged concerns that an activist approach to governance might lead to penalties for market abuse in instances where managers acquire inside information through their communications with the board. The Walker Review asserted that where advance notice is received by fund managers of an intended change in the board or in some aspect of the company's strategy, the fund manager should be rigorous in ensuring its compliance arrangements prevent the information being leaked to the relevant trading desk.[131]

The FSA published a letter to the ISC explaining how its rules on market abuse apply to activist shareholders who wish to work with other shareholders to promote effective corporate governance in companies.[132] The FSA also discussed how shareholders engaging in collective action would not necessarily be deemed to be acting in concert in relation to its rules on the disclosure of major shareholdings and change in control. Nevertheless, some major institutional shareholders are not satisfied that the FSA has provided enough clarity on these concerns.[133]

9.5.2 Adoption of the Stewardship Code

The Walker Review recognised that languishing shareholder engagement was partly a result of the structure of the stock

---

[130] Takeover Panel, Practice Statement No 26 on 9 September 2009.
[131] Walker Review, paragraph 5.14, p 73.
[132] FSA, Letter to Keith Skeoch, ISC Chairman, *Shareholder engagement and the current regulatory regime* 19 August 2009; FSA, Press Release, "FSA provides clarity for activist shareholders", 19 August 2009; *see* also, FSA Market Watch Issue No 20 May 2007.
[133] e.g. Response from BlackRock to the Financial Reporting Council's Consultation on a Stewardship Code for Institutional Investors, 16 April 2010, p 3.

market and modern investment management practices. While institutional investors manage more money than ever before, portfolio theory has encouraged portfolio diversification and low conviction investment strategies among managers.[134] Even so, the Walker Review may have underestimated the obstacles that stand in the way of a widespread adoption of the Stewardship Code by the investment community.

Whether or not the Stewardship Code is applied in practice by fund managers will ultimately depend on how it is received by end investors. The most obvious question is whether end investors are likely to forego real returns in order to support the promotion of less tangible gains in corporate governance. The needs and demands of investors differ enormously and it was recognised that the Stewardship Code would not be appropriate for all investors. The Walker Review believed that long-only institutions such as life assurance and pension funds where investors are looking for long-term returns would be the institutions most likely to adopt the Stewardship Code. Even here, however, the Walker Review may have been overly optimistic.

In the case of pension funds, managers' mandates will be decided by pension fund trustees. One might expect ensuring effective corporate governance to be relatively low down on trustees' list of priorities. Trustees' primary responsibility is to pay pensions for current and future fund members and this is the reason for their preoccupation with raising dividends and asset values, especially at a time when many pension funds are in actuarial deficit. Active engagement in corporate governance is likely to be an expensive exercise for managers, and trustees may not want these costs passed on to pension scheme investors.

The Walker Review also failed to recognise the decline in importance of UK institutional investors such as pension funds and insurance companies, the institutions most likely to adopt the Stewardship Code. Pension funds and insurance companies may long have held great sway over the UK stock market, but

---

[134] Walker Review, paragraphs 5.3 and 5.7.

there can be no doubt that the influence of UK-based institutional shareholders has been in decline over the course of the last 15 to 20 years. It is now questionable how powerful UK long-only institutions overall really are, particularly given the growing influence of overseas investors, hedge funds and sovereign wealth funds. The proportion of UK-listed companies owned by overseas shareholders reached 41.5 per cent in 2008. This is in contrast to 1990 when equivalent overseas holdings were just 11.8 per cent. Equally, pension funds and insurance companies' collective ownership of 52.1 per cent of the stock market has declined to just 26.2 per cent in the same period.[135] A recent survey by the Chartered Financial Analysts Institute suggested that foreign investors' interest in the stewardship of UK companies was particularly low in comparison to engagement among UK pension and insurance funds.[136] There has also been a rise in the number of index-tracker funds which account for a significant proportion of the investment in the FTSE 100 share index. These tracker funds are less incentivised than active fund managers to be concerned about the way in which their investee companies are governed.

The FRC sought responses from institutional investors about the Stewardship Code in its January 2010 Consultation Paper.[137] Most respondents identified the size of funds under management to be the biggest factor determining whether or not the Stewardship Code would be adopted. Funds of £1 billion or more were identified by the Chartered Financial Analysts Institute as most likely to adopt the Stewardship Code because of the size of their resources and influence and the fact that economies of scale would share out the burden of the costs of engagement among individual investors.[138] Several respondents recognised that smaller funds would only be able to commit themselves to corporate governance by outsourcing voting and other engagement activities to third parties.

---

[135] Institute of Chartered Accountants in England and Wales, Letter to Susannah Haan at the FRC, 13 April 2010, p 3.
[136] Chartered Financial Analysts Institute, Letter to Susannah Haan at the FRC, 30 April 2010, pp 6 to 7.
[137] FRC, *Consultation on a Stewardship Code for Institutional Investors*, January 2010.
[138] Chartered Financial Analysts Institute, Letter to Susannah Haan at the FRC, 30 April 2010, p 7.

Other major issues raised by respondents were that public disclosure of voting and engagement activities would cause concerns about confidentiality, and that there would be a danger of engagement becoming too compliance orientated. Concerns were raised that companies might actually prefer to engage with non-signatories to avoid having to disclose confidential information, and that the excessive use of tick-box compliance might lead to a deterioration in the quality of engagement, as in the case of the ERISA legislation in the US where "a rise in voting has not led to a rise in responsible ownership".[139]

Nevertheless, in spite of these concerns, there was an over-whelmingly positive response to the general desire and need for such a Stewardship Code. Most institutional investors who submitted responses to the FRC's consultation thought that having guidelines to encourage shareholder engagement was a good idea. Further, this positive approach to engagement may already have been having an effect even before the introduction of the Stewardship Code. Indeed, there are some encouraging signs that shareholder engagement in corporate governance is picking up.[140] There were a handful of successful shareholder protests in 2009, including the majority votes against remuneration reports at some large companies such as GlaxoSmithKline and Royal Dutch Shell. Whether shareholder activism and engagement in corporate governance is a blip or the start of a more permanent trend will depend on whether it can be shown that it really adds value to companies in the long term. The argument that active engagement in governance does add value, put forward by Myners and Walker, is a hard one to prove in practice; even so, it appears to be gaining some traction.

The success of the Stewardship Code will depend on it being able to bring about the fundamental behavioural change desired by the Walker Review. This will require institutional investors to

---

[139] ABI, Response to the FRC's Consultation on a Stewardship Code for Institutional Investors, p 4.

[140] Regular surveys conducted by organisations such as the NAPF and the Investment Management Association have shown a gradual but consistent increase in the resources devoted to engagement by institutions, and 70 per cent of respondents to the most recent NAPF survey felt that engagement had been at least partly effective. *See* FRC 2009 Review: Final Report, p 33 and NAPF, *Pension Funds' Engagement with Companies* June 2009.

take a long-term view on companies and, where they disapprove of management strategy, actively exert their influence on boards where otherwise they might simply have sold their shares.

9.6 The corporate governance implications of CA 2006

Aside from the developments of the Governance Code and the Stewardship Code, the previous Labour government's reforms in the field of corporate governance long tried to promote wider-participation of shareholders in the affairs of the companies in which they invest. Before the Stewardship Code, a number of legislative changes were introduced on the basis of "enhancing shareholder engagement and a long-term investment culture". These included the requirement for quoted companies to get shareholder approval for the annual directors' remuneration report, the requirement for a business review and the government's initiatives in response to the 2001 Myners report and the subsequent review of progress. Various of the changes under the CA 2006 have also been introduced with this objective of greater shareholder participation in mind.

In its White Paper in March 2005, the government commented that:

> "Shareholders have a key role to play in driving long-term company performance and economic prosperity. Informed, engaged shareholders – or those acting on their behalf – are the means by which the directors are held to account for business strategy and business performance and by which investment decisions are taken which reflect the best use of capital. However, the investment chain has become increasingly complex, with the result that communication up and down the chain, and the exercise of ownership rights and responsibilities have become more difficult."[141]

Improving shareholder participation has also been a goal of the European Commission. Its recently implemented Shareholder

---

[141] BIS's Company Law Reform, March 2005, p 15.

Rights Directive attempts to facilitate shareholder communication and increase their voting rights and rights to information.

9.6.1 *Shareholder communications*

Various changes have been introduced to improve the timeliness and transparency of company information and proceedings with a view to increasing shareholder dialogue and engagement.

They include the following provisions of particular relevance to public companies:

(a) A reduction in the time allowed for companies to file their annual accounts. This is intended to reflect improvements in technology and the increased rate at which information becomes out of date. For public companies it has been reduced from seven months to six months (Section 442(2)(b)).

(b) The requirement for AGMs to be held within six months of the end of the financial year for public companies (Section 336). This is intended to provide a more timely opportunity to hold the directors of a public company to account.[142] Conversely, the default provision is that private companies will no longer be required to hold an AGM.

(c) The publication of the full reports and accounts on the websites of quoted companies (Section 430).

(d) A public company is required to meet the cost of circulating resolutions received from members who hold not less than 5 per cent of the voting rights or at least 100 members holding an average of £100 or more in nominal amount of its paid-up share capital if received before the financial year end (Section 338).

(e) Enhanced rights for proxies to vote on a show of hands as well as a poll and to speak (Sections 284, 285, 324 and 329).

(f) The disclosure of the results of polls taken at general meetings by quoted companies on their websites (Section 341).[143]

---

[142] CA 2006, Explanatory Notes, paragraph 538.

[143] Section 341 was recently amended by the Companies (Shareholders' Rights) Regulations 2009 (SI 2009/1632) to give more detailed disclosure requirements for "traded companies", where traded companies are companies traded on regulated markets in the EEA, including the UK.

(g) The independent scrutiny of a polled vote where requested by a minority of members of a quoted company (members who hold not less than 5 per cent of the voting rights, or 100 or more members each holding an average of £100 or more in nominal amount of its paid up share capital (Section 342)). There is a period of a week to exercise the right, for example on a controversial resolution or where there appears to be a problem relating to voting procedures.[144]

(h) The grant of rights to indirect investors allowing them a greater role in company proceedings (Part 9 CA 2006).

9.6.2 Exercise of members' rights by non-members

Investors increasingly hold their shares through an intermediary or a chain of intermediaries. The UK government has accepted that there are advantages in this and that it is in any event sometimes a regulatory requirement. However, it is undoubtedly the case that such an approach does not facilitate shareholder engagement.

A number of measures have been adopted to overcome the problems which this can cause. The Explanatory Notes to the CA 2006 (the "Explanatory Notes") explain that the new provisions have been designed to make it easier for investors to exercise their governance rights fully and responsibly.

The CA 2006 contains provisions which allow all companies whose articles enable them to do so to extend certain rights to persons nominated by the registered member, including rights in respect of resolutions and meetings and to appoint a proxy.[145] Typically, any such nomination is expected to be in favour of a beneficial holder of the shares but the relevant section permits anyone to be nominated. However, only the member can enforce these rights and they do not affect the requirements for the transfer of a member's interest.

---

[144] CA 2006, Explanatory Notes, paragraph 342.
[145] Section 145.

The CA 2006 also contains special provisions for nominations in respect of information rights in listed companies.[146] A registered member of such a company will have the right to nominate a person on whose behalf he holds shares to receive communications sent to members and to require copies of accounts and reports. The enjoyment of such information rights by the nominated person may be enforced against the company by the member as if they were rights conferred by the company's articles.

A company will have an opportunity to check annually whether nominated persons wish to retain their information rights. A company will have the right to terminate a nominated person's information rights, if the company asks the nominated person if he wishes to retain such rights and does not receive a response within 28 days. However, only one such enquiry can be made in any 12-month period.

The Secretary of State may, by regulation, amend the provisions in relation to information rights to extend or restrict the classes of companies to which such provisions apply, make other provision as to the circumstances in which a nomination may be made or extend or restrict the rights conferred by a nomination.[147]

9.6.3 *Powers in relation to institutional investors*

Even before the Walker Review, the previous Labour government had long been concerned to ensure greater engagement by institutional shareholders. Under Section 1277 CA 2006, the Secretary of State and the Treasury have the power to make regulations requiring institutional investors to disclose information about the way in which shares held by them in quoted companies have been voted.[148] Section 1280 provides that the regulations made by the Secretary of State or the Treasury may require the institutions to which the section applies to disclose detailed information on, for example, the exercise or

---

[146] Sections 146 to 150.
[147] Section 157.
[148] Sections 1277 to 1280.

non-exercise of voting rights and any instructions given or delegation made relating to their exercise or non-exercise.

So far, this power has not been exercised. There is already a voluntary framework on voting disclosure published by the ISC in June 2007 and designed to operate in conjunction with the ISC Statement of Principles which now forms the Stewardship Code.[149] The voting framework works on a "comply or explain" basis where institutions can decide against making their voting record publicly available so long as they explain why they have done so. At the time of introduction, the ISC noted that a lot had already been achieved in recent years in terms of the improvement in voting disclosure.

Given the introduction of the Stewardship Code, it seems unlikely that these powers provided by the CA 2006 will be exercised soon. Instead, the provisions supply the government with an alternative line of attack if the voluntary framework is seen to be failing. Nevertheless, these provisions proved very controversial when debated in the House of Lords, where issues were raised similar to those discussed in the recent FRC consultation on the Stewardship Code. One such point was that compulsory disclosure might lead to a compliance-orientated approach to voting which might perversely result in a decline in the quality of engagement.

9.6.4 Electronic communications

For some companies – particularly those with large shareholder bases – the ability to communicate electronically with members and nominated persons can result in significant cost savings. The government also saw electronic communications as providing the opportunity to enhance the "immediacy and transparency of dialogue between companies and shareholders".[150]

Under the CA 2006,[151] a company may communicate by e-mail with persons who have agreed to receive documents via e-mail

---

[149] ISC, *Institutional Shareholders' Committee framework on voting disclosure*, June 2007.
[150] BIS's Company Law Reform White Paper, March 2005, p 18.
[151] Sections 1143 to 1148 and Schedules 4 and 5.

(or, in the case of communications with a company, if the company is deemed to have agreed to receive e-mail communications by a provision in the companies legislation).

The CA 2006 provides that a company may communicate by means of a website with persons who have agreed, or are deemed to have agreed, to receive such communications. A member or nominated person will be deemed to have agreed to receive communications by means of a website if:

(a) members of a company have resolved to approve the use of website communications or the articles of the company permit such communications; and

(b) the company requests the member or nominated person to agree to receive website communications and does not receive an answer within 28 days.

A member or nominated person will not, however, be deemed to have agreed to accept such communications, if the company's request does not explain clearly the consequences of failing to respond or the company seeks his agreement more than once in any 12-month period.

Where a member of a company has received information from the company otherwise than in hard copy form, he is entitled to require the company to send him a version of the information in hard copy form.

Electronic communications by quoted companies are also the subject of rules issued by the FSA for the purpose of implementing the Transparency Directive – the Disclosure and Transparency Rules. The rules provide that a decision to use electronic means to convey information (through either e-mail or website) must be taken in a general meeting of the company.[152] The use of electronic means must not depend on the residence of the recipient.[153] It had been thought that this will restrict the use of such means to cases where local securities laws do not make it necessary to restrict distribution. However, the

---

[152] DTR 6.1.8R(1).
[153] DTR 6.1.8R(2).

FSA has indicated that it would not regard the principle of equality of treatment of shareholders as being breached merely because an issuer does not offer to communicate electronically with shareholders where legal restrictions in certain jurisdictions mean that this is not possible.[154] Further, the written consent of direct shareholders or, in certain cases, indirect shareholders entitled to acquire, dispose of or otherwise exercise voting rights must be obtained to the use of electronic communications.[155] Consent is deemed to have been obtained if no objection is received within a reasonable period of time. The FSA has acknowledged that it is not ideal that both the CA 2006 and these rules apply. Its guidance indicates its view that the DTR should be applied in a way which is consistent with the CA 2006. For example, the FSA considers that the 28-day period for objections specified in the CA 2006 represents a reasonable time for the purposes of the relevant DTR provision.

The provisions in the CA 2006 dealing with electronic communications with shareholders came into force on 20 January 2007. This was a concession that was brought in seemingly as a response to business protests at the late extension of the provisions relating to business reviews.

9.6.5 Auditors and accounts

Reforms were introduced in the CA 2006 which were intended to allow limitation of auditors' liability, improve the quality of the audit process and simplify auditing and accounting procedures.

An auditor will be able to limit its liability in respect of the audit by agreement with the company. Agreements of this kind will be valid in respect of one financial year only and are subject to shareholder approval.[156]

---

[154] UKLA Publications, *List!*, Issue No 14, Updated April 2007. *See* also Stock Exchange AIM Notice, AIM 26, 12 January 2007, paragraph 3.

[155] Existing notifications of e-mail addresses are expressed to have effect as agreements to receive information in electronic form under the CA 2006 – paragraphs 4(1) and (2) of Part 2 of Schedule 5 Companies Act 2006 (Commencement No 1, Transitional Provisions and Savings) Order 2006.

[156] CA 2006, Part 16, Chapter 6.

The agreement may not limit the auditor's liability to less than the amount which is fair and reasonable in the circumstances, having regard to the auditor's responsibilities, its contractual obligations to the company and required professional standards. An agreement that purports to limit the auditor's liability to less than this amount takes effect as if it limited the auditor's liability to that amount. This provision allows the court to impose its view of what is fair and reasonable and thus involves a material element of uncertainty for auditors. The CA 2006 states that it is immaterial how a liability limitation agreement is framed, in particular, the limit on the amount of the auditor's liability need not be a sum of money, or a formula, specified in the agreement.

The debate over limitation of auditors' liability was one of the most highly publicised aspects of the CA 2006. The decision to allow auditors to limit their liability by contract was seen as balanced by the creation of a new criminal offence in relation to auditors' reports. This is committed where an auditor knowingly or recklessly causes its report on the company's annual accounts to include any matter that is materially misleading, false or deceptive.[157]

The provisions on the limitation of auditors' liability are broadly consistent with a recent European Commission proposal published in 2008 on measures to limit the civil liability of auditors and audit firms carrying out statutory audits of companies registered and listed in European Member States.[158] The position is less compatible with that of the SEC in the US, however, where the rules oppose firms entering into auditor liability limitation agreements. The FRC is soon to publish guidance on the impact of the SEC's rules on UK SEC registrants, and the GC 100 published an updated version of its guidance on the SEC rules in July 2009.[159]

New provisions designed to improve the value and quality of the audit include:

---

[157] Section 507.
[158] Commission of the European Communities, *Commission Recommendation concerning the limitation of the civil liability of statutory auditors and audit firms*, 5 June 2008.
[159] GC100 Update Note: Auditors' Limitation of Liability Agreements: Draft Revised June 2009.

(a) a power to make rules to require companies to disclose the content of audit engagement letters (Section 493);

(b) a right for a specified proportion of shareholders in a quoted company to require website publication of matters relating to the audit, or about the auditors ceasing to hold office, which the shareholders propose to raise at the next meeting of shareholders (Section 527);

(c) a requirement that the auditors of quoted companies must, on ceasing to hold office, make statements setting out the circumstances connected with their ceasing to hold office (Section 519); and

(d) the signature of the audit report by the "senior statutory auditor", who will be the individual identified by the audit firm (in accordance with EU guidelines or guidance issued by the Secretary of State) to sign the auditor's report on behalf of the firm (Sections 503 and 504).

9.6.6 Business review

Current requirements for a business review are set out in Section 417 CA 2006. A business review must:[160]

(a) contain a fair review of the company's business and a description of the principal risks and uncertainties facing the company;

(b) be a balanced and comprehensive analysis of the development and performance of the company's business during the financial year and the position of the company's business at the end of the year, consistent with its size and complexity; and

(c) to the extent necessary for an understanding of the development, performance or position of the company's business, the review must include an analysis using financial key performance indicators and, where appropriate, analysis using other key performance indicators, including information concerning environmental and employee matters. The key performance indicators are factors by reference to which the development, performance or

---

[160] Section 417.

position of the company's business can be measured effectively.

The CA 2006 provides that, for quoted companies, the review must, to the extent necessary for an understanding of the development, performance or position of the company's business, include:

(a) the main trends and factors likely to affect the future development, performance and position of the company's business and information about environmental matters, the company's employees and social and community issues. This must include information about any policies of the company in relation to these matters and the effectiveness of the policies; and

(b) provide "information about persons with whom the company has contractual or other arrangements which are essential to the business of the company". This was an additional and controversial requirement introduced into the CA 2006 at a late stage.

The CA 2006 contains a qualification about disclosure of information. Information will not have to be disclosed about impending developments or matters in the course of negotiation if the disclosure would, in the opinion of the directors, be seriously prejudicial to the interests of the company. Nor is disclosure required about a person if it "would, in the opinion of the directors, be seriously prejudicial to that person and contrary to the public interest".

The CA 2006 provides that a director is liable to compensate the company for loss suffered as a result of any untrue or misleading statement in the directors' reports (which would include the business review) or any omission from any report only if he knew the statement to be untrue or misleading or was reckless as to whether the statement was untrue or misleading or he knew the omission to be dishonest concealment of a material fact. Further, the director will not have liability to anyone other than the company.[161]

---

[161] Section 463. The section does not affect liability for a civil penalty or criminal offence or liability under the law of another jurisdiction.

The ASB published a report on the implementation of business reviews by listed companies in October 2009.[162] While satisfied with the standard of reporting in most areas, the report said that there were still significant opportunities for improvement, particularly in sections on principal risks and corporate social responsibility, as well as in "sustainability reporting". The ABI recommended that companies reduce the amount of "clutter" and make clear how information reported on corporate social responsibility and sustainability is actually relevant to their businesses. Meanwhile, the Climate Change Act 2008[163] and other regulations are placing ever more demands on businesses responding to an "evolving plethora"[164] of sustainability reporting requirements.[165]

Provision C.1.2 of the Governance Code recommends directors provide in the annual report an explanation of the company's business model and strategy for delivering the objectives of the company. The Governance Code states that it would be desirable if this explanation was located in the same part of the annual report as the Business Review.[166]

9.6.7 Codification of directors' duties

The CA 2006 codified directors' duties with a view to reflecting in statute the current common law position, but with some significant changes.

The CA 2006 provides that directors owe the following duties:[167]

---

[162] ASB, *Rising to the challenge. A review of narrative reporting by UK listed companies*, 29 October 2009.

[163] Section 85 Climate Change Act 2008 requires the Secretary of State to make regulations under Section 416(4) CA 2006 requiring directors' reports to disclose greenhouse gas emissions, or to explain why he has not done so, by 6 April 2012.

[164] The phrase is used in a report by Virtuous Circle, *Just how many greenhouse gas reporting (GHG) standards do we need?*, September 2009.

[165] As required by the Climate Change Act 2008, Defra and the Department of Climate Change and Energy published guidance on how to measure and report greenhouse gas emissions: *Environmental Key Performance Indicators: Reporting Guidelines for UK Business*, September 2009.

[166] Guidance as to the matters that should be considered in an explanation of the business model is provided at paragraphs 30 to 32 of the ASB's *Reporting Statement: Operating and Financial Review*.

[167] Sections 171 to 177 (both inclusive).

(a) to act in accordance with the company's constitution and for proper purposes;
(b) to promote the success of the company;
(c) to exercise independent judgment;
(d) to use reasonable care, skill and diligence;
(e) to avoid conflicts of interest;
(f) not to accept benefits from third parties; and
(g) to declare interests in proposed transactions or arrangements.

Whilst the detail of these duties are outside the scope of this Chapter, certain of the changes will be relevant in this context.

9.6.8   Duty to promote the success of the company

The statutory duty which caused the most heated debates in Parliament and the media is the duty of directors to promote the success of the company.[168] This duty requires a director to act in the way he "considers, in good faith, would be most likely to promote the success of the company for the benefit of its members as a whole".[169] In fulfilling this duty, a director is required to have regard (amongst other matters) to:

(a) the long-term consequences of any decision;
(b) the interests of the company's employees;
(c) the need to foster business relationships with suppliers, customers and others;
(d) the impact of the company's operations on the community and the environment;
(e) the desirability of the company maintaining a reputation for high standards of business conduct; and
(f) the need to act fairly as between members of the company.

The list is not exhaustive but it is intended that it:

> "highlights areas of particular importance which reflect wider expectations of responsible behaviour, such as the

---

[168] Section 172.
[169] This is subject to the directors' to consider or act in the interests of creditors in certain circumstances. *See* Section 172(3).

interests of the company's employees and the impact of the company's operations on the community and the environment".[170]

9.6.9 The meaning of "success"

The government stated that, for most companies, "success" is defined in commercial terms. In a debate in the House of Lords, the Attorney-General said the following:

> ". . . What is success? The starting point is that it is essentially for the members of the company to define the objectives that they wish to achieve. Success means what the members collectively want the company to achieve. For a commercial company, success will usually mean long-term increase in value. For certain companies, such as charities and community interest companies, it will mean the attainment of the objectives for which the company has been established.[171] But one can be more refined than that. A company's constitution and the decisions that a company makes can also go on to be more specific about what is the appropriate success model for the company. I have indicated that usually for a company it will be a long-term increase in value, but I can imagine commercial companies that would have a different objective as to their success."

9.6.10 "Enlightened shareholder value"

One of the main questions raised at the beginning of the Company Law Review process was whether directors' duties should continue to be owed solely to the company, except in limited cases, or whether directors should be required as a matter of law to account directly to third parties, e.g. employees, suppliers and local communities. The conclusion was that the existing position should remain: the CA 2006 provides that a director's duties are owed to the company rather than third parties.

---

[170] CA 2006, Explanatory Notes, paragraph 326.
[171] *See* Section 172(2).

However, the previous government favoured an approach known as "enlightened shareholder value". This requires a director to have regard to the interests of third parties in fulfilling his duties to the company. This approach is reflected in the new statutory duty to promote the success of the company. When fulfilling this duty, a director must have regard, among other things, to the interests of employees and the various other factors set out above.

The previous government's desire to introduce this list of factors as matters to which directors must have regard caused considerable debate. The government maintained consistently that directors will need to do more than pay "lip-service" to each of these factors when making decisions: directors will be required to give due and proper consideration to them. Indeed the Explanatory Notes state that the duty to exercise reasonable care, skill and diligence in Section 174 CA 2006 will apply. The Explanatory Notes emphasise that:

> "It will not be sufficient to pay lip service to the factors and in many cases the directors will need to take action to comply with this as part of the duty [in Section 172]."[172]

Critics expressed particular concern that this would make decision making more onerous. Further, critics claimed that these factors would increase the likelihood of directors' actions being challenged in the courts and would lead to greater judicial interference in business decisions particularly given the new statutory provisions relating to derivative claims. There was, therefore, concern that the increased risk of litigation will make directors more risk-averse.

Those in favour of the introduction of these factors, however, claimed that the risks which they pose to directors were exaggerated. They argued, first, that the director's basic duty remains a subjective one: the director must act in the way he considers, in good faith, would promote the success of the company. Further, a director is only obliged to have regard to

---

[172] CA 2006, Explanatory Notes, paragraph 328.

the factors listed above; a director is not required actively to promote the interests of the environment, the community and so forth.

The Explanatory Notes provide some support for this view stating that:

> "The decision as to what will promote the success of the company, and what constitutes such success, is one for the directors' good faith judgment. This ensures that business decisions on, for example, strategy and tactics are for the directors, and not subject to decision by the courts, subject to good faith."

and (having noted the duty to exercise reasonable care, skill and diligence in this context) go on to state that:

> "At the same time the duty does not require a director to do more than good faith and the duty to exercise reasonable care, skill and diligence would require, nor would it be possible for a director acting in good faith to be held liable for a process failure which would not have affected his decision as to which course of action would best promote the success of the Company."[173]

There were fears that there would be an increase in the amount of litigation faced by directors from activist shareholders seeking to test the courts' approach to these factors. One particular source of concern was that shareholders would be able to commence derivative actions using the new statutory provisions.[174] The CA 2006 put the old common law right to bring a derivative action on a statutory footing while removing some of the barriers that had previously made bringing a derivative action difficult for shareholders, such as the necessity to show that directors had personally benefited from the alleged wrongdoing. Derivative actions are brought by shareholders on behalf of the company for wrongs committed by directors in breach of their duties. As directors' duties are now codified, it was

---

[173] CA 2006, Explanatory Notes, paragraphs 327 and 328.
[174] CA 2006, Part 11.

thought that this would also make derivative actions easier, while the obligation to have regard to third parties such as employees and the community might increase the range of potential causes of action. At the same time, the government hoped that the drafting of the CA 2006 on derivative action would encourage greater shareholder activism.

However, while the long-term impact of the CA 2006 is not clear, fears that the floodgates of litigation would be opened to activist shareholders have so far proved ill-founded. There have been very few cases to date. This is partly to do with the procedure by which a shareholder must bring a derivative action. Shareholders must first get the permission of the court to bring a claim. Courts have so far been very restrictive in the way they have applied their own tests for allowing a derivative action.[175] One factor courts consider is whether a person acting in accordance with the director's duty to promote the success of the company would not seek to continue the claim. It is often hard to prove the action in question is in the interests of the company. Further, members may be dissuaded by the costs of losing an action to a company able to run up far greater legal expenses, especially since the benefit gained from a successful claim will go to the company rather than directly to shareholders. Success may be more likely under a contractual claim for a breach of the terms of any shareholder's agreement. Shareholders may also prefer to pursue their interests directly through an unfair prejudice petition.

So far, the record suggests that only the most committed "activist" shareholders convinced of the merits of their cause will bring a derivative action. The recent crisis, however, might have been thought to create the perfect conditions for such claims. It may be that, while the immediate aftermath of the implementation of the CA 2006 proved a false dawn for litigation against directors, the near future may yet provide some vindication for these fears.

---

[175] Cases where permission has been refused include *Mission Capital Plc* v *Sinclair* [2008] EWHC 1339 (Ch) All ER (D) 225 (Mar) (Floyd J; 17 March 2008), *Franbar Holdings Ltd* v *Patel* [2008] EWHC 1534 (Ch) [2008] All ER (D) 14 (Jul) [2009] 1 BCLC 1 (William Trower QC; 2 July 2008), *Stimpson* v *Southern Landlords Association* [2009] EWHC 2072 (Ch) (HHJ Pelling QC, 21 May 2009).

There were also concerns that directors' greater exposure to liability would increase bureaucracy and discourage risk-taking. There is no evidence so far that the CA 2006 has done either. The CA 2006 may have encouraged directors to record the reasons for their decisions and consider their duties more fully than before, but compliance with the legislation is unlikely materially to increase bureaucracy in a well-managed company. Further, the directors' duties are largely a codification of what existed in common law before, and so should not make directors any more risk averse than they were before the introduction of the CA 2006.[176]

9.6.11 Changes to the CA 2006 introduced by the Shareholder Rights Directive

The Shareholder Rights Directive (the "Directive") was implemented in this country on 3 August 2009 by the Companies (Shareholders' Rights) Regulations 2009 (the "Regulations"). The Directive hoped to improve shareholder participation by enabling shareholders to exercise their voting rights and rights to information more easily. It was also anticipated that its implementation across Europe would solve some of the problems associated with cross-border voting. The CA 2006 was already relatively advanced in terms of the rights given to shareholders. Rather than bring in new legislation, it was felt that the best response would be to introduce the parts of the Regulations that added weight to the CA 2006 in certain respects. ICSA has published guidance on the implications of the changes made to the CA 2006 in practice.[177]

Some changes to the CA 2006 apply to all companies, others to those traded on regulated markets in the EEA, including the UK ("traded companies").[178] Regulated markets in the UK include the LSE Main Market and the listed element of PLUS, but not AIM.

---

[176] Directors may wish to refer for guidance to GC 100, "Companies Act (2006) – Directors' duties", 7 February 2007, and GC 100, "Companies Act 2006 – Directors' conflicts of interest", 18 January 2008.

[177] ICSA Guidance on the Implementation of the Shareholder Rights Directive, 29 July 2009.

[178] Section 360C CA 2006.

9.6.11.1 Voting

Under the CA 2006 as amended, a proxy can now vote twice in the same meeting if representing more than one member.[179] This clarifies the position for proxies in a situation in which they are given conflicting instructions. If a proxy is appointed by several members with instructions to vote the same way, the proxy is entitled to vote only once, "for" or "against" as applicable. Where, however, one or more of the members instructs him to vote "for" and one or more member instructs him to vote "against", the proxy is then entitled to vote twice, both "for" and "against".

This is now the only stated exception to the general rule that a proxy only has one vote on a show of hands. It has been debated how this should be interpreted if a proxy has discretionary votes. If the proxy is given definite instructions both "for" and "against", it is uncertain whether the proxy would then be able to use a second discretionary vote the other way. The CA 2006 is subject to company articles, so companies will be able to change their articles to reflect their position on this if they so choose.

The Directive clarifies the position where a member appoints more than one proxy in respect of different shares within the same shareholding. In this case, each appointed proxy has one vote on a show of hands. This enables nominee shareholders to appoint the underlying beneficial owners as proxies in respect of those shares in which they have an interest.

The Directive also puts on a statutory footing the common law position that a proxy is required to vote in accordance with any voting directions provided by the appointing shareholder.[180] This introduces an extrastatutory duty for the proxy in addition to his common law duty as agent. As was the case before, if it is found that a proxy has not voted in accordance with instructions, this will not invalidate the results of the meeting.

---

[179] Section 285(2).
[180] Section 324A.

The Directive also permits companies to offer advance voting on a poll.[181] This is to enable members to cast a vote in advance of a meeting, separate to their rights to appoint a proxy. The provision was primarily designed for European Member States with no proxy systems or more restrictive proxy practices. It should be noted that this is a permissive provision so companies are not required to offer advance voting but may do through amending their articles if they wish.

9.6.11.2 *Notice of meetings*

The old CA 2006 distinction between the minimum requirements of 14 days' notice for a general meeting and 21 days' for an AGM has been modified slightly. Under the Directive, there is a general requirement that the notice period for all meetings of traded companies should be at least 21 days.[182] This is subject to an exception, however. A general meeting at a traded company (as opposed to an AGM) may be called on 14 days' notice so long as a special resolution has been passed at a previous meeting to that effect, and so long as the company offers the facility to allow shareholders to vote by electronic means. This will be met if the company offers the facility to shareholders to appoint a proxy by means of a website.

While the wording of this new provision in the CA 2006 affords flexibility to a company to call a meeting at 14 days' notice, voting guidelines issued by NAPF (supported by RiskMetrics) state that such notice should only be used sparingly by companies and in "limited circumstances" where it would clearly be to the advantage of shareholders as a whole. The NAPF guidelines provide that shareholders should consider voting against resolutions tabled at 14 days' notice "where the use of the shorter notice period has not been adequately justified by the company or the proposals are of such complexity that shareholders require more time to consider their voting decision".[183] Recent market practice has been for companies to propose enabling resolutions at their AGMs to allow general meetings to

---

[181] Incorporated into the CA 2006 in Section 322A.
[182] Section 307A.
[183] NAPF, Corporate Governance Policy, 2009/10 Policy Updates; RiskMetrics Group, European Corporate Governance Policy, 2010 Updates, November 2009.

be called on 14 days' notice. Where companies do so, NAPF encourages a statement in AGM circulars outlining "the circumstances in which a short-notice meeting may be called".

In addition to this change to the rules in the CA 2006 on the length of notice periods, there is also a new requirement that the matters set out in the notice for a meeting must be made available on a traded company's website.[184] There are also additional content requirements for notices of meetings. Traded companies must include the (newly introduced) voting record date,[185] the procedure on how to attend and vote and a statement of the member's right to ask questions (for more on which, *see* below), among other things.[186]

9.6.11.3 *Shareholders' rights to call meetings, have questions answered and add agenda items*

The original provisions of the CA 2006 allowed members of public companies to require directors to call a general meeting so long as they had the support of 10 per cent of the voting share capital of the company. The Directive has reduced this threshold to 5 per cent.[187]

The Directive also introduced a general right that shareholders must have their questions answered at general meetings. This was possibly the Directive's biggest statement of intent in relation to shareholder empowerment. Consequently the CA 2006, as amended, states that at a general meeting of a traded company, the company must cause to be answered any question relating to the business being dealt with at the meeting put by a member attending the meeting.[188]

This general principle that all questions should be answered is not without its drawbacks, however. If every question were to be answered it would add extra time and cost to meetings which would become side-tracked by a great deal of irrelevance. For

---

[184] Section 311A(1)(a).
[185] Section 360B(2).
[186] Section 311.
[187] Section 303.
[188] Section 319A.

this reason, exceptions to this general principle have been introduced and the CA 2006 provides that no answer needs to be given if it is undesirable in the interests of the company or the good order of the meeting.[189] Further no answer need be given if to do so interferes unduly with the preparation of the meeting, involves the disclosure of confidential information, or if the answer has already been given on a website in the form of an answer to a question.[190]

Shareholders also have a new right to require traded companies to add items to their AGM agendas.[191] This is in addition to existing rights under the CA 2006 to require the circulation of statements and resolutions.[192] The rules are the same as for requisitioned resolutions. Shareholders must have 5 per cent of total voting rights or 100 members entitled to vote with an average of at least £100 paid up share capital per member. The request must be received no later than six weeks before the meeting or if later, the time notice is given. The company must bear the cost of circulating the details of such agenda items if the request is received before the end of the financial year preceding the AGM.[193] As in the case of requisitioned resolutions, a company can refuse to include a matter in the AGM business if it is defamatory of any person, or frivolous or vexatious.[194]

Finally, amendments to the CA 2006 have removed the chairman's casting vote. The chairman will no longer be able to make the ultimate decision if there are equal votes on an ordinary resolution at a general meeting. Any provision giving the chairman a casting vote in a general meeting in a company's articles will be void.

9.7 Further power to legislate

The government took various powers to introduce further changes to companies legislation using subordinate legislation.

---

[189] Section 319A(2)(c).
[190] Section 319A(2)(a) and (b).
[191] Sections 338A, 340A.
[192] Sections 338, 339 and 340.
[193] Section 340B.
[194] Section 338A(2).

Of particular relevance to corporate governance, the government provided the FSA with the power for the UK Listing Authority ("UKLA") to make corporate governance rules relating to issuers whose securities have been admitted to a regulated market in order to take account of the UK's Community obligations.[195] In addition, the government took a similar power to make regulations for such issuers. These regulations may be made by reference to any specified code on corporate governance – which might include the Governance Code – and create new criminal offences punishable by a fine.[196] The government has already exercised these powers in connection with the implementation of the Statutory Audit Directive and the Company Reporting Directive in 2008.[197]

---

[195] Section 89O FSMA.

[196] Section 1273 CA 2006.

[197] BIS, European Company Law and Corporate Governance, *Implementation of Directive 2006/43/EC on Statutory Audits of Annual and Consolidated Accounts (8th Company Law Directive)*, March 2007.

Chapter 10

Directors Facing Disputes

Michael Hatchard

Partner
Skadden, Arps, Slate, Meagher & Flom (UK) LLP

This Chapter is divided into two parts. Section 10.1 covers disputes within the board of a company. Sections 10.2 to 10.4 cover disputes between the board and members of the company.

10.1 Disputes within the board

The actions and attitude of a board of directors reflect the sum of its parts. Individuals differ in their backgrounds, opinions and objectives. Diversity is a strength, but it is not surprising that one or more members of a board can sometimes find themselves at odds with others.

In practice, a board may continue running a company for years without rigid formality. There is nothing inherently wrong in this. Equally, differences will in general be resolved by a measure of compromise on all sides but situations can arise where compromise goes out of the window and irreconcilable positions are taken. It is these situations that this section addresses, first from the standpoint of the majority and then from that of the minority. It also addresses the position where the board is deadlocked.

10.1.1 Majority standpoint

The basic instinct of the majority of the board when faced with an objectionable director may be to exclude the director from board discussions or, ultimately, to remove the director from the board.

10.1.1.1 Exclusion from proceedings

Each director has the right:

(a) to be notified of a proposed board meeting in sufficient time to attend (or the meeting may be invalid); and
(b) to attend board meetings.

This right of attendance is fundamental, given the responsibilities associated with the office of director, and has proved to be enforceable by injunction.[1]

The procedures for notification of board meetings are likely to be provided in the articles of association and may be supplemented by practices generally observed by the company. Where relations are strained, reliance on formality with the aim of sidelining a particular director, for example not using readily available means of communication,[2] would be open to attack if it can be shown that a reasonable effort to give notice was not made and the consequences for the excluded director are material. Similarly, failing to supply information necessary to allow the directors to perform their functions will invite criticism.[3] Delegation of particular functions to committees or officers may operate in practice to limit participation but delegation is a fiduciary power that may not be improperly used to exclude a director from decision making and information flows. An over-riding consideration is the potential to invoke Section 994[4] (*see* Section 10.4.1.7(a) below).

10.1.1.2 Removal of directors

The articles can include procedures to remove a director, for example by conferring a power of removal on a specified

---

[1] *Hayes* v *Bristol Plant Hire Ltd* [1957] 1 WLR 499. Case holds that a director has a sufficient proprietary interest to maintain an action for the injunction. The underlying conclusion is founded on a Sir George Jessel, MR judgment that may itself have relied on an assumption that the relevant articles gave a right to attend meetings that must be upheld. *See* also *Pulbrook* v *Richmond Consolidated Mining Co* (1878) LR 9 Ch D 610, re-affirmed most recently in *Choudhary and others* v *Bhatter and others* [2009] All ER (D) 163 (Feb).
[2] *Mitropoulos* v *The Greek Orthodox Church and Community of Marrickville & District Ltd* (1993) 10 ACSR 134.
[3] *Official Receiver* v *Watson* [2008] All ER (D) 188, at paragraph 181.
[4] In this Chapter, all section references are to the Companies Act 2006 unless otherwise stated.

majority of the directors. In the absence of such a power, the board has no inherent right to remove a director from office (as distinct from termination of employment or curtailment of delegated authority). Without special provision in the articles, the directors are removable only by some action on the part of the members. This can be achieved either:

(a)   by exercise of a power conferred by or introduced into the articles; or
(b)   through use of the statutory procedure in Section 168.

Before starting the process to remove a director, it is worth checking to see whether he is already disqualified from holding office or whether there was any procedural defect in his appointment. The various bases of disqualification are reviewed in Chapter 2, Section 2.4.4.

Also consider whether there were any special terms of office conferred at the time of appointment and any implications of removal that need to be managed. Assess for example whether the board can function effectively without the relevant director, for instance as a result of quorum requirements or contractual commitments dictating board procedure. Review whether the relevant director exercises any delegated authority that must be cancelled. Determine whether removal of the director will trigger any breach of commitment and, if so, whether the rights of appointment are contractual or class rights.[5] The financial implications, especially in the case of executive directors, will also need to be anticipated.

The Section 168 procedure is reviewed and summarised in Chapter 2. The statutory procedure for removal of a director under Section 168 is inalienable and by its terms operates notwithstanding any agreement between the company and the director.[6] However, it does rely upon shareholders voting by the

---

[5] *Cumbrian Newspapers* v *Cumberland Co* [1987] Ch 1.
[6] Section 168. *See* also *Link Agricultural Pty Ltd* v *Shanahan* (1998) 28 ACSR 498, CA (Vic). The corresponding Section 303 CA 1985 also provided that the power to remove directors would operate notwithstanding anything in the company's Articles, but that reference has been omitted in Section 168 CA 2006 on grounds of redundancy on the premise that anything

necessary majority and the shareholders are free to fetter their voting rights contractually as they choose.[7]

Special notice is required of a resolution to remove a director under Section 168.[8] Section 312 contains the relevant provisions governing the giving of special notice, which appear incongruous in this context since it is in effect a warning procedure that serves a more helpful purpose where the resolution is being sponsored by a member rather than by the board. The board can of course give special notice to the company and otherwise ensure that the requirements in Section 312 are observed. While the Section 312 procedure would apparently require a meeting convened by the board to remove a director under Section 168 to be held on a minimum of 28 days' notice, the effect of the relief in Section 312(4) is to allow the meeting to be convened within a shorter period, provided notice of the intention to move the resolution has first been given to the company.

Section 169 imposes certain procedures for notification to the relevant director and confers rights on the director to publish a response of a reasonable length, at the expense of the company, save where the right to make representations is being abused. The board will be concerned to manage the surrounding publicity and will have the resources of the company at its disposal for that purpose. It will also have the initiative and in particular will control the timing and procedure of the meeting.

There is no particular form that the removal resolution must take although often expressed to the following effect:

---

contained in the articles that is contrary to the provisions of the Companies Acts, or against general law, will have no effect. *See Bushell* v *Faith* [1970] AC 1099, which remains instructive as an example of provisions contained in a company's Articles conferring weighted voting rights on shares held by a director in the event of a resolution being proposed to remove him as a director. The provisions were held to be effective with the result that the statutory power to remove the director was effectively circumvented. In *Criterion Properties Plc* v *Stratford UK Properties LLC and others* [2003] 1 WLR 2108 where provisions in an agreement with the company would give rise to significant, negative commercial consequences for the company in the event of removal of identified directors from office and thereby act as a fetter on the freedom of shareholders to remove directors under Section 303 CA 1985 (now substantially in Section 168), it was acknowledged that the approval of such an agreement might demonstrate an improper exercise of board power.

[7] *Holmes* v *Life Funds of Australia Ltd* [1971] 1 NSWLR 860.
[8] Section 168(2).

"THAT, special notice having been received by the Company, Mr X be removed as a director of the Company pursuant to Section 168 of the Companies Act 2006."

The director concerned, even if not a member of the company, is entitled to speak at the meeting, in addition to requiring his written representations to be read out (if not previously sent to members).[9]

Articles sometimes provide for the removal of a director by shareholder resolution. Such an article may be useful in bypassing the detailed statutory procedures that apply where reliance is placed on Section 168. However, while Section 168(5) provides that the statutory power does not derogate from any power to remove a director that may exist apart from Section 168, a power in the articles to remove a director by ordinary resolution might be open to question as subverting the statutory procedure. Hence, the practice has grown up that the articles permit shareholders by special resolution to remove a director as an effective alternative to the power and procedures in Section 168. That practice might be expected to continue. While Section 168 does not carry over from Section 303 CA 1985 the confirmation that the statutory right to remove a director applies notwithstanding anything in the articles, according to Explanatory Note 68 CA 2006, the omission was made on grounds of redundancy on the premise that anything contained in the articles that is contrary to the provisions of the Companies Acts, or against general law, will have no effect.

If a company's articles do not contain a provision for removal of a director, in the absence of any class rights to appoint and remove directors,[10] there is no reason why a general meeting should not pass two resolutions, the first a special resolution altering the articles to insert such a power, and the second implementing the removal.

Unless the vacancy created by the removal is filled at the shareholders' meeting, the board can fill it if so permitted by the

---

[9] Section 169(2) and (4).
[10] *Cumbrian Newspapers* v *Cumberland Co* [1987] Ch 1.

articles (*see* for example Article 17, Model Articles for Private Companies Limited by Shares (the "Model Articles")[11] but, if appointed at the shareholders' meeting, the appointee will assume the rotation features of the director he replaces whereas, if appointed by the board under a power to fill casual vacancies, the appointee will typically be subject to retirement at the next succeeding annual general meeting.[12]

Removal of a director under Section 168 or under a power in the articles does not, unless otherwise agreed, deprive him of any compensation or damages (*see* the discussion at Section 6.8 above) payable on termination either as a director or in respect of any appointment that terminates with his directorship.[13] It may also, in certain circumstances, be the foundation of a claim by the director under Section 994 (*see* Section 10.4.1.7 below).

In the case of a private company, the statutory written resolution procedure laid down in Section 288 is not available[14] to pass a resolution to remove a director under Section 168. In relation to articles permitting members' resolutions to be in writing, it is clearly not possible to rely on an article such as Regulation 5 of Part II of the 1948 Table A, which is expressly "Subject to the provisions of the Act", and it is questionable whether reliance can be placed on an article such as Regulation 53 of the 1985 Table A, even though not so qualified, because it is inconsistent with the statutory special notice provisions and the provisions of the Act conferring on the director concerned the right to speak in his own defence at the meeting.

---

[11] Companies (Model Articles) Regulations (SI 2008/3229).

[12] Section 168(3) and (4).

[13] Section 168(5)(a). While the entitlement to directors' fees may be qualified under the articles in the event of termination, entitlements under a contract of employment are unaffected save by their terms, certainly for early termination of a fixed-term contract. *Southern Foundries (1926) Ltd v Shirlaw* [1940] AC 701 (note the dissenting judgments in relation to the particular operation of the principle in circumstances where a controlling shareholder exercised rights conferred post-contract to remove a director rather than the company acting itself and the pragmatic if somewhat strained analysis supporting the majority conclusion that the actions of the shareholder and the company were either merged or interdependent); *Shindler v Northern Raincoat Co* [1960] 1 WLR 1038. See *Read v Astoria Garage (Streatham) Ltd* [1952] Ch 637 which may support the theory that where there is no specified contractual duration, termination by removal from office may not found a claim in damages for contractual breach if the terms of the contract provide for automatic termination of appointment on loss of directorship. Much depends on the terms of the contract in any particular case.

[14] Section 288(2)(a).

10.1.2   Minority standpoint

The position of the director who is in dispute with the other members of the board is to some extent the obverse of the above. The director has the right:

(a)   to be informed about the company's affairs;
(b)   to inspect the company's accounting records in accordance with Section 388[15] and a residual common law right.[16] The director is entitled to have the assistance of an expert when making such an inspection.[17] The ability to enforce such rights where removal from office is pending is, however, questionable;
(c)   to call a meeting of the board in compliance with the applicable notice provisions adopted by the Board or set out in the company's articles;
(d)   not to be excluded from board meetings.[18] Any director under threat of ejection should take care to give instructions for notification of board meetings that are both efficient and consistent with any notification provisions in the articles; and
(e)   in the case of a company that observes the UK Corporate Governance Code, to take independent professional advice, if necessary, at the company's expense.

As described above, the director also has the right to make representations to the members in the event that a resolution for his removal from office is proposed under Section 168,[19] and to speak at the meeting at which the resolution is proposed.[20]

---

[15]   Replacing Section 222 CA 1985.
[16]   *Conway* v *Petronius Clothing Co* [1978] 1 WLR 72. There is no clear basis to argue that the right to inspect extends beyond the scope of the statutory right under Section 388 to inspect accounting records. However, *see* Burn v *London and South Wales* (1890) 7 TLR 118, 9 Digest (Reissue) 197, 1190 which suggests a more general right of access to any document belonging to the company.
[17]   *West-Transvaalse Boeresake (Edms) Bpk* v *Pierterse* 1955 (2) SA 464, PD (Tvaal); *Conway* v *Petronius Clothing Co* [1978] 1 WLR 72.
[18]   *Hayes* v *Bristol Plant Hire Ltd* (above).
[19]   Section 169(3) and (4).
[20]   Section 169(2).

10.1.3   Boardroom deadlock

The board of a company may be deadlocked because one or more directors refuses to attend board meetings (so as to prevent there being a quorum) or because the directors are equally divided on a question and the chairman either does not have or is not prepared to use a casting vote.

As an alternative or perhaps an adjunct to removal of a director, the members in general meeting have an inherent default power to fill vacancies in the board[21] subject to any limit on the total number of directors imposed by the articles that cannot by its terms be adjusted by ordinary resolution. In addition, an article in the form of Article 17 of the Model Articles[22] empowers the general meeting to appoint additional directors.

The members can pass a special resolution to take the conduct of the business of the company away from the directors, but an ordinary resolution is insufficient except and to the extent that the articles require the directors to comply with directions given by the members in general meeting.[23]

Under articles that adopt or replicate Article 4(1) of the Model Articles,[24] the general meeting can give directions to the board by special resolution. Article 4(2) provides that no such resolution invalidates anything which the directors have done before the passing of the resolution.[25]

If the directors are unable by reason of dysfunction (e.g. because they cannot secure a quorum whether by reason of overall lack

---

[21] *Munster* v *Cammell Co* (1882) 21 Ch D 183; *Barron* v *Potter* [1914] 1 Ch 895 which distinguished *Blair Open Hearth Furnace Co* v *Reigart* (1913) 108 LT 665 in which it was held that if the directors have delegated power to fill vacancies that excludes any implied concurrent right of members; *see* also *Integrated Medical Technologies Ltd* v *Macel Nominees Pty Ltd* (1988) 13 ACLR 110, SC (NSW) in which it was held that any attempt in the articles to confer an exclusive power of appointment on the board must be clearly expressed. The principle in *Blair* was doubted by Lord Hanworth MR in *Worcester Corsetry Ltd* v *Witting* [1936] 1 Ch 640, although the ratio of the decision turned on construction of the particular articles.

[22] *See* also Regulation 78 of the 1985 Table A.

[23] *Automatic Self-Cleansing Filter Syndicate Co Ltd* v *Cunninghame* [1906] 2 Ch 34, CA; *The Gramophone and Typewriter Ltd* v *Stanley* [1908] 2 KB 89 at 105, CA, *dicta* of Fletcher Moulton and Buckley LJJ; *Quin & Axtens* v *Salmon* [1909] AC 442, HL.

[24] *See* also Regulation 70 of the 1985 Table A.

[25] *See* also Regulation 70 of the 1985 Table A.

of numbers or dispute) to exercise the powers given to them under the articles, the company in general meeting can perform the functions delegated to the board, certainly to appoint additional directors and perhaps to exercise other powers.[26]

The procedure by which to convene a general meeting in the absence of an effective board is addressed at Chapter 8.

As a last resort, a member may apply to the court to act either under its inherent power or under Section 37(1) Supreme Court Act 1981 for the appointment of a receiver to manage the affairs of the company. Alternatively, if the deadlock reflects a stalemate at the shareholder level, the remedy discussed in Section 10.4 below or a winding up on the just and equitable ground may provide the solution.

10.2 Disputes between the board and the members

The board of a company can find itself under attack from one or more of the members of the company for a variety of reasons, including claims that some action of the company has been taken in breach of a shareholder's personal rights; that the directors, or some of them, have committed some wrong against the company; or that the actions of the board have been unfairly prejudicial to one or more of the members.

The remaining parts of this Chapter examine this complex area of company law, and set out some practical guidelines in relation to the claims procedure for derivative and unfair prejudice complaints. The remainder of Section 10.2 considers first the rights that a shareholder has under the company's constitution, and the extent to which those rights can be enforced by the shareholder; then the rights which are conferred on the shareholder by particular statutory provisions. Section 10.3 below considers the circumstances in which a shareholder can bring an action in the name of the company to obtain redress for a wrong done to the company (a "derivative" action). Section 10.4

---

[26] *Barron* v *Potter* [1914] 1 Ch 895.

below addresses the right of a shareholder to bring an action under Section 994 to obtain a remedy for unfairly prejudicial conduct.

As an alternative to reliance upon the remedies considered in this Chapter, an aggrieved minority might instead draw the matters complained of to the attention of the Department for Business, Innovation and Skills or another body with powers of investigation. The alternatives are considered in Chapter 12.

10.2.1   Personal actions

This Section identifies a range of contractual and statutory rights and protections that form a key element of the minority shareholder protections. In exercising their powers, the directors need to be sensitive to the inherent limits on their authority and the potential for shareholders to intervene.

There is a complex interaction between a member's right to bring proceedings in an individual capacity and the derivative action discussed in Section 10.3 below where the acts complained of cause damage to the company. If the claimant can establish that the conduct has constituted a breach of some legal duty owed to him personally and the court is satisfied that such breach has caused him personal loss, separate and distinct from any loss occasioned to the company, a personal action can be mounted.[27]

10.2.1.1   Shareholders' personal rights

Section 33 creates a contract that is generally recognised as the basis of the legal relationship between the company and its members in addition to its operation as between the members themselves. The constitution of the company will bind the company and its members to the same extent as if there were covenants on the part of each member to observe the provisions of the constitution.

---

[27] *Jason Walker and others v James Nicholas Stones and others* [2001] QB 902, CA.

However, this does not mean that every shareholder necessarily has the right to enforce all of the rights that the contract appears on its face to confer. The decided cases are not entirely consistent and to some extent turn on their facts. Nonetheless, the general view is that the section gives contractual effect to a provision in the constitution only insofar as it gives rights to or imposes obligations on a member in his capacity as a member,[28] most certainly when in common with other members or a class of members ("insider rights") and not, for example, as a director[29] or as a professional adviser to the company[30] whether or not the director or adviser is also a shareholder ("outsider rights"). It is certainly the case that a member seeking to enforce a provision vested in him as a member should expect to succeed under established principle more readily than in an action to uphold a provision that does not touch on the member qua member. The difficulty in any attempt to uphold outsider rights by enforcing provisions in a company's articles has not been affected by the Contracts (Rights of Third Parties) Act 1999, which excludes Section 33 from its scope.[31]

Even if the provision of the company's constitution that has been breached is one that creates "insider rights", the member may not be able to bring a personal action to enforce it. This will in general be so if the breach involves only an internal corporate irregularity, such as an irregularity in the conduct of a meeting that is trivial or can readily be remedied by reconvening a meeting at which it is expected that a majority will prevail in a manner that renders the breach nugatory.

10.2.1.2 *Impact of the rule in Foss v Harbottle*[32]

The refusal by the courts to uphold personal actions by shareholders in respect of breaches of internal corporate irregularities

---

[28] *Hickman* v *Kent or Romney Marsh Sheep Breeders' Association* [1915] 1 Ch 881. For further analysis, *see* Section A Part 2 Law Commission Consultation Paper 142. *See* cases referred to in note 64 for discussion of the distinction between rights enjoyed by the company and those of individual shareholders.

[29] *Browne* v *La Trinidad* (1887) 37 Ch D 1; but *see John* v *Price Waterhouse* [2002] 1 WLR 953 – an appointment made "on the footing of the Articles" may have the effect of incorporating provisions of the articles into a director's terms of appointment.

[30] *Eley* v *Positive Government Security Life Assurance Co Ltd* (1875–76) LR 1 Ex D 88.

[31] Section 6(2) Contracts (Rights of Third Parties) Act 1999.

[32] (1843) 2 Hare 461, 67 ER 189.

stems from the "majority rule"[33] and "proper claimant"[34] principles generally attributed to the decision in *Foss* v *Harbottle*, set out in the case of *Edwards* v *Halliwell*[35] and restated in *Prudential Assurance Co Ltd* v *Newman Industries Ltd (No 2)*.[36] The "rule in *Foss* v *Harbottle*" is discussed in more detail in Section 10.3.1 below.

The courts have not always been consistent in relation to the ability of a shareholder to challenge internal corporate irregularities; in certain instances the line adopted has been to restrain individual action in reliance on an extension of the *Foss* v *Harbottle* principle while in other cases the courts have permitted a shareholder to enforce his contractual right under the articles. Shareholders have for example been allowed to bring personal actions involving defective or inadequate notice of meeting,[37] improper adjournment of meetings[38] or the right to have their votes counted,[39] but have been refused any remedy when a valid demand for a poll was wrongfully rejected by the chairman of the meeting even though, so it appears, the outcome of the particular poll would have reversed the result on a show of hands.[40]

If a general principle can be extracted from the authorities,[41] it may be that where a breach of internal procedure damages the company first and foremost and incidentally affects all members, it should be resolved by corporate action, save where an exception to the rule in *Foss* v *Harbottle* applies (*see* Section 10.3.1 below). Contrastingly, where the principal wrong is done to an

---

[33] The will of the majority of members of the company should in general prevail.

[34] A breach of duty owed to the company is a wrong for which the company and not its investors should seek a remedy. In determining whether to seek redress, the company may legitimately take into account balancing factors such as the relative return on investment of time and other resources in litigation.

[35] [1950] 2 All ER 1064.

[36] [1982] Ch 204.

[37] *Musselwhite* v *C H Musselwhite & Son* [1962] Ch 964.

[38] *Byng* v *London Life Association Ltd* [1990] Ch 170.

[39] *Pender* v *Lushington* (1877) LR 6 Ch D 70; *Oliver* v *Dalgleish* [1963] 1 WLR 1274.

[40] *MacDougall* v *Gardiner* (1874–75) LR 1 Ch App 606.

[41] *I* v *I* (above); *see* also *Burland* v *Earle* [1902] AC 83 at 93: "It is an elementary principle of the law relating to joint stock companies that the court will not interfere with the internal management of companies acting within their powers and in fact has no jurisdiction to do so." This rule is attributed by Lord Davey at p 93 to the decision in *Foss* v *Harbottle*.

individual member, that individual may seek redress unless the matter complained of is open to ratification by ordinary resolution. In cases of substantial wrongdoing, it is in any event likely to be appropriate to seek a remedy under Section 994.

10.2.1.3   *Transactions outside the company's powers*

The rule in *Foss* v *Harbottle* does not prevent a shareholder from bringing a personal action to restrain the directors from acting beyond their powers save in respect of acts done in fulfilment of a legal obligation that results from a prior act of the company.[42] While the principle was acknowledged in *Smith* v *Croft (No 2)*,[43] that a shareholder can have locus to bring an action to recover on behalf of a company property or money transferred or paid in an *ultra vires* transaction, and that an *ultra vires* act cannot be ratified by any majority of the members, it was held that if a majority of independent shareholders, acting in good faith, do not wish such an action to be continued, the will of that majority should prevail. This assumes that the shareholder promoting the action is not able to demonstrate a loss beyond that which is merely reflective of the loss suffered by the company as a result of the *ultra vires* transaction.

10.2.1.4   *Amendments to the company's articles*

A shareholder may be able to challenge a special resolution altering the company's articles on the grounds that the resolution was not passed *bona fide* (i.e. without fraud or malice) for the benefit of the company as a whole (i.e. the shareholders as a general body), or breached a class or special right or discriminated between majority and minority shareholders,[44] or (as discussed below) that the alteration was unfairly prejudicial to his interests for the purposes of Section 994.

---

[42] Section 40(4).
[43] [1988] Ch 114.
[44] *Allen* v *Gold Reefs of West Africa Ltd* [1900] 1 Ch 656; *Greenhalgh* v *Arderne Cinemas Ltd* [1951] Ch 286; cf. *Sidebottom* v *Kershaw, Leese & Co* [1920] 1 Ch 154, CA and *Shuttleworth* v *Cox Bros & Co* [1927] 2 KB 9, CA. In determining whether an amendment of the articles is *bona fide* for the benefit of the company, the test is by reference to the opinion of the shareholders; their *bona fides* will only be called into question if the circumstances are so oppressive or extravagant as to cast suspicion on their honesty. Benefit of the company will be assumed unless no reasonable man could consider it so (at 11, 17d *et seq.*).

The High Court of Australia decision in *Gambotto WCP Ltd*[45] adopted an interesting approach in relation to the assessment of validity of amendments made to the constitution of a company although not followed to date in the English courts.[46] The Australian court stressed the proprietary nature of a share and rejected a test based simply on the amendments being *bona fide* in the interests of the company as a whole. Instead, the court distinguished between amendments allowing expropriation by the majority of the shares of the minority or of valuable proprietary rights attaching to the shares and other amendments to the constitution giving rise to a conflict of interest. The court determined that the test applicable to the first category would be whether the power to alter the constitution had been exercised for a proper purpose and if so, whether the exercise of that power would not operate oppressively in relation to minority shareholders. For amendments falling into the second category, the court decided that, if regularly approved, such amendments would *prima facie* be fair, unless shown to be beyond a purpose contemplated by the constitution or oppressive.

10.2.1.5 *Shareholders' agreements*

Accepting that the law relating to enforcement of rights and obligations provided for in the articles is complex and, depending on what is intended, may not provide comprehensive protection for an individual shareholder, those wishing to regulate their relationship as shareholders should consider whether a shareholders' agreement is appropriate to supplement the constitution. A shareholders' agreement gives rise to specific contractual rights as between the parties that are enforceable in the normal course.[47]

If the company is a party to the agreement, then any restriction on its statutory powers contained in the agreement (such as a restriction preventing it from increasing its authorised share capital except by special resolution) will be void as far as the company is

---

[45] (1995) 182 CLR 432.

[46] *Constable* v *Executive Connections Ltd and others* [2005] 2 BCLC 638; *Citco Banking Corp NV* v *Pusser's Ltd and another* [2007] Bus LR 960.

[47] Provisions in a shareholders' agreement may also attach as class rights to shares; *see Harman* v *BML Group Ltd* [1994] 1 WLR 893.

concerned, but assuming the severability or disapplication of the provision in as far as it would otherwise bind the company, so as to avoid fettering the inalienable statutory powers of the company, parallel restrictions assumed by shareholders who are parties to the agreement will be enforceable amongst them.[48]

10.2.1.6 Statutory rights

The Companies Acts and the Insolvency Act 1986 provide shareholders with a disparate collection of other direct or indirect rights. The principal rights of shareholders in the Companies Acts,[49] which may in relevant circumstances be considered in parallel with the minority protection regime, are:

(a) to challenge a special resolution passed by a private company approving a payment out of capital for the redemption or purchase of its shares (Section 721);

(b) to apply to the court in the event that it proves impracticable to call or conduct a meeting by conventional means (Section 306);

(c) if representing not less than 5 per cent of the issued shares or any class thereof,[50] to challenge a special resolution of a public company to re-register as a private company (Section 98);

(d) if representing not less than 5 per cent of the total voting rights[51] of a public company, to require distribution of notice of a resolution to be proposed at the next annual general meeting (Section 338);

(e) if representing not less than 10 per cent of the total voting rights, to requisition an extraordinary general meeting (Section 303);

(f) if representing not less than 10 per cent of the shares,[52] to apply for the appointment of inspectors under Section 431

---

[48] *Russell v Northern Bank Development Corp Ltd* [1992] 1 WLR 588; applying the principle established in *Southern Foundries (1926) Ltd v Shirlaw* [1940] AC 701 at 739 and *Allen v Gold Reefs of West Africa Ltd* [1900] 1 Ch 656 at 671.

[49] Others can be found in Sections 125, 168, 229, 563, 803 and 981.

[50] Or being not less than 50 members.

[51] Or being not less than 100 members holding shares in the company on which there has been paid up an average sum, per member, of not less than £100.

[52] Or being not less than 200 members.

CA 1985, which may lead to the Secretary of State bringing a petition under Section 995 for an unfair prejudice remedy under Part 30 CA 2006 (*see* Section 10.4 below); and

(g) if representing not less than 15 per cent of the relevant class, to challenge a resolution varying the rights attaching to a class of shares passed in accordance with Section 630 (Section 633).

Principal rights available to shareholders under the Insolvency Act 1986 are:

(a) to object to a business or property transaction approved under Section 110 Insolvency Act 1986 (Section 111 Insolvency Act 1986); and

(b) to petition the court for the company to be wound up on the ground that it is just and equitable to do so (Section 122(1) Insolvency Act 1986) and a related restraining remedy under Section 126 Insolvency Act 1986.[53]

10.3 Derivative actions

A "derivative action" is a proceeding which a shareholder may bring to enforce a cause of action vested in the company. It has to be distinguished from a personal action of the type described in Section 10.2.1 above, which shareholders may bring in their own right to enforce a right vested in them personally.

Chapter 1 of Part 11 CA 2006 (derivative claims in England and Wales or Northern Ireland) sets out the legislative provisions relating to derivative claims that came into force with effect from 1 October 2007. The provisions largely reflect the recommendations of the Law Commission for a "new derivative procedure with more modern, flexible and accessible criteria for determining whether a shareholder can pursue an action".[54]

---

[53] Other rights that may be available to a contributory during a winding up can be found in Sections 133, 147, 155, 167, 168, 188 and 212 Insolvency Act 1986 and operate in addition to powers exercisable by the liquidator.
[54] Paragraph 6.15 Law Commission Report No 246.

The premise for a derivative action is based on the notion that an individual shareholder should only be able to bring such an action in exceptional and limited circumstances. The common law derivative action continues to apply in respect of events prior to 1 October 2007 and will inform the application of the statutory derivative action. Under the common law, as a generality a member cannot bring an action on behalf of the company for an injury done to the company; the company is the injured party and the action vests in it. The common law derivative action relied on an exception to this rule in circumstances in which the matter complained of constituted a fraud on the minority, including fraud proper as well as a breach by a director of fiduciary duty in circumstances in which the wrongdoers were in control of the company.

Since the introduction in 1948[55] of the prejudice remedy (now in Section 994) the significance of the common law derivative action diminished. The Law Commission, in its "Shareholder Remedies" Report 246, nonetheless identified in the derivative action a remedy that still serves a useful purpose in providing a mechanism for shareholders to intervene in the face of corporate wrongs. However, the common law remedy was complicated and unwieldy, employing archaic and uncertain concepts such as "wrongdoer control". Further, the common law action was available only to a minority shareholder if able to prove that the matter complained of had conferred a benefit on the controlling shareholders, or that the failure of the directors to bring an action constituted fraud on the minority. This narrowed the already limited circumstances in which a minority shareholder could bring a derivative action to circumstances of serious mismanagement. A derivative action based on negligence could only be brought if the majority had profited in some way from the negligence.

As a result, CA 2006 has introduced a new derivative procedure that has replaced the common law action (save for its transitional application to matters arising prior to 1 October 2007) and operates subject to tight judicial control with the objective

---

[55] Section 210 Companies Act 1948, now in Section 994.

of allowing justified actions to develop in stages. This offers the potential to mitigate the substantial costs typically associated with derivative actions while guarding against nuisance litigation.

Despite its limitations, a claimant in a derivative action has the advantage (when comparison is made with a Section 994 prejudice action) of not needing to prove unfairly prejudicial conduct by the defendants.[56] Furthermore, whereas Section 994 has to a substantial extent evolved as an exit remedy, the derivative action is designed to provide a solution for shareholders that wish to retain their investment.[57]

The right to bring the statutory derivative action is subject to obtaining the court's approval to allow the action to proceed, satisfying a two-stage test. First, the court must dismiss the application if the applicant cannot establish a *prima facie* case and secondly, the court may use its discretion to refuse or grant leave to continue a derivative claim taking into account specified matters. While the issues required to be taken into account by the court reflect principles developed in the common law derivative action, until experience in the application of the new procedure has developed further, it is uncertain whether this remedy will represent a means to meaningful redress for aggrieved shareholders. Rights have been reserved to alter or add by regulation to the circumstances that should be taken into account by the court in refusing or giving permission to bring or continue derivative claims.[58]

This Chapter contains a review in Sections 10.3.1 to 10.3.7 of the common law position because the common law criteria continue to be relevant in respect of causes of action that arise before I October 2007 and will influence the statutory derivative action described in Sections 10.3.8 and 10.3.9 below.

---

[56] The remedy under Section 995 is only available where the court is satisfied that an unfair prejudice has occurred.

[57] Paragraph 6.11, the Law Commission Report 246.

[58] Section 263(5). This section has been disapplied specifically in relation to entities taken into ownership by the Treasury.

10.3.1 The position under the common law—the rule in Foss v Harbottle

The derivative action has its origins in the principle of majority rule and the principle that the company that suffers the wrong-doing is the proper plaintiff, principles referred to as the rule in *Foss* v *Harbottle*.[59] This rule, substantially restated in *Prudential Assurance Co Ltd* v *Newman Industries Ltd (No 2)*[60] has operated according to the following principles:

(a) The proper claimant in an action in respect of a wrong alleged to be done to a corporation is prima facie the corporation.

(b) Where the alleged wrong is a transaction that might be made binding on the corporation by a simple majority of the members, no individual member of the corporation is allowed to maintain an action in respect of that matter because, if the majority confirms the transaction, *cadit quaestio* (the question is at an end); or, if the majority challenges the transaction, there is no valid reason why the company should not sue.

(c) The rule has no application if the alleged wrong is *ultra vires* the corporation, because the majority of members cannot confirm the transaction.

(d) The rule has no application if the transaction complained of could validly be undertaken or sanctioned only by a special or extraordinary resolution, because a simple majority cannot confirm a transaction which requires the concurrence of a greater majority.

(e) The rule has operated subject to a true exception where what has been done amounts to fraud or possibly oppression or unfairness[61] and the wrongdoers are themselves in control of the company.

At first instance in *Prudential Assurance Co Ltd* v *Newman Industries Ltd (No 2)*,[62] Vinelott J promulgated a broader exception

---

[59] [1843] 2 Hare 461; 67 ER 189.
[60] [1982] Ch 204.
[61] *MacDougall* v *Gardiner* (above); *Edwards* v *Halliwell* (above).
[62] [1981] Ch 257.

to the rule in *Foss* v *Harbottle*, so as to allow individual share-holder action whenever the justice of the case so required. This broad exception was rejected on appeal.[63] The decision at first instance that, as a result of a finding of fraud, individual share-holders were entitled to damages for the loss of value in their shares as a personal claim was also held to be misconceived in that the damage complained of was damage suffered by the company. To recover under a personal claim would require a case to be made of loss to personal assets caused by the fraudulent act, separate and distinct from the loss suffered by the company. No claim can be founded for personal loss that is merely a reflection of the loss suffered by the company unless the company has no cause of action to sue and recover the loss.[64] The foundation of the rule is the need to avoid double recovery and double jeopardy arising from the same facts, regardless of the capacity in which claims might be brought and to protect the company's creditors.[65]

This emphasises the scope and essential character of derivative action; it seeks relief to the extent and no larger than that which the company itself would have if it were the claimant. For this reason, a shareholder is able to assert a cause of action which

---

[63] [1982] Ch 204 at 221. This does not appear to be the case in Australia's *Biala Pty Ltd* v *Mallina Holding Ltd (No 2)* (1993) 11 ACSR 785.

[64] [1982] Ch 204 at 223; *see* also *Johnson* v *Gore Wood* [2001] 1 All ER 481 in which the House of Lords identified two circumstances in which an individual shareholder might sue, namely (i) where the company had no cause for action, the shareholder claim being measured by a reduction in the value of his shareholding and thus a reflective loss and (ii) where the share-holder had a separate cause of action distinct from that of the company in respect of a breach of duty owed independently to the shareholder, representing a personal loss that was sepa-rate and distinct from loss suffered by the company; *see* also *Giles* v *Rhind* [2003] Ch 618, which represents an attempt to introduce a wider exception where the wrong-doing had disabled the company, was doubted in *Gardner* v *Parker* [2004] EWCA Civ 781 and criticised in *Waddington Ltd* v *Chan* [2008] HKCU 1381; also *Day* v *Cook* [2003] BCC 256, *Ellis and another* v *Property Leeds (UK) Ltd* [2002] 2 BCLC 175 and *Shaker* v *Al-Bedrawi* [2003] Ch 350; the burden is on the defendant to establish that the whole claim is reflective and recoverable by the company.

In the US, where courts have held that directors and controlling shareholders of closely held corporations owe other investors a higher level of fiduciary duty that needs to be observed in the case of publicly held corporations, there is also precedent permitting a personal action as a means of providing direct compensation to a shareholder for loss sustained by a close corporation where all shareholders are joined in the action. However, this tendency to permit personal actions is more evident in states that do not make statutory provision for oppression actions. US courts have also been prepared to provide an individual remedy where the corporation is no longer a going concern or where there has been a change of control of the corporation and derivative action would not provide an adequate remedy.

[65] *Gardner* v *Parker* EWCA Civ 781.

arose before he became a shareholder because it is the company's and not his substantive right that is being enforced.[66]

This contrasts with claims under Section 994 when the conduct complained of is an unfair prejudice to some part of the members, not the company. In practice however, the distinction between the two procedures may become blurred. Notably, the new statutory derivative action may be brought pursuant to an order given under proceedings for protection of members against unfair prejudice.

10.3.2   Fraud on the minority

The common law exception described in Section 10.3.1(e) above was recognised because, without it, the minority's grievance could never have reached the court since the wrongdoers themselves, being in control, would not allow the company to sue.[67] To come within the exception, the claimant must show:

(a)   that what had been done amounted to fraud; and
(b)   that the wrongdoers were in control. However, an individual shareholder might be prevented from pursuing his action if an "independent organ" of the company did not wish the action to proceed.

In this context, "fraud" means "fraud in the wider equitable sense of that term, as in the equitable concept of a fraud on a power" and did not require proof of deceit.[68] Examples include:

(a)   attempts by the majority to sell worthless assets to the company, while concealing a commission paid to a director who procured the arrangement;[69]
(b)   the majority diverting business from the company to themselves in breach of their fiduciary duties;[70] and

---

[66]   *See* Section 260(4). *See* also *Seaton* v *Grant* (1866–67) LR 2 Ch App 459.
[67]   *Prudential Assurance Co Ltd* v *Newman Industries Ltd (No 2)* [1982] Ch 204 at 211.
[68]   *Estmanco (Kilner House) Ltd* v *Greater London Council* [1982] 1 WLR 2 at 12. Further held on the facts that the sum total of the facts represented such an abuse of power as to have the same effect as a fraud on the minority.
[69]   *Atwool* v *Merryweather* (1867–68) LR 5 Eq 464.
[70]   *Cook* v *Deeks* [1916] 1 AC 554 (PC).

(c) the majority compromising, on terms which were disadvantageous to the company, litigation against bodies in which the majority was interested.[71]

The fraud exception probably has no application where the wrongdoers did not themselves benefit. It certainly does not extend to mere negligence on the part of the directors,[72] unless the negligence was in failing to procure that the company take action against them (for their own benefit) and, even in such a case, if an independent majority could vote that proceedings not be taken, the action would fail.

In *Smith* v *Croft (No 2)*,[73] a case in which the purported wrongdoers had voting control, it was held that a minority shareholder's derivative action should not be allowed to continue if an "independent organ" of the company did not wish it to be pursued. The nature of an independent organ might vary from one company to another, but it could consist of a majority of the independent shareholders or directors (i.e. those not associated with the wrongdoers). The test of independence is whether the relevant parties were capable of reaching a determination as to a course of action that in their view was *bona fide* for the benefit of the company as a whole.[74]

It is also necessary for the claimant to show that the wrongdoers controlled the company. This might amount to a direct or indirect holding of a majority of the shares in the company, but could extend to a situation where control lay with the wrongdoers together with those likely to vote with them as a result of influence or apathy.[75]

A major problem for the claimant is the need to show that there was a *prima facie* case of fraud, and the element of control by the wrongdoers, at a preliminary hearing, as the court will make no

---

[71] *Menier* v *Hooper's Telegraph Works* (1873–74) LR 9 Ch App 350.
[72] *Pavlides* v *Jensen* [1956] Ch 565. However, in *Daniels* v *Daniels* [1978] Ch 406, the court suggested that if directors benefit personally from the negligence at the company's expense, this might constitute fraud on the minority.
[73] [1988] Ch 114.
[74] *Smith* v *Croft* (above) at 186.
[75] *Prudential Assurance* (above) at 219.

assumptions on these issues.[76] This could have the effect of turning the preliminary application into a mini trial, but has served to uphold the purpose of the rule, to avoid multiple claims where the company itself is competent to bring proceedings but might for its own reasons determine not to do so. It was even suggested in the *Prudential* appeal proceedings[77] that it might be right for a judge trying the preliminary issue to grant a sufficient adjournment to enable a meeting of shareholders to be convened, so that a conclusion could be reached in the light of the conduct of the members.

The fraud exception has been materially repackaged in the Section 260 derivative action that has replaced the common law exception with respect to matters arising on or after 1 October 2007. Transitional provisions restrict the scope of derivative action in respect of matters arising prior to 1 October 2007 substantially to circumstances that would have founded a derivative action under the common law exception to the rule in *Foss* v *Harbottle*.[78]

10.3.3   *Ultra vires transactions*

Alleged wrong that was *ultra vires* the company or illegal (such as the unlawful reduction of capital) or criminal provided a *prima facie* basis for the shareholder's common law derivative action without the need to show fraud on the minority.[79] To commence a derivative action under the statutory regime, it is necessary to demonstrate that a director has caused the company to undertake an action for an improper purpose in breach of duty.[80] In other circumstances, it is necessary to rely upon proceedings under Section 994 or to construct a claim based on breach of personal rights.

---

[76] ibid., at 221–222. This was described in *Smith* v *Croft* (above) at 139 as giving rise to a half-way house in this very special type of case.

[77] *Prudential* v *Newman* (above) at 222.

[78] Companies Act 2006 (Commencement No 3, Consequential Amendments, Transitional Provisions and Savings) Order 2007 (SI 2007/2194), Schedule 3, paragraph 20.

[79] *Smith* v *Croft* (above).

[80] Section 260(3).

10.3.4   *Where a special or extraordinary resolution is required*

A further limb of the rule in *Foss* v *Harbottle* (as set out in Section 10.3.1(d) above) provided, in effect, that a shareholder could bring an action to prevent the company from relying on an ordinary resolution to sanction a transaction if a special or extraordinary resolution was required by the Act or the articles.[81] Although traditionally packaged with the general concept of derivative action, this limb can now only be exploited as a personal action, in response to irregularities in voting procedure that represent breach of the contract to which the relevant shareholder is a party. In that respect, this limb has survived the introduction of the prescriptive statutory derivative claim under Section 260.

10.3.5   *Further obstacles*

Assuming that a complaint falls within one of the exceptions to the rule in *Foss* v *Harbottle*, a number of further tests would need to be satisfied to persuade the court to allow the common law action to proceed. Namely:

(a)   as referred to above, that no independent organ of the company must disapprove of the action;
(b)   whether the wrong complained of could, as a matter of law, properly be ratified;
(c)   whether the minority shareholder comes "with clean hands";
(d)   whether some other adequate remedy is available to the minority shareholder; and
(e)   whether the company was in liquidation.

Weight will continue to attach to the view of an independent organ of the company under the Section 260 derivative action procedure since the court is required to have particular regard to any evidence before it as to the views of members of the company with no personal interest in the matter.

In relation to ratification, the position has varied according to the nature of the defect. If the act complained of was lawful but

---

[81] *Pavlides* v *Jensen* (above).

ultra vires the company, then it could not be authorised in advance but might, as discussed in Section 10.3.3 above, be ratified (and the breach of authority by the directors absolved). If the act was within the powers of the company but outside the authority of the directors, then it could not be authorised in advance but might be ratified by subsequent ordinary resolution. However, if the act complained of amounted to a breach of fiduciary duty by the directors, whether or not the majority might seek to ratify the actions of the directors, should the effect be to transfer benefit from the minority to the majority or otherwise discriminate between the minority and the majority, the purported ratification would be no bar to the minority shareholder's common law action.[82]

The position is expressly addressed in the context of the Section 260 derivative action as described in Section 10.3.9.3 below. Notably, the court is required to refuse permission to bring a statutory derivative claim where the relevant act or omission was authorised by the company before it occurred or has been ratified by the company since it occurred. Where the wrong might yet be authorised or is ratifiable, the court is required to take into account the likelihood of authorisation or ratification but that prospect does not represent an absolute bar to the statutory derivative claim.

The common law derivative action was an equitable remedy and so the minority shareholder would be barred from bringing it if he had knowingly benefited from the relevant *ultra vires* act or misappropriation of assets. For the purposes of its determination whether to permit a Section 260 derivative claim to be brought, the court is required to consider whether the member is acting in good faith.[83]

---

[82] *Cook v Deeks* [1916] 1 AC 554, PC. Had a relevant majority previously determined to dissolve the company or that it should close its business, there would have been no breach of duty in subsequently taking the benefit of a contract personally; cf. *Regal (Hastings) Ltd v Gulliver* [1967] 2 AC 134 if a breach of fiduciary duty in the guise of a director making a profit from his position is not waived or ratified by a majority, the director will be liable to account; *see* also *Hogg v Cramphorn* [1967] Ch 254 and *Bamford v Bamford* [1970] Ch 212.

[83] Section 263(3)(a). *See* also *Nurcombe v Nurcombe* [1985] 1 WLR 370 at 378; *Barrett v Duckett* [1995] 1 BCLC 243.

The minority shareholder is prevented from bringing a derivative action if there is another remedy available.[84]

If the company is in liquidation, there is normally no need for a minority shareholder to bring a derivative action to obtain redress against the wrongdoers, as the liquidator can bring an action in the name of the company if there is a reasonable cause of action; and if he refuses, the shareholder may be able to obtain an order requiring the liquidator to bring the action[85] or an order permitting the shareholder to bring an action in the name of the company.[86]

10.3.6   Costs

A further, and potentially substantial, obstacle has been the burden of the costs of the action. It was held by the Court of Appeal in *Wallersteiner* v *Moir (No 2)*[87] that legal aid was not available to a shareholder bringing a derivative action, and legal aid is now largely unavailable anyway for money claims.[88] However, following *Wallersteiner* v *Moir (No 2)*, the claimant may apply for an indemnity out of the assets of the company for the costs incurred by him in bringing the action on the company's behalf (commonly called a Wallersteiner order).

The ability to apply for such an indemnity is now set out in the Civil Procedure Rules Part 19, Rule 19.9E.[89] Under this rule, the court may order the company "to indemnify the claimant against any liability in respect of costs incurred in the permission application or in the derivative claim or both".[90] The rule applies where the claim form for the derivative action was

---

[84] Section 263(3)(f). *See* also *Barrett* v *Duckett* above at 250.
[85] Sections 112(1) and 168(5) Insolvency Act 1986.
[86] *Barrett* v *Duckett* above at 255.
[87] [1975] QB 373.
[88] The Access to Justice Act 1999 set up alternative systems of funding for civil cases in England and Wales, including funding under the Community Legal Service, conditional fee agreements and litigation funding agreements.
[89] The new procedure was introduced by Rule 7 Civil Procedure (Amendment) Rules 2007, (SI 2007/2204).
[90] Rule 19.9E applies to derivative actions under the Chapter 1 of Part 11 CA 2006, whether issued or taken over by a member, and to claims by members of a trade union or by members of an incorporated body, to which Chapter 1 of Part 11 CA 2006 does not apply. This is further discussed in Section 10.3.7.

issued on or after 1 October 2007.[91] Where a claim was begun before 1 October 2007 the rules of court in force immediately before that date apply. Those rules are set out at Practice Direction 19C, paragraph 8(2).

According to the judgment in *Wallersteiner* v *Moir (No 2)*, providing it is reasonable and prudent in the company's interest for a claimant to bring a derivative action, and it is brought by him in good faith, the court may order an indemnity in favour of the claimant (whether the action ultimately succeeds or not).[92] The court may have regard to the ability of the claimant to finance the claim himself[93] and may order that part of the costs be borne by the claimant regardless of his means.[94] Where the company is a quasi-partnership, then the court may consider the granting of an indemnity by the company to be unjust since the successful claimant will be entitled to recover a proportion of his costs from the defendant and be entitled to a lien and an indemnity over the assets recovered for the remainder and, where the claimant is unsuccessful, it would be unfair for the company (in effect the successful defendant) to bear any of the costs.[95] Such principles shall be of continuing importance in guiding courts which now decide whether to order that a claimant be indemnified under Rule 19.9E of the Civil Procedure Rules.

The majority of the Court of Appeal in *Wallersteiner* v *Moir (No 2)*[96] considered that contingency fees (where the advisers to the petitioner are entitled to a share in the proceeds if the action is successful) could not be used as a mechanism to fund derivative actions. However, the introduction of new rules permitting conditional fee arrangements[97] (allowing recovery from losing

---

[91] *See* Rule 21 Civil Procedure (Amendment) Rules 2007 (SI 2007/2204).
[92] [1975] QB 373 at 392 and 403.
[93] *Smith* v *Croft* [1986] 1 WLR 580. In this case, Walton J suggested that it was for the claimant to show that he did not have sufficient resources to finance the action and that he genuinely needed an indemnity from the company. However, this more restrictive approach was not followed in *Jaybird Group Ltd* v *Greenwood* [1986] BCLC 319 at 327. *See* also *Iesini* v *Westrip Holdings Ltd* [2009] EWHC 2526 (Ch) at 125.
[94] *Smith* v *Croft* [1986] 1 WLR 580 at 597 to 598.
[95] *Halle* v *Trax BW Ltd* [2000] BCC 1020 as applied in *Mumbray* v *Lapper* [2005] BCC 990.
[96] [1975] QB 373 at 403.
[97] Under the Access to Justice Act 1999.

opponents of uplifted success fees, in addition to normal fees, and premiums for after-the-event legal expenses insurance) has heralded a new way by which a claimant may be able to protect himself from full exposure to costs unless and until he obtains an indemnity out of the assets of the company.

10.3.7 Procedure

Rules 19.9 *et seq.* Civil Procedure Rules state the procedure which must be adopted in bringing a derivative action. There also exists a new Practice Direction 19C which relates specifically to derivative claims. Rule 19.9 applies to claims brought under Chapter 1 of Part 11 CA 2006, whether issued by a member (*see* further CPR, Rule 19.9A) or taken over by a member (*see* further CPR, Rule 19.9B), "or otherwise". The reference to "or otherwise" includes claims brought in respect of corporate bodies to which Chapter 1 of Part 11 CA 2006 does not apply and such claims are dealt with expressly by CPR, Rule 19.9C.[98] Accordingly, the procedure to be adopted for the old common law derivative action is the same as that based on the relevant provisions of CA 2006. Rule 19.9 does not apply to claims made under Section 996 CA 2006.[99]

A claim under Rule 19.9 is started by issuing a claim form under Part 7 CPR. The company concerned must be made a defendant to the claim and the claim form must be headed "Derivative claim".[100] The claim form must be accompanied by a separate application for permission to continue the claim under Part 23 and a witness statement on which the claimant relies must be filed in support of this permission application.[101] Such an application is also required where a member wishes to take over a derivative claim initially brought by a company or other members, or where a derivative claim is brought by a member of a trade union or a body corporate to which Chapter 1

---

[98] This rule sets out the procedure for: (a) claims made by a member of a body corporate to which Chapter 1 of Part 11 CA 2006 does not apply; (b) claims made by a member of a trade union; or (c) claims which fall within (a) and (b) which a member wishes to take over.

[99] CPR, Rule 19.9(1).

[100] *See* CPR, Rule 19.9(3) and Practice Direction (Derivative Claims), paragraph 19, CPD.2, respectively.

[101] CPR, Rule 19.9A(2).

of Part 11 CA 2006 does not apply.[102] The principles which shall apply to the permission application are more fully discussed below. If the claimant seeks an order that the company or other body concerned indemnify the claimant against liability for costs incurred in the permission application or the claim, this should be stated in the permission application or claim form or both, as the case requires.[103]

After the claim form is issued the claimant may not take any further steps without the court's permission, unless this is permitted, required or is in order to bring an urgent application for interim relief.[104] Unless it is likely to frustrate some party of a remedy sought, the claimant must notify the company of the claim and the permission application by sending to the company a notice (in the form set out in Practice Direction 19C), copies of the claim form, particulars of claim, the application notice and evidence in support of the permission application.[105] The claimant is under an obligation to file a witness statement confirming that these steps have been carried out.[106]

10.3.8 *Derivative action under CA 2006*

Section 260 introduced a new statutory derivative action that replaced the common law derivative action and represents the sole basis for derivative claims in respect of matters occurring from 1 October 2007. Transitional provisions address the basis on which claims related to events preceding that date may be brought.[107]

The provisions of CA 2006 generally prescribe a wider range of circumstances in which a derivative action may be brought by a shareholder against a director[108] when compared with the

---

[102] *See* CPR, Rule 19.9B and 19.9C.
[103] Practice Direction (Derivative Claims), paragraph 19, CPD.2(2).
[104] CPR, Rule 19.9(4).
[105] *See* CPR, Rules 19.9A(4) and 19.9(7). If it is claimed that notification is likely to frustrate a remedy sought, the claimant must bring an application for an order of the court that this is the case. Such an application may be made without notice. For further details, *see* CPR, Rules 19.9(7)–(11). The requirement to provide notification (and the need to bring an application to avoid this) apply to claims brought under CPR, Rules 19.9B and 19.9C.
[106] Rule 19.9A(6). Similarly, this obligation applies to claims under CPR, Rules 19.9B and 19.9C.
[107] *See* note 79 above.
[108] *Iesini* v *Westrip Holdings Ltd* [2009] EWHC 2526 (Ch) at paragraph 75.

former common law derivative action, most particularly where a director's negligence is actionable. Also, the statutory derivative claim can be brought even if the director or directors have not benefited personally from the breach. Further, it is no longer necessary for the shareholder to show that those who have allegedly breached their duty control the majority of the shares in the company.[109] However, the statutory remedy is restrictive in comparison to the former common law claim in that a derivative claim under Chapter 1 of Part 11 CA 2006 may be brought "only in respect of a cause of action arising from an actual or proposed act or omission involving negligence, default, breach of duty or breach of trust by a director of the company",[110] or pursuant to an order in proceedings under Section 994. As such, a derivative claim will be available in the event of breach by a director or directors of the general duties as codified in Chapter 2 of Part 10 CA 2006, including the duty to exercise reasonable care, skill and diligence.[111]

Section 260 defines a "derivative claim" as comprising three parts. First, a derivative claim must be brought by a member of the company. It is immaterial whether the cause of action arose before or after the person seeking to bring or continue the derivative claim became a member of the company[112] and a "member of the company" includes a person who is not a member but to whom shares in the company have been transferred or transmitted by operation of law, for example where a trustee in bankruptcy or personal representative of a deceased member's estate acquires an interest in a share as a result of the bankruptcy or death of a member.[113] Secondly, a cause of action must vest in the company. Finally, the relief must be sought on behalf of the company (as opposed to the member).

Derivative claims may be brought against the directors (which includes shadow directors and former directors) themselves or against third parties. The statutory explanatory notes anticipate

---

[109] This nonetheless is a factor the court may take into account; *see Wishart* [2009] SLT 812 at paragraph 38.
[110] Section 260(3).
[111] Section 174.
[112] Section 260(4).
[113] Section 260(5)(c).

that derivative claims against third parties "would be permitted only in very narrow circumstances, where the damage suffered by the company arose from an act involving a breach of a duty etc. on the part of the director (e.g. for knowing receipt of money or property transferred in breach of trust or for knowing assistance in a breach of trust)".[114]

10.3.9 Procedure to bring a derivative claim under CA 2006

10.3.9.1 Application for permission to continue a derivative claim or continue a claim made by the company as a derivative claim

Pursuant to Sections 261 and 262, the court's permission (or leave, in Northern Ireland) must be obtained in order to continue a derivative claim or to continue a claim made by the company as a derivative claim. The court has a broad discretion to give directions as to the evidence that is required to be provided by the company in advance of the full hearing and as to the conduct of the proceedings generally, including powers to adjourn and give such directions as it thinks fit. The court is also given the power to exercise a broad discretion in determining the outcome of such an application and there is scope for significant judicial involvement in the process.

CA 2006 reflects the procedure under the Civil Procedure Rules for bringing a derivative claim by issuing a claim form under Part 7 CPR (*see* Section 10.3.7 above). There is no requirement to obtain the leave of the court prior to issuing the claim form. However, the member must then apply for leave to continue the claim thereby providing the court with the ability to assess whether a *prima facie* case exists and to develop a process for the conduct of the proceedings that is appropriate in the circumstances.[115]

---

[114] Companies Act 2006 Explanatory Notes prepared by the Department of Business, Innovation and Skills.

[115] For a review of this standard, *see* "Derivative Proceedings in a Brave New World for Company Management and Shareholders" by Andrew Keay and Joan Loughrey [2010] JBL, Issue 3.

If a *prima facie* case is not established, the court must dismiss the application and it may make any consequential orders it considers appropriate (e.g. a costs order against the member). The onus of proof is on the member to establish that a *prima facie* case exists on the evidence filed with the claim. If the court is satisfied on the strength of evidence filed by the member, it may give directions as to the evidence to be provided by the company and adjourn the proceedings meantime. On further hearing of the application, the court may give permission to continue the claim on such terms as it thinks fit, dismiss the application or adjourn the proceedings and give directions as it thinks fit.

Where a member wishes to apply for the permission (or leave) of the court to continue as a derivative claim a claim that has been brought by a company, the member must also convince the court that:

> "(a) the manner in which the company commenced or continued the claim amounts to an abuse of the process of the court;
>
> (b) the company has failed to prosecute the claim diligently; and
>
> (c) it is appropriate for the member to continue the claim as a derivative claim."

These requirements reflect the Law Reform Commission's concern to prevent undue interference by members with existing litigation. It was explained during the debates on the Companies Bill 2006 in Committee Stage in the House of Commons that an objective was to provide the member with a right to claim where a company has brought proceedings to prevent a derivative claim and the company has not prosecuted the claim diligently in the sense that it has not pursued the claim in a reasonable way without undue delay so as to have the effect of frustrating someone else's ability to bring a claim.

10.3.9.2 Application for permission to continue a derivative claim brought or continued by another member

Where a member wishes to apply for permission (or leave) of the court to continue a derivative claim brought or continued by another member, equivalent standards to those described above when convincing the court to permit a member to continue as a derivative claim a claim brought by the company will apply pursuant to Section 264. Similarly, if a *prima facie* case for giving permission (or leave) is not established, the court must dismiss the application and may make any consequential order it considers appropriate but, if the application is not dismissed, the court may give directions as to the evidence to be provided by the company and adjourn the proceedings meantime. On further hearing of the application, the court may give permission to continue the claim on such terms as it thinks fit, dismiss the application or adjourn the proceedings and give such directions as it thinks fit.

10.3.9.3 Court's discretion in determining whether to grant permission to continue a derivative claim

The court is granted a wide discretion to consider all relevant factors when determining whether a derivative claim should continue. CA 2006 specifies circumstances in which permission must be refused and the factors that the court must take into account in making its determination. Unless the parties otherwise agree, these further requirements should be addressed after permission (or leave) to continue a derivative claim has initially been granted, at a second stage when considering evidence developed by the company as directed after a *prima facie* case has been established. In practice, in assessing the *prima facie* case, there is likely to be a tendency to merge the assessment with some consideration of these further requirements.

In determining whether a *prima facie* case has been established, the existence of a good cause of action on the part of the company and negligence, default, breach of duty or trust by a director of the company must be established. At the second stage, the court must form a provisional view on the strength of the claim, considering the requirements in Section 263(2).[116]

---

[116] *Iesini* v *Westrip Holdings Ltd* [2009] EWHC 2526 (Ch).

Pursuant to Section 263(2), the court *must* refuse permission to continue a derivative claim under Sections 261 or 262 if it is satisfied:

> "(a) that a person acting in accordance with Section 172 (duty to promote the success of the company) would not seek to continue the claim, or
>
> (b) where the cause of action arises from an act or omission that is yet to occur, the act or omission has been authorised by the company, or
>
> (c) where the cause of action arises from an act or omission that has already occurred, the act or omission –
>
>> (i) was authorised by the company before it occurred, or
>>
>> (ii) has been ratified by the company since it occurred."

At one level, the court should only refuse permission if satisfied that no director would seek to continue the claim.[117] However, the court will consider the prospects of success, the ability of the company to recover damages, the disruption to the company's business, the costs and potential damage to the company's reputation, in effect some level of assessment as to reasonable business judgment.[118] Overall, the extent to which court will be prepared to form its own assessment as to the scope for a director to conclude that pursuit of a derivative claim is in the best interests of the company rather than defer to the decisions of incumbent directors is unclear.

As was the case for the common law derivative action, authorisation or ratification will also operate as a bar to continuation of a derivative claim. If not already authorised or ratified, the likelihood but not merely the possibility[119] that the company will authorise or ratify the matter complained of if invited to do so, is to be considered by the court under Section 263(3)(c).

---

[117] *Iesini* v *Westrip Holdings Ltd* [2009] EWHC 2526 (Ch) at paragraph 86.

[118] *Franbar Holdings Ltd* v *Patel and others* [2008] EWHC 1532 (Ch) at paragraph 36. *See* also at 30 and 36 for commentary that the lack of a fully developed case is not fatal to the ability of a director to determine that a claim should be continued. Also Wishart [2009] SLT 812 at paragraph 37.

[119] *Franbar Holdings* [2008] EWHC 1532 (Ch) at paragraph 47.

Provision for ratification of conduct by a director amounting to negligence, default, breach of duty or breach of trust in relation to the company is made in Section 239 and applies to conduct on or after 1 October 2007. Conduct prior to that date is subject to the law relating to ratification applicable immediately before that date. The section does not affect any enactment or rule of law imposing additional requirements for valid ratification including rules that certain acts are incapable of ratification.[120]

Section 239 imposes an additional restriction not applicable at common law, that a decision by a company to ratify conduct by a director must be made by the members without reliance on votes in favour of the ratification cast by the director or any member connected with him.[121] Ratification at common law does not exclude related party voting.[122] Moreover, Section 263(4) requires the court to take account of any evidence before it as to the views of members of the company who have no personal, direct or indirect, interest in the matter.[123] The court might be expected to require evidence from the company in that regard, in addition to the other factors it must take into account as described above and the discretionary considerations summarised below.

Having navigated the requirements in Section 263(2), the court must *take into account* the following considerations listed in Section 263(3) in making its determination:

(a) whether the member is acting in good faith;[124]

---

[120] Section 239(7) and *Franbar Holdings* [2008] EWHC 1532 (Ch) at paragraphs 44 and 45 although the basis for determination of what is incapable of ratification is confused. The full scope of what is incapable of ratification remains unclear although clearly including expropriation of company property and diversion of company opportunity: *Cook* v *Deeks* [1916] 1 AC 554.

[121] *See* Sections 252 and 254 defining connectedness for this purpose.

[122] *Regal Hastings* v *Gulliver* [1967] 2 AC 134 at 150.

[123] For an interpretation of the nature of interest for this purpose, *see Iesini* v *Westrip Holdings Ltd* [2009] EWHC 2526 (Ch) at paragraph 129.

[124] *See Nurcombe* v *Nurcombe* [1985] 1 WLR 370 at 376; *Goldsmith* v *Sperrings Ltd* [1977] 1 WLR 478; a dominant purpose to benefit the company is sufficient despite the existence of some collateral purpose unrelated to the benefit of the company – *Iesini* v *Westrip Holdings Ltd* [2009] EWHC 2526 (Ch) at paragraph 121. *See* also *Franbar Holdings* [2008] EWHC 1534 (Ch) at paragraphs 32 to 34 – an objective to enhance the buy-out value of a minority holding is not evidence of bad faith, nor is a poorly developed case. Note also that the claimant will be disqualified if he participated in the wrong to which the complaint relates: *Iesini* [2009] EWHC 2526 (Ch) at paragraph 122.

(b) the importance a person acting in accordance with Section 172 (duty to promote the success of the company) would attach to continuing the claim;

(c) whether the company is likely to authorise or ratify the matter;

(d) whether the company has decided not to pursue the claim;

(e) whether the act or omission in respect of which the claim is being brought gives rise to a cause of action that the member could pursue in his own right.

These factors do not entirely replicate the common law and are not clearly defined or weighted as to the importance the court should give them, providing inevitable scope for uncertainty and inconsistency. Notably, the considerations in Section 263(3) are discretionary, not mandatory, unlike the factors to be considered under Section 263(2). In addition, there is no guidance as to the sequence in which the factors in Sections 263(2) and (3) should be considered. As experience develops, the Secretary of State has authority to amend both Section 263(2) and (3), after consulting such persons as he considers appropriate.

Assembling the evidence required to demonstrate the likelihood of authorisation or ratification by the company in order to satisfy the consideration referred to in paragraph (c) above will impose an evidentiary burden on the company. That can however be addressed as a practical matter in the adjournment procedure envisaged in Section 261(3). The fact that weight is attached to the prospect of authorisation or ratification echoes the suggestion made in *Prudential Assurance Co Ltd* v *Newman Industries Ltd (No 2)*.[125] Obtaining authorisation or ratification might prove to be an expensive and inconvenient option but will only arise if a *prima facie* case has been made.

The attention required to be given to any decision of the company not to pursue a claim and the associated requirement in Section 263(4) to have regard to the views of members of the company who have no personal interest in the matter[126] may

---

[125] [1982] Ch 204.

[126] Those who are not implicated in the alleged wrongdoing, and who do not stand to benefit otherwise that in their capacity as members of the company. *Iesini* v *Westrip Holdings Ltd* [2009] EWHC 2526 (Ch) at paragraphs 129 and 130.

allow the court to bar a derivative claim for a breach of a director's duty even though incapable of ratification. It must however be recognised that these are discretionary factors only and embedded within them is full scope for the court to reach a determination based on the merits.

As to the last identified factor to be taken into account, the prospect of an alternative remedy available to the member arising out of the act or omission would include an unfair prejudice petition in the alternative to derivative action.[127] The common law required all remedies to be taken into account including those available to the company.[128]

Concern has been voiced that the statutory derivative claim inappropriately enhances the ability of minority members to bring derivative claims and exposes directors to more claims and liability. However, deterrent features in the statutory process include the requirement to establish a *prima facie* case at the outset and the broad discretion vested in the court to reject applications in the preliminary hearings or exploit the power to adjourn and give directions as circumstances dictate.[129] Historically, the courts have shown that they are reluctant to interfere with a decision of the board made in good faith, but it still remains to be seen how the courts will utilise the discretions conferred on them and whether a broad or narrow exception to the principle of majority rule will emerge.

The financial exposure of the petitioner to a costs order should circumstances merit remains unchanged and serves as a deterrent. Obversely, the scope for sequenced preliminary procedures while evidence is assembled offers the potential to allow for a more phased process than had emerged under the common law action. It remains the case that, should the shareholder be successful in a derivative action, any damages awarded are payable to the company and not to the shareholder.

---

[127] Where a Section 994 petition has been initiated, the prospect of success in seeking permission to bring a derivative action even on a consolidated basis is likely to be reduced; *see* *Franbar Holdings* [2008] EWHC 1534 (Ch) at paragraph 53.

[128] *Barrett* v *Duckett* [1995] 1 BCLC 243 at 372.

[129] *See Iesini* v *Westrip Holdings Ltd* [2009] EWHC 2526 (Ch) at paragraph 108.

All told, billed as "a weapon of last resort"[130] the procedure in relation to derivative claims maintains many strong deterrent elements. The multiplicity of considerations to be addressed by the court and the uncertain depth of consideration to be applied at the preliminary stages leaves plenty of scope for the courts to rejection applications. The introduction of the statutory derivative claim has not and is unlikely to result in a dramatic increase in litigation in this area.

10.4 Statutory unfair prejudice remedy (Section 994)

10.4.1 The requirements of Section 994[131]

Section 994(1) provides:

> "A member of a company may apply to the court by petition for an order under [Part 30 CA 2006] on the ground (a) that the company's affairs are being or have been conducted in a manner that is unfairly prejudicial to the interests of members generally or of some part of its members (including at least himself), or (b) that an actual or proposed act or omission of the company (including an act or omission on its behalf) is or would be so prejudicial."

This section comprises a number of elements, each of which is considered separately below. The remedy was first introduced in Section 210 Companies Act 1948 and related to conduct that was oppressive to some part of the members. The narrower concept of oppression was replaced by the requirement now reflected in Section 994[132] that the relevant conduct be unfairly prejudicial. The opportunity was also taken when replacing the remedy in the Companies Act 1980 to address other defects in Section 210.

Under Section 210 it was necessary to demonstrate that the facts would have justified a winding up on the just and equitable

---

[130] Hansard, HL, Vol 679 (Official Report) cols GC4-5 (Lord Goldsmith) 27 February 2006.

[131] Replacing Section 495 CA 1985 substantially without alteration with effect from 1 October 2007.

[132] Originally Section 75 Companies Act 1980 and then consolidated in Section 49 CA 1985.

ground. Section 994 imposes no such requirement.[133] It also makes clear that a single act or omission, and threatened conduct of a kind that would otherwise support a petition, can justify relief. Further, to supplement the fraud on the minority exception to the rule in *Foss* v *Harbottle*, the power of the court was extended to authorise proceedings to be brought against a third party in the name of the company and on such terms as the court should direct. Finally the right of persons entitled to shares by transmission to petition was specifically confirmed.[134] It was anticipated that the amendments now reflected in Section 994 should enable a petitioner to obtain relief where he could demonstrate a sufficient prejudice to his interests as a result of conduct that damaged the value of the company, as a result, for example, of negligence or abuse of corporate assets, but where the conduct complained of might fall short of fraud on the minority. Nonetheless there was a concern to achieve an appropriate balance such that the court should not interfere with *bona fide* commercial decisions taken on behalf of the company.

An amendment introduced in the Companies Act 1989 removed a defect that impeded reliance upon the remedy where the interests of some but not all of the members were unfairly prejudiced.

While successful petitions under Section 210 were rare, the remedy introduced in 1980 and now reflected in Section 994 has spawned a very high level of activity and has generally proved far more successful although a strong case for further reform has been made as reflected in the Law Commission "Shareholder Remedies" Report 246. In the event, no material reform has been introduced in CA 2006. In particular, the opportunity was not taken to adopt proposals for reform made by the Law Commission and summarised in Section 10.4.5 below.

The remedy was introduced as an alternative to a winding up on the just and equitable ground and is substantially relied

---

[133] *O'Neill* v *Phillips* [1999] 1 WLR 1092, HL at paragraphs 1098–1100; *Hawkes* v *Cuddy* [2009] EWCA Civ 291 at paragraph 104.
[134] These changes were all recommended by the Jenkins Committee Cmnd 1749 of 1962, *see* paragraphs 199 to 212.

upon as an exit mechanism for the damaged shareholder while not destroying the company. In distinguishing circumstances in which a claim under Section 994 is more appropriate than a derivative claim, if the substance of the claim relates to breach of duty or other conduct that is actionable by the company, a derivative claim is more suitable whereas a complaint relating to mismanagement of the company should be pursued on the grounds of unfair prejudice. However, reliance on Section 994 to address breaches of duty which have caused loss to the company has been successful even though the circumstances would warrant a derivative claim.[135] Evidently, should this trend develop, it opens the way to circumvent the need to pursue a derivative claim. Nonetheless, provided the remedy is corporate, the outcome can be rationalised with the core reflective loss presumption, that a shareholder cannot sue to make good a loss which would be made good if the company's assets would be replenished, through action against the party responsible for the loss.[136]

While the unfair prejudice claim applies to all Companies Act companies,[137] it has proved particularly relevant in the case of private companies, in circumstances where shareholders may also be directors and the distinction between the interests of an individual as an investor and his responsibilities as a director is blurred. Nonetheless, shareholders in private companies where disputes of the kind to which Section 994 applies are more likely to arise will generally be well served to anticipate dispute and make appropriate provision in shareholders' agreements or the articles. Such provisions should provide for controls over the conduct of the company's affairs, management of disputes and an exit solution in the event that issues in dispute cannot otherwise be resolved satisfactorily.

10.4.1.1 *The complainant must be a member*

In general, the petitioner must be a member at the time of bringing the petition, but it is unclear whether he must also

---

[135] *Re A Company (No 5287 of 1985)* [1986] 1 WLR 281 at 284.
[136] *Johnson v Gore Wood* [2001] 1 BCLC 313 at 337.
[137] Section 994(3).

have been a member at the time of the conduct to which the complaint relates. Any person to whom shares have been transferred or transmitted by operation of law is, although not a registered member, permitted to petition.[138] A former member is unable to petition under Section 994, even if he discovers that unfairly prejudicial conduct occurred while he was a member.

A separate, but similar, right is given by Section 995 to the Secretary of State to petition if he has received an inspector's report or obtained information by exercising his powers to do so, and it appears to him that the affairs of the company are being, or have been, conducted in a manner that is unfairly prejudicial to the interests of its members generally or of some part of the members or that any actual or proposed act or omission of the company (including an act or omission on its behalf) is or would be so prejudicial.

10.4.1.2 *The complaint must be made in the petitioner's capacity as a member*

The Section refers to members' interests including at least the petitioner. It has been held that, while the expression "interests" is wider than "strict legal rights",[139] those interests must be those of the petitioner qua member, and not in some other capacity; that is, the conduct complained of must adversely affect or jeopardise the value or quality of the shareholder's interest.[140] There may be circumstances where conduct affecting a member in some other capacity may nonetheless also affect the member as a member because it breaches a term on which he agreed to participate as a member. For example, where the value of membership is inextricably connected with a management role, removal from management may prejudice the member's interests as a member.[141]

---

[138] Section 994(2). *Re McCarthy Surfacing Ltd* [2006] All ER (D) 193 (Apr).
[139] *See Re a Company* [1986] BCLC 376 at 378; *Re JE Cade & Son Ltd* [1992] BCLC 213.
[140] *Re a Company (No 004475 of 1982)* [1983] Ch 178 at 189; *Re JE Cade & Son Ltd* (above); but *see* the remarks of Vinelott J in *Re a Company* [1983] 1 WLR 927. *See* also *O'Neill v Phillips* (above) which, while confirming that the prejudice must be suffered as a member, noted that the requirement should not be too narrowly or technically construed. *See* also commentary of Ralph Gibson LJ in *Nicholas v Soundcraft Electronics Ltd and another* [1993] BCLC 360.
[141] *O'Neill v Phillips* (above).

10.4.1.3   Effect on other members

The matter complained of need not affect the petitioner alone: it can affect all members (e.g. a fall in share value), even though the others do not complain.

10.4.1.4   Conduct of the company's affairs

It is not necessary for the conduct to be continuing at the time of presentation of the petition.[142] While the act complained of need not be continuing and a failure to act may prove sufficient,[143] if the offending conduct has been put right and cannot recur or can be remedied by the petitioner, no court-imposed remedy will be required or made available.[144] In effect, it is difficult to envisage circumstances in which persons in control of a company as directors and shareholders could bring a petition, even where relations with a minority shareholder have totally broken down, in an effort to squeeze out the minority in reliance on Section 994, notwithstanding some prior or even current improper conduct of the minority shareholder in any management role.[145]

There is no limitation period applicable to a petition under Section 994, and so historic conduct can be relied upon, but inexcusable delay may bar relief.[146]

Although Section 994 makes reference to a proposed act or omission of the company, proposed conduct of the company that is merely speculative may be insufficient.

10.4.1.5   Meaning of "the company's affairs"

The conduct complained of must be conduct by the defendant of the company's affairs, rather than conduct by shareholders of their own affairs or the exercise of their individual rights, and will

---

[142] *Re a Company (No 001761 of 1986)* [1987] BCLC 141 at 143.

[143] *Re a Company (No 001761 of 1986)* [1987] BCLC 141.

[144] *Re Legal Costs Negotiators Ltd* also known as *Morris and others* v *Hateley and another* (1999) [1999] BCC 547 or 1999 2 BCLC 171; and *see Grandactual Ltd, Re Hough* v *Hardcastle* [2005] All ER (D) 313.

[145] *Re Legal Costs Negotiators Ltd* (above).

[146] *Re a Company (No 005134 of 1986), Ex parte Harries* [1989] BCLC 383, at 397 to 398.

be construed liberally.[147] The offending conduct must be concerned with acts done by the company or those authorised to act on its behalf.[148] Conduct wholly in another capacity (even if that conduct affects the company) will not support a complaint.[149]

A refusal by a minority shareholder to sell shares, or disagreements between shareholders relating to their disposal of or dealings with their shares, will not constitute conduct of the company's affairs.[150] Similarly, disagreements as to the operation of a shareholders' agreement typically will not relate to the conduct of the company's affairs.[151]

Should controlling shareholders procure that a company takes no action to preserve its interests in the face of competing objectives of the controlling shareholders, or associated breach of directors duties, maintaining that policy of passive neglect of the company's interests will qualify as conduct of the company's affairs. Whether doing so is conduct that is unfairly prejudicial will turn on the facts.[152] The success of any petition under Section 994 based on a breach of duty is likely to depend upon evidence that the controlling shareholders have failed to act and that derivative action is not appropriate.

Particularly in a group context, where a subsidiary has an independent minority, the parent company must accept that, insofar as it competes with the interests of its subsidiary, there will be an obligation to conduct affairs so as to deal fairly with the subsidiary. Representative directors of the majority shareholder may find themselves in a delicate position where competing demands arise, but in those circumstances the burden will fall on the controlling shareholder to behave with evident fairness towards the minority shareholders and allow its representative directors to act in the best interests of their company. Exploiting control to guide the

---

[147] *Hawkes* v *Cuddy* (above) at paragraphs 49 and 50.
[148] *Re Legal Costs Negotiators Ltd* (above); *Arrow Nominees Inc and another* v *Blackledge and others* [2000] 2 BCLC 167.
[149] *Re a Company (No 001761 of 1986)* (above); *O'Neill* v *Phillips* (above).
[150] *Re Leeds United Holdings Plc* [1996] 2 BCLC 545.
[151] *Re Unisoft Group Ltd (No 3)* [1994] 1 BCLC 609; *Re Leeds United Holdings Plc* [1996] 2 BCLC 545, but *see Scottish Cooperative Wholesale Society* v *Meyer* [1959] AC 324.
[152] *Wilkinson* v *West Coast Capital and others* [2007] BCC 717.

company to a policy of inaction, restraint or omission is sufficient connection between the conduct of the controlling shareholders and the company's affairs for these purposes.

Where the affairs of members of a group of companies are to a significant extent treated as if they were a single enterprise, actions taken by the parent company in its own interests may be regarded as acts done in the conduct of the affairs of the subsidiary, even if the two companies are engaged in different types of business and despite general principles of separate corporate personality.[153] Obversely, conduct of the affairs of a wholly-owned subsidiary may give rise to allegations of unfair prejudice to the interests of members of the parent company.[154] This conclusion is justified by reference to the risk of diminution in value of the members' interests in the parent company that is reflective of the loss of value of the parent company's investment in the subsidiary as a result of the matters giving rise to the allegations. While this runs counter to the principle that a member should have no personal remedy and logically not enjoy any other personal cause of action when the loss is reflective, perhaps central to any determination whether a claim under Section 994 is appropriate in the alternative to a derivative action in such circumstances will be whether, following a derivative action, the relationship between the shareholders is such that an exit remedy under Section 994 would be more appropriate.

While the commercial realities will be an influential factor in determining the appropriate remedy, the mere capacity of one enterprise to exercise direct or indirect control over the affairs of another should not be expected to prove sufficient of itself to establish an adequate connection for this purpose.[155]

10.4.1.6   Meaning of "interests"

Although the expression "interests of members" in Section 994 limits the interests in question to those of the members qua members, it is not limited to strict legal rights under the company's constitution, and the court may have regard to

---

[153] *Nicholas v Soundcraft Electronics Ltd* [1993] BCLC 360, CA.
[154] *Re Citybranch Ltd, Gross and others v Rackind and others* [2005] 1 WLR 3505.
[155] *Grandactual Ltd, Re Hough v Hardcastle* (above).

wider equitable considerations.[156] However, the petitioner must usually show some breach of the terms on which the members have agreed or have an understanding that the affairs of the company should be conducted.[157]

This agreement need not necessarily be a formal agreement, but in appropriate circumstances can be a "legitimate expectation"[158] of the petitioner, breach of which might have formed the basis of a petition to wind up the company on the "just and equitable" ground set out in Section 122(1)(g) Insolvency Act 1986. In the case of *Ebrahimi* v *Westbourne Galleries Ltd*[159] (where the majority had exercised their legal right to remove the petitioner from his directorship) the House of Lords determined that it was both impossible and undesirable to give an exhaustive statement of the circumstances in which equitable considerations should be taken into account in determining whether a person's rights had been interfered with, but indicated that the circumstances might include one or probably more of the following elements:

(a) an association formed or continued on the basis of a personal relationship, involving mutual confidence – this element will often be found where a pre-existing partnership has been converted into a limited company;
(b) an agreement, or understanding, that all or (if there are sleeping shareholders) some of the shareholders shall participate in the conduct of the business;

---

[156] *See Re Macro (Ipswich) Ltd* [1994] 2 BCLC 354 at 404 – examples of interests included damage to the value of the company and the absence of independent directors; *Re Rotadata Ltd* [2000] 1 BCLC 122; *Gamlestaden Fastigheter AB* v *Baltic Partners Ltd and others (Jersey)* [2007] Bus LR 1521.
[157] *O'Neill* v *Phillips* (above) AT 1098 TO 1100.
[158] *Re Saul D Harrison* [1995] 1 BCLC 14, although this expression was qualified in *O'Neill* v *Phillips* (above) such that only to the extent equitable principles dictate should a remedy be available. Most US states provide a remedy in response to misconduct by those that control a corporation. A common theme in the development of such remedies is to relate them closely to breach of good faith and fair-dealing obligations by majority shareholders or, at its broadest, the frustration of "reasonable expectations" of shareholders. The reasonable expectations standard has enabled US courts to adapt the remedy to address the greater intimacy of business relationships that tend to exist in close corporations, permitting the court to assess the understanding of the parties and then determine whether the conduct of controlling shareholders is contrary to that understanding.

In determining the particular characteristics that bind participants in a close corporation, US courts have tended to distinguish subjective aspirations, frustration of which would not justify relief, and expectations that were known to and concurred with by other shareholders. In assessing expectations, the US courts have been prepared to look beyond rights and benefits anticipated by a shareholder in that capacity, to take account of an individual's collateral expectations as an officer or employee.
[159] [1973] AC 360, HL.

(c) a restriction upon the transfer of the members' interest in the company – so that, if confidence is lost or one member is removed from management, he cannot take out his stake and go elsewhere.

This parallel between circumstances in which an exercise of strict legal rights will nonetheless justify a remedy under Section 994 and the "just and equitable" ground for winding up is not intended to mean that the conduct complained of will not be unfair unless it would justify a winding up order on that ground. It is quite clear that whereas there was such a requirement in the former Section 210 Companies Act 1948, that standard is not replicated in Section 994. The parallel is not in the conduct that the court will treat as justifying the remedy but in the principles upon which it determines that the conduct is unjust, inequitable or unfair.[160]

The expression "quasi-partnership" has been used to describe companies in which some or all of the elements in paragraphs (a) to (c) above exist, and the distinction between companies which are quasi-partnerships and those that are not is important in understanding what attitude a court will take on a petition under Section 994. Where it is established that the company has the characteristics of a quasi-partnership, minority participants will in effect have an additional string upon which to rely, namely the breach of legitimate expectations that may go beyond the articles or agreements between shareholders, statutory obligations or directors' duties. However, it is not sufficient for the petitioner merely to establish that the company is a quasi-partnership in order to obtain a remedy under Section 994. He must also show either a breach of the legal terms on which the business of the company is to be conducted or, in the context of a quasi-partnership, use by the majority of their strict legal entitlements in a manner that equity would regard as contrary to good faith.[161]

---

[160] *O'Neill* v *Phillips* (above); also *Hawkes* v *Cuddy* (above) at paragraph 104.

[161] *O'Neill* v *Phillips* (above) at 1098 to 1100. The Law Commission, *Shareholder Remedies*, Report 246 at paragraph 4.11 references its suggestion that conduct could be unfairly prejudicial merely based on breaches of legitimate expectations, a concept adopted in *Re Saul D Harrison & Sons Plc* (above). In *O'Neill*, Lord Hoffmann qualified this broad interpretation on the basis that a balance must be struck between the breadth of discretion given to the court and the principle of legal certainty.

In identifying these hurdles, the House of Lords decision in *O'Neill* v *Phillips* represents a landmark limitation on excessive reliance upon Section 994 by shareholders petitioning on the strength of broad based disappointments. Section 994 does not provide a right to exit at will, even if it is possible to establish that the company is a quasi-partnership, simply because there has been a loss of trust, confidence or good relations.[162] Deadlock and the inability of the company to conduct its business as initially contemplated is not in itself sufficient.

Nonetheless, where an event occurs that puts an end to the basis upon which parties have entered into a quasi-partnership, making it unfair that some shareholders should insist upon the continuance of the association, the conduct of the majority to maintain that continuation in changed circumstances may be sufficient to support a petition.[163]

It will in general be difficult to demonstrate a quasi-partnership other than in small, possibly very small, companies. It is highly unlikely that a petitioner would be able to demonstrate that all members of a public company with a substantial number of shareholders were parties to some informal arrangement sufficient to qualify the contractual obligations and rights conferred by the constitution save perhaps in circumstances where there are two or more major shareholdings and there is a background of special cooperation or participation, for example, among founding shareholders.[164]

10.4.1.7 Meaning of "unfairly prejudicial"

This leads to a consideration of the meaning of the expression "unfairly prejudicial". There is a vast body of case law in the context of the Section 994 remedy, which is not surprising as the courts have acknowledged that the protection afforded by the Section has had to be worked out on a case-by-case

---

[162] *See* also *Hawkes* v *Cuddy* (above) at paragraph 108 rejecting *Re Guidezone Ltd* [2000] 2 BCLC 321.

[163] *Hawkes* v *Cuddy* (above) at paragraph 108 referring to *O'Neill* v *Phillips* (above) at 1101.

[164] *Re Blue Arrow Plc* [1987] BCLC 585; *Re Tottenham Hotspur Plc* [1994] 1 BCLC 655; *Re Astec (BSR) Plc* [1998] 2 BCLC 556 at 590; *CAS (Nominees) Ltd and others* v *Nottingham Forest FC Plc and others* [2002] 1 BCLC 613 at 627.

basis.[165] In its 1996 Consultation Paper,[166] the Law Commission analysed the petitions under the Section presented to the Companies Court at the Royal Courts of Justice between January 1994 and December 1995, and identified the following principal allegations pleaded (listed in order of frequency):

(a) Exclusion from management: by far the most common allegation was that the petitioner had been excluded from the management of the company,[167] and this exclusion would be likely to entitle the petitioner to relief if the court finds that he has a legitimate expectation to participate and that exclusion was unfairly prejudicial to his interests qua member.[168] The conduct of the petitioner, and the way in which he was excluded, would be relevant.[169] The Law Commission has recommended that in the case of a private company limited by shares, in which substantially all the members are directors, there should be a statutory presumption that the removal of a shareholder as a director or from substantially all his functions as a director is unfairly prejudicial conduct. While this recommendation is not reflected in terms in the CA 2006, as noted in *O'Neill* v *Phillips*, this would not seem very different in practice from the way in which the provision is interpreted. The key point, however, is that the unfairness is not so much in the exclusion alone as in the exclusion without a reasonable offer to buy out the relevant shareholder (*see* Section 10.4.2 below).

(b) Failure to provide information: although the failure to comply with the various requirements of the Companies Acts to provide members with information may be grounds for a petition under Section 994 (unless the failure is trivial), it is more commonly linked to an allegation of exclusion from management. However, a deliberate policy not to consult the petitioner on major issues on which he has a legitimate expectation to be consulted could amount to unfair prejudice.[170]

---

[165] Per Neill LJ in *Re Saul D Harrison & Sons Plc* (above) at 30.
[166] The Law Commission Consultation Paper No 142, Appendix E, Table 1.
[167] *Richards* v *Lundy and others* [1999] BCC 786.
[168] *Quinlan* v *Essex Hinge Co Ltd* [1996] 2 BCLC 417.
[169] *Re R A Noble & Sons (Clothing) Ltd* [1983] BCLC 273.
[170] Per Nourse J in *Re R A Noble & Sons (Clothing) Ltd* (above) at 289.

(c) Misappropriation of assets: there have been a number of successful petitions under the Section 994 remedy where the majority have been shown to have misappropriated the company's assets (often by selling them at an undervalue to a company controlled by them) or diverted business, which should have gone to the company, to another business owned by them or otherwise acted to run down the value of the company while transferring value to themselves.[171] These cases show that a petition under Section 994 is not barred even though the facts would have warranted the bringing of a derivative action or a personal action based on the directors' breach of fiduciary duties.

(d) Failure to remunerate/pay a dividend: the fact that a company's failure to pay a dividend affects all shareholders equally is no longer relevant following the amendments introduced by the Companies Act 1989 and reflected in Section 994. The petitioner will, however, have to show a legitimate expectation that dividends would be paid in order to overcome the objection that it is for the directors to decide what the company's policy should be on the retention or distribution of the company's profits. Failure to pay dividends is often linked to a complaint about excessive remuneration of the directors (*see* (f) below).[172]

(e) Mismanagement: the courts have been reluctant to interfere in the management of the company's business by the directors. Mere disagreement over the manner in which the business of a company is being operated or the policies of the board will not support action under Section 994. Section 994 will not provide an exit mechanism or financial top-up for a shareholder who is simply disappointed with the company's performance or disagrees with decisions of the board over the direction the company should take or who has fallen out with the majority. Generally, the courts have been alive to the potential to exploit the threat of litigation under the Section 994 remedy as leverage and as an instrument of oppression of a company and the controlling

---

[171] e.g. *Re London School of Electronics Ltd* [1986] Ch 211; *Re a Company* (No 5287 of 1985) [1986] 1 WLR 281; *Re Antoniades v Wong and others* [1997] 2 BCLC 419.

[172] *Shamsallah Holdings Pty Ltd v CBD Refrigeration and Airconditioning Services Pty Ltd* (2001) 19 ACLC 517.

majority.[173] However, it has been acknowledged[174] that serious or persistent mismanagement which the majority has done nothing to correct or which reflects a course of conduct previously accepted but nonetheless inconsistent with constitutional requirements that a shareholder is seeking to revive could amount to unfair prejudice.

(f) Excessive remuneration: if the remuneration paid to the defendant has clearly been in excess of what he deserved by comparison to his contribution to the company's business, that has been held to be unfairly prejudicial to the interests of the petitioner.[175]

Other commonplace allegations include oppressive conduct of board meetings,[176] breach of agreement, breach of statute,[177] improper allotment of shares,[178] breach of articles, decisions made for the benefit of related companies rather than shareholders in the company,[179] use of company funds to defend oppressive proceedings[180] and other breach of fiduciary duty.

The test of unfair prejudice is an objective one to be applied flexibly according to the circumstances in the context of the commercial relationship. It is not necessary for the petitioner to show bad faith or a conscious intention to prejudice the petitioner. Rather, the test is one of unfairness, not unlawful or even underhand conduct.[181] Indeed, as noted above, in the context of quasi-partnerships, the unfairness may consist of reliance on legal rights in circumstances where ethical considerations make it unfair to do so because the proposed exercise is outside either that which can fairly be regarded as having been in the contemplation of the parties when they became members or some later

---

[173] *Howard Smith Ltd* v *Ampol Petroleum Ltd* [1974] AC 821 at 832; *Rock Ltd* v *RSO Holdings Ltd* [2004] BCC 466; *see* also *Fisher* v *Cadman* [2006] 1 BCLC 499.

[174] *Re Elgindata Ltd* [1991] BCLC 959; *Re Macro (Ipswich) Ltd* [1994] 2 BCLC 354.

[175] *Re Cumana Ltd* [1986] BCLC 430, *see* also *Re Dalkeith Investments Pty Ltd* (1984) 9 ACLR 247.

[176] Young J in *John J Star (Real Estate) Pty Ltd* v *Robert R Andrew (Australasia) Pty Ltd* (1991) 6 ACSR 63 at 66.

[177] *DR Chemicals Ltd* (above).

[178] *DR Chemicals Ltd* (above) but *see* for contrast *CAS (Nominees) Ltd* v *Nottingham Forest FC Plc and others* [2001] 1 All ER 954. *See* also *Dalby* v *Bodilly and Coloursource Ltd* [2005] BCC 627.

[179] *See Brenfield Squash Racquets Club Ltd* [1996] 2 BCLC 184.

[180] *Re DG Brims & Sons Pty Ltd* (1995) 16 ACSR 559.

[181] *DR Chemicals Ltd* (above).

established understanding.[182] Thus, what may be fair between competing business people may not be fair in a quasi-partnership company context.

10.4.2 Obstacles

Even if the petitioner is able to demonstrate unfairly prejudicial conduct within the ambit of Section 994, there are further obstacles which he must overcome in order to obtain relief under Section 994. These are:

(a) Conduct of the petitioner: in contrast to the situation where the shareholder wishes to bring a derivative action (*see* Section 10.3 above), in the case of a petition under Section 994 it is not necessary for him to come "with clean hands". However, his conduct will be taken into account by the court in deciding whether conduct which was clearly prejudicial was also unfair.[183] Acceding to habitual breach of the constitutional procedures required to be observed in the conduct of a company's affairs may restrict the availability of a remedy in respect of those breaches.[184]

(b) Availability of an alternative remedy: this divides itself into three, namely: (i) the existence of pre-emption rights in the company's articles of association; (ii) in the absence of pre-emption rights, the existence of a fair offer by the other shareholder(s) to buy the petitioner's shares; and (iii) the availability of a ready market for the shares.

   (i) Pre-emption rights: if the company's articles contain (as the articles of many private companies do) provisions requiring (or entitling) a shareholder to offer his shares for purchase by the other shareholders (or, in some cases, by the company itself) before he can transfer them elsewhere, and he does not take advantage of those provisions, it might be argued that he has failed to exploit a remedy that is available in the

---

[182] *O'Neill v Phillips* (above).
[183] *Re London School of Electronics Ltd* (above); and *see Re DR Chemicals Ltd* (above). *See* also *Richardson and Wheeler v Blackmore* [2006] BCC 276.
[184] *Fisher v Cadman* (*see* above at note 174).

alternative to an order under Section 994. However, such provisions often require the shares to be valued on an "open market value" basis, and the value of a minority shareholding will often be valued on a discounted basis (i.e. at less than the *pro rata* value of the shares), and so to the disadvantage of the shareholder in contrast to the basis of valuation usually applied in the buy-out remedy available under Section 994. There may be other factors (such as the valuation procedures or the commercial impact of the conduct complained of) that render the provisions inappropriate as a fair alternative to a remedy under Section 994. It is now accepted that the existence of such provisions does not represent a bar to proceedings under the Section 994 remedy,[185] but an open offer to purchase the minority shareholder's shares at a fair price, which is calculated on a *pro rata* basis and otherwise fairly, will make it an abuse of process for the petitioner to continue an action.[186]

(ii) Offer to buy the petitioner's shares: a reasonable offer to buy the petitioner's shares at a fair price (to be determined by competent expert valuation if not agreed), with equality of access to relevant company information and a fair mechanism to deal with the petitioner's shares may be enough to prevent the petition under Section 994 from being successful. If the company is a quasi-partnership, the basis of valuation may need to be on a *pro rata*, rather than discounted, basis to be sure of success, although the court has a discretion in all cases.[187] There may be difficulties in deciding the date as at which the valuation is to be made, as this will need to be fair in context[188] and so will vary with the circumstances of the case but

---

[185] *See Belfield Furnishings Ltd, Paul Isaacs and others* v *Belfield Furnishings Ltd, Paul Millership and others* [2006] 2 BCLC 705.

[186] *Virdi* v *Abbey Leisure Ltd and others* [1990] BCLC 342, CA; *Re a Company* [1996] 2 BCLC 192; but *see Re Rotadata Ltd* (above) at 132.

[187] *Re Bird Precision Bellows Ltd* [1986] Ch 658 at 669; and *see O'Neill* v *Phillips* (above) also *North Holdings Ltd* v *Southern Tropics Ltd* [1999] 2 BCLC 625 at 639.

[188] *See Re London School of Electronics Ltd* (above). *See also Re Bee Tee Alarms Ltd* [2006] All ER (D) 157.

typically should be as close as possible to the actual date of sale and appropriately reflect an assessment of the impact of future events, whether positive or negative.[189] Failure to include in the offer terms a contribution to the costs incurred in disputing the claim may not be fatal but any assessment of the adequacy of the offer will have regard to what is reasonable in the circumstances. The respondent might expect a reasonable grace period following a breakdown in relations to frame an offer before he must necessarily also take into account the costs incurred by the plaintiff in seeking relief.[190]

(iii) An obstacle to proceedings under Section 994 that is particularly acute for a shareholder in a public company is the availability of a ready market for the shares.

(c) Costs: as with derivative actions (*see* Section 10.3.6 above) the issue of costs is pervasive. The old legal aid regime has been replaced by a new system of public funding that expressly excludes funding for matters relating to company law.[191] Moreover, as the petition is by the shareholder in his own right, the court has no discretion to grant the petitioner an indemnity out of the company's assets for his costs, a material point of distinction when compared with the derivative action. The Law Commission, in its 1996 Consultation Paper,[192] cites examples of the cost and length of proceedings seeking the Section 994 remedy, including the case of *Re Elgindata Ltd*,[193] in which the hearing of the petition lasted 43 days, costs totalled £320,000 and the shares, originally purchased for £40,000, were finally valued at only £24,600. In the case of *O'Neill* v *Phillips*,[194] the original petition was issued in January 1992

---

[189] *Bilkus* v *King* also known as *Re Clearsprings (Management) Ltd* [2003] All ER (D) 470 (Oct). *See* also *Wilkinson* v *West Coast Capital and others* [2005] All ER (D) 346 (Dec).

[190] *O'Neill* v *Phillips* (above).

[191] The new system was brought in under the Access to Justice Act 1999 (*see* note 89 above). Schedule 2 Access to Justice Act 1999 sets out services that are excluded from funding under the Community Legal Service regime.

[192] The Law Commission Consultation Paper No 142, p 104 *et seq*.

[193] [1991] BCLC 959.

[194] [1999] 2 BCLC 1.

and the House of Lords decision was handed down in May 1999. The new rules permitting conditional fee and litigation funding arrangements have now provided an alternative method of funding these petitions.[195]

10.4.3 Remedies available

Section 996 provides:

"(1) If the court is satisfied that a petition under [Part 30 CA 2006] is well founded, it may make such order as it thinks fit for giving relief in respect of the matters complained of.

(2) Without prejudice to the generality of subsection (1), the court's order may –

(a) regulate the conduct of the company's affairs in the future;

(b) require the company – (i) to refrain from doing or continuing an act complained of, or (ii) to do an act that the petitioner has complained it has omitted to do;

(c) authorise civil proceedings to be brought in the name and on behalf of the company by such person or persons and on such terms as the court may direct;

(d) require the company not to make any, or any specified, alterations in its articles without the leave of the court;

(e) provide for the purchase of the shares of any members of the company by other members or by the company itself and, in the case of a purchase by the company itself, the reduction of the company's capital accordingly."

Section 996 introduced as shown in paragraph (d) above an additional example order requiring the company not to make any, or any specified, alterations in its articles without the leave

---

[195] These alternative means of funding are referred to in Part II Access to Justice Act 1999.

of the court. The scope for such an order under the predecessor Section 461 CA 1985 was implicit from the references made to it in Section 461(3) CA 1985.

The decision as to the appropriate remedy is a matter of judgment, in the discretion of the court.[196] The court will take into account all relevant interests. The remedy is not limited to any remedies sought by the petitioner. The unacceptability to the petitioner of the relief that the court considers appropriate will be a major consideration but the court may make such order as it thinks fit.[197]

By far the most common form of relief sought is the purchase of the petitioner's shares.[198] In its 1996 Consultation Paper,[199] the Law Commission noted that, in petitions presented to the Companies Court at the Royal Courts of Justice between January 1994 and December 1995 seeking relief under the Section 994 remedy, 69.9 per cent[200] sought this form of relief. As noted in Section 10.4.2(b)(ii) above, difficulties can arise in such cases in relation to the basis of valuation of the shares (whether on a discounted basis, which is more likely where the shareholding is an investment,[201] or *pro rata* basis, which is likely where the relationship is a quasi-partnership)[202] and the date as at which the valuation is to be made.[203]

The courts have been prepared to grant relief to the company under a Section 994 petition on the basis that the broad discretion allowed to the court under Section 996 permits it to grant the same relief that it would have granted in a derivative claim.[204]

---

[196] *See Hawkes* v *Cuddy* (above) for a discussion at paragraphs 80–92.

[197] *Hawkes* v *Cuddy* (above) as paragraphs 85–91, clarifying paragraph 10.2 of the Law Commission Consultation Paper No 142 "Shareholder Remedies" as supporting only the proposition that the petition must specify the relief sought by the petitioner but that that is not to the exclusion of the court's discretion on remedies.

[198] But *see Re Brenfield Squash Racquets Club Ltd* (above); also *Re Planet Organic Ltd* [2000] 1 BCLC 366.

[199] The Law Commission Consultation Paper No 142 Appendix E.

[200] Taking into account that any given petition may include reference to more than one form of relief.

[201] *See Re Elgindata Ltd* (above). *See* also *Patricia Irvine and others* v *Ian Irvine and others* [2006] 4 All ER 102.

[202] *Strahan* v *Wilcock* [2006] 2 BCC 320.

[203] *See Bilkus* v *King* also known as *Re Clearsprings (Management) Ltd* (above) for a review of relevant considerations in selecting a valuation date; also *Profinance Trust SA* v *Gladstone* [2002] 1 WLR 1024 and *Re Cumana Ltd* (above).

[204] *Clark* v *Cutland* [2003] 2 BCLC 393 at paragraph 2.

Generally the courts will apply equitable considerations so as to arrive at a result that is, in all the circumstances, fair as between the parties.[205]

10.4.4 Procedure

In *Re a Company (No 004837 of 1998), North Holdings Ltd* v *Southern Tropics Ltd and others*,[206] the judges emphasised the need for active case management at an early stage in order to reduce the time and expense involved in ascertaining a fair price for the petitioner's shares, and for use of the power to require a joint expert or the appointment of an assessor, which would lead to a reduction in the number of striking out applications. This was an appeal concerning the former Section 459 action under earlier court procedure rules, but such cases shall continue to be of importance in light of the unchanged ethos behind the CPR.

Applications under Section 994 are now governed by the Companies (Unfair Prejudice Applications) Proceedings Rules 2009[207] (the "2009 Rules") and (as far as not inconsistent with

---

[205] *See Re Bird Precision Bellows Ltd* [1986] Ch 658 at 672; *Scottish Cooperative Wholesale Society* v *Meyer* [1959] AC 324 at 369; *Re Jermyn Street Turkish Baths Ltd* [1970] 1 WLR 1194 at 1208; *Guinness Peat Group Plc* v *British Land Co Plc and others* [1999] BCC 536, CA; *O'Neill* v *Phillips* (above); *Re Elgindata Ltd* (above). In terms of fashioning remedies, the US courts have provided a rich seam of alternatives for consideration. In addition to dissolution or buy-out, in many US states a court can appoint a provisional director to resolve deadlock and to enable the corporation to function. The appointment of a custodian represents an alternative that is more intrusive in the sense that a custodian need not operate with the approval or acquiescence of board members. Other remedies recognised in many US states include:

(a) alteration of the corporation's constitution;
(b) intervention in actions of the corporation;
(c) prohibition of planned actions;
(d) sale of assets;
(e) alterations to the board of directors;
(f) ordering an account of corporate assets or an investigation;
(g) requiring declaration of a dividend;
(h) identifying constructive dividends paid through controlling shareholder remuneration and directing a corresponding dividend to non-participating shareholders;
(i) ordering a rebalancing in the shareholding structure;
(j) treating related corporations as grouped for the purposes of determining appropriate relief;
(k) imposing damages payments;
(l) installation of effective accounting systems or management controls; and
(m) directing dissolution at a future date if differences have not in the meantime been resolved.

[206] [1999] 2 BCLC 625; and *see* also *Re Rotadata Ltd* (above).
[207] SI 2469/2009, made under Section 411 Insolvency Act 1986.

those Rules) the CPR, in particular Part 49 CPR (Specialist Proceedings) and the Practice Directions made under it.[208] The 2009 Rules replaced the Companies (Unfair Prejudice Applications) Proceedings Rules 1986 (the "1986 Rules"). The 2009 Rules shall not apply, and the 1986 Rules shall continue to apply, to any petition presented to the court before 1 October 2009.[209]

An application under Section 994 is made by petition in the form set out in the Schedule to the 2009 Rules ("with such variations, if any, as the circumstances may require"[210]). The petition must specify the grounds on which it is presented and the nature of the relief sought.[211] The court shall then fix a hearing for a day, i.e. " 'the return day", on which the petitioner and any respondent (including the company) shall attend before the registrar or district judge for directions, unless the court otherwise directs.[212] At least 14 days before the return day the petitioner must serve a sealed copy of the petition on the company and every respondent named in the petition.[213]

On the return day, or any time after it, the court shall give such directions as it thinks appropriate with respect to various matters.[214] Those matters include whether, and if so by what means, the petition is to be advertised, whether a stay (for any period) with a view to mediation or Alternative Dispute Resolution ("ADR") should be ordered, and any other matter in connection with the hearing and disposal of the petition.[215]

The petition may additionally ask for a winding-up order on "just and equitable" grounds under Section 122(1)(g) Insolvency Act 1986 in the alternative, relief which is not available under Section 994.[216] However, Section 125(2) Insolvency

---

[208] *See* the Chancery Guide 2009 issued by the Chancery Division, paragraphs 20.2 and 20.3.
[209] Rule 7 of the 2009 Rules.
[210] Rule 3(1) of the 2009 Rules.
[211] Rule 3(2) of the 2009 Rules.
[212] Rule 3(3) of the 2009 Rules.
[213] Rule 4 of the 2009 Rules.
[214] Rule 5 of the 2009 Rules.
[215] ibid.
[216] The Law Commission has proposed that the law should be altered to make a winding-up order available as a remedy in its *Shareholder Remedies* Report 246, paragraph 4.35. It also established that, in the period between January 1994 and December 1995, 37.3 per cent of petitions under Section 459 CA 1985 sought relief under Section 122(1)(g) Insolvency Act 1986 in addition (*see* Appendix J).

Act 1986 provides that the court is not to make a winding-up order on these grounds "if the court is . . . of the opinion both that some other remedy is available to the petitioners and that they are acting unreasonably in seeking to have the company wound up instead of pursuing that other remedy". The remedy of winding up is outside the scope of this Chapter, but it will be seen that there may be circumstances in which relief under Section 994 could be such an "other remedy". Since Section 124 Insolvency Act 1986 requires a winding-up petition to be brought by (among others) a "contributory", a member can only petition as such if he holds shares on which there is some liability, or if the company is solvent and there is some reasonable possibility of a surplus being available to the members.

The Practice Direction supplementing CPR Part 49[217] states:

> "(1) Attention is drawn to the undesirability of asking as a matter of course for a winding up order as an alternative to an order under [Section 459 CA 1985]. The petition should not ask for a winding up order unless that is the relief which the petitioner prefers or it is thought that it may be the only relief to which the petitioner is entitled."

A petition to wind up a company can lead to devastating consequences for the company, not least under its contractual commitments. Further, under Section 127 Insolvency Act 1986, any disposition of the company's property made after the commencement of the winding up is void unless the court otherwise orders; under Section 129 Insolvency Act 1986, the winding up is deemed to have commenced at the time of the presentation of the petition. The Practice Direction referred to above therefore provides:

> "(2) Whenever a winding up order is asked for in a contributory's petition, the petition must state whether the petitioner consents or objects to an order under Section 127 of the Insolvency Act 1986 in the

---

[217] Paragraph 1 of Practice Direction 49B to CPR Part 49.

standard form. If he objects, the written evidence in support must contain a short statement of his reasons.

(3) If the petitioner objects to a Section 127 order in the standard form but consents to such an order in a modified form, the petition must set out the form of order to which he consents, and the written evidence in support must contain a short statement of his reasons for seeking the modification.

(4) . . .

(5) If the petition contains a statement that the petitioner consents to a Section 127 order, whether in the standard or modified form, the Registrar shall without further inquiry make an order in such form at the first hearing unless an order to the contrary has been made by the Judge in the meantime.

(6) If the petition contains a statement that the petitioner objects to a Section 127 order in the standard form, the company may apply (in the case of urgency, without notice) to the Judge for an order."

Paragraph 7 of the Practice Direction sets out the terms of the standard order as follows:

"(Title etc.)
ORDER that notwithstanding the presentation of the said Petition

(1) payments made into or out of the bank accounts of the Company in the ordinary course of the business of the Company and

(2) dispositions of the property of the Company made in the ordinary course of its business for proper value between the date of presentation of the Petition and the date of judgment on the Petition or further order in the meantime shall not be void by virtue of the provisions of section 127 of the Insolvency Act 1986 in the event of an Order for the winding up of the Company being made on the said Petition Provided that (the relevant bank) shall be under no obligation to verify for itself whether any transaction through the company's bank accounts is in the ordinary course of business, or that it represents full market value for the relevant transaction.

This form of Order may be departed from where the circumstances of the case require."

10.4.5 Reform

In the past the Law Commission[218] has made a number of proposals with the aim of simplifying the unfair prejudice remedy and, in particular, ensuring active case management by the court.

Many of the Law Commission's proposals on procedure have been addressed by previous revisions of the CPR. For example, the court now has the power to strike out a claim or a defence which, in the court's view, discloses no reasonable grounds for bringing or defending the claim.[219] Another important innovation is that the CPR have given the court greater flexibility to make costs orders that take account of the way a party has conducted the proceedings and, in making an order for costs, the court must now consider whether it is reasonable for a party to raise, pursue or contest a particular allegation or issue.[220] Such increased powers should act as a deterrent to a party contemplating pressing ahead with weak or insubstantial allegations in a Section 994 case.

In addition to the above, the recommendation that ADR should be encouraged in shareholder disputes wherever appropriate and that an amendment be made to the 1986 Rules so as to include an express reference to its use is reflected in the possible directions which a court may give on or any time after the return day under the 2009 Rules.[221]

Other proposals for reform made by the Commission included:

---

[218] The Law Commission Report 246.
[219] CPR, Part 3, Rule 3.4. This rule refers to the ability of the court to strike out a "statement of case". Though this term is defined to cover formal pleadings such as a particulars of claim and a defence, a similar application of the rule can likely be achieved by the court in the case of petitions under Section 994, using its inherent power to make any order of its own initiative as part of the exercise of its case management powers (CPR Part 3, Rule 3.3).
[220] CPR, Part 44, Rule 44.3.
[221] Rule 5(f) of the 2009 Rules.

(a) the addition of winding up to the list of Section 996 reme-
    dies available in proceedings under Section 994;
(b) amendment to raise the following presumptions:

  (i) that in certain circumstances,[222] exclusion from partic-
      ipation in the management of a company will be
      presumed to be unfairly prejudicial (unless the respon-
      dent shows otherwise); and
  (ii) where the first presumption is not rebutted, and the
      court is satisfied that it ought to order a buy-out of the
      petitioner's shares, a presumption that the shares will
      be valued on a *pro rata* (rather than a discounted) basis;

(c) the introduction of a time limit for bringing a Section 994
    claim, although it was recommended that the time limit
    would apply only to the conduct which forms the basis of
    the unfair prejudice claim and that there should be no time
    limit imposed on other "background" matters to which the
    parties may refer in order to support or refute the claim;[223]
    and
(d) the amendment of Table A by the insertion of a new regu-
    lation providing a "no-fault" exit route for disgruntled
    shareholders so that they do not have to resort to bringing
    costly proceedings under Section 994 in order to have their
    shares bought out.[224] The inclusion of this new regulation
    would be optional and would allow the company to decide
    on the circumstances giving rise to the exit rights and the
    method of valuation of the shares in question.

None of these proposals is reflected in CA 2006 restatement and
marginal revision of the Section 994 remedy. In relation to the
recommendation referenced in (d) above, a structure to address
disagreement that is suitable in context should be developed
between shareholders and their representatives at the outset of

---

[222] The circumstances in which a presumption of unfair prejudice on exclusion from management will arise are set out in the draft Bill in Appendix A to the 1997 Report. The type of
companies envisaged are private companies limited by shares where substantially all the
members of the company are directors and where prior to his removal as a director or his
exclusion from management, the petitioner held, in his own name, at least 10 per cent of the
voting rights in the company (Law Commission Report 246, paragraphs 3.26 to 3.70).
[223] The Law Commission Report 246, paragraphs 4.22 and 4.23.
[224] The exit article is set out in draft regulation 119 in Appendix C to the Law Commission
Report 246.

a relationship or at least while harmonious relations prevail, whether in the constitution or the broader commercial framework regulating affairs between the members.

The trend referenced in Section 10.4.1 above to grant a corporate remedy in an unfair prejudice claim calls for clarification first to confirm that a corporate remedy should be made available under Section 996 and, in so doing, to establish suitable limitations. These might include a bar on a corporate remedy where the relevant conduct has been ratified or that other circumstances exist which indicate that a corporate remedy is not in the collective interest of the shareholders.

Chapter 11

Duties of Directors Facing Insolvency

Hamish Anderson

Partner
Norton Rose LLP

11.1   Introduction

Company directors who are facing the actual or prospective insolvency of their companies retain all of the duties they would have even if the company was fully solvent. Certain general duties hitherto based on common law rules and equitable principles have been brought within the ambit of statutory law by the Companies Act 2006 ("CA 2006"), replacing the Companies Act 1985, which nonetheless specifies that the newly codified rules shall be interpreted and applied according to the rules and principles on which they are based. However, the onset of insolvency imposes a further set of duties, mostly under the Insolvency Act 1986 ("IA 1986"), and adds a new dimension to the fiduciary duties of directors which reflects the significant position of the company's creditors as opposed to its shareholders when insolvency is in prospect. CA 2006 is silent on this matter except that the statutory duty for a director to "act in the way he considers, in good faith, would be most likely to promote the success of the company for the benefit of its members as a whole" (Section 172(1) CA 2006) is expressed to be subject to any rule of law requiring directors in certain circumstances to consider or act in the interests of a company's creditors. One of the considerations a director will have to take into account in discharging this duty is "the likely consequences of any decision in the long term". This is a provision, potentially open to wide interpretation, which could affect the criteria by which a company will be judged to be prospectively insolvent and therefore the point at which creditors' interests should take precedence over those of shareholders.

This Chapter deals with a number of statutory duties under the Insolvency Act 1986 which were enacted specifically to protect the creditors of insolvent companies, the cases surrounding the issue of directors' fiduciary duties when the company is insolvent or prospectively insolvent, and certain duties under the CA 2006 and the Financial Services Authority's Listing Rules and Disclosure and Transparency Rules which frequently become an issue on the prospective insolvency of the company. However, reference should be made to Chapter 13 for commentary on those sections of the Company Directors' Disqualification Act 1986 which deal with insolvency.

In considering their duties, directors should always keep it in the forefront of their minds that each company in a group is a separate legal entity and that they must discharge their duties to each company rather than the group as a whole. It may therefore be necessary to recognise and address conflicts of interest which arise between companies within a group.

11.2   Statutory duties under IA 1986

All of the provisions which are discussed in this part of this Chapter apply where a company has become subject to a formal insolvency procedure, either liquidation or administration. The liquidator or administrator then has the power to look back to the period shortly before a formal insolvency and bring proceedings, either for compensation against the directors personally or to undo certain transactions entered into by the directors during that period.

11.2.1   Wrongful trading (Section 214 IA 1986)

This provision only applies where a company goes into liquidation. The liquidator is entitled to apply to the court for an order making a person liable to contribute to the company's assets if the following conditions apply (Section 214(2) IA 1986):

(a)   the company has gone into insolvent liquidation;
(b)   at some time before the commencement of the winding up of the company, that person knew or ought to have concluded that there was no reasonable prospect that the company would avoid going into insolvent liquidation; and
(c)   that person was a director of the company at the time.

IA 1986 provides for a defence to proceedings for wrongful trading in the following terms (Section 214(3) IA 1986):

> "The court shall not make a declaration under this section with respect to any person if it is satisfied that after the condition specified in subsection (2)(b) [i.e. that that person knew or ought to have concluded that there was no reasonable prospect that the company would avoid going into insolvent liquidation] was first satisfied in relation to him that person took every step with a view to minimising the potential loss to the company's creditors as (assuming him to have known that there was no reasonable prospect that the company would avoid going into insolvent liquidation) he ought to have taken."

The section also provides guidance on the knowledge, skill and experience which is expected of directors in the following terms (Section 214(4) and (5) IA 1986):

> "(4) For the purposes of subsections (2) and (3), the facts which a director of a company ought to know or ascertain, the conclusions which he ought to reach and the steps which he ought to take are those which would be known or ascertained, or reached or taken, by a reasonably diligent person having both –
>
> (a)   the general knowledge, skill and experience that may reasonably be expected of a person carrying out the same functions as are carried out by that director in relation to the company, and
> (b)   the general knowledge, skill and experience that that director has.
>
> (5) The reference in subsection (4) to the functions carried out in relation to the company by a director of the

company includes any functions which he does not carry out but which have been entrusted to him."

The section defines "insolvent liquidation" as a "liquidation where the assets of the company are insufficient for the payment of its debts and other liabilities and the expenses of the winding up" (Section 214(6)).

11.2.1.1 Comments

There are relatively few reported cases in which this section has been considered. However, in an early but still important decision (*Re Produce Marketing Consortium Ltd (No 2)*)[1] Knox J characterised the method of establishing the quantum of the relevant director's liability as follows (at 553):

> "In my judgment the jurisdiction under s 214 is primarily compensatory rather than penal. Prima facie the appropriate amount that a director is declared to be liable to contribute is the amount by which the company's assets can be discerned to have been depleted by the director's conduct which caused the discretion under sub-s (I) to arise. But Parliament has indeed chosen very wide words of discretion . . . the fact that there was no fraudulent intent is not of itself a reason for fixing the amount at a nominal or low figure, for that would amount to frustrating what I discern as Parliament's intention in adding s 214 to s 213 in the 1986 Act, but I am not persuaded that it is right to ignore that fact totally."

Re Bank of Credit and Commerce International SA (in liq.); Morris v Bank of India[2] established that interest could be added to the award.

In the subsequent case of *Re DKG Contractors Ltd*,[3] the court simply ascertained the date on which the directors ought to

---

[1] [1989] BCLC 520.
[2] [2005] 1 All ER (Comm) 209.
[3] [1990] BCC 903.

have concluded that there was no reasonable prospect of avoiding insolvent liquidation and made an order rendering the directors liable to pay a contribution equal to the amount of trade debts incurred by the company after that date. Although a precise method of calculating the liability has not been established, the principle that it is compensatory and not penal is not in doubt. In the more recent case of *Re Continental Assurance Co of London Plc*,[4] it was held that it was not enough merely to say that, if the company had not still been trading, a particular loss would not have been suffered by the company. In order to impose liability on directors there must be sufficient connection between the wrongfulness of the directors' conduct and the company's losses.

In practice, if the directors of a company cease trading as soon as they reach the conclusion that there is no reasonable prospect of avoiding insolvent liquidation, then, assuming that their opinion was a reasonable one and they were not dilatory in reaching it, there should be little risk of a successful claim for wrongful trading being brought. This is because there will be no time for losses to accumulate between the directors reaching the relevant decision and the commencement of the liquidation or administration of the company. In *Re Continental Assurance Co of London Plc* (above), Park J considered the difficult position of directors balancing their wish to avoid liability for wrongful trading with making proper efforts to avoid liquidation if possible. He said (at 817):

> "An overall point which needs to be kept in mind throughout is that, whenever a company is in financial trouble and the directors have a difficult decision to make whether to close down and go into liquidation, or whether instead to trade on and hope to turn the corner, they can be in a real and unenviable dilemma. On the one hand, if they decide to trade on but things do not work out and the company, later rather than sooner, goes into liquidation, they may find themselves in the situation of the respondents in this case – being sued for wrongful trading. On the other hand, if the directors decide

---

[4] [2001] BPIR 733.

to close down immediately and cause the company to go into an early liquidation, although they are not at risk of being sued for wrongful trading, they are at risk of being criticised on other grounds. A decision to close down will almost certainly mean that the ensuing liquidation will be an insolvent one. Apart from anything else liquidations are expensive operations, and in addition debtors are commonly obstructive about paying their debts to a company which is in liquidation. Many creditors of the company from a time before the liquidation are likely to find that their debts do not get paid in full. They will complain bitterly that the directors shut down too soon; they will say that the directors ought to have had more courage and kept going. If they had done so, the complaining creditors will say, the company probably would have survived and all of its debts would have been paid. Ceasing to trade and liquidating too soon can be stigmatised as the cowards' way out."

Directors whose companies are facing financial difficulties should always have regular board meetings and at each meeting consider the prospects for the company and minute their reasons for the view they take and their reasons for any decision to continue trading. Up-to-date financial information must be available. In the context of disqualification proceedings, it has been held that a director must keep himself informed about the financial affairs of the company and play an appropriate role in its management (*Re Galeforce Pleating Co Ltd*).[5] This is directly relevant to the "functions" of the directors when applying the wrongful trading test. Ignorance of the financial position will not be a valid defence to any claim for wrongful trading. Directors are expected to apply the general knowledge, skill and experience that may reasonably be expected of a person carrying out the same functions as are carried out (or entrusted to) the relevant director in relation to the company. This point was also emphasised in *Re Produce Marketing Consortium Ltd (No 2)* above.

More recently, in *Re Hawkes Hill Publishing C Ltd (in liq.)*[6] it was held that whether a company has a reasonable prospect of avoiding an

---

[5] [1999] 2 BCLC 704.
[6] [2007] BCC 937.

insolvent liquidation cannot be determined on the basis of a snap-shot of its financial position at any particular time but must be based on rational expectations of what the future might hold. Helpfully, the judge added that directors are not clairvoyant and the fact that they fail to see what eventually comes to pass did not necessarily mean that they are guilty of wrongful trading.

Once the directors of a company have reached the conclusion that there is no reasonable prospect of avoiding an insolvent liquidation, they have a choice. Either the company must cease trading immediately and go into liquidation or another suitable insolvency procedure, or they may attempt to rely on the defence set out in sub-section (3), that the director took every step with a view to minimising the potential loss to the company's creditors as he ought to have taken.

This second option is a high-risk option for the following reasons:

(a) It is a defence to wrongful trading for the director to prove that he has taken these steps. In other words, the burden of proof shifts from the liquidator to the director himself.
(b) In the absence of detailed case law on this sub-section, it is unclear in practical terms what is meant by "every step he ought to have taken". One point which has been noted by many commentators is that there is no qualification to state that such steps should be reasonable. Consequently, the courts could insist on a very high standard for any director who wishes to rely on this section. Any director who considers that he will have to rely on this defence should take detailed legal advice at the time.

Practical problems often arise in relation to wrongful trading in circumstances where a period of continued trading may enhance the value of an asset which the company wishes to sell. It is some-times argued that, in such circumstances, the directors of a company have a positive duty to continue trading after reaching the point where they consider there is no reasonable prospect of avoiding insolvent liquidation. Such continued trading will, so the argument goes, have the effect of minimising the potential loss to creditors by a better value being achieved for the asset in question than would be achieved on a liquidation or other insolvency procedure. The author's view is that this interpretation is incorrect. As has been shown above, Section 214 IA 1986 does not impose a positive obligation upon directors to minimise the potential loss to creditors. The sub-section which refers to the concept of minimising potential loss to creditors is a *defence* to proceedings for wrongful trading. A director who manages to avoid any proceedings for wrongful trading being brought against him in the first place will not be relying on this sub-section. The usual and clearest way to avoid the possibility of proceedings for wrongful trading being brought is to cease trading as soon as it becomes clear that the insolvent liquidation of the company is inevitable.

Continuing to trade in order to enhance the sale proceeds of an asset may increase the actual proceeds of sale of the company's assets, but may not necessarily benefit the creditors of the company as a whole. It is often the case that secured creditors put pressure on company directors to maximise the proceeds of a particular asset by continued trading. However, if that continued trading involves incurring further credit from unsecured creditors, those unsecured creditors will in fact have suffered increased losses as a result of the continued trading. The directors will, effectively, have benefited one set of creditors at the expense of another set. Under such circumstances, the author sees no reason why the directors of the company should not be made liable for wrongful trading in respect of the losses caused to their unsecured trade creditors (and may also have exposed themselves to liability for fraudulent trading – *see* below). This point was, in fact, touched upon by Knox J in the *Produce Marketing* case in his comment (at 554):

> "The affairs of PMC were conducted during the last seven months of trading in a way which reduced the indebtedness to the bank, to which Mr David had given a guarantee, at the expense of trade creditors . . . the bank is, if not fully, at least substantially secured. If this jurisdiction is to be exercised, as in my judgment it should be in this case, it needs to be exercised in a way which will benefit unsecured creditors."

An issue which has been discussed in the case law surrounding wrongful trading is whether a director can plead Section 1157(1)

CA 2006 in his defence to wrongful trading proceedings. Section 1157(1) CA 2006 (which replicates the former Section 727 CA 1985) provides as follows:

"If in proceedings for negligence, default, breach of duty or breach of trust against –

(a) an officer of the company, or
(b) a person employed by a company as auditor (whether he is or is not an officer of the company),

it appears to the court hearing the case that the officer or person is or may be liable but that he acted honestly and reasonably, and that having regard to all the circumstances of the case (including those connected with his appointment) he ought fairly to be excused, the court may relieve him, either wholly or in part, from his liability on such terms as it thinks fit."

In an earlier judgment in the *Produce Marketing* case, Knox J held that in Section 727 CA 1985 a subjective test applied whereas in Section 214 IA 1986, particularly in sub-sections (3) and (4) an objective test applied. It was difficult to see how the two sections could be used in conjunction. Knox J therefore held that Section 727 CA 1985 was not available to the directors in wrongful trading proceedings (*Re Produce Marketing Consortium (No 1) Ltd*).[7] However, in the later case of *Re DKG Contracts Ltd* (above), Section 727 CA 1985 was pleaded. The judge held that the directors had acted honestly but not reasonably and declined to grant the relief sought. It is notable in this case that there were other breaches of duty in addition to wrongful trading and that the earlier decision of Knox J appears not to have been drawn to the attention of the court. In *Re Brian D Pierson (Contractors) Ltd*,[8] the court followed *Produce Marketing* in holding that Section 727 does not apply to wrongful trading claims. This was consistent with the court having a discretion as to the amount of any award under Section 214 and, in the author's view, the point should be regarded as settled.

---

[7] [1989] 1 WLR 745.
[8] [2001] 1 BCLC 275.

11.2.2   Fraudulent trading

Fraudulent trading is set out in Section 213 IA 1986. It is as follows:

> "(1) If in the course of the winding up of a company it appears that any business of the company has been carried on with intent to defraud creditors of the company or creditors of any other person, or for any fraudulent purpose, the following has effect.
>
> (2)   The court, on the application of the liquidator may declare that any persons who were knowingly parties to the carrying on of the business in the manner above-mentioned are to be liable to make such contributions (if any) to the company's assets as the court thinks proper."

The essential difference between fraudulent trading and wrongful trading is that fraudulent trading involves dishonest intent, described in this section as "intent to defraud". Fraudulent trading is also a criminal offence under Section 993 CA 2006.

Given the connotations of dishonesty in fraudulent trading, a strong measure of proof is required, and this section is consequently rarely used. But under Section 213, which covers the civil liability to pay compensation, it is also possible for the fraudulent acts of an employee to be vicariously attributed to the person of a company (*Morris and others* v *Bank of India*).[9]

The Court of Appeal has held that a business can be carried on with intent to defraud creditors even though only one creditor is actually defrauded by a single transaction (*Re Gerald Cooper Chemicals*).[10] However, *Morphitis* v *Bernasconi*[11] shows that the section does not apply in every case where an individual creditor is defrauded but only where the business has been carried on with intent to defraud.

---

[9]   [2005] EWCA Civ 693.
[10]   [1978] 2 All ER 49.
[11]   [2003] EWCA Civ 289.

Earlier, *Re Sarflax Ltd*[12] established that, even where the company is insolvent, preferring one creditor over another does not, per se, constitute fraud within the meaning of Section 213 (although it could constitute a breach of fiduciary duty and expose the director to a disqualification risk as well as giving rise to an action under Section 239, as to which *see* below).

It might be thought, in view of the lower standard of proof required in respect of wrongful trading, that the fraudulent trading jurisdiction has become redundant. This, however, is wrong for several reasons. Fraudulent trading is available as a civil claim against any person who is "knowingly a party to" the carrying on of the company business with intent to defraud. Thus on this aspect, liability under Section 213 is wider than liability for wrongful trading, because mere participants are potentially liable – for their involvement in the fraudulent act, while the only people being made liable under Section 214 are directors, albeit including shadow directors (*Re BCCI, Banque Arabe Internationale d'Investissement SA* v *Morris*,[13] in which the alleged participant was a bank).

The second circumstance in which fraudulent trading liability is more widely available than wrongful trading arises because the fraud does not have to be directed at the company itself or even the company's own creditors. If the business of the company is being conducted (a) with intent to defraud the creditors of another person or (b) for any fraudulent purpose the knowing participant is exposed to potential liability. This means that, unlike Section 214, the focus of the liability is not necessarily on the imminence of the company's liquidation and the putative defendant's awareness of that fact but rather it is on the propriety of undertaking liabilities.

Doubtlessly it will normally be proper to infer intent to defraud where a company continues to carry on incurring credit when the directors know that there is no reasonable prospect of the creditors receiving payment (*Re William Leitch Bros*)[14] but that is

---

[12] [1979] Ch 592.
[13] [2001] BCLC 263.
[14] [1932] 2 Ch 71, 77.

not the only circumstance in which fraud may be established. Thus it may be fraudulent to promise creditors that a parent company will stand behind its subsidiaries when the promisor knows that this is not true, even though he might genuinely, properly and reasonably consider that the subsidiary is sound (*Augustus Barnett & Sons*).[15] In that kind of case, wrongful trading would not be established, but fraudulent trading may be. Considerations of fraudulent trading could also arise where directors cause a company to incur new liabilities to suppliers which they know will not be paid in accordance with the terms of supply despite having a genuine belief that the company will be able to avoid insolvent liquidation, for example through some form of rescue or restructuring.

11.2.3 Misfeasance

Section 212 IA 1986 enables "misfeasance" proceedings to be brought against directors (and others) during the course of a company liquidation. This sometimes causes confusion. Although "misfeasance" is a convenient generic term for misconduct, Section 212 is purely procedural in that it enables action to be taken more efficiently but it does not create any additional obligations on the part of directors (or others). The subject-matter of misfeasance proceedings brought under Section 212 will always be breach of a duty identifiable elsewhere in the applicable legislation or under general law.

11.2.4 Transactions which can be overturned by liquidators or administrators

11.2.4.1 Transactions at an undervalue

Section 238 IA 1986 deals with transactions at an undervalue. The section applies where a company goes into administration or into liquidation. For the purposes of this section and for Section 239 (*see* Section 11.2.4.3 below) the administrator or liquidator is referred to as the "office holder".

---

[15] [1986] BCLC 170.

A company enters into a transaction with a person at an under-value if (Section 238(4) IA 1986):

"(a) the company makes a gift to that person or otherwise enters into a transaction with that person on terms that provide for the company to receive no considera-tion, or

(b) the company enters into a transaction with that person for a consideration the value of which, in money or money's worth, is significantly less than the value, in money or money's worth, of the consideration provided by the company."

The Act further provides, in sub-section (5), as follows (Section 238(5) IA 1986):

"The court shall not make an order under this section in respect of a transaction at an undervalue if it is satisfied –

(a) that the company which entered into the transac-tion did so in good faith and for the purpose of carrying on its business, and

(b) that at the time it did so there were reasonable grounds for believing that the transaction would benefit the company."

The question sometimes arises as to whether security given by a borrower for indebtedness which has been outstanding for a period before the giving of security could be characterised as a transaction at an undervalue. This point was considered in *Re MC Bacon Ltd*,[16] which has been the leading case on transactions at an undervalue and preferences. The case concerned a company which was in financial difficulties and had given security in respect of its existing overdraft at the time when it was insolvent. When the company subsequently went into liquidation, the liquidator commenced proceedings under Sections 238 and 239 to have the security set aside. Millett J held that a transaction of this type could not be a transaction at an undervalue, and stated:

---

[16] [1990] BCLC 324.

"In my judgment, the applicant's claim to characterise the granting of the bank's debenture as a transaction at an undervalue is misconceived. The mere creation of a security over a company's assets does not deplete them and does not come within the paragraph. By charging its assets the company appropriates them to meet the liabilities due to the secured creditor and adversely affects the rights of other creditors in the event of insolvency. But it does not deplete its assets or diminish their value. It retains the right to redeem and the right to sell or remortgage the charged assets. All it loses is the ability to apply the proceeds otherwise than in satisfaction of the secured debt. That is not something capable of valuation in monetary terms and is not customarily disposed of for value . . . in my judgment, the transaction does not fall within sub-s (4), and it is unnecessary to consider the application of sub-s (5) which provides a defence to the claim in certain circumstances."

In *Hill* v *Spread Trustee Co Ltd and Warr*,[17] however, doubt was cast on this part of the judgment in *MC Bacon* in the Court of Appeal and the point should now be regarded as open pending further consideration by the Court of Appeal. In principle, it seems that the grant of security will more easily withstand challenge as a transaction at an undervalue (and also as a preference, as to which *see* below) where it is given in return for forbearance (as was the case in *MC Bacon*). *Hill* v *Spread Trustee Co Ltd and Warr* concerned the more egregious situation of the grant of security being a transaction defrauding creditors (as to which also *see* below).

In *Barnes* v *Premium Credit Ltd*,[18] it was held that a re-grant of security where the previously granted security was void for want of registration did not amount to a transaction at an undervalue, but was a preference (*see* Section 11.2.4.3 below).

11.2.4.2   Relevant time

The court will not make an order in respect of a transaction at an undervalue unless the company entered into the transaction

---

[17]   [2006] EWCA Civ 542.
[18]   [2000] All ER (D) 39.

at a "relevant time" (Section 240 IA 1986). In order to have occurred at a relevant time:

(a) the transaction must take place at a time in the period of two years ending with the "onset of insolvency" (*see* Section 11.2.4.4 below) (or while an administration is pending); and
(b) at the time of the transaction the company must be unable to pay its debts within the meaning of Section 123 IA 1986 or become unable to pay its debts within the meaning of that section in consequence of the transaction.

Unless the contrary is shown, the second requirement is presumed where the person with whom the company enters into the transaction is connected with the company.

11.2.4.3   *Preferences (Section 239 IA 1986)*

This provision applies in similar circumstances to those relating to Section 238 IA 1986: that is, if a company goes into administration or liquidation. Section 239(4) describes the nature of a preference:

> "For the purposes of this section . . . a company gives a preference to a person if –
>
> (a) that person is one of the company's creditors or a surety or guarantor for any of the company's debts or other liabilities, and
> (b) the company does anything or suffers anything to be done which (in either case) has the effect of putting that person into a position which, in the event of the company going into insolvent liquidation, will be better than the position he would have been in if that thing had not been done."

For a company to "suffer" something to be done for these purposes, it must permit something to happen which it has the power to stop or obstruct: *Re Parkside International Ltd.*[19]

---

[19] [2008] EWHC 3654.

Under sub-section (5), the court shall not make an order unless the company which gave the preference was "influenced in deciding to give it by a desire to produce in relation to that person the effect mentioned in subsection (4)(b)".

The concept of a "desire to prefer" was introduced in the IA 1986 when the previous law of "fraudulent preference" was radically recast. The leading case on both transactions at an undervalue and preferences, *Re MC Bacon Ltd* (above), gives some guidance as to the interpretation of this sub-section. As mentioned in Section 11.2.4.1 above, the case concerned a company which had encountered financial difficulties. It gave security to its bank to secure its overdraft facilities, which were advanced to it before the security was given. This situation is clearly extremely common in the negotiations that companies have with their bankers when the company is in financial difficulties and facing insolvency. Millett J held that the giving of security in these circumstances was not a preference because the company was not "influenced by a desire to prefer" the bank. Millett J interpreted the concept of being "influenced by a desire to prefer" as follows (at 335 to 336):

> "It is no longer necessary to establish a *dominant* intention to prefer. It is sufficient that the decision was *influenced* by the requisite desire. That is the first change . . . The second change is made necessary by the first, for without it, it would be virtually impossible to uphold the validity of a security taken in exchange for the injection of fresh funds into a company in financial difficulties. A man is taken to intend the necessary consequences of his actions, so that an intention to grant a security to a creditor necessarily involves an intention to prefer that creditor in the event of insolvency. The need to establish that such intention was dominant was essential under the old law to prevent perfectly proper transactions from being struck down. With the abolition of that requirement intention could not remain the relevant test. Desire has been substituted. That is a very different matter. Intention is objective, desire is subjective. A man can choose the lesser of two evils without desiring either. It is not, however, sufficient to establish a desire to make the payment or grant the security which it

is sought to avoid. There must have been a desire to produce the effect mentioned in the sub-section, that is to say, to improve the creditor's position in the event of an insolvent liquidation. A man is not to be taken as *desiring* all the necessary consequences of his actions. Some consequences may be of advantage to him and be desired by him; others may not affect him and be matters of indifference to him; while still others may be positively disadvantageous to him and not be desired by him, but be regarded by him as the unavoidable price of obtaining the desired advantages. It will still be possible to provide assistance to a company in financial difficulties provided that the company is actuated only by proper commercial considerations. Under the new regime a transaction will not be set aside as a voidable preference unless the company positively wished to improve the creditor's position in the event of its own insolvent liquidation. There is, of course, no need for there to be direct evidence of the requisite desire. Its existence may be inferred from the circumstances of the case, just as the dominant intention could be inferred under the old law. But the mere presence of the requisite desire will not be sufficient by itself. It must have influenced the decision to enter into the transaction. It was submitted on behalf of the bank that it must have been the factor which 'tipped the scales'. I disagree. That is not what sub-s (5) says; it requires only that the desire should have influenced the decision. That requirement is satisfied if it was one of the factors which operated on the minds of those who made the decision. It need not have been the only factor or even the decisive one. In my judgment, it is not necessary to prove that, if the requisite desire had not been present, the company would not have entered into the transaction. That would be too high a test."

This approach was supported in *Re Fairway Magazines Ltd*,[20] where a company issued security for advances utilised to reduce an overdraft liability guaranteed by a director. It was held that the debenture was not a preference because the

---

[20]   [1992] BCC 924.

company was solely influenced by commercial considerations, namely the need to raise money from another source in order to continue trading. Mummery J made the point, however, that the desire to influence the creditor does not have to be the sole or decisive influence in making the decision.

Where the beneficiary of the preference is connected with the company otherwise than by reason only of being its employee at the time the preference was given, the desire to prefer is presumed (Section 239(6)) unless the contrary is shown.

This section also provides that the fact that something was done in pursuance of the order of a court is not enough to prevent the doing or suffering of that thing from constituting the giving of a preference (Section 239(7)).

As in the case of a transaction at an undervalue, IA 1986 provides that a transaction of this type will only be a preference if the company enters into it at a "relevant time". The "relevant time" is described as follows in Section 240 IA 1986:

(a) where the beneficiary of the preference is a person who is connected with the company (otherwise than by reason only of being its employee), at a time in the period of two years ending with the onset of insolvency;

(b) where the preference is not given in favour of a connected person, a time in the period of six months ending with the onset of insolvency (Section 240(1)); and

(c) in either case, when an administration is pending.

As for transactions at an undervalue, the company must be unable to pay its debts within the meaning of Section 123 IA 1986 at the time of, or as a consequence of, the preference.

11.2.4.4 *The onset of insolvency*

The "onset of insolvency" is relevant to both transactions at an undervalue and preferences and is defined in Section 240(3) which refers to the onset of proceedings rather than the financial condition of the company. The definition has become more complicated since its original enactment because of the expansion of the ways in which administration and liquidation can be commenced but, that aside, the rules are clear and the detail should be consulted in any case where the precise timing of a transaction is a critical factor. In summary, the overall effect is that the onset of insolvency will be no later than the formal commencement of the insolvency proceedings but may be slightly earlier, for example where liquidation or administration results from a court order in which case the relevant date is the date on which the application for the order was made.

11.2.4.5   *Effect of an order*

The court has a wide discretion as to the terms of the order it makes under Section 238 or Section 239, but the essential principle is that these are "clawback" provisions designed to restore the position to what it would have been if the impugned transaction had not occurred. The relevant office holder will be seeking to undo a transaction which has either depleted the assets of the insolvent estate (in the case of a transaction at an undervalue) or given one creditor a privileged position in relation to the general body of creditors (in the case of a preference). As such, the beneficiary of the transaction is the prime target of the proceedings (subject to the provisions of Section 241(2) to (3C) IA 1986 which provides protection for beneficiaries who did not have full knowledge of the circumstances of the transactions from which they benefited), rather than the director of the company responsible for entering into the transaction. However, the sanctions against directors who are responsible for procuring companies to carry out such transactions are equally significant and are set out in CDDA 1986, which is described in Chapter 13 below. It is therefore quite clear that these provisions have the practical effect of imposing on directors a duty not to enter into transactions of those types.

11.2.4.6   *Transactions defrauding creditors*

Directors should also be aware of Section 423 IA 1986 which concerns transactions defrauding creditors. This provision applies to all companies, whether or not insolvent (and applies to individuals as well as companies). The essential ingredients of a transaction defrauding creditors are as follows:

(a) a person must enter into a transaction at an undervalue. The definition of "transaction at an undervalue" is exactly the same as in relation to Section 238 IA 1986 except that it contains a further provision which is only relevant to individuals and not to companies (Section 423(1) IA 1986);

(b) the court may make an order under Section 423 if it is satisfied that the person entered into such a transaction for the purpose of:

(i) "putting assets beyond the reach of a person who is making, or may at some time make, a claim against him"; or

(ii) "otherwise prejudicing the interests of such a person in relation to the claim which he is making or may make" (Section 423(3) IA 1986).

The court may in such circumstances make such order as it thinks fit (Section 423(2) IA 1986) for:

"(a) restoring the position to what it would have been if the transaction had not been entered into, and

(b) protecting the interests of persons who are victims of the transaction."

Proceedings may be brought by the liquidator or administrator of the company, or by a victim of the transaction. A "victim", for these purposes, includes anyone who is prejudiced by the transaction, not just those creditors that the debtor may have had in mind when entering the transaction (*Sands* v *Clitheroe*).[21]

There is no requirement for a Section 423 application that the company be insolvent or go into liquidation or administration within a particular time limit from the date on which the company entered into the transaction. In order to obtain an order under Section 423, it is only necessary to show that the purpose was either to put assets beyond the reach of a creditor or creditors or otherwise to prejudice his or their interests. Although actual or pending insolvency need not be proved,

---

[21] [2006] BPIR 1000.

it will, in practice, be much easier for any person invoking Section 423 to prove this purpose where a company was in financial difficulty when the transaction occurred.

The Court of Appeal held in *Commissioners of Inland Revenue* v *Hashmi and another*[22] that prejudice to the creditor does not need to be the sole or even dominant purpose – it is enough if it is a real and substantial purpose of the transaction and not merely a consequence or by-product. Establishing purpose requires the court to have regard to the subjective state of mind of the transferor (*see Pagemanor Ltd* v *Ryan (No 2)*).[23]

Any transaction which could be attacked under Section 423 is likely, in the case of a company, also to be actionable by virtue of a breach of fiduciary duties by the directors, as is set out in more detail below. Although most of the reported cases on this section in fact relate to individuals, company directors need to be aware of it since the types of transaction it refers to, those which involve taking assets "out of the reach" of creditors, of course will almost inevitably end in the insolvency of the relevant company. Any deliberate attempt to try to make a company "judgment proof" can not only be attacked under Section 423 but can also easily lead to sanctions being taken against the directors under the CDDA 1986 (*see* again Chapter 13 below).

11.3 Fiduciary and statutory duties of directors

The fiduciary duties of directors are of crucial importance for all company directors, not just those whose companies are facing insolvency. However, where a company is insolvent, or prospectively insolvent, recent cases have emphasised the role of directors' fiduciary duties in protecting creditors as a class, not just shareholders, where it is the creditors as well as the shareholders of the company who stand to lose if the directors breach their duties.

---

[22] [2002] 2 BCLC 489.
[23] [2002] BPIR 593.

11.3.1 Nature of fiduciary and statutory duties

In exercising their powers, directors have a duty to act *bona fide* in the interests of the company (*Re Smith and Fawcett*).[24] If they do so, the courts will not interfere in their actions unless there are no reasonable grounds for that belief.

The CA 2006 has introduced a statutory statement of seven general duties which are set out in Sections 170 to 177. Those duties are:

- to act within powers;
- to promote the success of the company;
- to exercise independent judgment;
- to exercise reasonable care, skill and diligence;
- to avoid conflicts of interest;
- not to accept benefits from third parties; and
- to declare an interest in a proposed transaction or arrangement.

These duties are owed to the company, not to individual shareholders or creditors. Where the company is solvent, the company means shareholders as a class (*Regal (Hastings) v Gulliver*).[25] The shareholders as a class can therefore choose to approve the directors' acts. Shareholder approval of the transaction will be sufficient in the case of a solvent company to absolve the directors from liability for the breach (*Parke v Daily News (No 2)*).[26] However, if the company is insolvent its shareholders are not the only people concerned. Creditors also stand to lose if, for example, the directors procure that the company makes a gift to a third party.

11.3.2 Insolvent companies

This situation had to be considered in the decision of the High Court of Australia in *Walker v Wimborne*.[27] The company went

---

[24] [1942] Ch 304.
[25] [1967] 2 AC 134.
[26] [1962] 1 Ch 927.
[27] (1976) 137 CLR 1.

into liquidation and the liquidator challenged certain transactions which had taken place while the company was insolvent. These transactions included the payment of salaries to employees of other group companies and the making of an unsecured loan to another insolvent group member. It was held by the court that these acts amounted to misfeasance by the directors. Mason J made the following comments:

"In this respect it should be emphasized that the directors of a company in discharging their duty to the company must take account of the interests of its shareholders and its creditors. Any failure by the directors to take into account the interests of creditors will have adverse consequences for the company as well as for them . . .

The transaction offered no prospect of advantage to [the company], it exposed [the company] to the probable prospect of substantial loss, and thereby seriously prejudiced the unsecured creditors of [the company]."

One mistake sometimes made by the directors of companies facing insolvency is that they attempt to protect their position by obtaining a resolution of shareholders approving the transaction made in breach of their duties. Logically, if the breach of fiduciary duties has implications for creditors as well as shareholders, the shareholders' consent will be insufficient to absolve the directors of liability for breach of fiduciary duty. This point was considered in the Australian case of *Kinsela* v *Russell Kinsela Pty*.[28] In that case, the company leased its premises to its shareholders, at a time when it was insolvent, for a very low rent. The court held that the transaction was effected in breach of duty to the company and Street CJ made the following observation in relation to the ineffectiveness of authorisation by the shareholders:

"It is, to my mind, legally and logically acceptable to recognise that, where directors are involved in a breach of their duty to the company affecting the interests of shareholders, then shareholders can either authorize that breach in

---

[28] (1986) 4 NSWLR 722.

prospect or ratify it in retrospect. Where, however, the interests at risk are those of creditors I see no reason in law or in logic to recognize that the shareholders can authorize the breach. Once it is accepted, as in my view it must be, that the directors' duty to the company as a whole extends in an insolvency context to not prejudicing the interests of creditors . . . the shareholders do not have the power or authority to absolve the directors from that breach."

A similar point was considered in *West Mercia Safetywear Ltd* v *Dodd*.[29] In this case the company, West Mercia, was a wholly-owned subsidiary of AJ Dodd & C Ltd. Both companies were insolvent. Mr Dodd, a director of both companies, caused sums to be transferred by West Mercia to Dodd. This had the effect of reducing Mr Dodd's liability under a personal guarantee he had given in support of Dodd's overdraft. Clearly, the payment was made for the benefit of its shareholder. The Court of Appeal held that once a company was insolvent the interests of the creditors overrode those of the shareholders. Since West Mercia was known by Mr Dodd to be insolvent when the transfer took place and the transfer was a preference made to relieve Mr Dodd of his personal liability, Mr Dodd had breached his duty. The approval of the shareholders was in this case ineffective because creditors become prospectively entitled, through the mechanism of liquidation, to displace the power of the shareholders and directors to deal with the company's assets. (*West Mercia* has been cited in numerous subsequent cases and is generally treated as the leading English authority on the changed nature of directors' duties when insolvency supervenes.)

In *Gwyer & Associates Ltd* v *London Wharf (Limehouse) Ltd*,[30] the point was reinforced. Where a company is solvent the court has to ask itself "could an honest and intelligent man, in the position of the directors, in all the circumstances, reasonably have believed that the decision in question was for the benefit of the company". Where the company is insolvent, the question is asked with the substitution of "creditors" for "company".

---

[29] [1988] BCLC 250.
[30] [2002] EWHC 2748.

However, this does not restrict directors from acting inconsistently with the interests of a particular creditor where it is in the interests of the general body of creditors (*see Re Pantone 485 Ltd*[31]).

CA 2006 provides that the statutory duties are to be interpreted and applied in the same way as the common law or equitable principles on which they are based, and regard is to be had to those principles in applying them (Section 170(4) CA 2006). It can therefore be inferred that the duty to consider the interests of creditors on insolvency also applies.

11.3.3 Prospectively insolvent companies

A problem for directors emerges when considering at what point the creditors begin to become significant for the directors in considering their duties? This is a difficult question of both law and fact which eludes precise definition but the touchstone is the identification of whose economic interests are at stake. In a case such as *West Mercia Safetywear Ltd* v *Dodd*, where both companies were very clearly insolvent, there is no doubt that the creditors' interests must be taken into account. In *Facia Footwear Ltd* v *Hinchcliffe*,[32] it was held that where a company is in "a very dangerous financial position" the directors owed a duty to take account of the interests of creditors. However, it is not always easy for directors to assess whether the company's financial difficulties are sufficiently serious for the creditors' interests to become a legal issue. An interesting case on this point is *Aveling Barford Ltd* v *Perion Ltd*.[33]

In this case, a motion to set aside a judgment in default of defence was taken to the High Court. Aveling Barford Ltd was in liquidation. Perion Ltd was controlled by the same person as Aveling Barford (a Dr Lee). A property owned by Aveling Barford had been sold to Perion; and this fact was known to the directors of both Aveling Barford and Perion. The shareholders of Aveling Barford had consented to the transaction. Aveling Barford was solvent at the time but did not have any

---

[31] [2002] 1 BCLC 266.
[32] [1998] 1 BCLC 218.
[33] [1989] BCLC 626.

distributable reserves: it had an accumulated deficit on the profit and loss account. It would not have been able to make distributions to its shareholders.

Hoffmann J took the view that the directors of Aveling Barford had acted in breach of their fiduciary duty to the company by selling the property at an undervalue and that Perion had the necessary notice of the breach of fiduciary duty to be held a constructive trustee of the benefit. Hoffmann J also held that the consent of the shareholders was ineffective to waive the breach even though Aveling Barford was solvent at the time. His reasoning was based on the fact that the company did not have distributable reserves and was effectively a dressed up distribution to shareholders because of the close connection between Perion and Dr Lee, the company's ultimate shareholder.

This authority is interesting in that it appears to be saying that, where a company enters into a transaction for the benefit of a person connected with its shareholder, the directors must consider not just whether the company is solvent but also whether the company had distributable reserves, and that the approval of the controlling shareholder to a transaction benefiting an associate of the shareholder will not be sufficient to absolve the directors from liability if an equivalent dividend could not have been paid.

In the light of this decision, company directors should always consider the position of creditors if there is any prospect of entering into a transaction which benefits a party associated with a shareholder, even though the company may be technically solvent at the time.

This point was also discussed in the judgment of Cooke J in the New Zealand Court of Appeal in *Nicholson* v *Permakraft (NW) Ltd*.[34] This case considered a dividend which had been paid to shareholders where the company which had paid the dividend subsequently went into insolvent liquidation. The court considered the point as to whether the directors breached their fiduciary

---

[34] [1985] 1 NZLR 242.

duties when they recommended the distribution, in which case they would have been liable to refund the payment. In this case the New Zealand Court of Appeal held that the directors had not, on the facts, acted in breach of fiduciary duty. However, in the speech of Cooke J, some interesting *dicta* were made on the issue of the circumstances in which the shareholders could waive a breach of fiduciary duty by the directors. Cooke J made the following remarks at p 249:

> "The duties of directors are owed to the company. On the facts of particular cases this may require the directors to consider *inter alia* the interests of creditors. For instance creditors are entitled to consideration, in my opinion, if the company is insolvent, or near-insolvent, or of doubtful solvency, or if a contemplated payment or other course of action would jeopardise its solvency.
>
> The criterion should not be simply whether the step will leave a state of ultimate solvency according to the balance sheet, in that total assets will exceed total liabilities. Nor should it be decisive that on the balance sheet the subscribed capital will remain intact, so that a capital dividend can be paid without returning capital to shareholders. Balance sheet solvency and the ability to pay a capital dividend are certainly important factors tending to justify proposed action. But as a matter of business ethics it is appropriate for directors to consider also whether what they will do will prejudice their company's practical ability to discharge promptly debts owed to current and likely continuing trade creditors.
>
> To translate this into a legal obligation accords with the now pervasive concepts of duty to a neighbour and the linking of power with obligation ... in a situation of marginal commercial solvency such creditors may fairly be seen as beneficially interested in the company or contingently so."

Clearly, there are difficult issues to consider here. It may be that the English courts will develop a form of doctrine surrounding circumstances where a company may be solvent and have sufficient distributable reserves, but that it may not be prudent for a distribution to be made. In these circumstances, the creditors of the company will be the class who are most affected by such decisions, and shareholder approval of distributions or other transfers of value out of the company should not be effective to absolve the directors of their breach of duty. Whilst the law in this area is still developing, directors will always be well advised to consider carefully the interests of creditors if there is any possibility that the company may be prospectively insolvent.

Despite the uncertainties as to the scope of the duty to have regard to the interests of creditors, the better view is that in English law the duty remains a duty owed to the company and not to the creditors themselves. It will therefore only be actionable by or on behalf of the company (e.g. by an office holder), but a creditor could use the misfeasance procedure (*see* Section 11.2.3 above) to ensure that the company's claim was brought.

11.4 Public companies and listed companies: duties to shareholders

The duties of the directors of public companies and listed companies to their shareholders are complex and are covered elsewhere in this Guide. However, there are one or two legal provisions which, although relevant to all directors of such companies, tend to pose particular problems on insolvency and are therefore areas which the directors of such companies should always consider if there is any danger of insolvency approaching. These provisions include the maintenance of capital provisions under CA 2006 and (in relation to listed companies) the disclosure of information requirements under the Disclosure and Transparency Rules.

11.4.1 Serious loss of capital (Section 656 CA 2006)

Section 656 CA 2006 provides as follows:

"(1) Where the net assets of a public company are half or less of its called-up share capital, the directors must call a general meeting of the company to consider whether any, and if so what, steps should be taken to deal with the situation.

(2) They must do so not later than 28 days from the earliest day on which that fact is known to a director of the company.

(3) The meeting must be convened for a date not later than 56 days from that day.

(4) If there is a failure to convene a meeting as required by this section, each of the directors of the company who –

    (a) knowingly authorises or permits the failure, or

    (b) after the period during which the meeting should have been convened, knowingly authorises or permits the failure to continue, commits an offence.

(5) A person guilty of an offence under this section is liable –

    (a) on conviction on indictment, to a fine;

    (b) on summary conviction, to a fine not exceeding the statutory maximum.

(6) Nothing in this section authorises the consideration at a meeting convened in pursuance of subsection (1) of any matter that could not have been considered at that meeting apart from this section."

This provision is an important one for directors of public companies coming close to insolvency. The requirement to convene a meeting is, of course, a problem for directors who are in emergency negotiations for some scheme to save the company, since the publicity involved in convening a general meeting at this time may be inconvenient for the company. However, it is essential that directors are aware of their duty and convene the necessary meeting to avoid incurring penalties. The directors should also be aware that the section does not impose upon them a duty to remedy the situation in any way, but simply to call a meeting to consider what steps, if any, should be taken to deal with the situation.

11.4.2 The Listing Rules and the Disclosure and Transparency Rules

Where a company is listed on the London Stock Exchange, the directors must ensure that it continues to comply with its obligations under both the Listing Rules and the Disclosure and

Transparency Rules. Chapter 2 Disclosure and Transparency Rules, the purpose of which is to promote prompt and fair disclosure of relevant information to the market, needs careful consideration in this context. DTR 2.2.1R requires an issuer to notify a Regulatory Information Service as soon as possible of any inside information (as defined) which directly concerns it. However, an issuer may be able to delay the disclosure of inside information where the omission to disclose will not be likely to mislead the public and the information can be kept confidential.

Clearly, the obligation to disclose price-sensitive information can become a serious issue for the directors of listed companies where insolvency is in prospect. It is highly likely that the company's financial condition will be or become such as to warrant a notification under the Disclosure and Transparency Rules. Equally, the directors may well be reluctant to notify if they are involved in negotiations for a rescue of the company, since the announcement may prejudice the negotiations and worsen the company's problems. This dilemma is expressly addressed in the rules which provide that a company may be able to delay public disclosure of the fact that it is in rescue negotiations (or the substance of those negotiations) but the exception does not extend to permitting the company to delay public disclosure of the fact that it is in financial difficulty.

When a company to which the Listing Rules and the Disclosure and Transparency Rules apply is under financial pressure, these requirements need to be carefully and continuously monitored if the directors are to comply with their obligations.

11.4.3 *Financial Services and Markets Act 2000 ("FSMA")*

There are other provisions which, although of general application, may involve particularly difficult judgments when a company is experiencing any sort of solvency crisis – particularly where there the crisis is a short-term liquidity crisis and there are grounds for supposing that it is capable of resolution.

Sections 118 and 118A FSMA deal with market abuse. Examples of when market abuse will occur include the improper disclosure of inside information and the dissemination of misleading information. Where a director has engaged in market abuse or has permitted others to do so, the Financial Services Authority can impose civil penalties.

In addition, Section 397 FSMA provides criminal penalties for directors who (in summary) make a statement, promise or forecast that they know to be materially misleading, false or deceptive or who dishonestly conceal any material facts or recklessly make misleading, deceptive or false statements to induce dealings in a company's shares, or otherwise create a false or misleading impression as to the market in, price or value of the shares.

These matters are covered in more detail in Chapter 4.

11.5   Practical matters

The combined effect of the statutory provisions set out in this Chapter, together with the cases in the areas of fiduciary duties and the powers of the court to make disqualification orders against directors, require the directors of companies facing insolvency to take into account a wide range of responsibilities when carrying out their functions. Clearly, no two companies are the same and detailed legal advice should always be taken in relation to the circumstances of any particular company where an insolvency issue has arisen. However, directors of a company facing insolvency should always consider the following practical guidelines:

(a)   The board should convene regular meetings to consider the company's financial position and keep under constant review the issue of whether the company has a reasonable prospect of avoiding insolvent liquidation.

(b)   Every member of the board should ensure that he is adequately informed of the position of the company and should perform (and be seen to perform) his functions actively. Directors who leave other directors to cover for them can be penalised.

(c)   Ensure that all information about the company, in particular its financial details, is adequate and up to date and available to all directors.

(d) Careful consideration should be given to deciding whether all actions taken by the board are in the commercial interests of the company (having regard also to the matters specified in Section 172 CA 2006, as to which *see* Section 11.1 above).

(e) The effect of any proposed transaction on the interests of creditors should be considered. Even where the company is of doubtful solvency rather than clearly insolvent, the interests of creditors may become the determining factor in any allegations of breach of fiduciary duty. The board must never attempt to rely on shareholder approval to absolve it from a breach of fiduciary duty where the solvency of the company is in doubt.

(f) The board should consider the interests of all its creditors and not just a particular class (e.g. its bankers). It is not infrequent that boards of directors are pressed by certain powerful creditors to take action which is detrimental to other creditors. Directors can be penalised for acting in this way.

(g) Where the company is a listed company, the board should consider carefully its duties in relation to disclosure of information which could cause movements in the price of its shares.

(h) Each member of the board should consider his conduct carefully in relation to all relevant duties, not just those relating to insolvency. The insolvency of a company may be the trigger for scrutiny of the conduct of a director in relation to any aspect of his conduct.

(i) Where there is conflict amongst members of the board, each member must be seen to act positively to comply with his duties, since the sanctions relate to members individually not collectively. Where a member of the board disagrees with his co-directors, he should take active steps to make his views known and to obtain the information he needs to make the necessary decisions.

(j) All proceedings of the board should be carefully minuted and checked by each member of the board. In particular, the reasons for entering into any transaction and the reasons for the board's belief that the company can continue to trade should be recorded fully. Clearly the members of the board will need evidence that they behaved properly.

(k) If taking legal advice, the directors should consider taking that advice from advisers independent to those advising the company.

In a group situation, all the foregoing must be done in respect of each affected company and directors must be astute to consider the interests of the creditors of each company as separate constituencies. In the event of insolvency proceedings, their conduct will be considered on a company-by-company basis and even if several companies within a group, or the entire group, become subject to insolvency proceedings, it cannot be assumed that the same office holders will be responsible for all the companies and thus be able to understand any group-wide perspective.

Chapter 12

Regulatory Investigations

Angela Hayes

Partner
Mayer Brown International LLP

12.1   Introduction

Investigations are conducted in many different forms. The processes by which they operate impose a variety of obligations and duties which are enforceable in different ways. The focus of this Chapter is statutory investigations. The term "statutory investigation" includes any investigation conducted by a person whose authority to conduct such an investigation derives from statute and whose powers to demand information, whether by production of documents or by means of interview, are backed by sanctions imposed either by civil or criminal penalties, whether financial or custodial.

The common law right to remain silent has been under siege since compulsive powers to demand information were introduced into the bankruptcy legislation in the nineteenth century to enable creditors to identify and recover assets from a bankrupt's estate. Since then, there have been many examples of Parliament voting similar powers in support of other regulatory functions; for example, to the then Secretary of State for Trade and Industry (now deployed by the department of Business, Innovation and Skills) in support of his responsibilities to regulate companies; to the Commissioners of HM Revenue and Customs in support of their responsibilities to maximise revenue collection; to the Financial Services Authority (the "FSA") in support of its duty to regulate the conduct of banking, investment and insurance business in the UK and in its guise as the United Kingdom Listing Authority; and to the Director of the Serious Fraud Office ("SFO") in support of the duty to investigate and prosecute serious and complex fraud. Other important examples include the powers given to the Health and Safety Executive, the environmental agencies, marine and air accident investigators, office-holders appointed under the insolvency regime and the competition agencies.

The introduction of these various powers at different times for various purposes and in different political circumstances means that the substance and form of these powers vary considerably and it is not possible within the scope of this Chapter to give a comprehensive guide to all the various provisions to which a director of a company may possibly be exposed. By reference therefore to the more likely examples in the general commercial sector, namely the Companies Act 1985 ("CA 1985"), the Companies Act 2006 ("CA 2006"), the Financial Services and Markets Act ("FSMA"), and the Criminal Justice Act 1987 ("CJA 1987"), this Chapter seeks to identify the principal features which are common to most instances of statutory investigations. The main investigation powers in CA 1985 are not repealed and replaced by equivalents in CA 2006 but remain in force. This is why many of the statutory references given in this Chapter are still references to CA 1985 provisions. CA 2006 inserts into those surviving provisions additional powers for the Secretary of State to bring investigations to an end and to give directions to inspectors. We also look at what remains of the individual's common law rights and how they may be invoked in any given situation. This has become a particular issue with the incorporation into English law of the European Convention on Human Rights ("ECHR") as a result of the Human Rights Act 1998. This Chapter will conclude with some practical advice on how to respond to a statutory investigation.

The structure of this Chapter seeks to address the relevant issues in the order in which they are likely to occur in the course of the investigation. We examine:

(a) the potential scope of the investigation and the issues relating to the appointment of investigators, namely, the notice of appointment and the effect of the appointment;

(b) the confidentiality or otherwise of the investigation, the autonomy and the powers of the investigators and the sanctions for failure to cooperate and for obstruction;

(c) the limits on the powers and the rules of natural justice which apply; and

(d) the product of the investigation and what use can be made of its findings and the information which has been collected.

12.2 Scope of the investigation

The relevant statute will prescribe the circumstances in which and/or the purposes for which an investigator[1] can be appointed and the powers that the investigator can exercise during the conduct of an investigation. Statutes and specific provisions within them vary in the breadth of circumstances and purposes for which an investigator can be appointed; for example, the director of the SFO may exercise the compulsory powers to require information and documents under Section 2 CJA 1987 in order to "investigate any suspected offence which appears to him on reasonable grounds to involve serious and complex fraud" and in any case in which "it appears to him that there is good reason to do so for the purposes of investigating the affairs of any person";[2] the Department for Business, Innovation and Skills ("BIS") formerly known as the DTI can launch an investigation under the CA 1985 if there are circumstances suggesting that there is "fraud, misfeasance or other misconduct towards the company or towards its members" (Section 432(2) CA 1985); investigators may be appointed to investigate "the affairs of a company" (Section 431 CA 1985); the FSA may appoint investigators to investigate "the nature, conduct or state of the business of an authorised person" where

---

[1] The term "investigator" is intended to refer to all statutory investigators however described in the statute, for example, persons appointed under the CA 1985 are often described as "inspectors".

[2] The SFO's criteria for accepting a case for investigation are where: (a) there is a very significant public interest; (b) the sums at risk exceed £1 million; (c) the offences involve the public sector; (d) the evidence or the issues have an international dimension; (e) there is a highly complex and esoteric market where specialist market knowledge is needed; (f) the transactions themselves are particularly complex; (g) where accountancy help is essential; and (h) overall where it is felt that the conduct of the investigation should be in the hands of those responsible for the ultimate prosecution of the case.

it appears (to the FSA) that there is "good reason" for doing so (Section 167 FSMA). In contrast there are other examples where the scope of the investigation is more precisely prescribed. For example, under the CA 1985, BIS can launch investigations into the membership of a company (Section 442 CA 1985) or its investigation may confine itself to the books and records of a company (Section 447 CA 1985); under Section 168 FSMA investigators can be appointed for various specified purposes, such as investigating whether an authorised firm is carrying on a particular type of regulated business without FSA permission.

In theory, therefore, the legitimate scope of the investigation will be limited and there should be grounds for challenge if the circumstances of the appointment of an investigator and the scope of the investigation extend beyond what is permitted by the relevant statute. In practice, as the grounds for appointment are often so widely prescribed, it can be difficult to demonstrate good enough grounds for a challenge to succeed. In particular, there is very limited scope to challenge the decision to appoint investigators because the courts have held that there is no requirement on the appointing authority to disclose the material facts before it or the reasons for the appointment, provided it acts in good faith and does not use its discretion improperly. In *Norwest Holst Ltd* v *Secretary of State for Trade*[3] it was held, on appeal, that the wide discretion which had been conferred on the DTI to appoint inspectors to investigate a company's affairs and report to it, was exercised at a preliminary stage for the purposes of good administration, and carried with it no implication that there was any case against the company; accordingly, the rules of natural justice were, at that stage, inapplicable so that the appointment of inspectors could not be challenged where the DTI had acted in good faith and within the powers conferred by the relevant statute. It was further held that the court could not, and would not, review the exercise of that discretion where the company had not discharged the onus on it of showing that there was any lack of good faith on the part of the DTI.

---

[3] [1978] Ch 201. Also *see* the discussion of this decision in *R.* v *Secretary of State for Trade Ex parte Perestrello and another* [1980] 3 All ER 28.

Even though it is difficult successfully to challenge the appointment of investigators or the scope of an investigation, nevertheless it is crucial that a company's directors understand fully at an early stage the statutory basis of the investigation and its intended scope. In acting in the best interests of the company he or she serves, a director needs to ensure that the assistance given to investigators by the company and its directors is appropriately focused. That may well entail an exchange of views with an over-zealous investigator. One can often be successful in cutting back the scope of specific requests for information or documents by a timely challenge on whether particular materials are really relevant to the matters under investigation. Statutory investigations can be expensive and time consuming for target companies and their management. Investigators not infrequently request broad categories of documents and records without appreciating when they do so the volume of material they are asking for or the time it may take to compile. Initial requests for documents and information sometimes go well beyond what is reasonable in the context of the investigation being conducted. Directors need to be vigilant, therefore, to ensure that investigators' requests are reasonably and properly made.

12.3 The notice of appointment – the document

For the reasons stated above, this is an important document. Powers vest in investigators as a consequence of their appointment by the designated authority, for example, BIS or the FSA. Investigators ought to produce a notice of their appointment to any person in respect of whom they seek to exercise their powers. In some cases this is obligatory.[4] One would expect the notice to contain evidence of the identity of the appointing authority, the statutory provisions under which the appointment was made, the reasons for the appointment, the names of the individuals appointed and thereby authorised to exercise the powers prescribed and the date of the appointment (which

---

[4] Under Section 170 FSMA it is obligatory, save in exceptional circumstances, for the investigating authority to give written notice of the appointment of an investigator to the person who is the subject of the investigation and to give written notice to that person of any change in the scope of the investigation.

may, of course, substantially precede the date on which it is produced).[5] The statement of reasons for the appointment is usually very brief, often little more than a recital of the grounds prescribed by statute, but you should be looking for as much clarity as possible about which entities and/or individuals may be the target of the investigation. It is important to be clear whether you are being asked for information to assist an investigation into others or whether your company and/or individuals within it are or could become a target of the investigation. If the notice is not clear about this then further written confirmation should be sought.

Special powers exercisable by investigators in certain restricted circumstances to enter and search premises without notice will invariably only be granted by a justice of the peace and will be contained in a warrant.

12.4   Effect of the notice

The notice of investigation is important not just because of the insight it may give into the scope and purpose of an investigation, but also because receipt of it will impose on the recipient certain duties and obligations, which need to be recognised at an early stage. It will impose duties and obligations to ensure that all relevant information is preserved. An obligation to keep the investigation confidential may also be imposed. Often it will also be accompanied by a specific request for information and/or documents that must be responded to by a specific date. Sometimes, however, the notice of appointment is served first with a formal request for information following later.

All statutes providing for the appointment of investigators will have provisions reinforcing the inspector's powers by imposing criminal sanctions on those who falsify, conceal or destroy documents relating to the subject of the inquiry.[6] Each of the relevant enabling statutes will also impose obligations on those

---

[5]   Under Section 170(4) FSMA the notice of appointment must specify the provisions under which, and as a result of which, the investigator was appointed and state the reasons for his appointment.
[6]   Section 450 CA 1985; Section 177(3) FSMA.

who are the subject of an investigation to retain relevant material, but some statutes are more prescriptive than others.

Under Section 434 CA 1985, "When inspectors are appointed" it is the duty of all officers and agents of the company "to produce to the inspectors all documents of or relating to the company . . . in their custody or power". A strict interpretation would impose an obligation on the directors to disclose relevant material in their custody or power without needing a specific request once they have received notice that an appointment has been made. Where, however, it would be unreasonable to expect a director to be able to identify what is relevant to the investigation, in practical terms this can only be read as creating a duty to preserve all existing company material. In circumstances where the relevance of an important document is apparent, then under Section 434 a positive duty to produce it, without any specific request, would also arise. Under the FSMA, persons under investigation are only under a duty to produce documents or other information in response to a specific request by the investigator. But authorised persons under the FSMA are also bound to comply with FSA principles, under which they are bound to deal with the FSA in an open and cooperative manner and "to disclose to the FSA appropriately anything relating to the firm of which the FSA would reasonably expect notice". Breach of a principle by an authorised person is a disciplinary matter so that a failure by an authorised person to volunteer disclosure of relevant material would be a disciplinary matter under the FSMA.

12.5   Confidentiality of the investigation

The existence of a statutory investigation is rarely made public. BIS' practice, for example, is to commence its fact-finding enquiry with a confidential investigation using its powers under Section 447 CA 1985 to inspect the books and records of the company.[7] BIS will neither announce nor acknowledge the

---

[7]   This is the most widely used power of BIS and will almost always be used as a quick fact-finding exercise. For the year ended 31 March 2006 the DTI's Companies Investigation Bureau (now part of BIS's Insolvency Service) received over 3,702 complaints and, of these, approximately 593 were considered for potential use of statutory investigation powers and 148 were accepted for investigation. The vast majority of these were investigated under Section 447 CA 1985.

commencement of such an investigation nor will it give any notification of when it has been concluded. Any report produced will be confidential. Only on rare occasions now will BIS launch a full-scale investigation with the announcement of the appointment of inspectors under Section 432 CA 1985, the usual outcome of which is a published report.[8] Part XIV CA 1985 does give a discretionary power to the Secretary of State to direct the publication of reports following investigations conducted under the provisions of this part of the Act.

The FSA's policy is that it will not normally make public the fact that it is conducting an investigation or the findings of an investigation. It is bound by statutory restrictions under FSMA on the disclosure of confidential information (Section 348) and on the publication of its decisions (Section 391). Under the latter both the FSA and recipients are prohibited from publishing details about an FSA warning notice or decision notice. The FSA is only entitled to publish information about its decision when that decision takes effect (when a final notice or effective supervisory notice is issued). However, in exceptional circumstances the FSA will publish the fact that an investigation is under way, for example if this is desirable to maintain public confidence, such as where the matters under investigation have become the subject of public concern, speculation or rumour. In doing so it must still have regard to the statutory restrictions.[9]

Where the existence of a statutory investigation has not been announced by the appointing authority, that information itself will be considered confidential within the meaning ascribed to it by the statute.

SFO investigations, if not formally announced, are publicly acknowledged following an initial period in which investigations are made for the purposes of assessing whether or not it is a suitable case for the SFO to take on.

---

[8] This is a rarely used power. However, one example of the appointment of inspectors under this section is the Transtec investigation. Another is the appointment of investigators in May 2005 to investigate the affairs of MG Rover Group.

[9] Examples of investigations that the FSA has acknowledged include Marks & Spencer Plc and Shell Transport and Trading Company Plc.

12.6 The autonomy of the investigators

One feature of an investigation which may affect the way in which it is likely to be conducted is the degree of autonomy given to the investigator by the authority appointing him/her.

Statutory investigations fall broadly into two categories: those which are essentially conducted by or on behalf of the authority itself, such as investigations under Section 447 CA 1985 or Section 165 FSMA, and those which are conducted by investigators appointed by the authority (usually in these circumstances referred to as "inspectors") to investigate and report back (e.g. Sections 167 and 168 FSMA and Section 432 CA 1985). As far as the latter are concerned, the earlier statutes provided for limited formal means of control exercisable by the appointing authority over the direction of the investigation. No doubt the intention was to ensure that the inquiry would be seen as being independent and objective. However, the regulators are being increasingly empowered to limit the period of the investigation or confine it to a particular matter. Significantly in the FSMA, specific provisions enable the FSA to give directions to the investigators to control the scope of the investigation, the period during which it is to be conducted, the conduct of the investigation and the reporting of the investigation.[10] Carrying on this trend, CA 2006 gives powers to the Secretary of State to take appropriate action where an investigation appears to be taking too long and to give directions to inspectors with which they are obliged to comply (new Sections 446A and 446B CA 1985).

One type of investigation carried forward from the Banking Act 1987 to the FSMA is the power of the FSA to require an authorised person under the Act to provide the FSA with a written report by a suitably skilled person nominated or approved by the FSA about any aspect of the business including that relating to other members of the group or partnership of which that person is a member.[11] The advantages of this to the regulator are

---

[10] Section 170 FSMA.
[11] Section 166 FSMA.

that the costs of the exercise are borne by the institution and the regulator retains control over the "form" of the report. The Bank of England's practice was to use this power on a routine basis as a way of auditing discrete areas of a bank's business such as accounting and internal control systems or the bank's financial returns. It is likely that the FSA will continue to use it in the same way, but it is now available across the full spectrum of the financial services industry rather than confined just to banks.

12.7 Powers of the investigators

The powers themselves, sometimes described as draconian, are broadly consistent across the spectrum of legislation. There are basically two: the power to require the production of documents and the power to require persons to answer questions. In addition, some statutes make provision for the power to take evidence on oath, the power to require the production of information "without delay", that is, then and there,[12] and the power to require the production of original documents as opposed to just copies.

These powers will usually be reinforced by the invasive powers of entry, search and seizure pursuant to warrants issued by justices of the peace.[13] Warrants will only be issued if the justice of the peace can be satisfied that certain preconditions are met. These will typically comprise reasonable grounds for believing either:

(a) that documents which a person has failed to provide pursuant to a previous request are to be found on the premises; or

(b) that documents on the premises of an authorised person (for the purposes of the FSMA) or any person's premises (if a relevant indictable offence has been or is being committed) are likely to be removed, tampered with or destroyed if a request for them was made.

---

[12] Section 165(3) FSMA; under Section 447(3) CA 1985 the BIS may authorise an officer to require the production "forthwith" of any specified documents.
[13] Section 448 CA 1985; Section 176 FSMA.

12.8   Sanctions

12.8.1   Sanctions for failure

Failure to cooperate with a statutory investigation may result in any number of possible sanctions (unless a defence of reasonable excuse can be made out, *see* Section 12.9 below).

Usually a failure to cooperate will itself be a criminal offence punishable with imprisonment or a fine. Under Section 2(13) CJA 1987 a person may be liable on summary conviction to imprisonment for a term not exceeding six months and/or a fine not exceeding level 5 on the standard scale. Directors beware! A recurring theme throughout this regulatory legislation, which applies not only to the conduct of investigations but to all substantive matters dealt with in this legislation, is the statutory liability of directors for offences committed by the company if it can be shown that the offence had been committed with the director's consent or connivance, or it was attributable to any neglect on his/her part.[14]

Some statutes, however, provide for the investigators to refer any failure to cooperate to the court which will then be required to decide whether such failure amounts to a contempt of court punishable by imprisonment or a fine.[15] This is the approach adopted under FSMA. Such referrals are rare and, when they occur, the court's usual initial response, where it judges the failure to be unreasonable, is to give the defendant a second chance.

Authorised persons under FSMA will have obligations to cooperate with their regulator pursuant to the FSA's Principles and rules which govern their business, breach of which will render them liable to disciplinary action by the regulator. They can be fined or, in the worst cases, removed temporarily or permanently from the register of authorised persons.

---

[14] Section 1121 CA 2006 (Section 733(2) CA 1985); Section 400 FSMA.
[15] Sections 436 and 453C CA 1985; Section 177(1) and (2) FSMA.

With regard to investigations concerning share ownership under the CA 1985,[16] where there is difficulty in finding out the relevant facts about shares, BIS may impose restrictions on dealings in those shares under Part XV CA 1985.

12.8.2 Sanctions for obstruction

The provision of false or misleading information is a criminal offence. It is not necessary to prove that it was intentional. It will be enough to prove that it was done recklessly. The FSMA does not contain an equivalent provision to the offence under the Banking Act 1987 (now repealed) of withholding of information. However, as explained above, to do so could lead to disciplinary sanctions.

The falsification, concealment, destruction or disposal of documents will similarly attract criminal sanctions and it will be enough to prove that a person caused or permitted this to happen.

12.9 Limits on the powers of investigators

An investigator's statutory powers will be subject to certain limitations. Any offence of failing to provide information pursuant to requirements imposed by any legislation will typically permit a defence of reasonable excuse. What amounts to a reasonable excuse will always be judged by reference to the facts of the particular case, but by implication it imposes on investigators a duty to respect the rules of natural justice, to act fairly and to act in accordance with their terms of reference.

12.9.1 The duty to act fairly

Investigators are obliged to act fairly. In exercising information-gathering powers and, in particular, in relation to the examination of witnesses, there is a duty not to impose unreasonable demands on a person in terms of the time to be expended or the expense to be incurred in preparation.

---

[16] Section 442 and Section 444 CA 1985.

Kevin Maxwell succeeded in persuading the Vice Chancellor, Sir Richard Scott, that, in the exceptional circumstances applying to his case, the potential burden that the questioning proposed by the inspectors imposed on him risked going beyond that which an unrepresented individual could be required to accept. The court therefore held that, until steps were taken by the inspectors to reduce that burden, his refusal to answer questions did not constitute a breach of his statutory obligations.[17] Inspectors may not, therefore, place demands on persons that are unreasonable whether as to the time they have to expend, or the expense they have to incur in preparation but it is likely that these demands will have to be exceptional before a court will respond sympathetically.

A witness should be given reasonable notice that he/she is required to attend before the investigators for examination. Advance notice in general terms of the matters on which the witness is to be examined is also appropriate. Witnesses will be allowed to attend with a legal adviser, but legal advisers will not be permitted to answer on behalf of the witness. As the process of a statutory investigation is inquisitorial, a witness will not have the right to cross-examine other witnesses or to see the transcripts of evidence of other witnesses. Witnesses should not be led to believe that the evidence they give will be confidential; investigators may wish to put their evidence to other witnesses or include it in a report. Witnesses will normally be supplied with a transcript of their evidence which they will be invited to review for transcription errors. They should be invited to correct any errors in the information provided and add any additional information or comments. SFO and FSA interviews will also usually be taped and a transcript of the tape provided following the interview.

12.9.2   *The duty to act within the terms of reference*

The investigators will be bound by the terms of reference of their appointment. They will not be permitted to ask for

---

[17] *Re an Inquiry into Mirror Group Newspapers* [1999] 1 BCLC 690. Kevin Maxwell's circumstances were highly unusual given the interrogations over 61 days that he had already undergone and his criminal trial and acquittal.

information which extends beyond that which could conceivably be relevant. Often, it will be difficult for the recipient of a request for information to form a view as to relevance and thereby legitimately challenge any such request, especially in the more wide-ranging, large-scale BIS investigations. But where, for example, inspectors have been appointed to look into a narrow issue, they should not be allowed to extend the scope of their inquiry to other matters unless specifically authorised to do so.

12.9.3   Legal professional privilege

Information (whether in documentary form or otherwise) which falls within the scope of a person's legal professional privilege is usually (but not always) exempt from production, but not all communications between a lawyer and his/her client are necessarily privileged. In broad terms, there are two types of legal professional privilege:

(a)   *legal advice privilege*: these are confidential communications between a lawyer and his/her client which come into existence for the purpose of giving or getting legal advice;[18] and
(b)   *litigation privilege*: when litigation is contemplated or pending, any communications between the client, his/her lawyer or agent and a third party will be privileged if they come into existence for the sole, or dominant, purpose of giving or getting advice in relation to the litigation or collecting evidence for use in the litigation.

Communications falling into either of these two categories will not be covered if they occurred for the purpose of committing a fraud or a crime. Lawyers will however usually be required to furnish details of their client's name and address. The precise application of legal professional privilege to particular documents can sometimes be difficult to judge. Furthermore, regulatory statutes may themselves modify the concept of legal professional privilege. In particular, FSMA has a specific definition of "protected items" that a person is not obliged to produce

---

[18]   The scope of common law legal advice privilege has now been set by the House of Lords in *Three Rivers DC v Bank of England (Disclosure) (No 4)* [2004] UKHL 48.

to investigators. Although it appears broadly to mirror the common law definition, in some respects it is unclear and will need careful interpretation.

12.9.4   *Other obligations of confidentiality*

Documents and other information in respect of which a person owes an obligation of confidentiality by virtue of carrying on the business of banking also usually attract a degree of privilege. No one can be required to disclose such information unless:

(a)   he/she is the person under investigation or a member of that person's group;
(b)   the person to whom the obligation is owed is the person under investigation or a member of that person's group;
(c)   the person under investigation consents; or
(d)   the making of the requirement has been specifically authorised.[19]

12.10   Privilege against self-incrimination

The privilege against self-incrimination is the common law right of any individual not to be required to give evidence against himself/herself. The right has been significantly eroded by regulatory statutes enabling investigators to compel a person to answer questions or produce information. However, the position has changed as a result of the decision of the European Court of Human Rights in the *Saunders*[20] case and the incorporation of the ECHR into domestic law in October 2000. Since then amendments to regulatory statutes have been introduced by the Youth Justice and Criminal Evidence Act 1999 to bring them more expressly into line with ECHR principles. Prior to these developments the English courts had held that the privilege was overridden by statutes providing that questions must be answered under compulsion, so that evidence provided under compulsion could be used in any proceedings,

---

[19]   Section 452 CA 1985; Section 175(5) FSMA.
[20]   [1997] BCC 872.

including criminal proceedings, against the person who had given it.

The position now is that a distinction needs to be drawn between the right to remain silent in response to questions and the restrictions on the use that can be made of answers given under compulsion in subsequent proceedings. An "inviolable" common law right not to incriminate oneself still exists only in respect of criminal proceedings, where a qualified right of silence remains.[21] In regulatory investigations the right of silence has generally been abrogated completely by the statutory compulsory powers but answers to questions so obtained cannot be used (with two exceptions discussed below) as evidence in criminal proceedings against the person giving them. In fact, even before *Saunders* this was the position in relation to evidence obtained by the SFO pursuant to their Section 2 CJA 1987 powers as a result of express protections in that Act.

In civil proceedings generally (as distinct from statutory investigations using compulsory powers) a privilege against self-incrimination can be claimed to enable a person to refuse to answer a question or to refuse to allow inspection of a document if answering the question or producing the document would expose that person or their spouse to criminal proceedings or to proceedings for the purpose of recovering a penalty. However, the privilege can only be claimed if the criminal offence or penalty concerned is under UK law, it cannot be claimed as against foreign criminal proceedings.[22] In fact it is very hard to persuade a court that the privilege can rightly be claimed. The court will be looking for evidence that the person's likelihood of being involved in criminal proceedings will be significantly greater if the information is provided. The claim of privilege will not succeed if the person is already in real danger of criminal proceedings bring brought.

---

[21] The Detention Code prescribes the following caution:

"You do not have to say anything. But it may harm your defence if you do not mention when questioned something which you later rely on in court. Anything you do say may be given in evidence."

See Section 34 Criminal Justice and Public Order Act 1994.

[22] *Arab Monetary Fund* v *Hashim and others* [1989] 3 All ER 466. *AT&T Istel Ltd* v *Tully (1992)* 3 All ER 522.

Article 6 ECHR,[23] which addresses the issue of procedural fairness in the determination of both "criminal charges" and "civil rights and obligations", guarantees the right to a fair hearing by an independent and impartial tribunal. Article 6 has been interpreted as not permitting the use in evidence in criminal proceedings of answers given in response to compulsory questioning. In *Saunders* the European Court of Human Rights confirmed that the use by the prosecution at his criminal trial of transcripts of statements made by Saunders to DTI inspectors appointed under Sections 432 and 442 CA 1985 was in breach of Article 6 such that Saunders had been denied a fair hearing. Following this decision the government's policy changed, with an acceptance that even in cases where there were express statutory provisions to the contrary (such as Section 434(5) CA 1985) answers obtained in response to compulsory questions could not be used as evidence in criminal proceedings (apart from the two exceptions). Since then, as mentioned above, specific statutory amendments have been made by the Youth Justice and Criminal Evidence Act 1999 (including the addition of a new sub-section (5A) to Section 434 CA 1985). The two exceptions are first, where evidence relating to answers given by a person under compulsion is adduced or questions relating to them are asked in the criminal proceedings by or on behalf of that person; secondly, they can be used in proceedings the purpose of which is to prove the falsity of those answers.

The Article 6 protection does not extend to the conduct of BIS investigations themselves as distinct from any criminal proceedings which might follow. The court ruled in *Fayed* v *UK*[24] that DTI inspectors did not make legal determinations as to civil or criminal liability and the findings of DTI inspectors were not dispositive in any way. The court went on to hold that if the protections available under Article 6 were to be applied to DTI investigations it would "unduly hamper the effective regulation in the public interest of complex financial and

---

[23] Article 6 states: "In the determination of his civil rights and obligations or of any criminal charges against him, everyone is entitled to a fair and public hearing within a reasonable time by an independent and impartial tribunal . . .".
[24] [1994] 18 EHRR 393.

commercial activities". The same principles would apply to all statutory investigations.

12.11 The product of the investigation

Statutory investigators fall into two broad categories:

(a) those who have been appointed to investigate and report; and

(b) those whose powers to investigate are ancillary to statutory functions whether these be to prosecute serious fraud (the SFO), to regulate financial services business (the FSA), or to collect revenue (the Commissioners of HM Revenue and Customs).

As regards the former, the report may itself only be a prelude to prosecution or other enforcement action in which case the opportunity to respond to the content of that report or challenge the veracity of the evidence on which its conclusions are based will arise in the context of the legal or disciplinary process which ensues.

Where, however, the report is to be published, the investigators' duty to act fairly requires that those who are the subject of criticism in the report be given an opportunity to respond to that criticism. This principle was established through the late Robert Maxwell's challenges to DTI inspectors' powers before the Court of Appeal in 1970 and 1974 arising from investigations into Pergamon Press. In the first case, he argued that he should not be compelled to give evidence to DTI inspectors unless he also had the right to read the transcripts of the evidence of other witnesses and, if necessary, meet any allegations by evidence or by written or oral submissions. On the second occasion, following completion of the report, he argued that the inspectors had acted in breach of the rules of natural justice in failing to give him an opportunity to answer any tentative criticisms they were minded to make of him in the final report or put to him any relevant statements made by other witnesses or in documents which were prejudicial to him.

In the first case it was held that Mr Maxwell's refusal to give evidence was unjustified. Although the proceedings before the inspectors were only administrative, and not judicial or quasi-judicial, the characteristics of the proceedings required the inspectors to act fairly, in that if they were disposed to condemn or criticise anyone in a report they must first give him a fair opportunity to correct or contradict the allegation. However, for this purpose an outline of the charge would usually suffice and, save for the requirement to act fairly, the inspectors should not be subject to any set rules of procedure but should be free to act at their own discretion. As a matter of fact, the court found that the inspectors had shown that they intended to act fairly and had given every assurance that could reasonably be required.

In the second case, it was held that a clear distinction was to be drawn between an inquiry based on a charge or accusation and one such as that on which the inspectors had been engaged in which they were asked to establish what had happened and, in the course of so doing, to form certain views or conclusions. Having heard the evidence and reached their conclusions, the inspectors were under no obligation to put to a witness such of those conclusions as might be critical of him. All that was necessary was that the inspectors should put to the witness the points that they proposed to consider when he first came to give evidence. Once the inspectors had heard the evidence they were entitled to come to the final conclusions which would be embodied in their report. The inspectors had conducted the enquiry fairly; the fact that certain matters of detail had not been put to Robert Maxwell when he was giving evidence was not a ground for impugning the report. Nevertheless, the DTI's policy and practice did change following this decision, to offer more than these minimum safeguards. The DTI's "Notes for the Guidance of Inspectors" (published in 1990 in its Investigations Handbook, now out of print) suggested that, even where a witness has had the substance of the evidence against him put to him at interview, it might be appropriate when the inspectors have prepared a first draft of their report to write to a witness setting out any intended criticisms and inviting him to respond within a fixed period. Subsequently it may be appropriate in fairness to the witness to include the response in the report either in whole or in part.

12.12 How may the information be used?

12.12.1 *Criminal proceedings*

As we have seen, Article 6 ECHR has had an impact on the admissibility of compulsorily acquired testimony against self-interest in the context of criminal proceedings. It is now established that answers obtained in response to compulsory questioning cannot (apart from the two exceptions mentioned in Section 12.10 above) be used in evidence in criminal proceedings against the person giving them.

The issue that remains, which determines the extent of the protections under Article 6, is whether a matter will be characterised as "civil" or "criminal". These concepts are autonomous ECHR terms and, if a matter is categorised under the ECHR as criminal, then additional protections will apply. So even if a matter is characterised as "civil" in the UK, it could still be "criminal" under the ECHR. Where there is a power to imprison someone for the offence involved, this is generally determinative of it being a "criminal" matter. Proceedings which include a power to impose large financial penalties (e.g. tax evasion proceedings)[25] could also be classed as criminal proceedings. How are regulatory investigations generally to be classified?

This issue was widely debated during the Bill phase of the FSMA and a distinction has been drawn in the FSMA between enforcement action taken for breach of the market abuse provisions, which can be taken against any person, and enforcement action taken for breach of the FSA rules or principles, which could only be taken against an authorised person. The FSA's policy is to treat the former as criminal proceedings for the purposes of Article 6 and the defendants are therefore entitled to all the procedural safeguards provided under Article 6 for criminal proceedings. The latter are viewed by the FSA as regulatory civil proceedings and the full protections provided by Article 6 will not apply. The rationale for this is that, although in both cases unlimited financial penalties may be imposed and

---

[25] *Bendenoun v France* (1994) 18 ECHR 54.

in respect of an authorised person his/her authorisation and potentially, therefore, his/her livelihood can be removed, the authorised person has volunteered to be subject to the enforcement regime. The subsequent decision of the Court of Appeal in the *Fleurose*[26] case tends to confirm that the FSA's policy as regards disciplinary proceedings is correct. The Court of Appeal had to consider the correct classification for the purposes of the ECHR of disciplinary proceedings under the rules of the former financial services regulator, the Securities and Futures Authority. It held, applying the principles set out in *Han & Yau*,[27] that the SFA's disciplinary proceedings had been civil in nature so that the full Article 6 protections did not apply. The English court has also expressed a view on this point in the context of proceedings under the Company Directors Disqualification Act 1986 ("CDDA 1986").[28] The court was asked to consider whether, in the circumstances of disqualification proceedings, the use in evidence of information provided by the respondents under Section 235 Insolvency Act 1986 ("IA 1986") was permissible under Article 6. The court held that directors' disqualification proceedings were regulatory civil proceedings not "criminal" proceedings in ECHR terms; and that, although evidence obtained under Section 235 IA 86 was obtained under compulsion, its use in evidence in regulatory civil proceedings would not, except perhaps in rare cases, make the hearing unfair for the purposes of Article 6 of the ECHR.

12.12.2   *Civil proceedings*

Although Article 6 ECHR has restricted the use that can be made of compulsorily acquired evidence in criminal proceedings, such evidence could still be used in civil proceedings. In *British and Commonwealth Holdings Plc (in admin)* v *Barclays de Zoete Wedd Ltd and others*[29] one of the parties applied for inspection of the transcripts of evidence given to DTI inspectors appointed under Section 432 CA 1985. The court held that the

---

[26] *Fleurose* v *Disciplinary Appeal Tribunal of the Securities and Futures Authority Ltd* [2002] IRLR 297.

[27] *Han & Yau and others* v *Customs and Excise Commissioners* [2001] EWCA Civ 1048.

[28] *Re Westminster Property Ltd, The Times*, 19 January 2000.

[29] [1999] 1 BCLC 86.

fact that the evidence had been given in circumstances which were confidential and that the transcripts contained evidence which had been given under compulsion were no reasons why they should not be produced for inspection in the civil proceedings. The civil court has a discretion whether to admit such evidence.

Directors should therefore be aware that evidence given to BIS inspectors may be used in civil proceedings. However, before the transcripts may be produced, they may be edited (or "redacted") in two important respects: first, witnesses who are not parties to the civil proceedings and whose evidence is quoted in the transcripts should be notified and given the opportunity to object to the disclosure of their evidence (*Soden* v *Burns*)[30] and second, the transcripts may contain provisional criticism material and such material may validly be the subject of a public interest immunity certificate (*Re Atlantic Computers Plc*).[31]

Under Section 441 CA 1985, a copy of any report of inspectors appointed under Part XIV CA 1985 which is certified as a true copy is admissible in any proceedings as evidence of the inspectors' opinion on any matter in their report.

12.13 To whom may the information be disclosed?

Confidential information received during a statutory investigation, whether by the authority conducting the investigation or by those to whom information has been imparted for the purposes of conducting the investigation, will generally be subject to restrictions on its further disclosure, breach of which can attract criminal sanctions.

Confidential information is defined under the FSMA as information which relates to the business or other affairs of any person and which is received under or for the purposes of the Act. There is a general prohibition on disclosure of such confidential information. Under the CA 1985 the restrictions on disclosure attach to information received pursuant to specified

---

[30] [1996] 2 BCLC 636.
[31] [1998] BCC 200.

investigatory powers. Each statute then provides for circumstances in which confidential information may lawfully be disclosed. These include with the consent of the person from whom the confidential information was received or, if different, the person to whom it relates; or because at the time of disclosure the information is already available to the public from other sources; or because the information is in the form of an anonymous summary or collection of information such that information relating to any particular person cannot be ascertained from it. Each statute provides for a large number of exceptions to the disclosure restrictions which typically include disclosure to other bodies exercising similar regulatory functions. These exceptions are colloquially known as "gateways". There is no obligation to disclose confidential information where a gateway applies; the gateways are permissive rather than mandatory. It is an offence to disclose such information other than in accordance with the gateways.

It is stated BIS policy to treat the transcripts of evidence before inspectors appointed under the CA 1985 as confidential but available for release in certain circumstances (at the discretion of BIS). These circumstances include:

(a) release to the Director of Public Prosecutions, the SFO and other prosecuting authorities and the police where to do so will assist the investigation and prosecution of crime;
(b) on an application for a disqualification order under the CDDA 1986;
(c) to the liquidators of companies being investigated for the purposes of civil proceedings as a result of an application by the liquidator to the court under Section 236 IA 1986; or
(d) in any circumstance in which or for any purpose for which disclosure is permitted under Section 449 CA 1985.

Any such disclosure is discretionary and BIS may impose preconditions for its release and/or redact passages which BIS considers that it would not be in the public interest to disclose. As such, witnesses who give evidence to inspectors appointed under the CA 1985 can have no assurance that their evidence will remain confidential.

The permissive gateways available to the FSA under the FSMA are set out in a statutory instrument[32] (the "Gateways Regulations"). The pattern of permitted disclosures and purposes for which that disclosure can be made under the Gateways Regulations is complex. This is because EU directives applicable to various of the FSA's activities impose their own specific restrictions on the UK implementing legislation in relation to the disclosure of information. The Gateways Regulations consequently draw a distinction between directive information and non-directive information and the FSA can disclose the latter for a wider range of purposes. The gateways include:

(a) disclosure for the purposes of any criminal investigation or proceedings whether in the UK or elsewhere;

(b) for the purposes of certain specified civil proceedings, including under the Company Directors Disqualification Act 1986;

(c) broadly the information covered by the single market directives or the UCITS Directive can be disclosed to a long list of designated persons and bodies set out in Schedule 1 Gateways Regulations for the purposes of their particular functions specified there. These include central banks, monetary authorities, recognised investment exchanges, the Panel on Takeovers and Mergers, the Director General of Fair Trading, the Competition Commission, designated professional bodies and investigators, auditors and actuaries appointed under the FSMA;

(d) other information, not covered by directive restrictions, can also be disclosed to the bodies and persons listed in Schedule 2 for the purposes of their wider functions specified there and to a prescribed disciplinary proceedings authority.

12.14 Practical considerations

Having examined the principal features of statutory investigations, we conclude by considering some of the practical issues

---

[32] Financial Services and Market Act 2000 (Disclosure of Confidential Information) Regulations 2001 (SI 2001/2188) as amended by the Financial Services and Markets Act 2000 (Disclosure of Confidential Information) Regulations 2006 (SI 2006/3413) and more recently Financial Services and Markets Act 2000 (Disclosure of Confidential Information) Regulations 2009 (SI 2009/2877).

which arise for directors when a statutory investigation is commenced. However, the approach to the investigation will depend on the particular circumstances of the case. This list of practical issues will therefore have to be tailored to suit the particular facts of each case.

Throughout the course of the investigation, it is important to bear in mind that as much reputational damage may result from the way in which a person responds to an investigation as can arise from the underlying complaint itself.

12.14.1 Conflicts of interest

Following the appointment of investigators, the director's first duty should be to consider whether there is any risk of a conflict between his/her personal interests and those of the company. If there is such a risk it will need to be properly managed. This can be achieved either by excluding himself/herself from the responsibility of managing the company's response to the investigation or, if alternative appropriate representation is not available, by relying on independent external advice. A director who is not himself in a conflict situation should, together with the other directors, take steps to ensure that no other director who has any such conflicts remains involved. In some circumstances, it may be necessary to rely on the non-executive directors to perform the role of ensuring that the investigation is properly dealt with from the company's perspective.

12.14.2 Centralise management

Consideration will need to be given to how the investigation is to be dealt with by the company. It is usually sensible for one person at board level to be charged with overall responsibility for dealing with the investigation and coordinating responses to the investigators' requests for documents and information.

It may also be necessary and appropriate to establish a team to deal with the investigation. Typically, as the investigation proceeds, the range and mix of skills required will change. In addition to the obvious need to involve senior management, lawyers, accountants and compliance, it may also be appropriate to involve a non-executive director, who may provide someone with sufficient independence and authority but may also be perceived by the investigators to be impartial in relation to the matters under investigation.

The number of company staff assisting with the investigation should be kept to a minimum to ensure that confidentiality can be maintained and that tight control can be kept of evidence and material gathered and created during the investigation, in particular internal communications generated (*see* Section 12.14.9 below).

If the investigation has been announced publicly, it is likely that it will attract press comment. It may be appropriate to appoint PR advisers to deal with press enquiries and to monitor the press for adverse publicity.

Prompt consideration may need to be given to whether it is appropriate to suspend or dismiss any employees.

12.14.3   External advisers

In appropriate cases some regulators (e.g. the FSA) may be prepared to hold off from commencing their own formal investigation to allow a company time to conduct internal investigations and produce a report. This can happen in cases where there is no ongoing misconduct or no immediate danger to interested parties and the regulator can see that the company is taking its responsibilities seriously and has engaged appropriate external professional expertise. This can be a sound reason for directors to bring in professional advisers early.

In any event there can be difficult questions of judgment and interpretation involved in ensuring, in the best interests of the company, that a regulator's requests are reasonable and that the company does not go further than it needs in responding to them. This means it will usually be in the best interests of the company to take legal advice. Commonly where the investigation relates to matters of a financial nature the directors' first reaction will be to call on the company's usual accountants to assist. However, this could create material disclosable to the regulator as their work may not be covered by legal professional privilege unless a company's in-house legal team or external legal advisers are involved at the outset. A firm's usual accountants may also have a conflict of interest with the company in relation to the matters under investigation. Directors will also need to consider whether it is appropriate to engage the company's usual external legal advisers or whether a new team is needed. That may be the case if the company's usual lawyers have in the past advised on the matters under investigation or been aware of them in giving other advice, which means that a conflict of interest between the company and its lawyers could arise.

Any directors or other company staff who may be called upon to assist in an investigation but may have a conflict of interest with the company should be advised to obtain independent legal advice. The company may wish to fund the costs of that independent legal advice but directors will need to consider carefully whether that is in the best interests of the company and whether it is permissible within the limitations of the CA 2006.[33] The extent to which legal and professional costs of the investigation are covered under Directors and Officers ("D&O") liability insurance is also relevant (*see* below).

12.14.4   *Insurance*

If there is D&O insurance cover in place, consideration will need to be given to the terms of the policy and whether the insurers should be notified. Underwriters may wish to be involved and it is sensible to obtain their consent to the steps being taken and to inform them regularly of developments.

Similarly, in cases where there has been a substantial loss to the company as a result of, for example, a fraud, consideration will need to be given to notifying the company's insurers. It is usually prudent to do so at an early stage.

---

[33] Section 234 CA 2006 allows a company to indemnify a director against third-party claims provided the indemnity is a qualifying third-party indemnity with sub-section (3). This is a significant change from CA 1985 where under Section 310 a commitment in advance to indemnify legal costs was invalid unless it was contingent on a successful defence.

D&O policies in the past have tended to be unclear as to how far costs of legal advice in relation to regulatory investigations are covered and there is considerable variation between insurers in the policy wording that has been used. Where the potential legal costs are significant, insurers not infrequently seek to rely on policy interpretation to avoid covering those costs. Such arguments are open to challenge but this often means that costs must start being incurred with these issues unresolved, which can put directors and officers in a difficult position if they must be self-funding.[34]

12.14.5 Notification

The Disclosure and Transparency Rules require listed companies to notify a Regulatory Information Service as soon as possible of any information that is not public knowledge and which when disclosed would be likely to have a significant effect on the price of its listed securities. Listed companies will need to consider whether the matters that an inspector has been appointed to investigate are something that should be disclosed to the market or even whether the fact of the appointment itself should be announced. The latter will not be appropriate if the investigation itself is confidential but a listed company may need to seek guidance from the Listing Authority, particularly if there are rumours or press speculation.

The appointment of investigators may trigger an obligation to notify the company's regulator. For example, under Rule 15.3.15 of the FSA's Supervision Manual, a firm must notify the FSA immediately if it becomes aware that any statutory or regulatory authority, professional organisation or trade body has started an investigation into its affairs.

12.14.6 Preservation of evidence

At the outset, every possible step needs to be taken to secure and preserve all the evidence which could be relevant to the

---

[34] Also *see* note 33. Section 233 CA 2006 (replacing Section 310 CA 1985) allows a company to insure its directors against action by the company or third parties. The City of London Law Society, ICSA, the ABI and BIBA have issued guidance, which includes the risks that should be covered and a checklist of major issues that directors should consider.

investigation. This will entail identifying the key players and the documentation which they may have and where it might be. It will also be necessary to establish how far-reaching the problem is within the company.

All possible sources of evidence will need to be identified. Immediate steps may need to be taken to avoid evidence being inadvertently lost through a routine destruction policy or being recorded over or even deliberately tampered with.

12.14.6.1   Documents

Consideration will need to be given to what classes of documents (such as correspondence, notes, minutes, diaries, internal memoranda, audit documentation and e-mails) may have been created and which need to be preserved.

12.14.6.2   Telephones

Often telephone calls will have been taped, particularly in cases involving the securities industry. Tapes will need to be retrieved and transcribed. Telephone logs of calls made and received and voicemail messages sometimes provide useful evidence.

12.14.6.3   Computer records

Specialist IT assistance will be required to ensure that computer records (including e-mails) are not lost and that computers are effectively quarantined and the forensic integrity of the evidence is preserved. The overriding factor in the securing of computer evidence is time. The faster the relevant computers are taken out of use or their hard disks copied (imaged), the greater the chance of recovering usable evidence from them.

All these types of documentation will need to be collated and held in a single, secure place. Records will need to be kept of the source of each file or document and procedures may need to be introduced to ensure that accurate records are kept if files are removed from the central collation point. Ideally, if a document is required for use, a photocopy should be used.

12.14.7   Production of evidence

As stated above, investigators have wide powers to require the production of documents and to require witnesses to attend interviews. Information (whether documentary or oral) which falls within the scope of legal professional privilege is usually – but not always – privileged from production so it is necessary to consider carefully each request for information from the investigators to ensure that privileged information is not disclosed.

The law in this area is complex and, in places, uncertain. As a result, it is a very real reason why legal advice should be sought at the outset of the investigation.

A practice used by some authorities when exercising search warrants is for independent counsel to be appointed to review documents for which a claim is asserted. The practice was considered and approved by Moses J in *R. v Commissioners of Inland Revenue Ex parte Tamosius*.[35]

12.14.8   Witnesses

The investigators will usually also require witnesses to attend interviews. It will be necessary to consider whether an individual should obtain separate legal representation. If it appears that the interests of the individual may be at variance with those of the company, the individual should be advised to obtain separate legal representation.

12.14.9   Material gathered during the investigation

It is very important to monitor and control communications generated during the course of the investigation about the subject matter of the investigation. As much as possible of the work a company does in its own internal investigations and in gathering information to be provided to the inspectors should be prepared in such a way that it is covered by legal

---

[35] *The Independent*, 12 November 1999.

professional privilege. Such privileged materials should be segregated. Materials not covered by privilege will potentially be disclosable to the inspectors and "idle gossip" could potentially be very damaging.

It is also important to monitor the information which is passed to the investigators so that a full record is retained of the documents and information which has been handed to them. Consideration should also be given to seeking to agree with the investigators, to the extent possible, restrictions on the use which may be made of the material disclosed to them.

Chapter 13

Disqualification of Directors

David Allison and Stephen Robins

3–4 South Square

13.1   Introduction

The power of the court to make a disqualification order prohibiting a person from being concerned in the management of a company was first introduced by Section 75 Companies Act 1928 on the recommendation of the Greene Committee. The powers of the courts to make disqualification orders were extended incrementally over the years and are now contained in the Company Directors Disqualification Act 1986 ("CDDA"). The purpose of the statutory regime for the disqualification of directors has always been perceived as the two-fold objective of the protection of the public from future misconduct and the prevention of the misuse or abuse of the privilege of limited liability.[1] Although the majority of disqualification orders and undertakings relate to directors of insolvent companies, the fact that a company is solvent and profitable is no bar to disqualification, as it is the conduct of the director which determines whether disqualification is appropriate, not the success or otherwise of the company. Judicial decisions in disqualification proceedings are highly relevant to a proper understanding of the duties to which directors are subject and the standards of behaviour which the courts expect from them, and it should therefore come as no surprise that a book addressing the subject of directors' duties contains an analysis of this subject matter.

---

[1] *See*, e.g. *Re Atlantic Computers Plc* (unreported, 15 June 1998) per Timothy Lloyd J, as quoted in *Secretary of State* v *Sullman* [2008] EWHC (Ch) 3179, per Norris J, and the cases mentioned in note 16 below.

13.2 Grounds of disqualification by the courts

The CDDA provides the statutory basis for the commencement of disqualification proceedings. Section 1 CDDA prescribes the scope of the disqualification order which can be made by the court. The CDDA separates those sections which make provision for the basis for a disqualification order into three broad categories:

(a) general misconduct in connection with companies;[2]
(b) unfitness to act as a director of a company;[3] and
(c) other cases.[4]

13.2.1   The first category: general misconduct

Section 2 CDDA provides for disqualification where a person is convicted of an indictable offence "in connection with the promotion, formation, management, liquidation or striking off of a company, or with the receivership or management of a company's property". The court which convicts the person may make a disqualification order of its own motion.[5] In the event that the criminal court does not impose a period of disqualification, Section 16(2) CDDA provides that an application for a disqualification order may be made to a court having jurisdiction to wind up the company. The period of disqualification which the court may impose is dependent upon which court makes the order. Where the disqualification order is made by a court of summary jurisdiction, a period of up to five years may be imposed. In any other case a period of up to 15 years may be imposed.[6] The principles which the criminal courts apply when determining whether to make a disqualification order and the period of such order should be consistent with those applied by the civil courts.[7]

---

[2] Sections 2 to 5 CDDA.
[3] Sections 6 to 9 CDDA.
[4] Sections 9A, 10, 11 and 12 CDDA.
[5] *See*, e.g. *R.* v *Georgiou* [1988] 4 BCC 322; *R.* v *Goodman* [1993] 2 All ER 789; *R.* v *Myatt* [2004] EWCA Crim 206; *R.* v *Scragg* [2006] EWCA Crim 2916.
[6] Section 2(3) CDDA.
[7] *SOS* v *Tjolle* [1998] 1 BCLC 333 at 336e to g.

Section 3 CDDA provides for disqualification of up to five years where a person has been "persistently in default in relation to provisions of the companies legislation requiring any return, account or other document to be filed with, delivered or sent, or notice of any matter to be given, to the registrar of companies". Section 3(2) CDDA provides that the required persistent default can be conclusively proved if the director is found guilty of three or more defaults in any five-year period.

Section 4 CDDA provides that a disqualification order of up to 15 years may be made where in the course of the winding up of a company it appears that the director has been guilty of fraudulent trading under Section 993 Companies Act 2006[8] or any other fraud in relation to the company.[9] Disqualification orders may be made in respect of conduct in relation to a solvent company under this section. Where the company is insolvent, the proceedings will likely be brought under Section 6 CDDA.

Section 5 CDDA enables the court to make a disqualification order of up to five years where a person has been convicted of an offence due to "a contravention of, or failure to comply with, any provision of the companies legislation requiring a return, account or other document to be filed with, delivered or sent, or notice to be given, to the registrar of companies"[10] and during the five years preceding the conviction the person has had three or more default orders and offences within Section 5.[11]

13.2.2 *The second category: unfitness to act as a director*

Section 6 CDDA obliges the court to make a disqualification order if it is satisfied that the defendant's conduct as a director of a company which has become insolvent makes him unfit to be concerned in the management of a company.[12] Section 9

---

[8] Section 4(1) CDDA.
[9] Section 4(2) CDDA.
[10] Section 5(1) CDDA.
[11] Section 5(3) CDDA.
[12] Section 6(1) CDDA. Where the court is satisfied that unfitness has been established, disqualification is mandatory; the court has no discretion to decline to make an order. The introduction of mandatory disqualification gave effect to a recommendation of the Cork Committee in 1982.

CDDA sheds some light on the concept of "unfitness" by requiring the court to have regard specifically to the matters specified in Schedule 1 CDDA. This issue is considered below.

Section 7(1) CDDA provides that an application for a mandatory order under Section 6 can be made only if it appears to the Secretary of State that it is expedient in the public interest that such an order should be made. The Secretary of State is under a continuing duty to keep the position under review. Proceedings can be brought and continued only if it appears, and continues to appear, to the Secretary of State that it is expedient in the public interest that an order be made. An application for a mandatory order must be made by the Secretary of State or, if the Secretary of State so directs in a case where the person against whom the order is sought is or has been a director of a company which is being wound up by the court in England and Wales, by the Official Receiver. As originally enacted, this meant that, if the winding up had been completed and the company dissolved, the application could be made only by the Secretary of State. Accordingly the words "is being wound up" were amended by the Insolvency Act 2000 to read "is being or has been wound up".

Section 8 of the Act provides for the Secretary of State to make an application for a disqualification order if he believes it to be in the public interest to do so based on reports following, or documents obtained during, an investigation into the affairs of a company. The maximum period of disqualification which the court can impose under Section 8 is 15 years. There is no need for the company to have become insolvent for a disqualification order to be made under Section 8.

13.2.3   The third category: other cases

Section 9A, which was added by Section 204(2) Enterprise Act 2002 and came into force on 20 June 2003, obliges the court to make a disqualification order against a person provided that two conditions are satisfied in relation to him.

First, the company of which he is a director must be shown to have committed a breach of competition law. Section 9A(4) defines the phrase "breach of competition law" by reference to the Competition Act 1998 and Articles 81 and 82 EC Treaty establishing the European Community (Articles 101 and 102 Lisbon Treaty).

Secondly, the court must be satisfied that his conduct as a director makes him unfit to be concerned in the management of a company. For the purpose of Section 9A, the court is expressly forbidden from considering the matters mentioned in Schedule 1. Instead, the court is required to consider:

(a) whether the director's conduct contributed to the breach of competition law;
(b) whether the director had reasonable grounds to suspect that the conduct of the undertaking constituted the breach and he took no steps to prevent it; and
(c) whether the director did not know but ought to have known that the conduct of the undertaking constituted the breach.

The court is also permitted to have regard to the director's conduct as a director of a company in connection with any other breach of competition law. The maximum period of disqualification under Section 9A is 15 years. The Office of Fair Trading is permitted to apply for a disqualification order under Section 9A.

Section 10 CDDA provides that where a court has made an order under either Section 213 or Section 214 Insolvency Act 1986 ("IA 1986")[13] that a person is liable to contribute to the assets of a company, the court may, of its own motion, make a disqualification order of up to 15 years.

Section 11 CDDA makes it an offence for an undischarged bankrupt or a person subject to a bankruptcy restrictions order "to act as director of a company or directly or indirectly to take part in or be concerned in the promotion, formation or management of a company" without the permission of the court which adjudged him bankrupt.[14] The offence of acting as a company

---

[13] For fraudulent trading and wrongful trading respectively.
[14] Section 11(1) CDDA.

director while bankrupt or subject to a bankruptcy restrictions order is an offence of strict liability. Whether a defendant has been concerned in the promotion, formation or management of a company will be a question of fact for the jury and will not depend on the defendant's own view of his actions.[15]

This Chapter's limited examination of law of directors' disqualification will focus on the law and procedure applicable to applications for disqualification orders under Sections 6 and 8 CDDA on the grounds of unfitness.

13.3   The purpose of disqualification

The primary purpose of disqualification is the protection of the public.[16] Disqualification proceedings do not amount to a criminal charge.[17] The protection conferred upon the public by disqualification has two constituent elements:

(a) the prohibition imposed upon an unfit director from undertaking a position in the formation, promotion or management of a company without the permission of the court;[18] and
(b) the deterrent effect of disqualification, which is intended to raise the standards of conduct of company directors generally.[19]

13.4   Territorial limits of the CDDA

The CDDA has extra-territorial effect. Section 22(2)(b) CDDA 1986 provides that the word "company" includes any company which may be wound up under Part V IA 1986. By virtue of

---

[15] *R.* v *Doring* (2002) Crim LR 817.
[16] *See*, for example, *Re Blackspur Group Plc* [1998] 1 WLR 422 at 426; *Re Atlantic Computers Plc* (unreported 15 June 1998) per Timothy Lloyd J; *Shuttleworth* v *Secretary of State* [2000] BCC 204; *Re Pantmaenog Timber Co Ltd* [2004] 1 AC 158 at paragraph 74 and paragraphs 77 to 79; *Secretary of State* v *Sullman* [2008] EWHC (Ch) 3179 per Norris J.
[17] *R.* v *Secretary for State Ex parte McCormick* [1998] BCC 379.
[18] *Secretary of State* v *Bannister* [1996] 1 All ER 993.
[19] *Re Swift 736 Ltd* [1993] BCLC 896, at 899; *Re Grayan Building Services Ltd* [1995] Ch 241 at 253G; *Re Westmid Packaging Services Ltd* [1998] 2 BCLC 646 at 654; *Re Landhurst Leasing Plc* [1999] 1 BCLC 286 at 344d.

Sections 220 and 221 IA 1986, companies incorporated in foreign jurisdictions may be wound up by the English courts.

To wind up a foreign company, the court must be satisfied:

(a) that the company's centre of main interests is in England and Wales; or
(b) that the company has an establishment in England and Wales; or
(c) if the company's centre of main interests is outside the European Union, that there is:

  (i) a sufficient connection with the jurisdiction;
  (ii) a potential benefit to creditors; and
  (iii) at least one creditor subject to the jurisdiction.[20]

Pursuant to Section 6 CDDA, the court can make a disqualification order in respect of any person who is or has been a director of a foreign company that may be wound up under Part V IA 1986. Similarly, the prohibition in a disqualification order against acting as a director of a company extends to prohibit the disqualified person from undertaking directorships of any company that may be wound up under Part V IA 1986.

The court may grant permission to serve disqualification proceedings on defendants out of the jurisdiction.[21] There is nothing to prevent foreign nationals from being made the subject of disqualification proceedings. Extra-territoriality is necessary to ensure that the CDDA is effective in the context of cross-border transactions and communications. Electronic means of communication enable companies to be controlled across borders, and therefore Parliament must be presumed to have intended Section 6 CDDA to extend to foreigners who were out of the jurisdiction and to conduct which occurred out of the jurisdiction.[22] In exercising its discretion to order service out of the jurisdiction, the court will need to be satisfied that the claimant has a good arguable case against the defendant.

---

[20] *See* (where the company's centre of main interests is within the European Union) the EC Regulation on Insolvency Proceedings and (where the company's centre of main interests is outside the European Union) *Re Latreefers Ltd* [2001] BCC 174.
[21] Rule 5(2) Disqualification Rules and paragraph 7.3 of the Practice Direction.
[22] *Re Seagull Manufacturing Co Ltd (No 2)* [1994] 1 BCLC 273.

13.5   Procedure

The vast majority of applications for disqualification are brought under Section 7 CDDA for an order under Section 6 CDDA. Proceedings under Section 7 CDDA can be commenced by the Secretary of the State or, in circumstances where the company is being wound up by the court, by the Official Receiver at the Secretary of State's direction.[23] The application must be made to the court which is winding up the company or, if the company is not being wound up by the court (e.g. because it is in administration or because it is in creditors' voluntary liquidation), to the court which would have jurisdiction to wind it up (or, where the company has been dissolved under paragraph 84 of Schedule B1 IA 1986, to the court which would have jurisdiction to wind it up, had it not been dissolved).[24] Proceedings commenced in the wrong court are not invalid, and proceedings commenced in the wrong court may be retained in that court.[25]

13.5.1   The relevant procedural rules

The relevant procedural rules for an application for a disqualification order will be determined by the section under which the application for disqualification is made. The sources of the procedural rules for disqualification proceedings are the Practice Direction on Directors' Disqualification Proceedings (the "Practice Direction"), the Insolvent Companies (Disqualification of Unfit Directors) Proceedings Rules 1987[26] (as amended) (the "Disqualification Rules") and the Civil Procedure Rules ("CPR"). The procedure for disqualification proceedings for orders under Sections 6 and 8 CDDA is provided for by both the Disqualification Rules and the Practice Direction.[27] The Disqualification Rules apply the provisions of the CPR to proceedings, except where the provisions of the Disqualification Rules are inconsistent with the CPR,[28] and the application of the

---

[23] Section 7(2) CDDA.
[24] Section 6(1) CDDA and *Secretary of State* v *Arnold* [2007] EWHC 1933 (Ch).
[25] Section 3B CDDA, *see* also *Secretary of State* v *Shakespeare* [2005] 2 BCLC 471.
[26] SI 1987/2023.
[27] Paragraph 1.3(1)(d)(e) of the Practice Direction.
[28] Rule 2(1) Disqualification Rules; CPR 2.1(2).

CPR is also subject to the application of the appeal and review procedure under Rules 7.47 and 7.49 IA 1986.[29]

13.5.2 Pre-action prima facie case recommendations to the Secretary of State under Section 7(3) CDDA

In cases where the company is insolvent, it is the office-holder who is likely to discover grounds capable of supporting a finding of unfitness. He is the person who will discover the information which the Secretary of State will need to consider when determining whether to commence disqualification proceedings. Section 7(3) CDDA requires the office-holder[30] of an insolvent company who is of the opinion that a director, past or present, of the company is unfit to act as such, to report his view to the Secretary of State.[31] The Court of Appeal has held that, in proceedings under the CDDA, there is an implied exception to the strict rules of hearsay evidence and opinion evidence and that reports obtained by the Secretary of State pursuant to his statutory powers are admissible in evidence in proceedings under the CDDA.[32]

Section 7(3) CDDA is supplemented by Section 7(4) CDDA which enables both the Secretary of State and the Official Receiver, where he is not the office-holder, to require the office-holder to provide such information or documents as the Secretary of State reasonably requires to determine whether to bring proceedings for a disqualification order. The Secretary of State has no absolute right to production of the documents. The court exercises its discretion when determining whether

---

[29] Rule 2.4 Disqualification Rules.

[30] The office-holder will be the official receiver in relation to all companies being wound up by the court. The obligation remains on the official receiver even when his appointment as liquidator is superseded by the appointment of another liquidator. The office-holder will be the liquidator in creditors' voluntary liquidations. In administration and administrative receivership, the office-holder will be the administrator and the administrative receiver respectively.

[31] The reporting obligation placed upon office-holders is governed by the Insolvent Companies (Reports on Conduct of Directors) Rules 1996. These rules also require the office-holder to provide returns detailing the identities of all directors and shadow directors.

[32] *Secretary of State* v *Aaron* [2008] EWCA Civ 1146. *See* also *Re Travel & Holiday Club* [1967] 1 WLR 711; *Re Armvent* [1975] 1 WLR 1679; *Re St Piran Ltd* [1981] 1 WLR 1300; *Re Rex Williams Leisure Plc* [1994] Ch 1; *Secretary of State* v *Ashcroft* [1998] Ch 71 and *Secretary of State* v *Stojevic* [2007] EWHC 1186 (Ch).

to order the office-holder to comply with the request of the Secretary of State.[33]

The purposes of liquidation, administration and administrative receivership include obtaining information on the conduct of the affairs of the company and of those responsible for it during its trading history, with the consequence that the duty to report such information to the Secretary of State under Section 7(3) should be readily complied with. The authorities provide some useful guidance:

(a) In *Re Polly Peck International Plc*,[34] interviews of officers of the company had been conducted under Section 236 IA 1986 on the basis that the joint administrators had assured the interviewees that the information would only be used for the purposes of the administration. It was held that disclosure of the transcripts of the interviews to the Secretary of State would be in accordance with the undertaking, as it would be in furtherance of the purposes of the administration.

(b) In *Re Westminster Property Management Ltd*,[35] it was held that the use of statements obtained under Section 235 IA 1986 in disqualification proceedings did not necessarily involve a breach of Article 6 European Convention on Human Rights ("ECHR").

(c) In *Re Pantmaenog Timber Co Ltd*,[36] the House of Lords held that the court may make an order under Section 236 IA 1986 requiring third parties to disclose documents and provide information to the Official Receiver where the Official Receiver's sole purpose is to obtain evidence for use in the disqualification proceedings.

(d) A report compiled by the office-holder will not be subject to legal professional privilege. Therefore the court can order disclosure of the report to a defendant to disqualification proceedings.[37] In contrast, the working papers of the office-holder or inspector will not be admissible or disclosable.[38]

---

[33] *Re Lombard Shipping and Forwarding Ltd* [1993] BCLC 238 at 245.
[34] [1994] BCC 15.
[35] [2001] BCC 121.
[36] [2004] 1 AC 158.
[37] In *Re Barings Plc* [1998] Ch 356, Scott V-C held that disclosure of the report was necessary in the interests of fairness and to save costs.
[38] *Re Astra Holdings Plc* [1998] 2 BCLC 44.

The Secretary of State is entitled to use information which has come into his possession by means other than the report of the office-holder when determining whether an application for a disqualification order should be made. The Secretary of State will form his own view on the relevant report and is under no obligation to act in accordance with the opinion of the office-holder. The Secretary of State will commence proceedings where he believes that it is in the public interest to do so. The decision of the Secretary of State to commence proceedings is one which, in theory at least, is susceptible to judicial review, but the prospects of succeeding in such an application are likely to be very low.[39]

13.5.3 *Procedure on an application for a disqualification order*

Section 16(1) CDDA provides that "a person intending to apply for the making of a disqualification order by the court having jurisdiction to wind up a company shall give not less than 10 days' notice of his intention to the person against whom the order is sought".[40]

In previous cases, the courts have had to consider whether this provision is intended to be mandatory or directory. In the event that it were held to be mandatory, the failure to comply with the 10-day notice period would render the proceedings a nullity, whereas the failure to comply with a directory provision would merely constitute a procedural irregularity which the court has a discretion to excuse. In *Re Cedac Ltd*,[41] the Court of Appeal held that failure to give notice was a procedural irregularity and therefore did not render the proceedings a nullity.

The notice does not need to contain any indication of the grounds upon which a disqualification order will be sought; it needs only to state the intention to make an application for a

---

[39] As displayed by the decision in *Secretary of State* v *Davies (No 2)* [1997] 2 BCLC 317.

[40] The period of 10 days is calculated excluding both the date on which the notice is given and the date on which the proceedings are issued. This provision is only applicable to those cases where the application is made to the court with jurisdiction to wind up a company and is not applicable where the court is empowered of its own motion to make a disqualification order or where the application is before a court which does not have jurisdiction to wind up a company: *Re Cedac* [1991] Ch 402.

[41] [1991] Ch 402.

disqualification order.[42] In fact, the notice is unlikely to be of any practical use to the director unless he can show that it is a case of mistaken identity. The respondent should attempt to use this period to obtain legal representation.

Applications for disqualification orders are to be made by the issue of a claim form and the use of Part 8 CPR.[43] All disqualification proceedings are to be allocated to the multi-track.[44]

Upon issuing the claim form, the claimant will be given a date for the first hearing, such date to be at least eight weeks after the date of issue.[45] At the time of issuing the claim form, the claimant shall file his evidence in support of the application.

There is an obligation on the claimant to set out in the affirmation in support the main parts of the evidence on which he intends to rely, which is all the more important where there are no particulars of claim to identify the key facts upon which the court will be asked to exercise its powers. Fairness to the respondent demands that he be informed not only of the allegations of unfitness but also the essential facts which are to be relied on in support of them. The more serious the allegations made against the director, the more important it is for the case against him to be set out clearly and with adequate particularity. That applies in all cases where serious wrongdoing is alleged, particularly where it is asserted that the director knew his acts were wrongful or improper.[46]

It is for the claimant to effect service of the claim form, and the affidavit evidence upon which he relies,[47] which shall be accompanied by an acknowledgment of service. Service of the claim

---

[42] *Re Surrey Leisure* [1999] 1 BCLC 731.
[43] Paragraph 4.2 of the Practice Direction; Rule 2(2) Disqualification Rules. Part 8 CPR is to apply to disqualification applications, subject to the provisions of the Practice Direction and the Disqualification Rules.
[44] Paragraph 2 of the Practice Direction. Accordingly the rules relating to allocation questionnaires and track allocation do not apply.
[45] Paragraph 4.3 of the Practice Direction.
[46] *Secretary of State* v *Swan* [2003] EWHC 1780 (Ch).
[47] All evidence in disqualification proceedings is to be by affidavit, subject to the exception that when the official receiver is a party, his/her evidence may be in the form of a written report.

form by first class post shall be deemed to be effective on the seventh day after posting, unless the contrary is shown.[48]

Upon receipt of the claim form, the defendant should ensure that he files and serves the acknowledgment of service form within 14 days after service of the claim form. This acknowledgment of service form shall state whether:

(a)   he contests the application on the grounds that he was not a director or shadow director of a named company at the time of the conduct which forms the basis of the application, or that he disputes that his conduct was as alleged by the claimant;

(b)   in the case of any conduct which he admits, he disputes that such conduct renders him unfit; and

(c)   while not intending to defend the application for his disqualification, he intends to adduce mitigating factors with a view to reducing the period of disqualification which is to be imposed.[49]

Where a defendant fails to file and serve an acknowledgment of service form within the prescribed period, he is entitled to attend the hearing of the application, but is not entitled to take part in the proceedings unless the court gives him permission to do so.[50] Within 28 days of service of the claim form upon him, the defendant must file and serve any evidence in opposition to the application upon which he wishes to rely. In the event that the claimant wishes to put in evidence in reply, such evidence must be filed and served within 14 days after receiving the defendant's evidence. At all times before the first hearing of the application, it is open to the parties to extend the time for service of evidence by written agreement.[51]

At the first hearing of the application, the registrar (or district judge in a county court) will either determine the case or give directions and adjourn the application. It is advisable to seek

---

[48]   Rule 5(1) Disqualification Rules; paragraph 7.2 of the Practice Direction.
[49]   Rule 5(4) Disqualification Rules; paragraph 8.2 of the Practice Direction.
[50]   Paragraph 8.4 of the Practice Direction.
[51]   Paragraph 9.7 of the Practice Direction.

all necessary directions at this first hearing, as it is intended that disqualification applications should be determined at the earliest possible date. Furthermore, it will be in the defendant's interests to do so in order to minimise the costs of the proceedings.

On applications under Sections 7 or 8 CDDA, the court may hear and determine the application summarily on the first hearing of the application, without further notice to the defendant. In the event that this approach is taken by the court, the maximum period of disqualification which may be imposed by the court is five years. In circumstances where the court is of the view that a period in excess of five years would be appropriate, it will adjourn the application to be heard at a later date that will be notified to the defendant.[52] The registrar will also take the course of adjourning the application where he is of the view that there are questions of law or fact which are not appropriate for summary determination.[53] Where the registrar adjourns the application, he will direct whether the application is to be heard by a registrar or a judge, and give any further directions for the case management of the application.[54] In contested applications, such directions are likely to include fixing of a pre-trial review of the case after the close of evidence.

13.5.4 Applications under Section 7(2) CDDA to commence proceedings for an order under Section 6 CDDA out of time

Pursuant to paragraph 17 of the Practice Direction, an application for permission to bring Section 6 proceedings out of time is made by Application Notice under Part 23 CPR to the court that would ordinarily have jurisdiction had the proceedings been issued in time. Applications under Section 7 CDDA should be brought within two years after the company became "insolvent" within the meaning ascribed to the term by Section 6(2)

---

[52] Rule 7(4)(a) Disqualification Rules; paragraphs 6.1(4) and 10.5 of the Practice Direction.
[53] Rule 7(4)(b) Disqualification Rules; paragraph 10.5(2).
[54] Rule 7(5) Disqualification Rules; paragraph 11 of the Practice Direction. In *Lewis* v *Secretary of State* [2001] 2 BCLC 597, the court established guidelines for the factors to be taken into account when considering whether a disqualification application should be tried before a registrar or a judge.

CDDA.[55] When the application is made outside this period, the permission of the court is needed. The application for permission should be made to the court which would have jurisdiction over the disqualification proceedings under Section 6(3) CDDA if permission were to be given and the proposed respondent must be made a party. The Secretary of State will bear the burden of showing a good reason for the extension of the period. When permission is not obtained prior to the issue of a claim form outside this time limit, the defendant will be entitled to have the proceedings struck out, as the permission must be obtained prospectively, rather than retrospectively.

The case law reveals that the imposition of a two-year period for the issue of proceedings by Section 7(2) CDDA has two main objectives:

(a) to enable those who have been directors of insolvent companies the ability to organise their affairs once the two-year period has passed free of the risk of future disqualification; and

(b) to protect the public interest, as it is obviously wrong that a person whom the Secretary of State considers to be unfit to act as a director should be left free to act as one any longer than is necessary.[56]

Factors which the court will take into account when considering an application to commence proceedings out of time[57] include the length of the delay,[58] the reasons for the delay,[59] the prejudice

---

[55] Where more than one event of insolvency occurs, the two-year period begins to run from the time of the first event: *Re Tasbian* [1989] BCLC 720. The case law supports the proposition that the day on which the company became insolvent within Section 6(2) is to be included when calculating the relevant period of two years. There is no time limit in relation to applications for orders under Sections 2 to 5, 8 and 10. For the purposes of the CDDA, proceedings to disqualify company directors are "brought" on the day when the request and claim form are received by the court office, rather than on the date that the form was issued by the court: *Secretary of State v Vohora* [2007] EWHC 2656 (Ch).

[56] *Re Blackspur Group Plc (No 2)* [1998] 1 WLR 422; *Re Noble Trees Ltd* [1993] BCLC 1185 at 1190; *Re Polly Peck International Plc (No 2)* [1994] 1 BCLC 574 at 590.

[57] *Re Probe Data Systems Ltd (No 3)* [1992] BCLC 405, at 416.

[58] *Re Manlon Trading* [1995] 4 All ER 14 at 23: the public interest in the disqualification of unfit directors does not diminish with the passage of time, but it must be balanced against the right of the director to carry on without the threat of disqualification proceedings for an unreasonable period.

[59] *Re Copecrest Ltd* [1994] 2 BCLC 284: permission was given where the delay was attributable to the conduct of the directors. Where the delay is not due to the conduct of the director, the reasons for such delay should be explained by the Secretary of State.

caused to the director by the delay[60] and the strength and seriousness of the case against the director (the public protection factor).[61] These factors, although important, are not exhaustive, and all relevant factors will be taken into account. The court will then carry out a balancing exercise to determine whether the grant of permission is appropriate on the facts of the case, and in doing so its discretion is unfettered.[62]

Article 6(1) ECHR incorporated into English law by the Human Rights Act 1998 provides the right to a fair trial within a reasonable time.

The rationale for the reasonable time requirement is that defendants should not be subjected to "prolonged uncertainty and anxiety in learning whether their opponents' claims will be established or not".[63] The relevant question is whether having regard to all the circumstances of the case, the time taken to determine the person's rights and obligations was unreasonable.[64] The relevant period will begin at the earliest time at which a person is officially alerted to the likelihood of proceedings against him. Where a delay between the official notification of the likelihood of proceedings and the hearing of the matter is such that the hearing is likely to be unfair, the court or tribunal should dismiss the proceedings.[65]

These principles have been applied in disqualification cases. In *Davies v United Kingdom*,[66] for example, the European Court of Human Rights ("ECtHR") held that the state was responsible for the greater part of the five and a half years it took to dispose of

---

[60] *Re Polly Peck International Plc (No 2)* [1994] 1 BCLC 574: illness of the director may, on suitable facts, be taken to represent so serious a prejudice as to bar an extension. The prejudice caused by disqualification proceedings on the director's livelihood may be taken into account. The weakening of the director's evidence with the passage of time may also be taken into account as a form of prejudice.

[61] *Re Stormont Ltd* [1997] 1 BCLC 437; *Re Packaging Direct Ltd* [1994] BCC 213.

[62] The unfettered nature of the discretion is illustrated by *Re Stormont Ltd* [1997] 1 BCLC 437, in which the court held that it would be appropriate to give permission in relation to the claim against one of the directors but exercised its discretion to stay the proceedings on the basis of undertakings offered by the director.

[63] *Attorney-General's Reference (No 2 of 2001)* [2004] 2 AC 72 at 85.

[64] *Porter v Magill* [2002] 2 AC 357 at 496.

[65] *Attorney General's Reference (No 2 of 2001)* [2004] 2 AC 72 at 89.

[66] [2006] 2 BCLC 351.

the proceedings. In all the circumstances the proceedings had not been pursued with the diligence required by Article 6 and the failure to determine the applicant's "civil rights and obligations" within "a reasonable time" amounted to a violation of Article 6.

In *Eastaway* v *United Kingdom*,[67] the disqualification proceedings against the applicant lasted almost nine years. The applicant himself was largely responsible for the last period of some three and a half years because of his unmeritorious application for judicial review to the High Court and appeals to the Court of Appeal and House of Lords. However, the ECtHR held that the state authorities were responsible for a substantial part of the delay prior to that period. Applying the principles that the reasonableness of the length of proceedings was to be assessed in the light of the circumstances of the case and that special diligence was called for in bringing disqualification proceedings to an end expeditiously because of the considerable impact which they had on a company director's reputation and ability to practise his profession, the ECtHR held that the proceedings against the applicant had not been pursued with the diligence required by Article 6 and that the failure to determine the applicant's "civil rights and obligations" within "a reasonable time" amounted to a violation of Article 6.[68]

13.6 Determining unfitness

Three factors must be present for the court to make an order under Section 6: (a) the defendant must have been a director of the company; (b) the company must have become "insolvent"; and (c) the defendant's conduct as a director of that company must be shown to have been such as to make him unfit to be concerned in the management of a company.

13.6.1 Who is a director?

The reach of the CDDA extends to apply to:

---

[67] [2006] 2 BCLC 361.
[68] *See*, by way of comparison, *Re Blackspur Group Ltd* [2001] 1 BCLC 653, in which it was held that there had been no breach of the defendant's right to a hearing "within a reasonable time" even though proceedings against him under Section 6 CDDA had been on foot for over eight years.

(a) directors properly appointed in accordance with the articles of association of the company;
(b) shadow directors as defined in Section 22(5) CDDA; and
(c) *de facto* directors.

The first category is straightforward and requires no comment; the second and third categories have proved more difficult in their application.

13.6.1.1 Shadow directors

The statutory definition in Section 22(5) CDDA provides that a shadow director is someone on whose directions and instructions the company's board is accustomed to act. But a person is not deemed a shadow director by reason only that the directors act on advice given by him in a professional capacity. The meaning of the definition of shadow director was considered by the Court of Appeal in *Secretary of State* v *Deverell*,[69] in which Morritt LJ summarised the law in a number of propositions as follows:

(a) The definition of a shadow director is to be construed in the normal way to give effect to the parliamentary intention ascertainable from the mischief to be dealt with and the words used. In particular, as the purpose of the CDDA is the protection of the public and as the definition is used in other legislative contexts, it should not be strictly construed merely because it also has quasi-penal consequences in the context of the CDDA.
(b) The purpose of the disqualification legislation is to identify those, other than professional advisers, with real influence in the corporate affairs of the company. But it is not necessary that such influence should be exercised over the whole field of its corporate activities.
(c) Whether any particular communication from the alleged shadow director, whether by words or conduct, is to be classified as a direction or instruction must be objectively ascertained by the court in the light of all the evidence. In that connection it is not necessary to prove the

---

[69] [2000] 2 All ER 365. *See* also *Secretary of State* v *Aviss* [2007] 1 BCLC 618.

understanding or expectation of either giver or receiver. In many, if not most, cases it will suffice to prove the communication and its consequence. Evidence of such understanding or expectation may be relevant but it cannot be conclusive. Certainly the label attached by either or both parties then or thereafter cannot be more than a factor in considering whether the communication came within the statutory description of direction or instruction.

(d) Non-professional advice may come within that statutory description. The proviso excepting advice given in a professional capacity appears to assume that advice generally is or may be included. Moreover the concepts of "direction" and "instruction" do not exclude the concept of "advice" for all three share the common feature of "guidance".

(e) It will, no doubt, be sufficient to show that in the face of "directions or instructions" from the alleged shadow director the properly appointed directors or some of them cast themselves in a subservient role or surrendered their respective discretions. But it is not necessary to do so in all cases. Such a requirement would be to put a gloss on the statutory requirement that the board are "accustomed to act" "in accordance with" such directions or instructions.

(f) If the directors usually took the advice of the putative shadow director, it is irrelevant that on the occasions when he did not give advice the board did exercise its own discretion.

(g) If the board were accustomed to act on the directions or instructions of the putative shadow director it is not necessary to demonstrate that their action was mechanical rather than considered.

13.6.1.2   *De facto directors*

Section 22(4) CDDA provides that the definition of the word "director" includes "any person occupying the position of director". This makes clear that the jurisdiction to make a disqualification order extends to a person occupying the position of a director, by whatever name called.

Persons who undertake the functions of directors, even though not formally appointed as such, are called *de facto* directors or directors in fact. But the authorities are not entirely consistent in defining a *de facto* director. The critical issue, and the jurisprudential difficulty, is to distinguish a *de facto* director from someone who acts for, or otherwise in the interests of, a company but is never more than, for example, a mere agent, employee or adviser.

The correct approach is for the court to ask whether the individual in question assumed the status and functions of a company director so as to make himself responsible as if he were a *de jure* director, i.e. whether he was part of the corporate governing structure.[70]

13.6.1.3   Mutually exclusive concepts?

Formerly, it had been suggested that the two concepts of *de facto* director and shadow director were mutually exclusive. But it has now been held that there is no conceptual difficulty in concluding that a person can be both a shadow director and a *de facto* director simultaneously. He may, for example, assume the functions of a director as regards one part of the company's activities (say, marketing) and give directions to the board as regards another (say, manufacturing and finance).[71]

13.6.2   When does a company become insolvent?

A company becomes "insolvent" for the purposes of Section 7 CDDA on the happening of any of the events mentioned in Section 6(2) CDDA, namely:

(a) the company goes into liquidation at a time when its assets are insufficient for the payment of its debts and other liabilities and the expenses of the winding up;
(b) the company enters administration; or
(c) an administrative receiver of the company is appointed.

The event of insolvency may occur "whether while he was a director or subsequently": Section 6(1)(a) CDDA. For

---

[70] *Re Kaytech International Plc* [1999] BCC at 390. *See* also *Secretary of State* v *Hollier* [2007] BCC 11 and *Secretary of State* v *Hall* [2009] BCC 190.
[71] *Re Mea Corp Ltd* [2006] EWHC 1846 (Ch) at paragraph 89.

the purposes of determining whether a liquidation was insolvent:

(a) the assets and liabilities should be valued as at the date of liquidation, and not according to what is subsequently realised;

(b) interest accruing on debts after the liquidation and statutory interest under Section 189 IA 1986 is not to be taken into account; and

(c) the "expenses of the winding up" must be construed as if the word "reasonable" were included immediately before the phrase.[72]

It will not be open to the director to challenge the validity of the insolvency proceedings, by reason of which the company is deemed to be insolvent, within the disqualification proceedings. The validity of the insolvency proceedings must be determined in other proceedings, pending the outcome of which the disqualification proceedings may be adjourned or stayed.[73]

13.6.3   What is "unfitness"?

In *Re Sevenoaks Stationers Ltd*,[74] Dillon LJ said that the words contained in Section 6 CDDA "are ordinary words of the English language and they should be simple to apply in most cases. It is important to hold to those words in each case . . . [T]he true question to be tried is a question of fact-what used to be pejoratively described in the Chancery division as a jury question". As Hoffmann LJ put it in *Re Grayan Ltd*,[75] the court must decide whether the conduct in question, "viewed cumulatively and taking into account any extenuating circumstances, has fallen below the standards of probity and competence appropriate for persons fit to be directors of companies".

Section 9 and Schedule 1 CDDA provide a non-exhaustive list of guidance on the matters that the court may "have regard

---

[72] *Re Gower Enterprises Ltd* [1995] BCC 293.
[73] *Secretary of State v Jabble* [1998] 1 BCLC 598, at 601.
[74] [1991] Ch 164 at 176 B to G
[75] [1995] Ch 241 at 253E

in particular"[76] when assessing whether a respondent is unfit.[77] The matters listed in Schedule 1 CDDA to which the court may have regard in particular include any breach of fiduciary duty, misapplication of the company's assets, failure to comply with the obligations in the Companies Act 2006 in relation to keeping proper records, extent of responsibility for the insolvency of the company, extent of responsibility for the company entering into transactions liable to be set aside as preferences or transactions at an undervalue[78] and a failure to comply with the obligations placed on a director by the IA 1986. However, it is clear that the provisions of Section 9 and Schedule 1 CDDA are not exhaustive and the court can consider any misconduct of the director in deciding whether he is unfit.[79]

In each case it will be a question of fact for the court whether the conduct amounts to unfitness. Jonathan Parker J summarised the position in *Re Barings Plc (No 5):*[80]

> "In considering the question of unfitness, the respondent's conduct must be evaluated in context – 'taken in its setting' . . . It follows . . . that the court will assess the competence or otherwise of the respondent in the context of and by reference to the role in the management of the company which was in fact assigned to him or which he in fact assumed, and by reference to his duties and responsibilities in that role. Thus the existence and extent of any particular duty will depend upon how the particular business is organised and upon what part in the management of that business the respondent could reasonably be expected play (*see Bishopsgate Investment Management Ltd (in liq.)* v *Maxwell*

---

[76] Section 9(1) CDDA. These words and the phrase "conduct in relation to any matter connected with or arising out of the insolvency of that company" in Section 6(2) CDDA, show that the court may take any misconduct into account: *Re Landhurst Leasing Plc* [1999] 1 BCLC 286.

[77] Only the factors listed in Part I of Schedule 1 will be relevant on an application for a disqualification order under Section 8 CDDA. On an application for an order under Section 6 CDDA both Part I and Part II of Schedule 1 will be applicable. Schedule 1 will not be applicable in applications under Section 9A.

[78] Sections 238 to 240 IA 1986.

[79] *See,* for example, the observations of Neuberger J in *Re Amaron Ltd, Secretary of State* v *Lubrani (No 2)* [2001] 1 BCLC 562 at 568.

[80] 1999] 1 BCLC 433 at 483g and 484c to g

(*No 2*) [1993] BCLC 1282 at 1285 per Hoffmann LJ) . . . Thus while the requisite standard of competence does not vary according to the nature of the company's business or to the respondent's role in the management of that business – and in that sense it may be said that there is a 'universal standard' – that standard must be applied to the facts of each particular case. Hence to say that the Act envisages a 'universal' standard of competence applicable in all circumstances takes the matter little further since it says nothing about whether the requisite standard has been met in any particular case. What can be said is that the court, whilst taking full account of the demands made upon a respondent by his management role, will recognise incompetence in whatever circumstances and at whatever level of management it occurs, from the chairman of the board down to the most junior director."

Although the determination of whether a director's conduct was such to render him unfit will always be a question of fact, an analysis of the case law discloses the following guidelines:

(a) Misconduct by the director which has the consequence of conferring a benefit upon him personally to the detriment of the company is likely to lead to a finding of unfitness. An obvious example is where a director causes a company to enter into a transaction which constitutes a preference within Section 239 IA 1986 or a transaction at an undervalue within Section 238 IA 1986, the beneficiary of which is the director. In *Re Funtime*,[81] for example, a company director who knowingly entered transactions that were improper preferences in favour of himself and his associates was declared to be unfit to be a director.

(b) Criteria of competence, discipline in complying with the duties regarding records, accounts and returns, and honesty are highly relevant in assessing fitness or unfitness. However, the question for the court is the much broader issue of applying to the facts of the case the standard of conduct laid down by the courts appropriate to a

---

[81] [2000] 1 BCLC 247.

person fit to be a director, that being a question of mixed law and fact. In particular, unfitness by reason of incompetence may be established without proof of a breach of duty. On the other hand, although dishonesty is not the acid test, the court must be very careful before holding that a director is unfit because of conduct that does not amount to a breach of any duty (whether contractual, tortious, statutory or equitable) to anyone, and is not dishonest.[82]

(c) The companies legislation does not impose on directors a statutory duty to ensure that their company does not trade while insolvent; nor does the legislation impose an obligation to ensure that the company does not trade at a loss. Directors may properly take the view that it is in the interests of the company and of its creditors that, although insolvent, the company should continue to trade out of its difficulties. They may properly take the view that it is in the interests of the company and its creditors that some loss-making trade should be accepted in anticipation of future profitability.[83] If, with hindsight, it is clear that this decision was the wrong one, it does not follow automatically that the directors should be disqualified. The evaluation of risk is to some extent a subjective matter[84] ordinary commercial misjudgment is not in itself sufficient to justify disqualification.[85]

(d) However, causing a company to trade, first, while it is insolvent and, secondly, without a reasonable prospect of meeting creditors' claims is likely to constitute incompetence of sufficient seriousness to grant a disqualification order. But it is important to emphasise that it would usually be necessary for both elements of that test to be satisfied. In general, it is not enough for the company to have been insolvent and for the director to have known it. It must also be shown that he knew or ought to have known that there was no reasonable prospect of meeting creditors' claims.[86]

---

[82] *Secretary of State* v *Goldberg* [2004] 1 BCLC 597.
[83] *Secretary of State* v *Gash* [1997] 1 BCLC 341.
[84] *Secretary of State* v *Aaron* [2009] EWHC 3263 (Ch) at paragraph 39.
[85] *Re Lo-Line Electric Motors Ltd* [1988] Ch 477 at 486 per Sir Nicolas Browne-Wilkinson V-C.
[86] *Secretary of State* v *Creegan* [2001] EWCA Civ 1742, [2002] 1 BCLC 99 at 101. *See also Re Uno Plc* [2004] EWHC 933 (Ch).

(e) Non-payment of Crown debts is no more serious than a failure to pay other creditors and it cannot be treated as automatic grounds for disqualification. However, in some cases it might be evidence of a policy of unfair discrimination between creditors which would merit disqualification.[87]

(f) A history of repeated failure, whether ignorant or intentional, to comply with the statutory obligations to prepare and file financial statements, annual returns and other statutory documents will usually lead to a finding of unfitness.[88] The principal reason behind the attitude of the court to this type of misconduct is that compliance with the statutory provisions should enable the company to detect and address financial difficulties at an early juncture. The failure to detect such matters at an early stage is likely to have the consequence of increasing losses sustained by creditors.

(g) Directors should be careful before seeking to transfer the assets and goodwill of an ailing company to a new company prior to the ailing company entering into a formal insolvency procedure. Apart from the personal liabilities which can arise out of such facts, it is very likely that the director will be found to be unfit, particularly if the transferee company subsequently becomes insolvent.[89]

(h) A director of a company which becomes insolvent is obliged, under the IA 1986, to cooperate with and give assistance to the office-holder appointed over the insolvent company's affairs. This cooperation is essential for the office-holder to be able to identify and recover the company's assets. A repeated failure on the part of a former director to comply with his duty to cooperate is likely to result in a finding of unfitness.[90]

It is no answer for a defendant in disqualification proceedings to assert that he had little or no involvement in the company's

---

[87] *Re Sevenoaks Stationers (Retail) Ltd* [1991] BCLC 325; *Verby Print for Advertising Ltd, Fine* v *Secretary of State* [1998] 2 BCLC 23 at 39; *Official Receiver* v *Dhaliwall* [2006] 1 BCLC 285; *Official Receiver* v *Key* [2009] BCC 11.

[88] *Re Swift 736 Ltd* [1993] BCLC 896; *Re Promwalk Services Ltd, Frewen* v *Secretary of State* [2003] 2 BCLC 305; *Re NCG Trading Ltd* [2004] EWHC 3203 (Ch).

[89] *Re Keypak Homecare Ltd (No 2)* [1990] BCLC 440; *Secretary of State* v *Walker* [2003] 1 BCLC 363.

[90] *Secretary of State* v *McTighe (No 2)* [1996] 2 BCLC 477.

business and no real knowledge of its affairs. A director is under a continuing duty to keep himself fully informed about the company's affairs, and this duty will not be satisfied where the director maintains only a negligible actual involvement in the affairs of the company.[91] As long as an individual continues to hold office as a director, he is under a duty to inform himself as to the financial affairs of the company and to play an appropriate role in the management of its business. In the event that a director is not prepared to discharge these responsibilities properly, the appropriate course is for him to resign his directorship.[92] There are several cases where a director has, in effect, been disqualified on grounds of complete non-participation, and the courts have made clear repeatedly that a lack of knowledge (or alleged lack of knowledge) will not prevent a finding of unfitness.[93]

A non-executive director will also be under an obligation to inform himself of the affairs of the company, and to read and understand the company's accounts, and inquire as to any difficulties.[94] This approach is necessary to ensure that the practice of appointing respected city figures as directors to improve investor confidence has appropriate safeguards.

Under Schedule 1 CDDA, the court is required to consider the relative responsibility of the respondent for the defaults of the company. In practice, this will involve both the consideration of each director's involvement in the particular acts relied upon to establish unfitness, and an investigation of the division of work within the company, and the experience and particular expertise of each board member.

The fact that a director has professional advisers who fail to draw attention to the impropriety of transactions might negate a finding of unfitness or be a mitigating factor in the period of

---

[91] *Re Wimbledon Village Restaurant Ltd* [1994] BCC 753; *Secretary of State* v *Thornbury* [2008] 1 BCLC 139; *Secretary of State* v *Hall* [2009] BCC 190.

[92] *Re Galeforce Pleating Co Ltd* [1999] 2 BCLC 686.

[93] *Re Barings Plc* [1999] 1 BCLC 433; *Re Park House Properties Ltd* [1997] 2 BCLC 530; *Re Burnham Marketing Ltd* [1993] BCC 518 at 526 to 528; *Secretary of State* v *Thornbury* [2008] 1 BCLC 139; *Official Receiver* v *Key* [2009] BCC 11.

[94] *Re Continental Assurance Co of London Plc* [1997] 1 BCLC 48.

disqualification to be imposed. However, any reliance on such advice must be reasonable.[95]

The delegation of certain functions is a necessary element of the affairs of most companies, and directors are clearly entitled to order the company's affairs in this manner. While this is a perfectly reasonable act, the mere act of delegation will not absolve a director from any responsibility for that particular part of the business. When delegating the functions a director will be entitled to trust the competence and integrity of the person to a reasonable extent, in the absence of any facts putting him on inquiry, but he and the other members of the board of directors, will remain responsible for supervising the conduct of the person in fulfilling the delegated duties.[96] The extent of supervision which is necessary will be dependent on the facts of the particular case, and it is likely to be a different standard for executive and non-executive directors.

There are certain duties, however, which cannot be delegated to others. For example, statutory duties such as maintaining proper financial statements, and fiduciary duties cannot be delegated to others. Furthermore, all directors, including non-executive directors need to keep themselves informed of the company's financial position.

A director will not simply be able to assert that another director had responsibility for the area of the business which led to the failure of the company. The board of directors as a whole remains collectively responsible for the supervision of the conduct of the individual director in carrying out the delegated functions.[97] A non-executive director will be able to rely on what he is told by the executive directors, but must ensure that he evaluates the information given in a critical and objective manner.[98]

---

[95] *Re Bradcrown* [2001] BCLC 547.
[96] *Re Barings (No 5)* [1999] 1 BCLC 433 at 586e to f; *Re Polly Peck International Plc (No 2)* [1994] 1 BCLC 574; *Re Westmid Packing Services* [1998] 2 All ER 124.
[97] *Re Landhurst Leasing Plc* [1999] 1 BCLC 286 at 346f; *Secretary of State* v *Bairstow* [2004] EWHC 1730 (Ch). *See* also the general duties of company directors in Sections 171 to 177 Companies Act 2006.
[98] *Re TLL Realisations Ltd* (unreported 27 November 1998) (upheld on appeal, [2000] 2 BCLC 233).

It is imperative for the less senior directors to question the actions of those more senior to them and not simply be blindly led by an autocratic chairman. The duties to which directors are said to require them to act with "independence and courage".[99] An employee who has been promoted to the board of directors must ensure that he satisfies his responsibility for supervising the conduct of the more senior members of the board. In the event that he is not consulted on, for example, financial matters and the other members of the board refuse to consider the matter at his request, the appropriate course may be to resign unless he remains in office to continue to challenge the conduct of the other directors. If the other directors continue to pay insufficient attention to financial matters, the director may have a duty to inform the non-executive directors of the misconduct, or even the company's auditors.

Regardless of the size or structure of the company in relation to which the conduct alleged to render the director unfit is said to have occurred, the court must decide whether that conduct is such to render the respondent unfit to be concerned in the management of companies in general, regardless of size or structure.[100]

The court is also able to consider the defendant's conduct in relation to other companies when determining whether the defendant is unfit, and such companies need not be insolvent.[101] There is no need for the conduct relied upon in relation to the collateral companies to be the same as or similar to that adduced in relation to the "lead company". The only connection necessary is that the defendant had been a director of the collateral companies and that his conduct as a director of the collateral company tended to show unfitness.[102] The conduct of the defendant in relation to collateral companies will only be looked at cumulatively with those matters in relation to the insolvent company for the purpose of finding additional matters of complaint. The respondent will not be able to set up his conduct as a director

---

[99] *Re Landhurst Leasing Plc* [1999] 1 BCLC 286 at 353g.
[100] *Re Polly Peck International Plc (No 2)* [1994] 1 BCLC 574.
[101] Where a collateral company is solvent, the factors listed in Part II of Schedule 1 CDDA will not be relevant.
[102] *Secretary of State* v *Ivens* [1997] 2 BCLC 334.

in relation to other companies which have been successful in the period running up to his trial in order to prevent a disqualification order being made.[103]

In *Re Surrey Leisure Ltd*,[104] the Court of Appeal rejected the argument that there could be only one "lead company" in an application for an order under Section 6 CDDA. The decision was based upon there being no provision in the CDDA which imposed a limit on the number of lead companies on which the applicant for a disqualification order could rely. It was held that it would be inappropriate for the court to impose a maximum on the number of lead companies in these circumstances as it would not advance the cause of public protection, and permitting more than one lead company would not give rise to any unfair procedure.

The burden of proving unfitness lies on the Secretary of State. Although the standard of proof is the civil standard, that is to say on the balance of probabilities, the seriousness of the allegation is reflected in the need for evidence of appropriate cogency to discharge the burden of proof.[105]

13.7 Period of disqualification

In the event that the court finds a director unfit on an application made under Section 6 CDDA, it is obliged to impose a disqualification period of at least two years. In contrast, where a director is found unfit on an application brought under Section 8 CDDA, the court can exercise its discretion against making a disqualification order in an appropriate case.

In the leading case of *Re Sevenoaks Stationers (Retail) Ltd*,[106] the Court of Appeal laid down the following guidelines, dividing the possible 15-year period into three brackets:

(a)   The minimum bracket of two to five years is for those cases where, though disqualification is mandatory, the case is not very serious.

---

[103] *Re Bath Glass* [1988] BCLC 329; *Re Grayan Building Services Ltd* [1995] Ch 241.
[104] [1999] 2 BCLC 457.
[105] *Re Living Images Ltd* [1996] 1 BCLC 348 at 355 to 356; *Re H* [1996] AC 563 at 586 to 587.
[106] [1991] Ch 164.

(b) The middle bracket of six to ten years is for those cases which are serious but do not fall within the top bracket.

(c) The top bracket of over 10 years is for particularly serious cases, e.g. where a director who has been disqualified once already is subsequently disqualified again.

The Court of Appeal has stated that it is not appropriate or necessary to perform a detailed comparison with the facts of other cases when determining the period of disqualification.[107] Generally speaking, however, it may be said that cases involving misappropriation are always serious, since creditors will legitimately feel aggrieved at others, particularly those responsible for the management of the company, benefiting at their expense.[108]

When determining the appropriate period of disqualification, the court will take into account any mitigating factors which are present. These factors can either be extenuating circumstances accompanying the misconduct such as reliance on professional advice or an absence of personal gain, or factors which are unconnected to the misconduct such as a low likelihood of re-offending or personal loss in the failure of the company (the former type of mitigating factor will have more weight).

13.8 Disqualification undertakings and the *Carecraft* procedure

The Insolvency Act 2000 ("IA 2000") came into force on 2 April 2001. One of the main changes effected by this Act was the amendment of the CDDA so as to permit the Secretary of State to accept disqualification undertakings from directors without the need for a court hearing.[109] This new procedure avoids the need for the costly *Carecraft* procedure that the courts had developed previously.[110]

---

[107] *Re Westmid Packaging Services Ltd* [1998] 2 All ER 124.
[108] *Secretary of State* v *Blunt* [2005] 2 BCLC 463. *See* also *Secretary of State* v *Gee* [2007] EWHC 350 (Ch) and *Secretary of State* v *Poulter* [2009] BCC 608.
[109] The general background history to the introduction of undertakings is set out in the judgment of Chadwick LJ in *Re Blackspur Group (No 3), Secretary of State* v *Davies and others (No 2)* [2001] EWCA Civ 1595, [2002] 2 BCLC 263.
[110] *Re Carecraft Construction Co Ltd* [1994] 1 WLR 172.

13.8.1   *Disqualification undertakings*

Section 1A CDDA as amended provides that in the circumstances specified in Sections 7 and 8 CDDA the Secretary of State may accept a "disqualification undertaking". A disqualification undertaking is an undertaking by a person that, for a period specified in the undertaking, the person will not be a director of a company, act as receiver of a company's property or in any way, whether directly or indirectly, be concerned or take part in the promotion, formation or management of a company unless (in each case) he has the leave of a court, and will not act as an insolvency practitioner.

The maximum period which may be specified in a disqualification undertaking is 15 years, and the minimum period which may be specified in a disqualification undertaking under Section 7 is two years.[111] Where a disqualification undertaking by a person who is already subject to such an undertaking or to a disqualification order is accepted, the periods specified in those undertakings or (as the case may be) the undertaking and the order are to run concurrently.[112]

In determining whether to accept a disqualification undertaking by any person, the Secretary of State may take account of matters other than criminal convictions notwithstanding that the person may be criminally liable in respect of those matters.[113]

A disqualification undertaking corresponds in terms to the order which the court may make under Section 6 CDDA and has the same consequences. The director will be prohibited by the undertaking from acting as a director or as a receiver of a company's property or as an insolvency practitioner for the period stated in the undertaking and any breach of the undertaking during the period of disqualification would constitute a criminal offence under Section 13 CDDA.

---

[111] Section 1A(2) CDDA.
[112] Section 1A(3) CDDA.
[113] Section 1A(4) CDDA.

The preliminary considerations are also the same. Section 7(1) CDDA requires the Secretary of State to form the view that it is expedient in the public interest that a disqualification order should be made against a person under Section 6 before initiating proceedings for such an order. Section 7(2A) of the Act provides as follows:

> "If it appears to the Secretary of State that the conditions mentioned in Section 6(1) are satisfied as respects any person who has offered to give him a disqualification undertaking, he may accept the undertaking if it appears to him that it is expedient in the public interest that he should do so (instead of applying, or proceeding with an application, for a disqualification order)."

The Secretary of State must form the opinion that the conditions specified in Section 6(1) are satisfied before becoming entitled to accept a disqualification undertaking. He must therefore apply his mind to the evidence of conduct and unfitness in precisely the same way as the court is required to do when considering an application for a disqualification order. Section 9(1A) CDDA provides that, in determining whether he may accept a disqualification undertaking from any person, the Secretary of State shall, as respects the person's conduct as a director of any company concerned, have regard in particular to the matters mentioned in Part 1 of Schedule 1 CDDA and, where the company has become insolvent, to the matters mentioned in Part II of Schedule 1. Before the Secretary of State can determine whether it is expedient in the public interest that he should accept the undertaking which is offered, he must first satisfy himself that the necessary basis for disqualification is made out.

The CDDA as amended also contains provisions for the release or modification of any disqualification undertakings that are accepted. Section 1A CDDA makes the prohibition contained in the undertaking subject to the leave of the court and Section 17 CDDA sets out the procedure to be followed in cases where application for leave is made. On the hearing of an application for leave for the purposes of Section 1(1)(a) or 1A(1)(a), the Secretary of State must appear and call the attention of the court to any matters which seem to him to be relevant, and may himself give evidence or call witnesses.[114]

A director who has given a disqualification undertaking may also apply to the court under Section 8A for the period of disqualification to be reduced or for the undertaking to cease to be in force. On an application under Section 8A, the applicant is not permitted to challenge any facts recorded in the agreed statement of unfit conduct, unless either some ground was shown which would be sufficient to discharge a private law contract or some ground of public interest was shown which outweighed the importance of holding a party to his agreement.[115] On the hearing of an application under sub-section (1), the Secretary of State shall appear and call the attention of the court to any matters which seem to him to be relevant, and may himself give evidence or call witnesses: *see* Section 8A(2) CDDA.

The Secretary of State is entitled to refuse to accept a disqualification undertaking if it is not accompanied by an acceptable statement of unfit conduct.[116] He has power to require such a statement and is entitled to refuse to accept a disqualification undertaking if an acceptable statement is not provided.

Section 9B CDDA, as inserted by Section 204(2) Enterprise Act 2002, provides for "competition disqualification undertakings". It applies where:

(a) the Office of Fair Trading ("OFT") thinks that a company has committed or is committing a breach of competition law; and
(b) the OFT also thinks that a director of that company is unfit to be concerned in the management of a company; and
(c) the director in question offers to give the OFT a disqualification undertaking.

The OFT has a discretion to accept a disqualification undertaking from the director instead of applying for or proceeding

---

[114] Section 17(5) CDDA.
[115] *Secretary of State* v *Jonkler* [2006] 2 All ER 902, [2006] 2 BCLC 239.
[116] *Re Blackspur Group Plc* [2001] 1 BCLC 653.

with an application for a disqualification order. The maximum period that may be specified in a disqualification undertaking is 15 years.

13.8.2   The Carecraft procedure

Where the parties are able to agree the wording of a statement of unfit conduct but fail to reach agreement in respect of the period of disqualification, the *Carecraft* procedure may be used.

The adoption of the *Carecraft* procedure is dependent upon the parties being able to draft an agreed statement. This statement will be placed before the court, and the court will be requested to exercise its discretion to make an order based only upon the facts in the statement. The use of the procedure is now enshrined in paragraph 13 of the Practice Direction. The Practice Direction further provides that where the court makes a disqualification order under the *Carecraft* procedure, the *Carecraft* statement should be annexed to the order.

The ultimate discretion as to whether to make an order on a *Carecraft* basis lies with the court, and this gives rise to need for the statement to provide for its status in the event that the court refuses to deal with the application on this basis. This should ensure that any admissions of fact made by the director in the statement cannot be used at the full hearing of the application.

There is no critical time by which a director must agree to the use of the *Carecraft* procedure or otherwise face a full trial of the application for his disqualification. In the interest of costs, however, it will be prudent for the director to determine whether he is amenable to compromising the proceedings by use of the *Carecraft* procedure at the earliest opportunity. To this end the defendant should prepare his evidence at the earliest possible stage in order to evaluate the relative strengths and weaknesses of the case against him. The Secretary of State will not usually be prepared to enter into negotiations until after he has received the director's affidavit evidence in opposition to his application. It is advisable that all negotiations which are focused upon agreeing a *Carecraft* statement should be conducted on a without prejudice basis. This will ensure that in the event that the parties are unable to reach an agreement, the negotiations will not be available to the court at the full trial of the application.

In addition to setting out those admitted or undisputed facts which are said to justify a finding of unfitness, the *Carecraft* statement should also set out any mitigating circumstances relied upon by the parties. The willingness of the director to adopt the *Carecraft* procedure may, in itself, constitute a mitigating factor.

13.9   Discontinuance of proceedings

The Secretary of State may discontinue disqualification proceedings at any time by filing and serving a notice of discontinuance on each defendant specifying against which defendants the claim is discontinued.[117] The costs incurred by the director in defending the proceedings up to the date of service of the notice will, unless the court otherwise orders, be paid by the Secretary of State.[118] When the director has filed a defence prior to the discontinuance of the proceedings and the Secretary of State seeks to make another claim arising out of the same or substantially the same facts, the Secretary of State will need the permission of the court to make the claim.[119] The fact that a defendant to disqualification proceedings has previously successfully resisted disciplinary proceedings will not necessarily be a bar to the commencement of subsequent disqualification proceedings against him.[120]

13.10   Appeals

A defendant may appeal against a disqualification order on the ground that it should not have been made or on the ground that the period of disqualification is excessive. An appeal may also be made by the Secretary of State on the ground that the period

---

[117] CPR Part 38. In circumstances where any party to the disqualification proceedings has given an undertaking to the court, the Secretary of State will need the permission of the court to discontinue the proceedings.
[118] CPR 38.6.
[119] CPR 38.7.
[120] *Re Barings Plc (No 3)* [1999] 1 BCLC 226.

of disqualification is too lenient. An appeal from an order made by a county court judge, or a district judge, or a registrar of the High Court will lie to a single judge of the High Court. Permission to appeal is required.[121] Appeals from a High Court judge will lie to the Court of Appeal. Again, permission is required.

The appeal will be a true appeal rather than a hearing *de novo*, with the result that the appellate court will not depart from the trial judge's findings of primary fact on the oral evidence of the witnesses unless such finding was perverse. In *Re Grayan Building Services Ltd*,[122] Hoffmann LJ explained the general principle in the following terms:

> "The [trial] judge is deciding a question of mixed fact and law, in that he is applying the standard laid by the courts (conduct appropriate to a person fit to be a director) to the facts of the case. It is in principle no different from the decision as to whether someone has been negligent . . . On the other hand, the standards applied by the law in differing contexts vary a great deal in precision and generally speaking, the vaguer the standard and the greater the number of factors which the court has to weigh up in deciding whether or not the standards have been met, the more reluctant an appellate court will be to interfere with the trial judge's decision . . . I agree with the way in which the matter was put in *Re Hitco 2000 Ltd* [1995] BCC 161: 'Plainly, the appellate court would be very slow indeed to disturb such conclusion as to fitness or unfitness. In many, perhaps most, cases the conclusion will have been so very much assisted and influenced by the oral evidence and demeanour of the director . . . that the Appellate Court will be in nowhere near as good a position to form a judgment as to fitness or unfitness than was the trial judge. But there may be cases where there is little or no dispute as to the primary facts and the Appellate Court is in as good a position as the trial judge to form a judgment as to fitness. In

---

[121] *See* paragraph 17.6 of the Practice Direction on Insolvency Proceedings, which has the effect of reversing *Secretary of State* v *Paulin* [2005] 2 BCLC 667 on this point.
[122] [1995] Ch 241 at 254.

such cases the Appellate Court should not shrink from its responsibility to do so, and, if satisfied that the trial judge was wrong, to say so'. . .".[123]

Similarly, the actual order or period of disqualification will not be interfered with unless the trial judge can be shown to have erred in principle. In *Re Deaduck Ltd*,[124] Neuberger J gave the following guidance in relation to appeals concerned with the length of a period of disqualification:

> "In this connection care must be taken before an appellate court interferes with the period of disqualification imposed by an inferior court. To use a term sometimes invoked in connection with criminal appeals, it is normally inappropriate for the appellate court to tinker with the period imposed. Nonetheless, where the appellate court is satisfied that a period of disqualification imposed was too great to a significant extent, or where the appellate court considers that appropriate factors were not or cannot have been taken into account, it is right, indeed, it is only fair on the director concerned, for the appellate court to interfere."[125]

It is possible, in theory, for a disqualified person to seek a stay of the order pending his appeal. However, the courts have repeatedly held that a disqualification order should not be stayed save in exceptional cases and that the correct course of action for the disqualified director will be to apply for permission to act as a director notwithstanding the disqualification, pending the hearing of the appeal.[126]

13.11   The effect of disqualification orders and undertakings

Disqualification orders and undertakings are recorded in a public register kept by the Secretary of State, which also

---

[123] *See* also *Kotonou* v *Secretary of State* [2010] EWHC 19 (Ch).

[124] [2000] 1 BCLC 148.

[125] For a recent example of a successful appeal against the length of the period of disqualification, *see R.* v *Randhawa* [2008] EWCA Crim 2599.

[126] *See Secretary of State* v *Bannister* [1996] 1 WLR 118 and *Secretary of State* v *Sainsbury* [2009] EWHC 3456 (Ch).

includes details of any relevant permission to act granted by the courts. A disqualified person must resign from any offices which he is prohibited from holding.[127]

13.11.1 *The extent of disqualification*

Section 1(1) CDDA provides that a disqualification order is one that prevents the person subject to the order from acting as a director,[128] liquidator or administrator,[129] a receiver or manager of a company's property,[130] or being directly or indirectly concerned or taking part in the promotion, formation, or management of a company.[131] Section 1 CDDA was amended by the IA 2000 to prevent disqualified directors from acting as insolvency practitioners. Section 1A(1) CDDA, which relates to disqualification undertakings, replicates the provisions of Section 1(1) as amended by the IA 2000.

Upon the making of a disqualification order, the court does not have jurisdiction to order that the disqualified person is prohibited only from doing certain of the acts specified in Section 1(1); it is an all or nothing situation.[132] There is no jurisdiction to limit a disqualification order to the holding of directorships in a public company.[133] Furthermore, the court does not have jurisdiction to impose additional prohibitions upon the disqualified person.

A company for the purposes of Section 1(1) CDDA includes any company which may be wound up under Part V IA 1986. As explained above, this has the effect of extending the prohibition to foreign companies susceptible to being wound up here as unregistered companies.[134]

---

[127] Articles of association often require a director to resign upon becoming "prohibited by law from being a director".

[128] Section 1(1)(a) CDDA.

[129] Section 1(1)(b) CDDA.

[130] Section 1(1)(c) CDDA.

[131] Section 1(1)(d) CDDA.

[132] *Re Gower Enterprises Ltd (No 2)* [1995] 2 BCLC 201; *R. v Bramley* [2004] EWCA Crim 3319.

[133] *R. v Ward, The Times*, 10 August 2001.

[134] The prohibition imposed upon an undischarged bankrupt is rather more narrow in scope, as the foreign company must have an established place of business in Great Britain (Section 22(1) CDDA).

Where a disqualification order is made, the disqualification period takes effect from the date of the order, but unless the court otherwise directs, the prohibition imposed by the order begins on the twenty-first day after the day on which the order is made.[135] The prohibition will apply to companies limited by guarantee and unlimited companies, as well as private and public companies limited by shares.[136] The prohibition does not, however, extend to preventing the disqualified person from carrying on business as a partner in a partnership, since carrying on business as a partnership does not allow those concerned to take advantage of the concept of limited liability.[137]

The disqualified person will be prohibited from acting as a director regardless of the title he uses, with the result that he will be in breach of the order or undertaking if he is acting as a director even if the title he uses is, for example, "trustee".[138] It is also irrelevant whether the person is a *de jure* director or a *de facto* director. Furthermore, disqualification on the grounds of unfitness will result in the person being prohibited from acting as a shadow director in relation to a company.[139] Disqualification will also prevent the person from acting as a director of a building society,[140] a member of the committee of management or officer of an incorporated friendly society,[141] a director or officer of an NHS foundation trust,[142] a charity

---

[135] Rule 9 Disqualification Rules, paragraph 16 of the Practice Direction.

[136] This is the effect of Section 22(9) CDDA.

[137] The Insolvent Partnerships Order 1994 fails to make any provision for disqualification from acting as a partner, although it specifically provides the CDDA so that an order under Sections 6 to 10 CDDA may be based upon conduct in relation to an insolvent partnership. The courts have frequently emphasised that disqualification exists to deal with directors who abuse the privilege of limited liability: *see*, e.g. *Re Probe Data Systems (No 3) Ltd* [1991] BCLC 586 at 593 and *Wilson v Whitehouse* [2006] EWCA Civ 1688 at paragraph 52.

[138] Section 22(4) CDDA.

[139] Section 22(4) CDDA. The term "shadow director" is defined in Section 22(5) CDDA as "a person in accordance with whose directions or instructions the directors of the company are accustomed to act (but so that a person is not deemed a shadow director by reason only that the directors act on advice given by him in a professional capacity". Although the CDDA does not expressly provide that persons who are disqualified on grounds other than unfitness are prohibited from acting as shadow directors, it is suggested that such conduct would fall within the prohibition being concerned in or taking part in the management on the company.

[140] Section 22A CDDA.

[141] Section 22B CDDA.

[142] Section 22C CDDA.

trustee,[143] or a trustee of an occupational pension scheme established under a trust.[144]

The other prohibition in Section 1(1) CDDA which merits further consideration is that of being directly or indirectly concerned or taking part in the promotion, formation or management of a company. There is no statutory definition for the terms "promotion", "formation" or "management". Interpretation of these terms is left to the courts. The protective purpose of disqualification is likely to result in a liberal interpretation of these words.[145] The concepts of "taking part in" promotion, formation and management and being "concerned in" promotion, formation and management are distinct and either may be satisfied by direct or indirect conduct.[146]

It is likely that any involvement in the internal or external management of a company will constitute a breach of a disqualification order or undertaking. Therefore a person who is unsure whether his proposed conduct would amount to a breach of the terms of disqualification should consider applying to the court for permission to act in such a manner.

An insolvency practitioner who is subject to a disqualification order or undertaking is automatically disqualified from acting as an insolvency practitioner.[147] It is an offence under the IA 1986 to act as an insolvency practitioner without the relevant qualifications.

13.11.2 *Criminal and civil sanctions*

A person who acts in breach of a disqualification order or undertaking is liable to both criminal and civil sanctions.

---

[143] Section 72(1)(f) Charities Act 1993.
[144] Section 29(1)(f) Pensions Act 1995.
[145] *R. v Campbell* (1984) 78 Cr App Rep 95.
[146] ibid.
[147] Section 390(4) IA 1986. The effect of this provision is that the impact of the order will be wider than that envisaged by Section 1(1) CDDA. The prohibition will extend to acting, e.g. as a provisional liquidator, administrative receiver, trustee in bankruptcy and supervisor of a corporate or individual voluntary arrangement.

Criminal sanctions are provided by Section 13 CDDA, which provides that a person who acts in breach of a disqualification order or undertaking is liable on conviction on indictment, to imprisonment for not more than two years or a fine or both,[148] and on summary conviction to imprisonment for not more than six months or a fine not exceeding the statutory maximum or both.[149] The offence committed by acting in breach of a disqualification order or undertaking is one of strict liability, with the consequence that an honest belief that the acts did not breach the order (or, as the case may be, undertaking) will not be a sustainable defence.[150]

Where a body corporate which is subject to a disqualification order or undertaking acts in contravention of the order or undertaking and it is proved that the offence occurred with the consent or connivance of, or was attributable to any neglect on the part of any director, manager, secretary or other similar officer, or any person purporting to act in such a capacity, he is also guilty of the offence.

Civil sanctions are provided by Section 15 CDDA, which provides for civil liability in circumstances where a person acts in breach of a disqualification order or undertaking. By virtue of Section 15(1)(a) CDDA, such a person will be personally liable for all the debts and other liabilities of the company which are incurred at a time when he was involved in the management of the company.[151] Section 15(1)(b) imposes civil liability on others involved in the management of the company who act, or are willing to act, on instructions given by a disqualified person without permission of the court if they know the person to be disqualified. The liabililty imposed is personal liability for all the debts and other liabilities of the company which are incurred at a time when the person was acting or was willing to act on instructions given by the disqualified person.[152] For this purpose, once it is shown that the person acted, or was willing

---

[148] Section 13(a) CDDA.
[149] Section 13(b) CDDA.
[150] *R. v Brockley* [1994] 1 BCLC 606.
[151] Section 15(3)(a) CDDA.
[152] Section 15(3)(b) CDDA.

to act, on the instructions of a person who he knew to be subject to a disqualification order or undertaking, there is a rebuttable presumption that he was willing at any time thereafter to act on any instructions given by the disqualified person.[153]

The liability imposed by Section 15 is joint and several liability with the company and any other person who may be personally liable for the company's debts. Those who are appointed directors in place of the disqualified person should be particularly aware of this potential liability. They must ensure that they do not merely act as the nominee for the disqualified person, or act in any way which enables the disqualified person to play a role in the management of the company.

Where a company, acting by a disqualified director, enters into contracts, it is not possible to contend that those contracts are void for illegality; rather, they will be valid and enforceable. This is because the policy underlying Section 11 CDDA is the protection of the public from untrustworthy individuals being involved in the management of a limited liability company. The protected class includes those who extended credit to the company. If a company were unable to sue on its contracts, the company's debtor book would be destroyed, and the very persons whom the legislation was designed to protect would thereby be prejudiced.[154]

13.12 Applications for permission to act by a disqualified director

Although a disqualification order or undertaking prohibits the director from engaging in any of the conduct specified in Sections 1A(1) and 1(1) CDDA, this prohibition is expressly subject to "the leave of the court".[155] This ensures that in appropriate cases a person will not be prevented from acting as a director for the entirety of the period of his disqualification.

---

[153] Section 15(5) CDDA.
[154] *Hill* v *DEFRA* [2006] 1 BCLC 601.
[155] The disqualification imposed upon an undischarged bankrupt by Section 11(1) CDDA and under Section 12(2) CDDA, is also expressed to take effect "except with leave of the court".

The procedure which governs an application for permission to act is found in Section 17 CDDA. The Practice Direction provides that the application will be made by a Part 8 claim form,[156] or by an application notice in existing disqualification proceedings.[157] If possible the application should be made immediately upon disqualification, or at least within the period before disqualification commences, as this will enable the applicant to request permission to continue to act in the proposed capacity pending the hearing of his application.[158] The respondent to an application for permission will be the person who made the application for the disqualification order.[159]

When considering an application for permission, the court will be mindful not to grant permission too freely for fear of undermining either the protection of the public[160] or the deterrent effect served by disqualification.[161] The case law dealing with applications by disqualified directors for permission to act reveals that the court will not usually entertain an application for the prohibition to simply be lifted; rather, the court will normally only grant permission in relation to a specific company or companies.

The applicant will bear the burden of proof in establishing that the case is one in which it is appropriate for the court to give permission. In cases where the court is prepared to give permission, it will only do so subject to conditions which it believes are necessary to give the public sufficient protection.[162] The court is likely, on balance, to be less ready to grant permission to the

---

[156] A claim form issued pursuant to Part 8 CPR.

[157] Paragraph 20 of the Practice Direction.

[158] The evidence in support of the application must be by affidavit: paragraph 22 of the Practice Direction.

[159] In circumstances where the applicant for the disqualification order was not the Secretary of State, the Secretary of State should also be made a respondent to the application. For the avoidance of doubt, paragraph 23 of the Practice Direction provides that in all applications the claim form or application notice and supporting evidence must be served on the Secretary of State.

[160] *Re Barings Plc (No 4)* [1999] 1 All ER 1017; *Re Servaccomm Redhall Ltd* [2006] 1 BCLC 1; *Kluk v Secretary of State* [2007] EWHC 3055 (Ch).

[161] *Re Tech Textiles Ltd* [1998] 1 BCLC 259; *Kluk v Secretary of State* [2007] EWHC 3055 (Ch).

[162] Although there is no provision in the CDDA which gives the court power to attach conditions to the grant of permission, the case law reveals that the courts have consistently adopted such a course. Conditions commonly ordered include the imposition of controls at board level, for example by the appointment of an independent accountant as a finance director, an obligation to hold board meetings at monthly intervals, and an obligation to have the monthly management accounts inspected by the auditors.

applicant to act if the disqualification order made against him was in the "higher bracket". The adoption of this approach by the courts reflects the need for protecting the public from the conduct of the individual which justified disqualification in the first place. The cases show that the chances of the application being successful are enhanced where the application relates to a company with which the applicant was involved at the time of disqualification but his conduct in relation to the company did not form part of the disqualification proceedings.

The court will look to all the circumstances of the case when determining whether to give permission, and its discretion is not fettered in any way.[163] The case law reveals that two factors will have an important bearing on the exercise of the court's discretion:

(a) whether there is a need for the applicant to act contrary to the prohibition imposed by Section 1(1) CDDA; and
(b) whether the public would be adequately protected in the event that the court gives permission.

The applicant will need to address the grounds upon which his original disqualification was based to show that there are sufficient controls in place at the company in respect of which he seeks permission to act as a director, to convince the court that the misconduct is unlikely to occur again. The court will wish to be informed of the financial position of the company to be satisfied that it is trading successfully, to be satisfied that the company has adequate financial controls; to be informed of the risks inherent in the company's business, and that the company is being managed in accordance with the standards prescribed by the relevant legislation and the courts.[164]

In *Re Barings Plc (No 4)*,[165] for example, Scott V-C heard an application by the former chief executive officer of Barings for permission to act as a non-executive director in respect of three

---

[163] *Re Dawes & Henderson (Agencies) Ltd (No 2)* [1999] 2 BCLC 317; *Kluk v Secretary of State* [2007] EWHC 3055 (Ch).
[164] Including the numerous requirements imposed by the Companies Act 2006.
[165] [1999] 1 BCLC 262.

private companies. The application was made prior to the disqualification order was made against Mr Norris. There were no allegations of dishonesty or fraudulent impropriety; only allegations of incompetence. Scott V-C granted permission as he held that there was no risk of the recurrence of the defects apparent in Mr Norris's previous conduct. This was especially so in a case where the applicant was not seeking to be given permission to exercise any executive responsibilities in relation to the companies. Permission was therefore given on the condition that Mr Norris remained an unpaid non-executive director and that he be barred from entering into a service contract with the companies. Scott V-C stated:

> "The improprieties which have led to and required the making of a disqualification order must be kept clearly in mind when considering whether a grant of Section 17 leave should be made. If the conduct of a director has been tainted by any dishonesty, if the company in question has been allowed to continue trading while obviously hopelessly insolvent, if a director has been withdrawing from a struggling company excessive amounts by way of remuneration in anticipation of the company's collapse and, in effect, living off the company's creditors, and if a disqualification order were then made, these circumstances would loom very large on any Section 17 application. The court would, I am sure, have in mind the need to protect the public from any repetition of the conduct in question. That conduct, and the protection of the public from it, would have been the major factor requiring the imposition of the disqualification."[166]

He rejected the submission that the applicant had to show a "need" to act as a prerequisite for success, and held that the balancing exercise was between the protection of the public and the desire of the applicant to act as a director.

In *Re Brittania Homes Centres Ltd*,[167] the registrar's decision to grant leave was overturned on appeal on the grounds that it

---

[166] At 265c to e.
[167] [2001] 2 BCLC 63.

undermined the effect of the disqualification order. Leave would have meant that the disqualification order had no practical effect whatsoever because the respondent would have been trading in the same way having previously managed a series of one-man companies, all of which had gone into liquidation.

In the event that the applicant is successful, the order of the court granting permission to act, along with any conditions imposed, must be notified to the Secretary of State for entry on the disqualification register. Conditions which will commonly be attached to the grant of permission include the appointment of an independent accountant as a finance director, an obligation to hold regular board meetings, the auditing of monthly management accounts and the removal of the applicant from the company's bank mandate.

13.13   Conclusion

Disqualification is an essential part of the statutory mechanism for the prevention of abuse of limited liability. Directors of companies must ensure that they are fully aware of their duties and that they act in accordance with them. In the event that directors fail to conduct themselves in the required manner, disqualification plays an important role in the protection of the creditors and exists to deter others who hold the office of a director from engaging in similar conduct.

Index

593